Decorating the 'Godly' Household

RELIGIOUS ART IN POST-REFORMATION BRITAIN

TARA HAMLING

PUBLISHED FOR THE PAUL MELLON CENTRE FOR STUDIES IN BRITISH ART
BY YALE UNIVERSITY PRESS · NEW HAVEN AND LONDON

For my parents

PAT and JOHN HAMLING

who made it all possible

Designed by Sarah Faulks

Printed in China

Library of Congress Cataloging-in-Publication Data
Hamling, Tara.
Decorating the godly household : religious art in post-reformation Britain / Tara Hamling.
p. cm.
Includes bibliographical references and index.
ISBN 978-0-300-16282-0 (cl : alk. paper)
1. Art in interior decoration–Great Britain. 2. Decoration and ornament, Architectural–Great Britain. 3. Christian art and symbolism–Great Britain--Modern period, 1500– 4. Home–Great Britain–Religious aspects–Christianity. 5. Protestants–Great Britain–Social life and customs–16th century. 6. Protestants–Great Britain–Social life and customs–17th century. 7. Great Britain–Religious life and customs. I. Title.
NK2115.5.A77H36 2010
704.9'482094109031–dc22
2010027341
A catalogue record for this book is available from The British Library

Frontispiece: View of the plasterwork ceiling of c. 1636 in the long gallery of Lanhydrock House, Cornwall. Photograph: © The National Trust

Pg. vi: Judith with the head of Holofernes, detail, painted panel from the long gallery ceiling at Dean House, Edinburgh, 1627. © scotlandsimages.com / National Museums Scotland

The distinction we make between 'mere' decoration and function is unwarranted; decoration is intrinsically functional, or else its presence would be inexplicable.

Alfred Gell, *Art and Agency* (Oxford, 1998), p. 74

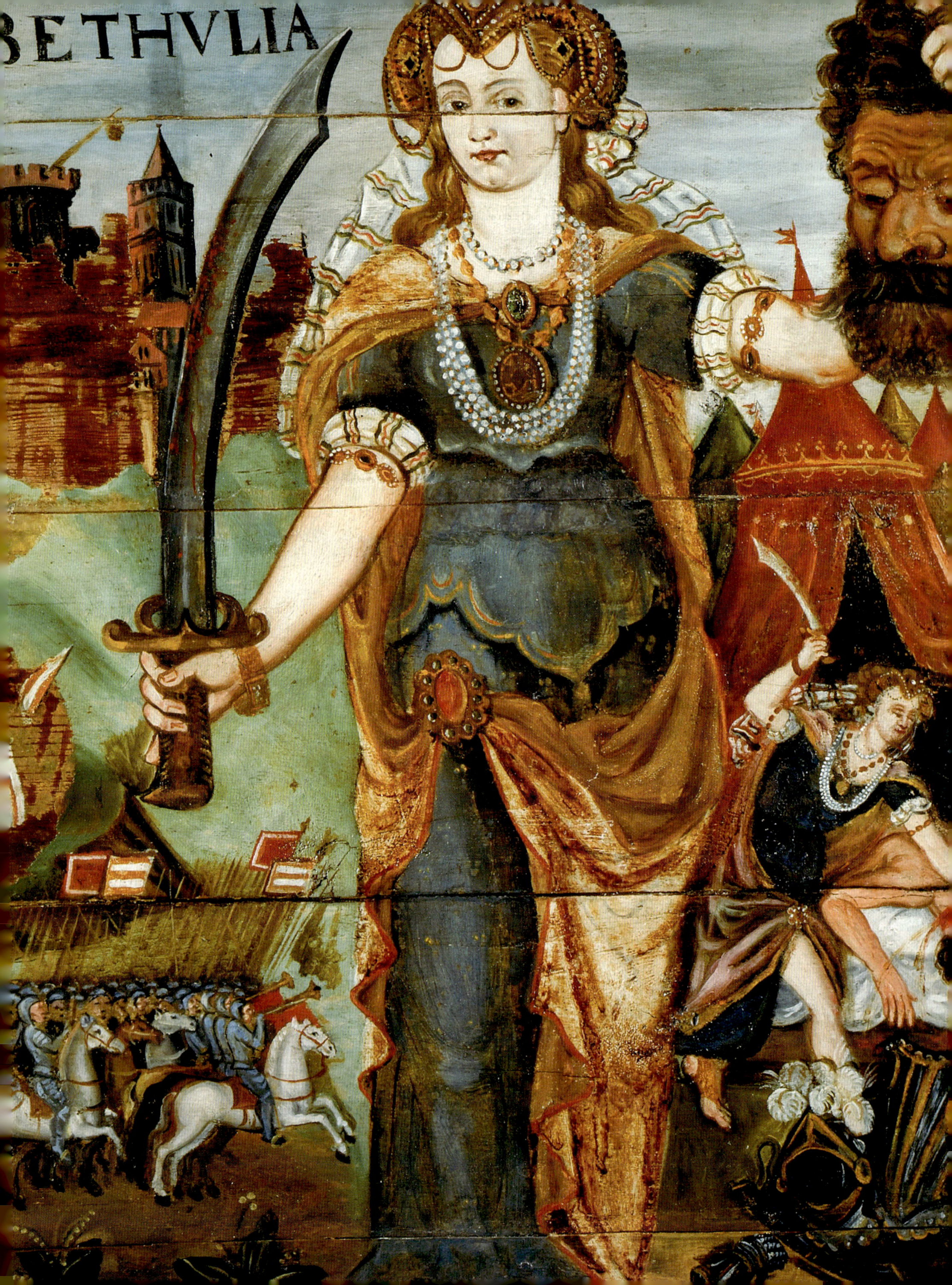
BETHVLIA

Contents

Acknowledgements

This project has evolved over the last twelve years and in the context of degrees and fellowships at four universities. During that time I have been privileged to work with truly inspirational tutors, supervisors, mentors and colleagues.

The genesis of the project was an undergraduate dissertation at the University of Leicester and I am grateful to Philip Lindley for his infectious enthusiasm and encouragement which gave me the confidence to continue to postgraduate study. My M.Phil studies at the University of Birmingham were enriched by the sparky intelligence of Tim Barringer and Shearer West who supported my interests and pointed the way forward.

Most of the research towards this book was undertaken in the context of doctoral and post-doctoral study in the Art History Department at the University of Sussex. During the eight years I spent at Sussex the Art History Department was populated with a raft of exceptional scholars who also happened to be great people, which meant that my time there was not only intellectually stimulating but personally rewarding. I am immensely grateful to Nigel Llewellyn for being open to my ideas and for providing exemplary supervision, expert guidance and ongoing support. My work and confidence has also benefited greatly from the expertise and generosity of Maurice Howard who has been an unfailing mentor, advisor and friend. I am grateful to all former colleagues at Sussex for many kindnesses but especially wish to acknowledge Meaghan Clarke, Craig Clunas, Liz James, Michelle O'Malley and Evelyn Welch, who have all helped to support my studies and early career. I am proud to acknowledge Margaret Aston's role as the external examiner for my doctoral thesis and I am greatly indebted to her for the many ways she has helped support the development of my work. Steve Wharton, my study-buddy, has generously read and commented on the various manifestations of my research over many years.

The interdisciplinary nature of the book has benefited from my move in 2007 to the History Department at the University of Birmingham. The Centre for Reformation and Early Modern Studies and the Shakespeare Institute, where I have been based, have provided stimulating and supportive environments for research on the early modern period. I am grateful to Richard Cust and Catherine Richardson (now at the University of Kent) in particular for being dedicated mentors to a junior scholar, in looking out for my interests and for reading and commenting on drafts of my work.

For their generosity in sharing research and helping in various ways I thank Michael Bath, Claire Gapper, Ian Green, Kate McLuskie, the late Annabel Ricketts, Kate Rumbold, Richard Simpson, Richard L. Williams, Lucy Worsley and Anthony Wells-Cole. Thanks are due to my students at Sussex and Birmingham for helping me think through various aspects of the project and to all those members of audiences who asked questions following public airings of the research as it progressed. Their interest has kept my enthusiasm alive. I am also grateful to the anonymous readers for Yale University Press, whose astute suggestions helped me to improve the manuscript in many significant ways.

The process of research towards this book has relied on the generosity and goodwill of the many owners of historic properties who have allowed me access to their homes and given permission for me to publish photographs of their property. I am also indebted to the various House Managers for properties owned by the National Trust, the National Trust for Scotland, English Heritage, Historic Scotland and other independent trusts for allowing me access to their buildings outside public opening times. Staff at the National Monuments Record Centre have provided helpful and efficient service and I am grateful to Alyson Rogers for her help with image permissions.

The financial support provided by scholarships has enabled me to undertake the various stages of research that have informed this book. I gratefully acknowledge the following awards: a British Archaeological Association Ochs Scholarship to support my M.Phil studies; an Arts and Humanities Research Council Postgraduate Studentship and a Paul Mellon Doctoral Fellowship to support my doctorate; a British Academy Postdoctoral Fellowship to support the wider research project that informs this publication. Fieldwork costs have been supported by travel grants from the Society of Architectural Historians; the Graduate Research Centre for the Humanities at the University of Sussex and a British Academy Small Research Grant. For generous contributions towards the costs of images I am grateful to the Paul Mellon Centre for Studies in British Art, the University of Birmingham (Research and Knowledge Transfer Award) and the Society of Architectural Historians of Great Britain (Dorothy Stroud and Margaret Ramsden bursaries).

I would like to thank Michelle O'Malley for her help in bringing the book to publication and Gillian Malpass at Yale University Press for her guidance and support throughout the process. I am also grateful to Katharine Ridler for her painstaking copy-editing and Sarah Faulks for her skilled work on the design.

Finally, I must try to express the enormous gratitude I feel towards my family. I met my husband Bill Bigge mid-way through research when I was grappling with some methodological issues. His intellectual outlook, which combines approaches from science and the creative arts, encouraged imaginative insights I would never have achieved on my own. His practical creativity has also improved this book in numerous ways; he is responsible for much of the photography and all of the diagrams. The book came together thanks to my daughter, Darcy May Bigge, whose presence soothed me as I put the pieces in place in the spring and summer of 2008.

My wonderful Mum and Dad have been the source of endless practical, emotional and intellectual support throughout the lifespan of this project. They provided financial support for a protracted process of higher education because they trusted me and believed in my abilities. They fostered my enthusiasm for this subject, acted as sounding board and actively participated in the practicalities of research so that I have the memories of many shared adventures and discoveries to cherish. I hope this book reflects our journey and goes some way to honour their belief in me.

Note to the Reader

Original spelling and punctuation for early modern sources has been retained except for u/v and i/j which have been modernised throughout.

Brief biographical details including an indication of the religious outlook of significant Protestant authors are provided in the notes. The reader is encouraged to consult the *Oxford Dictionary of National Biography* for more detailed information.

Quotations from the Bible are taken from the King James Authorised Version of 1611, unless otherwise indicated.

ABBREVIATIONS

BL	British Library, London
ODNB	*Oxford Dictionary of National Biography*
OED	*Oxford English Dictionary*
NMR	National Monuments Record Centre
NMS	National Museums of Scotland
RCHME	Royal Commission on the Historical Monuments of England
RCAHMS	Royal Commission on the Ancient and Historical Monuments of Scotland
SBT	Shakespeare Birthplace Trust, Stratford-upon-Avon
V&A	Victoria and Albert Museum, London

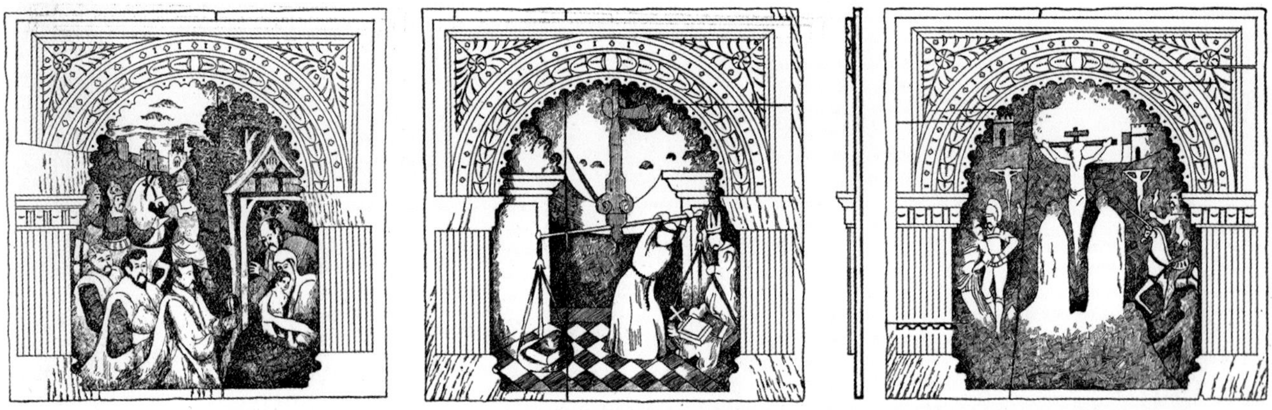

Subject : the Adoration.

Showing the Bible in one scale outweighing the ornaments of the Church of Rome.

Subject : the Crucifixion. With section of woodwork.

THREE PANELS FROM AN OVERMANTEL AT UCKFIELD.

1 Drawing of three panels from an overmantel from a house in Uckfield, Sussex, as published in *Sussex Notes and Queries*, 1929

Introduction

One of the better-known aspects of the Reformation and its aftermath in England and Scotland is the destruction of images, particularly those forms of imagery associated with devotional behaviour, such as altarpieces and statues of religious figures. The image of the axe-wielding Puritan iconoclast stripping churches of their glories is a familiar stereotype that has entered the popular consciousness (Fig. 2). Less well known is the fact that a great wealth of art with religious subject matter continued to be made and displayed in the century after the Protestant ascendancy in Britain, but in a domestic context. A drawing published in 1929 in the journal *Sussex Notes and Queries* illustrates one of the forms this imagery might take (Fig. 1). It records the appearance of an Elizabethan chimneypiece from a town house in Uckfield, Sussex, with an overmantel consisting of three painted wooden panels within a carved frame. The style of the work suggests that it dates from the 1590s. On the left is a scene of the Three Kings adoring the Christ Child (the Adoration) and on the right is the Crucifixion. In the journal's accompanying text the scene in the centre is described as the Bible in one scale outweighing the ornaments of the Church of Rome.[1] Although the back-

2 Woodcut showing Puritan soldiers stripping churches, from John Vicars, *True Information of the Beginning and Cause of all our troubles* (1648)

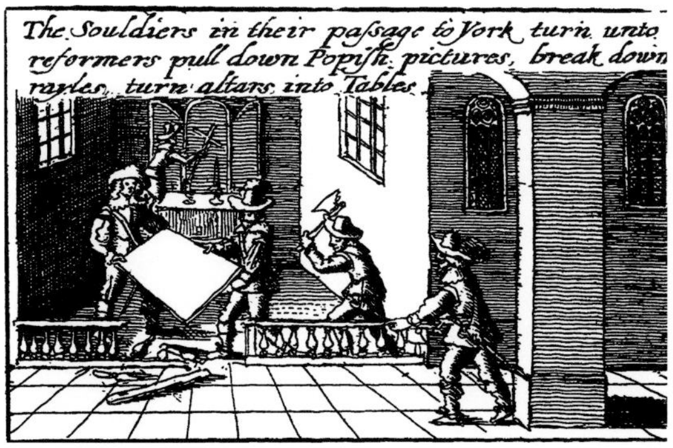

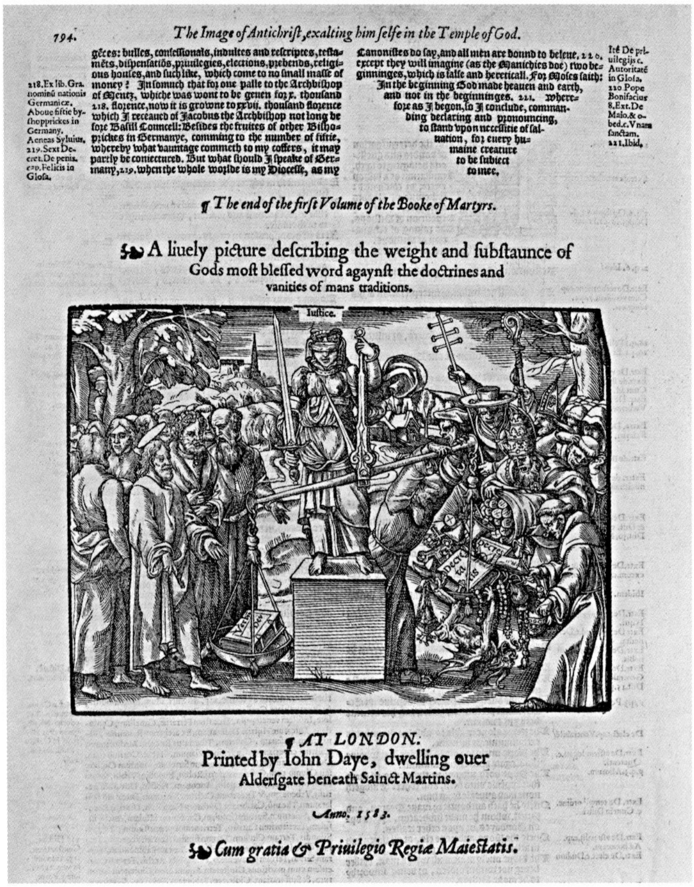
194. The Image of Antichrist, exalting him selfe in the Temple of God.

gēces: bulles, confessionals, indultes and rescriptes, testamēts, dispensatiōs, priuilegies, elections, prebends, religious houses, and such like, which come to no small masse of money? Insomuch that for one palle to the Archbishop of Mentz, whiche was wont to be geuen for x. thousand 218. florence, now it is growne to xxvij. thousand florence which I receaued of Iacobus the Archbishop not long before Basill Councell: Besides the fruites of other Bishoprickes in Germanye, comming to the number of fiftie, whereby what vauntage commeth to my coffers, it may partly be coniectured. But what should I speake of Germany, 219. when the whole worlde is my Diocesse, as my Canonistes do say, and all mē are bound to beleue, 220. except they will imagine (as the Manichies doe) two beginninges, which is false and hereticall. For Moses saith: In the beginning God made heauen and earth, and not in the beginninges. 221. Wherefore as I begon, so I conclude, commanding declaring and pronouncing, to stand vpon necessitie of saluation, for euery humaine creature to be subiect to mee.

218. Ex lib. Grauominū nationis Germanicæ. Aboue fiftie byshoppricks in Germany. Aeneas Syluius. 219. Sext Decret. De penis. cap. Felicis in Glosa.

Itē De priuilegijs c. Autoritatē in Glosa. 220 Pope Bonifacius 8. Ext. De Maio. & obed. c. Vnam sanctam. 221. Ibid.

¶ The end of the first Volume of the Booke of Martyrs.

A liuely picture describing the weight and substaunce of Gods most blessed word agaynst the doctrines and vanities of mans traditions.

¶ AT LONDON.
Printed by Iohn Daye, dwelling ouer Aldersgate beneath Sainct Martins.

Anno. 1583.

Cum gratia & Priuilegio Regiæ Maiestatis.

3 'A lively picture describing the weight and substance of God's most blessed word against the doctrines and vanities of mans traditions.' Woodcut from John Foxe, *Actes and Monuments* (the 'Book of Martyrs'), London, 1583 edn, vol. 1, p. 794

ground is quite damaged, the figures on the left can be identified as a monk and a bishop attempting to add their weight to tip the scale against the Bible. It might seem extraordinary that in late Elizabethan England traditional religious imagery, familiar from devotional altarpieces of the pre-Reformation past, was newly created and displayed alongside a Protestant allegory emphasising the superiority of the Word of God over man-made instruments of worship. The religious iconography is unchanged from medieval tradition. Even the form of the mantelpiece recalls medieval art; the three panels resemble the conventional triptych arrangement of devotional altarpieces. Yet the new, reformed context for this imagery is indicated by the fact that the principal, central position – traditionally occupied by a cultic image such as the Crucifixion, Virgin and Child or the Trinity – is replaced with an emblem of Protestantism.

In fact, the origin of this pictorial allegory strengthens the Protestant credentials of the chimneypiece. It seems that the imagery is adapted from a woodcut first published in John Daye's *Whole Works of William Tyndale* of 1573 but also used in the 1576 edition of Foxe's 'Book of Martyrs' and subsequent editions (Fig. 3). The scales and the figures on the right of the scene are faithful to the woodcut. Damage to the upper section of the painted panel means that no figure of Justice is legible but that she was originally included in the composition is suggested by the linear shape recorded faithfully by the twentieth-century artist, which compares with the position of Justice's sword in the woodcut. The present location of the panels is not known but the appearance and content of this Elizabethan chimneypiece as recorded in the drawing demonstrate that traditional religious imagery was not incompatible with reformed faith. Rather, this work represents a fusion of old and new iconographies. Traditional religious imagery is not avoided, censored or replaced; instead, it is cast in a supporting role to the central message of Protestant supremacy. In this way the Uckfield chimneypiece usefully introduces the central theme of this study – the ways in which traditional religious imagery could be employed to support and advance the Protestant faith. This overmantel also establishes a connection between imagery in domestic decoration and Protestant printed texts; the nature and implications of this relationship is a theme explored throughout this book.

The chimneypiece from Uckfield is just one example of a great body of decorative art with religious subject matter created during the century or so after the Protestant religious settlements of England and Scotland. From about 1560 to 1660 it was common for scenes and characters from the Old and New Testaments to be painted, carved and sculpted on the walls and ceilings of manor houses and the town and rural houses built by merchants and prosperous farmers. Large-scale surface decoration still survives *in situ* in hundreds of houses dating from this period and many more examples of now lost work are recorded in antiquarian literature and in the archives of the National Monuments Record Centre and the Royal Commission on the Ancient and Historical Monuments of Scotland. Biblical imagery also adorned a range of moveable items, such as furniture, textiles and ceramics; the extant objects are now dispersed across museum and private collections. It is clear that what survives today represents only a fraction of a once ubiquitous trend in interior decoration. If such material was ubiquitous it was also prominent; it adorned significant spaces in the grander rooms, as well as high-status fittings, furniture and objects designed for conspicuous display in specific locations within the interior.

It is striking that this fashion for large-scale religious imagery coincided with the aftermath of the Reformations in England and Scotland, a period of ongoing debate and controversy about the status and role of religious paraphernalia in Protestant culture. Histories of the period often cast early Protestantism as an austere religion of the word and relate how its proponents were obsessively anxious about the corrupting power of the image. Yet the existence of this decorative art as a body of material demonstrates that traditional religious iconography remained an important, and highly visible, part of reformed culture. Why biblical imagery should become popular in domestic houses at a time when attempts to control access and response to religious imagery resulted in the destruction of comparable art in churches is something of a conundrum.

The fact that these new religious images were created for a domestic setting is significant because for the most part it was images in churches and other devotional contexts that excited reformers and thus became the focus of official censure and action. As I discuss in detail in Chapter 1, attitudes towards images fluctuated over the course of the period 1560 to 1660 and the picture is further complicated by the great diversity of opinion on this issue across the religious spectrum. In terms of official policy, there was an initial clampdown on images and associated devotional paraphernalia in churches in the 1560s[2] followed by renewed pressure on images as evidence of popish sympathies under the threat of a Catholic uprising in the 1570s and 80s.[3] The advent of the Stuart dynasty left official policy unchanged but during the first decades of the seventeenth century a degree of acceptance of certain religious images emerged under the influence of an anti-Calvinist trend of opinion which favoured the re-introduction of some aspects of traditional ceremony to church worship.[4] A limited but significant resurgence of religious art was achieved through the so-called Laudian reforms of the 1630s when many parish churches were 'beautified' with traditional imagery; this then contributed to a counter-wave of hostility towards images among stricter Protestants which culminated in an official campaign by Parliament in the 1640s to remove and deface not only the recently introduced fixtures and imagery but also surviving remnants from the pre-Reformation past. However, all but the very strictest prohibitions were selective; only those images that obviously contravened the Second Commandment by representing the Godhead or were tainted by association with devotional activity were targeted. In short, therefore, there was no consistent line of development and many degrees of opinion on the matter of church art. There was, however, a considerable degree of unanimity on the status of images in secular contexts. The consensus among Protestant theologians within the Established Church was that biblical imagery was permissible outside churches and other places of worship, as long as it was used only for civil, rather than religious, purposes. This view was expressed even by William Perkins, the Puritan divine, who declared in an oft-quoted passage: 'We hold the historical use of images to be good and lawful: and that is, to represent to the eye the acts of histories, whether they be human or divine; and thus we think the histories of the Bible may be painted in private places'.[5] Yet, while it is evident that such imagery was acknowledged to be permissible in a domestic context, it is not clear why it was desirable. How could Protestant patrons reconcile the making and viewing of this imagery with cultural anxieties about the dangers of religious images as an affront to God and a worldly diversion from pure devotion and habits of thought? This and other questions surrounding the purpose of religious imagery in reformed, domestic space, how it was viewed, how it was understood and how it was treated by its audience have yet to be addressed.

My book engages with these questions to provide the first detailed account of the nature, meaning and function of religious imagery in the decorative arts of post-Reformation Britain. It not only documents and collates the body of material evidence but also analyses its significance in relation to the religious and cultural context of the period by focusing on practices of religious observance within the 'godly' household. The term 'godly' is here used in its broadest sense to mean 'pious' or 'devout'.[6] While some of the patrons for this kind of imagery can accurately be described as members of 'the godly' – a contemporary term adopted by more zealous Protestants in preference to the derogatory label of 'puritan' – the evidence suggests that most individuals responsible for commissioning this type of decoration were members of the confirming majority who accepted the version of Protestantism adopted by the state.[7] Although the decorative art that forms the subject of this study is here presented as a body of material representing a widespread fashion for religious imagery in the home, this 'fashion' was never co-ordinated but represents a range of responses to the processes of religious change and consolidation and reflects different varieties of Protestant thought, which diverged more and more as the period progressed. The various examples of work discussed here were no doubt designed to fulfil a range of specific, as well as general, functions to cater to the individual beliefs and needs of particular patrons and families. It appears, however, that this sort of imagery was most popular among members of society who wanted to appear and to act as good and pious Christians within the official religion.

THE VIEW FROM ART HISTORY

The subtitle to this book, 'Religious Art in Post-Reformation Britain', might raise a few eyebrows. It is generally thought that 'religious art' did not exist in Britain in the period 1560–1660 and certainly not as any significant category. Standard art-historical accounts relate how the Reformation of the 1530s and 40s caused an almost immediate halt to the production of religious art and the destruction of all existing religious images. As the Tate Gallery's *Companion to British Art* published in 2001 explains:

> the onset of the Dissolution of the monasteries . . . inaugurated more than a hundred years of intermittent iconoclasm, the destruction of religious art and artefacts in England . . . The effect of this destruction and of the dismantling of Roman Catholic authority and liturgy which initiated it on the visual arts in England can hardly be exaggerated. Some commentators estimate that up to ninety-five per cent of religious art was destroyed by 1650 . . . The battle over imagery commenced and left a deep scar on the canvas of British art history.[8]

This 'deep scar on the canvas of art history' is vividly evoked by material evidence such as defaced paintings and sculptures, the result of Reformation iconoclasm. The gouges scraped into the painted surface of the late fifteenth-century panel depicting the Virgin from an Annunciation scene in the Victoria and Albert Museum (Fig. 4) amply testifies to the hostility felt by reformers towards this kind of potential idol. However, iconoclasm is only one part of the story of the impact of the Reformation on the visual arts in Britain. Although the subject of iconoclasm has received a considerable amount of attention in the historiography of the period and has captured the public imagination, recent scholarship has begun to detail the complex processes of survival, censorship, assimilation, modification and innovation which resulted in the emergence of a specifically Protestant visual culture.[9] Important studies have focused on particular categories of imagery or object, including buildings; print; portraits; funeral monuments and other visual culture associated with the death ritual; ceremony; and the form, decoration and use of private chapels.[10] Yet evidence for religious art has been harder to find and has reinforced the impression that it was incompatible with reformed ideology.

A few religious pictures produced during the Elizabethan period, such as the *Allegory of Man* of about 1596, have received some degree of attention, largely because of their high-profile presence in national collections (Fig. 5). Yet this painting, which includes a scene of the resurrected Christ in heaven, is usually cast as something of an anomaly. Commentary on this work explains that British paintings of religious subjects are rare because Protestant unease about images meant it would have been highly controversial to display religious paintings.[11] This suggests that there was little demand for art with religious subject matter. In fact, the rarity of this kind of painting can be explained in relation to its medium rather than its subject matter. Paintings in oil on panel were not widely produced in early modern Britain, partly because there was a shortage of native artisans skilled in this craft. Nevertheless, during the same period an enormous amount of religious imagery in a range of other media was produced. This includes the so-called 'decorative arts' such as wall painting, plasterwork, carved wood and painted panelling, as well as crafted objects such as textile hangings, furniture, cushions, embroideries, silverware and ceramics. That this body of material has not yet received sustained scholarly attention in relation to its historical context reflects the traditional prejudices of the discipline of art history.

An overwhelming emphasis on the significance and influence of Renaissance art in Italy, coupled with a disciplinary bias towards the so-called 'high arts' of painting in oils and sculpture in stone, has directed the activities of art historians away from the decorative arts of Britain, especially the crafts produced in and for a domestic setting. Traditionally preoccupied with the history of 'great' art in grand settings, conventional art-historical accounts mourn the demise of church art and focus instead on the court and elite culture for evidence of artistic inspiration and innovation. Outside the academy, work into the decora-

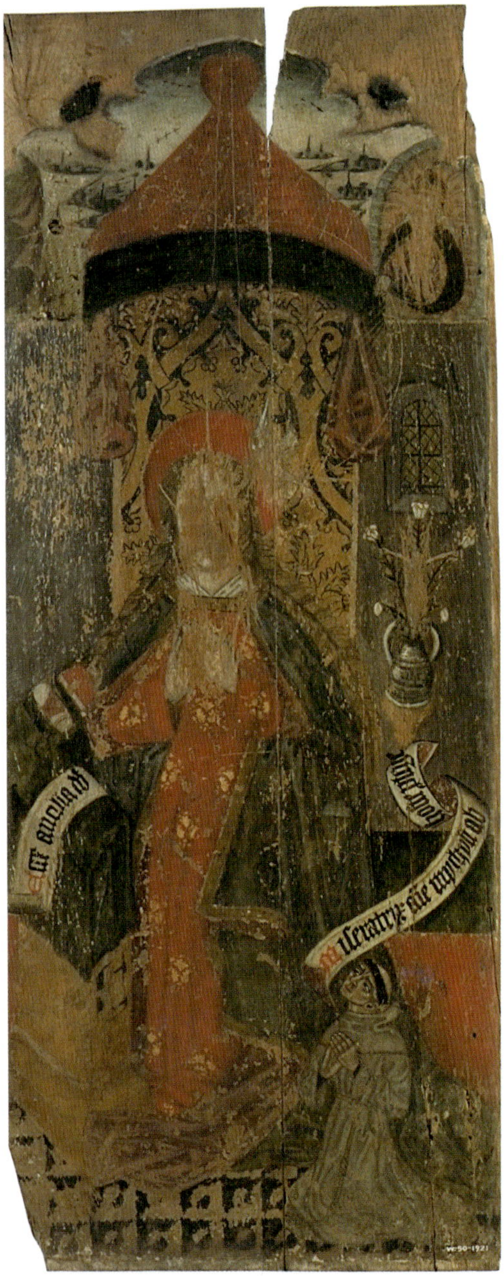

4 The Virgin from an Annunciation scene, 1470–90, oil on oak panel. Victoria and Albert Museum, London. Notice how the iconoclast has defaced only specific areas: the face and hands of the Virgin and the figure of Christ crucified on the right. The face of the figure near the top right has also been defaced; this might represent God the Father

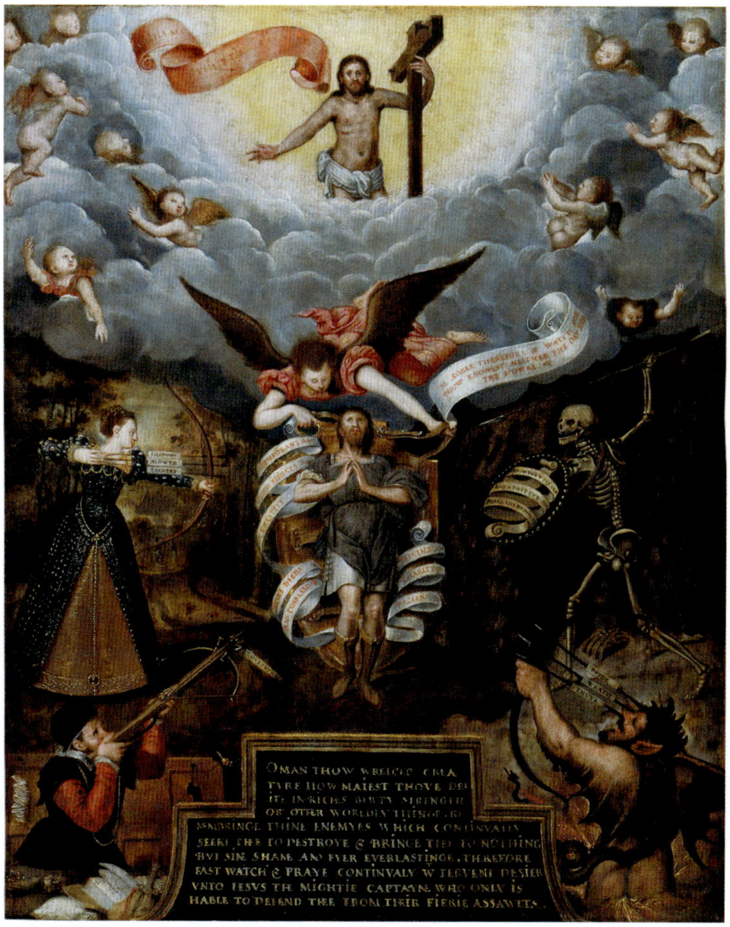

5 British School, *Allegory of Man*, 1596 or after, oil on wood, Tate Collection, London. Although this sort of oil painting on panel is rare in post-Reformation England, the religious subject matter (including Christ in Heaven) was not incompatible with reformed thought as long as the image was not abused by worship

tive arts has been conducted mainly by museum practitioners and this has shaped the nature of research. Most significantly, decorative art is generally catalogued, studied and published according to museological categorisation by media and technique so that ceramics, textiles, silverware and furniture are each considered as a distinct group of objects.[12] This has prevented an overall comparison of recurring themes and subject matter across the decorative arts and so, once again, no clear overview of the impact of the Reformation on the wider visual culture has emerged.

With an absence of art-historical publications on this subject, the idea that post-Reformation Protestantism was a barren or austere culture of the Word has dominated the historiography of the Reformation in England and Scotland. This view was cemented in the mid-1980s when Patrick Collinson put forward his brilliantly catchy but ultimately flawed notion of iconophobia.[13] According to Collinson's original formulation, between the first and second generation of Protestant reformers in England there was a shift from iconoclasm, 'characterised by the attack on unacceptable images but consistent with the enjoyment of good images', to 'iconophobia', defined as 'the total repudiation of all images' irrespective of either subject matter or context. This momentous shift in Protestant mentality was dated to around the year 1580. Furthermore, this transformation was not restricted to the radical wing of English Protestants but, so Collinson argued, swept across the population as a whole to create 'a society suffering from severe visual anorexia.'[14]

It could be argued that one of the reasons that this concept of iconophobia has been so influential and still persists despite the publication of subsequent research which undermines its central premise is because the discipline of art history has itself been slow to acknowledge the existence and significance of visual art created outside the context of the church or the court.[15] Art historians have traditionally been somewhat sniffy about secular art produced lower down the social scale, which is generally dismissed as mere 'popular' or 'folk' art with little aesthetic or intellectual value. There are a few notable exceptions including James Ayres's *Domestic Interiors* which charts the evolution of design, fixtures and fittings.[16] Generally, it has taken a new wave of interdisciplinary interest in the domestic environment to draw attention to this context for the making and display of art and craft and to make connections with patterns of daily life, although it is perhaps fair to say that an interest in 'Renaissance' themes still dominates approaches to the study of the early modern domestic interior.[17]

POST-REFORMATION VISUAL CULTURE IN ENGLAND AND SCOTLAND

This study is concerned with the long post-Reformation period and begins in 1560. From that year onwards England and Scotland were, in effect, Protestant states. The Elizabethan Settlement of 1559 in England and the Scottish Confession of Faith approved in 1560 established reformed versions of church organisation and doctrine. Although the degree of unanimity between the English and Scottish Churches after 1559 is open to debate, it is fair to say that both settlements put forth broadly similar Calvinist-influenced tenets.[18] The processes of consolidation initiated in England in 1559 and Scotland in 1560 followed separate trajectories with distinct paces of change but, for the purposes of this book, the cultural impact of these processes can be seen to have encouraged similar responses in relation to the visual arts.

The particular form of Protestant visual culture that emerged in England and Scotland is especially evident after the union of the two crowns under James VI and I in 1603. A fashion in both countries for religious scenes in domestic decoration gained pace during the first decades of the seventeenth century and reached a peak in the period 1620–40. There was a decline in occurrences throughout Britain during the Civil War and interregnum which requires little explanation considering the social and economic instability of the period, which effectively called a halt to investment in domestic building. The cut-off point for this study is 1660 as the Restoration of Charles II inaugurated a new fashion for baroque style in the French manner. Nevertheless, in provincial areas older traditions endured so that an example of the Sacrifice of Isaac in a plasterwork ceiling at

Coalharbour Farm in Ham, Somerset, is dated 1679, long after such decoration would have been considered *démodé* in more courtly circles.

The shared characteristics of domestic decoration in England and Scotland during this period was no doubt partly a response to artistic influence from the Netherlands – in the form of imported printed imagery as well as the availability of skilled foreign craftsmen – combining with native traditions; this Netherlandish influence had a great impact on the architecture and decorative arts across Britain during the later Renaissance period.[19] It is also possible that the interest in religious subject matter as decoration in the home in both countries can be understood in relation to their religious settlements. The state religion of both countries adopted a relatively uncompromising position in relation to devotional art in churches but failed to resolve questions about the status and function of religious imagery in the wider culture. Meanwhile, official advice in both countries emphasised the central importance of religious observance in the domestic sphere. As Jane Dawson has observed: 'Most protestants in England and Scotland read the same key religious texts and, crucially, the same Bible. There was also considerable overlap in the personnel who spread religious ideas which helped to produce a common outlook.'[20] This common outlook, I suggest, contributed to a shared interest in decorating houses with religious imagery.

My argument is not, however, that the situation in Britain was completely distinct from that in other reformed countries. Indeed, it is possible to suggest that a connection between Protestantism and an emphasis on biblical themes in the decoration of houses was not restricted to Britain but extended throughout northern Europe. Andrew Morrall has shown how religious imagery used as decoration for domestic ceramics in sixteenth-century Europe connected with specific social rituals and reinforced the moral instruction central to the Protestant household. He explains that 'a very wide variety of biblical themes were used in large quantities throughout the sixteenth century by the potteries of the Rhineland'.[21] The objects produced by these potteries would have been exported throughout Europe.[22] Morrall's study focuses on drinking and dining rituals but he also suggests how an interest in biblical subjects extended to larger furnishings including the great tiled stoves found in the larger German households of the sixteenth century – a centrepiece equivalent to the fireplace in Britain. In the Protestant Netherlands the establishment of Calvinism as the official religion resulted in the plain church interiors with whitewashed walls familiar from the paintings of Pieter Saenredam, Emanuel de Witte and other specialists in this genre. Yet there was still a demand for paintings with religious subject matter for domestic display and stories from the Old and New Testaments were fairly common throughout the sixteenth and seventeenth centuries.[23] Given that England, Scotland and the Protestant Netherlands adopted Calvinist settlements and that Netherlandish style influenced the visual arts of Britain, it might be expected that all three countries would exhibit similar trends in interior decoration. However, despite sustained investigation I have found little extant evidence for a widespread fashion for fixed surface decoration incorporating religious imagery in Dutch houses of this period; perhaps the thriving market for paintings in oil meant that there was little demand for large-scale imagery in other media.[24] So while it seems that an interest in religious imagery for domestic display was common throughout reformed Europe, the forms in which this interest materialised responded to the particularities of the religious settlements, artistic traditions and domestic arrangements of different areas.

SOURCES: THE VISUAL AND MATERIAL EVIDENCE

The body of visual and material evidence that forms the primary focus of this study comprises roughly a hundred examples of fixed surface decoration (painting on walls and panelling, carved stone and wood, plasterwork) plus a range of moveable objects including furniture, ceramics and textiles. Some of the visual material discussed in this book will be familiar, having been documented in other studies, but other material is little known because it has only been described in relatively inaccessible sources such as antiquarian literature, regional society journals, or publications dedicated to a particular category of decorative art. Several works are published for the first time (certainly in modern times) yet the originality of this study is not in the documenting of individual examples but in analysing this wealth of fixtures and objects as part of the wider cultural context. Existing accounts of the decorative arts often serve to separate items from their original historical and physical context. Decorative art was never experienced in isolation but as part of the collection of objects, images and textures that made up the furnishings of a room, or suite of rooms, within a particular house. Choices made about such decoration responded to prevailing cultural fashions and expectations as well as the particular functions of specific rooms within the early modern house.

My interest in the original context for decorative art means that this study focuses on examples of fixed surface decoration which can be identified with a particular setting, house and owner. Unlike many of the smaller moveable items, decoration applied to the surface of walls and ceilings becomes part of the fabric of the building and is difficult to remove without considerable expense and inconvenience. The depiction of religious imagery on the surfaces of walls and ceilings therefore represents a significant decision on behalf of the patron that the chosen subject matter will remain appropriate or fashionable. Given the religious turbulence of the long Reformation period, it is perhaps surprising that religious subject matter should be depicted using decorative media that constituted a more or less permanent addition to a building and could not easily be modified to accommodate the winds of change. The types of houses in which such material can be found ranges from the greater country houses belonging to the 'elite' class of nobility (such as Hardwick Hall and Bolsover Castle); the country houses of the gentry (Montacute, Chastleton, Little Moreton); town houses built or renovated by prosperous merchants or tradesmen (the urban elite) such as 90 High Street in Oxford or 5 Widemarsh Street in Hereford; and larger farmhouses owned by prosperous yeomen ('The Batch' in Sidbury, Shropshire; 'The Springs' in Meadle, Buckinghamshire). In general, however, biblical subject matter is found mainly in the houses of the gentry and so-called 'middling sort', by which is meant the more prosperous merchants, citizens and yeomanry of the middle class.[25] These members of society contributed to a widespread 'building boom' in the period covered by this study, which included the construction of new and fashionable dwellings as well as the extension and modification of existing buildings. This building activity is the subject of Chapter 2. A rise in the amount of interior decoration created across a much broader range of housing reflects the increased prosperity and swelled ranks of the middle classes but why biblical themes were favoured remains to be addressed.

It seems that elite patrons generally preferred figures and scenes from classical mythology as the subject for decoration in their houses. These patrons were also able to afford the most expensive medium of carved marble or alabaster. Architectural historians have focused to a large extent on these greater country houses built by the nobility and upper gentry and classical subject matter in the decorative arts has been interpreted as evidence for the influence of Renaissance ideals in Britain.[26] Yet the decoration of these houses was not typical. By focusing on the more humble houses owned by gentry, merchants and yeomen, this study draws attention to a group of lesser buildings, about which comparatively little is known, and a different set of interests.

Much of this fixed surface decoration is still *in situ* in historic houses in private ownership or in the hands of a heritage organisation. This creates various problems in relation to access, security and privacy and I am greatly indebted to the various owners who have been extraordinarily generous in granting me and my camera access to their homes. In some cases I have not disclosed the location of decoration out of respect for the privacy of the property owner. The decoration that survives in place is probably just a small percentage of the amount created; much has been lost over the centuries as fashions changed and before the introduction of building regulations limited the 'improvement' of dwellings and insisted on the preservation of earlier material. In the twentieth century a thriving trade in architectural salvage might have encouraged the preservation of material but has resulted in fixtures such as chimneypieces or overmantels being sold off and re-installed at unrelated properties or in museums.[27] Accurate documentation of such movements is rarely kept and it has been no small task to trace either the original location or the current whereabouts of some items.

As well as being moved, re-installed (sometimes in odd locations) or destroyed, the appearance of surviving material has often been altered considerably from its original condition, through later 'restoration', general wear and tear or creative embellishment. The Victorians enthusiastically adapted surviving material, especially carved wooden panels, by incorporating fragments of earlier pieces within more extravagant confections. Much wall painting has been 'restored', sometimes I suspect with a permanent marker and felt-tip pens. The over-painting or resurfacing of wall painting, plasterwork and carving over several centuries means that it is necessary to be careful in making judgements about the original treatment or appearance of the surface.

My interest here is on the native production of decorative art, that is, work produced within Britain, though not necessarily by native craftsmen (indeed, the names of craftsmen where known often indicate northern European origins or descent). I have excluded, for the most part, imported objects in order to contain the parameters of the study and because moveable items are harder to contextualise in relation to specific locations and the beliefs of the patron. I am less interested in 'shop-bought' goods than decoration and objects made to order for identifiable locations. Most of the moveable items included here such as delftware chargers or woven items such as hangings or cushions include the initials of a patron indicating a specific commission rather than being speculatively made. While I focus on native production, I acknowledge the influence of foreign style and iconography disseminated through prints, through the training and skills of émigré artisans and through the direct exposure to fashionable imported crafts. In larger households wares produced by local craftsmen would have been displayed alongside more exotic imported crafts and the dialogue between different objects, textures, styles and motifs must have created a certain kind of visual dynamic.

CONTEXTUALISING THE EVIDENCE: HISTORY AND METHOD

This monograph is in no way meant to serve as a comprehensive or exhaustive survey of British decorative art of the sixteenth and seventeenth centuries with religious subject matter. My purpose is not to produce a catalogue of extant examples but to analyse what this 'fashion' reveals about the cultural values and practices of the society that produced it. In order to support my claim that this trend was widespread across Britain, I have plotted on a map the geographical locations for the fixed surface decoration mentioned in this book (Fig. 6). This map shows how examples of decorative art with religious subject matter can be found in most of the counties of England and Scotland but it also indicates important variations in the dates and media of extant work across the various regions. These regional variations are the result of a multitude of factors, including greater quantities of surviving material in rural areas which have experienced less building development. I think there are two key factors that account for the spread of examples shown here: one is methodological and results from my research strategy, the other is historical and relates to craft practice. I shall consider each in turn.

Firstly, the spread of material plotted on the map is patchy because the evidence to identify the existence and location of material is patchy. One of the challenges of this project was to overcome the logistical and methodological difficulties associated with the study of such a broad-ranging, disparate and under-researched body of material. In the early stages of my research I made use of the Pevsner *Buildings of England* series, the reports of the RCHME and RCAHMS, the *Country Life* archive, antiquarian literature, regional society journals and word of mouth. I have followed up references to examples wherever I have come across them but my approach has not been systematic enough to scour each county in turn and I have paid much greater attention to some areas where abundant material survives and neglected some counties entirely. That is not to say that material does not exist in those areas, just that I am not aware of them. Part of this is due to the un-

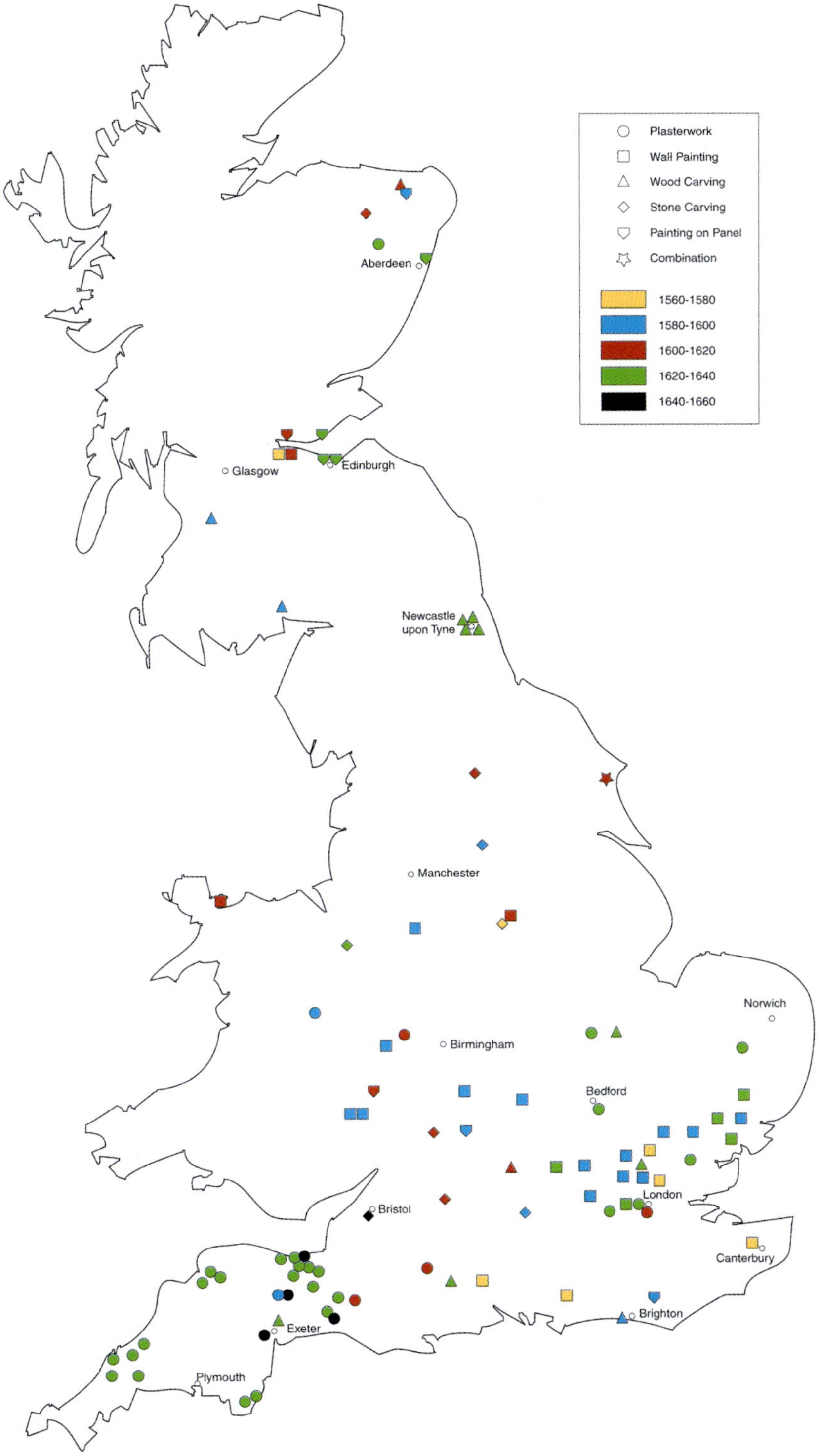

6 Map showing the locations of domestic buildings with interior decoration mentioned in this book. This illustrates the original locations, where known

evenness of data across the various Pevsner volumes, an invaluable resource to identify or verify the existence and location of interior decoration. There is considerable disparity across the original volumes as to the amount of detail provided for decorative fixtures, especially work that predates the eighteenth century. The updated editions usually provide much fuller and richer information about the appearance of interiors, although the most comprehensive coverage of the latest editions is not yet available for every county.

In addition to these sources, I have relied on some exhaustive, micro-scale studies of region and media by other scholars, which has contributed to concentrations of examples in particular areas. Wall painting in Essex and in the counties of the Welsh Marches has been the subject of studies by Muriel Carrick and Kathryn Davies respectively.[28] Wall painting in Hertfordshire is the subject of a meaty article by E. Clive Rouse.[29] A detailed survey and catalogue of decorative painting in Scotland by Michael Bath introduced me to many of the examples there.[30] The counties of the West Country have been a particular focus of my own research, which has built on and extended earlier studies of plasterwork in the region including John and Jane Penoyre's study of plasterwork in Somerset.[31] Finally, and most significantly, my knowledge of the extant material across the counties of England owes a great deal to Anthony Wells-Cole's comprehensive and meticulous study of the influence of continental prints on art and decoration in Elizabethan and Jacobean England.[32] His identification of a Newcastle-based wood carving workshop has resulted in a cluster of examples there.

Another reason for the clusters on the map is that different crafts flourished in different regions and at different times. This accounts for certain trends across the geographical range and date span covered by this study. I should point out that craft practice is not the focus of this book; I am less concerned with the processes of production than the 'social life', or functions, of decorative imagery once created. But to understand these trends in media and date, it is necessary to provide a brief overview of craft organisation and operation.

CRAFT PRACTICE

While much of the decorative art discussed and illustrated here might seem crude and unsophisticated to modern aesthetic tastes – Pevsner often referred disparagingly to the examples he recorded in the *Buildings of England* as 'rustic' – it represents the professional crafts of early modern Britain and was created by skilled artisans regulated by various craft guilds. In London these craft guilds were usually highly specialised and fiercely territorial as the sheer number of craftsmen active in the capital put pressure on trade and encouraged the rigorous defence of prerogatives. The records of the Painter-Stainers' Company of London, who were responsible for painting on solid surfaces and on cloth, document prolonged disputes during the seventeenth century with the Heralds at the College of Arms and with the Plasterers. The Heralds complained that Painters were encroaching on their turf by painting coats of arms while the Plasterers complained that the Painter-Stainers were stealing their trade by applying colour to plastered walls and ceilings.[33] Most cities could not support such specialised guilds and so crafts that were more or less allied banded together to create companies of several trades. In Shrewsbury, for example, was the 'Company of Saddlers, Painters, Plumbers, Glaziers, Lorimers [makers of intricate metal pieces such as for a horse's bridle], Fuysters [the ancient name for Carpenters] and Spurriers'.[34] In Salisbury in 1617 a new Charter established the 'Companye of the Joyners, Whellers, Worsteed Makers, Bookbinders, Carpenters, Millwrightes, Coopers, Free Masons, Rough Masons, Paynters, Instrument Makers, Ropers, Turners, Saweyers, and Bellowe-makers'. Despite this catch-all organisation for the building trades, competition between the crafts led to numerous disputes including quarrels between the carpenters and painters and the carpenters and joiners.[35]

Clusters of material in a given area can also be explained by the existence of regional centres for specific crafts. Bristol was a centre of production for carved limestone chimneypieces; only one as far as I am aware is still *in situ*, in the lodge built in about 1590 on the Colston estate in Bristol (now known as Red Lodge). This early (Elizabethan) example does not include biblical imagery but later examples from the mid-seventeenth century include religious subject matter; one dated 1670 has a simple, shallow relief carving of the Sacrifice of Isaac with the arms of Sir Robert Cann, who was mayor of Bristol in 1662 and 1675. It is said to have been removed from 'a house in Bristol'. The present whereabouts of this chimneypiece is not known and the only record of its appearance is an old illustration provided in C. J. Charles's *Old English Interiors* of 1919.[36] Another carved chimneypiece associated with this Bristol workshop represents a remarkable adaptation of the ancient iconography of the Weighing of Souls, now installed in the great hall of Sutton Place in Surrey; a full discussion is reserved until the final pages of this book. It seems that Yorkshire was another centre for stone carving in the late sixteenth and early seventeenth centuries; examples illustrated here include the chimneypiece in the great chamber of Fountains Hall and that in the great hall at Burton Agnes depicting the parable of the Wise and Foolish Virgins (both about 1610). At Heath Old Hall, another carved stone chimneypiece, originally in the great chamber, depicts the Death of Jezebel, illustrating 2 Kings 9 (Fig. 7). The work is dated 1584 and from a Protestant perspective can be understood to celebrate the downfall of an evil ruler who led her people into idolatry and immorality.[37]

A wood carving workshop in the Newcastle area was identified by Wells-Cole and is associated with the carved woodwork at Burton Agnes and a group of overmantels salvaged from houses in Newcastle.[38] One chimneypiece allegedly from the Mansion House in Newcastle was moved to Clervaux Castle and then sold from there in about 1980. The two main panels depicting the Adoration and the Presentation in the Temple are now in private collections but are illustrated in *Art and Decoration*.[39] Another, originally in Derwentwater House in Newcastle and now at Haughton Castle in Northumberland, contains scenes of Cain and Abel and David and Goliath. The same workshop is responsible for the overmantel dated 1636 in the Merchant Adventurers Hall in the Guildhall in Newcastle. Two further allegorical overmantels are associated with this workshop; one from a merchant's house on Sandhill (later the Beehive Inn) includes a group of Lot and his Daughters while the other, now at Chipchase Castle in Northumberland,

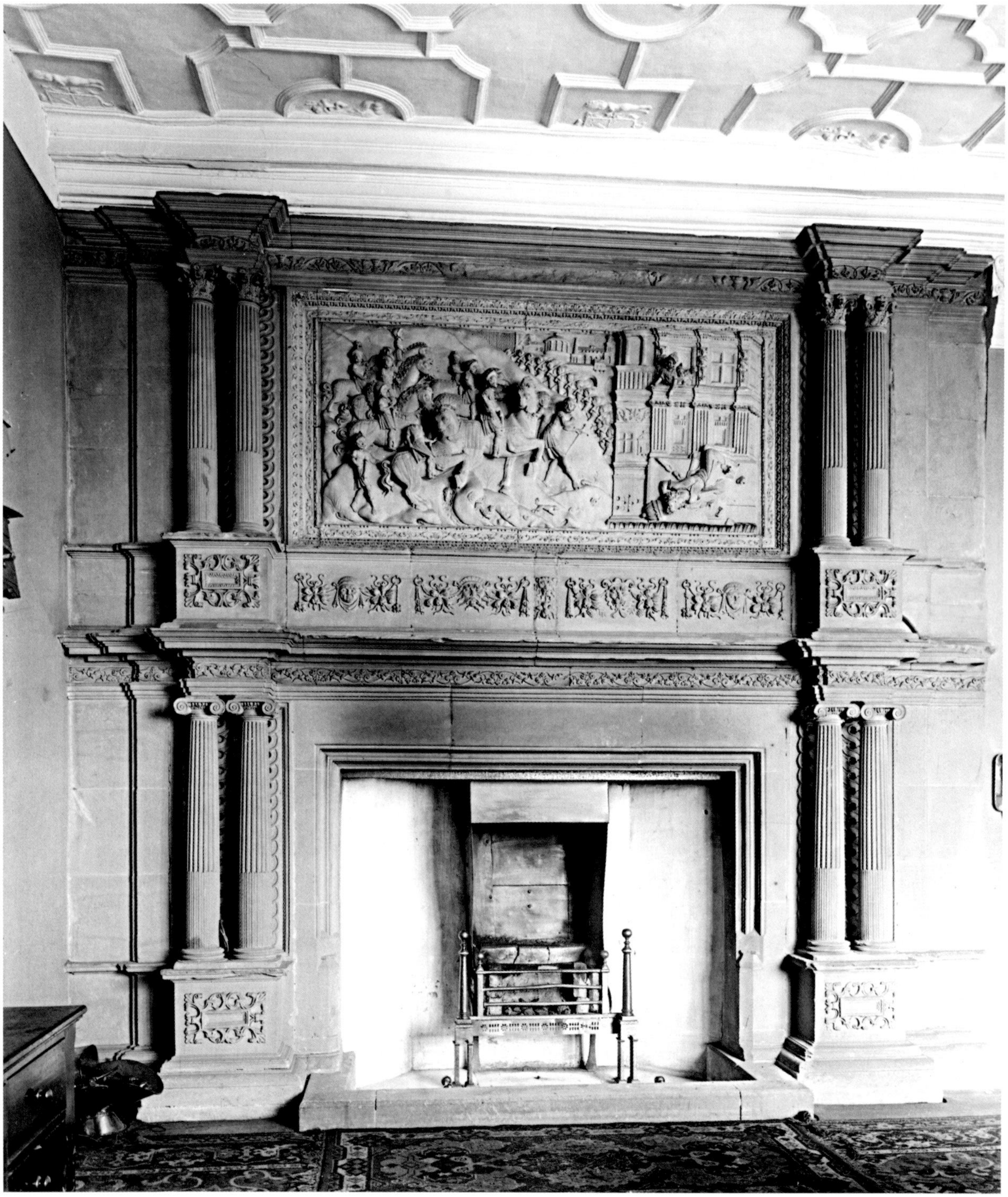

7 The Death of Jezebel, carved stone chimneypiece from Heath Old Hall, Yorkshire, now at Hazlewood Castle Hotel, dated 1584. This image of the archetypal 'pride before a fall' depicts the downfall of an idolatrous queen, which suggests that it may have had political as well as religious significance

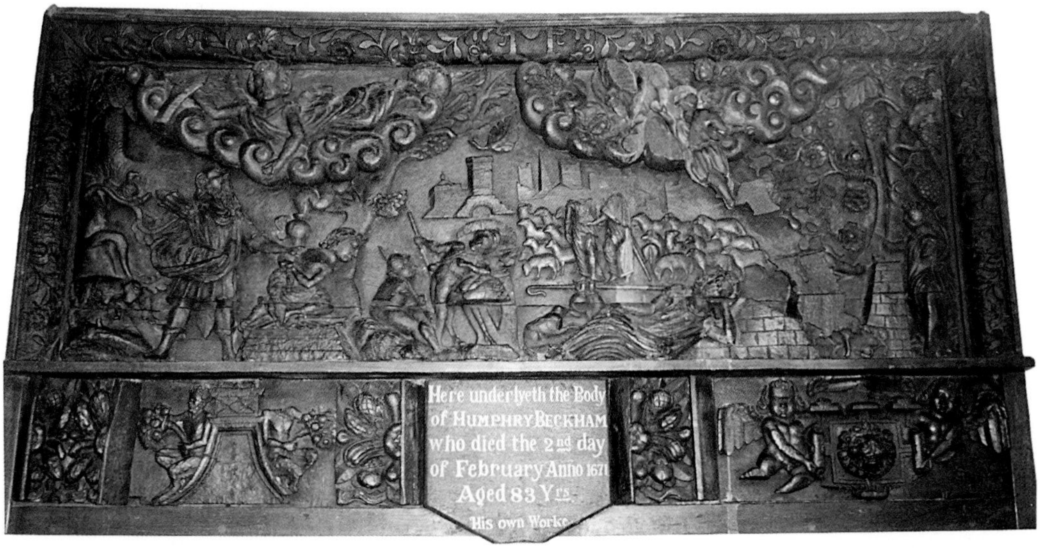

8 Memorial to Humphrey Beckham, carved wood panel with scenes from Genesis, c. 1630–40. St Thomas's Church, Salisbury. This panel carved by Beckham was probably originally intended as a domestic fireplace overmantel

depicts an allegory of the passing of time. Another wood carving workshop was centred on Salisbury. This provides one of the few occasions when extant decoration can be connected with the name of a particular craftsman. In St Thomas's Church in Salisbury is a carved wood panel with an inscription identifying the panel as a memorial to Humphrey Beckham, who died, aged 83, in 1671. The panel, which depicts several scenes from Genesis, is described as 'his Owne Work' (Fig. 8). The rectangular form and size of the panel suggests that it was originally intended as a fireplace overmantel and probably dates from the 1630s or 40s. Humphrey Beckham was a chamberlain and warden of the Joiners' Company early in the seventeenth century, as was his brother John. Presumably, they were members of the same workshop. Based on this identifiable example of Humphrey's work it is possible to attribute the chimneypiece at 8 Queen Street in Salisbury, which includes a scene of the Sacrifice of Isaac, to him or his workshop (see Fig. 152).[40]

The abundance of plasterwork in the counties of the West Country (mainly Cornwall, Devon and Somerset) is often associated with the so-called 'Abbott family' of plasterers from Frithelstock in Devon. However, the only supporting documentary evidence about a plasterer by the name of Abbott relates to one John Abbott (1639–1727) who was active in the second half of the seventeenth century. The attribution of plasterwork of Elizabethan and Jacobean date in the region to John Abbott's father or grandfather is now accepted as a commonplace but it turns out that the evidence for this attribution is flawed. In the Exeter Record Office is a curious manuscript book of crude plasterwork designs once owned by John Abbott.[41] For many years this manuscript was described as a working pattern book of designs added to and passed down from father to son over three generations in the Abbott family of plasterers.[42] This thesis has been overturned by Michael Bath who analysed the watermarks in the book and found that its pages were manufactured in the 1650s.[43] Bath re-positioned the Abbott book as a 'copy book' whereby all its contents were copied into it by the plasterer John Abbott in the 1650s or 60s. This calls into question the attribution of plasterwork in the region to John Abbott's ancestors and no other evidence has come to light to confirm the identities of local craftsmen active prior to the mid-seventeenth century. From the wide date span and the considerable variation in style and quality across the region, it seems clear that a number of separate workshops and craftsmen were active in various parts of the West Country during the late sixteenth century and the first half of the seventeenth century.

Essex, Hertfordshire, Herefordshire and Oxfordshire are particularly rich in Tudor wall painting with some examples stretching into the seventeenth century. Extant wall painting is not confined to these areas but a concentration of examples there might reflect the existence of particularly active and prolific workshops, or the lack of available craftsmen in other trades.[44] Finally, the art of large-scale decorative painting on wooden panels flourished in Scotland throughout this period. Michael Bath has documented examples dating from the early sixteenth century through to the mid-1600s and, as he points out, the use of this particular medium makes the Scottish tradition somewhat exceptional.[45] The art of plasterwork seems to have been employed in Scotland somewhat later than in England and although both crafts were employed at some sites, figurative work in plaster is rare.[46] Perhaps the high incidence of decorative painting results from the absence of plasterers or carvers able to provide an alternative medium for figurative work.

Another issue to address is that different crafts were popular at different periods across the date span. While the interest in biblical subject matter remains constant, there are dips and peaks in the quantity and nature of decorative art produced at various intervals. Most of the examples I have recorded of biblical imagery in surface decoration prior to 1590 are in the medium of wall painting in England. This reflects the fact that in the second half of the sixteenth century the most common forms of decoration were the associated crafts of wall painting and painted cloths (and possibly printed wares). Unfortunately, all are subject to a high rate of deterioration. For members of society outside the elite there was little choice since no other affordable forms of surface decoration existed that could accommodate complex figurative iconography. Wall painting and painting on cloth were allied crafts, executed by the same body of craftsmen, but wall painting has endured considerably better than the more fragile medium of painted cloth. Those cloths that survive can rarely be connected with a specific location. It seems that the fashion for painting on walls and cloth declined after about 1600, although Stow's observation in his *Survey of London* of 1598 in relation to the Painter-Stainers Hall in Trinity Lane, 'for so of olde time were they called, but now that workemanship of stayning is departed out of use in England', probably exaggerates the extent of this decline even in the capital, and it endured for longer outside London.[47]

The waning of the fashion for painting directly on wall or cloth coincided with the development of other crafts. Most of the earlier large-scale pictorial images in plasterwork and wood carving date from the 1590s and incidences reach a peak during 1620–40. Native tapestry production was not established until the 1560s or 70s and it took time to expand the level of production, so that most extant examples date from the later sixteenth and seventeenth centuries. The art of figurative plasterwork, in particular, seems to have replaced wall painting as the most popular choice of décor for middle-class patrons. In a comprehensive analysis of the records of the London Plasterers' Company, Claire Gapper has noted:

> The years between 1609 and 1620 witnessed a phenomenal growth in the number of plasterers from 176 to 287, an increase of 63%. This rapid rise in the size of the company coincides with the emergence of the fashion for increasingly complex decorative plasterwork in domestic interiors and probably reflects the growing demand for craftsmen with the requisite skills.[48]

Thus, the development and expansion of certain crafts responded to an increased clientele of middle-class patrons as well as a shift in fashion (and the two factors are probably not unconnected). The art of plasterwork could be enjoyed by a new group of customers in the form of increasingly prosperous (but not rich) merchants such as Mark Hawkins, the builder of the Butterwalk in Dartmouth, Devon. Having decorated the interiors of his new houses with religious scenes in plasterwork (illustrated in later chapters), Hawkins over-stretched his resources and was forced to sell his newly built property. It is not difficult to understand why plasterwork, described as a 'cheap piece of magnificence' by Sir Henry Wotton in 1624,[49] should have been the form of decorative art favoured by patrons in this middling social group.

A final pattern or trend to note in relation to craft production is that while stories from the Old Testament were common throughout 1560–1660, New Testament subject matter before 1600 is rare and most examples date from 1610–40. This trend can perhaps be explained as a gradual subsidence of fears about the danger of idolatry and an emerging consensus about what imagery was deemed acceptable. As I describe in Chapter 3, some imagery in decorative art was copied from printed Protestant books, this provenance presumably underlining its permissibility. It is possible that the appearance of New Testament imagery in decorative art can be attributed to growing anti-Calvinist attitudes followed by the cultural influence of the so-called Laudian reforms under Charles I which encouraged a revival of some aspects of traditional church art and ceremony. However, it should not be assumed that all patrons for New Testament imagery were of high-church persuasion, as the more godly leanings of some individuals suggest that the opposite is true and this complicates the picture further. As I argue in Chapter 5, the idea that more 'sacred' imagery in the form of New Testament subject matter was avoided in the sixteenth century and revived in the first half of the seventeenth century is too simplistic and it is only possible to reconcile these shifts in emphasis with changes in religious policy if the functions such imagery served are understood. It is also the case that an increase in New Testament subject matter cannot be explained solely in relation to the religious climate but reflects a complex interplay of artistic, economic and social factors. More building activity and the artistic trends outlined above, including the greater availability of craftsmen with the requisite skills to execute figurative work and a greatly expanded clientele, facilitated a general rise in the quantity of material produced from 1600 to 1640, so a rise in occurrences of New Testament subject matter should be set within this more general increase in craft production.[50] The increase in New Testament subject matter might also reflect the greater availability and accessibility of printed imagery to serve as templates; this is another issue discussed in detail in Chapter 3.

THE PROCESSES OF DESIGN

The emphasis throughout this study is on the beliefs and intentions of the patron rather than on the artistry of craftsmen. It is assumed that the principal householder (usually male) was responsible for commissioning and defining the nature of decoration for his home. This is because what is known about craft practice in early modern Britain suggests that the patron, rather than the craftsman, defined the content and appearance of decorative art.[51] Craftsmen made work to order and followed the directions of their employers. Wells-Cole has established that craftsmen working in all media relied on European printed wares as a source for designs, motifs and iconography.[52] The reader is encouraged to consult his monograph alongside this study for information about the printed sources employed for works of decoration discussed here. Presenting additional discoveries about the printed sources used for decorative work is not a major concern of this book, although identifying such connections can be useful in assessing the intended function of the iconography once transferred to the walls and ceilings of domestic interiors. I suggest in Chapter 3 that the copying of imagery from the pages of English Protestant conduct manuals suggests that decoration was intended to serve an analogous function to these texts in promoting and directing Protestant piety within the domestic sphere.

It seems likely that patrons directed craftsmen to selected printed material to serve as a model for decorative designs. This reliance on printed material was no doubt partly a response to fashion – the most commonly pilfered material was in the mannerist style of Netherlandish art, which seems to have suited British tastes – but was also a necessity since craftsmen in Britain did not have access to training in draughtsmanship and so struggled to create figurative work without recourse to a template. There is evidence that craftsmen did not entirely understand the iconography they copied from prints. An example is the wall paintings from Stodmarsh Court, Kent, partly preserved in the Victoria and Albert Museum, where the monogrammed signature of the engraver, Virgil Solis, from within the print was duly copied into the painted version.[53]

In his discussion of the circumstances surrounding the building of Elizabethan and Jacobean country houses, Malcolm Airs describes how the usual procedures for the design and execution of building work involved a series of dialogues between the patron, surveyor (master mason), and various craftsmen and that drawings, called 'platts', based on these discussions were often produced for the patron to approve before beginning work.[54] Unfortunately, such platts for decorative art rarely survive and I have found none which relate to decoration with biblical subject matter. An explanation for this is provided by one extant platt in the archive of Longleat House. This is a pen and ink drawing with a design for a plaster ceiling, possibly for Ramsbury Hall in Wiltshire, and dates from about 1580–1601.[55] The design shows a geometric pattern marked out by ribs, with floral and fleur-de-lis motifs. At the centre of the design is a square box filled with handwriting, a message from the craftsman to the patron: 'Right honerable in this place did I mean to drawe my lordes armes But this plase is so troublesome unto me that I Can not do it unto my mind But y will work your honer this Pece of work that the lyk shall not be in England'. In other words, I cannot *draw* your coat of arms but I can *work* it in plaster.[56] It is also possible that the widespread use of printed sources eliminated the need for hand-drawn platts to delineate the proposed form and appearance of decoration, because patrons could simply direct the craftsmen to copy the print. While this is only speculation it does account for the apparent paucity of original designs for decorative art in the historical records.

References to payments for completed decorative art crop up in extant household account books from the period but the nature of this source means that entries are usually perfunctory and so rarely provide much insight into the nature and appearance of decoration or the processes surrounding its production. A notable exception is the account book kept by Sir Edward Pytts relating to the building of Kyre Park between 1588 and 1618, which provides an unusual amount of information surrounding the commission of two marble chimneypieces representing the stories of Susannah (from the Apocrypha) and Mars and Venus. This source records that Pytts hired a Dutch carver named 'Garrett Hollyman' (presumably Garret Hollemans, better known as a sculptor of monuments) to undertake the work and that several payments were made to Garret between March 1592 and July 1594, including £15 in total for the chimneypiece of Mars and Venus. It is clear from his record book that Pytts defined the subject and content of the decoration, including an inscription to accompany the story of Mars and Venus.[57] Although this reveals much about the circumstances surrounding decorative work of the highest quality for a wealthy client, the extent to which this can be taken as representative of the processes involved in crafts produced for members of the middle classes remains opaque.

SOURCES: PRINTED TEXTS

Despite the existence of a few manuscript sources to provide some evidence about the circumstances surrounding the making of decoration or the acquisition of decorative items, it is deeply frustrating that documentary evidence to suggest how people thought about, and responded to, decoration once it was installed in the home is distinctly lacking. We might expect historical sources such as letters and diaries to provide evidence of people's engagement with domestic furnishings but it seems this was a subject contemporaries rarely wrote about, at least in these contexts. Although few first-hand written documents have come to light to provide a context for the material evidence, how contemporaries might have engaged with domestic imagery can be assessed through printed sources. Contemporary literature is employed throughout this study to elucidate the meanings and significance of iconography. This includes scenarios and quotations from dramatic texts, although the theatrical context should make one cautious in making straightforward connections between staged situations and domestic environments in real life. Nevertheless, as Catherine Richardson has shown, ideas about the domestic environment as represented in dramatic texts played on the material and moral meanings of the early modern house as understood by contemporaries.[58]

My main textual source employed alongside the visual material is the genre of printed text dedicated to describing and advancing Protestant religious practice. This category of self-help manual was designed to aid the godly in the pursuit of 'correct' behaviour and thought on a daily, even hourly, basis. Their prescriptions are therefore concerned to a large extent with religious activities in the context of the home. The range of practices associated with religious observance within the post-Reformation household is a surprisingly little studied topic, with most attention focusing on the personal (often introspective) activities of Puritan individuals. My study is concerned with the more social or public practices involved in performing and supporting Protestant piety in a domestic context. To explore the connections between religious imagery in domestic decoration and prescribed forms of Protestant behaviour, my discussion incorporates extracts of advice from devotional and conduct literature. A key focus is the relationship between images in decorative art and spiritual activities, collective and individual, taking place within the home.

There is, however, a problem in attempting to connect the ideal modes of behaviour and thought as prescribed in Protestant literature with the real, lived experience of individuals on a daily basis. It cannot be assumed that the advice put forward in such texts reflected actual practice. However, the popularity of this genre of self-help religious manual suggests that many householders and pious individuals aspired to the ideal and it seems likely that the creation of decorative art formed part of concerted efforts to construct a pious identity, in the same way that buying printed conduct books expressed a dutiful commitment to prescribed modes of behaviour. There is evidence that the more godly householders attempted to act on such advice. The London lathe worker and Puritan Nehemiah Wallington (1598–1658) bought a copy of the popular manual *Of Domestical Duties* by William Gouge (first published in 1622) and consulted a range of other godly texts including John Dod and Richard Cleaver's influential *A Plaine and Familiar Exposition of the Ten Commandments* (1604 and many subsequent reprints). More to the point, Wallington's notebooks reveal how he put such advice into practice as, for example, when he drew up a list of '31 articles for my family for the reforming of our lives', to which family members and servants put their mark.[59] We might wonder if, once endorsed, the document was pinned up in the home as a rule and reminder. Thus, the fairly extreme patterns of religious behaviours recommended by these manuals filtered through society to be implemented with zeal by the hotter sort of Protestant. If the less zealous chose not to put all aspects of the advice literature into practice, the ideal provided a general framework of approved behaviour for dutiful householders to perform in part. Therefore, in the chapters that follow I suggest that religious imagery as decoration in the home can be understood to have served the same set of functions as Protestant devotional and conduct literature. That is, to help fashion and publicise a 'godly' identity, to place spiritual concerns at the heart of domestic life, to regulate behaviour and habits of thought and to prompt and facilitate pious meditation.

THE STRUCTURE OF THIS BOOK

The final task of this introduction is to outline the structure of the book. Chapters 1 and 2 set out the cultural context in which the fashion for religious imagery in domestic decoration developed. The first chapter examines the religious changes of the period and how this affected attitudes to images and practices surrounding them. It establishes the nature of the Reformation critique of the image and identifies those iconographies and objects that were outlawed by the mid-sixteenth century but it also describes the range of images considered broadly acceptable within mainstream Protestant culture and indicates the diversity of thought on this issue across the religious spectrum. Chapter 2 describes the nature of the building boom of the early modern period which encouraged those members of society with disposable income to invest in domestic decoration and furnishings as part of a general trend for the improvement of houses. It sets out the architectural developments of this period and describes how this influenced living standards and the social functions of sub-divided interior space. Chapter 3 synthesises the themes of the previous chapters by focusing on practices of Protestant piety within the domestic context. It establishes a connection between the spiritual activities involved in household religious observance and the nature of decoration in the principal areas of domestic space. This serves to introduce the largest chapter (4), the greater part of which is in the style of a 'virtual' tour through the public rooms of a typical gentry house: hall, parlour, staircase, great chamber, bed chamber and gallery. I explore the relationship between the functions of rooms within larger houses in England and Scotland and the character of the imagery that decorated them. The type of religious subject matter commonly employed in the surface decoration of these rooms is evoked through discussion of numerous examples of decorative art still *in situ* in historic buildings throughout Britain. This chapter also provides a brief overview of the range of moveable objects that were adorned with biblical stories and figures. In the last two chapters I suggest how the display of religious imagery in specific locations in the domestic interior might operate to affect thought and behaviour. Chapter 5 focuses on the decoration of fireplaces and interprets the significance of popular Old Testament iconography in relation to the practice of godly meditation. The final chapter is concerned with perception and response; it speculates about the psychological impact of the presence of large-scale religious imagery in the home to suggest that it could simultaneously be comforting (to offer spiritual 'protection') and discomforting (to regulate behaviour).

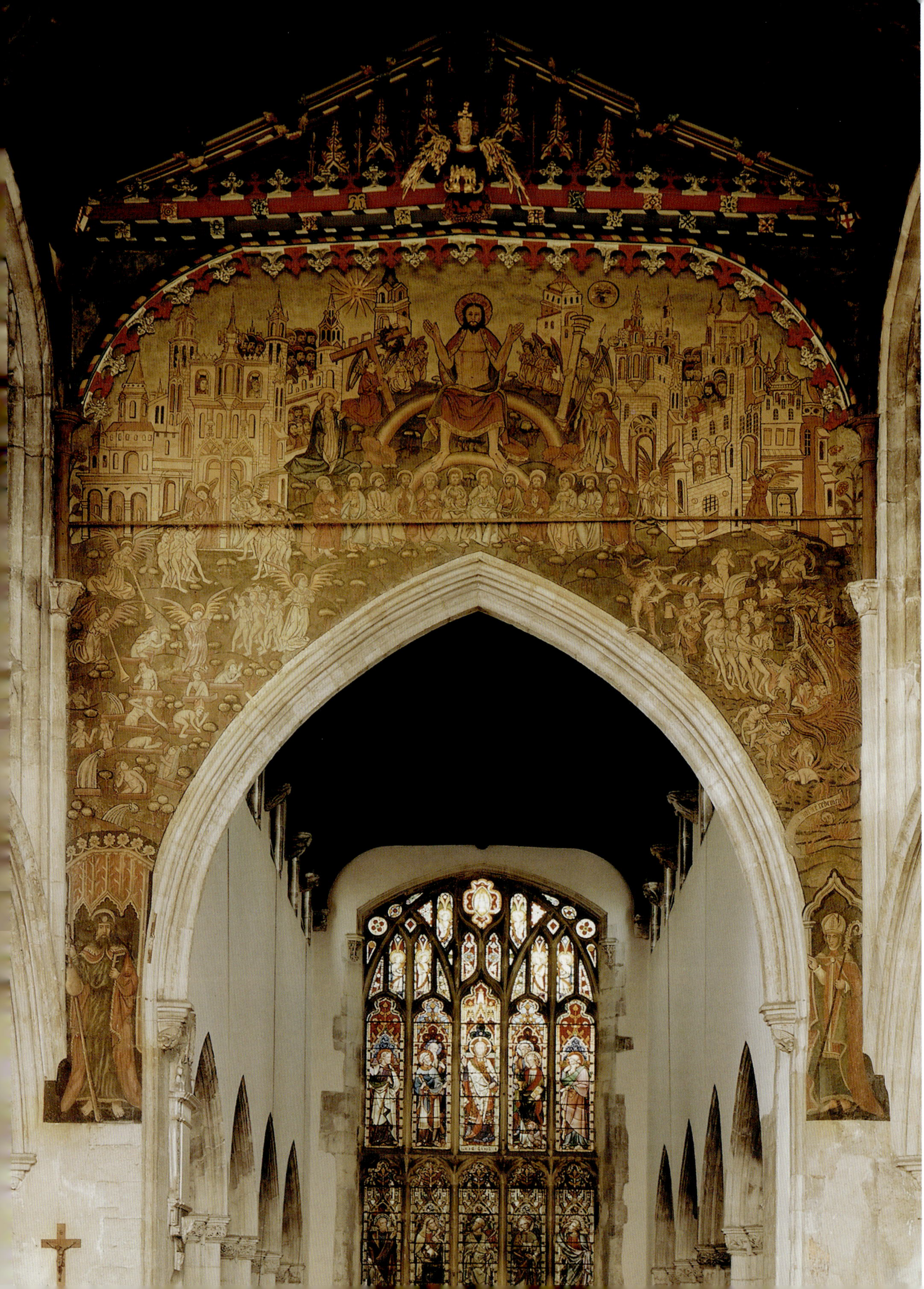

I

Religious Imagery in Britain, c. 1400–c. 1660

This chapter explores how the religious and visual culture of late medieval Britain was transformed by the process of reformation in the sixteenth century. Traditional accounts of the subject have established as a commonplace that the Reformation was a calamitous event in terms of cultural development; the rich artistic heritage of the medieval past is contrasted with an austere and barren Protestant culture of the Word. A view of the Reformation as a violent rupture with the past has been encouraged by important studies of iconoclasm – the removal, destruction and defacing of religious images. The material evidence of mutilated paintings and headless statues seems to confirm that the advent of Protestantism represented a sudden and complete break with the visual and material culture of the medieval period. In recent years, however, a new wave of scholarship has emphasised that the story of reformation in Britain is one of continuity as well as change. Studies of the visual arts have drawn attention to the survival and preservation of traditional artistic forms as well as the creative processes of assimilation and modification which contributed to the emergence of a recognisably Protestant visual culture.[1]

Here, I set the scene for the rest of the book with a brief overview of the role of religious imagery in pre-Reformation culture in Britain to establish where images were seen, the subject and nature of popular imagery and how images and related objects were experienced and used by believers. I then describe the impact of reformed ideology on the status and use of images in theory and in practice. It is not my purpose to provide a detailed account of late medieval religious practices involving images or the impact of the Reformation on these practices. Other authors have provided comprehensive and authoritative surveys and analyses of these subjects.[2] It is, however, impossible to assess the extent of continuity and change in the production, nature and use of religious images in

9 (FACING PAGE) Last Judgement or 'Doom' painting above the chancel arch, c. 1470–1500, church of St Thomas, Salisbury

post-Reformation culture without first establishing a sense of the visual and spiritual world of the preceding period. The first part of the chapter outlines the range of physical settings where religious images were encountered in the later medieval period and describes the most popular subject matter for devotional use. It then describes the nature of the Reformation assault on images and details the official prohibitions surrounding religious images in churches, before providing an overview of post-Reformation writings that comment on the strictures of the Second Commandment. This identifies a broad consensus in the Established Church on the general distinctions between lawful and illegitimate images but also underlines the lack of unanimity on the issue of images across the spectrum of religious belief. The chapter concludes with a survey of the making and breaking of religious images in post-Reformation Britain in order to provide a sense of the wider visual culture in which domestic decoration was created and viewed.

RELIGIOUS IMAGERY IN PRE-REFORMATION BRITAIN

Religious imagery dominated the visual culture of late medieval England and Scotland, as it did throughout Christian Europe.[3] Experienced in the richest profusion in places of worship, religious imagery was also part of daily life; it was worn on the body or viewed in the street and, as will be seen, it also featured in the decoration and furnishings of both large and relatively humble domestic houses. The various functions of these images were bound up with specific aspects of Catholic ritual and belief and it is important not to generalise about the role of religious imagery in worship and in wider visual culture. There was a difference between didactic imagery crafted for the purposes of information and instruction, and devotional imagery which supported collective and individual communication with heavenly figures. This distinction between didactic and devotional imagery is highly significant for the present study as it was emphasised by sixteenth-century reformers and reiterated by Protestant commentators throughout the seventeenth century.

Settings for Images

For most ordinary people religious imagery was experienced primarily in the context of their parish church. Late medieval churches were adorned and filled with all manner of religious image. The body of the church was dominated by the great rood figures of Christ on the cross flanked by the Virgin Mary and St John; these statues were usually carved in wood and mounted on the rood beam across the chancel arch. Underneath, the rood screen separating the nave from the holy chancel area was richly decorated and often contained panels painted with numerous figures from the heavenly hierarchy including saints, angels, patriarchs, prophets and sibyls.[4] Niches, supports and brackets throughout the body of the church held statues of holy figures and saints, some bedecked with rich clothing and jewels. Most of these rood and niche statues had candles set before them. Three-dimensional statues in alabaster, stone or wood also stood on altars. Great churches had many altars and even parish churches had additional altars in the nave for the celebration of guild and chantry masses.

As the ritual focus for collective worship and the performance of mass, the chief or 'high' altar was embellished with the most impressive imagery. The altar itself was adorned with richly embroidered draperies and frontals reflecting the liturgical calendar. In the later medieval period there was a trend for grand and imposing reredoses set behind the high altar. An example is the altar screen of about 1360 at Christchurch Priory church in Dorset which – along with a Tree of Jesse and a scene of the Adoration of the Christ Child – contains numerous niches for statues of saints (Fig. 10). Also in the chancel on the north side of the altar was the Easter sepulchre; more ornate versions were carved with depictions of the Corpus Christi (the dead Jesus held in the arms of the Father with the Dove of the Holy Spirit above) or Resurrection, to refer to the sepulchre's function as part of the symbolic re-enactment of the entombment, in which the consecrated host was placed in or on the sepulchre on Good Friday and taken out on Easter Sunday to be placed on the altar.[5]

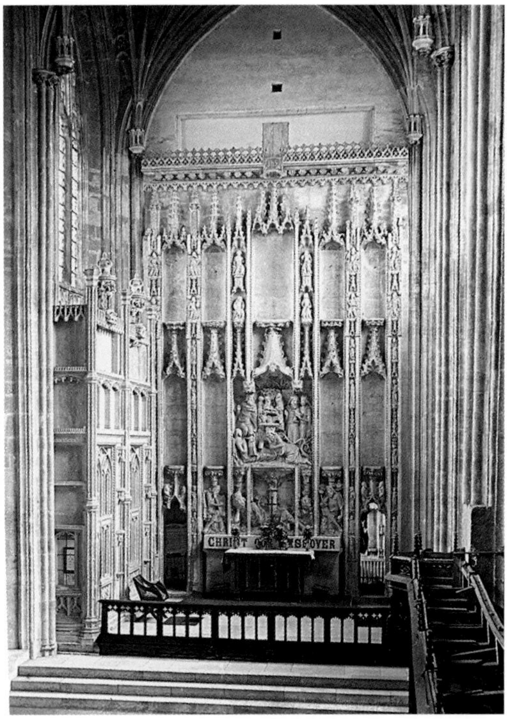

10 The fourteenth-century altar screen at Christchurch Priory church in Dorset

The walls of churches were often painted with extra-large figures of favoured saints such as St Christopher or St George, as well as series of narrative scenes depicting the lives and martyrdoms of saints.[6] At Breage church in Cornwall a great painted mural dating from late in the fifteenth century includes the figure of St Christopher and a 'Christ of the Trades' (Fig. 11). Many mural cycles contained dozens of separate scenes. Favoured subjects were the life of the Virgin or the life and Passion of Christ. The painted Passion Cycle, like the Passion sequences that were a vital part of the English Mystery Plays, depicted the narrative of Christ's Passion and death, sometimes continuing to the Resurrection and beyond. A particularly well-preserved set of wall paintings on the Passion from the fifteenth century can be seen in Pickering parish church in North Yorkshire. The lives, martyrdoms and miracles of various saints were also common in narrative series. Subjects such as the Deadly Sins and the Three Living and Three Dead provided warnings against sin and reminders of mortality.[7]

In stained glass too the same range of narrative series was employed. The windows of churches were a particular focus for display and most carried comprehensive iconographical programmes. An example is the scheme of twenty-eight windows made in about 1480 at St Mary's Church in Fairford, Gloucestershire, which provides a visual account of the Bible from the Creation to the Last Judgement along with scenes from the life of the Virgin Mary and figures of saints. Such narrative schemes in stained glass usually cul-

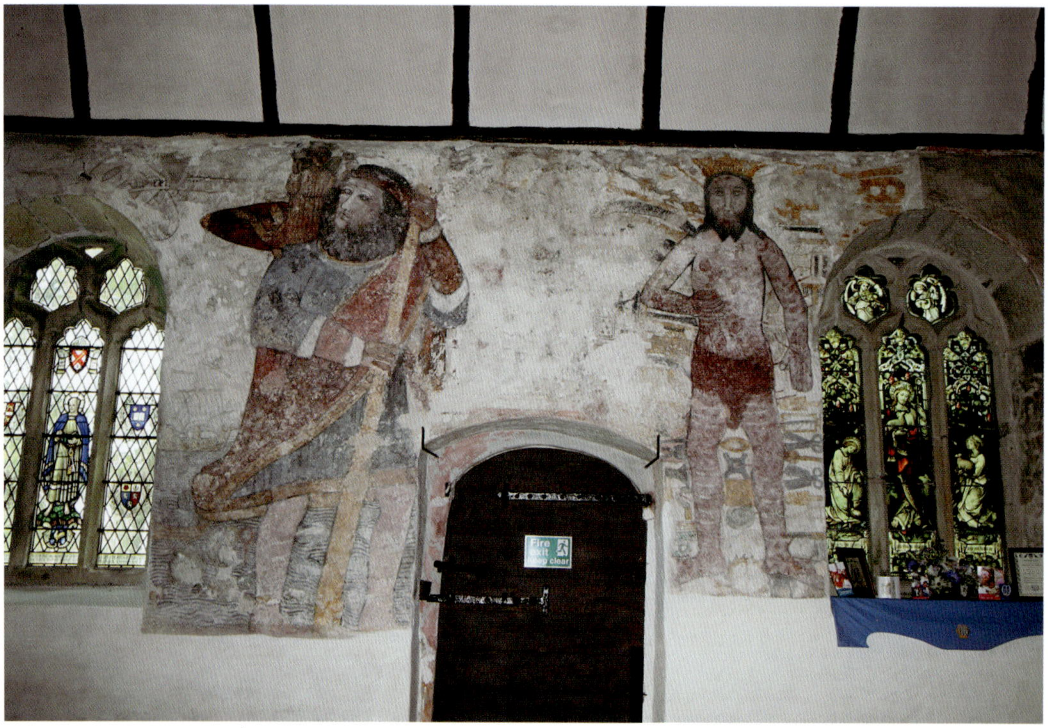

11 St Christopher and 'Christ of the Trades', fifteenth-century wall paintings at Breage church in Cornwall

minated in the great window at the east end which portrayed the most sacred imagery of the Passion and Resurrection. It was common to pair episodes or figures from the New Testament with parallel events and personages from the Old Testament as a manifestation of the Christian concept of types and anti-types. This ancient method of biblical interpretation held that the coming of Christ as saviour was prefigured or foreshadowed by episodes in the lives of the Old Testament patriarchs. The depiction of Old and New Testament scenes as types and anti-types respectively was popularised in the later medieval period through printed versions of the *Biblia Pauperum* and the *Speculum Humanae Salvationis*; these illustrated books informed all the visual arts. Typological cycles were especially suitable for stained glass because a series of windows with each divided into numerous panels provided ample space to develop elaborate pictorial schemes.[8]

Most churches had a Doom painting, a vivid and ominous depiction of the Day of Judgement and the sending of souls to heaven and hell. Doom paintings were usually situated towards the east end of a church, often on the Chancel arch itself, so that it would be constantly in view of worshippers as they looked towards the priest during services. Late medieval Doom paintings painted over at the Reformation have been uncovered at Holy Trinity Church in Coventry (about 1430–40), the Guild Chapel in Stratford-upon-Avon (about 1500) and the church of St Thomas in Salisbury (about 1470–1500; Fig. 9).

The furniture of the church was also adorned with imagery: font, lectern, pulpit and bench ends were often carved with scenes and figures (Fig. 12). Even the roof space might be decorated with carved statues or painted figures, with angels particularly common (see Fig. 25). The sculptural programme of about 1444 in the nave roof at St Mary's in Bury St Edmunds, Suffolk, includes forty-two carved wooden figures of prophets and saints, and fifty-eight angels, including eighteen life-size angels projecting inwards on the hammer beams.[9] All these fixtures and furnishings of the church were supplemented during services with additional paraphernalia for worship including the vestments worn by priests, which were often embroidered with holy figures, and ritual objects such as the chalice and pax-board (an image of the Crucifixion kissed by worshipers during mass).

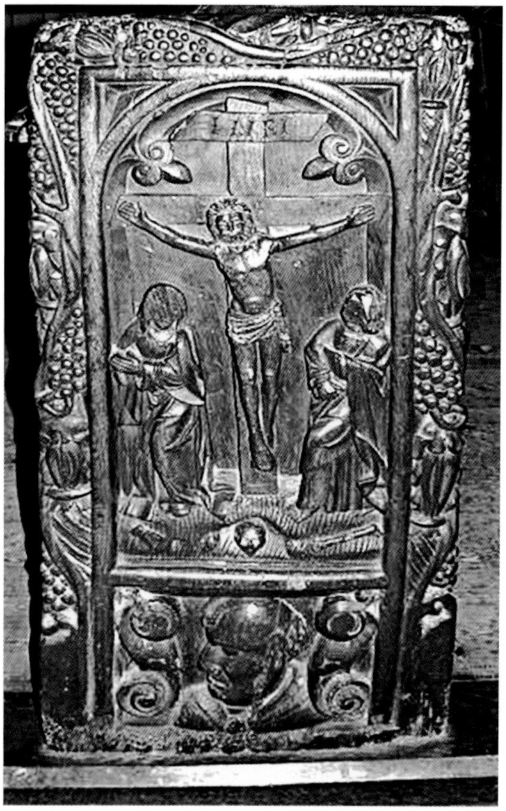

12 The Crucifixion, carved bench end, early sixteenth century, at Abbotsham church, Devon

Church ceremony often extended outside the church into the churchyard and beyond. Funeral and burial ceremonies involved the wider community as did perambulations such as the Rogationtide processions accompanied by banners, crosses and the ringing of hand bells to cast out evil spirits and protect the parish community. Mystery, or miracle, plays were dramatic performances of Bible stories acted out to public audiences on festival days. These theatrical productions brought the iconography of church imagery into the civic realm.

Outside the infrastructure of the ecclesiastical establishment – the cathedrals, monastic buildings and chantry chapels of late medieval Britain – religious imagery was also ever present in the urban and rural landscape. Apart from crosses, which could be seen everywhere, the exterior of buildings in towns and villages might be decorated with holy figures. A large wooden figure of St Peter once formed the corner post on the exterior of an Exeter town house,[10] while monuments such as market crosses were sometimes adorned with schemes of religious iconography. The wider physical landscape beyond the churchyard wall and outside the precincts of abbeys, cathedrals and convents was punctuated with crossroad crosses and venerated sites such as holy wells, trees, springs, caves and rocky outcrops.[11]

Pilgrimage practices formed an important part of the late medieval experience of images. Visitors to holy shrines and sites would not only view ornately decorated structures and objects in which the highlight was usually a famous religious image, they would leave behind votive objects as offerings while taking away a souvenir such as a pilgrim's badge (Fig. 13) or paper object like a prayer card. These objects might be worn or carried about the person or alternatively could be displayed in the home.

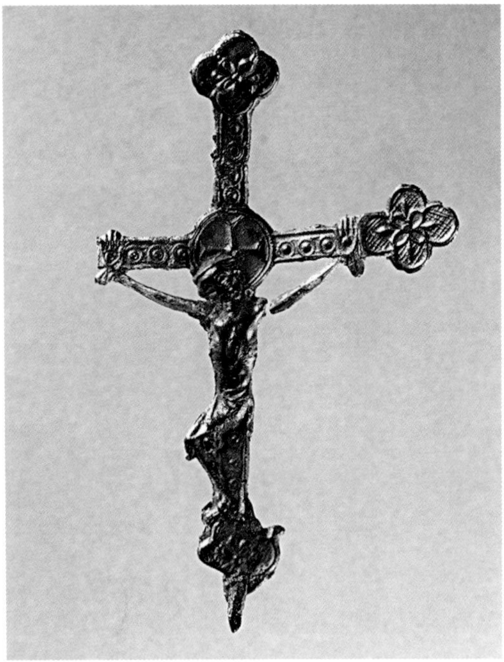

13 Pilgrim badge of lead alloy showing a crucifix with nimbed figure of Christ. British Museum, London

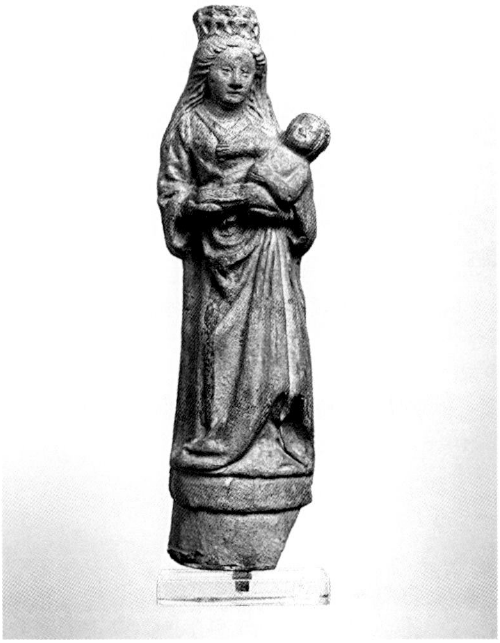

14 Virgin Mary and Child pipe-clay figurine, c. 1466–1535. Museum of London, London. Found in archaeological excavations in London, this figurine was probably imported from Germany or the Netherlands. It was once brightly coloured; there are remains of red pigment on the dress

Turning to the domestic sphere, most larger houses incorporated richly decorated private chapels and oratories containing a similar array of religious images and objects as found in churches. Larger devotional paintings or sculpture were placed on an altar and the walls were draped with hangings, while other images and objects often incorporated relics. A 1541 inventory of goods at the Vyne, an early Tudor house in Hampshire, records a lavish appointment of plate, altar cloths, hangings and vestments for priests as well as 'two large tablets of the pictor of our lorde' which might refer to paintings or sculpture in any one of several different media.[12]

Religious imagery was not confined only to chapels in larger private houses. Inventories record such imagery as the subject of paintings, hangings, sculptures and paper items in the principal rooms such as the hall and parlour.[13] Painted cloths and small devotional alabasters were particularly common. Few examples of the once ubiquitous painted cloth have survived and none of early date has religious iconography. These hangings were often large in scale, offering a cheaper alternative to tapestry, and examples mentioned in inventories suggest that subject matter included Old and New Testament stories and religious figures.[14] Common subjects included the Virgin Mary, the Passion and various saints. In the later fifteenth and early sixteenth centuries small-scale alabaster reliefs were mass-

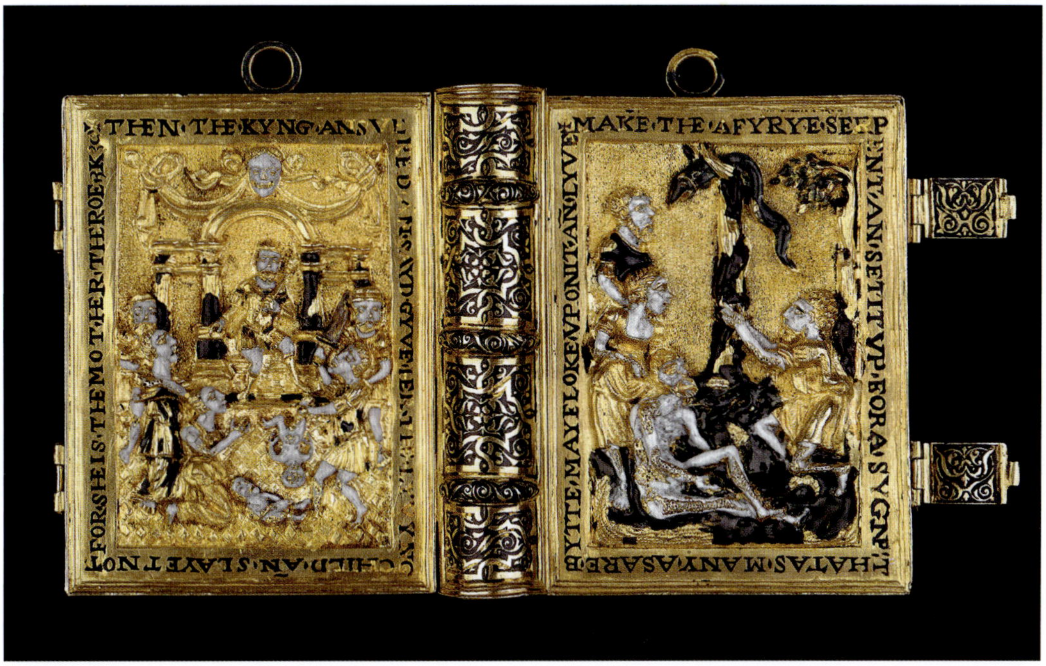

15 Gold prayer book case, c. 1540–45 with scenes of the Judgement of Solomon and the Brazen Serpent. British Museum, London

produced and the relatively inexpensive cost (often less than one shilling) allowed a wider public to acquire such items. A popular subject in alabaster was the decapitated head of John the Baptist.[15] Further down the social scale, small pipe-clay figurines, often of the Virgin Mary, offered cheaper alternatives to alabaster sculptures (Fig. 14). Printed single-sheet devotional images were also readily available.[16] These woodcut images were often associated with indulgences, which granted on performance of a prayer a period of relief from the pains of purgatory (see Fig. 19). Netherlandish paintings give some clue as to how small devotional statues and prints might be displayed in domestic space: two paintings associated with Robert Campin (1375–1444) show sacred figures in interiors furnished with religious images. In a version of the Annunciation, the Virgin sits before a fireplace on which is pinned a piece of paper, possibly a hand-coloured print, with an image of St Christopher, while in the right wing of the Werl Altarpiece St Barbara sits beside a similar fireplace with a small statue of the Trinity.[17] In the left wing the donor kneels in an anteroom with a statue of the Virgin and Child placed on a corbel above the door.

Small Books of Hours and primers exemplify how religious imagery for devotional use was transported through domestic space and used in different physical contexts. These prayer books for private devotions were lavishly illustrated with schemes of imagery.[18] Prayer books could be worn on the body and might be housed in a decorated case hung from the girdle; an exceptionally fine example dating from 1540–45 illustrates the Old Testament stories of the Judgement of Solomon and the Brazen Serpent (Fig. 15).[19] Religious imagery and texts adorned other clothing accessories and jewellery such as wrist straps, hat pins and pendants.[20] Jewellery for devotional use could include a sophisticated iconographical programme: the Middleham Jewel of the mid-fifteenth century shows scenes of the Nativity, Trinity and fifteen saints as well as magical texts, while the 'Coventry Ring' of similar date portrays Christ standing in the tomb (the image of Pity) with other signs related to the Passion and the Five Wounds.[21] Other items of jewellery bear the more simplified cultic symbolism of the Holy Name of Jesus (IHS).[22] The cost of such objects was out of reach for ordinary people but pilgrims' badges could also provide a focus for devotion (see Fig. 13).

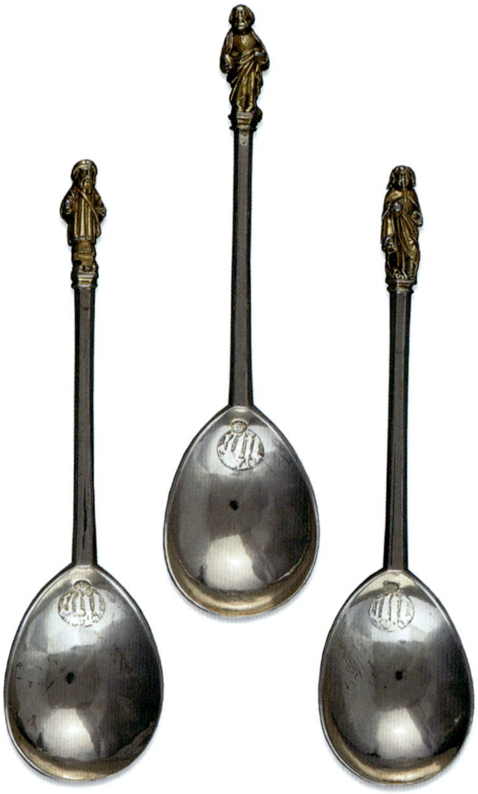

16 Three of a set of silver 'Apostle' spoons made in London, 1536–37. British Museum, London

From the evidence of material remains it seems that other 'domestic' objects such as pottery tiles, vessels and tableware were sometimes decorated with religious imagery or symbols. Increasingly in the late medieval period wealthy gentry and merchants could afford to have ornate domestic objects for their personal use. These would include display pieces for dining, such as spoons, flagons and cups. Shallow drinking bowls called mazers were sometimes adorned with religious inscriptions and motifs on the rim and in the base of the bowl. 'Apostle' spoons with figures of the Apostles on the handle were usually in sets of thirteen, one for each of the twelve Apostles and the thirteenth with the figure of Christ. The spoons symbolised the Last Supper of Christ in the company of the Apostles. An early Tudor set is also adorned with the sacred monogram IHS in each of the bowls (Fig. 16). Such items could be stored in a wooden chest which might also bear religious imagery; an early sixteenth-century panel from the front of a wooden chest, now on display at Hever Castle in Kent, includes several scenes from the book of Genesis.[23]

As well as portable furnishings and objects, there is evidence that the principal rooms in late medieval dwellings were decorated with religious imagery in more permanent materials. Some hammer-beam roofs in the halls of greater houses included carved figures of angels comparable to their counterparts in churches; those at Rufford Old Hall in Lancashire were created in the mid-sixteenth century on the very eve of the Reformation. A set of large wooden panels dating from the 1530s was probably made as part of the wall decorations of Cardinal David Beaton's apartments in St Andrew's Castle in Fife.[24] The panels include scenes of the Annunciation, the Tree of Jesse and the 'Arma Christi', a heraldic display of the wounds suffered by Christ during his Passion (Fig. 17).

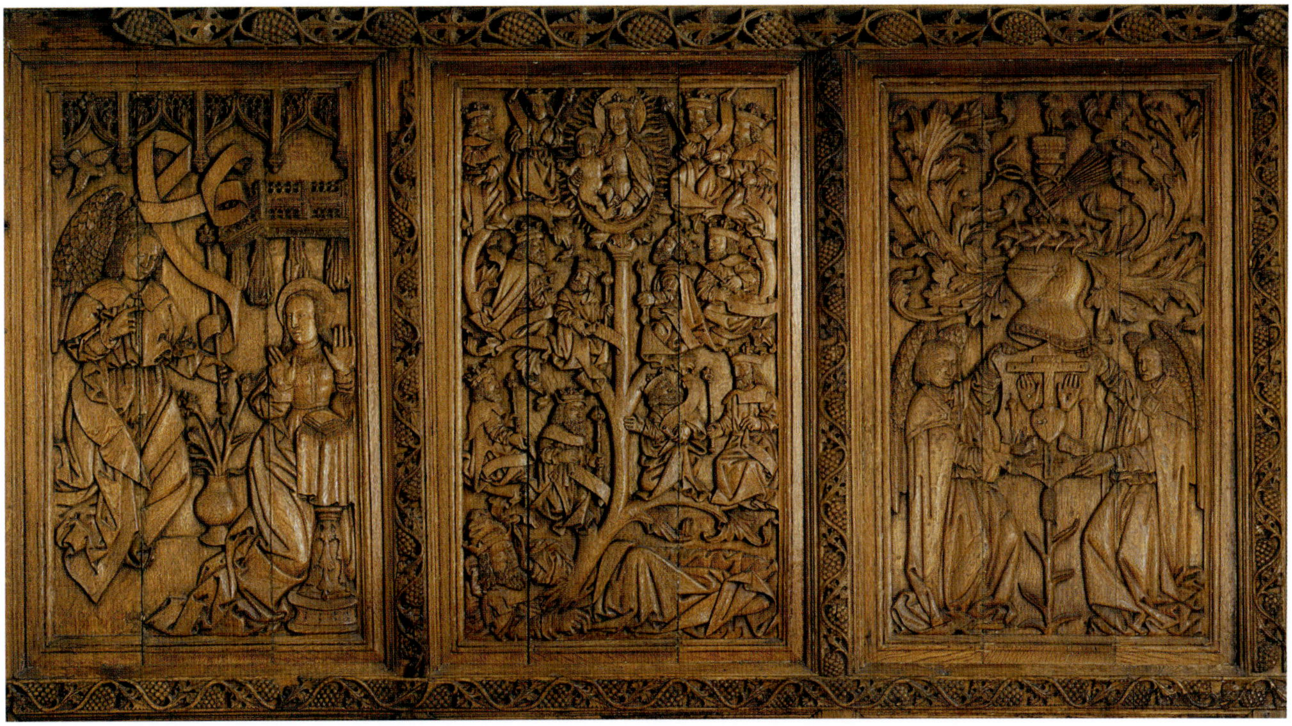

17 Annunciation, Tree of Jesse and 'Arma Christi', three of the carved oak panels of the 1530s commissioned by Cardinal David Beaton for his apartments in St Andrew's Castle, Fife

Remains of late fifteenth-century wall paintings at Cothay Manor in Somerset include a Virgin and Child and a scene of the Annunciation.[25] A row of cottages at Piccotts End in Hemel Hempstead was originally one dwelling of importance containing a great hall open to the roof. This room was decorated with wall paintings of about 1470–1500 including Christ in Majesty, the baptism of Christ, a Pieta (the Virgin mourning over the dead Christ) along with Sts Peter, Clement, Catherine and Margaret of Antioch. A third example is provided by the Rochford Tower in Boston, Lincolnshire, where traces of early sixteenth-century wall paintings on the first floor include scenes of the Annunciation, St Anne with the Virgin, St Michael, St Anthony and a coat of arms supported by angels.[26] The painted walls dating from the 1550s in the grand south room on the first floor of Kinneil House, Bo'ness, West Lothian, include six scenes illustrating the parable of the Good Samaritan along with depictions of St Jerome in the Wilderness and the Penitent Mary Magdalene.[27] This fashion for permanent religious decoration was not restricted to grander houses. The hall screen in the modest fifteenth-century dwelling now known as Marker's Cottage in Devon is painted with the fashionable grotesque-work of the early sixteenth century and religious figures, including St Andrew.[28] A traditional longhouse built in the 1480s in Cornwall has the remains of wall paintings in the hall including representations of St James of Compostella and St George and the Dragon.[29]

Subject matter: popular 'cultic' imagery

It is clear from this brief overview that religious imagery was omnipresent in life in pre-Reformation Britain and that the most common forms of religious imagery related to Christ's Passion, the Virgin and saints. Having surveyed the settings in which people experienced religious imagery, I can now concentrate more specifically on the popularity of certain subject matter and how this imagery was actually used in the daily devotional life of individuals.

Traditional theory about the utility of religious images was as teaching aids to instruct the faithful and as reminders of the honour due to heavenly figures. Pope Gregory the Great's pronouncement in the sixth century that images functioned as books for the illiterate (laymen's bibles) remained the standard official explanation of the role of religious images in the Established Church.[30] By the later medieval period, however, images had multiplied, diversified and developed additional functions. Increasingly, images were used not only to inform and trigger devotional activity but also became the practical focus for individuals' communication with heavenly figures. The proliferation of images designed to aid an affective, personal piety was a feature of late medieval religion.

The type of image that attracted this kind of devotional attention can be defined crudely in terms of its form.[31] Narrative images depicting an event or series of events were unlikely to attract the concentrated attention of the pious. Images of individual personages, however, in realistic or symbolic form, whether painted on flat surfaces or carved in three dimensions, evoked the presence of the represented figure and thus prompted use as the focus of prayer. There was still a degree of overlap and narrative scenes could also function as devotional images. One way to distinguish devotional imagery from the vast majority of scenes in wall paintings, hangings, carvings and stained glass is that the particular attention bestowed on the devotional image was manifested by actions performed before it, such as the setting up of lights, the presentation of gifts or the prolonged gazing associated with directed prayer.

Another way to identify devotional imagery is through its relationship with liturgical and ritual use. The use of images in the context of public worship, such as the kissing of the pax or 'creeping to the cross' (a Good Friday ceremony in which parishioners would approach a crucifix on their knees and kiss it), encouraged belief in the mediating efficacy of the image itself as a channel or gateway to the holy personage it represented, so that honour paid to the sign passed on to the signified. This was important because of belief in the intercessory power of Christ, the Virgin and saints to mediate between God and believers and effect change in the lives of people by, for example, alleviating sickness or offering protection from harm. Images of these figures allowed the faithful to concentrate their individual prayers and requests on an appropriate visual focus. Any beneficial effects experienced during or after such dedicated prayer fostered and supported belief in the miracle-working powers of certain cult images. Popular forms of behaviour surrounding images suggested that believers were confusing the nature of their communication with holy figures and were mistakenly assigning autonomous agency to the image itself. It was the elision, in practice, between signifier and signified that worried critics of images.

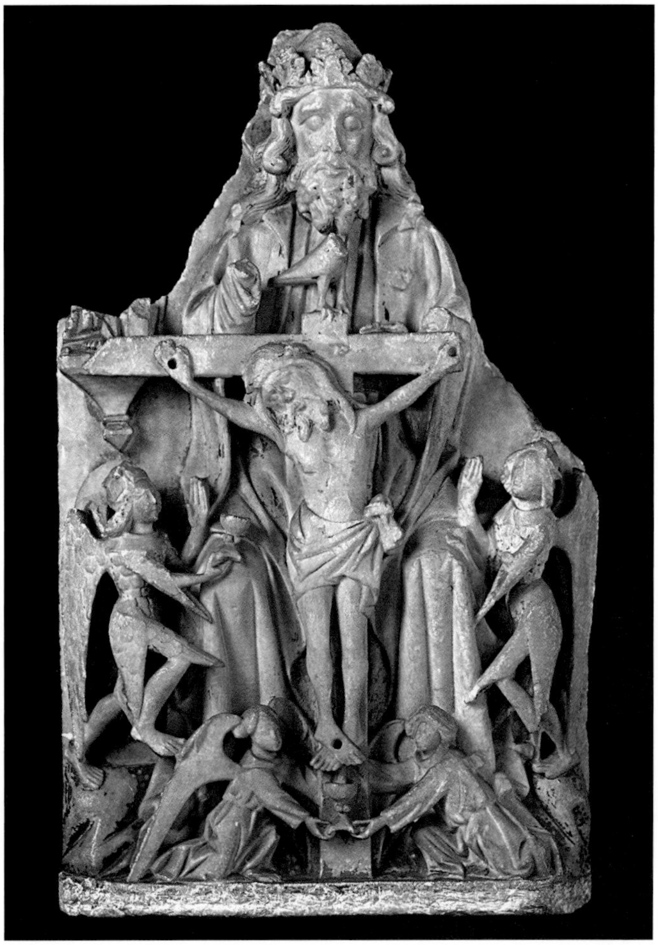

18 The Trinity, late fifteenth-century alabaster panel. Victoria and Albert Museum, London

Among the popular devotional images was that of the Trinity, a representation of the Godhead in its three persons of God the Father, Christ the Son and the Holy Spirit. The usual iconography, as depicted in a late fifteenth-century alabaster panel (Fig. 18), showed God the Father as an old man with a beard wearing a crown and robe and sometimes seated on a throne. This large figure holds his arms outstretched to support a crucifix before him. A dove, representing the Holy Spirit, stands or hovers between or above Father and Son.

The crucifix itself was, of course, ubiquitous. From its lofty position on the rood it dominated the space of great and parish churches and featured in church ceremonial. Crosses too, could be seen everywhere, in church, on the street and at country crossroads. By far the most popular images for personal devotional use in the late medieval period were those associated with the events of Christ's Passion. Eamon Duffy has argued that the liturgical centrality of the crucifix in the surroundings of late medieval English men and women was matched by a similar emphasis on the Passion and related iconography as the centre of private devotion.[32] Affective prayer and meditation on the Passion

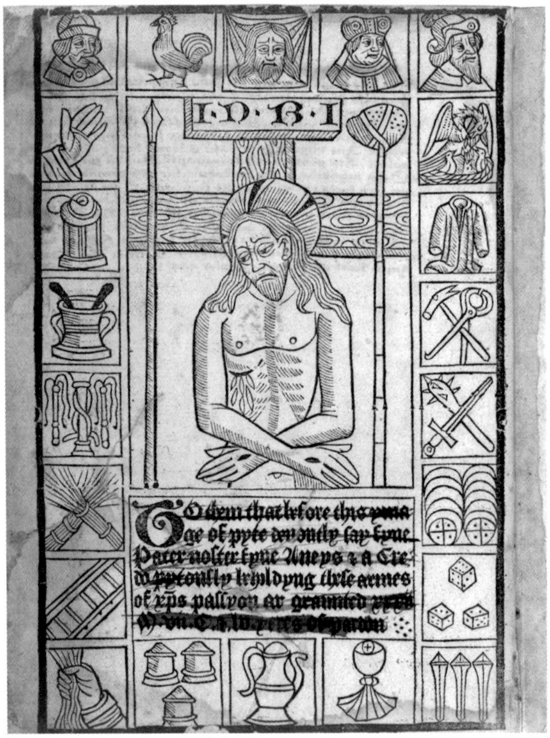

19 Christ as Man of Sorrows ('Image of Pity'), woodcut, English, c. 1499. Bodleian Library, Oxford. The inscription granting an indulgence on performance of a prayer before the image has been crossed out, presumably at the time of the Reformation

of Christ was fundamental to late medieval piety. This form of devotional activity involved the detailed imagining of the events of the Passion and the tortures inflicted on Christ in order to generate a tender appreciation of the extent of God's love for humankind. Empathy with the horrors of Christ's sufferings prompted an emotional engagement which facilitated a spiritual connection with God. For many, the practice of affective devotion required the support of visual illustrations so that, alongside images of the Crucifixion, new iconographies associated with Christ's sufferings and sacrifice emerged in the fourteenth and fifteenth centuries.

The most common of these new symbolic images included the Arma Christi (the Five Wounds of Christ; see Fig. 17), the Pieta and the Image of Pity, or Man of Sorrows, in which the crucified Christ displays his wounds (Fig. 19). Usually, the Cross featured in the background of the Pity and the Pieta and both iconographies often included the symbols of the Passion. The Image of Pity was associated with a legend in which Pope Gregory I while celebrating Mass experienced a vision of Christ standing in his tomb displaying his wounds and surrounded by the Instruments of the Passion. A kneeling Pope Gregory is sometimes included before an Image of Pity to refer to this miracle; an example in wall painting can be seen at Slapton church in Northamptonshire. All these iconographies related to the Passion were popular across all media of representation in ecclesiastical and domestic contexts and the imagery in print was usually accompanied by lavish indulgences for those who prayed before it.[33] The poignancy of these images of the broken body or wounds of Christ was especially suitable for affective devotion, which operated through the stirring of emotions, especially compassion, to enable the believer to come closer to Christ through empathy with his human suffering.

Especially potent in prompting affective response was the Pieta, where the Virgin holds her dead son on her lap. This Marian iconography was enormously popular throughout Christian Europe and proliferated in all media in the fourteenth and fifteenth centuries in England and Scotland.[34] The iconography combined the Lamentation over the dead Christ at the foot of the Cross, with the emotive power of the focus on the grieving mother holding the broken body of her dead son. Viewers could identify with the human anguish of Mary's loss while sharing her acceptance of Christ's sacrifice as the source of

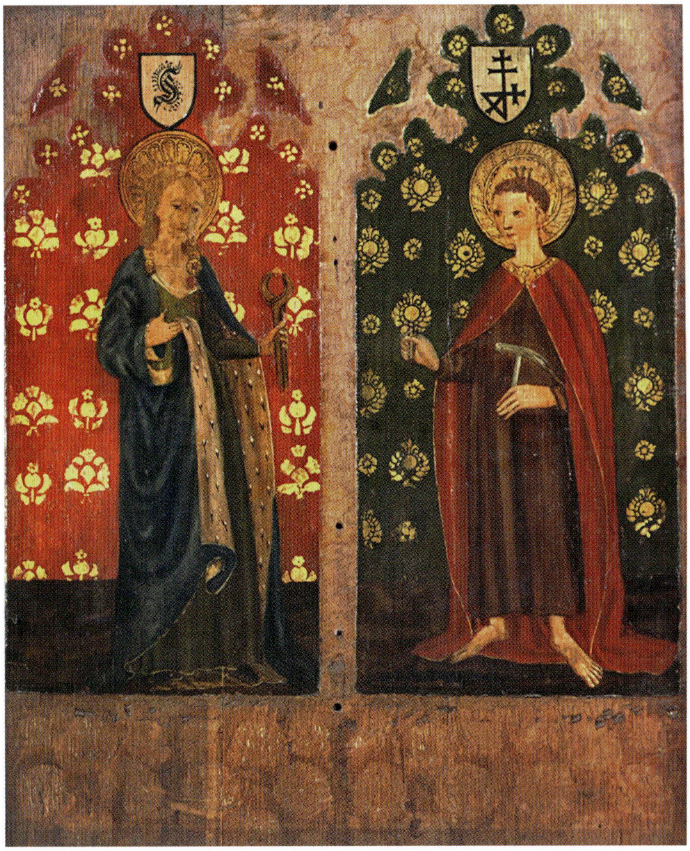

20 St Agatha and St William of Norwich, painted panel from a rood screen, 1450–70, commissioned by Ralph Segrym for the Chapel of St Mary in St John's Church, Maddermarket, Norwich. Victoria and Albert Museum, London

salvation for humanity. In this way the iconography emphasised Mary's role as mediator for humankind. The role of Mary as intercessor also encouraged the popularity of other scenes in the Virgin's life. Prayers and meditations on the Joys and Sorrows of the Virgin formed a major part of Marian piety.[35] While the Pieta encapsulated the Sorrows of the Virgin, scenes of the Annunciation, Nativity, Resurrection, Ascension (of the Virgin) and Coronation (of the Virgin) depicted her Joys. All these scenes were particularly popular in carving, painting and glass. The cult of the Virgin was second only to that of Christ himself and she was venerated by both sexes. It is clear, however, that she had a particular appeal for women. Images of the Pieta, Annunciation and Nativity had special resonance for women and statues of the Virgin holding the infant Christ allowed women to associate maternal feelings with the practice of affective devotion (see Fig. 14).

Images of saints could be seen everywhere in late medieval England and Scotland.[36] Most parish churches had numerous statues of saints, some housed in chapels or on altars, others distributed in niches or on brackets in the body of the church. Those singled out for special honour in public spaces were regional and parish patron saints or family saints (Fig. 20). St George and St Andrew were commonly depicted because of their significance as national patron saints for England and Scotland respectively, while certain saints had a universal appeal, such as St Christopher as the patron saint of travellers. Although the faithful were expected to honour the whole company of saints, they were also encouraged to adopt individual saints for special attention in their personal devotions. These special saints might share the same name or occupation or might be adopted due to their specialisation in a particular field of ordeal or injury. St Margaret (of Antioch) was popular as the patron saint of pregnancy; St Erasmus of stomach disorders and disease; St Apollonia of toothache. Unlike the distressing emotional impact of devotional images associated with Christ's Passion, many images of saints functioned as kindly companions. Saints were perceived as friendly helpers and their images in a personal and domestic context emphasised their role as part of an extended family providing comfort and hope through their efforts in mediating on behalf of humans in the heavenly sphere.

THE REFORMATION ASSAULT ON IMAGES

The religious reformations that took place during the sixteenth century transformed the visual culture of much of northern Europe. Reformers argued that certain aspects of Christian belief and ritual had become corrupted by false doctrines and malpractice. An assault on images was not initially a principal element of the reformers' agenda but became significant as part of the attack on other aspects of Roman Catholic piety including the elaboration of church ceremonial, the doctrine of justification through works (reformers insisted that salvation was achieved through faith not action) and popular cults of devotion, particularly to Mary and the saints.

Early reformers voiced specific grievances against the cult of saints, images and relics. Over time the range of images singled out for condemnation expanded to embrace any visual representation of holy figures in a devotional context. The popular devotional icons of God, the Virgin, saints and imagery associated with Christ's Passion were particularly offensive from a reformist perspective because the excesses of worshipful behaviour they attracted indicated that believers confused the image with the heavenly prototype for which it stood, as if the image itself possessed divine agency, while the proliferation of images of Mary and the saints used in relation to intercessory prayer undermined Protestant emphasis on the mediating sacrifice of Christ. Reformers maintained that an image used as the focus of worship was idolatry (false worship). It was a corruption of the practice of true and pure religion and an insult to God as it contravened His commandments.[37] Yet, early reformers differed in the detail of their attitudes towards images, contributing to the emergence of different Protestant churches. While all Protestants agreed that idolatrous worship directed to the image rather than its prototype was forbidden by God's own law, some maintained that images were acceptable, even beneficial, as long as they were not abused by worship. The father of the Reformation, Martin Luther, was not hostile to images; he argued that images were 'indifferent things' of themselves and only detrimental if abused. Not only did he accept the traditional justification of images as teaching aids and reminders of holy things but he also recommended the painting of Bible stories in churches if the imagery served to instruct.[38] A more extreme position was adopted by Luther's contemporaries Andreas Karlstadt and Ulrich Zwingli but it was the Swiss reformer John Calvin who had the greatest influence in advancing a more radical Reformed position on images.[39] Calvin dedicated a chapter to the issue of images in his *Institutes of the Christian Religion* (1559):

> we know too well from experience that the moment images appear in churches, idolatry has as it were raised its banner; because the folly of manhood cannot moderate itself, but forthwith falls away to superstitious worship. Even were the danger less imminent, still, when I consider the proper end for which churches are erected, it appears to me more unbecoming their sacredness than I well can tell, to admit any other images than those living symbols which the Lord has consecrated by his own word: I mean Baptism and the Lord's Supper, with the other ceremonies. By these our eyes ought to be more steadily fixed, and more vividly impressed, than to require the aid of any images which the wit of man may devise.[40]

Given the transcendence of God, Calvin rejected the human attempt to create signs and symbols of God's presence on earth, especially the statues, images and paintings present in Roman Catholic churches. Man-made symbols could not assist communication between the human and the divine because material props prevented access to the immaterial, spiritual realm. According to this formulation, religious images and other worldly paraphernalia were not just utterly redundant for devotional purposes but led people away from God.

The Roman Catholic Church responded to the reformers' assault on images in the decisions reached by the Council of Trent. In the final, twenty-fifth session in December 1563 the Council reasserted the ancient case for ecclesiastical imagery. It acknowledged that practices involving images should be carefully regulated to prevent abuses but restated the traditional justifications for images in churches: first, to instruct the people, second, to prompt them in remembering the Articles of Faith and the gifts of God and third, to provide exemplars of spiritual and moral behaviour. The Catholic Church also defended the devotional use of images, stating that outward gestures of honour paid to the image were transferred to the prototype, so that:

> the images of Christ, of the Virgin Mother of God, and of the other saints, are to be had and retained particularly in temples, and that due honour and veneration are to be given them; not that any divinity, or virtue, is believed to be in them, on account of which they are to be worshipped; or that anything is to be asked of them; or, that trust is to be reposed in images, as was of old done by the Gentiles who placed their hope in idols; but because the honour which is shown them is referred to the prototypes which those images represent; in such wise that by the images which we kiss, and before which we uncover the head, and prostrate ourselves, we adore Christ; and we venerate the saints, whose similitude they bear.[41]

In practice these different positions on the issue of images contributed to a splintering of the Catholic Church and the emergence of several distinct Protestant churches. The changes to religion brought about by the process of reform varied greatly across different areas of Europe and similarly the pace and extent of the destruction and preservation of images was unique to each of the emergent Protestant states. In some areas popular support for reform led to outbreaks of unofficial iconoclasm – the violent removal and destruction of images from churches. Mob-led iconoclastic riots took place in Zürich (in 1523), Strasbourg (1524), Copenhagen (1530), Münster (1534), Geneva (1535), Augsburg (1537) and Scotland (1559). The Seventeen Provinces of the Netherlands were hit by a wave of Protestant iconoclasm in the summer of 1566. These unofficial purges often paved the way for official proscriptions and action. In most cases, however, images were removed from churches in an orderly manner by official authorities in the newly reformed cities and territories of Europe.[42]

The different patterns of change resulted in a range of outcomes in relation to the appearance of Protestant churches. Lutheran Germany adopted a tolerant stance on images so that much religious imagery – including altar reredoses and wall painting – could remain in churches.[43] In the Protestant Northern Netherlands where the Reformed or Calvinist position was adopted, church interiors were whitewashed and stripped of adornments but a culture of religious tolerance meant that there was no impediment to the continued production of religious paintings for display in secular contexts.

In England and Scotland the process of reformation in the first half of the sixteenth century followed different trajectories and the detail of this falls outside the parameters of my study. Wholesale state iconoclasm had occurred in England during the reign of Edward VI and this set the stage for Elizabethan policy but the stripping of the churches had been reversed under the Catholic Mary Tudor. A turning point for both countries came around 1560 with the establishment thereafter of Protestantism as the state religion. England and Scotland each experienced iconoclastic purges of churches in 1559; in Scotland this was unofficial mob action while in England for the most part the removal of church images was conducted in an organised fashion according to government directives. After these initial waves of iconoclasm the authorities of both countries adopted a relatively radical position on images in churches. Following the more extreme Reformed position advanced by Calvin, religious imagery and ceremonial accoutrements were removed from churches and the walls were whitewashed to obscure earlier paintings.

The Elizabethan Injunctions of 1559 set out detailed instructions to the English church hierarchy on how to implement the new religious settlement. These instructions were based on the earlier Edwardian Injunctions of 1547, with some significant changes to reflect the more conservative position of the queen compared to her brother.[44] The 1559 Injunctions formed the basis of the law for the rest of the reign and several items dealt specifically with the issue of images. Injunction 2 explained that images were superfluous items of superstitious belief, incapable of any independent agency:

> to the intent that all superstition and hypocrisy crept into divers men's hearts may vanish away, they [the clergy] shall not set forth or extol the dignity of any images, relics,

> or miracles; but, declaring the abuse of the same, they shall teach that all goodness, health, and grace ought to be both asked and looked for only of God, as of the very Author and Giver of the same, and of none other.

Injunction 23 concerned more practical iconoclastic action. It ordered the clergy to:

> take away, utterly extinct, and destroy all shrines, coverings of shrines, all tables, candlesticks, trindals, and rolls of wax, pictures, paintings, and all other monuments of feigned miracles, pilgrimages, idolatry, and superstition, so that there remain no memory of the same in walls, glass windows, or elsewhere within their churches and houses; preserving nevertheless, or repairing both the walls and glass windows; and they shall exhort all their parishioners to do the like within their several houses.

This extension of the prohibitions to the private sphere was followed up in a later Injunction (no. 35): 'Item, that no persons keep in their houses any abused images, tables, pictures, paintings, and other monuments of feigned miracles, pilgrimages, idolatry, and superstition.'[45]

Having established the official position which required the physical removal of images from places of worship, the next stage in the process of reform was to effect a change in the mentality of believers so that no desire for images remained. To that end the issue of images formed a major part of the second book of Homilies published in 1563. The Homilies were officially endorsed sermons intended to be read to congregations to instruct and safeguard against error. The new 'Homily against peril of idolatry, and superfluous decking of churches' consolidated and enshrined the strands of reformed thinking about images in determining that images of God, Christ, the Virgin Mary, the Apostles, Martyrs and 'other of notable holiness' were most dangerous in relation to the peril of idolatry but extended what was forbidden to all images in churches, for good measure. It expounded the official position that: 'Images placed publicly in Temples, cannot possibly be without danger of worshipping and idolatry, wherefore they are not publicly to be had or suffered in Temples and Churches'.[46] The lengthy discussion provided a comprehensive and rigorous denunciation of religious images in the context of worship.

Official iconoclasm as outlined in the Elizabethan Injunctions indicates the kinds of church fixtures and furnishings that were removed from most parish churches by the mid-1560s. The great rood was dismantled and the carved figures destroyed. Painted murals and woodwork throughout the body of the church were hidden by whitewash and sometimes the newly blank walls were re-painted with texts. Statuary was removed leaving empty niches and brackets. Narrative scenes in stained glass were removed (although the Injunction's direction to preserve the fabric of the church allowed imagery in glass to remain longer than in other art forms). The new visual emphases were the pulpit and the boards displaying the texts of the Ten Commandments; both were imposed by official proclamation and these furnishings symbolised the significance of the Word in Protestant worship. These newly stripped and relatively bare churches provided the public space for worship for the majority of churchgoers who conformed to the new state religion. Churchgoers were also taught through sermons to reject images as tools for their personal devotions but the extent to which the austere reality of the new church spaces shaped the attitudes of the wider public is unclear. Although affection for traditional images is impossible to quantify it certainly existed, manifested in a lack of pre-emptive image-destruction ahead of official visitations and the hostility of some parishioners to the iconoclastic actions of officials.[47] While outward conformity to the new forms of worship was required by the state, the official religions of England and Scotland were sufficiently elastic to embrace a wide range of beliefs and ideological perspectives. This diversity of belief across the religious spectrum resulted in continued debate and disagreement over the status and role of images in religious practices and in wider culture.

While most scholars agree that a spectrum of religious belief existed in early modern Britain, there is considerable debate about the nature, size and composition of the various groups within the scale. These debates need not be detailed here. It is clear that at each end of the spectrum were non-conformists; recusant Catholics at one extreme to Puritan Separatists at the other. All but these extreme positions, however, were accommodated within the established church.

After 1560 in Scotland the changes associated with the Reformation were gradual and far from rigid. In general, the majority conformed to the Reformed version of Protestantism laid down in the Confession of Faith, although large parts of the Highlands and islands remained Catholic. Recusancy was never a great problem although in the towns Catholics were prevented from holding civic office. Popular Protestantism in the early stages was a largely urban affair and radical Protestantism was never more than a minority movement until the 1630s when popular resistance to royal intervention in Scottish religious affairs resulted in the pro-reform National Covenant of 1638.[48]

Similarly the English church embraced a wide range of religious ideologies. At one end of the spectrum of belief within the Established Church were the conservative 'church papists' who outwardly conformed to the Established Church yet inwardly remained Roman Catholics.[49] At the other end were those moderate Puritans who desired further reform and purification of the Established Church.[50] The majority of churchgoers in between were probably ambivalent in the early years of state Protestantism but it has been argued that by the turn of the seventeenth century a sizeable number of laypeople were committed to the Church of England's liturgy as enshrined in the Book of Common Prayer.[51] According to some historians these 'Prayer-Book Protestants' or 'parish Anglicans' formed the bedrock of mainstream Protestantism between the Reformation and the Civil War.[52] During the first half of the seventeenth century the two strands of Protestantism, which can be described crudely as 'high church' (conservative) and 'low church' (favouring further reform) perspectives, became more pronounced and had a greater impact on the experience of ordinary churchgoers.[53] In the early decades of the seventeenth century a more tolerant approach to aspects of traditional Catholic ceremony gained momentum in the Established Church leading to the so-called Laudian reforms of the 1630s, which re-introduced some of the abandoned Catholic ceremonial and church adornments.[54] The impact of these counter-Reformation changes to the nature of public worship – which included the decoration of churches as part of an emphasis on the 'beauty of holiness' – angered committed Protestants and encouraged more extreme forms of Puritanism, as manifested in renewed iconoclasm carried out under Parliamentary orders in the 1640s.[55] This wide spectrum of belief across as well as outside the Established Church meant that the status and role of images remained a matter of debate and controversy throughout the period 1560–1660. To understand these debates it is useful to focus on the text of the Second Commandment as this provided the foundation for most Protestant image theory in Britain.

INTERPRETING THE SECOND COMMANDMENT

The section of God's Commandments that dealt with the prohibition of idolatry assumed a position of major doctrinal importance during the Reformation as it was a key point of difference between Protestantism and the rejected Roman Catholic Church. Its command against the making and worshipping of images, which had originally formed part of the stipulations attached to the First Commandment, was emphasised by reformers to the point of being separated out as a distinct, Second Commandment.[56] This is the text of the Commandment as provided in the King James Bible of 1611 (Exodus 20: 4–6):

> Thou shalt not make unto thee any graven image, or any likeness of any thing that is in heaven above, or that is in the earth beneath, or that is in the water under the earth. Thou shalt not bow down thyself to them, nor serve them: for I the LORD thy God am a jealous God, visiting the iniquity of the fathers upon the children unto the third and fourth generation of them that hate me; And shewing mercy unto thousands of them that love me, and keep my commandments.

The promotion of the text which formed the Second Commandment in Protestant religion is illustrated by the Commandments triptych of the late sixteenth century in Preston St Mary Church in Suffolk (Fig. 21). This painted triptych, which borrows the three-panel format of medieval altarpieces for the emblazoned written word, lists the Ten Commandments in the central panel. The Second Commandment is written in larger and more freely spaced text compared with Commandments One and Three, which are squeezed into the top and bottom of the left-hand tablet. The six remaining Commandments Four to Ten are squashed into the right-hand tablet. Thus the Second Commandment is emphasised visually and spatially in the list, as it was emphasised in Protestant belief.

Controversy arose, however, because the Second Commandment did not specify what type of imagery was forbidden beyond the vague and ambiguous 'graven image' and 'likeness'. This ambiguity led to vast differences in theological opinion and contributed to the emergence of sects within the church. Any analysis of the Protestant image question must therefore acknowledge a wide divergence of opinion. Some radical groups favoured a literal interpretation, eschewing all man-made imagery, while others, more realistically,

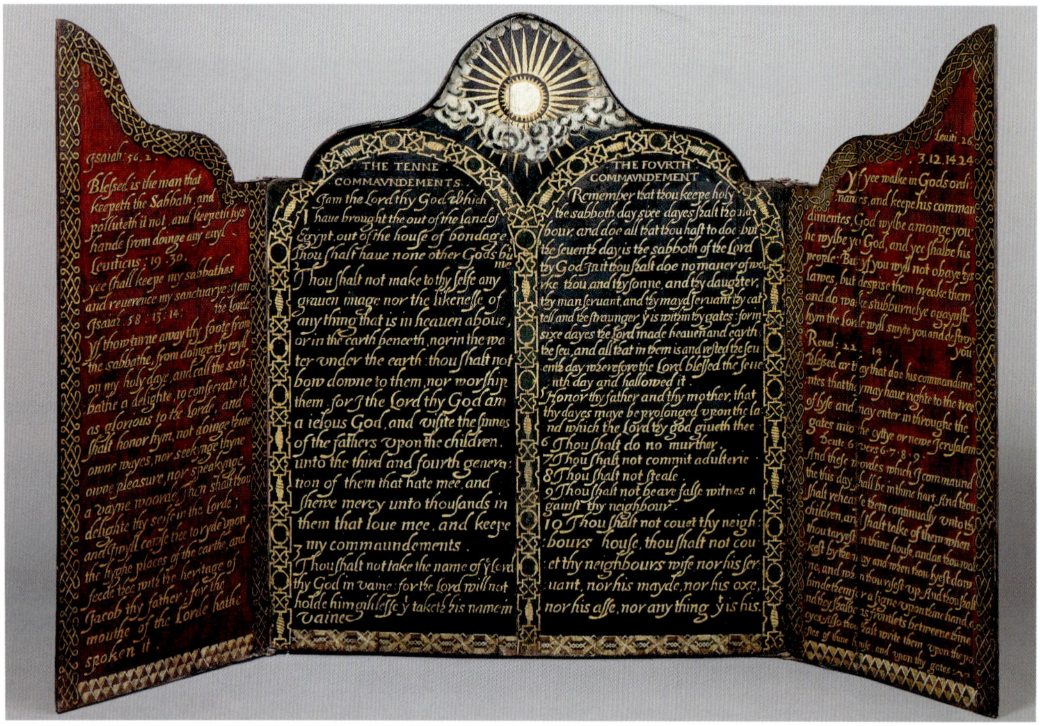

21 Triptych painted with the Ten Commandments, late sixteenth century, Preston St Mary Church, Suffolk

adopted a moderate stance and attempted to limit the Commandment to certain types of religious image in specific contexts.

The moderate position, which was adopted by official policy, hinged on several key distinctions between images that were likely to be 'abused' by worship and those which were not. Based on the text of the Commandment, Protestant theologians and commentators focused on the interconnected issues of use, location, media and subject matter. The principal issue was how an image might be used. 'Thou shalt not bow down thyself to them, nor serve them' highlighted that of reception and was identified as prohibiting only those religious images that might prompt worship – the adoration of a man-made (and therefore inherently false) representation of holy figures. This led to attempts to define the nature of worshipful behaviour. William Perkins, an influential churchman of moderate Puritan persuasion, explained that 'Adoration in generall, is an outward Worship, signifying and testifying the inward worship of the heart. More specifically, by it we must conceive, the bowing of the head, and knee; the bending and prostrating of the bodie; the lifting up of the hands, eyes, and such like.'[57] A few years later the godly radical Henry Ainsworth explained the range of bodily gestures embraced by this command: '*not bow down* or, *not worship*: under this one, all other gestures of reverence are forbidden; as bowing the knee, *1 King.19.18.* kissing, *Hos.13.2.* lifting up of the eyes, *Ezek.18.6.*

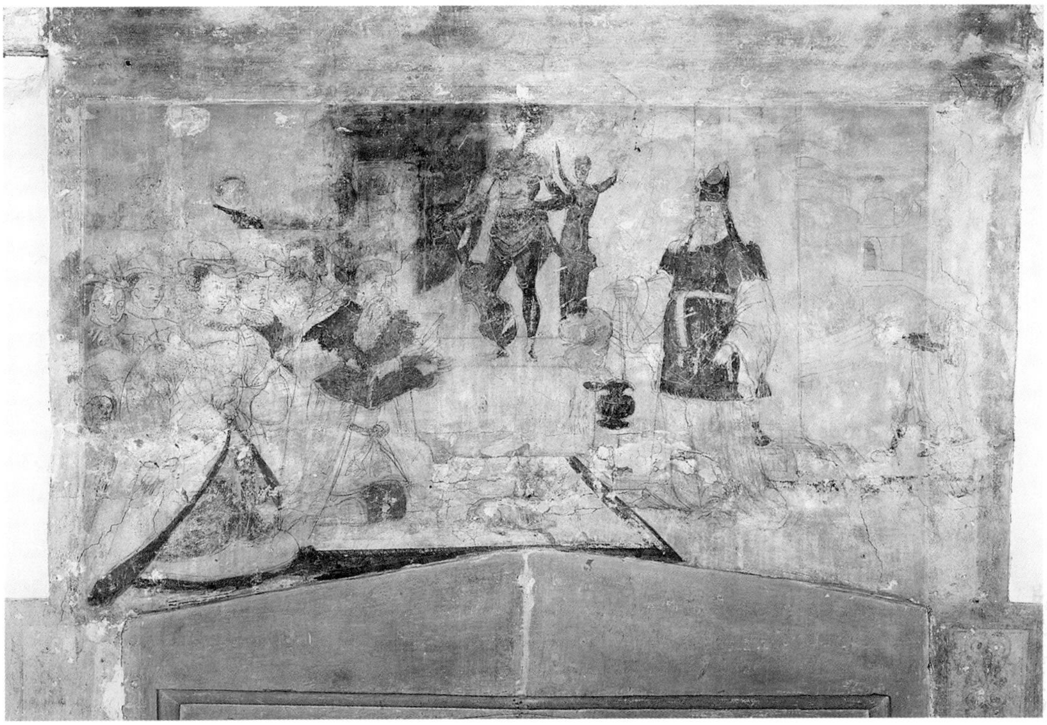

22 King Solomon worshipping false gods, wall painting of c. 1585–90 at Queen Hoo Hall, Tewin, Hertfordshire

spreading out of the hands, *Psal.44.23* and the like'. However, he continued, 'to bow down unto men, for civill honour, is lawfull'.[58] Some authors argued that not only external gestures of reverence were forbidden but also attitudes of the mind. In a treatise published in 1625 the Puritan churchman Edward Elton described the 'inward idolatry of the heart' as 'when men misconceiving God, and imagining him to be that which he is not, do worship him according to that conceit, and foolish imagination: for then they worship an idol of their own brain'.[59]

Idolatry as the outward worship of images is depicted in wall paintings dating from the 1580s at Queen Hoo Hall in Tewin, Hertfordshire, a small Elizabethan country house substantially altered between 1584 and 1589. A painting above the fireplace in the main first-floor room shows King Solomon with his wives worshipping and sacrificing to false gods (Fig. 22).[60] The king is shown on his knees before an altar, on which are two painted statues of strange appearance. Before the altar lies a dead animal as a sacrifice. A priest, holding burning incense, officiates over proceedings. This Old Testament story was employed by Protestant authors as an anti-exemplar – how not to behave – and as a warning of the ease by which one might fall into this sin committed by even the wisest biblical patriarch. The Elizabethan 'Homily against peril of idolatry' explains:

Solomon suffering his wanton Paramours to bring their Idolles into his Court and Palace, was by carnall harlots perswaded, and brought at the last to the committing of Spirituall Fornication with Idolles, and of the wisest and godliest Prince, became the most foolishest and wickeddest also. Wherefore it is better even for the wisest to regard this warning . . . Let him that standeth, beware lest he fall, rather then wittingly and willingly to lay such a stumbling blocke for his owne feet and others.

It can be assumed that the representation of this story in decorative art also functioned as a warning, reminding viewers to beware their own inclination towards idolatry. Fortitude against committing the sin of idolatry was also a central message of the story of the Three Men in the Fiery Furnace and Daniel in the Lions' Den; examples of these stories depicted in seventeenth-century plasterwork are discussed in detail in Chapter 5.

The story of King Jeroboam from I Kings 13 provided another Old Testament example warning against the worship of false gods. This story is depicted in particularly well-preserved wall paintings at Canons Ashby in Northamptonshire. The paintings are in grisaille (using only shades of grey and brown) and decorate a partition wall of what was once the withdrawing room connecting with the great chamber. They probably date from the late 1580s or 90s when the house was extended by Sir Erasmus Dryden, a committed Puritan. Dryden's credentials as a zealous Protestant are confirmed by his support of John Dod, the Puritan clergyman and co-author of *A Plaine and Familiar Exposition of the Tenne Commandements* (1604), by inviting Dod to become the family's chaplain after he had been ejected from his living for non-conformity.[61] Dryden's choice of subject matter for the decoration of this more intimate space for entertaining reflects and communicates his religious convictions. The paintings depict in two scenes the fate of the man of God in an idolatrous land. In a scene on the left, King Jeroboam is shown sacrificing at the altar of Bethel when he is denounced for his idolatry by the man of God (or prophet) who had come from Judah. Jeroboam reaches out his hand to order that the man be arrested but his hand withers and the altar fractures. A larger scene on the right shows the man of God lying dead alongside a lion and an ass (Fig. 23). The biblical account explains that he was killed by a lion as divine judgement for his disobedience in accepting hospitality from a deceitful prophet in Bethel when God had commanded against it. That his corpse and the ass which he had been riding were not eaten by the lion was an indication of the miraculous nature of his death. Both scenes therefore depict miraculous events resulting from God's judgement against transgressions. The message of this story can be understood to underline the need for fortitude against sin and obedience to God's command, as well as the mortal danger of fraternising with members of an idolatrous land. There can be little doubt that this subject was chosen to comment on England's religious situation by a patron eager for further reform. The emphasis on the miraculous might seem traditional in recalling the pre-Reformation depictions of saints' lives but it may be significant that the painting is in grisaille and not coloured; perhaps Dryden was attempting to keep the imagery muted to avoid any idolatrous transgression of his own.[62]

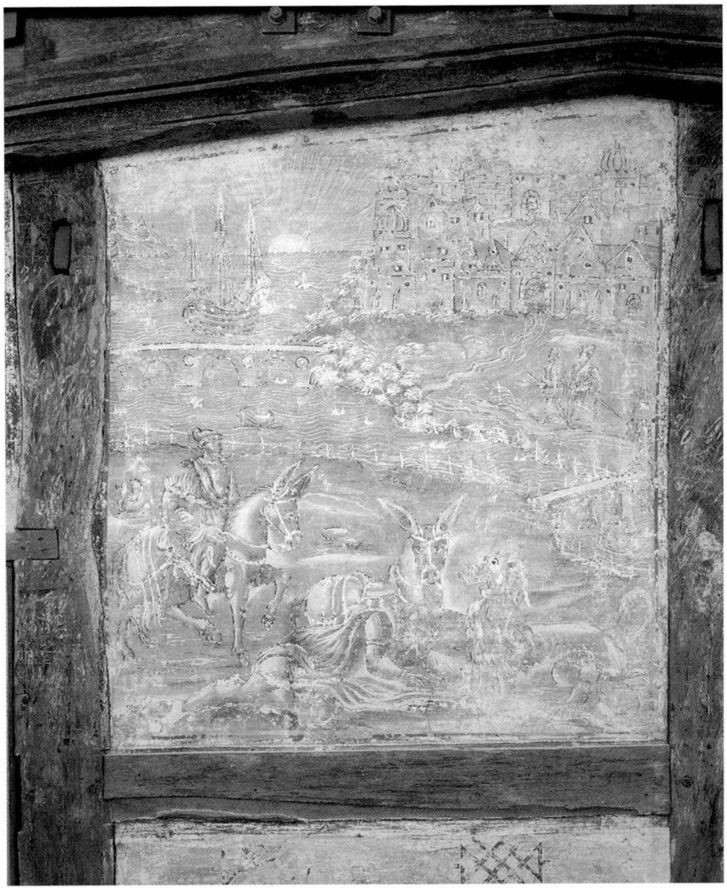

23 The man of God lying dead, wall painting at Canons Ashby, c. 1590

Having digressed slightly with these cautionary illustrations of idol-worship in decorative art I now return to the intricacies of Protestant image theory. The principal issue of use was bound up with that of location. Images in churches were most likely to be worshipped, given the sacred function and associations of the building. The Elizabethan Homily against idolatry of 1563 drew a distinction between images used outside the purposes of religion, which were tolerable, and images in public spaces for worship, which always presented the risk of idolatry: 'Images used for no religion, or superstition rather, we mean Images of none worshipped, nor in danger to be worshipped of any, may be suffered. But Images placed publicly in Temples, cannot possibly be without danger of worshipping and idolatry, wherefore they are not publicly to be had or suffered in Temples and Churches.' As it was impossible to police the actions and thoughts of the faithful, it was generally agreed that the official ban on all religious images in churches was the safest course of action. Nevertheless, some divines maintained that even in churches images might be kept if the people were taught how to use them properly. John Donne acknowledged that pictures for the purposes of instruction were not necessary wherever there was frequent preaching but suggested that 'if the true use of Pictures be preached unto them [the people], there is *no danger* of an abuse; and so as *Remembrances* of that which hath been taught in the Pulpit, they may be retained'.[63] Lancelot Andrewes offered a similar view: 'To have a story painted for memories sake we hold not unlawful, but that it might be well enough done, if the church found it not inconvenient for her children'.[64]

It is the status of religious images in the context of domestic settings that is at issue for the present study but this status was always much less rigidly defined than for images in places of worship. As has been seen, the 1559 Injunctions, which remained the basis of official proscriptions thereafter, recommended the removal of only abused images from private houses, that is, images that had been or could be used as a focus for devotion. This probably referred to salvaged images and objects from churches as well as devotional objects for domestic use. The Elizabethan visitation articles of the same year provided more detail on the concerns about images in private settings.[65] Article 45 asked the clergy: 'Whether you know any that keep in their houses undefaced any images, tables, pictures, paintings, or other monuments of feigned and false miracles, pilgrimages, idolatry and superstition, and do adore them, and especially such as have been set up in churches, chapels, or oratories.' The explicit concern here was with images used in devotion and this could be determined largely through their location in private chapels and oratories. For other forms of imagery in the domestic sphere the position is less clear. Realistically, any proscription of imagery in private houses would not only have been impossible to police or enforce, it was also less justifiable than the ban on images in churches. A firm body of opinion held that images in domestic settings were permissible because they were unlikely to be abused by worship. In a text published in 1579 the moderate Puritan William Fulke argued that 'the painting of stories in clothes or galleries &c.', 'were in no use of religion, and without all daunger of worshipping, therefore not prohibited by this [second] commaundement'.[66] The consensus of opinion agreed with this and the line adopted by William Perkins, who was opposed to biblical images in churches but found them acceptable elsewhere: 'We hold the historicall use of images to be good and lawful: and that is, to represent to the eye the acts of histories, whether they be human or divine; and thus we think the histories of the Bible may be painted in private places.'[67]

In another treatise, Perkins explained that one of the lawful uses of images was 'when images are made for the beautifying of houses either publike or private, that serve only for civill meetings'.[68] The 'beautifying' of houses suggests a decorative function and three decades later, in 1635, Simon Birckbek's defence of the English Church also emphasised the acceptable role of images as ornament:

> for we mislike not pictures or Images for historicall use and ornament; now this distinction and disparitie between making and worshipping, is confirmed by the example of the Brazen Serpent, made by Gods owne appointment; for when the same was onely made, and looked upon, it was a Medicine, when it was worshipped, it became a poison, and was destroyed.[69]

However, even in secular settings only certain kinds of religious imagery were permissible. Perkins defined lawful images as 'the acts of histories' from the Bible and this points to a third key issue in Protestant image theory, that is, the nature of the image (its form and materials) and its historical usage.

The Elizabethan 'Homily against peril of idolatry' explained that:

> men are not so ready to worship a picture on a wall, or in a window, as an embossed and gilt Image, set with pearl and stone. And a process of a story, painted with the gestures and actions of many persons, and commonly the sum of the story written withal, hath another use in it, then one dumb idol or image standing by it self. But from learning by painted stories, it came by little and little to idolatry . . .

Thus the Homily distinguished between narrative stories painted on walls or in windows and individual images of holy figures. The reference to 'one dumb idol or image standing by itself' indicates three-dimensional carved sculpture in the round. Form and material properties of images were considered relevant to the debate because reformers recognised that the degree of realism and richness of an image affected the viewer's response.[70] Free-standing jointed wooden carvings were condemned by early reformers for their realistic appearance and seemingly magical movements which deceived worshippers into belief that the image was animate. Similarly, images that were gilded or enriched with ornate clothing and precious stones suggested special qualities that encouraged veneration. Realism and rich materials seduced the viewer into affection and admiration for mundane objects. A literal interpretation of 'graven images' in the Second Commandment as 'carved' and 'cast' images provided another important restriction on the range of images open to attack. The godly separatist Henry Ainsworth, however, represents the more extreme position; he extended the range of prohibited art forms by defining 'a graven-thing' as 'any thing hewen, graved, cut or carved . . . And the holy Text elsewhere expressly condemneth *Images*, *Ezek.16.17.* and not onely *graven*, but *molten*, *Hos.13.2.* or *painted*, *Ezek.8.10.* So under this one particular, all pourtratures, and human devices are forbidden, not onely things made with hand, but with hart and thought'.[71]

Subject matter or iconography was also assessed according to the risk it posed in prompting worship. The majority of commentators agreed with the Homily and distinguished between narrative images, which represented biblical histories or stories, and images of individual figures isolated from a narrative context. One way to distinguish between narrative images and idols was the notion of scriptural fidelity: if the image could be justified as a literal depiction of historical events as recorded in the scriptures. Images with invented elements that went beyond descriptions provided in biblical texts were identified as false and lying deceptions that directed believers away from God's truth. As James Calfhill explained in 1565, 'since our Religion ought to be grounded upon truth, Images which can not be without lies ought not to be made, or put to any use of Religion'.[72]

I have mentioned that statues and carvings of central holy characters, God the Father, Christ, the Virgin Mary and saints, were deemed especially dangerous because they were beloved by believers and prompted demonstrably incorrect behaviour. Here again, the Homily against idolatry provided the lead:

> the greater the opinion is of the maiestie and holiness of the person to whom an Image is made, the sooner will the people fall to the worshipping of the said Image. Wherefore the images of God, our Saviour Christ, the blessed virgin Marie, the Apostles, Martyrs, and other of notable holiness, are of all other images most dangerous for the peril of Idolatry, and therefore greatest heed to be taken that none of them be suffered to stand publicly in Churches and Temples.

Reformers unanimously agreed that the image of God the Father was forbidden in any context because, in the words of Gervase Babington in 1583, 'he may not be imagined to be like either man or woman, or any other creature. He never was seene, and therefore can not be painted or pictured like any creature, but with a breach of this [second] commandment'.[73] Protestant commentators reserved special disdain for the image of God the Father as an old man, most often seen in the Trinity (see Fig. 18). In 1624 Peter Barker described the Trinity in relation to the Roman Catholic dependence on images:

> let the Papists therefore (as they did in their common prayer bookes in the Reigne of Queene Mary) figure the image of the Trinity with three faces, let them figure, as in many church-windowes the Father like an old man, with a long grey beard and a furred robe; his son sitting by him, with a Dove between them: those men doe but feed their eies and adore the pictures with dis-honour of God and injury to his divine nature, and is no likeness of God, but onely an imagination of man.[74]

In his manual of drawing published in 1612, Henry Peacham echoed contemporary theological treatises in warning that 'a painter [is] not priviledged to draw what hee list'. Certain images were forbidden, including: 'The picture of the Trinitie, as commonly it is drawne, first God the Father like an old man, between his knees Christ upon the Crosse, and over his Head a Dove resembling the holy Ghost. I hold it blasphemous, and utterly unlawful.'[75] Peacham's disapproval of this image is firmly stated and yet his familiarity with the iconography suggests that images of the Trinity could still be seen fifty years after they had, supposedly, been removed from churches. The image of the Trinity was found to be false and unlawful because it attempted to visualise in material form the unimaginable mystery of the Godhead. This meant that not only the figure of God the Father but the other elements of the Trinity – the figure of Christ on the Cross and the dove of the Holy Spirit – were also flawed.

Some authors based their criticism of the crucifix on the historical use of the image as the focus of devotion. Edmund Gurnay, writing at the end of the 1630s when Puritan image-fever was heating up in response to Laudian reforms in the Established Church, observed: 'And such a kind of Image (called the Crucifix) hath been found by experience to be so powerfull unto devotion, as that many beholders have not been able to withhold from tears at the sight thereof'.[76] While many authors writing during the long post-Reformation period agreed that the image of Christ on the Cross was dangerous, some asserted that the depiction of Christ as man prior to the Crucifixion was acceptable as long as it was used only as an illustration of historical events. William Perkins argued that

> it is not unlawfull to make or to have the Image of Christ, two caveats being remembered. The first, that this Image be onely of the manhood: the second, that it be out of use of religion. For if otherwise it be made to represent whole Christ, God and man: or, if it be used as an instrument or a signe in which, and before which men worship Christ himselfe, it is . . . a flat idol . . .[77]

Lancelot Andrewes agreed that it was not 'unlawful to paint or make any portraiture of Christ in his humane nature, as at his passion &c. Provided, no religious worship be given to it'.[78] Others rejected the idea that it was possible to depict Christ only as man. James Calfhill, responding to John Martial's argument that 'the image of the Sonne, because he is made man for our sakes may (as a man) be sette forth unto us', countered that 'the Divinitie of Christ can not be separate from his humanitie'.[79] Similarly, in objecting to representations of Christ in art, Andrew Willet, writing in 1608 asserted: 'Some thinke, that privately to have the image of Christ it is not unlawfull . . . But I rather approve herein the judgement . . . that Christ should not be pictured at all . . . because Christ being God and man, the image of Christ must needs be a lying image, which cannot express his Godhead'. He continued: 'Beside, who seeth not that there is great peril of adoration in having an image of him, who in that humane shape was worshipped?'[80]

Henry Peacham again followed the moderate line of official policy in directing his gentlemanly readers that 'Neither by any meanes may the picture of our Sauiour, the Apostles and Martyrs of the Church be drawne to an Idolatrous use, or be set up in Churches to be worshipped' but, he added, in an echo of the ancient justification of images, these subjects were legitimate for historical uses in churches and domestic houses:

> That pictures of these kindes may be drawne, and set up to draw the beholder *ad Historicum usum*, and not *ad cultum*, I hold them very lawfull and tolerable in the windowes of Churches and the private houses, and deserving not to bee beaten downe with that violence and furie as they have beene by our Puritanes in many places.[81]

The image of the Cross was a point of contention throughout the sixteenth and seventeenth centuries. Although crucifixes were finally condemned as superstitious in a statute of 1606, official policy on crosses was unclear and this resulted in much controversy on the matter.[82] Opinion was divided but Henry Peacham in his treatise on drawing cautiously allowed that empty crosses might be depicted if 'not for any superstitious use'[83] and many public crosses such as those in churchyards or market squares were not removed by official iconoclasts and remained intact unless local radicals took the law into their own hands.

This discussion of Protestant writings based on the text of the Second Commandment illustrates that there was no blanket ban on religious imagery in post-Reformation Britain. There were varying attitudes among those who regarded themselves as good Protestants and all but the most extreme agreed that only certain kinds of imagery were problematic and only then in churches and other places of worship. The distinction between permissible and prohibited imagery hinged on whether the function, context, form and subject matter signalled legitimate status. Lawful images were defined as the illustration of 'histories', which were justified in terms of the ancient theory that imagery functioned as a reminder of spiritual things. The picture is complicated, however, by changes in official policy during the period 1560–1660 which fostered more extreme responses among those who felt marginalised by the position of the Established Church.

MAKING AND BREAKING RELIGIOUS IMAGERY IN POST-REFORMATION BRITAIN

Having established that there was a wide range of opinion on the issue of images across the religious spectrum and across the period covered by this study, in this final section I turn to the status and use of religious images in practice. How did the various theories about what constituted permissible and prohibited images, as expressed in Protestant writings, impact on the production and destruction of visual art? What follows describes the kinds of religious imagery made and displayed in various settings in post-Reformation Britain, alongside some examples of acts of iconoclasm by Puritan opponents to images. This brief survey is intended to provide a sense of what was acceptable and objectionable in the wider visual culture; the focus is on the nature and reception of religious imagery outside the domestic sphere although there is some discussion of private chapels and pictures in domestic settings. People experienced religious images in a variety of forms and spaces in post-Reformation Britain and this would have informed attitudes to the creation and display of imagery in the home. This overview therefore sets a wider context for the focus on interior decoration in the following chapters.

Contrary to what many authoritative histories on the subject assert, religious imagery could still be seen in post-Reformation Britain. In fact, certain kinds of religious imagery helped support the Protestant message, even in churches. Although the principal concern here is with the creation of new work, it is first necessary to acknowledge that the visual and material legacy of the late medieval period formed a significant part of post-Reformation visual culture. As Maurice Howard has recently pointed out, the material remains of former monastic buildings were incorporated into the post-Reformation landscape as part of domestic and urban architecture.[84] The people of post-Reformation Britain used the built and crafted fabric of the past by re-shaping as occasion demanded, adapting what they possessed to new circumstances. Certain religious objects made of rare materials and thus of intrinsic value were adapted to new uses or moved to legitimate spaces.[85] For example, some time before 1608 the Cutt family transferred the medieval glass depicting the Passion of Christ from their former seat at Horham Hall in Essex to the east window of their new chapel at Childerley in Cambridge.[86] The rich materials contained in embroidered priests' vestments were recycled and turned into domestic hangings; Bess of Hardwick used dismantled copes for some of the Elizabethan hangings still on display at Hardwick Hall in Derbyshire.[87] Other objects simply moved through the Reformation period without incident; it is known from wills and inventories that inherited pictures, tapestries and painted cloths made before the Reformation continued in circulation and were displayed in private houses. The survival and deliberate preservation of certain kinds of traditional imagery must have informed public perceptions of what was acceptable in Protestant culture.

Secondly, it is important to acknowledge that there are fluctuations in the amount of new visual material created across the period considered here. The greater proportion of religious art made during 1560–1660 was created during the first decades of the seventeenth century. Considerably less material dating from the Elizabethan period exists. While this may be a coincidence of survival or the result of the expansion over time of the prosperous middle class which created more patrons for the visual arts, it seems likely that the advent of the seventeenth century coincided with the subsidence of a culture of prudent circumspection in relation to images. It might be assumed that during the decades following the religious settlement there was widespread uncertainty about the status of images in Protestant culture which discouraged the manufacture of new work. In the early years of the Protestant settlement the sin of idolatry loomed large on the mental horizon of believers as a result of state iconoclasm and reformist propaganda. By the turn of the century a second generation of Protestants who had not witnessed the official iconoclasm of the first half of the sixteenth century were perhaps less cautious about the strictures surrounding images. It was, perhaps, an easing of this culture of anxiety that encouraged a rise in the production of religious imagery. The type of imagery created during this period reveals much about new attitudes to the role of the visual in Protestant culture and reflects the emergence of new varieties of Protestant thought. Similarly, instances of iconoclasm indicate where the line of acceptability was crossed.

It is also important that the changed religious and political situation of the period 1625–40 created a particular set of circumstances for the making and breaking of images which complicates any chronological overview. Under the Laudian ascendancy from the late 1620s into the 30s the creation of new religious imagery was encouraged by official policy as part of a high-church agenda to re-introduce aspects of traditional church ceremonial and furnishings.[88] Unauthorised iconoclastic activity during that period can be read as part of Puritan opposition to this agenda, so that the issue of images is bound up with wider concerns about the policies of the crown and the liturgy of the Established Church.[89] The campaign of official iconoclasm in the 1640s under the Puritan government not only reversed the changes of the Laudian period but also targeted a wider range of images. A House of Commons order of 1641, followed by parliamentary ordinances in 1643 and 1644, ordered the destruction of all crucifixes and crosses, images and pictures of any person of the Trinity, of the Virgin Mary or of saints, not only in churches but also in other public places.[90] From records produced during the process of implementing these orders it is clear that religious imagery in churches had not been entirely eradicated under the Elizabethan visitations. The iconoclastic activities of William Dowsing in the 1640s indicate the amount and range of pre-Reformation imagery that had been allowed

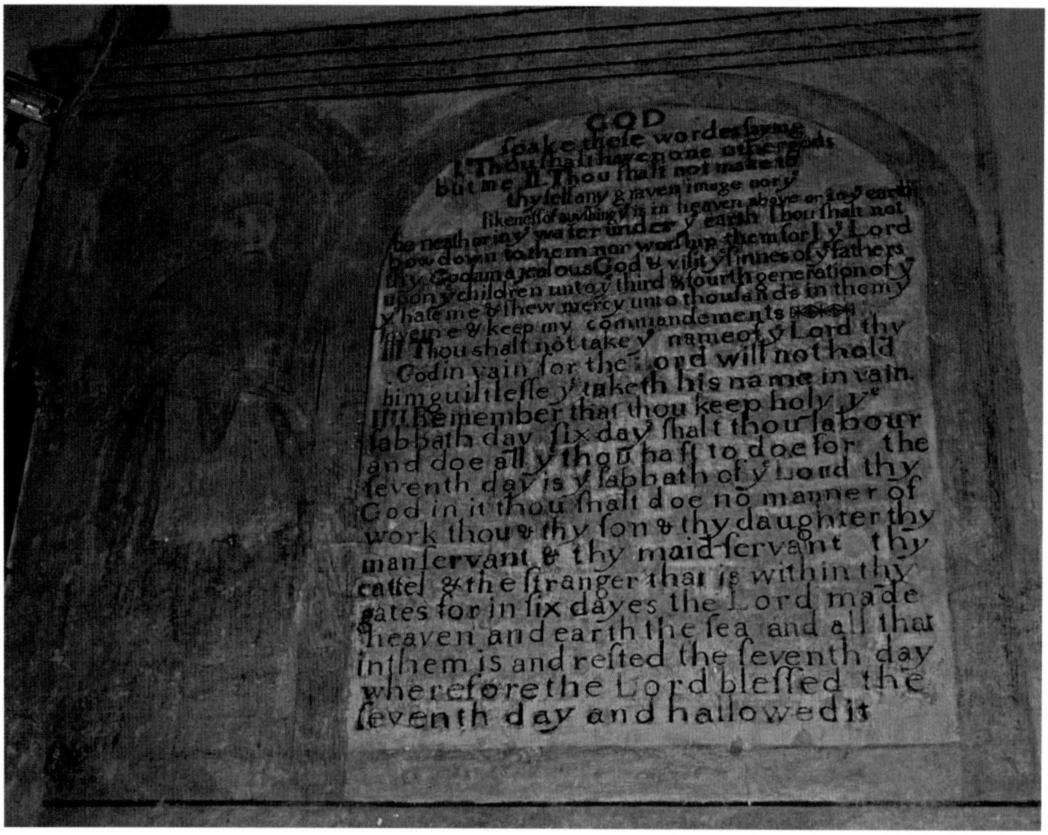

24 The Ten Commandments, late seventeenth-century wall painting at Stokesay church, Shropshire

to remain on display in churches in East Anglia. He oversaw the destruction and mutilation of 'popish' or 'superstitious' images of God the Father, Christ, crucifixes, crosses, the Virgin Mary, saints and angels in stained glass, in roofs and fonts and on the exterior of churches. The material targeted by Dowsing was in the most part imagery in the decorative fixtures of churches and his removal or defacing of the offending fabric often required considerable determination in reaching inaccessible locations.[91]

Alongside these late medieval survivals, some parish churches had been decorated with new paintings and fixtures after 1560. A royal order of 1561 required the setting up of the Ten Commandments in all churches. In some cases these texts were accompanied by the figures of Moses and Aaron, as in the late seventeenth-century paintings on the north of St John the Baptist Church in Stokesay, Shropshire (Fig. 24). These paintings combine the Protestant emphasis on the Word with images of venerable Old Testament figures which were unlikely to prompt worship. Other examples of Old Testament figures in post-Reformation wall painting include the Twelve Patriarchs, or sons of Jacob, painted on the walls of the nave at Burton Latimer church in Northamptonshire. The paintings were created in about 1600 and the design includes a scriptural reference underneath each figure. In this way the decoration represents the new Protestant interest in Old Testament history which replaced the pre-Reformation emphasis on saints' lives; elsewhere in this church wall paintings depicting the martyrdom of St Catherine had been covered by whitewash. On the west wall of Launcells church in Cornwall is a painting dating from the mid-seventeenth century of the Sacrifice of Isaac. The great figure of Abraham can be compared in terms of scale and impact to pre-Reformation wall paintings of St Christopher. A lengthy inscription underneath the Launcells painting is a characteristic feature of Protestant decoration; the text serves to underline the scriptural fidelity and therefore the legitimacy of the image.[92] Meanwhile at Walsoken church in Norfolk two large carved wooden statues of King David playing his harp and King Solomon hang above the east and west ends of the nave. They appear to date from about 1620 and the Solomon carving forms the centre of a painting of the Judgement of Solomon of similar date.

These examples of post-Reformation parish church decoration do not appear to represent any high-church leanings; the choice of subject matter is entirely in keeping with the Protestant emphasis on Old Testament history. More unusual is the ceiling of the nave at Muchelney parish church in Somerset which was decorated in about 1600 with colourful paintings of the heavens opening to reveal angels bearing scrolls with mottos such as 'Wee praise thee O God' and 'Praise the Lord's name' (Fig. 25).[93] That angels were an acceptable form of ecclesiastical decoration might have been suggested by the survival of pre-Reformation carved angels in the roof space of other churches, as at Long Sutton, just four miles away (Fig. 26).[94]

With all these examples it is assumed that the work was carried out on behalf of the parish community, not least because of its presence in the nave. By contrast, a scheme of plasterwork in the chancel of St Mary's in East Knoyle, Wiltshire, was designed by one man, Dr Christopher Wren, who was later presented to the Puritan Parliamentary Commission in 1647 for 'heretical practices' including, it seems, commissioning this artwork.[95] The figurative plasterwork was created in 1639 and includes angels, cherubim, scenes from the story of Jacob's Ladder, Christ's Ascension and a man praying to the Ascension with a dove above. Some of this programme of decoration, including a plaster ceiling decorated with cherubim, was removed in the nineteenth century but other parts of the figurative work show a pattern of damage (focusing on the figure of Christ and the heads of most of the other figures) which suggests deliberate mutilation. Wren himself ordered one of his church wardens before the commission in 1647 to take down 'certaine pictures in the chancel at Knoyle wch might prove scandalous'. These might have included an image of the Trinity over the communion table 'with the glory about it' which was part of Wren's original design.[96]

This imagery was problematic partly because of its presence in the main body of the community church. Imagery in family chapels within the parish church was less controversial because it arrogated as 'reserved' semi-domestic space sections of places of worship that were otherwise parochial. In fact, a similar scheme of plasterwork decoration to that at St Mary's in Wiltshire was created in 1633 in St Martin's Church in Exminster, Devon

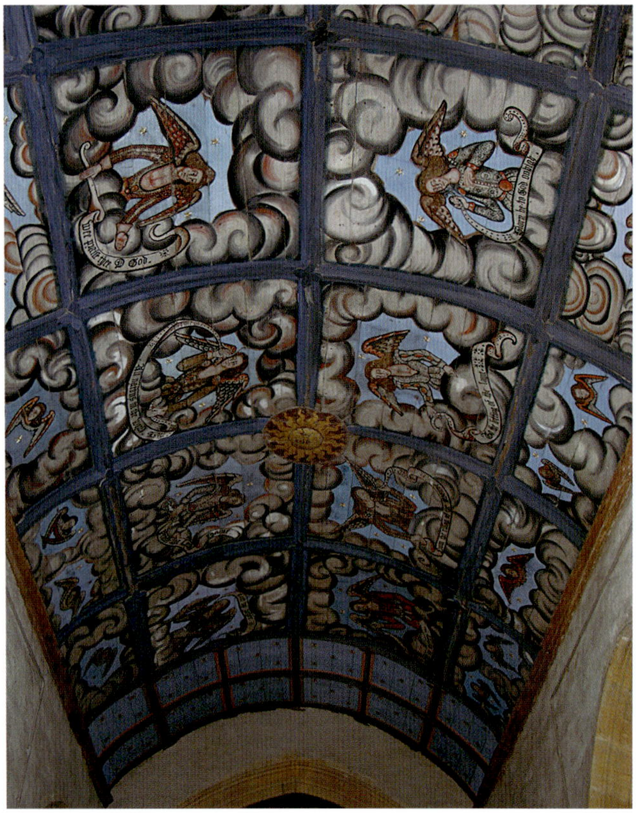

25 Painted ceiling, c. 1600, parish church of St Peter and St Paul, Muchelney, Somerset

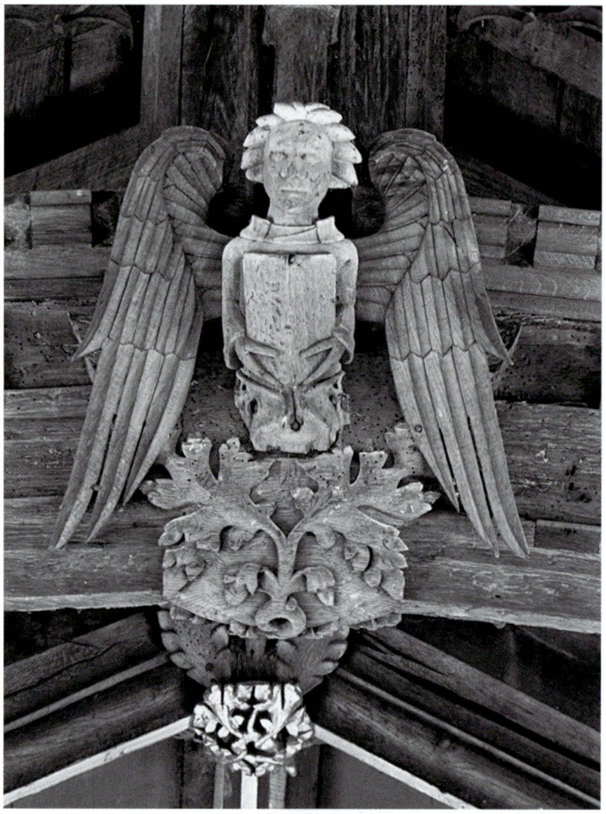

26 One of the angels from the late fifteenth-century carved roof decoration of Holy Trinity Church, Long Sutton, Somerset

(Fig. 27). That this work was considered appropriate and that it still survives intact today is perhaps due to its location in the family chapel of the Tothills of Peamore House, which occupies a separate area to the south side of the main chancel. The barrel-vaulted ceiling is decorated with representations of the Apostles, Evangelists and a great angel, which hovers above the entrance to the chapel. On the wall above the altar is a series of scenes in sculpted plasterwork depicting Christ carrying the Cross, his Crucifixion, Resurrection and Ascension. Although it seems extraordinary that images of Christ's Passion should have been created in a church setting at this date, it is possible that the semi-private location, combined with the plain finish of the unpainted white plaster, kept this imagery on the cusp of acceptability.

While the physical location and materials used for the Exminster ceiling suggest a concession to Protestant image theory, the painted ceiling at St Mary's Church in Grandtully, near Aberfeldy in Scotland, shows how traditional iconography was modified to conform to Protestant requirements. The ceiling was created as part of refurbishments carried out in 1636 by Sir William Stewart, the eleventh laird of Grandtully, who was the

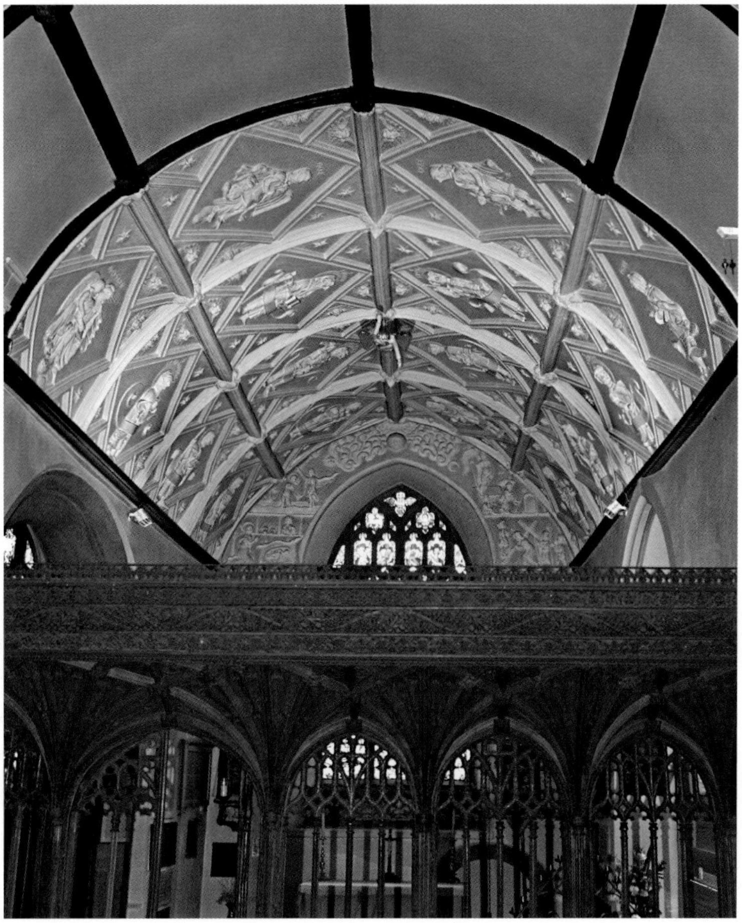

27 View of the plasterwork decoration of the Tothill family chapel in Exminster church, Devon

Sheriff-Principal of Perth under Charles I.[97] Its imagery reflects a general revival of church decoration during the Laudian period but also illustrates how Protestant concerns about religious imagery affected traditional iconography. The ceiling design includes heraldic and floral motifs, figures of Virtues and the Four Evangelists (Fig. 28). At the centre of the ceiling is a Protestant version of the Last Judgement (Fig. 29).[98] The scene shows a dying man in a canopied bed with the figure of Death as a skeleton standing over him alongside a grieving relative. Above the deathbed atop the clouds and either side of a blazing sun two angels sound their trumpets to call the dead to rise to judgement. On the right-hand side of the scene corpses rise from their graves. The figure of Christ in Heaven is conspicuously absent, such a departure from the conventional iconography no doubt in response to Protestant image theory. This revised Last Judgement iconography might reflect an intention to use the space as a memorial chapel, housing a tomb monument.

Another memorial chapel, to the Mildmay family at St Leonard's Church in Apethorpe, Northamptonshire, is decorated with a Jacobean stained-glass window dated 1621

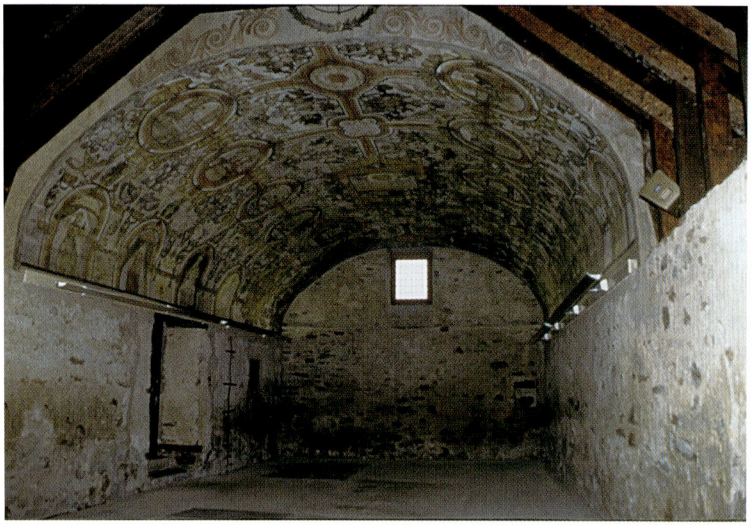

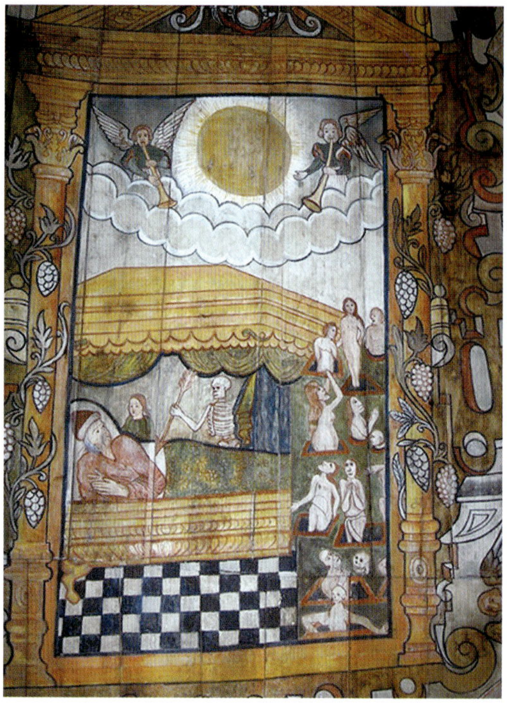

28 (ABOVE) The painted ceiling of Grandtully church, near Aberfeldy, Scotland

29 (RIGHT) Detail of the central 'Last Judgement' scene from the painted ceiling of Grandtully church, Scotland

which also has traditional imagery updated to conform to Protestant strictures. It includes scenes of the Creation and Temptation, Crucifixion, Resurrection and a re-working of the Last Judgement (Fig. 30). In this last scene, heaven is depicted as a sphere of orange light surrounded by patriarchs with the Tetragrammaton (the four Hebrew letters that correspond to YHWH (God's name, Yahweh) at the centre. Along the bottom of the window are didactic texts such as 'Love not your owne pleasures more then your owne soules' and 'Happie is he who is kept blameless to this Saviours cominge'.

The Grandtully ceiling and Mildmay window demonstrate that newly made religious imagery in churches was not unacceptable as long as it avoided the most controversial elements as identified by reformers. Fidelity to the rules was necessary because stricter Protestants were vigilant in identifying and destroying prohibited imagery. In 1629 Henry Sherfield, the recorder of Salisbury, took it upon himself to break a pre-Reformation stained-glass window depicting the Creation in the church of St Edmund in Salisbury because it included the figure of God as an old man.[99] The modified iconography of the Creation and Last Judgement scenes in the Mildmay window avoided the depiction of God in human form, employing the Tetragrammaton instead.

Such imagery in family chapels reflects the conservative religious persuasion of high-church patrons who nevertheless strove to conform to the requirements of reformed ideology in the detail of the artistic works they commissioned. The fact that the imagery was allowed to remain in a public church indicates that it successfully negotiated the line between acceptable and prohibited imagery. If such imagery could be tolerated in public

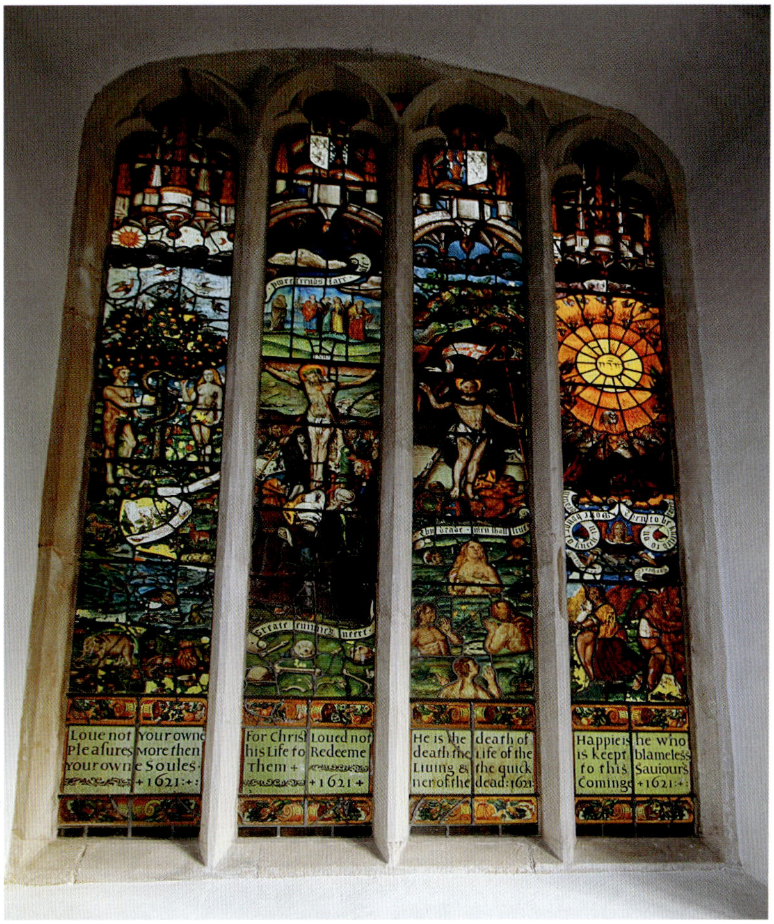

30 Stained-glass window dated 1621 in the Mildmay memorial chapel at St Leonard's, Apethorpe, Northamptonshire

spaces of worship, there was even less restriction on the making or display of imagery within the private sphere of the home.

Religious imagery in domestic chapels had always been less rigorously restricted than in public spaces of worship. Queen Elizabeth herself caused consternation among stricter Protestants by retaining a crucifix, with lights, on the altar in the royal chapel. Daring iconoclasts twice took direct action to destroy the offending object, first in 1562 and again in 1567. After this second act the crucifix was replaced with a tapestry of the Crucifixion, a concession in that the three-dimensional icon was replaced with a narrative depiction of a historical event.[100] The Chapel Royal provided a model for loyal citizens so that Bess of Hardwick's chapel at Hardwick Hall in 1601 also had 'a Crucefixe of imbrodered worke' along with 'too pictures of our Ladie the Virgin Marie and the three Kinges' and 'the salutation of the Virgin Marie by the Angle [the Adoration and Annunciation]'.[101]

In 1609–10 Robert Cecil had a series of twelve scenes from the Old Testament created in stained glass for the windows of his new private chapel at Hatfield House in Hertfordshire.[102] The scheme includes inscriptions in Latin which identify each Old Testament

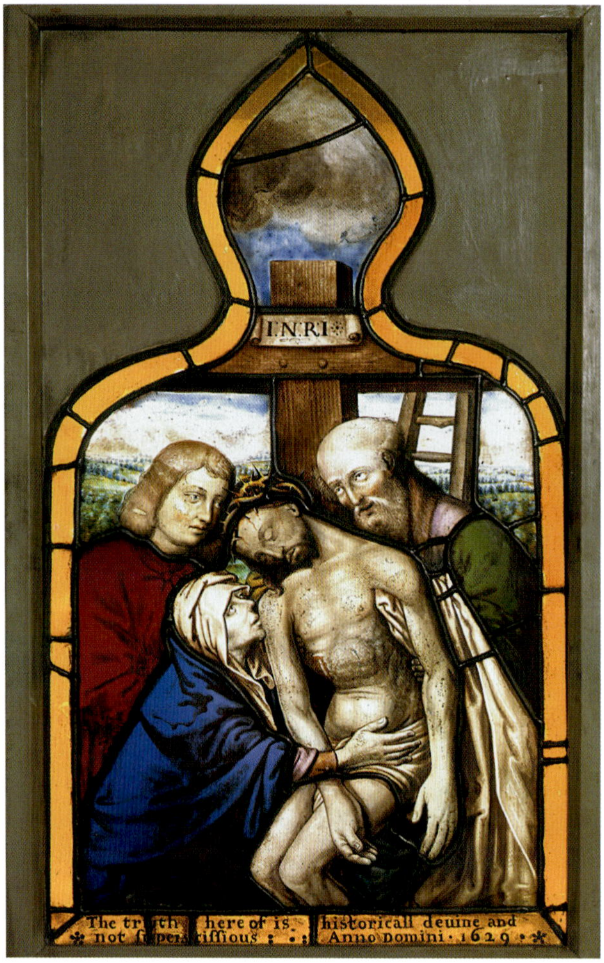

31 The Deposition, stained-glass panel dated 1629 from Hampton Court in Herefordshire. Victoria and Albert Museum, London

scene with a New Testament parallel, continuing the medieval tradition of typological pairing. Pauline Croft has described how Cecil's doctrinal and aesthetic sensibilities developed in the direction later associated with Laudianism, and the decoration of his chapel is used as evidence for this religious outlook.[103] However, this scheme of stained glass should not be seen as an 'un-Protestant innovation', as suggested by another author,[104] but a response to contemporary image theory which, as William Perkins asserted in the passage quoted earlier, found scenes of biblical history in private settings acceptable. In one sense, Cecil was simply exploiting the elasticity in contemporary thought surrounding this issue. The chapel at the manor house of Hampton Court in Herefordshire was also decorated with a series of biblical scenes in stained glass, including subjects from the New Testament. One panel dated 1629 depicts the Deposition (Fig. 31). Since this represents the figure of the dead Christ, it was thought necessary to include an inscription along the bottom of the panel to defend it against potential criticism: 'The truth here of is historicall devine and not superstitious'.

Religious hangings and pictures in other areas of the home were apparently unproblematic since they posed little risk of idolatrous abuse. Some idea of what subjects were on view and where they were displayed may be gained from occasional references in household inventories and wills, although these sources are limited by the demands of their function as legal documents. It seems that religious pictures were most often displayed as part of a picture collection in one of the main reception rooms or, in larger houses, a gallery. Robert Dudley, Earl of Leicester, was a leader of the radical Protestant faction at court and yet he had thirteen religious pictures in his possession at his death in 1588. His collection included a picture of 'Christ taken from the Cross' at Wanstead in Essex and a Nativity at Leicester House 'with 2 leaves to fould and unfoulde', indicating a triptych. The latter sounds like a pre-Reformation altarpiece yet a large proportion of Leicester's subject pictures were not inherited but acquired after 1580.[105] John Donne's will of 1631 is unusual in listing not only the subject matter of paintings but also their location in his home. He left his religious pictures to his friends including a picture of 'the blessed Virgin Marye which hangs in the little dining chamber', a picture of Adam and Eve in the great chamber, a Mary Magdalen in his (bed?) chamber and a Virgin with Joseph in his study.[106]

Only Puritan zealots objected to biblical pictures in a domestic setting but accounts of rare iconoclastic attacks on domestic pictures serve to illustrate the contemporary divisions on attitudes to religious imagery. In a publication of 1644 Samuel Torshell remembers one hypocritical man who:

> set out like John against corruptions, and over-ran even good manners, in some houses that entertained him, so that he would teare and deface any Devotionall picture (as they call it) wheresoever he came; and out of his detestation of Images would scarce endure a crosse in a Gentlemans Coate of Armes; who afterward when a favourable Prebend-wind had cool'd him, came to be active for superstitious innovations, and of a bitter spirit against the godly minded.[107]

The identity of this man is not known but he must have been active in defacing pictures in the houses of his hosts in the 1620s ahead of his conversion to the 'superstitious innovations' of the Laudian years. His behaviour can be compared to that of Sir William Springett who as a deputy lieutenant for the county of Kent in the 1640s 'expressed great zeal against superstition; encouraging and requiring his soldiers to break down all idolatrous statues and pictures, and crosses'. This zeal extended beyond his searches of 'popish houses' to the homes of his Puritan colleagues. His wife Mary described in her autobiography an episode of image destruction that took place when Springett visited the house of another deputy lieutenant. She describes how:

> passing through the hall he espied several large, fine, superstitious pictures; as of the crucifixion of Christ, of his resurrection, &etc. They were thought very ornamental to the hall, though removed thither out of the parlor by way of manifesting their neglect of them. But my dear husband thought it a very inconsistent, unequal thing, to de-

stroy those things in popish houses, and leave them in the houses of their opponents. He therefore, with his sword, put them all out of the frames, and putting them thereon, carried them into the parlour; and the woman of the house being there, he said, 'What a shame it is that your husband should be such a persecutor of the Papists and yet spare such things as these in his own house!'[108]

The description of this episode, though anecdotal, is revealing in several respects. Springett had a point about the inconsistency involved in the application of proscriptions; in 1584 'a picture of Christ upon canvas' was among a group of suspect items confiscated from the house of the Catholic Sir Thomas Tresham at Hoxton but, as noted, pictures of Christ's Crucifixion and Resurrection could and did remain in the homes of owners with good Protestant credentials.[109] This story also suggests, however, that the location of such pictures within the house was considered important. Here the owners had moved the pictures from the relatively intimate, familial space of the parlour to the grand and public entranceway of the hall, to indicate their 'neglect' of them, which can be taken to mean a lack of too much interest or care. This report of Springett's scruples underlines once again the importance of the setting of an image in directing the response of viewers.

The meaning of the term 'picture' was fluid in the early modern period and although it usually referred to an individually framed work of art it might describe imagery in a wide range of materials including painted or carved panels, hangings and prints. Printed pictures were another kind of imagery displayed in a domestic context. These might be detached from printed books or purchased as a poster-size single sheet that was always designed for display. Although religious imagery was not particularly common in print after 1560, Tessa Watt's major study of cheaper printed wares has shown that biblical scenes were still a significant part of the presses' output.[110] An example of traditional imagery in a post-Reformation printed broadside designed for display is a Nativity scene entitled 'Christus Natus Est' of 1631.[111] The central scene is surrounded by symbols of the Passion and this imagery is supported by detailed texts including an account of 'The History of Christ his Life and Death'.

Religious themes also feature prominently among the thousands of ballads produced during this period. Ballads are rhymed accounts set to popular folk tunes and were sung on street corners and other public places. Copies of the lyrics – commonly known as broadsides because they were printed on one side of a single broad sheet of paper – were displayed in various locations, including bookstalls, alehouses and domestic dwellings. In addition to the texts and the titles of the music to which the lyrics should be sung, these broadsides also featured woodcut illustrations. 'An excellent ballad of Joseph the Carpenter and the Sacred Virgin Mary' (of about 1630) includes a woodcut of the Virgin and Child between angels, while 'A most godly and comfortable Ballad of the glorious Resurrection of our Lord Jesus Christ (to the tune of *Rogero*)' printed in 1640 has a large woodcut of Christ rising from the tomb (Fig. 32).[112] Such printed pictures were accessible to a wide public and could be pinned to the wall or displayed above chimneypieces in a similar manner to pre-Reformation devotional prints. Images in print also provided

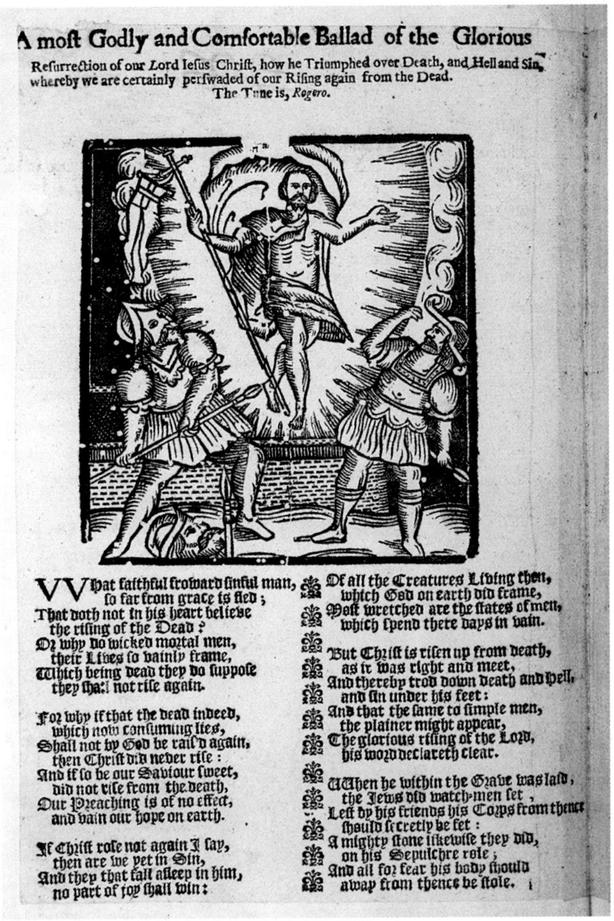

A most Godly and Comfortable Ballad of the Glorious Resurrection of our Lord Iesus Christ, how he Triumphed over Death, and Hell and Sin, whereby we are certainly perswaded of our Rising again from the Dead.
The Tune is, *Rogero.*

VVhat faithful froward sinful man,
so far from grace is fled;
That doth not in his heart believe
the rising of the Dead?
Or why do wicked mortal men,
their Lives so vainly frame,
Which being dead they do suppose
they shall not rise again.

For why if that the dead indeed,
which now consuming lies,
Shall not by God be rais'd again,
then Christ did never rise:
And if so be our Saviour sweet,
did not rise from the death,
Our Preaching is of no effect,
and vain our hope on earth.

If Christ rose not again I say,
then are we yet in Sin,
And they that fall asleep in him,
no part of joy shall win:
Of all the Creatures Living then,
which God on earth did frame,
Most wretched are the states of men,
which spend there days in vain.

But Christ is risen up from death,
as it was right and meet,
And thereby trod down death and hell,
and sin under his feet:
And that the same to simple men,
the plainer might appear,
The glorious rising of the Lord,
his word declareth clear.

When he within the Grave was laid,
the Jews did watch-men set,
Lest by his friends his Corps from thence
should secretly be fet:
A mighty stone likewise they did,
on his Sepulchre role;
And all for fear his body should
away from thence be stole.

32 The Resurrection, woodcut from 'A most godly and comfortable Ballad of the glorious Resurrection of our Lord Jesus Christ' (1640)

a template for decorative imagery on walls and ceilings.[113] This is discussed in detail in Chapter 3.

This book is concerned with the status and function of religious imagery in large-scale interior decoration in the domestic sphere. Such imagery falls outside the range of proscribed imagery identified in Protestant writings. As William Perkins argued, painted histories from the Bible were acceptable in private places. Yet even fixed surface decoration in a domestic context might attract criticism or hostility if its location was tainted by associations with Roman Catholicism.

For example, the carved stone entrance porch at Huntly Castle in Aberdeenshire was created in 1602 for George Gordon, the first Marquis of Huntly and leader of Scotland's Roman Catholics (Fig. 33). The porch once incorporated traditional religious imagery which was defaced by the Covenanters' army who occupied the house in 1640 while the second marquis was imprisoned for supporting the king. Originally, the upper sections of the porch included the Five Wounds of Christ with the instruments of his Passion and two supporting figures, probably St Mary and St John; above this a circular panel once displayed the risen Christ in glory. At the apex of the porch was the figure of St Michael

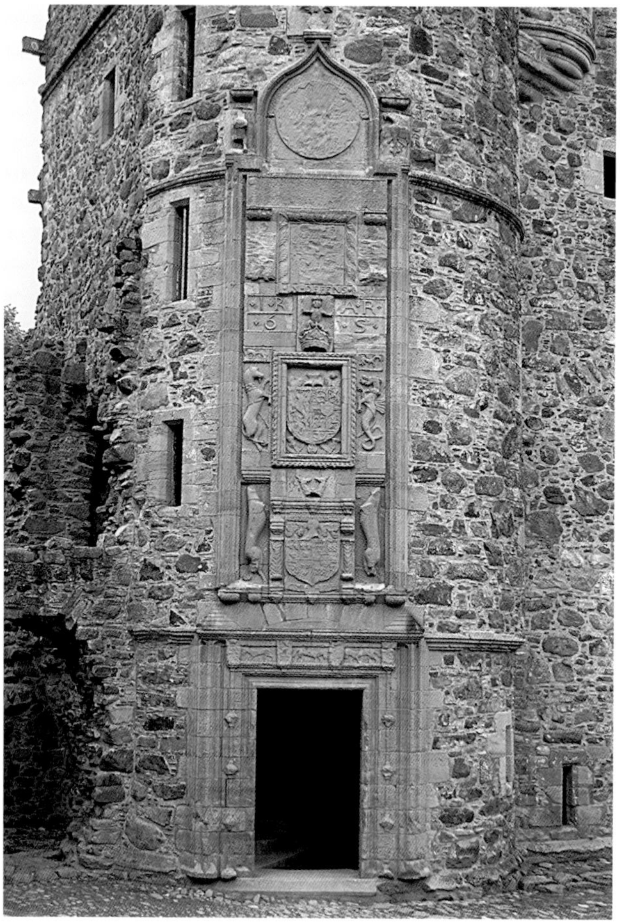

33 Carved stone entrance porch at Huntly Castle in Aberdeenshire. Created in 1602, the religious symbolism of this porch was defaced by iconoclasts in 1640

triumphing above Satan. Only this religious iconography was defaced, leaving the heraldic imagery in the lower registers intact. A contemporary witness described how the house 'was preserved from being rifled or defaced, except some emblems and imagerye, which looked somewhat popish and superstitious lycke; and therefore, by the industry of one captain James Wallace, wer hewd and brocke doune off the frontispiece of the house; but all the rest of the frontispiece containing Huntly's scutcheon, etc, was left untouched'.[114] This episode shows how iconoclasts could be discerning in destroying only the objectionable elements of imagery.

In conclusion, this chapter has shown how the process of the Reformation in Britain caused the removal and destruction of only certain kinds of religious image from places of worship. While Protestant emphasis on the Second Commandment led to the stripping and whitewashing of churches, a significant amount of traditional religious imagery could remain until the more comprehensive clampdowns of the 1640s. During the period 1560–1660 there was no unanimity on the question of the utility or danger of images in other contexts. Most Protestant theologians within the established church agreed that biblical imagery was permissible outside churches and other places of worship, as long as it was used only for civil, not religious, purposes. There were shifts in thinking over time and in the early decades of the seventeenth century new religious imagery was created even in church settings, but the beautification of churches with images aggravated tensions between those of high church persuasion and their godly adversaries. Given this highly charged atmosphere of shifting doctrines and attitudes and the friction between different groups, it is not clear why good Protestant patrons chose to create new religious images for their homes. This is explored in later chapters. First, it is necessary to establish the physical context in which interior decoration was made and viewed. The next chapter provides an overview of developments in architectural design, building techniques and interior arrangements in domestic buildings during this period, with reference to examples of houses built by gentry, merchants and yeomen.

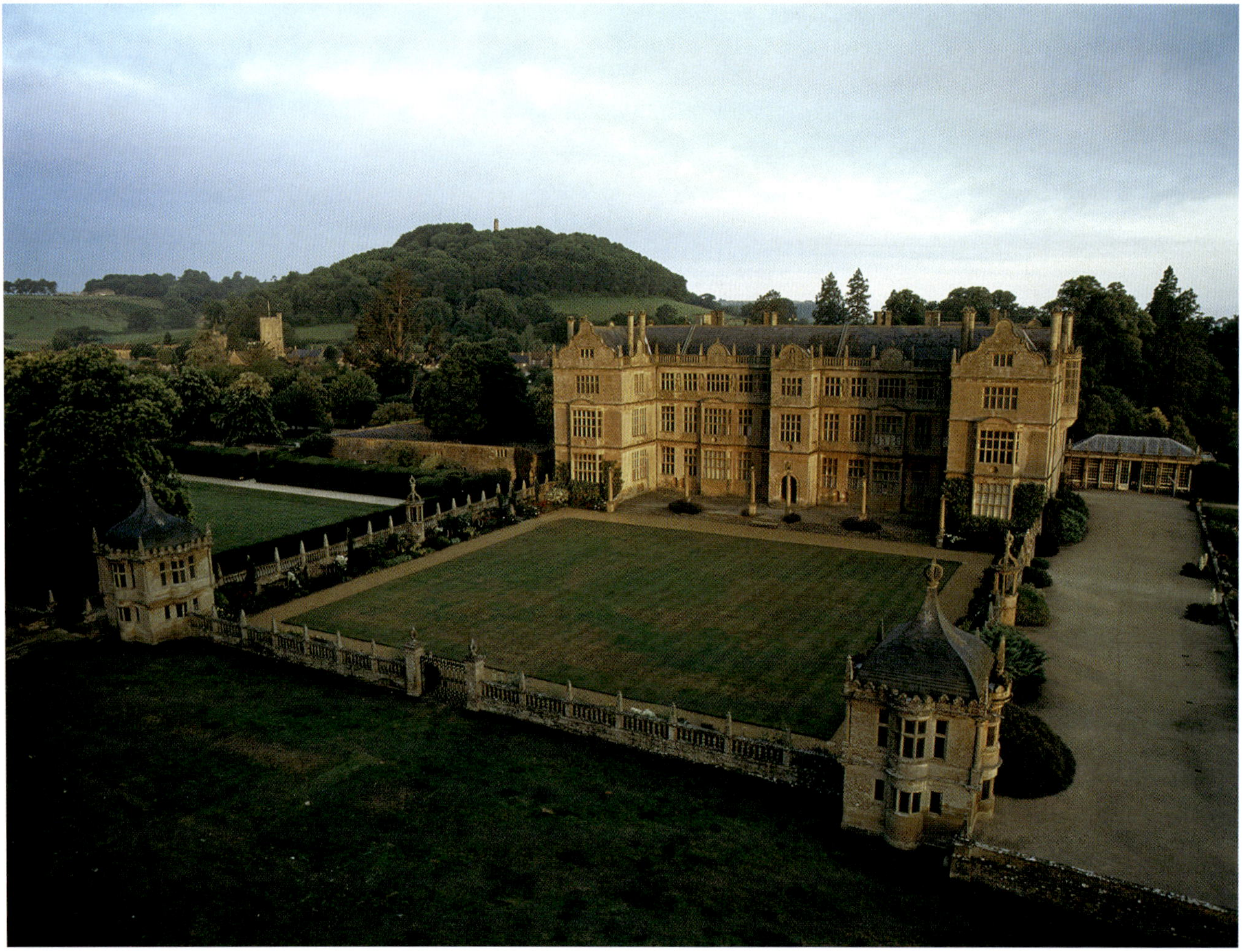

34 Aerial view of Montacute House, Somerset, completed in 1601

2

Building 'Gorgeous' but Godly Houses

The changes to ecclesiastical buildings wrought by official iconoclasm had involved the stripping away of interior fixtures and this often left the fabric of churches at risk of decay. There was certainly little new investment in ecclesiastical architecture until the 1620s and 30s. Yet, at the same time, secular architecture flourished in the post-Reformation period. This shift in building activity was noted by Elizabeth I, among others. She observed: 'It breedeth no small offence and slander to see and consider, on the one part, the curiosity and costs bestowed by all sorts of men upon their private houses, and the other part, the unclean or negligent order, or sparekeeping of the house of prayer, by permitting open decays, and ruins of coverings, walls and windows.'[1]

Modern scholars have agreed that between about 1570 and 1640 there was a secular building boom on an unprecedented scale. In the first serious account of this 'great rebuilding' published in 1953, W. G. Hoskins argued that increased building activity in rural England assumed the proportions of a 'revolution in the housing of a considerable part of the population'.[2] The consensus is that an unprecedented degree of building activity took place during the sixteenth and seventeenth centuries, although there is some debate as to the extent and nature of the 'boom' and the date parameters during which it occurred.[3] It is undoubtedly true that this was a period of great building activity that affected much of society, a fact remarked on by contemporaries. This activity included the construction of new buildings in town and country as well as the extension and modification of existing structures. A range of socio-economic factors stimulated this building boom: stable government, a flourishing economy, increased social mobility and a general rise in living standards. The form and appearance of buildings changed dramatically as a result of technical developments, improvements in the native manufacture of construction materials and the influence of new styles from the continent. All these factors contributed to a social and economic environment in which more people were in a position to build than ever before. Noblemen built palatial houses in the (often vain) hope of entertaining the monarch, while members of the gentry built grand mansions in the centre of their country estates, prosperous merchants and tradesmen built fashionable town houses and freeholder yeomen built or extended large farmhouses, but everywhere new or improved buildings pronounced the status and wealth of their owners.

Clearly, the motivations for building were manifold but desire for increased comfort in living conditions as well as aggrandisement of the owner were among the chief concerns in the design and execution of new building work. In consequence, interior decoration played an important part in the great rebuilding as it contributed to improved living conditions (in insulating and ornamenting the interior) while providing a medium for the public demonstration of wealth and social position. This combination of practical and social considerations in the use of decoration is described by the Puritan commentator Phillip Stubbes in 1583: 'for as cloth of gold, arase, tapestrie, and other riche ornaments, pendices, and hangings in a house of estate serve not onely to manuall uses and servile occupations, but also to decorate, to bewtifie, and become the house, and to showe the riche estate and glorie of the owner.'[4]

What were the results of this building craze? The first, and most obvious, answer is that more buildings resulted in more walls and therefore more physical space for the application of decoration. Yet, the mere existence of more wall space does not in itself result in the use of applied decoration. Another consequence of the building boom which had a more significant effect on the nature of interior decoration was the advent of more permanent living conditions.

In the medieval period, only the upper echelons of society lived in large, solidly constructed buildings and fairly frequent moves from one residence to another meant that the most usual form of decoration consisted of textiles that could be packed up, transported and re-hung relatively quickly and easily. Moreover, rooms in medieval houses were multi-functional and needed to be decorated accordingly. As Peter Thornton observed, 'furnishings made of textile materials – wall-hangings, cushions, carpets, bed hangings, padded chairs and canopies . . . could quickly transform a bare interior into one of accommodating comfort and visual delight, and could contrive settings appropriate to each occasion'.[5] In lesser manor houses, the emphasis on the main hall as the functional heart of the household meant that this was often the only room to receive applied decoration; as seen in Chapter 1, this often consisted of mural paintings of religious figures.

By the sixteenth century a sustained period of peace and stable government had resulted in a more static and secure way of life but the consequent shift towards more permanent living conditions emphasised the inconvenience and discomfort of medieval buildings. The construction of new buildings conceived as an entirety allowed for a general re-evaluation of the design and functions of domestic houses to enable more convenient internal layouts. As a result of this re-evaluation, the sequence of spaces in most of the larger domestic buildings from the period 1560–1660 follow certain set patterns based on a core of principal rooms, with each dedicated to specific functions. This development is most evident in the greater houses of aristocracy and gentry where there were fewer economic or spatial restrictions on the size or design of the building.[6] Nevertheless, the same tendency towards formalised internal layouts to maximise the comfort of day-to-day living is also evident in the more modest houses newly built or improved by merchants and farmers.[7]

In this chapter I provide a brief overview of the design and interior layout of houses built or remodelled by owners at the level of gentry, yeoman and merchant in country and town, with reference to representative examples. This offers a sense of the appearance of domestic buildings and the spatial arrangement of interior space in a series of rooms which, over the course of the period, increasingly became dedicated to specialised functions. The discussion concludes with an account of the social and religious sanctions for ostentatious display, which I suggest could have encouraged godly builders to select religious imagery as the subject of decoration in their houses.

THE GENTRY HOUSE

The great number of country houses built or improved over 1560–1660 mirrors the dramatic swelling of the gentry class in the early modern period.[8] Alongside the hereditary lords of manors, a new group of country house builders emerged, as individuals made wealthy through trade, industry and the law invested in land and an impressive country seat in order to consolidate and advance their status in the community.[9] The country houses of gentlemen varied greatly in size and architectural pretension, reflecting the various degrees of rank within this class as well as the number of people the building needed to accommodate. Gentry households, which included family and servants, could number between ten and forty people.[10] The actual number of servants attached to a gentry household depended to a large extent on the financial circumstances and social status of the gentleman and the scale of the building matched the size of the retinue. Some of the houses built by members of the landowning gentry approach the ambition and magnificence of the great courtier houses; these were built by members of the upper levels of the gentry, that is, the minor aristocracy and wealthy new men with connections at court. Montacute House in Somerset falls into this category.

Montacute was built at the very end of the sixteenth century and completed in 1601 for Sir Edward Phelips, a lawyer made rich and powerful through a career in politics and court appointments. The up-and-coming status of Phelips may be seen in the design of his house which, despite being brand new is reminiscent of traditional manorial architecture and thus pretends an ancient pedigree for a recently elevated family. At the same time Phelips's connections at court are indicated by references to the latest fashions. Montacute is an outward-looking house, with an abundance of windows puncturing the façade and articulating the current atmosphere of security and assurance. The multiplication and expansion of windows, a major feature of Elizabethan and Jacobean architecture,

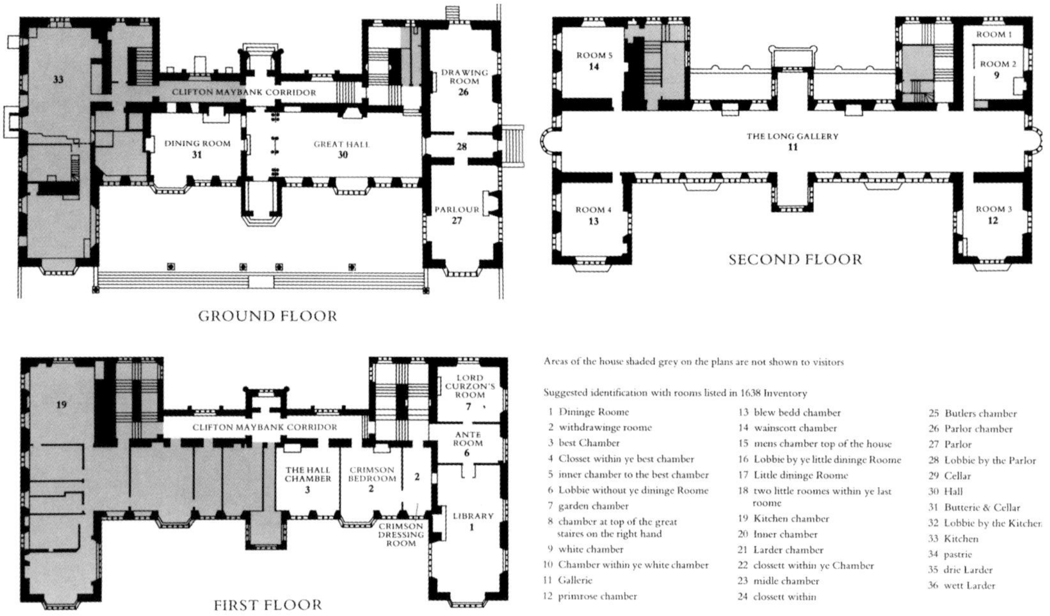

35 Floor-plans for Montacute House

shows off extravagant expense on the costly material of glass. Montacute's design incorporates elements of Italian and Netherlandish style represented by the ordered symmetry and regularity of the façade, the incorporation of classical motifs (such as columns, obelisks and shell niches) and the Dutch curved gables (Fig. 34). Despite these references, the overall effect is restrained and typically English, in keeping with Phelips's own background, education and status. A balustraded wall round an outer court recalls the fortified forecourts of medieval manors. The third storey, containing a great gallery, 172 feet long, is embellished on the principal façade with carved statues of the Nine Worthies. Although dressed in Roman costume, these sculptures are naïve in execution, betraying their English manufacture, and resemble the stone figures of warriors atop the battlements of medieval castles (as for example at Alnwick in Northumberland). In this way, the architectural style of Montacute perfectly encapsulates the character and social pretensions of its builder.

The internal design of Montacute represents one of the more common floor-plans for country houses of the Elizabethan and early Stuart periods, the E-plan, so called because with its wings projecting from a main block and a central, emphasised porch it resembles the letter E (Fig. 35). Montacute, like other large E-plan houses, actually forms a double E, placed back to back. This is also called the H-plan, with the sideways H formed by projecting wings at all four corners and a central horizontal block. The E-plan represents an expanded and developed version of an established and successful arrangement of internal space common in medieval manor houses, based round a great hall in the central block.

Montacute is typical of country houses built during this period in accommodating an ideal sequence of state rooms including hall, parlour, a grand staircase, great chamber, principal bedchamber and long gallery as well as various withdrawing rooms attached to these state rooms and additional lodgings for guests.[11] The various social functions of these rooms are discussed in full in Chapter 4. There were also many more modest rooms for daily use by family and servants and a suite of service rooms. The rooms of state lead on from one another in a ceremonial route through the public areas of the house. Montacute's floor-plans show the typical division of service rooms (on the left-hand side of the building) and reception space on the right-hand side (Fig. 35). From the grand entrance through a central porch, the ground floor is dominated by the great hall, which leads to two reception rooms: the parlour, used for family dining, and the parlour chamber, originally used as a guest bedroom. At the other end of the hall are the service rooms including a large buttery, cellar and kitchen. The scale of these working rooms indicates the size of the household they serve and the degree of hospitality offered, so that these areas also represented the status and character of the owner.

Back on the ceremonial route, a great stone staircase leads from the hall to the first floor where the principal reception rooms mirror the arrangement of rooms below. The great chamber, the most important room of state used for formal hospitality, sits directly above the parlour. A small lobby outside provides space for servants and guests to gather before entering the room of state. A doorway from the great chamber leads to a withdrawing room for greater intimacy which itself connects to the principal bedchamber. On the second floor an imposing long gallery runs the length of the building, with four chambers at each corner of the building providing additional lodgings. All the main reception rooms were decorated with fixtures and furniture appropriate to their importance, including decorative and figurative plasterwork and wood panelling in most rooms. The great chamber had the most expensive and lavish decoration including a carved stone fireplace and stained glass in the windows. In this way Montacute incorporated all the necessary trappings of a great country mansion, with the quantity, order, scale and decoration of the state rooms reflecting the estate of the owner.

In Scotland the houses of this class of builder adopted a widely different appearance and layout in the form of the tower house, which incorporated a similar suite of reception rooms but rising vertically over many floors.[12] Craigievar Castle in Aberdeenshire provides an example (Fig. 36). It was built between 1610 and 1626 by William Forbes, a merchant who gained his fortune through the Baltic trade. Forbes made use of an existing castle on the site but the new mansion he created round it proclaimed his wealth by accommodating the latest fashions and the requisite state apartments arranged over five floors. Within these Scottish tower houses, the great hall was the most important room of state. Usually situated on the first floor, this room combined the function of the hall and great chamber in English houses. As at Craigievar, a smaller withdrawing chamber leading from the hall provided a more intimate space, much like the parlour in the Eng-

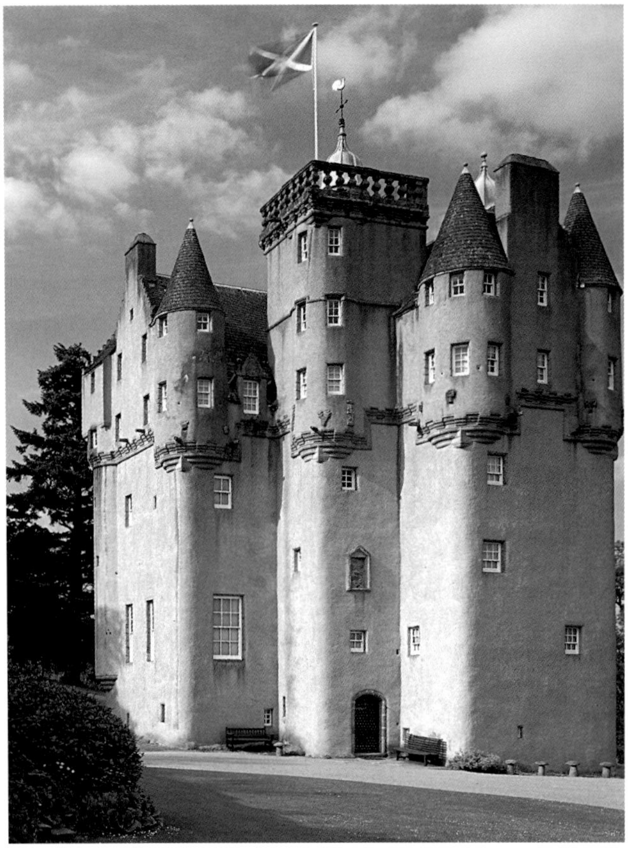

36 Craigievar Castle, Aberdeenshire, built 1610–26

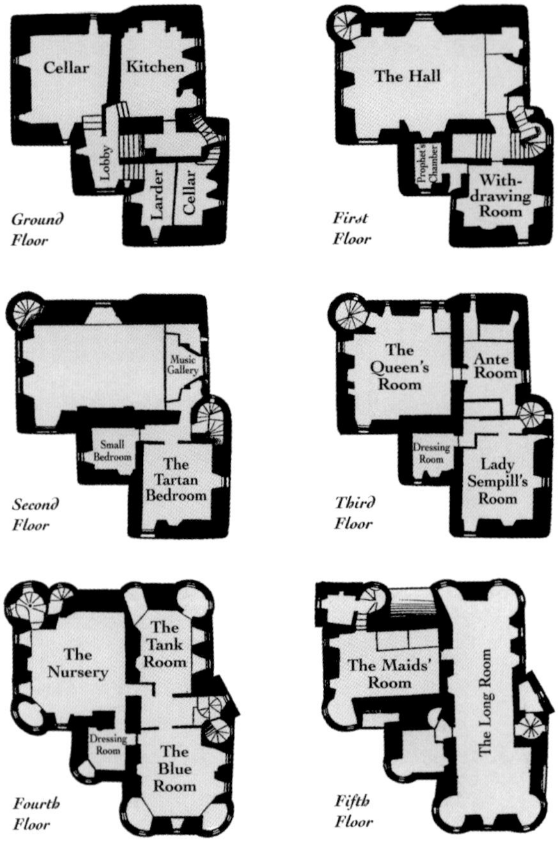

37 Floor-plans for Craigievar Castle

lish plan. At Craigievar the service rooms are housed on the ground floor below the hall, the second, third and fourth floors provided lodgings, while the fifth floor accommodated a gallery (Fig. 37). This space is a truncated form of the galleries in houses of equivalent status in England but perhaps the exercise gained in climbing five flights of stairs left less need for an extensive gallery for the purposes of walking. It was fashionable during this period for larger houses to have 'prospect' chambers for surveying the gardens and outdoor entertainments and the gallery at Craigievar must have commanded extensive views over the surrounding estate land. Craigievar was among the earlier tower houses to be decorated with plasterwork ceilings and ornament, as this trend arrived in Scotland a couple of decades later than in England. Other tower houses, such as the nearby Crathes Castle, were decorated during the same period with brightly coloured painted ceilings including texts on moral themes and figures of virtuous heroes and heroines.

Montacute and Craigievar represent the kind of mansions constructed at the top end of gentry building. In general, however, the form and appearance of houses built by members of the gentry were restricted by several factors. Large-scale building was limited by social and economic constraints, the scale of the household and the nature and extent of the owner's education and experience.[13] Firstly, as with other forms of visual and material display, the social code of decorum dictated that the scale, form and ornamentation of houses must be appropriate to the social class of the builder. Sir Henry Wotton expressed this code in his *Elements of Architecture* published in 1624: '*Décor*[um] is the keeping of a due *Respect* betweene the *Inhabitant*, and the *Habitation*. Whence *Palladius* did conclude, that the principall *Entrance* was never to be regulated by any certaine *Dimensions*; but by the dignity of the *Master*'.[14] While this concept of the relationship between architectural form and the dignity of the owner encouraged the building of new country houses to attest the status of important men, it also imposed limitations on the scale and grandeur of gentry houses. Stepping beyond the bounds of decorum was considered vulgar and pompous. Sir William Wentworth's letter of advice to his son, written in 1604, warned:

> Take hede of superfluitye in Building, for that is a monument of a gentleman that wanted discrecion and judgement. Let your house be too little for a daie or twoe, rather then too greate for a yeare; and for the furniture of your house, lett it be decent, not costlie, as also your apparel which otherwise wise men will hould vanitye.[15]

Allied to this social constraint was the practical limitation of expense. Economic constraints caused gentry builders to rely on locally available materials in the building of new extensions and complete houses, resulting in great regional diversity. Where possible, builders at this level employed the more permanent materials of brick and stone, often replacing earlier timber-framed structures. The use of durable materials offered increased protection from weather and fire but perhaps also symbolised the intended permanence of the structure and the social status it represented. Builders at all levels of society were encouraged to make use of existing structures and recycle materials wherever possible; Fountains Hall in Yorkshire, for example, was built for Stephen Procter between 1598 and 1604 on dissolved monastic lands, partly with stone robbed from the ruins of Fountains Abbey.[16]

For many of the builders at gentry level the extension of an existing medieval dwelling offered clear economic advantages, although incorporating older structures and fabric limited the degree of innovation possible and prevented a cohesive overall design.[17] With these buildings, improvements tended to be piecemeal or periodic. Sir John Moreton embarked on a series of improvements to his fifteenth-century timber mansion at Little Moreton in Cheshire between 1559 and 1580. The nature of the alterations underlines the restrictions imposed by attempting to update an existing building. Lacking space in the main house to incorporate a fashionable long gallery, Moreton squeezed one into the top floor of a three-storey gatehouse wing. The result, from the outside at least, is of a precarious and top-heavy mass of glass and timber (Fig. 38). Improvements inside the house included a new decorative scheme in the parlour, with wood panelling incorporating a frieze of text and scenes on the story of Susannah and the Elders, discussed in Chapter 4.

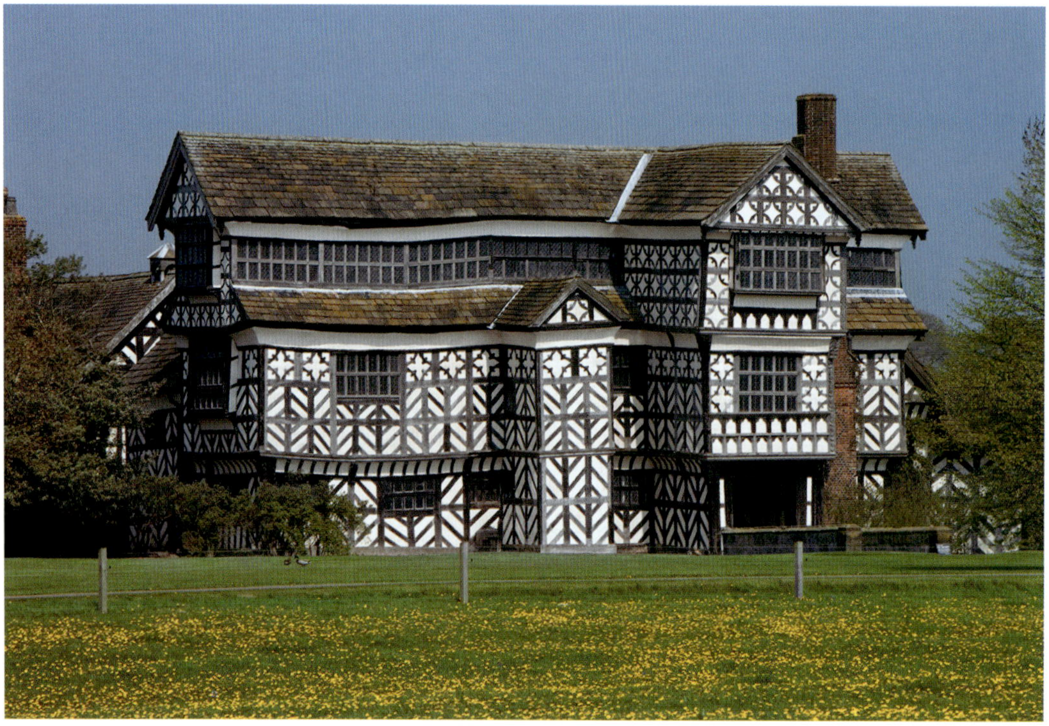

38 The gatehouse and south wing of Little Moreton Hall, Cheshire, fifteenth century with Elizabethan additions

Where funds allowed, the building of new country houses enabled members of the gentry to incorporate the latest fashions in design and decoration. An example is Chastleton House in Oxfordshire, constructed between 1607 and 1612 for Walter Jones, a lawyer who invested his wealth in acquiring the lordship of a manor. Chastleton represents another common ground-plan for gentry houses, known as the compact plan. It is built of local Cotswold stone round a small, central courtyard. Although the exterior elevations are quite plain, the design emulates late Elizabethan great houses such as Wollaton Hall in Nottinghamshire and Hardwick Hall in Derbyshire through projecting and receding planes and, as at Hardwick, the number of window lights visible on the exterior expresses the status of rooms within (Fig. 39). The main indicator that this is the house of a gentleman, not a courtier, is the restricted use of applied ornament on the façade. Despite the more compressed plan, the interior has a full complement of state rooms arranged over two floors with the luxury of two staircases contained in projecting towers, and a long gallery extending the width of the second floor (Fig. 40). Here the service rooms are pushed into the basement rather than out to one side of the building. The great chamber on the first floor is decorated with carved panelling with an inset frieze of twenty-four painted roundels representing the twelve Old Testament prophets and the twelve sibyls.[18]

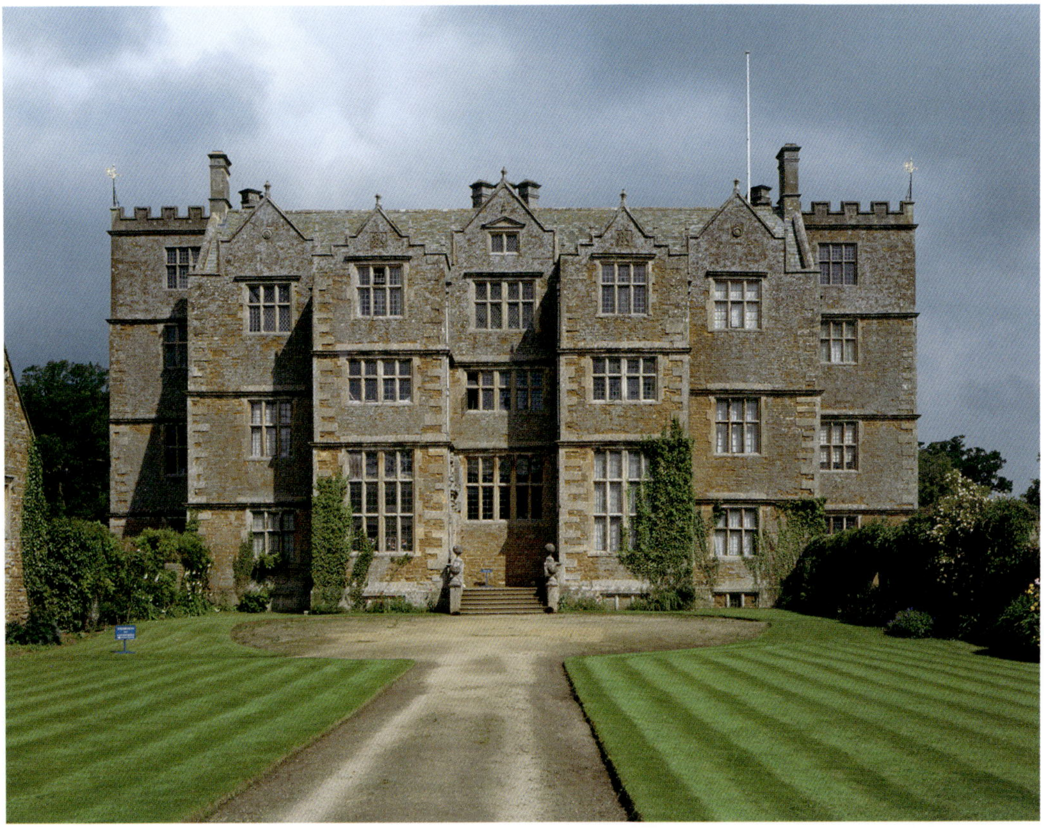

39 Exterior of Chastleton House in Oxfordshire, completed in 1612

Along with the social sanctions of decorum to restrict the amount and character of surface decoration, another constraint on the form and appearance of country houses was the extent of education and experience possessed by the builder. Most members of the gentry were tied to their own native traditions and local communities and they rarely had first-hand experience of courtly taste or continental travel. Lacking direct engagement with continental models or knowledge of foreign-language architectural treatises, gentry builders relied on the available printed sources of style, such as John Shute's *First and Chief Grounds of Architecture* (1563), which introduced English readers to the classical orders, and a series of engraved volumes by Jan Vredeman de Vries, which spread a taste for Netherlandish mannerist ornament throughout northern Europe. Influenced by these printed sources, gentry builders adopted a free interpretation of classical orders and motifs. This was combined with a native evolution of late Gothic forms and the application of strapwork and grotesque decoration, which pervaded all the visual arts during this period. A combination of education and reliance on printed sources also influenced the choice of subject matter in interior decoration. The use of biblical stories reflects the nature of gentlemanly education during the early modern period. Alongside the Bible,

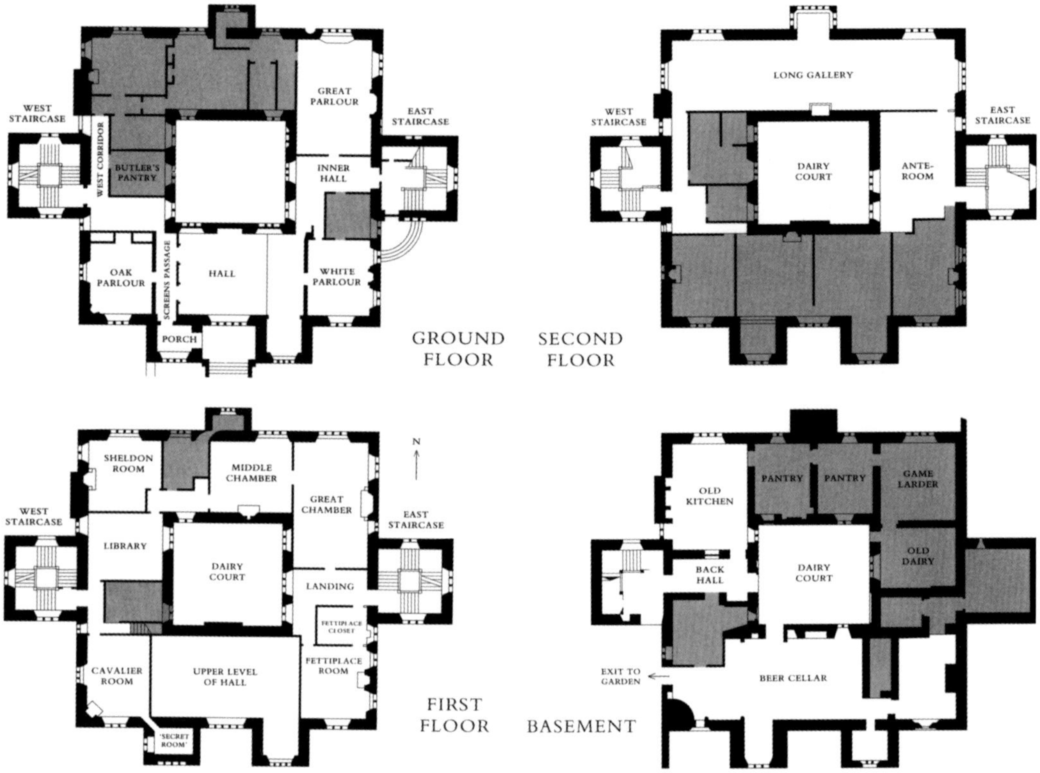

40 Floor-plans for Chastleton House

scenes from Ovid's *Metamorphoses* were sometimes depicted in the decoration of houses of the gentry. A fine example is the carved oak panels dated 1619 from the parlour of the 'Grange' in Devon, now installed in the Speed Art Museum in Louisville, Kentucky, which depict several scenes from this text including the stories of Hercules and Cerberus, Actaeon and Diana and Pyramus and Thisbe.[19] The popularity of stories from this text in the decoration of gentry houses was no doubt largely due to the fact that it was, from 1567, readily available in English in Arthur Golding's translation but also perhaps because Golding cast these stories within a Protestant moral framework that appealed to members of this social group.

In general, therefore, the architectural forms favoured for the gentry house represent an essentially insular development. By and large, gentry houses were built to express and assert the status and wealth of the owner in his community through the simple language of new or updated living accommodation incorporating all the latest indicators of social status: use of permanent construction materials; large and glazed windows; multiple, emphasised chimneys; a suite of reception rooms (including a long gallery) on two or more floors connected by a joined staircase; plasterwork, panelling and textiles to adorn the interiors.

THE FARMHOUSE

These developments in the design of country houses were emulated by builders further down the social scale. Indeed, it is fair to say that the middling ranks of the social spectrum experienced the most profound improvement in housing conditions. The steep rise in food prices in the sixteenth century meant that the freeholders and tenant farmers of rural England were able to invest surplus income in remodelling their houses. This potential for investment in building occurred at the same time that technological developments facilitated a revolution in the arrangement of domestic space.

Yeomen, who owned and farmed their own land, occupied a broad middle class below the ranks of the gentry but above husbandmen.[20] There were, however, marked variations in wealth between landowning farmers at this level. In terms of standard of living, the wealthiest yeomen could equal or surpass the lesser gentry, while poorer yeomen were closer to the ranks of prosperous husbandmen. Yeomen typically employed non-family labour and the most well-to-do had several servants. The variations in wealth between yeomen can be read in the size rather than the style of farmhouses. Although regional variations in design and use of materials encouraged different internal layouts, there was a general consistency in the character and use of interior space in yeoman homes. The difference between the houses of richer and poorer yeomen was mainly in the number of rooms and, of course, in the quantity and quality of interior furnishings. Whether they built new houses or developed existing structures, this class of builder focused on two goals: to improve the quality of internal space and to create more of it. This was achieved thanks to the increased availability of two materials in particular, brick and glass. The most fundamental change was the creation of chimneystacks – often the only part of a farmhouse built in brick. An allied development was the increased size and number of glazed windows.

Throughout the medieval period the more humble rural dwellings consisted of one large room (the hall) open at the roof to allow ventilation of a central hearth. In extended structures, bays at each end of the central hall provided additional areas for services, storage and living accommodation but the hall was the only heated room and therefore the functional focus of daily life. Even where the end bays comprised two storeys, the use of this space was restricted by limited access. The central position of the double-height hall prevented direct movement between these two areas and so ladders were needed at each end.

In the sixteenth century the increased use of brick allowed the insertion of a chimneystack into existing buildings, so that the central hearth was moved to one side of the hall and the smoke vented through a flue. With the space of the hall freed from its traditional function, it could be floored over to create an upper storey with extra rooms. The creation of additional fireplaces with flues off the main chimneystack, or the addition of more stacks, increased the comfort of other rooms which also benefited from the insertion or creation of larger, and glazed, windows. Now that the upstairs was brought into use for storage or as potential accommodation, more permanent staircases were required to provide easy access. A sturdy wooden staircase incorporated within the building not

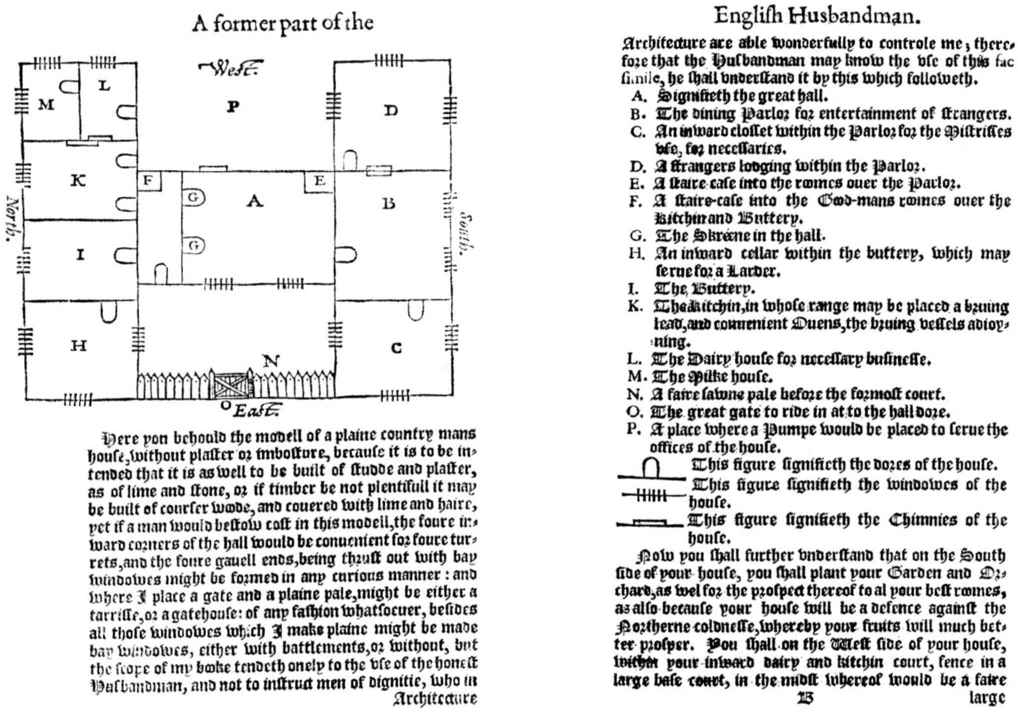

A former part of the

Here you behould the modell of a plaine country mans houſe, without plaſter or imboſture, becauſe it is to be intended that it is as well to be built of ſtudde and plaſter, as of lime and ſtone, or if timber be not plentifull it may be built of courſer wode, and couered with lime and haire, yet if a man would beſtow coſt in this modell, the foure inward corners of the hall would be conuenient for foure turrets, and the foure gauell ends, being thruſt out with bay windowes might be formed in any curious manner: and where I place a gate and a plaine pale, might be either a tarriſſe, or a gatehouſe: of any faſhion whatſoeuer, beſides all thoſe windowes which I make plaine might be made bay windowes, either with battlements, or without, but the ſcope of my booke tendeth onely to the vſe of the honeſt Huſbandman, and not to inſtruct men of dignitie, who in Architecture

English Husbandman.

Architecture are able wonderfully to controle me; therefore that the Huſbandman may know the vſe of this fac ſimile, he ſhall vnderſtand it by this which followeth.

A. Signifieth the great hall.
B. The dining Parlor for entertainment of ſtrangers.
C. An inward cloſſet within the Parlor for the Miſtriſſes vſe, for neceſſaries.
D. A ſtrangers lodging within the Parlor.
E. A ſtaire-caſe into the roomes ouer the Parlor.
F. A ſtaire-caſe into the Good-mans roomes ouer the Kitchin and Buttery.
G. The Skreene in the hall.
H. An inward cellar within the buttery, which may ſerue for a Larder.
I. The Buttery.
K. The kitchin, in whoſe range may be placed a bruing lead, and conuenient Ouens, the bruing veſſels adioyning.
L. The Dairy houſe for neceſſary buſineſſe.
M. The Milke houſe.
N. A faire ſawne pale before the formoſt court.
O. The great gate to ride in at to the hall dore.
P. A place where a Pumpe would be placed to ſerue the offices of the houſe.

This figure ſignifieth the dores of the houſe.
This figure ſignifieth the windowes of the houſe.
This figure ſignifieth the Chimnies of the houſe.

Now you ſhall further vnderſtand that on the South ſide of your houſe, you ſhall plant your Garden and Orchard, as wel for the proſpect thereof to al your beſt roomes, as alſo becauſe your houſe will be a defence againſt the Northerne coldneſſe, whereby your fruits will much better proſper. You ſhall on the Weſt ſide of your houſe, within your inward dairy and kitchin court, fence in a large baſe court, in the midſt whereof would be a faire

B

large

41 Floor-plan of 'the model of a plaine country mans house' from Gervase Markham's *The English Husbandman* (1613)

only improved communication between the various upper and lower rooms but also eliminated the need for the hall to function as a thoroughfare.

This subdivision of internal space greatly improved standards of comfort and privacy. Liberated from smoke and gloom, the interiors of farmhouses were airier and brighter and the creation of new and distinct internal spaces allowed rooms to develop more specialised functions. The preparation and cooking of food could shift from the hall to rooms at one end of the house while at the other end the parlour was given over to social and living space. As the main reception space for the provision of hospitality, the parlour was the most richly decorated and usually contained the best bed but the upper floor was increasingly used for sleeping as well as storage.

The optimum development of the hall-house plan was illustrated in a book aimed at the aspiring yeomanry, Gervase Markham's *The English Husbandman* of 1613. Markham provides a floor-plan of what he calls 'the model of a plaine country mans house' (Fig. 41). The plan is of a fully developed, H-plan house with a central hall, five service rooms in one projecting wing and three larger rooms for entertaining in the other. Markham's plan is a representation of the ideal (as realised at Montacute) and this number of rooms, the two staircases and three chimneys would have been beyond the means of most farmers. However, it broadly reflects the type of home lived in by the gentry and wealthier yeo-

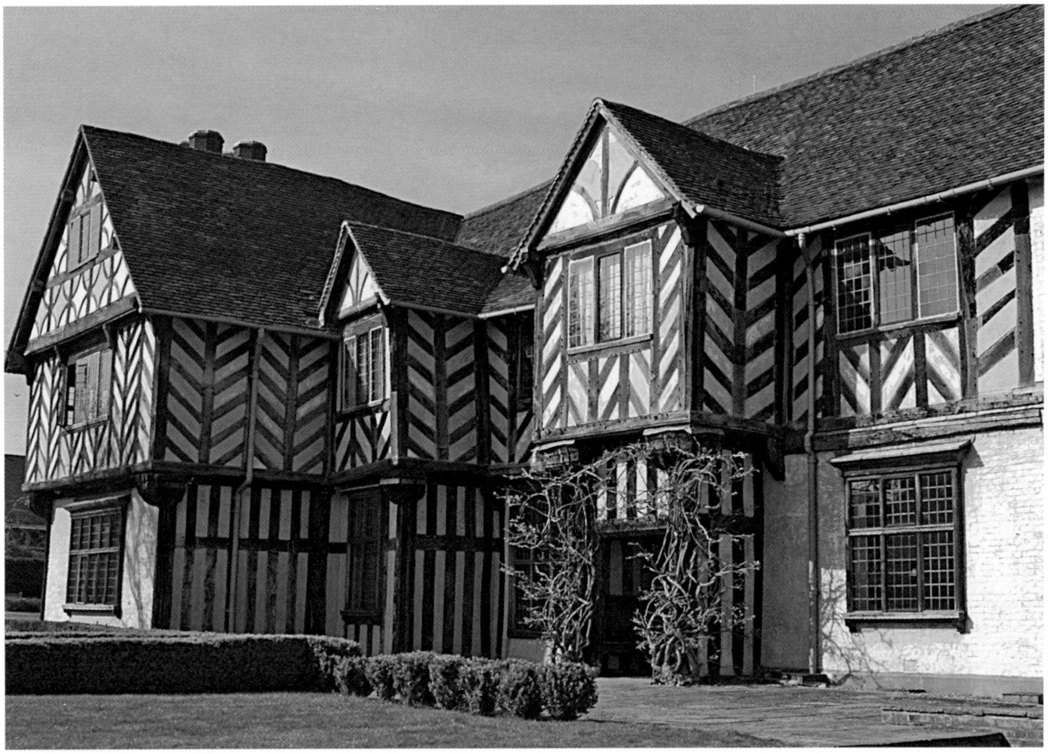

42 Blakesley Hall, Birmingham, built c. 1590

manry. Blakesley Hall, in the outskirts of Birmingham, is an example of a rural house which sits on the threshold between a gentry and a yeoman house (Fig. 42). Built in about 1590 by Richard Smalbroke, a successful Birmingham merchant who moved to Blakesley to adopt the lifestyle of a country gentleman, this timber-framed house, it is fair to say, has delusions of grandeur. The house does not quite achieve the full H-plan but its L shape still reflects the evolution of the hall-house plan with the main block housing the hall and the service rooms, while the reception rooms extend into the lateral wing. Blakesley Hall's interior has remains of decorative wall paintings with textual inscriptions and on the first floor there is a long corridor which might have been styled as a gallery, indicating how builders at this level of society attempted to mimic the innovations of larger gentry houses. Just a few miles away is a similar timber-framed building known as Stratford House (originally Camp Hill Farm) which was built in 1601 as the farmhouse of one Ambrose Rotton.[21] Apart from the pretensions to gentrified status indicated by Blakesley's 'gallery', these houses are roughly comparable in size and aspire to the fully developed hall-house plan illustrated by Markham.

It is evident that certain floor-plans proved most convenient in adopting the new architectural and design features. Alongside the development of the formerly open-hall house, other plans evolved. Perhaps the most simple, yet sophisticated, response to the

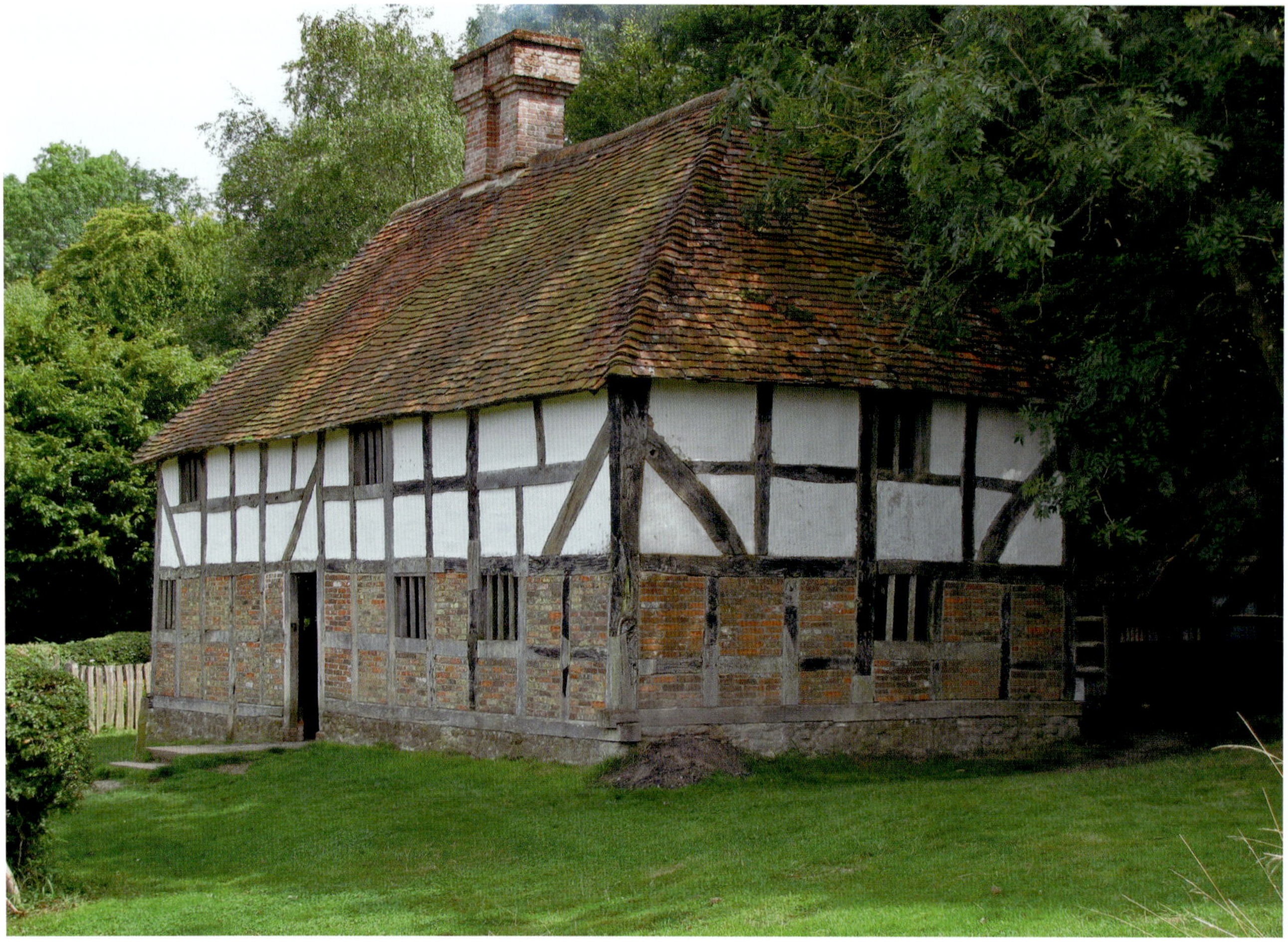

43 ‘Pendean’ farmhouse from Midhurst, Sussex, built c. 1609 as a small yeoman farmhouse

incorporation of chimneystacks was the lobby-entry house. This became increasingly common in the timber-framed areas of the country. An example is ‘Pendean’ farmhouse from Midhurst in Sussex, built in about 1609 as a small yeoman farmhouse and now re-erected in the grounds of the Weald and Downland Open Air Museum in West Sussex (Fig. 43). The lobby-entry house centres on one large chimneystack, with an entrance at the front and a staircase at the rear (Fig. 44). This chimneystack provides fireplace openings on both sides over two floors, an economical and effective use of just one chimney. Such a basic unit could be extended with the addition of bays at each end, although these required additional chimneystacks to heat the outer rooms.

An increase in chimneys meant that more houses, and more rooms in houses, had a fireplace and chimneybreast as an architectural feature and focal point. Embellishing this new feature highlighted the modernity of the improvements to the building. Unlike gentleman builders, yeomen were rarely able to invest in cohesive schemes of decoration

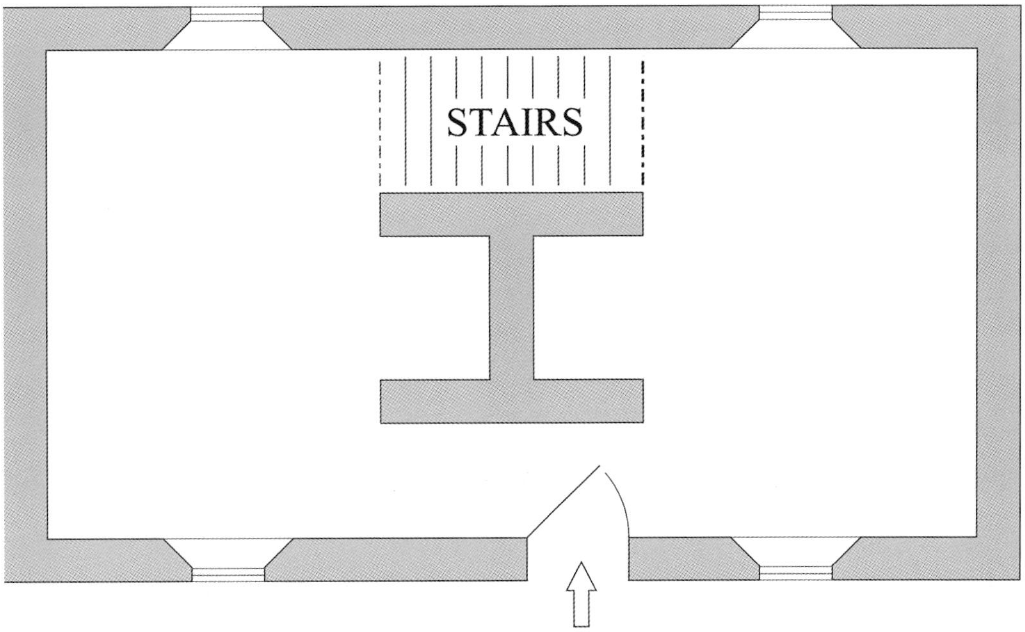

44 Floor-plan for the basic lobby-entry house

through several rooms but focused instead on one or two main rooms, usually the hall and parlour. At the level of the farmhouse, the chimneybreast might be the only feature in a room to receive permanent surface decoration. Decoration of the chimneybreast was usually carried out at the same time as improvements to the house, on the occasion of inheriting a property or on marriage. The significance of the chimneybreast as a site for decorative imagery is discussed in detail in Chapter 5.

Comparison between Markham's drawing and the 'Pendean' floor-plan shows how the scale of farmhouses could vary according to the wealth and social ambitions of individual builders. If the larger houses built by prosperous yeomanry approached the scale and architectural sophistication of the houses of the lesser gentry, this reflects the new fluidity between these classes in early modern society.

THE TOWN HOUSE

Building activity in towns boomed from the later sixteenth century onwards as trade prospered and an increase in population put pressure on existing dwellings. More significantly, the rapid rise in the status of merchants led to higher expectations concerning living standards. New money desired convenient and comfortable housing but also wanted to stamp its mark on the urban community through the highly visible display of a new town house. The kinds of town houses built during the early modern period varied according to the

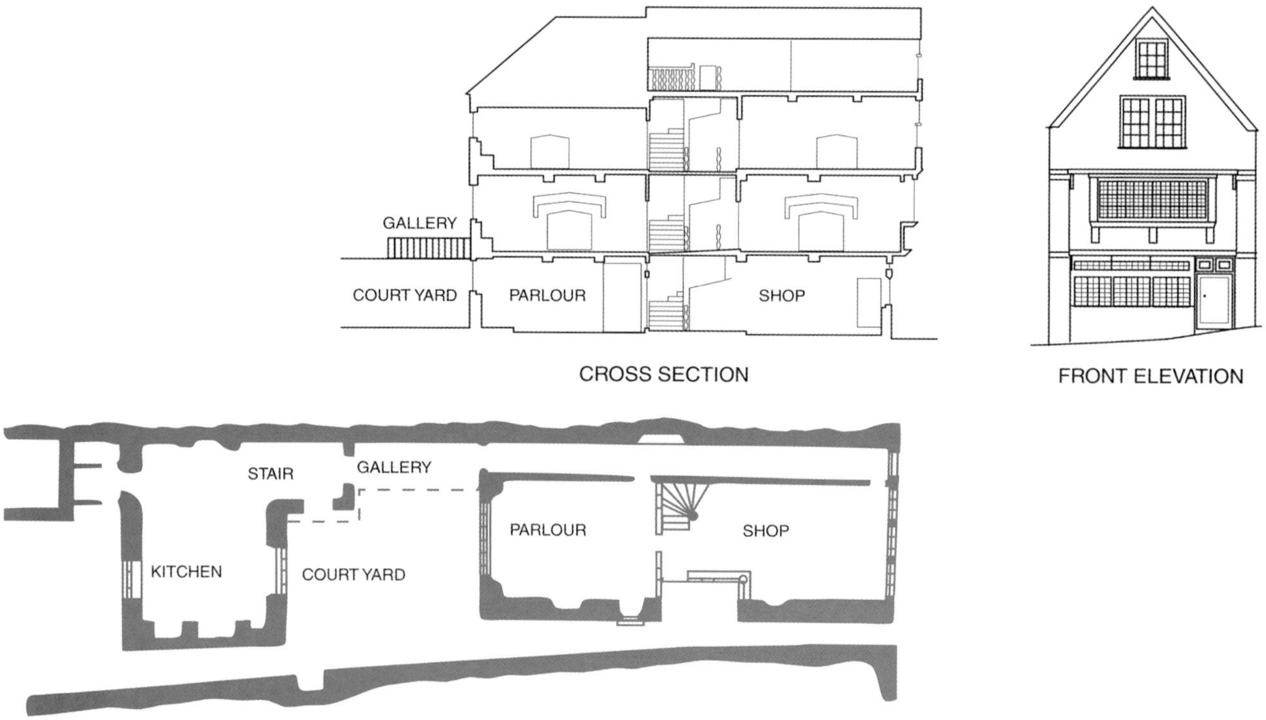

45 This diagram for a town house built c. 1575 in Totnes, Devon, illustrates a typical plan in response to the narrow plots of towns and cities

locality and the requirements of individuals. For the largest town houses the basic plans conformed to two main types. First, the town mansions of the urban elite, which were essentially country mansions set down in an urban environment making no concession to pressure on space through compactness of plan. There are two examples of this kind in Scotland: Culross 'Palace' in Fife and Provost Skene's House in Aberdeen.[22] Culross was built in 1597 for George Bruce, a local merchant and mine owner, and extended with an additional wing in 1611, the year after Bruce received a knighthood. The later, north wing included improved and additional accommodation reflecting Bruce's elevated status. On the east wall of one of the first-floor reception rooms is the fragmentary remains of a huge wall painting of the Judgement of Solomon. Provost Skene's House in Aberdeen was first built in the sixteenth century but was bought and renovated in 1622 by Matthew Lumsden, a wealthy merchant. Among various improvements he made to the house was the creation of the painted ceiling in the gallery, discussed in Chapter 4.

The most common plan for domestic buildings in the cities and towns was what might be called the narrow, stacked house. This arrangement developed from a common medieval type and was ideally suited to the increasing demands on space in the prosperous towns of the early modern period. Constructed of timber, the narrow stacked house maximised the space available on a narrow footprint by ascending vertically over several storeys. Wealthy merchants and tradesmen particularly favoured this plan because even a massive house could occupy a prime position in the town centre, offering the potential to exploit commercial possibilities as well as the high-profile location.

A diagram for 70 Fore Street in Totnes, Devon, illustrates the typical plan (Fig. 45). This house was built around 1575 for Walter Kell, a cloth merchant. The ground floor usually consisted of a shop off the street with a parlour (in the larger houses) and a detached kitchen block reached through a small courtyard at the rear. Incorporating a shop left no space for a sizeable hall on the ground floor so that the grandest reception room (the great chamber) was on the first floor, with bedrooms stacked in floors above and possibly a garret in the attic. The great chamber was embellished with the most impressive decoration; this room in a similar house at 18 Fore Street in Taunton is decorated with an ornate plasterwork ceiling and a fireplace overmantel of about 1620 depicting the Sacrifice of Isaac. Eight rooms ascending over four storeys were incorporated by the design, thanks in part to a compact newel staircase (a spiral stair round a central pole) at the centre of the building.

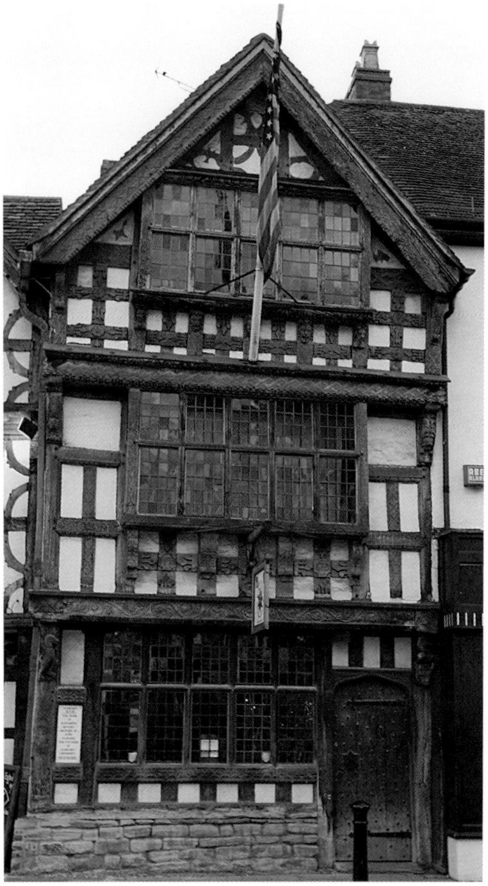

46 Timber-framed town house known as 'Harvard House' in Stratford-upon-Avon, built in 1596 for Thomas Rogers

Projecting upper storeys, jettied over the street or rear, is one of the characteristic features of this type of town house, as another means to maximise the available floor space inside. Bay windows on the street frontage also steal a few more feet of internal space while asserting the wealth and status of an owner who could afford excessive amounts of glazing. The grander houses were exercises in self-promotion, for the purposes of trade and social status, and the elaboration of features such as windows and corbels to support jettied upper storeys served to proclaim the status of the occupant. In addition to the pattern created by exaggerating the structural features of the visible wooden frame, the timber frontages of these houses were often adorned with decorative carving. 'Harvard House' in Stratford-upon-Avon provides an example. Built in 1596 for Thomas Rogers, a butcher and cattle merchant, the elaborately carved façade includes this date with Rogers's initials and those of his wife and son, a scrolling vine pattern, Tudor roses and a bull's head – presumably a reference to the owner's trade (Fig. 46).

The house known as 'Gladstone's Land' in Edinburgh represents the 'narrow stacked' town house in Scotland. A merchant called Thomas Gledstane and his wife Bessie Cun-

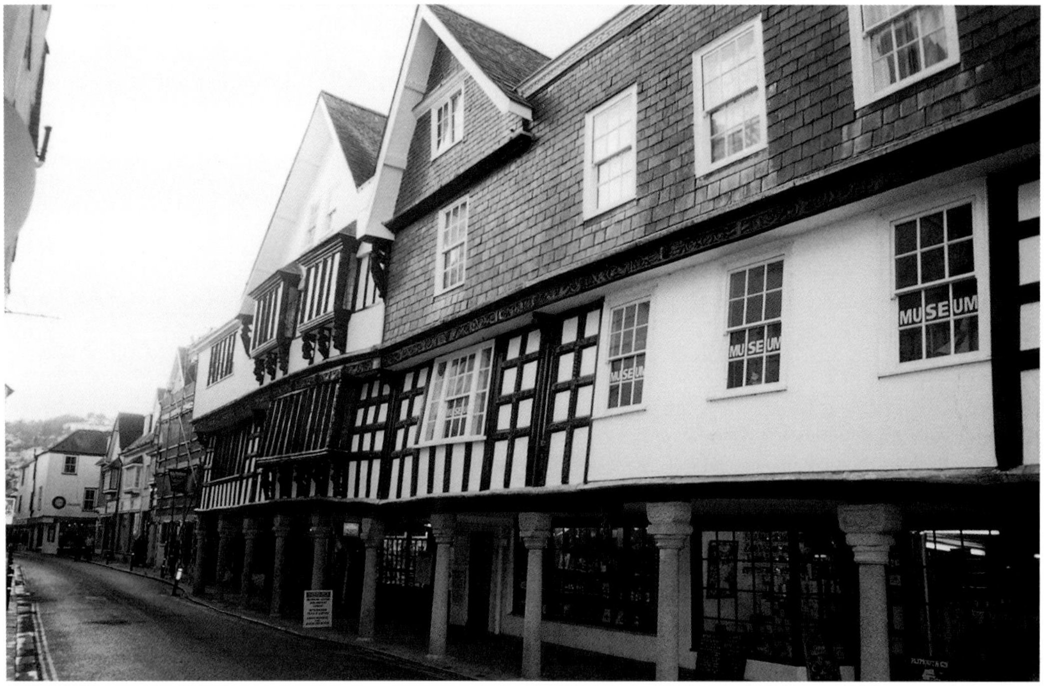

47 The houses of the Butterwalk in Dartmouth, Devon, built between 1635 and 1640 by a fish merchant who dabbled in speculative building

ningham together bought a town house on this site in 1617 and set about improving the original dwelling by adding a large stone extension on the front, which created an additional room on each floor.[23] Their improved building follows a similar internal plan to the Totnes house, with a shop on the ground floor and five floors (including an attic) housing reception and lodging rooms above. The principal reception room on the first floor is decorated with colourful painted beams and walls.

With a practical limit on the number of storeys that even the loftiest houses could support, the wealthiest citizens chose to multiply this plan sideways over additional plots to double, triple or even quadruple the accommodation. These mansions with their uniform appearance capped by rows of gables on the street frontage often resemble a row of separate houses despite being constructed as single mansions. A group of town houses built by clothiers in Shrewsbury represent these grander mansions. Owen's mansion dated 1592 is double-fronted; Sherar's mansion was built before 1573 as a triple-fronted, three-storey house, while another, known as 'Ireland's Mansion', was constructed around the same time as a quadruple plan.[24] Sketches made in the eighteenth century of 'New Place', the grand residence acquired by William Shakespeare in Stratford-upon-Avon, suggest that it had an impressive quintuple frontage.[25]

Other builders chose to speculate with additional dwellings alongside their own plot to be sold once completed. The Dartmouth Butterwalk in Devon is an example of this kind of speculative building (Fig. 47). It originally consisted of two town houses built between 1635 and 1640 by Mark Hawkins, a fish merchant. One house was built as his own residence and another, finished five years later, was leased to one John Budley, who became the town mayor.[26] Both houses were decorated with religious scenes in plasterwork; in the best first-floor chamber in the mayor's house was a fireplace overmantel depicting the Judgement of Solomon.[27] The decoration in Hawkins's house is discussed in later chapters.

DECORATING THE DOMESTIC INTERIOR

It is clear from these buildings that the prosperous middle classes of early modern Britain lavished considerable attention and expense on the exteriors and interiors of their new and improved houses. The fashion for fixed surface interior decoration as a permanent addition to a building was a relatively new development in houses outside the courtly elite. What facilitated this fashion?

There is little doubt that a cultural shift towards more permanent housing and ways of living encouraged the development of fixed surface decoration within the domestic interior. The design process and permanent use of a building encouraged a higher degree of material comfort and visual elaboration. Since internal fixtures and fittings were usually undertaken at the same time as building work, the building of a complete house enabled the creation of a cohesive programme of decoration throughout the interior, while the addition of an individual piece of fixed surface decoration provided one means of improvement or modification by an owner wanting to impress his own mark on an existing building. This was often carried out at the time of inheritance or acquisition, or to commemorate a marriage (evident through the inclusion of the couple's initials). More formalised and specialised use of internal space meant that decoration no longer had to be adaptable (and thus moveable) but could depict subjects and themes reflecting the primary purpose of a given room. Moreover, the employment of fixed surface decoration can be seen as an integral part of this process of re-evaluating the internal layout of domestic buildings because it could be used to help articulate and define the nature and function of different spaces within the interior. In his treatise on Italian classicism, *The Elements of Architecture*, Wotton advises his readers that the disposing of pictures within interiors should 'bee as *properly* bestowed for their *quality*, as *fitly* for their *grace*: that is, *chearefull* Paintings in *Feasting* and *Banquetting* Roomes; *Graver Stories* in *Galleries*, *Landschips*, and *Boscage*, and such *wilde* workes in open *Tarraces*, or in *Summer houses* (as we call them) and the like.'[28] Although Wotton is referring to paintings rather than fixed surface decoration, his comment indicates an understanding that the nature of decoration reflected, and influenced, the character of the room.

Although there are few first-hand comments relating to specific works of decorative art, there are contemporary sources that testify to the richness and visual impact of domestic interiors in the sixteenth and seventeenth centuries. A now well-worn (but, in relation to this study, immensely pertinent) quotation from William Harrison's *Description of England* (1577) records the abundance of objects in 'the houses of knights, gentlemen, merchantmen, and some other wealthy citizens' where 'it is not geason [uncommon] to behold generally their great provision of tapestry, Turkey work, pewter, brass, fine linen, and thereto costly cupboards of plate'.[29] Harrison goes on to remark on the rise in wealth and living standards of those lower down the social scale:

> so in times past the costly furniture stayed there, whereas now it is descended yet lower, even unto the inferior artificers and many farmers, who, by virtue of their old and not of their new leases, have for the most part learned also to garnish their cupboards with plate, their joint beds with tapestry and silk hangings, and their tables with carpets and fine napery.

Therefore, a much larger proportion of society than ever before was in a position to invest in luxury goods for the home. Harrison's comments refer to moveable items of furniture and furnishings and it is extremely frustrating that there is a lack in the documentary sources of any detailed mention of fixed surface decoration, which is known from the surviving material evidence to have been ubiquitous. Harrison is more concerned with practical matters in his discussion of the decorative arts:

> the walls of our houses on the inner sides in like sort be either hanged with tapestry, arras work, or painted cloths, wherein either divers histories, or herbs, beasts, knots, and suchlike are stained, or else they are ceiled [panelled] with oak of our own or wainscot brought hither out of the East countries, whereby the rooms are not a little commended, made warm, and much more close than otherwise they would be.[30]

While the reference to 'divers histories' indicates the range of narrative subject matter employed it is frustratingly generalised and throwaway, typical of remarks concerning decorative art found in commentaries on the art and architecture of the period. However, Harrison was writing in 1577, an early date at the very start of the fashion for narrative imagery in domestic decoration and while plaster was still mainly 'laid on so even and smoothly as nothing in my judgement can be done with more exactness'.[31]

Household inventories of the period 1560–1660 record in great detail the rise in costly household goods and furnishings. Lists of items in a given property, usually carried out following the death or attainder of the owner for purposes of probate, constitute a rich source of information for historians interested in material culture.[32] Unfortunately, however, inventories are of limited use for this study. The difficulty with inventories is that because they were usually occasioned by the need to establish the extent of property and list saleable commodities, they tend only to record moveable items and furnishings and leave permanent fixtures, which cannot readily be traded, unrecorded. Wills which itemise domestic goods as bequests present much the same problem. In both sources therefore one finds much emphasis on textiles (especially painted cloths and other hangings, coverlets, table-carpets and cushions) and occasional references to pictures, usually meaning individually framed paintings, but little mention of fixed surface decoration such as plasterwork, wood carving and wall painting, except in cases where these fixtures were considered detachable and therefore saleable. Hence wooden panelling (wainscot) is occasionally included in inventories, presumably where it was considered possible and profitable to strip it from the walls.

Similarly, and of particular significance for the present study, the subject matter or iconography of decorative items was rarely recorded, probably because it was not relevant to the costing procedure, although it is surprising that subject matter was not used as a method of identifying objects for the purposes of listing. It is, however, understandable that the recorders, with matters of valuation in mind, would have been more likely to identify objects in terms of their materials (which contributed greatly to their value) rather than subject matter (which presumably did not). Thus a typical inventory entry stresses the material quality of objects, as with the following list of goods in the 'Chamber over the Wyne Seller' at Wadley in Berkshire in 1596: 'Itm, the hanginges of the Chamber wth gilded lether, one greene cussyn of velvet, one covering of yelowe damaske and silver lace, and yelowe taffitie curtyns'.[33] Another common method of identification was to indicate the size of objects, as with this entry from the inventory of goods owned by Lord Wharton at Healaugh Manor in Yorkshire: 'Item in the litell Chambre by the Closet five peces of hanginges of tappastrie in length xv yeardes and in depth ij yardes iij quarters'.[34]

The mode of identification varied, however, according to the type of objects being recorded and, in some cases, the subject matter of the decoration is provided. Both the size and the pricing in entries such as: 'syxe peces of hanginge five of the storie of Jepthae conteyninge seven score sticks & 17 at 5/-the sticke', valued at the high sum of £39 7s 6d, indicate that the 'hanginges' were sets of Flemish tapestries.[35] There are several reasons why the iconography of large-scale Flemish tapestries is more often noted within inventories than that of other forms of decorative art. Firstly, tapestries were often the most expensive items to be listed, so that more detail is provided for these prestigious goods. Secondly, the sheer size of most Flemish tapestries would have meant that it would have been hard for any observer to fail to register the iconography, which the recorder then included in the records. In addition, it is probable that identifying the subject matter of such tapestries helped to differentiate between separate sets of tapestries within the same household or the number of pieces of tapestry in a particular set.

On occasion, individual entries can shed some light on iconography, such as the 'table' 'of death and pride' and 'one of death more in woode' found in 'the Greate Gallerie' in the inventory of William Lovelace of 1577, indicating an interest in allegories in the *memento mori* tradition, perhaps executed in carved wood relief.[36] General observations can also be made from inventory sources, such as the naming of two rooms after the subject matter of the decoration contained within them, as listed in the inventory of Hardwick Hall made in 1601. Presumably, the recorder followed a popular convention in the household when he used the name 'Tobies Chamber' for the room in which was hung 'Fyve peeces of tapestrie hanginges of the storie of Tobie Tenn foote deep', and 'Prodigall Chamber' for the room hung with 'three peeces of tapestrie hanginges of the storie of the Prodigall sonne, Eleven foote deep'.[37] This seemingly playful recording of the biblical personages depicted in the decoration as the 'occupants' of the room indicates a high degree of familiarity with, even affection for, the subject matter of imagery.

THE RIGHT USE OF RICHES

Despite the fact that a large proportion of society was lavishing attention on their new and improved houses, this type of activity was not unanimously approved. A tension existed between this widespread investment in domestic buildings and religious values. Social conventions required individuals to express their rank through conspicuous display – dress, behaviour, land, property and belongings. Such visible expression of wealth was especially important for those seeking social advancement. At the same time, the religious and moral values of the Protestant faith rejected worldly ambition, vanity and luxury and instead demanded a demonstration of humility and modesty. Embellishing the home was therefore a potentially problematic activity for more committed Protestants.

Godly authors condemned the building of costly houses. In his biography of the Puritan householder John Bruen, William Hinde contrasts Bruen with 'such Gentlemen and others, as being rich in this world . . . had rather bestow an hundred pounds in building and beautifying their owne houses, than an hundred pence towards the laying of the foundation, or building up of the walles or windowes of Gods house amongst them'.[38] Gervase Babington also warns against the enjoyment of riches in this world in his exposition of the Commandments first published in 1583. He observes disdainfully: 'To build and inhabite great and goodlie houses how manie bewitched with vanitie, delight in it, and with much care and cost applie themselves unto it'.[39] Babington offers the example of the biblical Solomon who recognised the folly and vanity of all his earthly enterprises. Likewise in his revised *Workes* of 1612 Richard Greenham invokes the example of Solomon for, 'as all good writings agree excessive building was the beginning of his falling away. He was building the Lords house seven years, but in building his owne house hee was thirteen years'.[40] Such vanity would not go unpunished, Greenham warns, for money should be put to serve God's glory not man's pride: 'for this cause the Prophets tell us, that the wood and stones of our houses shall come and give witnesse against us at the great day, for turning them violently to another use than God hath ordained them'.[41] In his 1613 account of *Indecorum* or unseemly behaviour, Stephen Egerton warns his readers against pride during life, 'whereby is meant worldly honour and preferment, great attendance, brave attire, gorgeous houses, stately service and other things of that kind which are as nets & snares to the ambitious'.[42] Building and inhabiting 'gorgeous houses' was thus cast as potentially perilous for the soul.

William Gouge in 1622 blames those wives who 'bring their husbands into debt, and weaken, if not cleane overthrow their estate, by gorgeous decking and adorning their houses, by brave and costly apparel, by dainty fare'.[43] Several godly authors attack pride in outward display by focusing on the lively topic of apparel. Clothing was another area in which an aspiring member of the middle class could attempt to better themselves but

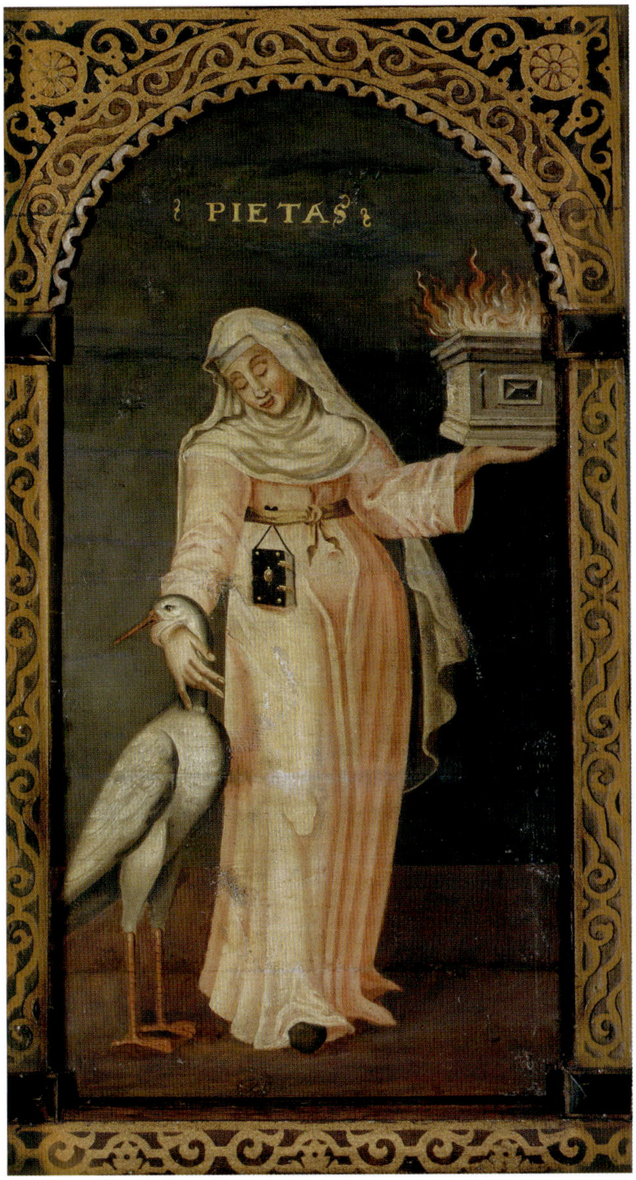

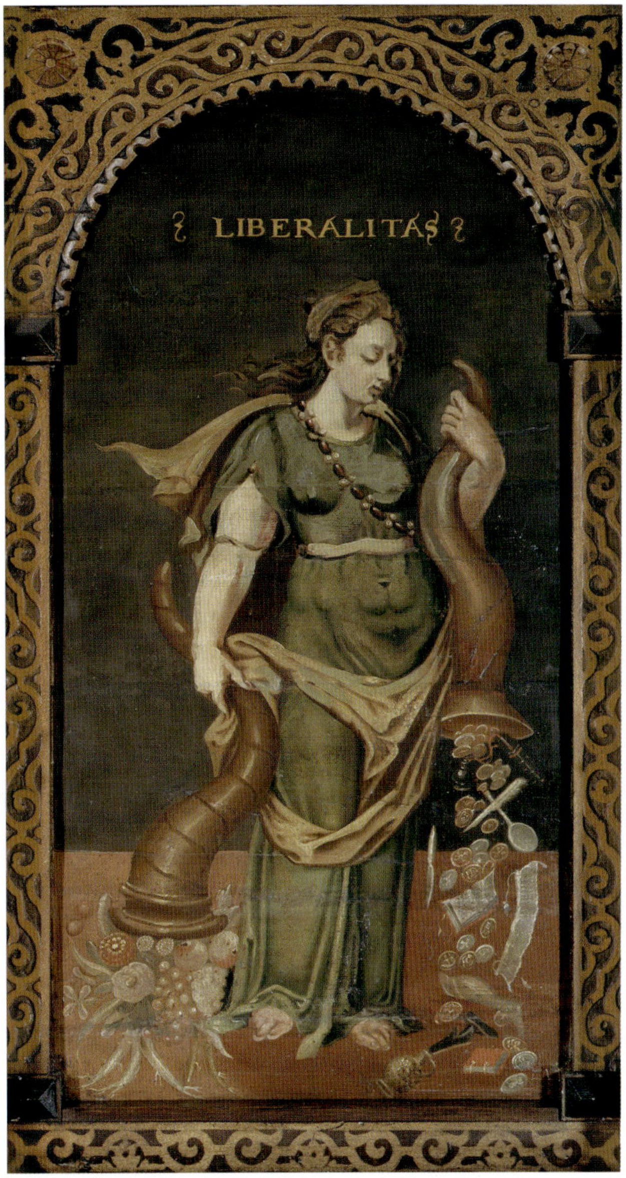

48 'Pietas' and 'Liberalitas', painted panels of c. 1620. These allegorical figures were possibly part of a decorative chimneypiece in Edward Alleyn's house, now Dulwich College

the delight of contemporaries in rich materials and exaggerated fashions attracted the attention of moralists. As Phillip Stubbes rages, only men of birth and office should wear fine clothes for 'the pride of apparel, remaining in sight, as an exemplaries of evill, induceth the whole man to wickednes and sinne'.[44] In his 1608 description of 'the right, lawful and holy use of apparel', William Perkins recommends plain dress to his godly audience: 'Our care for apparel, and the ornaments of our bodies, must be very moderate . . . the garments that we make to cover our bodies, must be such as may express the virtues of our minds; specially the virtues of Modesty, Frugality, Shame-fastness.'[45] Some members of the godly certainly followed this advice in rejecting ostentatious and colourful dress as well as the more extreme fashions of the time and adopted instead plain and sober dress, usually in black fabric with simple white linen details at the collar and cuffs.[46] In a sermon 'On Apparelling' delivered in the 1650s James Durham extended the strictures on clothing to the domestic sphere more generally:

> Next to what has been said of dressing the body, somewhat may not inappositely be spoke to anent [about] dressing and decking of houses and beds, and anent household furniture or plenishing, wherein there may be an evil concupiscence and lust, and an inordinate affection; our minds being often by a little thing kindled and set on fire.[47]

While Protestant commentators were unanimous in condemning superfluous adornment of the self or the greedy acquisition of luxury possessions, most agreed that ownership of material goods and outward ornament was permissible, even desirable, if put to the service of religion, to honour God and to promote godliness. William Perkins states that 'men must not voluntarily forsake their riches, and so bring sorrow to themselves' but establishes as a 'rule' that 'we must so use and possesse the goods we have, that the use and possession of them, may tend to Gods glorie, and the salvation of our soules.'[48] Egerton also argues that the worldly blessings of wealth should be used to the glory of God and to assist the path to salvation. He writes: 'O that the Lord would endue me with this holy discretion, that hee would give me a believing and religious heart, and make all these outward ornaments, and common gifts, instruments of grace, and spurres to godliness.'[49]

Upwardly mobile members of society therefore had to strike a delicate balance between potentially contradictory social and religious expectations when investing in their houses. This tension is reflected in the painted allegorical figures set in a fireplace overmantel at Dulwich College, south London, which was possibly part of the domestic fixtures of Edward Alleyn's mansion.[50] The two figures represent Piety and Liberality (see Fig. 48). While liberality was considered a virtue of the wealthy gentleman in relation to the provision of generous hospitality, here the virtue is cast in a negative light. The personification of this attribute has not one but two horns of plenty. She upturns these cornucopias so that flora and fruit (symbolising fecundity and prosperity) flow out from one while money and domestic items flow from the other. Piety, meanwhile, holds aloft what must be the burning light of faith or truth. It appears, therefore, that the qualities of Piety and Liberality are here cast as opposites and that the waste involved in liberal spending and acquisition of goods is considered contrary to pious living.

One way to achieve a balance between self-promotion and a show of modesty was through the use of religious imagery as decoration in the home. Interior decoration improved the appearance and status of the building and thus aggrandised the owner, while the depiction of biblical stories indicated that the householder was concerned with spiritual, rather than worldly matters. In this way the decoration of houses with religious imagery served as a badge of social and godly identity to advertise the status and piety of the household.

It can be concluded, therefore, that religious imagery used as decoration in the principal rooms of newly modernised houses could express the self-fashioned identity of the godly householder as part of the material, outward display presented to guests and the wider community. Yet in the form of decorative fixtures these images were on permanent display in the household where they were viewed repeatedly by its members. This raises the question of how these images functioned in relation to the more routine aspects of daily life. The following chapters consider how religious imagery in the domestic interior could serve in practical ways in Egerton's terms as 'instruments of grace, and spurres to godliness' to support daily household religious observance and to ensure the spiritual salvation of members of the family.

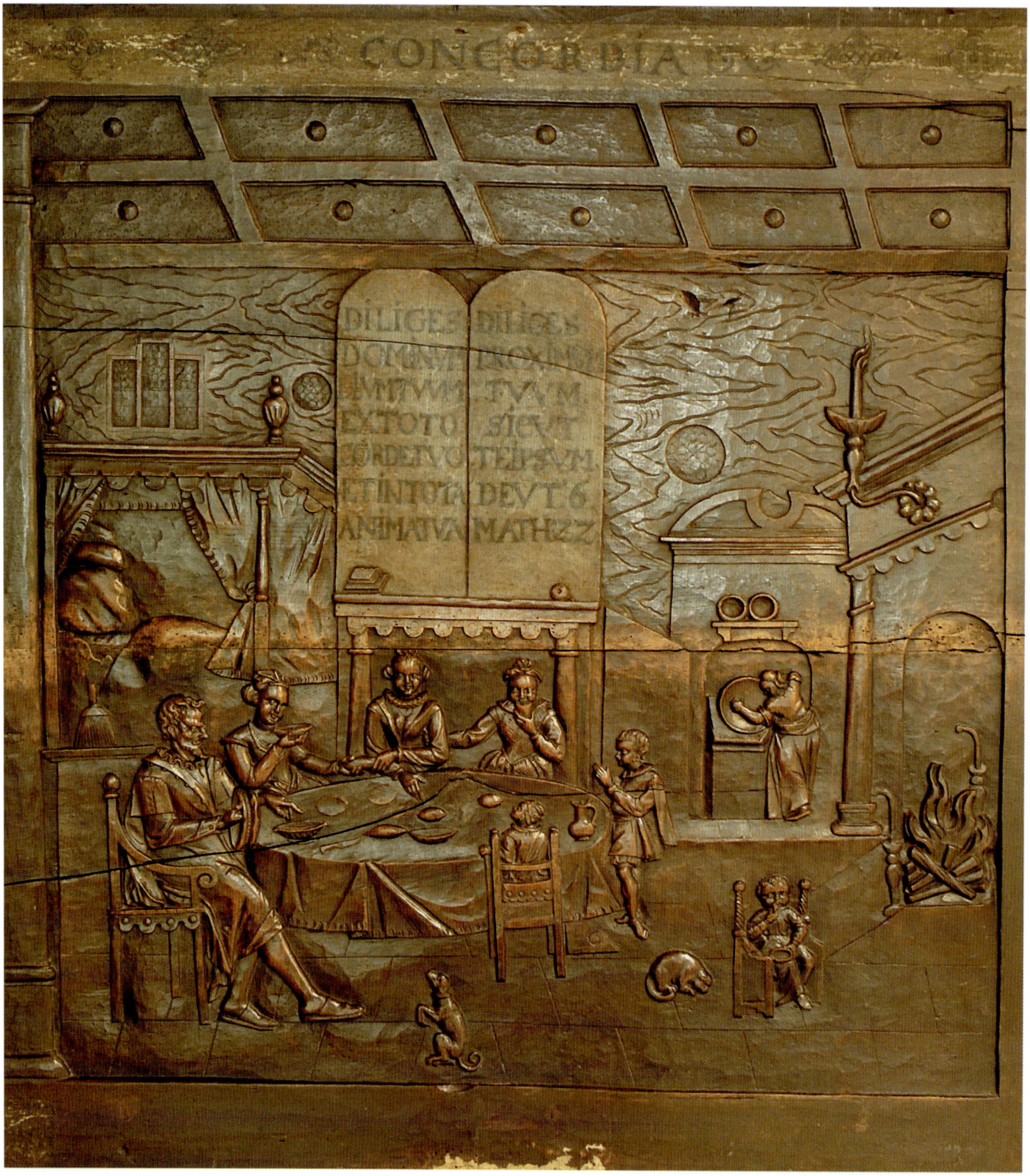

49 Allegory of 'Concordia' (Concord) expressed as an ordered god-fearing household, sixteenth-century Flemish carved wood panel

3

The Spiritualisation of the Household

Having established what kinds of houses were being built during the period 1560–1660, this chapter is concerned with the daily activities of the households contained within them. It focuses in particular on the nature of Protestant religious observance in the household and examines the relationship between godly devotional and conduct literature and religious imagery in domestic decoration. It is now widely accepted that images in print served as a source of design and iconography for the visual arts of early modern Britain. As Anthony Wells-Cole has shown, most of the printed material employed in England was produced on the continent, especially in the Low Countries.[1] It is the case, however, that a small but significant amount of the iconography depicted in domestic decoration was copied from the illustrated title pages of Protestant books, including the best-selling guides to 'godly' behaviour which offered advice on approved religious practices and habits of thought. What follows examines the implications of this connection between printed imagery from godly literature and religious imagery in interior decoration and speculates about the functions of the iconography once transferred from the printed page to the context of the domestic interior.

The early modern household in Britain comprised members of family and servants in a hierarchy of relationships: husbands and wives, parents and children, masters and servants. Servants and apprentices were considered integral members of families. A daily routine of activities provided a formal framework for domestic life and regulated the nature of interaction between these groups. Each household was presided over by the male householder, whose responsibilities included the maintenance of order and discipline within a God-fearing atmosphere of piety. The ideal of the ordered, well-run household is illustrated in a Flemish carved wood panel dating from the sixteenth century (Fig. 49).[2] In faded lettering along the frame at the top is written the word 'Concordia' (Concord)

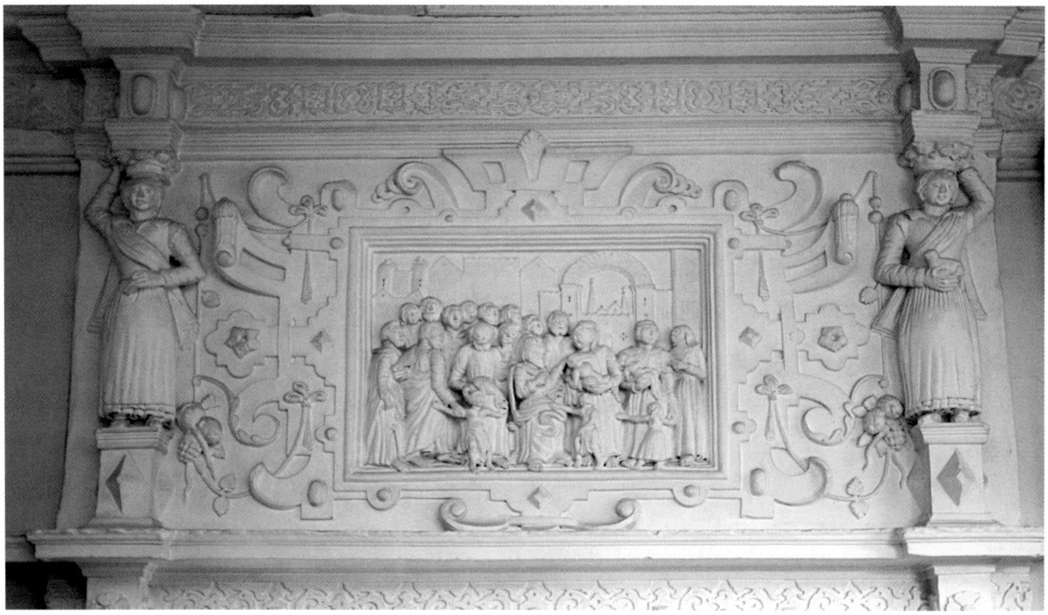

50 Christ blessing little children, plasterwork overmantel at the Court House, East Quantoxhead, Somerset, c. 1629

and underneath is a scene of domestic harmony, with a well-to-do family seated round the dinner table and a servant busy in the kitchen.[3] The key to this family concord, the viewer is given to understand, is fidelity to God's commandments, represented in two great tablets displayed over the fireplace. The references to Deuteronomy 6 and Matthew 22, written on the tablets, underline the importance of living under God's commandments. These texts in Latin quote the commands to 'love the Lord God with all thine heart, and with all thy soul' and to 'love thy neighbour as oneself'. This chapter describes similar examples from houses in early modern Britain where God's word is emphasised visually within the decoration of domestic rooms.

There is a shortage of documentary sources to shed light on the relationship between decoration in the domestic interior and patterns of life taking place around it. It is rare to find evidence in the historical record on the circumstances surrounding the creation of decorative art or the personalities involved in commissioning and viewing it. This is because it is often difficult to identify the owner of a property at the time decorative work was carried out. It is useful therefore to begin with a particular case where such evidence does exist, by way of introducing the relationship between religious imagery in decorative art and the duty of the good Protestant householder to instruct his family in the reformed faith.

In 1622 George Luttrell of Dunster Castle in the county of Somerset married his second wife, a lady named Silvestra Capps. This was not a particularly illustrious match and seems rather rash on the part of the sixty-one-year-old Luttrell. His first wife had been dead less than a year and his new wife already had two, apparently illegitimate, daugh-

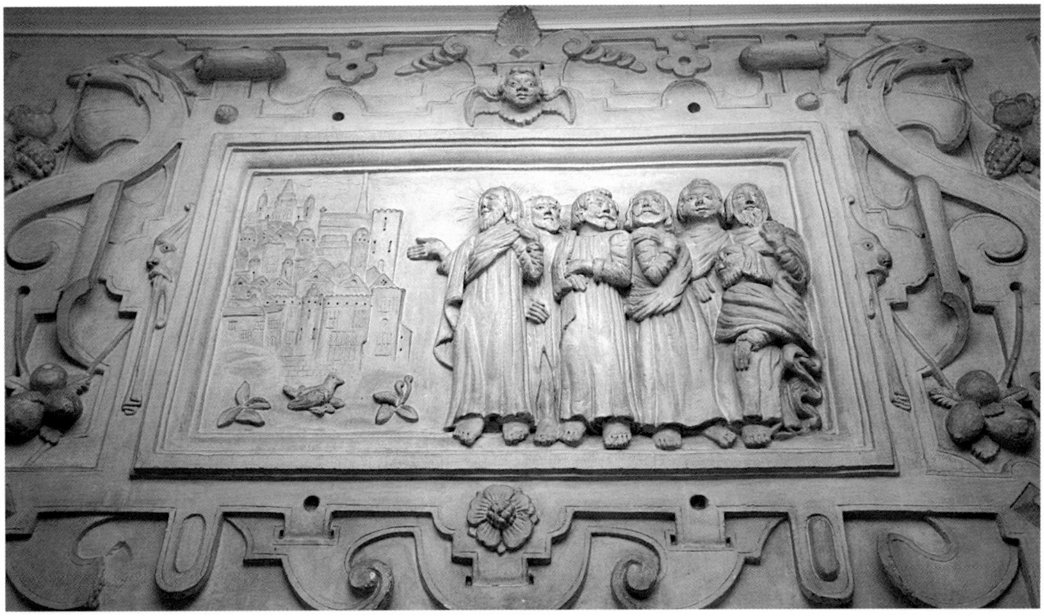

51 Christ laments Jerusalem's failure to foster the faith, plasterwork overmantel of c. 1629 at the Court House, East Quantoxhead

ters. The speed of the courtship and the generous provision made for these girls in his will suggests that Luttrell may have been the father.[4] Whatever the background to the alliance, Silvestra did extremely well out of the marriage settlement. Along with three other manors her jointure included the manor house of East Quantoxhead and it was presumably with a view to Silvestra's future comfort that Luttrell spent the last years of his life renovating and beautifying this house. A lead pipe on the exterior of the building records the initials of the couple and the date 1628. At about the same time, Luttrell commissioned decorative work for the interior of the house. Four of the main reception rooms were adorned with chimneypieces in high-relief plasterwork, depicting scenes from the life of Christ.[5] The chimneypieces are still extant today: in a large ground-floor parlour is a scene of Christ blessing little children, illustrating Matthew 19.13 (Fig. 50) while an overmantel in a first-floor room depicts a passage from Matthew 23.37, where Christ laments over Jerusalem's failure to foster the faith and compares himself to a hen gathering her chicks under her wings (a symbolic hen with her chicks is included in the foreground of the scene; Fig. 51). In another first-floor reception room is a scene of the Agony in the Garden (Fig. 52) and in the largest first-floor room, probably the old great chamber, is a scene of Christ being taken down from the Cross (the Deposition) (Fig. 53).[6]

This imagery is unusual in depicting the figure of Christ including scenes relating to his sacrifice and it may indicate that Luttrell was a fairly relaxed kind of Protestant, possibly leaning towards the high-church end of the religious spectrum. Luttrell's stated position, though, makes it clear that he had no sympathy with the Roman Catholic faith.

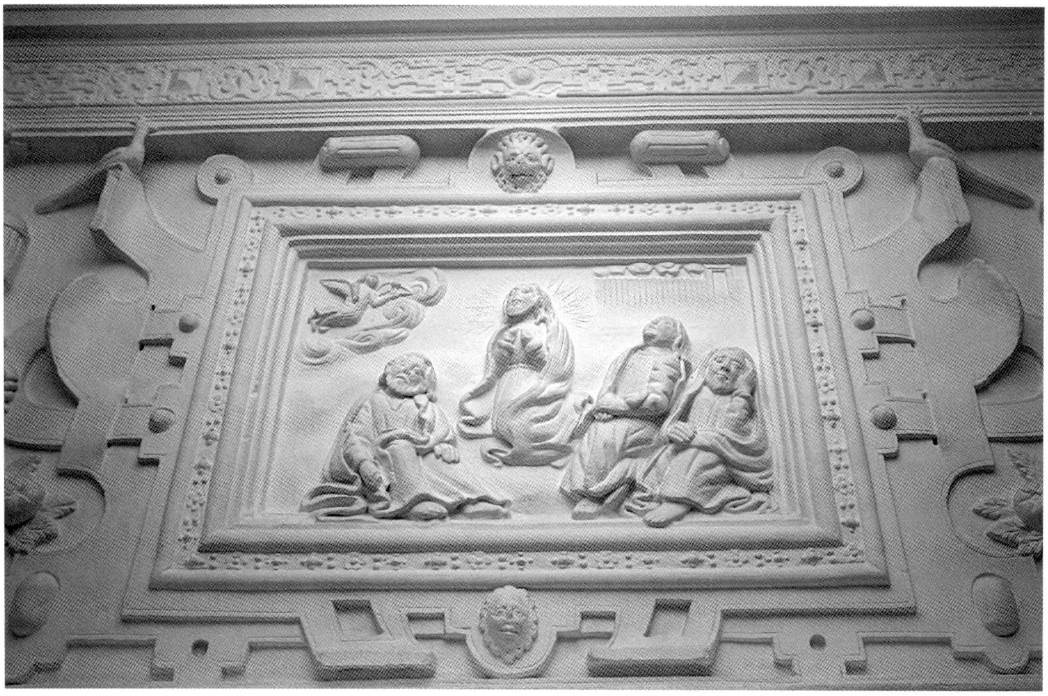

52 The Agony in the Garden, plasterwork overmantel of c. 1629 at the Court House, East Quantoxhead

53 The Deposition, plasterwork overmantel of c. 1629 at the Court House, East Quantoxhead

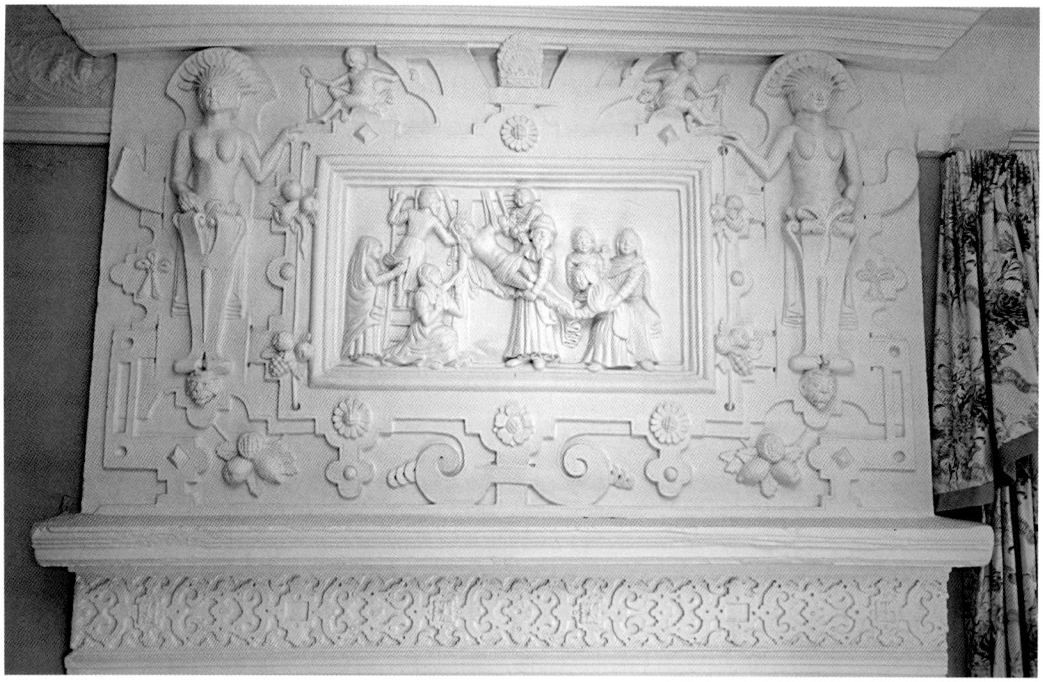

A few years earlier Luttrell had gone to some pains to express his hostility to members of the old faith. In 1621 he made a formal declaration that one of his daughters, Elizabeth, should have the sum of 1400 pounds bequeathed to her by her mother, his first wife, provided that she did not marry a Popish Recusant or the son of a Popish Recusant, or any other without his own consent.[7] This declaration was obviously intended to prevent an undesirable match but it confirms Luttrell's conformity to the state religion.[8] The episode serves to prove that the traditional religious imagery depicted at the Court House should not be understood as evidence of popish sympathies but that Protestant patrons within the Established Church could desire and create new images of Christ for display within their home.

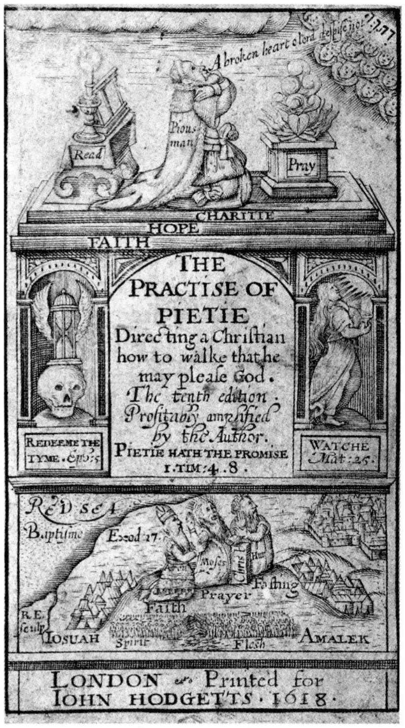

54 Lewis Bayly's best-selling guide to godly behaviour was Silvestra Skory's sole inheritance from her second husband. This title page is from the 1618 edition. British Museum, London

Anthony Wells-Cole has shown that the scenes in the overmantels at the Court House are copied from an engraved book illustrating the *Vita, Passio, et Resurrectio Jesu Christi* (Life, Passion and Resurrection of Jesus Christ), published in Antwerp by Adriaen Collaert in 1566.[9] This was a picture-book intended to aid prayer and devotion. Perhaps Luttrell hoped that the spiritual atmosphere created by this imagery would provide an environment conducive to a sedate and pious widowhood for his younger wife. If so, he was mistaken. Following Luttrell's death in 1629 Silvestra was remarried, after just nine months, to Sir Edmund Skory. But it seems this marriage was far from happy: family legend tells how Silvestra pushed Sir Edmund out of one of the ground-floor windows of the Court House during one of their many blazing arguments. In support of this oral history, there are pointed references to Silvestra's tempestuous nature in Sir Edmund's will of 1632. He first bequeathed the sum of 20 shillings to his servant who, he claimed, 'hath lived under the tyranny of my wife, to the danger of his life'. Then he recorded the following barbed bequest: 'to my wife, Dame Silvestra Skory, whom I hartely forgive all her wicked attempts against mee, a praier booke called The Practise of Piety, desiring that she better love and affect the same than hitherto she had done it'.[10]

The book bequeathed to Silvestra was one of the publishing sensations of the seventeenth century. *The Practise of Pietie* written by Lewis Bayly was published in at least thirty-three editions between 1613 and 1636 (Fig. 54).[11] The book is designed as a practical guide to Protestant piety of the more extreme variety and offers a comprehensive account of approved behaviour and habits of thought.[12] Sir Edmund's bequest was no doubt intended to publicise that Silvestra had fallen short of this ideal. Silvestra, presumably angered by this slur and the lack of any financial bequest, tried unsuccessfully to prove that her husband was of unsound mind.[13] She married for a third time in 1634 and was still in possession of the manor house in 1655.[14]

The story hinted at by these historical details brings into focus a relationship between the religious decoration in the manor house at East Quantoxhead and the spirit of strict religious observance prescribed in Protestant conduct literature, as exemplified by *The Practise of Pietie*. Two husbands attempted to impose spiritual concerns on Silvestra, one through religious art and the other through devotional literature. In doing so, these husbands were fulfilling the role of Protestant patriarch.

THE GODLY PATRIARCH

During this period the head of the household, assumed to be male, had ultimate authority over all matters relating to the household. As William Perkins explained in his *Christian Oeconomie*, published in 1609, 'he is *Paterfamilias*, the father and chiefe head of the familie: to him therefore the true right and power over all matters domestical, of right appertaineth'.[15] The role and responsibilities of the male householder were emphasised in Protestant literature as part of a wider preoccupation with what Christopher Hill, writing in 1964, termed the 'spiritualisation of the household'.[16] Hill argued that this self-conscious form of household religion was most enthusiastically embraced in Puritan circles. While it is the case that the spiritualisation of the household was implemented with zeal by stricter Protestants, it is clear that mainstream Protestants also emphasised the religious duties of householders.[17] In the later sixteenth century and through the first half of the seventeenth century Protestant theologians consistently defined the home as the central unit in fostering the reformed faith: 'If ever we would have the church of God to continue among us', wrote Richard Greenham, 'we must bring it into our households and nourish it in our families'.[18] As Perkins declared: 'Those families wherein the service of God is performed are, as it were *little churches*, yea even a paradise upon earth'.[19] William Gouge echoed Perkins in his manual on domestic duties published in 1622: 'a familie is a little Church, and a little commonwealth'.[20] The family, agreed John Downame, is like 'a particular church . . . and the master of the family representeth the minister and the rest of the house the people in the congregation'.[21]

As these comments indicate, the good Protestant patriarch was expected to provide not only for the material needs of his household but also for their spiritual welfare. The primary duty of the godly householder as identified by almost all contemporary writers was to lead his household in the reformed religion. His foremost duty, as Perkins explained, was: 'To beare the chief stroke [responsibility], and to be the principal agent, directer and furtherer of the worship of God within his familie . . . And this he doth partly by praying for & with his household, and partly by instructing them in the holy Scriptures, and in the grounds of religion'.[22] Most authors agreed with Perkins in identifying two essential duties: providing religious instruction and leading the family in public and private worship. In this way Protestant householders were expected to be active leaders in the knowledge and worship of God within the home. Ideally this was achieved through a daily round of activities including Bible readings, catechising, prayer, blessing and thanksgiving at mealtimes and the singing of psalms. In addition, householders were in-

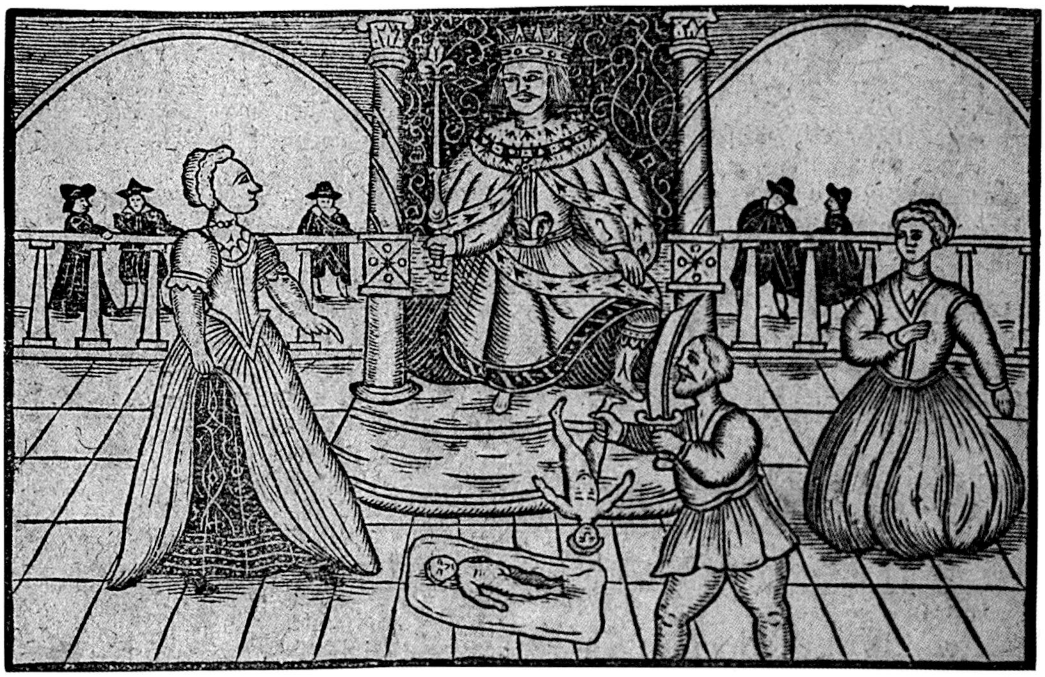

55 The Judgement of Solomon, woodcut from a printed ballad, c. 1630

structed to enforce Sunday religious observance strictly by leading the family to public worship at church and questioning them on their understanding of the sermon afterwards. In theological and conduct literature, Protestant householders were compared to Old Testament patriarchs such as Abraham, Solomon, Joshua and, particularly, David. These patriarchs were invoked time and again as models for the authority and behaviour of the 'godly' householder.

The Image of the Godly Patriarch

One iconography provided a particularly appropriate means to express the wise and just governance of a godly patriarch: the Judgement of Solomon, illustrating 1 Kings 3.16–28. This story functions as a parable of wisdom. Solomon had to judge which of two women claiming to be the mother of an infant was the genuine mother. He ordered that the child should be cut in half, with half going to each woman. On hearing this, one woman cried out that she was the impostor and to let the other woman keep the child. In this way Solomon identified the true mother, who would rather give away her child than see it harmed. The popularity of the tale is illustrated by its appearance in a printed ballad of about 1630. This ballad, which versifies the story to be sung to the tune of 'the Ladies fall', includes a relatively crude woodcut of the scene of Judgement which is comparable to many depictions of the subject in decorative art (Fig. 55).

There are numerous scenes of the Judgement of Solomon across various decorative media and throughout the period of this study. An illustration of this story within domestic space served to construct a particular kind of patriarchal and judicial identity for the master of a household and to reflect and reinforce his role as arbitrator in domestic disputes. It set out the 'natural' order of men's authority over women while allowing women to trust in the wisdom and fairness of God's appointed servants (men) in settling domestic disputes. Solomon provides an appropriate role model because, as William Gouge stated, the master of the household 'is a king in his owne house: as a king is to see that land well governed where he is king, so he that is the chiefe ruler in an house'.[23] This model of wise governance was also particularly appropriate for those householders who held an official position in the wider community, such as Justice of the Peace or service as a member of a town corporation.

An early example of this subject in wall painting is in the building known as the Forge in Much Hadham, Hertfordshire. The Forge, a relatively modest building, was once part of a medieval hall house on an H-plan and a small room in the south wing fronting the street is decorated with wall paintings depicting the Judgement of Solomon (Fig. 56) paired with an extremely elaborate representation of the royal arms of Queen Elizabeth I (Fig. 57).[24] Based on the evidence of the costumes, the paintings appear to date from about 1575–80. On the west wall is painted the royal arms and the slogan 'God Save the Queen'. What is strikingly unusual is the elaboration of the arms to include further royal iconography. The arms are supported by two yeomen of the guard holding halberds and wearing the Royal Badge, and throughout the background there are little white and red roses to represent the Tudor union of Lancaster and York.

Not only is this depiction of the royal arms unusually sophisticated for wall painting at this level of society but there is another departure from convention in the composition and character of the Judgement of Solomon scene on the north wall. This scene departs from the usual formulaic symmetrical composition, with the mothers arranged either side of Solomon on his throne (as depicted in the ballad) and instead is horizontally disposed with Solomon enthroned to the left, his councillors and attendants arranged round him, while the mothers kneel and stand to the right of the scene. It depicts the dramatic climax when Solomon halts the soldier from slicing the infant in half. The additional details of the architectural setting and the extravagant costume show more care for verisimilitude than is usual in domestic wall painting and this, together with the elaborate royal arms of Elizabeth I, evoke a contemporary courtly environment. Elizabeth was often compared to Solomon in state propaganda to support her identity as a wise and godly Protestant ruler. She is depicted in this guise, for example, in the frontispiece to the *Christian Prayers and Meditations* (1569) where a portrait of the queen kneeling in prayer is supported by a Latin text underneath quoting the prayer uttered by Solomon after his completion of the Temple (2 Chronicles 6.14).

If the elaborated iconography of the royal arms and the courtly setting of the biblical scene in the wall paintings at the Forge were intended to evoke the court of Elizabeth I, one might wonder why the patron took pains to gesture towards royal favour in this way.

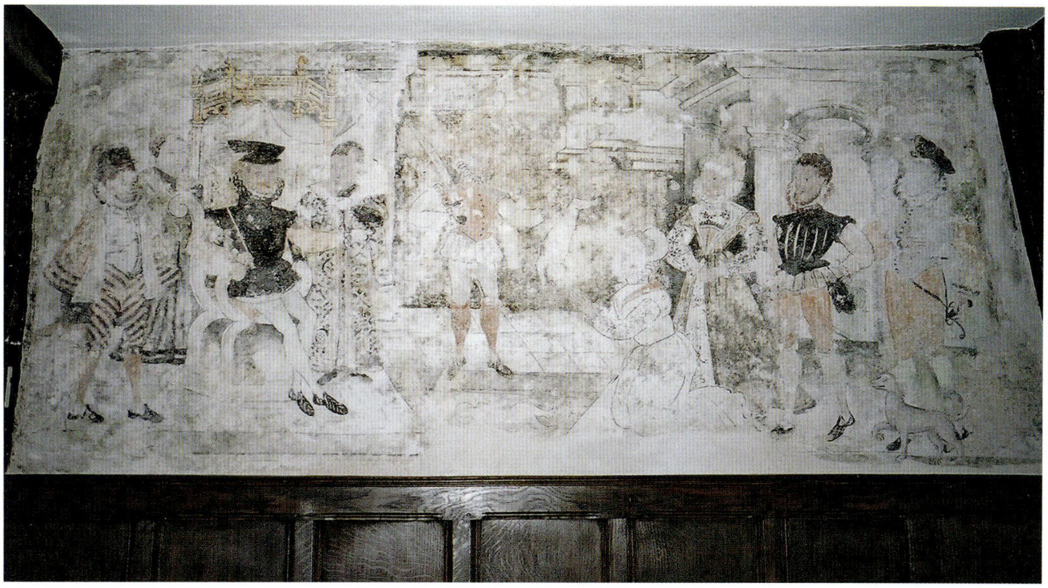

56 The Judgement of Solomon, wall paintings of c. 1575–80 at the Forge, Much Hadham, Hertfordshire

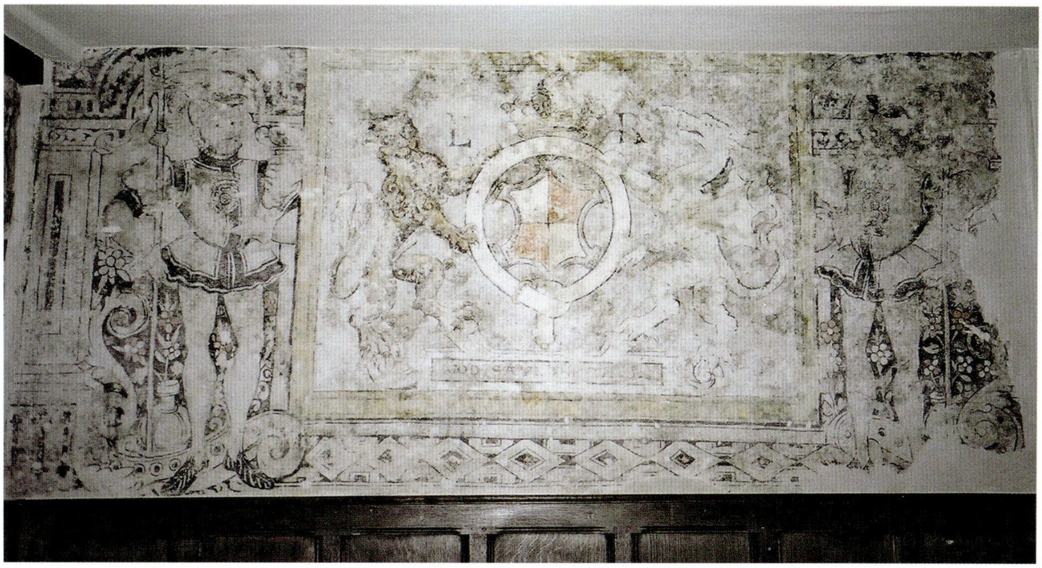

57 The royal arms, wall paintings of c. 1575–80 at the Forge, Much Hadham

The painted decoration in black and white on the east wall with its window onto the street includes two shields with the Newce coat of arms, so the work may be associated with Clement Newce, who died in 1579, or his son William (who died in 1610 or 11), although William is a less likely candidate for the work, as he was resident from 1572 in a newly built house where the present Much Hadham Hall stands. Clement Newce is described within his funerary brass in the parish church as 'of Muche Hadham in the Counttye of Hertford esquier somtymes Cyttezin and Mercer of London'. He acquired manorial lands and was confirmed in his elevation to the gentry by the granting of arms in 1549. Is it possible that Newce hoped to receive the queen during one of her many progresses?[25] In fact Elizabeth I did stay at nearby Hadham Hall, the seat of Henry Capell, from 13 to 16 September 1578 as part of her planned route back to London from the summer progress to Norfolk.[26] There is no record of her activities in the area during her stay but it is certainly possible that local dignitaries hoped to receive her and carried out decorative work accordingly. One might wonder if a similar motivation prompted Sir George Bruce to choose a painting of the Judgement of Solomon (now barely visible) to grace his newly constructed north wing at Culross Palace in Scotland, built in 1611. James I visited Bruce at Culross in 1617 and the king, like Elizabeth, was associated with the wise Solomon in royal propaganda.[27]

As a celebration of wise government, images of the Judgement of Solomon could allude to the virtues of householders or their monarch. In relation to self-fashioning, it is possible to understand why this iconography appealed to men like Sir Stephen Procter (1562–1619), the builder of Fountains Hall in Yorkshire. Procter had purchased the Fountains estate by 1598 and set about constructing a new mansion, completed in about 1604. The carved stone chimneypiece in the great chamber of around that date includes a large scene of the Judgement of Solomon (Fig. 58). This allusion to wise and just rule fits what is known about Procter's biography.[28] As a Justice of the Peace, he appears to have acted as a zealous protector of the Protestant faith. He was particularly determined in hunting out recusants and investigating possible popish sympathies. Already in 1602 he had exhibited in the Star Chamber a bill against Sir William Mallory alleging that by his 'countenance and remissness, the county hereabouts had relapsed into disobedience in religion'. After 1605 he was involved in investigating the Gunpowder Plot in London and Yorkshire. He was employed as a revenue official to collect debts to the crown and his zeal in pursuing the perceived religious and financial misdemeanours of his neighbours rattled the cages of powerful men, prompting complaints alleging his abuse of office. In 1614 he was charged in the Star Chamber with 'scandal and conspiracy' in 'endeavouring unjustly to involve two Yorkshire Knights in trouble about the Powder Plot and for slandering the Lord Privy Seal'.[29] This brought about a fall in reputation and retirement from office and he died heavily in debt three years later. The image of Solomon presiding over a courtroom setting was, one may suppose, a projection of Procter's self-image as a godly judge.

Judgement of Solomon iconography became so common that it could be pared down to its essential elements and yet still be readily identifiable. At Barrington Court in Somerset a crude version of the story in a plasterwork overmantel of about 1625 includes a circular scene including only the king seated on his throne, the two mothers kneeling before him and the soldier with his sword aloft holding the infant, all floating in undefined space (Fig. 59). The work was possibly carried out at the time that one William Strode, a clothier, acquired the property.[30] While this image in plaster may not offer

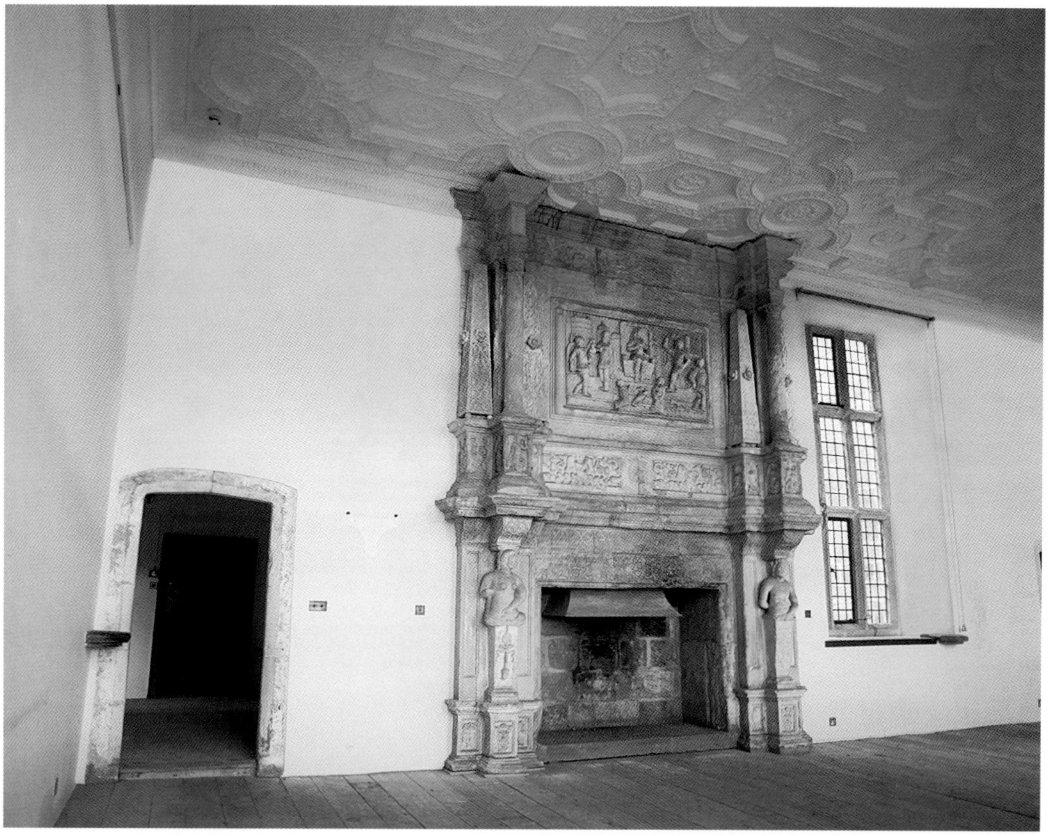

58 The carved chimneypiece in the great chamber of Fountains Hall in Yorkshire, c. 1604

much pictorial detail or artistic merit as decoration for one of the principal rooms of a country seat, it seems to have fulfilled its purpose in expressing a godly, just and wise identity for Strode as he set about establishing himself as master of this larger and grander home.

PRACTICES OF HOUSEHOLD RELIGIOUS OBSERVANCE

As a religious role model responsible for the spiritual welfare of all under his care, the godly patriarch was advised by most prescriptive texts to convene the whole household for guided prayers every morning and evening. Ideally, the householder would lead the twice-daily communal gathering with a reading from the Bible or a set prayer designed specifically for this purpose from a devotional book. In his devotional manual, *The Practise of Pietie*, Lewis Bayly explained:

> if thou desirest to have the blessing of God upon thy selfe and upon thy familie: eyther before or after thine owne private devotion, call every morning all thy familie to some

59 A simplified version of the Judgement of Solomon in plasterwork at Barrington Court, Somerset, c. 1625

> convenient roome; and first, eyther reade thy selfe unto them a Chapter in the word of God, or cause it to be read distinctly by some other. If leasure serve, thou maist admonish them of some remarkeable good notes; and then kneeling downe with them in reverent sort . . . pray with them.[31]

While Bayly does not specify which 'convenient room' might be used for these prayer meetings, contemporary sources record that the main reception and living rooms such as the great hall, great chamber and parlour were used for this purpose in many Protestant houses. In his account of the exemplary life of the godly gentleman John Bruen, William Hinde noted that Bruen's servants would continue praying to God for a blessing on their desires and labours, 'which they ordinarily performed in the kitchen, more privately, after prayer in the Parlour with the whole family'.[32] In a letter dated 12 May 1626, Lady Brilliana Harley, the wife of the Puritan politician Robert Harley of Brampton Bryan in Herefordshire, recorded: 'this day I have bine so fare as the parler to give thankes with my family for his mercy to me. And as I have doun it this day so I pray god I may doo it all my life in obedience to him which [is] the best sacrifis we can offer to the lord'.[33] The young William and Mary Springett conducted their own form of household prayers in their lodgings while boarding with Springett's uncle in the 1630s. Later in life Mary recorded that William 'would use no form of prayer in the house; but prayed morning and evening in our chamber, with me and our servants, which wrought great discontent in the family'.[34] Presumably, Springett's radicalism led him to eschew his uncle's religious direction and conduct his own brand of household observance.

Ordinary rooms in the house were used for family prayers even in some larger country houses with internal chapels. This practice reflects a change in the use and status of domestic chapels in response to the reformed faith's emphasis on simplicity and purity in the practice of worship. As the late Annabel Ricketts has shown, it was no longer considered necessary to use the special and secluded (often consecrated) space of the chapel for the daily routine of Protestant religious observance.[35] For many householders, it was more practical, appropriate and efficient to hold daily religious meetings in general domestic space and thereby avoid the ceremonial implications of services in chapels. Where a chapel was provided in new houses built by loyal Protestants, it was treated as a room of assembly with few distinguishing features. It might also be sited on the main circulation route through the house, rather than in a more secluded space set apart from the main reception rooms.[36]

William Hinde described the typical form of daily religious service in the household of John Bruen. The ringing of a bell called the household to gather together in the parlour. First Bruen would read a short prayer in a set form, after which it was usual for everyone to sing some psalms. Then Bruen would 'read a chapter himselfe out of the Bible, to make his family better acquainted with the order, and matter of the scriptures'. Finally, the whole company would kneel in prayer 'making their requests knowne unto God, in all manner of supplications with thanksgiving'. This same routine was performed each evening, 'much after the same manner, saving that then he tooke some more paines with them . . . out of that portion which he tooke in the chapter, read at that time unto them, propounding and applying some wholesome doctrine, profitable for their godly edification.'[37]

Although male householders were expected to take the lead in such activities, it is clear that the mistress of the house was also responsible for maintaining the daily routine of instruction and prayer. Lady Margaret Hoby frequently recorded in her diary of 1599–1605 how she catechised her servants, heard their repetitions of the Sunday sermons or read to them from godly literature.[38] Several decades later, the diary of the Puritan clergyman Ralph Josselin makes it clear that his wife played an active role in the religious observance of the household.[39]

The ubiquitous direction for Protestant householders to provide 'godly edification' is usually defined in terms of active instruction, such as the preaching of the Word, catechising and guided prayer. Historians, following Hill, have overwhelmingly focused on the role of active instruction in the spiritualised household.[40] However, it is likely that householders interpreted their responsibilities much more widely. In particular, it seems that some masters wanted to provide tools for spiritual practices that could operate at any time during the day, and beyond the group activities he supervised. In order 'to exercise the minds and hearts of his own family (and such as might by occasion come to his house) unto godliness and good things', John Bruen 'brought in, and set up upon a deske, both in his Hall, and in his Parlour, two goodly faire Bibles of the best Edition, and largest Volume . . . and these hee placed to be continuall residentiaries, the bigger in the Parlour, and the lesser in the Hall'.[41]

In setting up Bibles for the continual exercise of the hearts and minds of his household, Bruen was acting in accordance with the advice of Protestant prescriptive authors to provide constant edification, not only through teaching but also by making God's Word visible on the fabric of houses. Richard Brathwaite offers the following instruction, 'as you are to use touching spirituall affaires, being Masters of Housholds in your private families':

> And wee are taught what wee must doe, returning from Gods house to our owne: and what wee are to doe sitting in our houses, even to lay up Gods word in our heart and in our soule, and binde it for a signe upon our hand, that it may be as a frontlet betweene our eyes. And not only to be thus instructed our selves, but to teach them our children, speaking of them when thou sittest in thine house, and when thou walkest by the way, and when thou liest downe, and when thou risest up. And not so onely, but thou shalt write them upon the posts of thine house, and upon thy gates. Whence you see, how no place, time, or occasion is to be exempted from meditating of God: but especially in Housholds and Families ought this exercise of devotion to be frequently and fervently practised; for a Blessing is pronounced upon the performance.[42]

This rehearses the biblical instruction given in Deuteronomy 6.4–9 and 11.18–12 to write God's Word on the 'posts' of the houses so that no place, time or occasion is exempted from meditating on God. Many other commentators, including Robert Cleaver, also mention this Commandment:

> And this is the meaning of that Law, which Moses gave to the Israelites, Commaunding them to write the word of God upon the Postes of their houses, and upon their Gates. Whereby all under government, were taught, what should be required of them so long as they lived in those houses, namely, to serve God: and all governours were taught, what specially to looke after in all them that went in and out of their gates, and lived under the roofe of their houses, even to serve the Lord in all parts of his worship, for which end he hath given them such authoritie over them.[43]

The sense that the godly householder was fulfilling God's command to write his Word on the posts of his house might have been the motivation for domestic decoration incorporating religious texts and mottos. A wall painting over a fireplace at Feering House in Feering, Essex, actually quotes the original text from Deuteronomy 6.4–9.[44] Although the painted text is in a poor condition, it seems to follow the translation given in the Tyndale Bible of 1537:

> Heare Israel, the Lorde thy God is Lorde only and thou shalt love the Lorde thy God with all thyne harte, with all thy soule and with all thy myght. And these wordes which

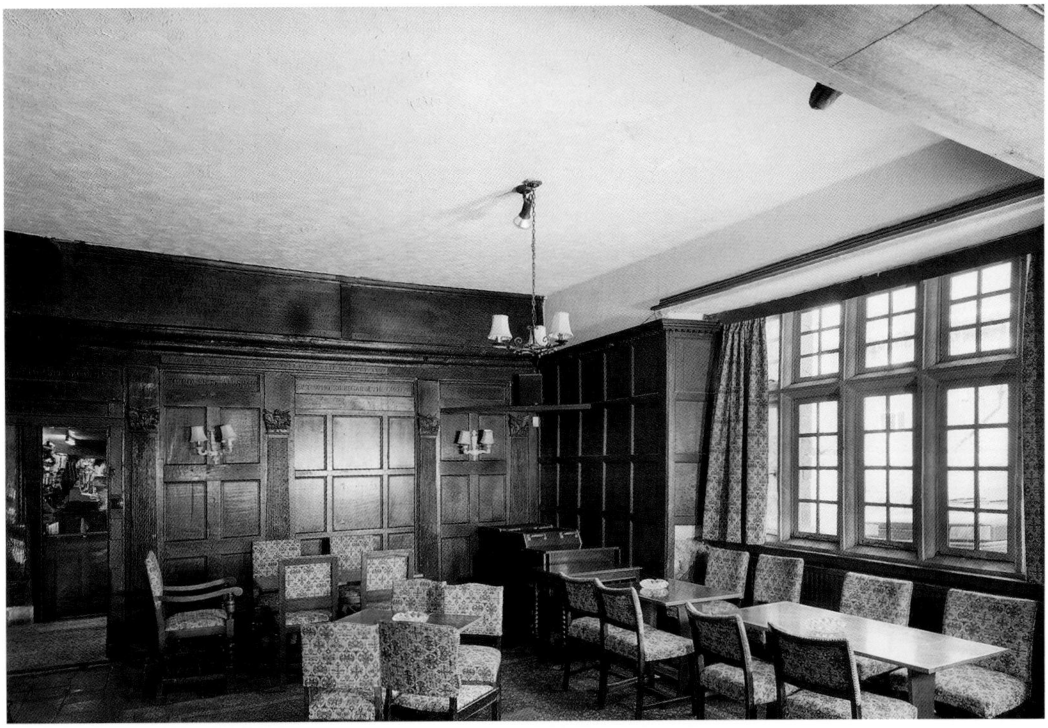

60 View of the sixteenth-century screen incorporating panels with the texts of the Ten Commandments in the former great hall of Hangleton Manor, East Sussex

> I commaunde the this daye, shalbe in thine herte and thou shalt whett them on thy childern, and shalt talke of them when thou art at home in thyne housse and as thou walkest by the waye, a[n]d when thou lyest doune and when thou rysest upp: and thou shalt bynde them for a sygne uppon thyne hande. And they shalbe papers off remembraunce betwene thyne eyes, and shalt write them uppon the postes of thy housse and uppon thy gates.

At Hangleton Manor in Sussex the upper section of the decorated wooden screen dividing the entrance passage from the great hall is carved with a version of the Ten Commandments (Fig. 60).[45] This domestic screen resembles a rood screen dividing the nave of a church from the holy chancel area. The setting up of the Ten Commandments in churches was required by royal order in 1561 and thus became an approved form of post-Reformation church ornament. To judge from the style of the carved decoration which includes five bays of fluted Corinthian pilasters, the wooden screen must date from the later part of the sixteenth century. The owner of the house between 1565 and 1592 was Richard Bellingham, the head of a large family including thirteen children.[46] It is possible to imagine the family gathered for prayers in the hall, with these texts providing an appropriate and functional backdrop. The Ten Commandments formed a central element of Catholic and Reformed catechisms and Ian Green has shown how catechising played an important

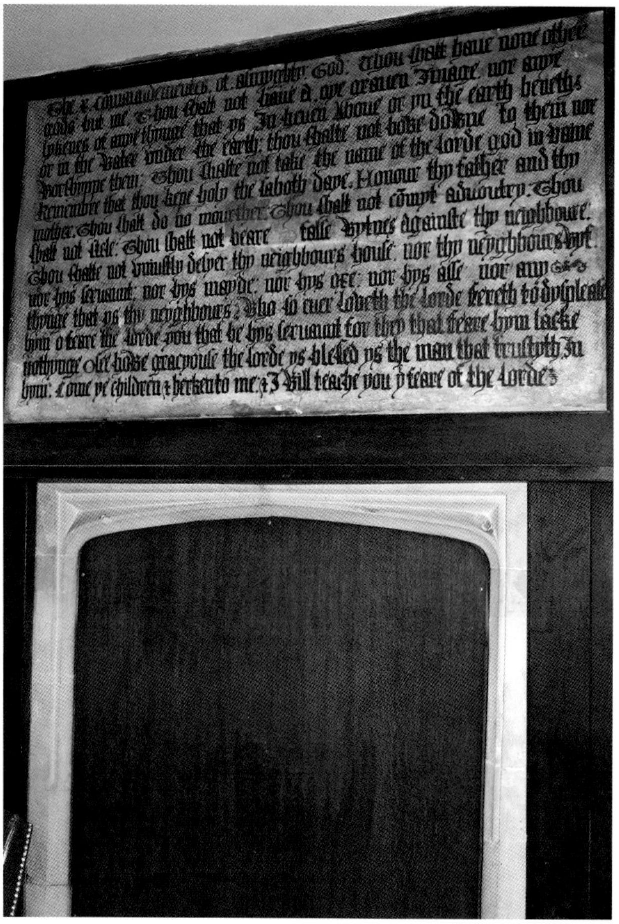

61 The Ten Commandments painted above the fireplace in an upstairs room of 'St Martin's Priory' in Canterbury, Kent, c. 1550s

part in advancing literacy as well as religious belief.[47] The texts at Hangleton might therefore have assisted reading ability as well as comprehension of God's commands. That the screen was used as part of collective religious observance is indicated by an additional text from Proverbs 13.18, carved in one long inscription beneath the Commandments panels. The text, taken from the Tyndale Bible of 1537, reads: 'He that thinketh scorn to be reformed, cometh to poverty and shame: but who so receiveth correction, shall come to honour'. The addition of this particular text turns the hall screen into a vehicle of reform, indicating the householder's role in instructing his family and servants.

Similarly, the Ten Commandments are painted above the fireplace in a first-floor room at 'St Martin's Priory' in Canterbury, Kent (Fig. 61).[48] This house was originally built for one John Wilde in the 1550s on ex-monastic land. The text is written in black letter and includes the Commandments as well as extracts from the Book of Psalms. Its final line quotes Psalm 34.11: 'Come ye children and herken to me and I will teache ye feare of the Lorde'. Again, the emphasis is on the teaching of God's Word.

There was a great fashion for religious and moral texts in wall painting of the Elizabethan period. Often the inscriptions formed a frieze around the top of painted walls, with decorative scrollwork, fruit and flowers, or geometrical designs adorning the main body of the wall. An example is at Ansells End Farm, Kimpton in Hertfordshire.[49] This is dated 1605, a fairly late instance of this kind of decoration. From the records it seems that the fashion for writing texts in painted decorative borders on walls was at its height in the later Elizabethan years, that is, roughly 1570–1600. Examples are documented at Pirton Grange in Hertfordshire and Pekes Farmhouse in Chiddingly, East Sussex, among numerous others.[50] Juliet Fleming has shown that many of these texts are taken from Thomas Tusser, *A hundred good poynts of husbandry* (1570), which included a series of 'Husbandly Poesies' broken down room by room: 'Poesies for the hall', 'Posies for the Parler', 'Posies for the gest's Chamber' and 'Posies for thine own bed Chamber'.[51] The Books of Proverbs, Ecclesiastes and the Psalms were also favourite sources. Even Bess of Hardwick, who preferred classical to biblical subject matter for the interior decoration of Hardwick Hall, chose a pious inscription as the subject of the overmantel dated 1597 in the principal chamber of her own suite of apartments which would have been used on a daily basis (unlike the grander state apartments on the floor above). The inscription reads: 'The conclusion of all thinges is to feare God and keepe his commandments'.

In Scotland there was a similar taste for moral texts in decoration not just in the interiors of houses but inscribed at the doorways. The house built by Clement Cor in Advocate's Close in Edinburgh in 1590 has two entrances at ground-floor level with pious inscriptions on the lintels: 'Spes Altera Vitae' (hope in another life) and 'Blissit be God of al his Giftis'.[52] A group of painted ceilings in Scotland use inscriptions as a form of decoration, as in the 'Rohaise Room' of Delgatie Castle in Aberdeenshire (Fig. 62). The painted wooden ceiling, dated 1597, includes numerous mottos adapted from biblical proverbs running along the inside face of the beams.[53]

At other locations moral or religious texts are accompanied by images. In a deep painted frieze of about 1600 in a first-floor chamber of a town house in Hereford (now the Black Lion pub), the text of the Decalogue is accompanied by scenes from the Old Testament that illustrate the breaking of these Commandments (Fig. 63). The wall paintings that survive today depict Commandments Four to Seven but it is probable that in the original scheme all ten were represented. Among the scenes still visible is Joab's murder of Amasa (2 Samuel 20.9) underneath the text 'Thou shalt doo noe Murder' (Fig. 64). It is possible to imagine the householder using these images as part of his daily instructions to remind his family of the dire consequences of sin and disobedience.

It seems therefore that religious and moral texts written on the posts and walls of domestic houses provided an appropriate setting for collective religious observance and served to reinforce and extend the householder's instruction. A means of constant edification was provided, which operated throughout each day and when the master was away from home. In this way the decoration could function not only as instruction but also as a form of social control.

Another essential duty of the good householder was the maintenance of order and discipline. The patriarch was directed to regulate behaviour in his household and prevent any member from engaging in forms of behaviour 'that tend to Gods dishonour'.[54] How

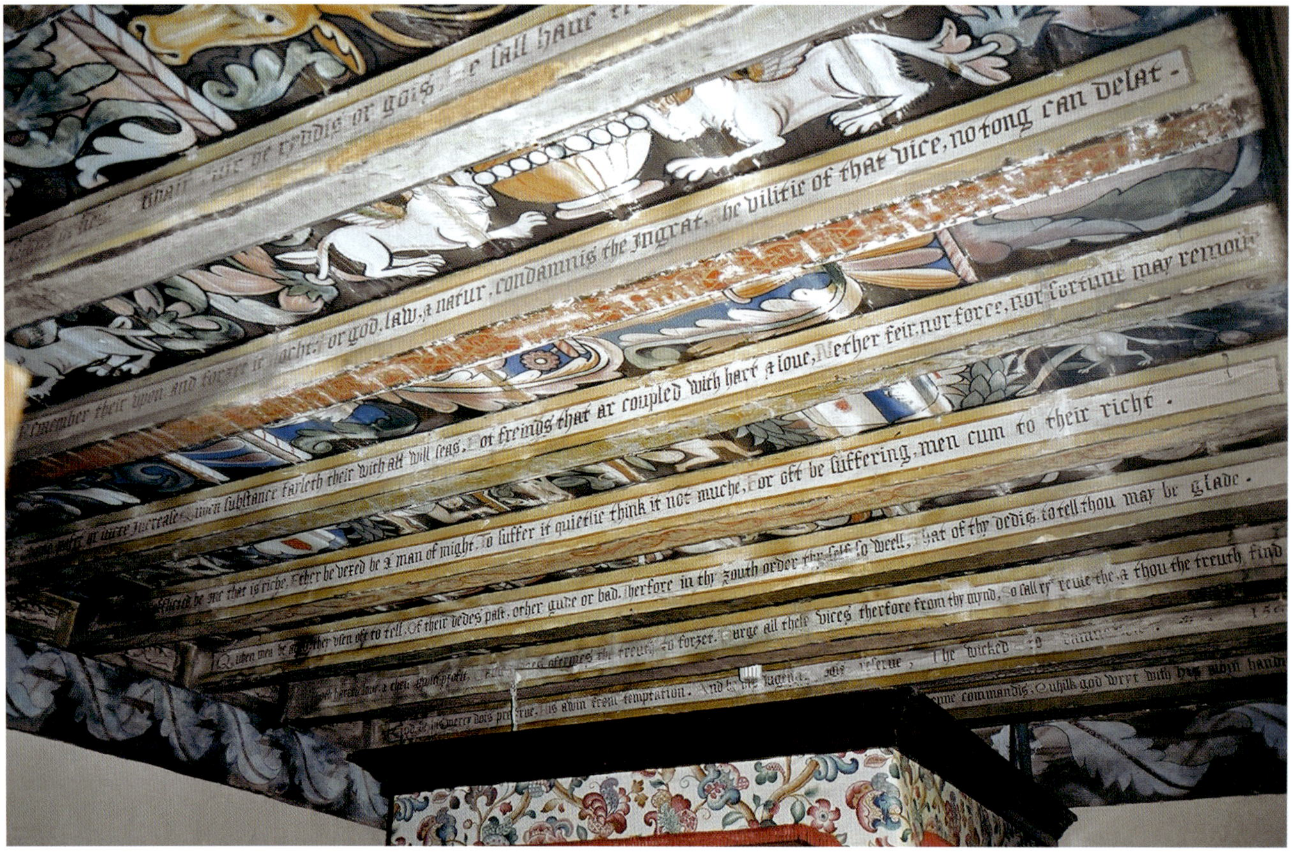

62 The painted wooden ceiling of the 'Rohaise Room' at Delgatie Castle in Aberdeenshire, dated 1597

might such control have been achieved? In enforcing discipline, the godly patriarch could invoke a higher authority. As William Gouge observed: 'For there is no such meanes to stirre up servants to doe all good dutie, as the feare of God planted in their hearts.'[55] One way to ensure that fear of God was planted in the heart of each member of the household was to invoke his presence before them. Edward Dering's 'Morning prayer for private houses and Families' of 1578 contains the appeal:

> We beseech thee, O Lorde, that in all our consultations, wordes & workes this daye, and the whole course of our lyfe, we maye alwayes have thee present before our eyes, knowing that thou seest even the very deepe thoughtes in our hartes, which alwayes maye be able to pull us backe, that we neyther [do?] nor yet consent unto any sinne or wickednesse.[56]

Knowledge that the all-seeing God knows every thought and action is cited in this prayer as a means for the prevention of sin. Another way to 'alwayes have thee [God] present before our eyes' was to provide visual reminders of God's presence. In his 1621 sermon on

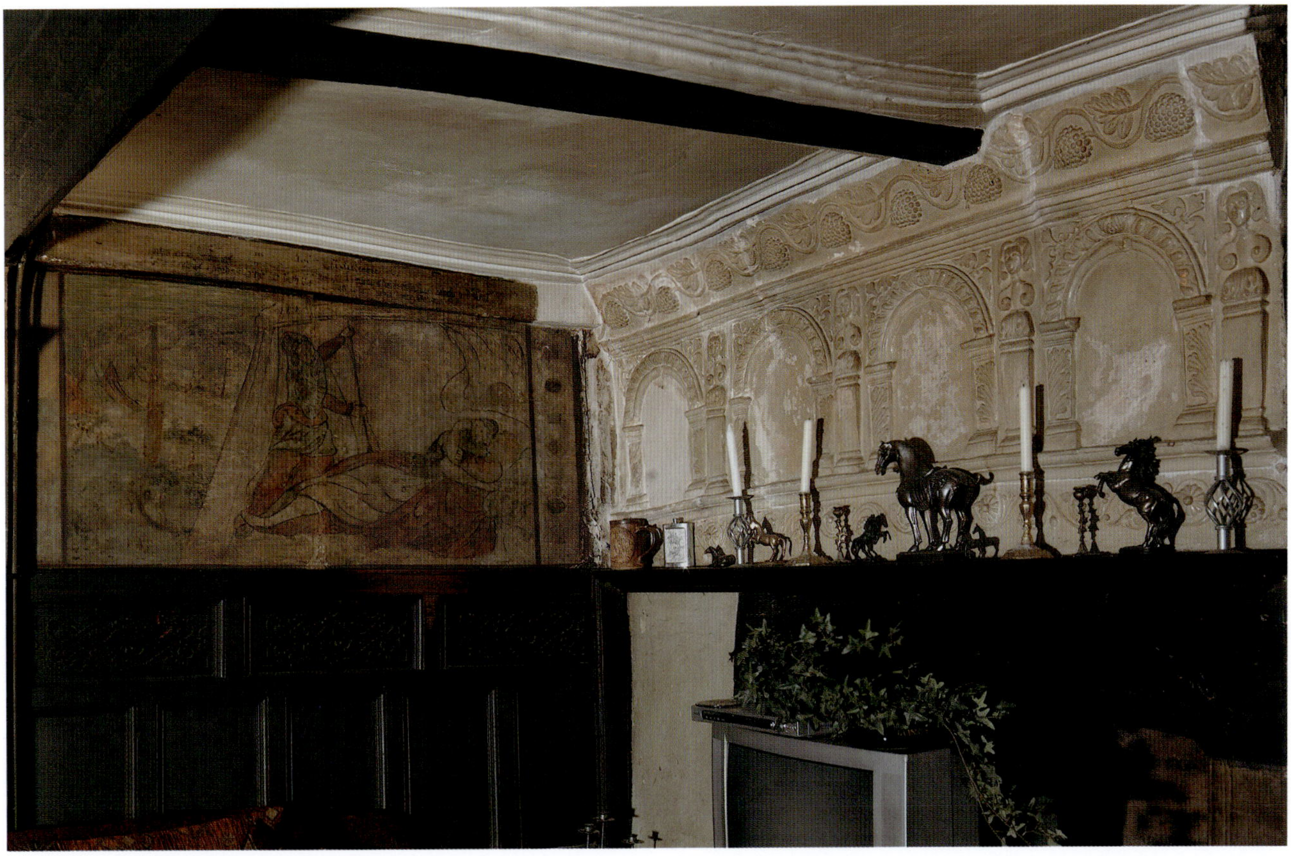

63 View of the painted frieze of c. 1600, in the first-floor room of a town house in Hereford (now the Black Lion public house)

the religious duties of leaders, George Hakewill reminded his audience that even in private places God sees all:

> It were good, then, to write upon their walls, and to engrave upon their windowes, that short Motto (which as short as it is, yet our memories are shorter); *Cave, Deus videt*, Take heed, God sees it. But then should wee chiefly call it to minde, and make use of it, when, being inclosed within our wals, sequestered from company, occasion and opportunity invite us to sinne.[57]

Here again, the use of inscriptions written on walls (or engraved in windows) within domestic settings was recommended as a constant warning and prevention against sin. The illustration of stories from scripture was perhaps intended as the pictorial equivalent of writing God's Word on the fabric of the building. It seems likely that the use of religious texts as decoration in the home evolved to include the use of images. This dynamic between text and image is suggested especially where imagery in domestic decoration is copied from the pages of godly literature.

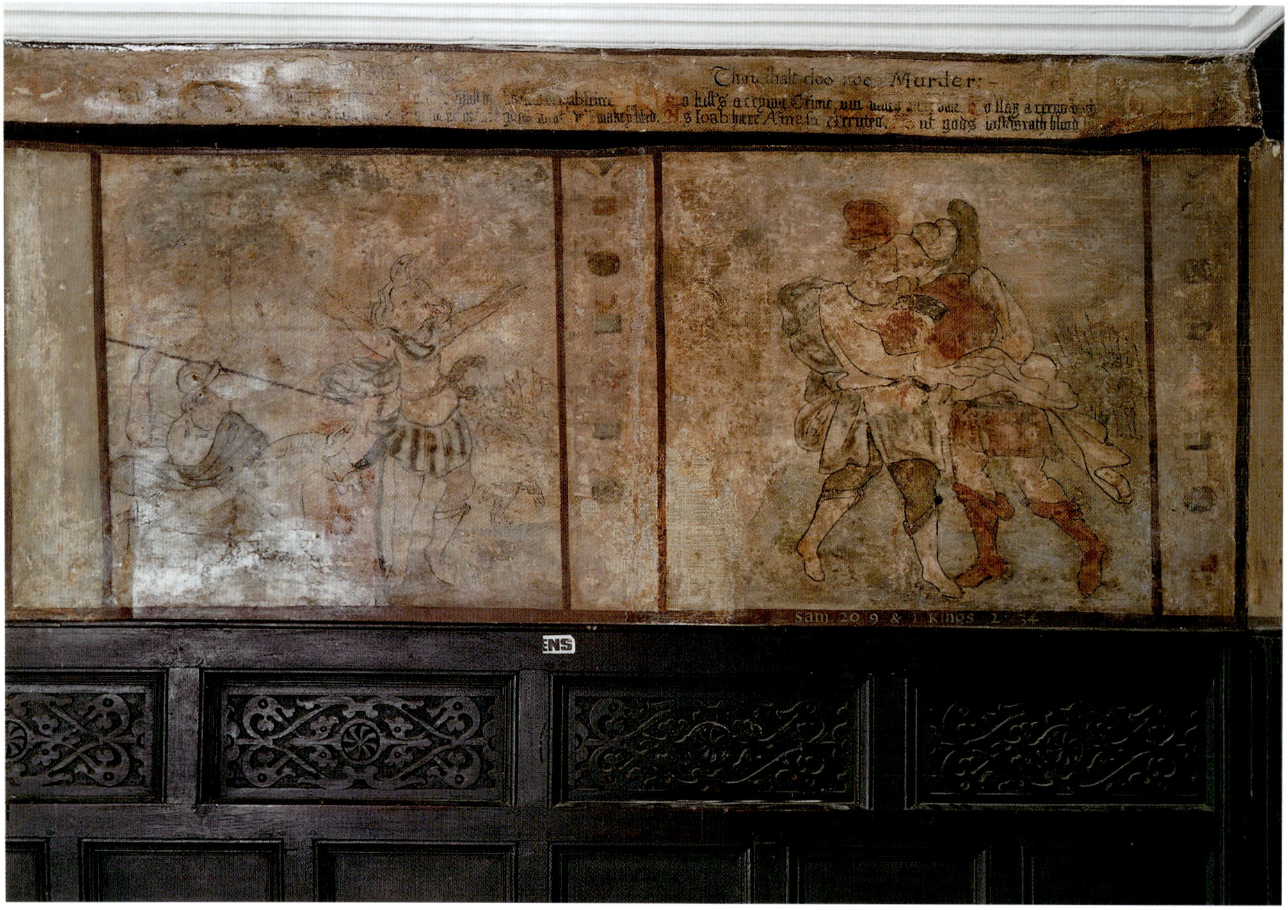

64 Detail of the painted frieze in the Black Lion

'GUIDES TO GODLINESS': FROM PAGE TO WALL

In response to the emphasis on household religious observance, edifying and devotional literature for domestic use found a ready market as householders sought practical aids to inform and support religious activities and habits of thought in the home. Ian Green has shown how treatises on the theme of godly living sold in higher than average quantities compared to other types of treatise and continued to sell well in the two centuries after the Reformation.[58]

One of the early devotional manuals designed specifically for a reformed audience was the *Christian Prayers and Meditations*, printed in 1569 with a revised version published as *A Booke of Christian Prayers* in 1578. This book provided a Protestant version of the medieval Book of Hours, with prayers and meditations for every moment of the day from 'our first waking' in the morning to 'when we be ready to sleep' at night. Despite its intended function as part of a wider campaign to promote the reformed faith, the book includes a wealth of traditional religious illustrations in wide decorative borders on each page. In this way, the book served to preserve and circulate traditional pre-Reformation religious iconography long after it had been banished from the walls of churches. The title page to both the 1569 and 1578 editions published by John Daye depicts the ancient iconography of the Tree of Jesse, an illustration of the genealogy of Christ, which includes the Virgin and Child at the apex (Fig. 65). This same image was employed as the subject for decoration dating from about 1635 in a three-storey house forming part of the Butterwalk in the harbour town of Dartmouth in Devon (Fig. 66). The house was built by a fish merchant named Mark Hawkins, who was a member of the staunchly Puritan Town Corporation during the 1630s. A plasterwork ceiling in the largest, first-floor chamber of Hawkins's house depicts a Tree of Jesse, with images of the Four Evangelists at the corners. The design includes the recumbent figure of Jesse, with twenty-eight little patriarchs encircled in the branches of the vine and the Virgin and Child at the top. This ceiling is discussed in greater detail in Chapter 6 but what is of interest here is the similarity between the imagery in print and plaster. That this design derives from *A Booke of Christian Prayers* is indicated by the inclusion of a particular detail, the name 'Jesse' written along the sleeve of the recumbent figure. A small-scale illustration from the title page is here writ large, expanded to cover the whole ceiling of the room.

The *Christian Prayers* also supplied the iconography for two allegorical figures in a carved overmantel dating from 1614 at Postlip Hall in Gloucestershire (Fig. 67). Two female figures at the sides of the overmantel are copied from the illustrated margins of the 1578 edition (Fig. 68). This allows the figures to be identified as personifications of Temperance and Courage. It is interesting that the carver chose not to reproduce the vomit issuing from the subdued figure of Intemperance in the woodcut; perhaps this was considered too graphic for representation in the great chamber as a formal room used for dining in state.

Such use of this printed prayer book as a source for imagery in domestic decoration establishes an explicit relationship between decorative art and the genre of Protestant devotional literature. There are other examples of such connections. A chimneypiece dating from about 1650 in what was the parlour of Cowick Barton Manor (now an inn), just outside Exeter in Devon, is copied from the illustrated title page to John Downame's *A Guide to Godlynesse*, first published in 1622 (Figs 69 and 70). This book falls within the same genre as *The Practise of Pietie*, as a particular type of Puritan conduct manual targeting a godly readership early in the seventeenth century. The upper section of the title page, the narrative scene with its surrounding decorative cartouche and the figures of Charity and Humility were transferred to the chimneypiece. Identifying the particular printed source makes it possible to ascertain that the figure on the right of the chimneypiece, which lacks any specific attributes, is meant to represent the virtue of Humility. At some point the overmantel acquired some gaudily painted decoration but originally it would have been left plain and unadorned. The scene illustrates verse 14 from Philippi-

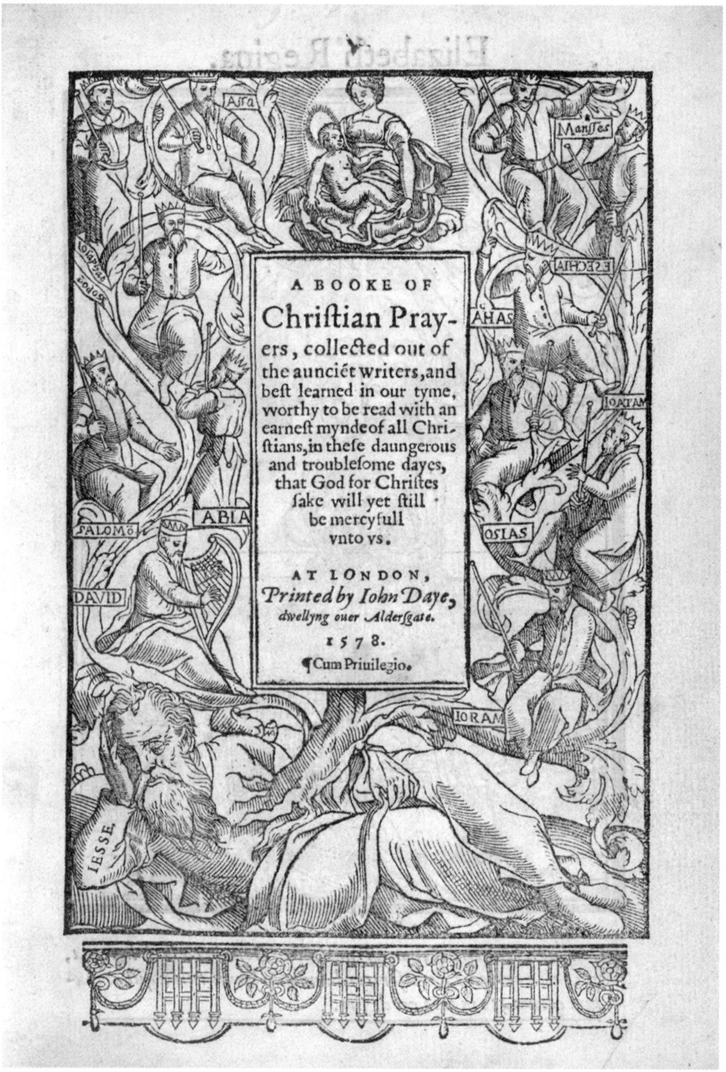

65 The Tree of Jesse, title page to *A Booke of Christian Prayers* (1578)

ans 3: 'I press toward the mark for the prize of the high calling of God in Christ Jesus'. Following Jean Calvin's own commentary on Philippians, Protestant authors frequently quoted this scriptural verse as an allegory of godly perseverance in applying all efforts towards the goal of salvation.[59] Another overmantel with the same scene but lacking the flanking figures and, it seems, the devil bringing up the rear, is at Holcombe Burnell Barton in Devon (Fig. 71). Other examples where imagery in domestic decoration can be identified with printed Protestant literature are mentioned in the following chapters.

It is a common research strategy to seek and locate borrowings from printed sources in decorative art. Often, however, the use of imagery in print as a template for pictorial embellishments in other crafts is treated only in terms of working practice and method. This neglects issues surrounding the motivations for, and implications of, the borrowing

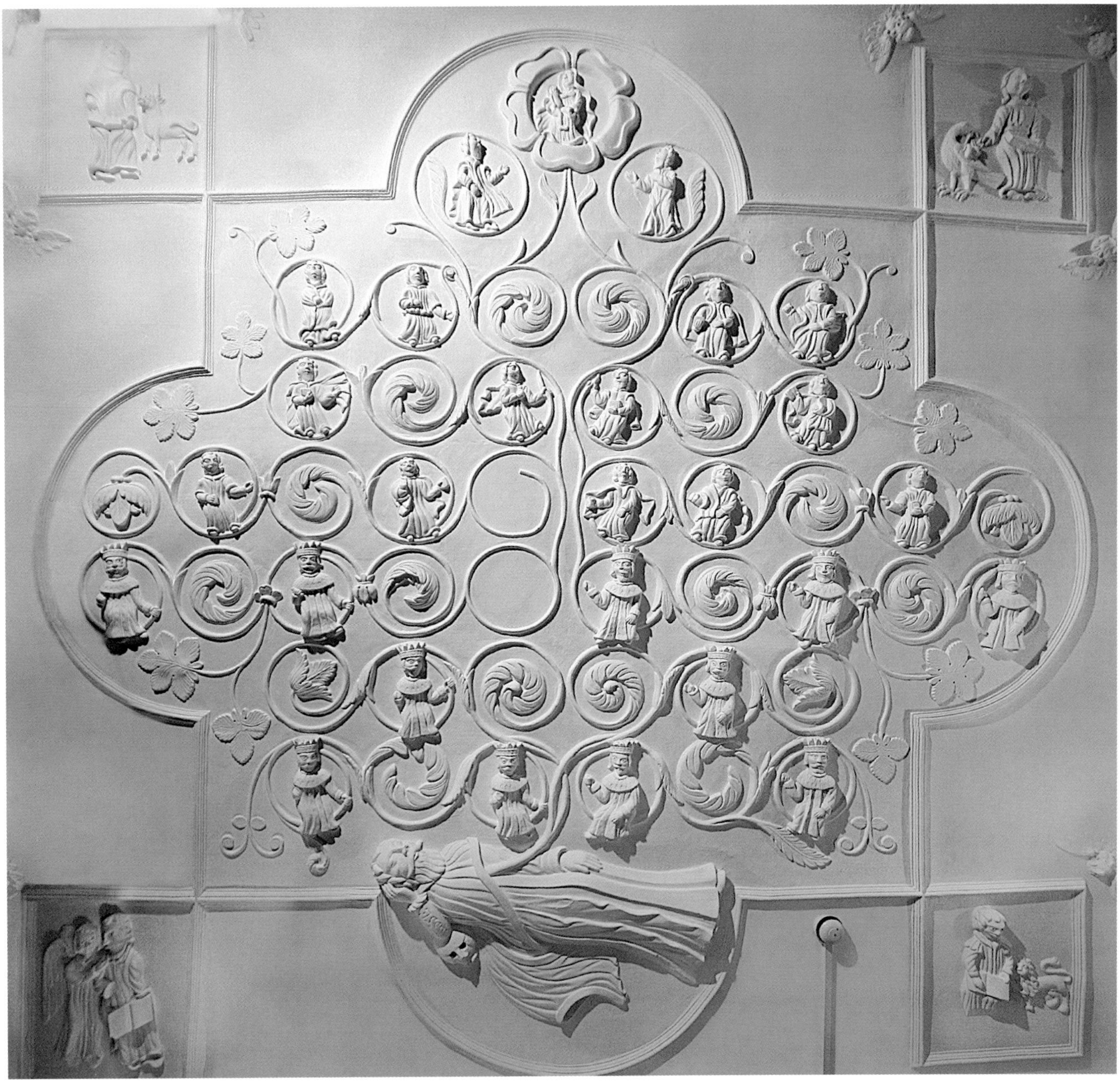

66 The Tree of Jesse depicted in plasterwork on a ceiling in the Dartmouth Butterwalk in Devon, c. 1635

in relation to the ideology of the patron and the belief systems of the intended audience. It seems likely that patrons would have considered these printed illustrations alongside, and as an index to, the contents of the book. Copying such imagery indicates that the patron approved of the book to the extent that it was desirable to transfer its imagery to the more visible and public arena of the household. Indeed, the transmission of imagery

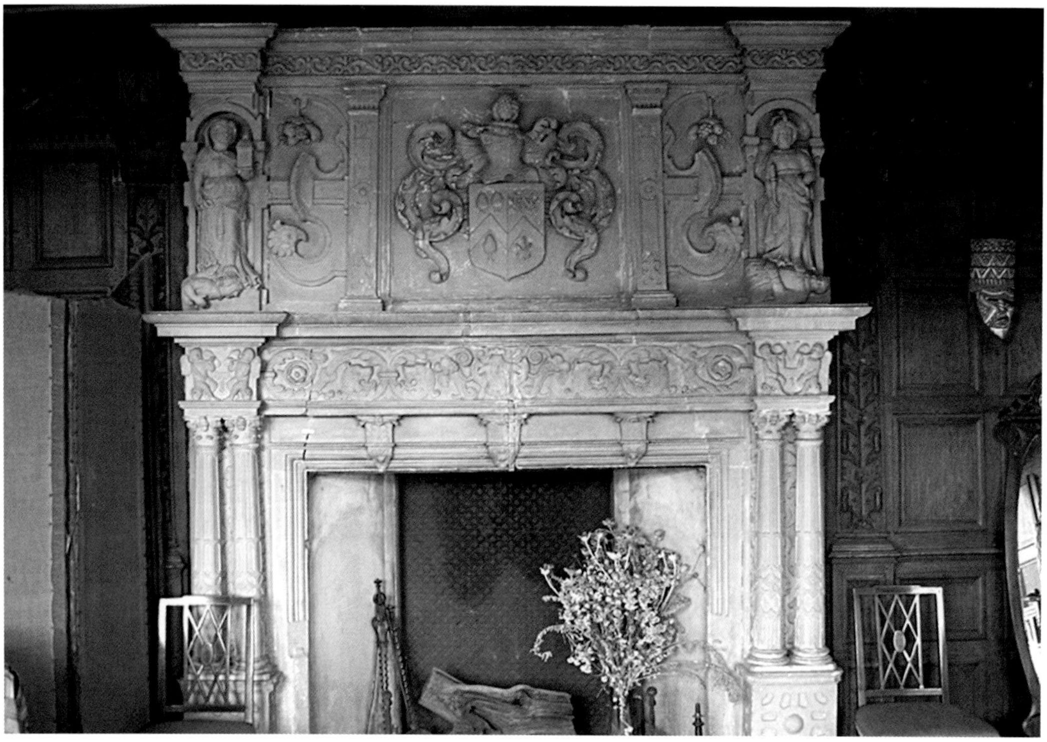

67 Allegorical figures of Temperance and Courage flanking a coat of arms, carved overmantel of c. 1614 in the old great chamber, Postlip Hall, Gloucestershire

68 Pages from *A Booke of Christian Prayers* (1578), showing the figures of Temperance and Courage in the margins alongside details of the figures from the Postlip overmantel

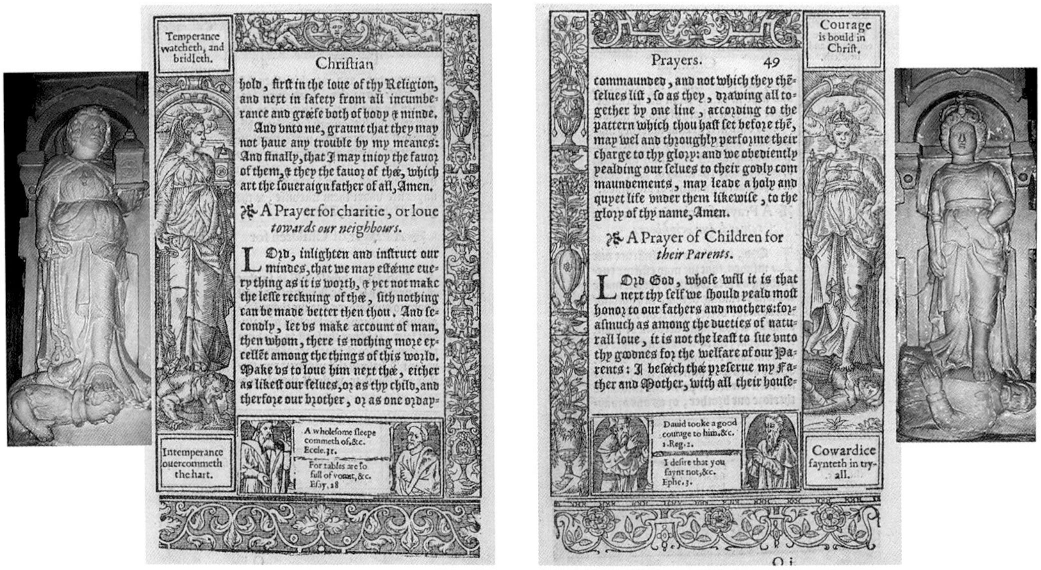

Temperance watcheth, and bridleth.

Christian

hold, first in the loue of thy Religion, and next in safety from all incumbe-rance and grefe both of body & minde. And vnto me, graunt that they may not haue any trouble by my meanes: And finally, that I may inioy the fauor of them, & they the fauor of thee, which art the soueraign father of all, Amen.

A Prayer for charitie, or loue *towards our neighbours.*

LOrd, inlighten and instruct our mindes, that we may esteeme euery thing as it is worth, & yet not make the lesse reckning of thee, sith nothing can be made better then thou. And secondly, let vs make account of man, then whom, there is nothing more excellent among the things of this world. Make vs to loue him next thee, either as likest our selues, or as thy child, and therfore our brother, or as one ordayn-

A wholesome sleepe commeth of, &c. Eccle. 31.

For tables are so full of vomit, &c. Esay. 28

Intemperance ouercommeth the hart.

Courage is bould in Christ.

Prayers. 49

commaunded, and not which they themselues list, so as they, drawing all together by one line, according to the pattern which thou hast set before thee, may wel and thoroughly performe their charge to thy glory: and we obediently yealding our selues to their godly commaundements, may leade a holy and quyet life vnder them likewise, to the glory of thy name, Amen.

A Prayer of Children for *their Parents.*

LOrd God, whose will it is that next thy self we should yeald most honor to our fathers and mothers: forasmuch as among the dueties of naturall loue, it is not the least to sue vnto thy goodnes for the welfare of our Parents: I beseech thee preserue my Father and Mother, with all their house-

Dauid tooke a good courage to him, &c. 1. Reg. 2.

I desire that you faynt not, &c. Ephe. 3.

Cowardice faynteth in tryall.

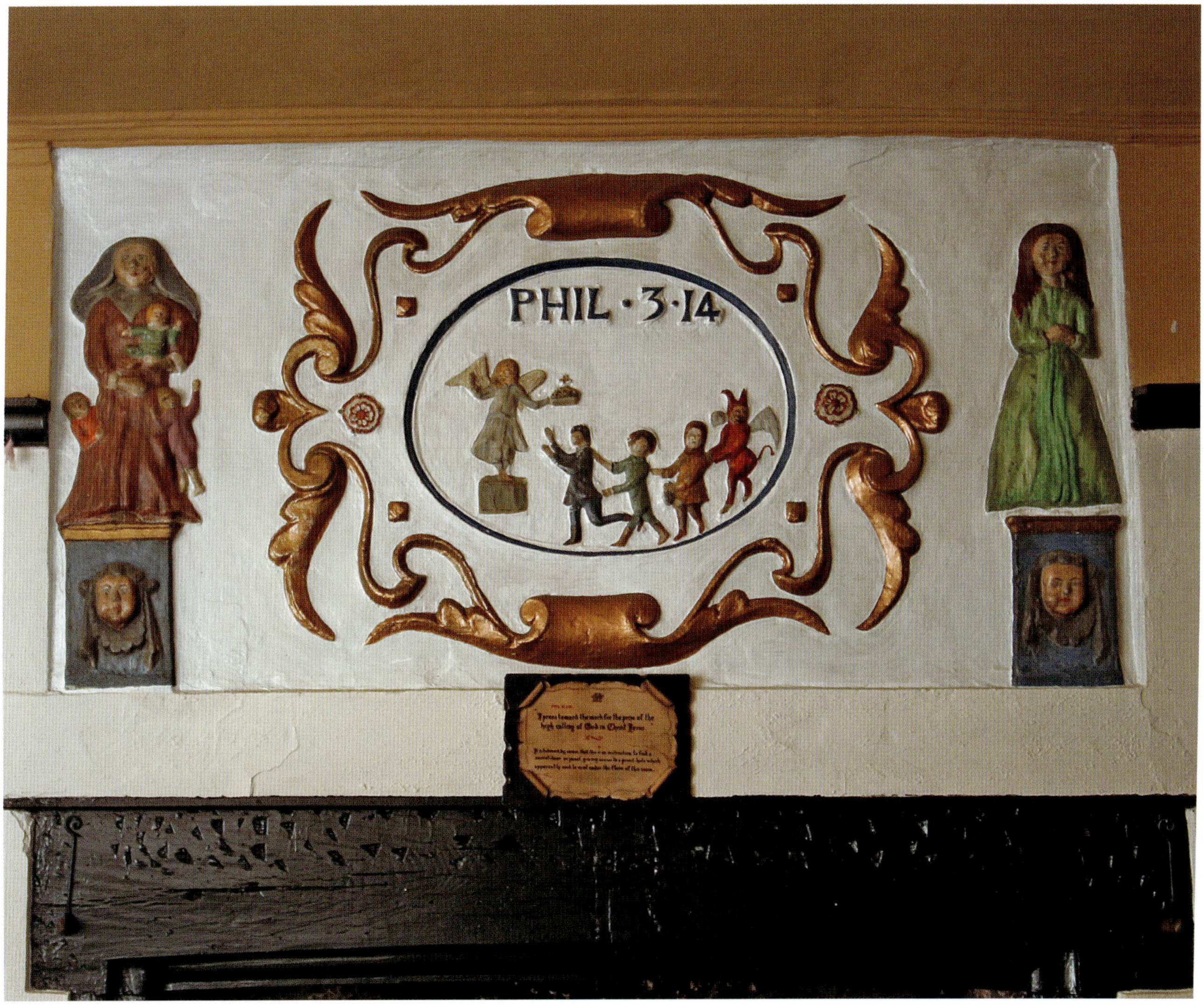

69 Allegory illustrating Philippians 3.14 in the plasterwork overmantel of c. 1650 at Cowick Barton Inn, Exeter, Devon

from the title pages of Protestant advice manuals to the walls and ceilings of houses suggests that the decoration was intended to serve an analogous function in promoting and directing Protestant piety within the domestic sphere.

❦

To conclude, I have suggested that biblical texts and images in decorative art supported the pattern of religious observance in the spiritualised household; it created an appropriate setting for collective religious observance including gatherings of the household twice

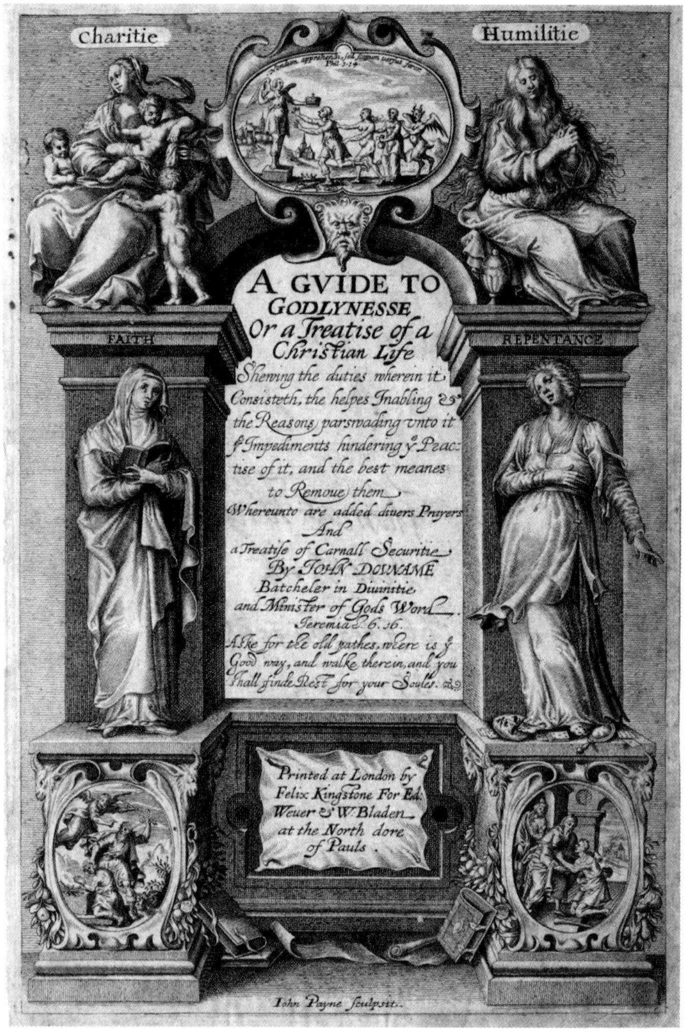

70 The illustrated title page to John Downame's *A Guide to Godlynesse* (1622)

daily for prayers, Bible readings and the singing of psalms. The permanent presence of this decoration served to extend the instruction and guidance provided by the master of the household, acting as a continual reminder of spiritual matters throughout the day. In this way, text and imagery in decorative art helped to maintain order and discipline and provided the wider household with a constant means to salvation. In pursuing these themes, the next chapter is concerned with the relationship between religious imagery in decorative art and the practical functions of specific rooms in the domestic interior in order to assess how large-scale religious imagery might have operated in the daily life of the household. The type of religious subject matter commonly employed in the decoration of these rooms is evoked through discussion of examples of decorative art still *in situ* in historic buildings throughout Britain.

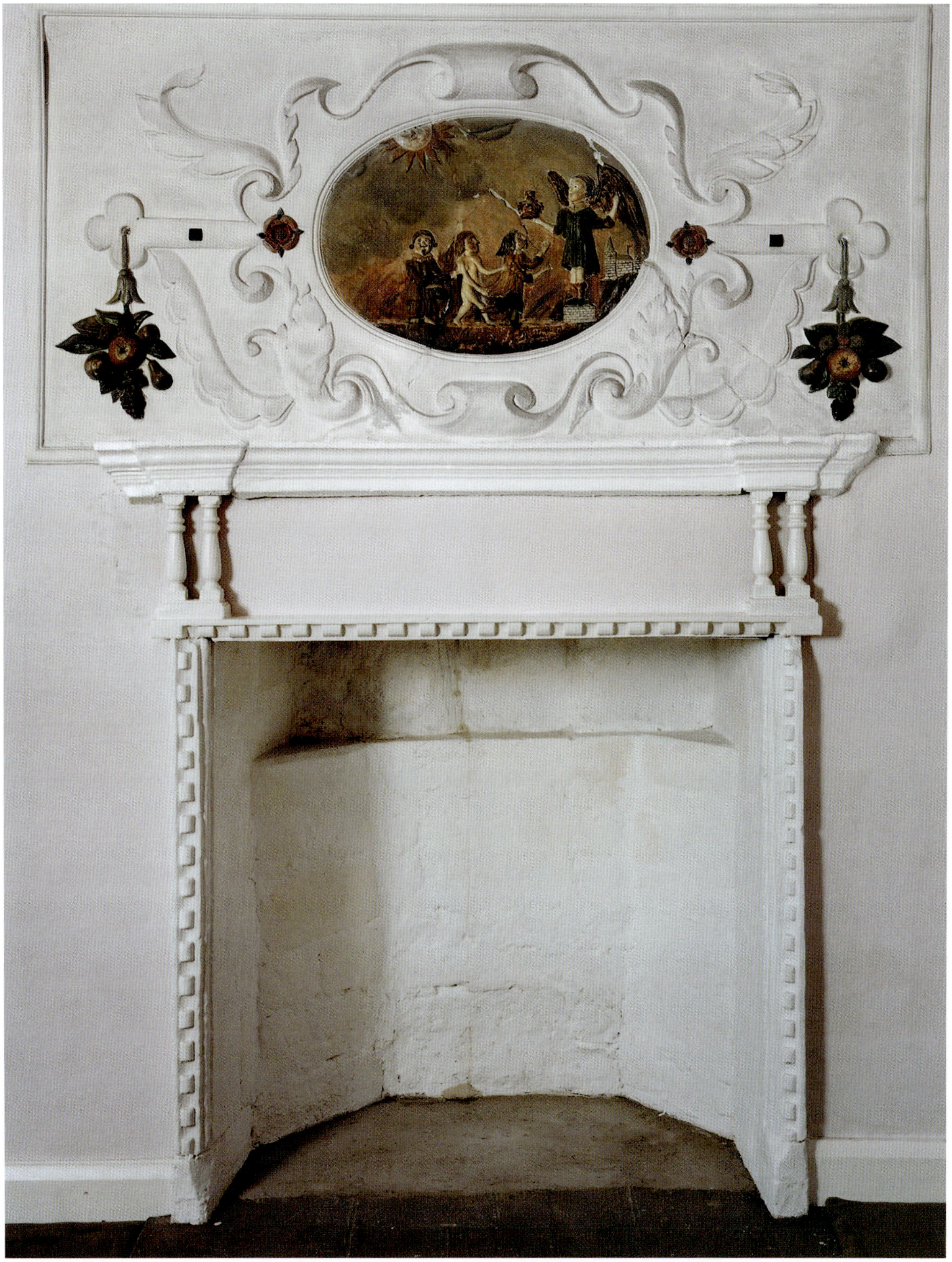

71 Another version of the allegory illustrating Philippians in a chimneypiece of c. 1650 at Holcombe Burnell Barton, Devon

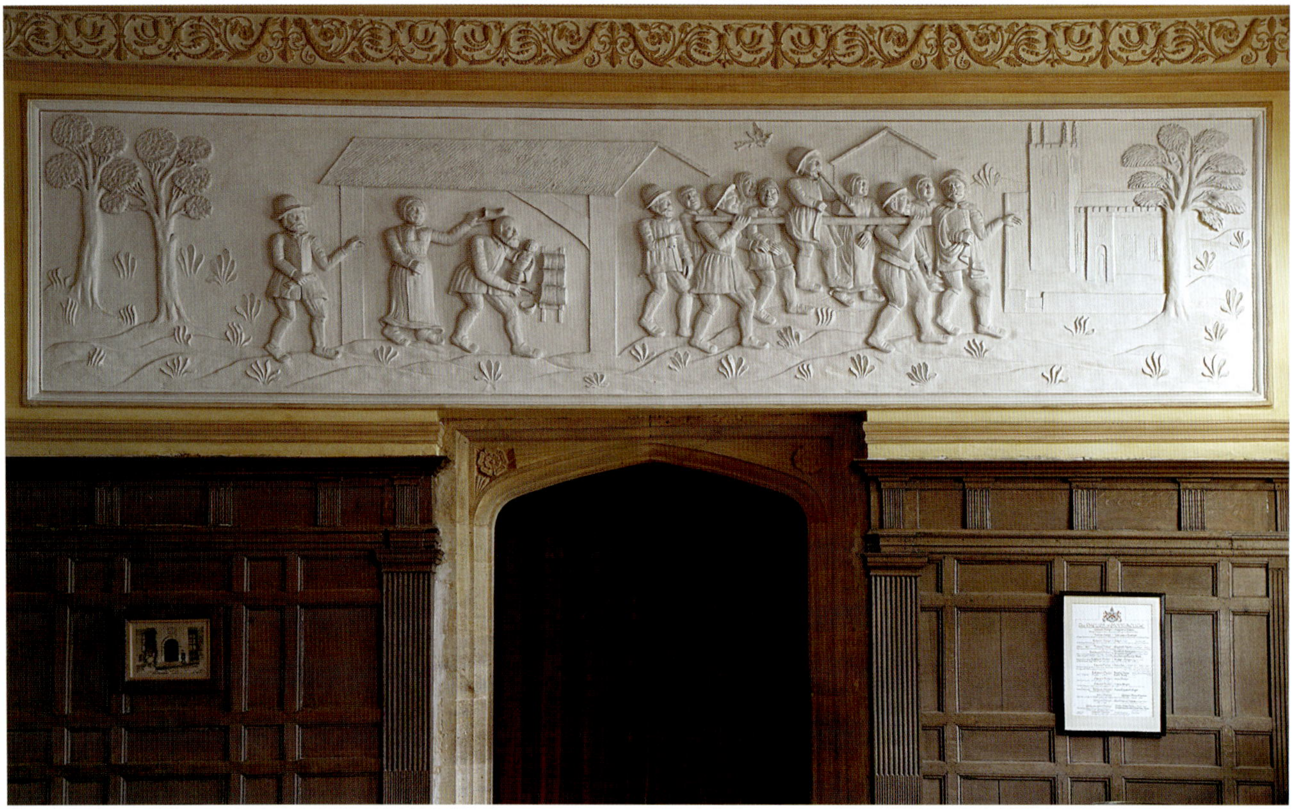

72 'Riding the Skimmington', plasterwork panel of c. 1600 in the great hall at Montacute House, Somerset

4

Decorating the Protestant Household

It was established in Chapter 2 that the arrangement of rooms in the larger houses of early modern Britain followed set patterns. Rooms were laid out according to a convention that developed from a practical need to separate the functional, service areas of the house from family and entertaining space. The division of domestic interiors into areas used by staff and rooms for use by the family acquired symbolic associations relating to class differentiation and the formalities of etiquette. Thus, the family areas developed into a ceremonial suite of formal rooms reflecting the public persona of the house. The standardisation of this sequence of spaces meant that a visitor encountering any given domestic interior for the first time would know what to expect in terms of orientation and conduct according to the situation and status of each room.

While some noble patrons at the top of the class hierarchy experimented with innovative modifications to the conventional floor-plan, this kind of experimentation for the purposes of architectural innovation rarely occurred lower down the social scale. Conforming to established models provided an opportunity for aspiring landowners and merchants to demonstrate inclusion in elite quarters. Where discrepancies in the standard layout occurred, it was usually the result of constraints on space or materials.

This standardisation of design means that it is possible to construct a 'virtual' tour of formal rooms that serves as a typical arrangement reflecting most houses of size built or modified during the sixteenth and seventeenth centuries. The sequence consists of hall, parlour, staircase, great chamber, bedchamber and gallery.[1] While many houses lacked one or more of these rooms – especially in the case of town houses, with their more compact design[2] – and greater houses incorporated numerous ancillary spaces, this sequence represents the ideal core provision for most patrons building at this time. What follows is an account of the practical and social functions of each room in relation to the types of decoration employed, with reference to specific examples of extant decoration in historic houses throughout England and Scotland. This offers an insight into the relationship between the functions of rooms and the nature and role of decoration. The chapter concludes with a brief discussion of the kinds of decorated moveable objects commonly displayed alongside large-scale decorative fixtures in these formal rooms.

THE HALL

On entering the house the first room experienced was the hall; in larger houses this room is often described, for obvious reasons, as the 'great' hall. It was usually located at the centre of the ground floor, the notable exception to this rule being the design of Scottish castles, where the hall is invariably located on the first floor with the service rooms beneath, rather than to the side.[3] Some smaller Scottish castles and town houses in England and Scotland lacked a large, formal hall and instead contained a more modest entranceway with an impressive reception room (the principal first-floor chamber) above. Nevertheless, in the larger rural houses of England, the hall was second only to the great chamber as the most prestigious reception room. This is often reflected in the common arrangement of situating the great chamber directly above the hall, sharing the same interior dimensions.

The high status of the great hall within the hierarchy of rooms in early modern domestic architecture was a legacy from the medieval period.[4] During the Middle Ages the hall was the functional heart of the house and in addition to serving multiple practical functions it also acquired symbolic status in representing the idea and structure of the institution of the household. As the largest room at the centre of the house it accommodated the whole household for dining, entertainment and lodging. Since the size of the hall reflected its capacity for gatherings of the whole household it came to represent the size of the establishment (that is, the number of servants) and therefore the social position of the owner. As the room used to dispense hospitality, in the form of food and lodging, it symbolised the owner's virtue of largesse. In larger houses the hall was magnificently decorated, in token of the owner's ability to provide not just for his household but also as an indication of the lavish quality of hospitality provided to high-ranking guests.

During the period 1560–1660 the great hall retained the symbolic functions of the medieval period, even while some of the practical functions were under review. With the addition of extra, specialised rooms, the hall was no longer required to accommodate the whole household, except on special occasions. Yet, if space permitted, a huge hall suggested the high social status and virtues of the owner and could be used for large-scale entertainment, such as the performance of a masque. A large hall also served as a suitably impressive initial reception space for guests. Meantime, it often continued in use as a dining room but increasingly only for the lower members of the household, while the owner and his family removed to another, more exclusive and intimate space. In country houses this was usually the parlour or, on formal occasions, the great chamber, while in town houses the principal first-floor chamber would be used for family dining, with lower servants dining in the service areas below.

As the size of the hall continued to symbolise the capacity of the entire household and because it was a space used by members of all ranks, this room more than any other represented the institution of the household. It also provided a forum for direct and indirect communication on behalf of the master to his extended family. This is illustrated by the inscription above the fireplace in the great hall at Aston Hall in Birmingham, a large mansion built between 1618 and 1635 by Sir Thomas Holte.[5] The inscription is a communication from the master of the house to his servants, who would have had the best opportunity to study this text during communal meals. It reads:

If service be thy meane to thrive
Thou must therein remain
Both silent, faithful, just, and true
Content to take some paine
If love of vertue may allure
Or hope of worldly gaine
If feare of God may thee procure
To serve do not disdaine

An inscription on the fireplace overmantel dated 1683 in the old hall of Kilravock Castle in Croy, Inverness, also reminded the extended family that the household operated in the fear of God: 'RELIGION JUSTICE TRUTH MERCIE/AND THE EXERCISE OF THE FEAR OF GOD/ARE SURER PRESERVERS OF A FAMILIE/THAN ALL THE OTHER METHODS AND MEASURES/IN THE WORLD . . . KILRAVOCK BOOK. 1683'[6] Similarly, the use of imagery in the decoration of the great hall could communicate the ideology of the owner. In the great hall of Montacute House in Somerset, built by Edward Phelips in the last years of the sixteenth century, is the celebrated 'Skimmington Ride' panel which stretches across the wall at the ceremonial 'high' end of the room (Fig. 72). The high end of the hall, farthest from the kitchens, was the traditional location of the high table where the master and his family would preside over communal dining in medieval times. While such communal dining rarely occurred after the mid-sixteenth century, the symbolic association of the high end of the hall with the identity of the owner remained. Therefore the location of the Skimmington panel directly above the traditional position of the high table and facing the body of the hall, indicates that it should be interpreted as a communication on behalf of the owner, Phelips, to his household.

The plasterwork panel depicts a scene of a custom known as 'Riding the Skimmington', a ritualised punishment imposed by a village community on a man for allowing himself to be dominated by his wife.[7] This ritual involved the unfortunate husband being paraded round the streets on a long pole known as the 'skimmington'. The panel at Montacute depicts two scenes as cause and effect: on the left the man is portrayed within his home holding a baby while carrying out domestic tasks and cowering before his wife who beats him over the head with a shoe. On the right the same man is astride the skimmington pole, being carried round the village by his neighbours. While the scene is depicted in a lively and light-hearted manner, the actual imposition of this public humiliation must have been extremely unpleasant and a matter of great shame for the victims; it was obviously considered so ruinous to the reputation of a couple from Suffolk that they left the village and sought retribution in the Star Chamber.[8]

The ritual of the skimmington and the associated panel at Montacute has been interpreted as a means of reinforcing the political and social concept of patriarchy by ridiculing those who subvert the 'natural' authority of husband over wife.[9] If this is the purpose of the image, it is significant that the patron at Montacute felt the need to assert the importance of patriarchy within the decoration of his home and chose to do so through a scene of a peasant custom. Patriarchy defined the relationship not only between genders but also between classes. As has been seen, the head of the household, assumed to be male, was responsible for the well-being of his wife and family and also the many servants and estate workers under his charge. Depiction of this particular subject in the great hall – a room associated with the wider rank and file of the household – serves perhaps as an attempt by the patron to establish an ideological connection between himself and his inferiors. This rather positive representation of an often riotous folk custom – the faces in the crowd are smiling – suggests that the image was intended to endorse and extend the life of the spectacle. In this way the householder demonstrated his support of the ritual and underlined the importance of its function, thus reinforcing his own position. Significantly, the scene shows the spontaneous self-regulation of a community from within its own ranks. The community of a household similarly had to regulate the behaviour of its own members.

In addition to communicating messages to individuals within the household, the great hall was also a reception room for guests and as the first room experienced by a visitor, it was designed to communicate information about the status and wealth of the owner. Halls served an important political function in the self-fashioning of the owner as they provided a stage for his public identity. The decoration of this room was therefore required to impress and sometimes led to extravagant and ostentatious decoration. However, as observed in the previous chapter, good Protestant householders were instructed to restrain themselves in the display of outward ornament to avoid the sins of vanity and pride. Selecting appropriate decoration for the hall exemplifies the dilemma for godly householders in demonstrating their social position through outward display while simultaneously indicating their humility before God. One way to balance these various and potentially contradictory messages was through the use of religious imagery as decoration.

At Burton Agnes Hall in Yorkshire is an exceptional survival of religious imagery employed as decoration in the great hall. Burton Agnes Hall was built during the first decade of the seventeenth century by Sir Henry Griffith, who had recently been appointed to the Council of the North. Profits from this appointment contributed towards the building of Burton Agnes Hall as his new seat in the region.[10] The great hall is dominated by its decoration, with traditional religious imagery in carved wood, plaster and alabaster (Fig.

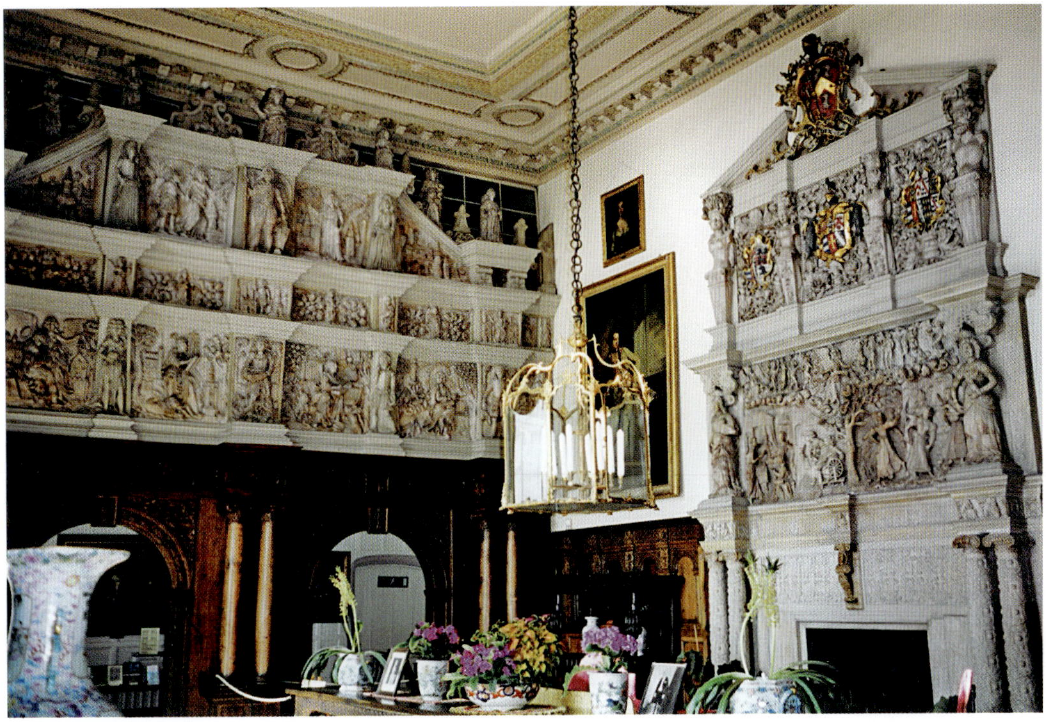

73 View of the great hall at Burton Agnes Hall in East Yorkshire, built c. 1610

73). A huge carved wood and plasterwork screen of about 1610, with its assemblage of Old Testament patriarchs, Apostles, Evangelists, angels and virtues, arranged in tiers extending right up to the ceiling, represents the heavenly hierarchy (Fig. 74). It resembles the style and traditional imagery of late medieval rood screens, the effect of which Eamon Duffy has described as 'a sense of being surrounded and assisted by the "whole company of heaven"'.[11] Meanwhile, the carved alabaster overmantel illustrates the parable of the Wise and Foolish Virgins in Matthew 25.

There can be little doubt that the overall effect of this scheme of decoration is awe-inspiring and is certainly an effective way to demonstrate the status, wealth and virtues of the owner. However, the choice of religious iconography and holy figures as subject matter refers to higher, spiritual authority and therefore represents a sophisticated response to the potential risk of overstepping the required degree of modesty and humility before God. Furthermore, the religious subject matter of the decoration can also be understood as a response to the practical functions of this room as the assembly and dining space for lower members of the household.

In keeping with the Protestant emphasis on constant self-examination and moderation, eating (along with other forms of bodily activity) was loaded with moral and spiritual overtones. The potential for members of the household to act inappropriately during meals was remarked on by most of the stricter Protestant commentators. As Lewis Bayly

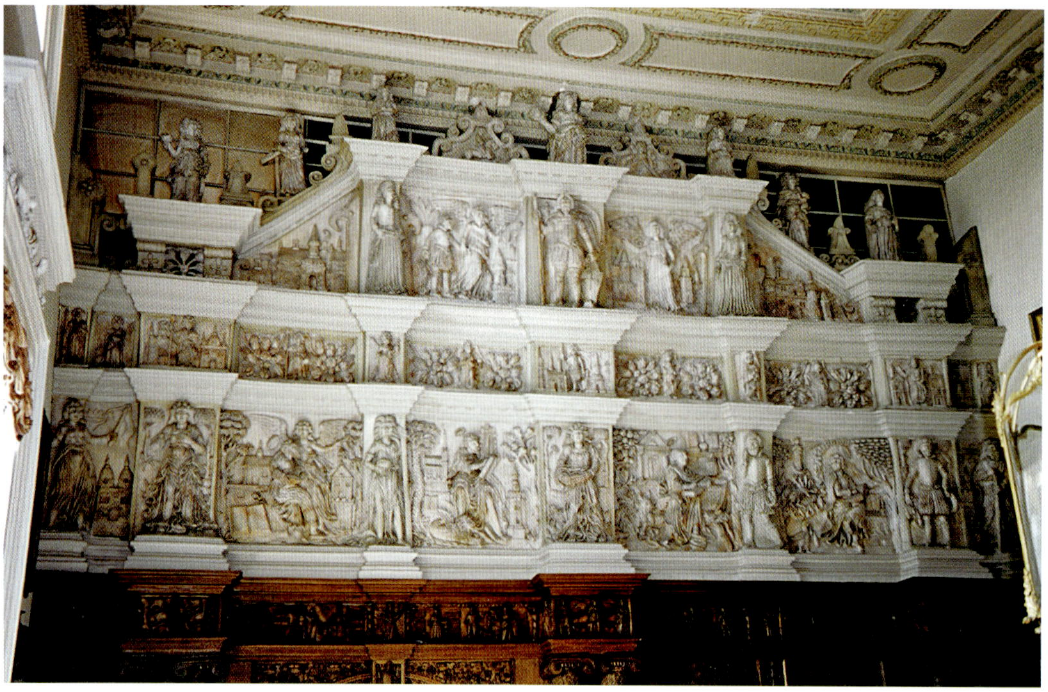

74 The heavenly host of biblical figures depicted in the plasterwork and carved wood screen in the great hall at Burton Agnes Hall, c. 1610

warned his readers: 'And as no one action . . . makes a man more to resemble a beast, then eating or drinking: so the abuse of eating and drinking to surfeiting, drunkennesse and spewing; makes a man more vile then a beast.'[12] Similarly, John Downame, in *A Guide to Godlynesse* warned:

> For as the devill layeth in every place baites and snares to intrap us, so especially upon our tables, and mingleth the poison of sinful corruption with our meates and drinkes, that if we doe not use them in the feare of God, and keepe a narrow watch over our selves that we offend not in them, they will proove no lesse dangerous to our soules, then necessary . . . for the refreshing of our bodies.[13]

In order to prevent such indulgence and abuse of God's bounty, householders were advised by Protestant authors to lead the household in prayer before each meal and in thanksgiving afterwards, as well as encouraging individual meditation during the meal. Yet during this period, as noted, the head of the household, with family members and upper servants, dined separately in the parlour or great chamber. The removal of the master from communal dining in the hall created a need to provide some means to control behaviour in his absence. In this way the holy figures staring down from the carved screen at Burton Agnes onto the space of the hall served as useful overseers, to monitor the behaviour of members of the household engaged in everyday activities in the space of the room.

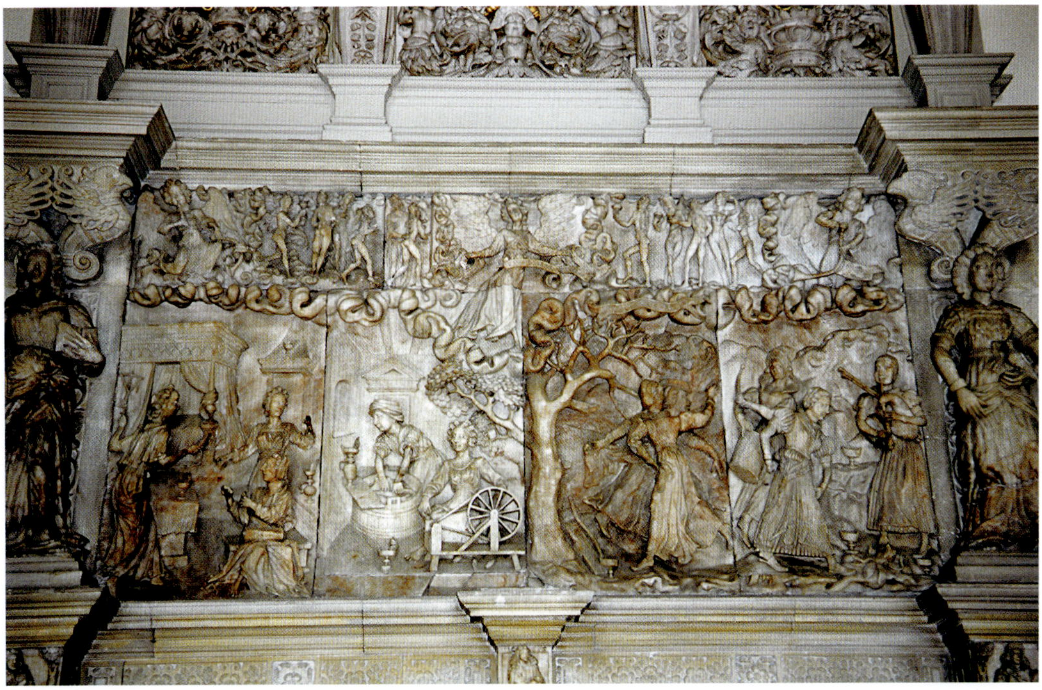

75 The Wise and Foolish Virgins, carved alabaster chimneypiece in the great hall at Burton Agnes Hall, c. 1610

Meanwhile, the carved alabaster overmantel, illustrating the parable of the Wise and Foolish Virgins, served as an example of good behaviour and as a warning against indulgence in trivial pastimes (Fig. 75). The imagery includes scenes of domesticity: on the left the Wise Virgins are depicted dutifully engaged in various domestic tasks such as sewing, spinning and laundry. In contrast, the Foolish Virgins, on the right, waste their time with music and dancing. This parable was understood, in line with its original meaning, as an allegory of the Last Judgement and its message underlined the importance of constant preparedness for the day of reckoning.[14] Thus, at the top of the scene the two groups of Virgins are shown lining up at the door to the marriage feast (a metaphor for the kingdom of heaven). The Wise Virgins are welcomed at the open door by the Groom (symbolising Christ), while at the top right of the scene the Foolish Virgins find the door closed. In this way the viewer is instructed that industrious workers will be welcomed into the kingdom of heaven while the idle will be denied entry. That this image was an appropriate instruction on behalf of the master to the servants in his household is obvious. As an allegory of the Last Judgement this image is also a form of *memento mori*, a reminder to meditate on death even during the prime of life in order to ensure readiness for judgement. This might seem unsuitable imagery to serve as a backdrop to eating and yet can be understood as the visual equivalent of Lewis Bayly's instruction to meditate on death during meals. He advised: 'Meditate, that thy body which thou doest now so dain-

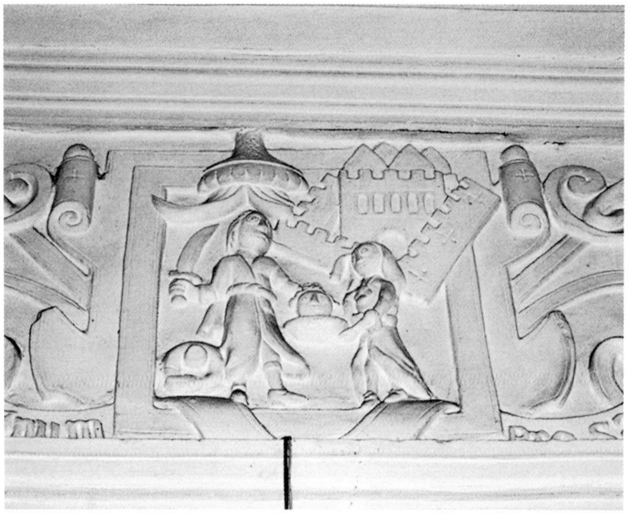

76 The Presentation of the Head of John the Baptist to Salome, detail of the plasterwork frieze of c. 1640 in the hall at Gaulden Manor, Somerset

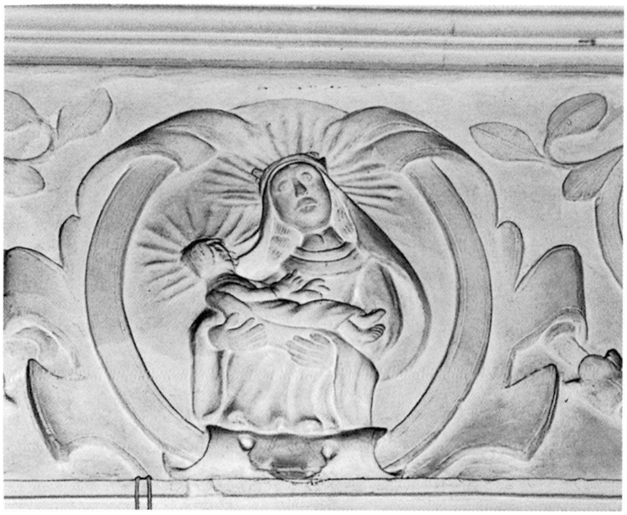

77 The Virgin and Child, scene from the plasterwork frieze of c. 1640 in the hall at Gaulden Manor

tily feede, must be (thou knowest not how soone) meate for Wormes'.[15] Thus, this choice of subject matter provided an ideal model of behaviour alongside a warning of the spiritual consequences of bodily fulfilment. The message of the imagery is duty, moderation and spiritual preparedness.

A similar function is served by the imagery depicted in the plasterwork ceiling of the hall at Gaulden Manor in Somerset, a relatively modest country house enriched in about 1640 by its new owner, John Turberville.[16] The decoration includes four religious scenes set within the deep plaster frieze and two figures at the centre of oval cartouches in the body of the ceiling. In the frieze are scenes of Adam and Eve's fall, the Presentation of the Head of John the Baptist to Salome, St Martin giving his coat to a beggar and the Virgin and Child (Figs 76 and 77). Two ceiling panels depict the figures of King David playing the harp and an angel sounding the trumpet on Judgement Day above a recumbent skeleton (Figs 78 and 79). A clue to the meaning of this imagery is offered by inscriptions in Latin on scrolls issuing from the mouths of the figures. The Latin words 'spoken' by King David can be translated as 'Praise [Him] with harp and with lute', while the angel states 'Arise from the Dead and come to Judgement'.[17]

Once again, it is instructive to relate this imagery to the functions of the room. As a space for occasional entertainment, the hall might have been used as a venue for musical activities. The practice of music as a secular recreation became fashionable in upper-class households during the sixteenth century. Playing musical instruments, with the associated singing and dancing, provided a focus for social interaction and performed a key role in rituals of courtship. For this reason the hotter sort of Protestant was vociferous in attacking such frivolous, and potentially amorous, activity. In his rather fanatical account of

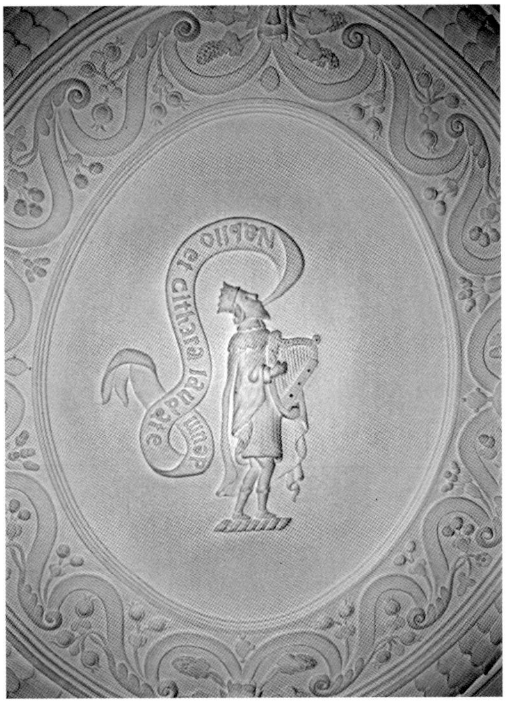

78 King David, detail of the plasterwork ceiling of c. 1640 in the hall at Gaulden Manor

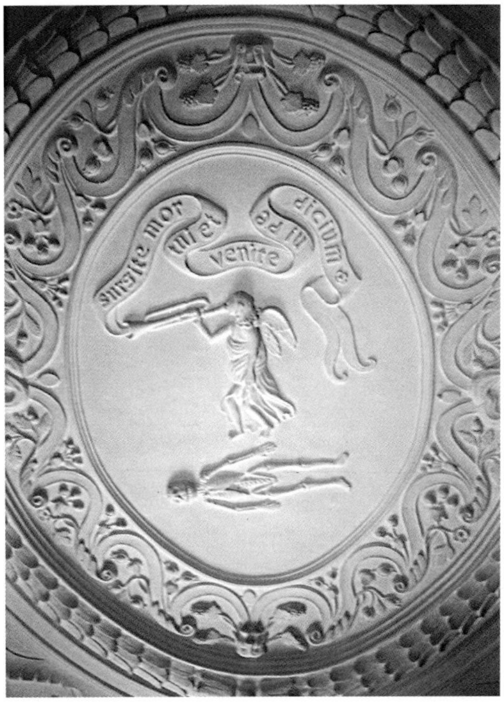

79 Angel sounding the trumpet on Judgement Day, detail of the plasterwork ceiling of c. 1640 in the hall at Gaulden Manor

moral and religious abuses, published in 1583, the Puritan Phillip Stubbes granted the merits of music as a tool to praise God but denounced the use of music 'in public assemblies and private conventicles, as directories to filthie dauncing, thorow the sweet harmonie and smoothe mellodie therof, it estraungeth the mind, stirreth up filthie lust, womanisheth the minde, ravisheth the hart, enflameth concupisence, and bringeth in uncleannes'.[18] The title page of William Daman's *Psalms of David in English meter* of 1579 proclaims that the book was intended for 'the use of godly Christians for recreating themselves, in stede of fond and unseemely Ballades'. Among the godly the only permissible music-making was the singing of psalms, which were believed at the time to have been written by the biblical King David. The figure of King David in the ceiling decoration at Gaulden Manor can be understood to authorise such musical activity, while reinforcing its purpose in Christian worship. Meanwhile, the *memento mori* in the form of the angel sounding the trumpet on Judgement Day in the parallel ceiling panel helped to ensure that recreation of the body through music did not result in neglect of the soul.

These decorations in the great halls of Burton Agnes and Gaulden Manor therefore represent highly sophisticated responses to the multiple and potentially contradictory functions of the room, and the responsibilities of the good Protestant householder: specifically, to be self-effacing in the display of status and wealth and to provide for the spiritual welfare of his household. The imagery not only reflects the activities taking place in the room but also helps to define and control the nature of behaviour.

The two decorative schemes described above are rare survivals but there are written accounts of similar decoration in the halls of other country houses. Two descriptions of country houses written by nineteenth-century travellers in the county of Cornwall suggest that large-scale religious imagery was relatively common in the great hall. In 1817 a visitor to Trewan, a manor house near St Columb, recorded: 'the grand hall is lofty and curiously finished . . . It has a handsome circular ceiling, the basement of which rests on a cornice whereon are exhibited in figures formed of plaster of paris, the principal events recorded in the book of Genesis'.[19] Meanwhile, fourteen miles away at Trewane Manor in St Kew (the similarity in name is a coincidence), a description from 1820 records that the hall was 'ornamented with some curious carved work, and many composition figures' including 'Justice, Abraham and King Solomon with numerous attendants'.[20] These descriptions call to mind the barrel-vaulted plasterwork ceilings in two other Cornish mansions, Lanhydrock House and Prideaux Place, and indicate that a specialised workshop was active in the area.[21]

During nineteenth-century alterations to Trewane Manor the plasterwork in the hall was destroyed but at a nearby farmhouse, less than two miles from Trewane, is a somewhat battered plasterwork overmantel *in situ* in the old hall, with the remains of a depiction of Adam and Eve's fall. Although in poor condition, it is still possible to discern the figures of Adam and Eve standing either side of the Tree of Knowledge. This work indicates how religious imagery was also employed as decoration in the hall of lesser rural houses but was more limited in scale, occupying just the focal point of the room, above the fireplace. Such a limitation meant that the owner had to be more selective in his choice of subject. It is significant that the scene chosen was the moment of Adam and Eve's fall from grace, a reminder to the company in the hall of the essential sinfulness of man.

At a manor house of similar status, Horsepits House near West Bergholt in Essex, a wall painting above the fireplace in the old hall depicts Abraham sacrificing Isaac, illustrating Genesis 22, flanked by two female characters from the Old Testament and Apocrypha, Judith and Esther. These solid and formidable female figures stand between paired columns and are identified by their attributes of sword (Judith) and sceptre (Esther). Although the painting is in fragmentary condition, it is clear that the figure of Judith has her sword raised in a gesture mirroring the raised arm of Abraham in the centre. The wall painting appears to date from 1628, when the house was lived in by Thomas Dibney, a clothier.[22] While it was common to depict female personifications of virtues as supporting figures on either side of a central narrative scene, the representation of specific biblical characters is more unusual. It suggests an allusion to their virtue of self-sacrifice. Muriel Carrick, who has examined the painting as part of a study of wall paintings in Essex, has observed how both characters served as intercessors acting on behalf of their people.[23] Esther risked her own death to plead the cause of her people to her husband, King Ahasuerus, while Judith slew the tyrant Holofernes to liberate her people. These female heroines are paired with the example of personal sacrifice provided by the male patriarch, Abraham, at the centre of the painting, while the theme of intercession is continued with the angel who intercedes to prevent Isaac's sacrifice. The choice of iconography relating to the virtue of selflessness is certainly appropriate for representation in a room that symbolised the community of the household.

THE PARLOUR

In the standard sequence of principal rooms, the next important reception room usually located on the ground floor was the parlour.[24] The room that became known as the parlour developed as a withdrawing room from the hall, offering more privacy and comfort, and traditionally adjoined the hall at the 'high' end, sometimes with a connecting passageway or landing (as at Montacute; see the floor-plan illustrated in Chapter 2).[25] In some Scottish castles, this room was known as the 'chamber of dais' and, like the hall, was on the first floor, but otherwise the room served similar functions to the parlour in England. Despite their close proximity, the character of the parlour was in complete contrast to the hall. Whereas the hall was open to persons of all ranks, the parlour was reserved for those of higher status, serving as a family room for sitting and dining and for receiving guests of some position. The character of the parlour as a withdrawing room to the hall, filtering down large gatherings to more select and intimate companies, is illustrated by a comment in Thomas Wilson's 'godly treatise' of 1620:

> I may compare our hearts to a great large house, whose hall is love, and the parlour brotherly kindnesse: as then a great man admits all friends, strangers, one and other into his hall, so our love is to lie open unto all men, without respect or difference; but our brotherly kindnesse we communicate onely to such as our even Christians, as we doe allow our nearest acquaintance onely to have accesse into our parlour.[26]

This symbolic concept of the house as a metaphor for the body (and vice versa) was fairly common in early modern literature but this passage also evokes the nature of access to the parlour as an exercise in social differentiation. Moving from the hall into the parlour signalled a distinct shift in atmosphere. If one purpose of the hall was to intimidate and awe, the parlour had to be conducive to comfort and recreation. The hall was grand and lofty while the parlour was smaller, less ostentatiously decorated and fitted out for comfort; it was often wainscoted for warmth and furnished with comfortable chairs and side tables.[27]

Contemporary literature often mentioned the parlour as the location for conversation. In Act 3 Scene 1 of Shakespeare's *Much Ado about Nothing*, Hero tells Margaret 'run thee to the parlour. There shalt thou find my cousin Beatrice Proposing with the Prince and Claudio'.[28] Similarly, in his 1601 discourse on spirits and devils, styled as a conversation between a group of gentlemen, John Deacon staged much of the action in the host's parlour. This was evidently the room considered most suitable for conversation; the host, Orthodoxus, suggests to his guests: 'let us now . . . keepe close in my parlour, with ful purpose to proceede in our conference till dinner be ready'.[29] The phrase 'keepe close'

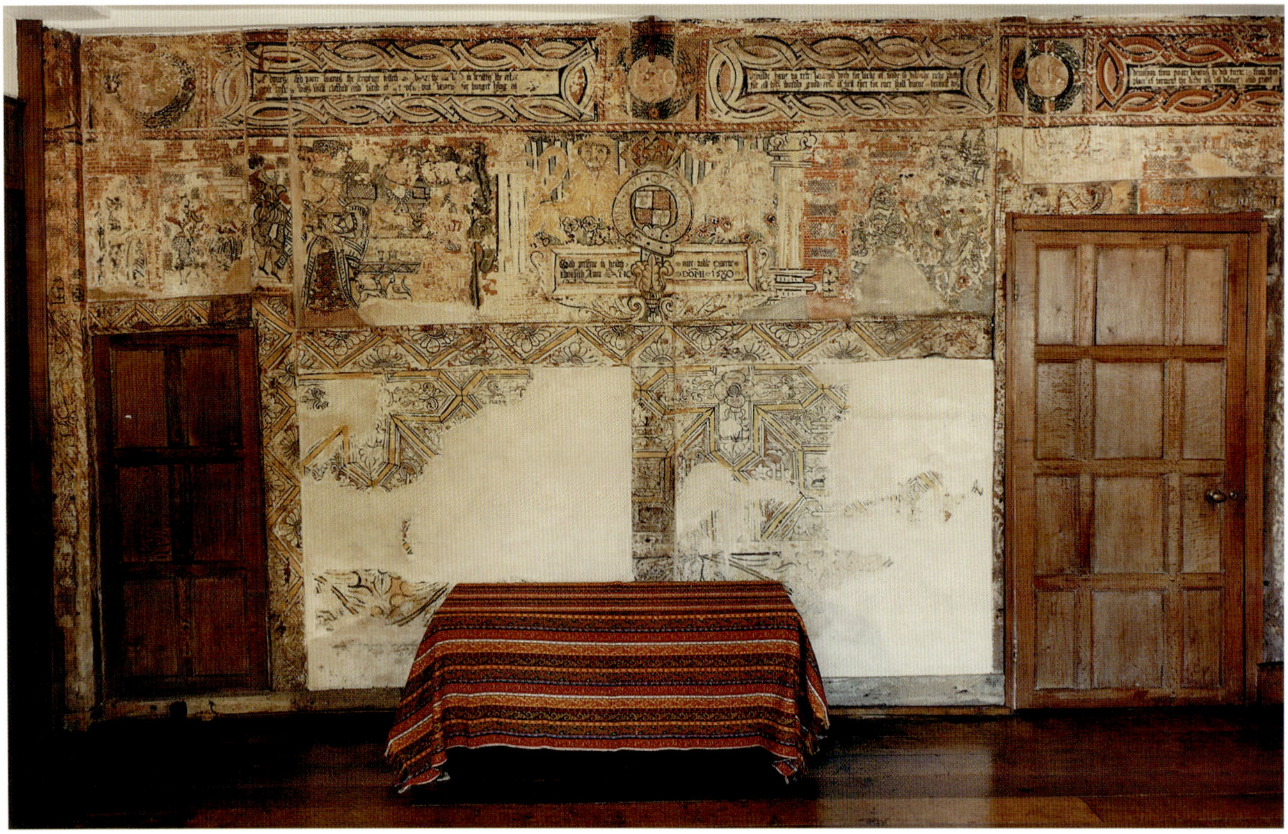

80 Wall paintings of 1580 in the old parlour at Pittleworth Manor, Hampshire

suggests an intimate, cosy environment and yet later, after supper, Orthodoxus complains that he is weary with sitting and announces: 'let us go walke a turne or two in my parlour. And having revived our spirits by the singing of psalmes: returne againe to our purpose [the discussion]'.[30] This suggests a parlour of some size to accommodate walking to stretch the legs. It also indicates the nature of the room as a multi-function space; along with walking, another form of recreation, the singing of psalms, also took place in the parlour.

The company in Deacon's treatise do not eat in the parlour but instead remove there after dining, probably because as a group of gentlemen not well acquainted, the company would dine more formally in the great chamber. That great chamber, on the first floor, was a grander room used for dining and entertaining on formal occasions (as discussed later in this chapter). In smaller houses just one room would function as both parlour and great chamber and, where possible, was on the first floor. However, in larger houses, two rooms were provided for the same functions, one for everyday use, one for special occasions, one informal, one grand. This is sometimes reflected in the internal floor-plan, with the great chamber situated directly above the parlour, rather than the hall.[31]

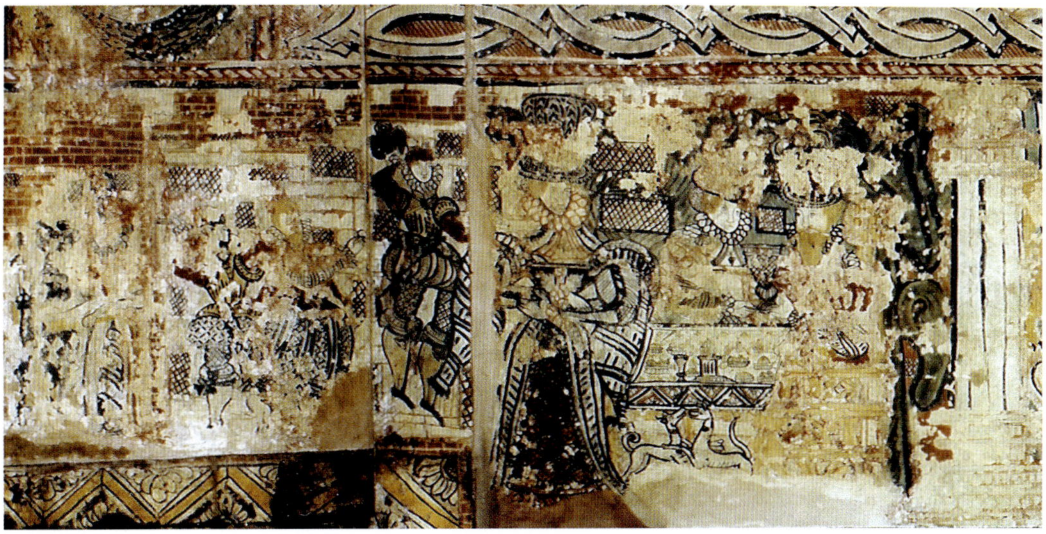

81 Dives and his family dining, detail of the wall paintings of 1580 in the old parlour at Pittleworth Manor

Owning a separate parlour and great chamber was a luxury and a sign of status. It allowed for the separation of comfort and state. Larger houses often had several parlours, each with a specific purpose.[32] Smaller houses had to manage with just one room, which combined practical and ceremonial functions. Even in houses with a separate great chamber, it is clear that it was the parlour that was used for everyday, informal dining and for dining with familiar guests, so that references to the 'dining parlour' is common in contemporary documents. The household accounts kept by John Willoughby of Leyhill, Devon, in 1604 list seven additional guests invited to dine in the parlour, while two male servants, presumably attendants to the guests, ate in the hall. Willoughby also recorded the costs of this hospitality, allowing 6d a piece for those sitting at the family table and for those at the servants' table 4d a piece.[33]

As a room used by family members and upper servants on a daily basis and for entertaining guests informally, the decoration of the parlour served very different functions from that of the hall. In keeping with the informal role of the room as a dining and sitting room for the family, subject matter in figurative decoration tended to focus on familial themes and domestic activities, such as eating. An example is the parlour at Pittleworth Manor in Hampshire, decorated with colourful wall paintings dated 1580.[34] The decoration includes two scenes from the parable of Dives and Lazarus, illustrating Luke 16, depicted on either side of the royal arms of Elizabeth I (Fig. 80). In the pictorial scene on the left, a small company of sumptuously dressed figures is gathered round a table laden with dishes of food (Fig. 81). In the companion scene on the right is a single figure, representing Lazarus, who is shown lying on the ground outside the house with dogs licking his sores. Above these scenes are explanatory inscriptions and other moral texts such as: 'Repent amend and synn no more: aske grace and mersye and pittey the poore'.

The parable of Dives and Lazarus seems a particularly fitting subject for depiction in a domestic setting, reflecting the use of the room for dining, and serving as a reminder of the responsibilities of householders to provide charity to the poor. In this way the decoration engaged in wider cultural trends. As Paul Slack observed: 'It was commonplace in the sixteenth and early seventeenth centuries to compare the lot of rich and poor, of Dives and Lazarus, in order to determine the ideal type of each, and hence their reciprocal obligations'.[35] The story underlined a specifically Christian form of charity, with acts of mercy towards the poor as much a tribute to Christ as a recognition of dearth and hardship.

Throughout the medieval period, private almsgiving had been understood as an essential religious and social duty of the wealthier classes. However, attitudes to charity and provision for the poor were renegotiated during the sixteenth and seventeenth centuries as a response to rapid political, religious, social and economic change. By 1580, when the wall paintings at Pittleworth were created, the traditional operation of private charity was perceived to be in decline. As Slack demonstrated, a widespread condemnation of the idle or 'undeserving' poor, coupled with the growth of towns (especially London) which took householders away from their estates, were factors in the erosion of old charitable ideals.[36] The Dives and Lazarus subject matter at Pittleworth Manor might, therefore, comment on wider social and political change. It could be seen to represent a reaffirmation of the Christian virtues of private almsgiving during a time when a wave of state legislation (consolidated in the Poor Law of 1601) made welfare provision the responsibility of parishes rather than individuals.

As well as a form of social commentary, the decoration at Pittleworth communicates spiritual concerns. It has already been noted how eating was an activity loaded with spiritual significance and, as with the parable of the Wise and Foolish Virgins depicted in the hall at Burton Agnes, the parable of Dives and Lazarus had two levels of meaning. On one level it reinforced the charitable obligations of wealthy householders. On another it alluded to death and judgement, warning of dire consequences resulting from negligence in this duty. As Tessa Watt has observed: 'The image of the poor beggar functioned much like a skull on the desk, which warned one in the fullness of life to be thinking of death. In fact, such a *memento mori* appears as a moral text on another wall in the same room: "Thus lyving all ways dred wee death and diing life wee doughte".'[37] Once again there is a high degree of sophistication in the choice of decorative subject matter, which utilises themes and imagery centring on scenes of everyday domestic activity, while simultaneously communicating spiritual messages concerning the need for self-regulation and examination as preparedness for death and judgement.

A similar degree of sophistication in the choice of imagery for depiction in applied decoration can be seen in the parlour at Little Moreton Hall in Cheshire, where a set of paintings illustrate the story of Susannah and the Elders from the Apocrypha. Little Moreton Hall was renovated and improved in the 1580s by John Moreton, a wealthy landowner. Moreton was evidently keen to be seen as a good Protestant in observing the ban on religious images in spaces used for worship. During his renovations, the walls of

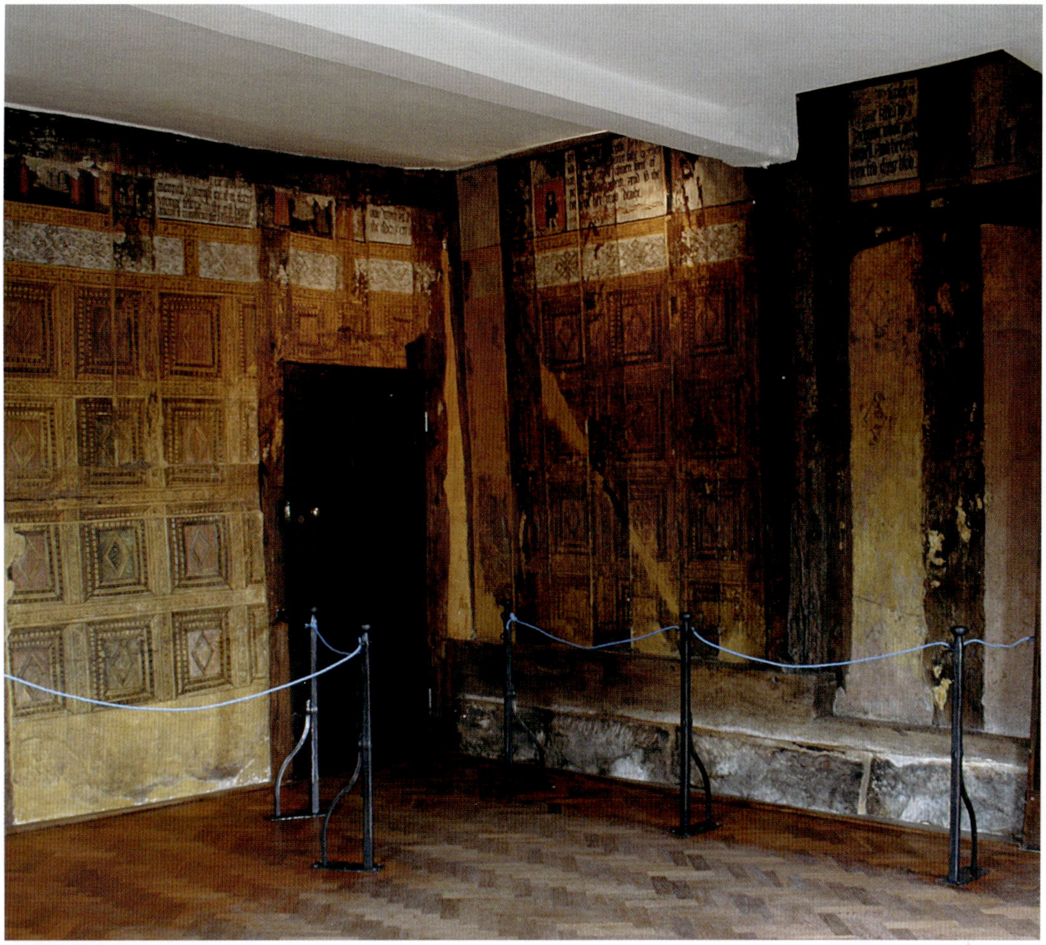

82 View of the painted decoration, 1580s, in the parlour at Little Moreton Hall, Cheshire

the chapel at Little Moreton Hall were decorated with paintings of texts taken from the Tyndale Bible of 1537 and it was his parlour that was enriched with religious images. The story is communicated through image and text within a deep frieze at the top of the walls (Fig. 82). Six narrative scenes are visible, interspersed with panels of black-letter text summarising verses 15–46 of the History of Susannah. The pictorial paintings are fragmentary (the ceiling has been lowered thus obscuring the upper part of the frieze) and in a state of decay but considering their age, and the fact that they were depicted on paper and pasted onto the wall, it is amazing that they have survived at all.[38]

The story – about a woman who stalwartly refused the sexual advances of powerful men, even when faced with the prospect of losing her own reputation and life – was a popular theme throughout Europe during the Renaissance period, not least because the moral of the subject matter served as an excuse for erotic depictions of the female nude. A painting of this subject executed in 1607 by the Flemish artist Peter Paul Rubens (in

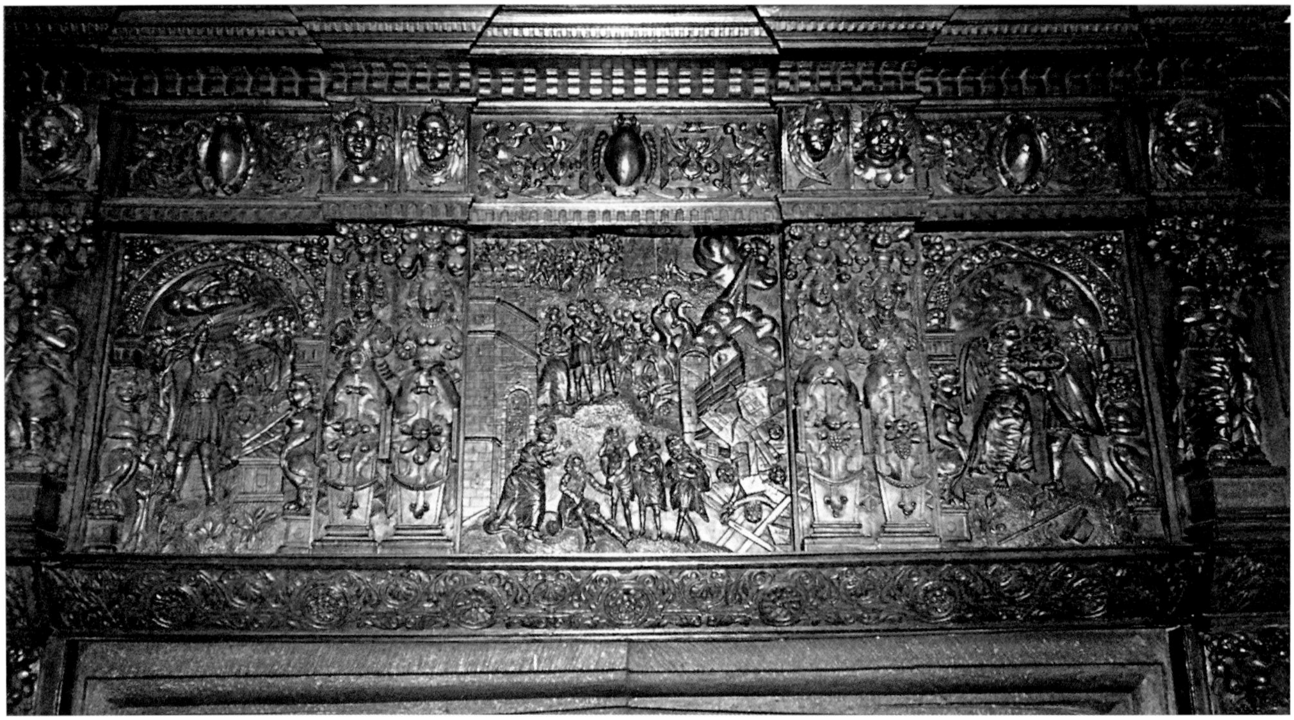

83 The carved wood overmantel of 1630–40 in the parlour at Bradninch Manor, Devon

the Galleria Borghese, Rome), delights in the treatment of the naked figure of Susannah, which occupies most of the canvas, offering a sensual representation of pink flesh and curving form. By contrast, in a version of the subject painted in 1647 by Rembrandt (in the Gemäldegalerie, Berlin), working in the Protestant northern Netherlands, the figure of Susannah is smaller in scale and most of her body is covered by drapery. This more modest interpretation of the subject was influenced by the tastes of a Protestant market that was uncomfortable with flagrant displays of sexuality.

In the version at Little Moreton Hall, there is little hint within the imagery of the more titillating aspects of this story. Unlike the European convention focusing on the moment of the proposition, with a semi-nude Susannah at the centre of the composition, the emphasis here is on the entirety of the story, with a series of scenes forming a narrative sequence that would originally have culminated in scenes of the judgement, punishment and death of the lecherous and deceitful elders.[39] This underlines that decorative art in the domestic interior in Post-Reformation Britain was not primarily intended for the purposes of aesthetic enjoyment. Rather it was the message, associations and mood of the imagery that took priority in the design and execution of the decoration. The imagery chosen for decoration in this parlour communicates complex messages about gender roles, sexual desire and restraint, judgement, punishment and death. It may be significant that the owner of Little Moreton Hall was the head of a large family. John

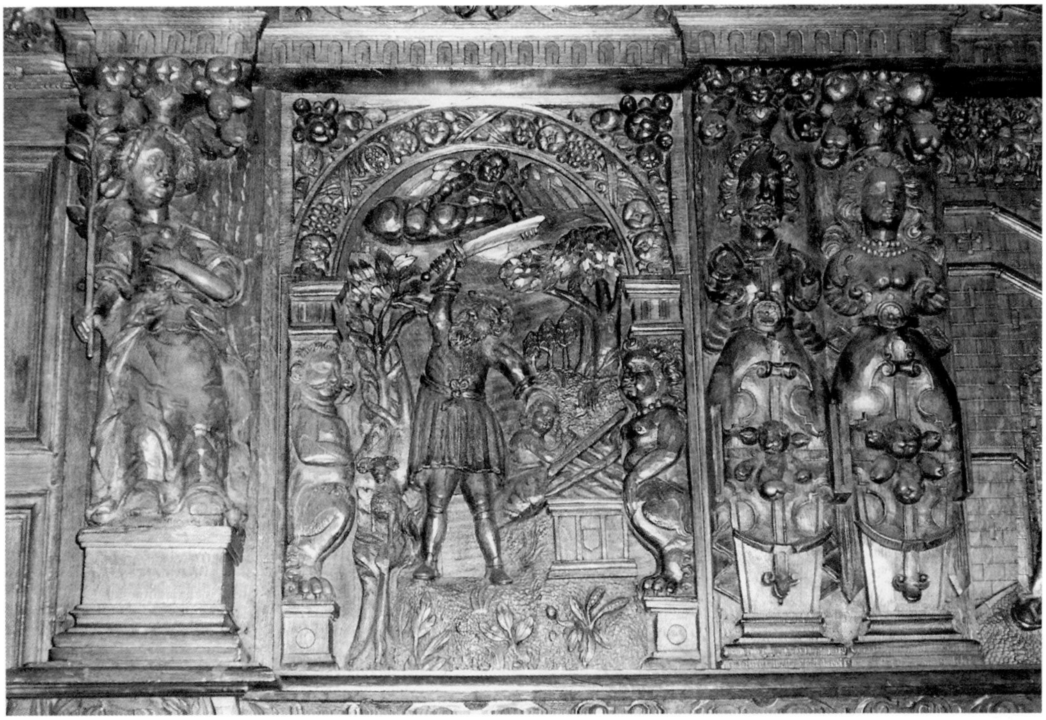

84 The Sacrifice of Isaac, detail of the overmantel in the parlour at Bradninch Manor

Moreton married four times and had ten children, including several daughters.[40] Perhaps he chose the story of Susannah as the subject of decoration in the parlour with his daughters' moral education in mind.

The stories of Dives and Lazarus and Susannah and the Elders share a theme – to accept humbly the suffering of trials, tribulations and hardship in the hope of eventual deliverance. In the case of the pauper Lazarus, the deliverance comes after death when he gains access to heaven. For Susannah the deliverance comes earlier when Daniel (the boy sent by God) steps in to secure her reprieve, and this was understood as an analogy for deliverance through faith.[41] Similarly, the three stories from Genesis depicted in a carved wood overmantel above the fireplace in the ground-floor parlour at Bradninch Manor in Devon can be understood to show these same themes of trials and deliverance.[42] The overmantel, dating from about 1630–40, includes three narrative panels, separated by paired male and female caryatids (Fig. 83). On the left under an arch is the Sacrifice of Isaac (Fig. 84). In the centre is a larger panel with a continuous narrative depicting various calamitous episodes from the Trials of Job, including the dramatic illustration of his home falling to the ground and killing his children (Fig. 85). On the right-hand side of the overmantel Jacob wrestles with the Angel (Fig. 86).

All three stories depicted in the Bradninch overmantel are concerned with trials, temptation and deliverance. These trials are all explicitly concerned with familial relationships.

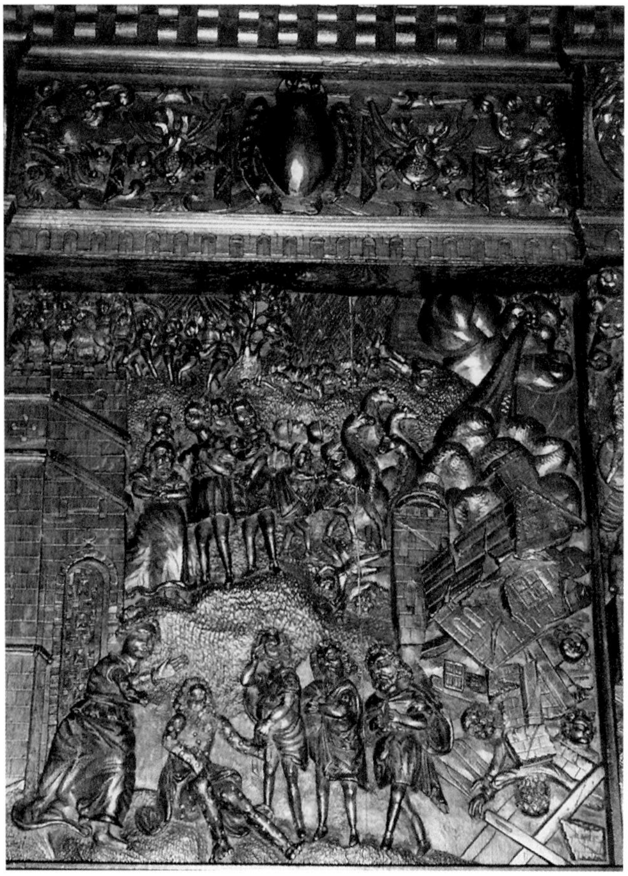

85 The Trials of Job, detail of the overmantel in the parlour at Bradninch Manor

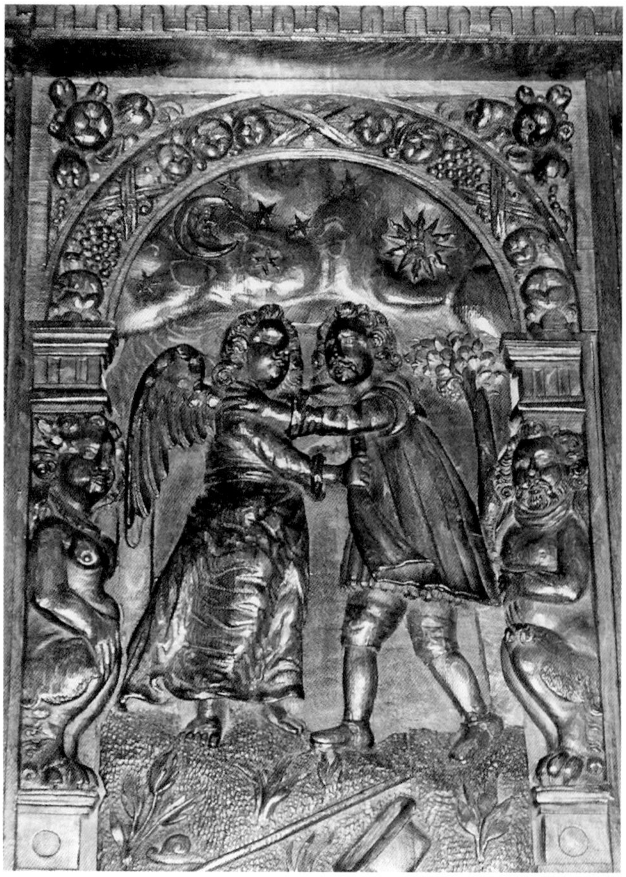

86 Jacob wrestling with the Angel, detail of the overmantel in the parlour at Bradninch Manor

Abraham was ordered to sacrifice his only son, Isaac, to God but on demonstrating his intention to obey, was prevented at the last moment from harming Isaac through the intervention of an angel. Job's ordeal involved the loss of his goods, home, children and health and yet he refused to blame God for his afflictions. Jacob wrestled with a man of God through the night before a meeting with his estranged brother and, though wounded in the battle, he emerged the stronger and was able to be reconciled with his brother and thereby avoid military confrontation. The Bradninch overmantel does not include an inscription to indicate the intended meaning of this imagery but one can assume that the original audience would have approached such images with contemporary exegesis in mind. The theme of trials of faith shared by all three stories was expounded by William Cowper in his *Triumph of a Christian* of 1608 which seems to offer the textual equivalent of the iconographic message in the Bradninch overmantel. Cowper's treatise was concerned with the nature of affliction and adversity as the path to deliverance through faith. He wrote at length on the story of Jacob wrestling with the Angel as a model of faith, obedience and patience, which he specified as 'necessary for those who are troubled in conscience'. He also invoked other biblical models and dwelt at length on Abraham and Job in particular. In his advice to the reader on how to behave in response to temptation, he wrote:

> Thou therefore whose heart is set to seeke the Lord, & in this perplexitie wouldst know what to doe and how to behave thy selfe, I can no better way resolve thee, then to send thee to looke unto Abraham, Jacob, Job, and the rest of these [examples], who have been exercised with the like tentations [temptations] before thee.[43]

While Cowper's instruction to 'look unto' the examples of Abraham, Jacob and Job was no doubt intended to be followed in relation to reading these stories in the Bible, the representation of these particular episodes in the overmantel at Bradninch allowed the opportunity literally to look on their example. Thus these three biblical patriarchs served as the ideal models of faith and patience through terrible affliction and spiritual doubt. The overmantel and Cowper's treatise can be understood to have served the same function: to provide comfort and guidance to the godly during periods of difficulty, with a promise of eventual deliverance through faith and obedience.

It is undoubtedly significant given the domestic setting that all three examples represent familial relationships and, more specifically, caution the onlooker to overcome family ties and love in order to come closer to God and secure salvation. In this sense it is important that the overmantel is in the parlour, used as a sitting and dining room for the family. The imagery proclaims and supports the identity of a Protestant husband and father who puts his obedience to God above all else. Meanwhile he fulfils the role of dutiful patriarch by providing a source of spiritual guidance and comfort for his family and household.

To conclude this discussion of imagery in parlours I want to consider a remarkable scheme of wall paintings dated 1623 in the ground-floor living room of a large yeoman's house known as 'Roger's Farmhouse' in Newton, Suffolk. The paintings were documented by the Reverend G. Montagu Benton in the 'Notes' section of the *Antiquaries Journal* of 1941 when they were described as in fragmentary condition.[44] Benton's description of the wall paintings as visible in 1941 was accompanied by black and white photography which is unfortunately of insufficient quality to reproduce here. The building is now in private ownership and so my account is based on Benton's description and the evidence provided by the accompanying photographs.[45]

The scheme of painting at 'Roger's Farmhouse' depicts two subjects: the life of Samson from the Old Testament and the Martyrdom of St Stephen from the New Testament. Benton suggested that the decoration must originally have extended across the four walls but the painting visible in 1941 was confined to the east and west walls. Across the upper part of the east wall is a series of scenes from the life of Samson. At the far end of the west wall a group of three figures is just a fragment of a larger scene that once extended along this wall and above the fireplace. Above this remaining fragment of painting are the concluding words of an inscription and the date for the work, which read: 's Saull, ACTS: 7: 56.1623'. Although the inscription mentions only verse 56, the piece of text ending with 's Saull' concludes verse 58 so it can be inferred that the text for verses 56 to 58 of Acts 7 once ran along the top of the wall from end to end. These verses read as follows:

> 56 And said, Behold, I see the heavens opened, and the Son of man standing on the right hand of God. 57 Then they cried out with a loud voice, and stopped their ears, and ran upon him with one accord, 58 And cast him out of the city, and stoned him: and the witnesses laid down their clothes at a young man's feet, whose name was Saul.

Benton therefore identified the remaining portion of painting with its three figures as Saul and two of the witnesses from the Martyrdom of St Stephen. This means that there can be little doubt that in the space above the fireplace was once depicted St Stephen's vision of Christ and a scene of him being cast out of the city and stoned to death. Indeed, Benton recorded that he could make out faint traces of a kneeling figure of St Stephen and a Christ in Glory.

It is striking that an image of St Stephen's martyrdom by stoning and his vision of Christ in Glory was depicted in a prominent position above the fireplace in the principal room of a yeoman's farmhouse in 1623. Images of saints and depictions of Christ were identified in the 'Homily against peril of idolatry' of 1563 as especially likely to prompt idolatry and this was reiterated by many Protestant commentators. According to traditional devotional practice, images of the sufferings endured by saints provided a stimulus for affective devotion and St Stephen's experience of a holy vision could serve as a point of access for the viewer's own devotional visualisation of Christ, operating in much the same way as scenes of the mass of St Gregory. How then can one explain the presence of this imagery in reformed, domestic space? First, as a narrative depiction which adheres to the biblical account, this imagery can be understood as a representation of history and therefore fell within the range of permissible imagery as defined by William Perkins and other commentators. But what is the significance of these particular stories? In order to identify the meaning of the imagery for its Protestant audience, it is necessary to consider the whole scheme of decoration in the room. On first consideration, it looks as if the stories from the life of Samson and the Martyrdom of St Stephen are unrelated but there is a thematic thread connecting the two. The climax of the sequence of scenes about Samson in the wall paintings is a depiction of his pulling down the pagan temple. An explanatory inscription in black letter above reads: 'Samson being set in ye mids of ye multitude breaketh downe ye temple of dagon & s[l]ayeth them & himselfe'. St Stephen was martyred after reprimanding the council of Jewish elders for the betrayal and murder of Christ. However, a central theme of his discourse as provided in Acts 7 was to reject the building of temples as necessary to faith because, like the Mosaic Law, this was a temporary institution always intended to be superseded by the teachings of the Messiah and fulfilled by the coming of Christ. Both biblical figures, therefore, sacrificed their lives to attack, in practice or in theory, the building of false temples.

The 'iconoclasm' of Samson and the theme of St Stephen's discourse therefore both served to underline the essential Protestant tenet that man should have a direct relationship with God unhindered by any worldly paraphernalia. In addition, St Stephen, along with St Paul (previously Saul, as depicted in the wall paintings), was one of the founding fathers of the new, Christian faith which was born from the Jewish religion, in the same way that Protestants could view themselves as the founders of a new religion purified of the corruptions of the Roman Catholic faith. The decoration at 'Roger's Farmhouse' can thus be understood to express overtly Protestant ideology yet, somewhat paradoxically, the message is communicated through traditional religious imagery which was itself criticised by reformers as a worldly distraction from pure faith and an obstacle to the direct worship of God. Analysis of the wall paintings at this farmhouse suggests how a high level of iconographical sophistication could underpin the choice of subject matter for the decoration of even a fairly unprepossessing dwelling.

From the examples discussed here, it is clear that in general the tone of the decoration of parlours was far from cheerful. Rather, the atmosphere was decidedly sombre. This counteracted the potentially upbeat atmosphere associated with the functions of the room – gatherings of company, feasting and after-dinner recreation. However, the intimate, informal nature of the room as a family dining and sitting room suggests that such imagery was aimed at a relatively sophisticated audience, capable of understanding the meaning of the imagery with reference to contemporary literature. In this way, decoration was not only a form of visual ornament but also an important mode of communication and an influence on behaviour.

THE FORMAL STAIRCASE

The nature and status of the staircase underwent radical change from the mid-sixteenth to the late seventeenth century.[46] During medieval times, staircases in larger houses had been tucked away, often in turrets at the extremities of buildings, while in smaller farmhouses and humbler dwellings stairs had often been no more than simple ladders.[47] In both cases stairs had been purely functional and steep, cramped and usually unadorned. From the middle of the sixteenth century large, spacious staircases became a focal point in most houses of status. This development resulted from two principal factors. First, the separation of service areas from high-status reception space required a separate, formal stairway within the ceremonial route. Second, developments in architectural theory, design and expertise facilitated the conception and construction of staircases of comparable impact and status to the reception rooms they connected.

As a significant part of the ceremonial route through the principal rooms of the house, the main staircase could provide a stately and impressive vehicle for ascent. In English country houses the great stair usually led off the high end of the hall, opposite the parlour, so that it connected the principal reception rooms on the ground floor with the great chamber on the floor above. This standard arrangement is illustrated in Gervase Markham's diagram of 'a plaine country mans house' (see Fig. 41), where the principal stair is located at the high end of the hall, adjoining the parlour, providing access to the high-status reception rooms on the first floor.

The size and quality of the staircase gave an indication of the scale and comfort of the building as a whole. But consideration was also paid to the experience of climbing. Inspired by Italian architectural theory based on classical models, Sir Henry Wotton in his *Elements of Architecture* offered the following recommendations to his English readers:

> To make a compleate *Staire-case*, is a curious peece of *Architecture*: The vulgar Cautions are these. That it have a very liberall *Light*, against all Casualtie of *Slippes*, and *Falles*. That the space above the *Head*, bee large and *Airy* . . . as it were good *Ventilation*, because a man doth spend much breath in mounting. That the *Halfe-paces* bee well distributed, at competent distances, for reposing on the way.[48]

Wotton's recommendations signal a fundamental change in attitudes to the nature of moving through spaces in the interior. The success of a staircase here rests on the quality of the experience in climbing it. Thus, the area round the staircase should be light and airy, with plenty of landings for 'reposing on the way'. Once the staircase was conceived as a vehicle for stately and leisurely ascent, with spaces to pause *en route*, it was exploited for the purposes of visual display.

At Montacute House in Somerset, the principal staircase of about 1600 is made from stone, turned in broad flights round a stone newel. This type of stone stairway is found in the grandest houses of the second half of the sixteenth century, including Burghley House in Lincolnshire (1560) and Hardwick Hall in Derbyshire (1590–97). Stone staircases were also common in Scottish castles throughout the sixteenth and seventeenth centuries, where various design innovations allowed more spacious and grand formal stairways, which stretched at least up to the hall and associated reception rooms on the first floor.[49] Such staircases tended to be left relatively plain and unadorned. Their impact relied to a great extent on the impressive nature of the sweeping flight of narrow treads, from which applied ornament might detract.[50]

Early in the seventeenth century improved techniques of joinery meant that elaborate wooden staircases became common in larger houses as well as in houses of middling status. In fact, wooden staircases became extremely desirable as fashion responded to interest in new building techniques. For town houses and less prestigious houses where space was at a premium the staircase was kept simple and compact, with a modest newel staircase or a straight flight of timber steps. In houses of any pretension, however, where space allowed, the open-well wooden staircase offered an opportunity to improve the comfort, appearance and status of the building. Wooden staircases, constructed by specialist carpenters, permitted the incorporation of carved ornament and so encouraged a fashion for figurative carving within the structure which reached a peak during the first half of the seventeenth century.

In his essay 'Of Building' published in 1612, Francis Bacon recommended the new fashion for crafted wooden staircases incorporating carved imagery. He advised: 'The Staires likewise, to the upper Roomes, let them bee upon a Faire open Newell, and finely raild in, with Images of Wood, cast into a Brass Color: And a very faire Landing Place at the Top.'[51] What Bacon probably had in mind when recommending 'images of wood' within the

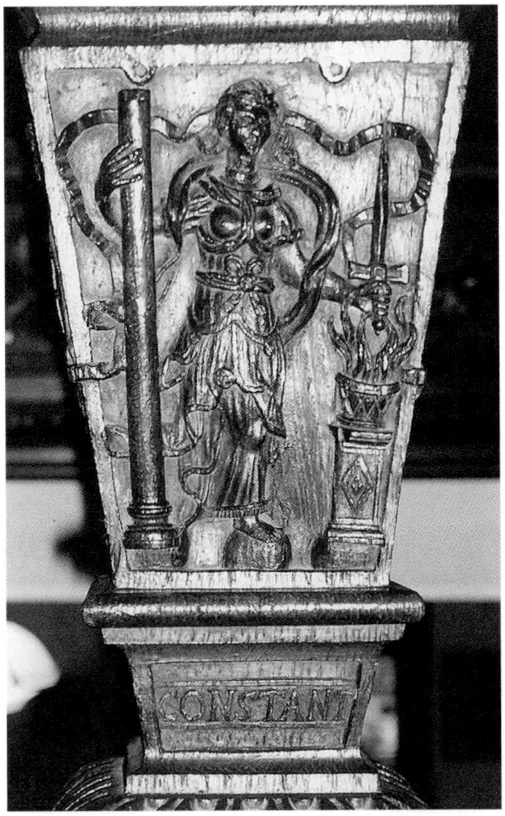

87 The Virtue of Constancy, detail of the carved staircase of c. 1600 from Slaugham Place, Sussex, now in Lewes town hall

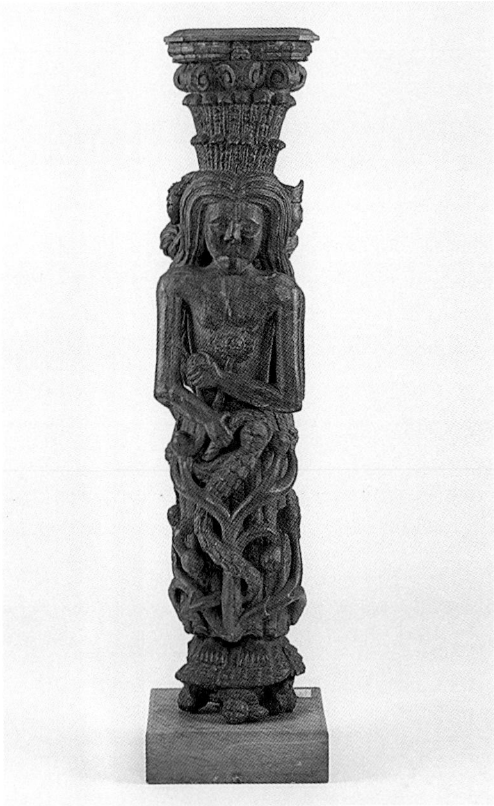

88 The figures of Adam and Eve carved in a wooden post, c. 1600–20. Victoria and Albert Museum, London

staircase can still be seen at Hatfield House in Hertfordshire, the palatial mansion built by Robert Cecil, Chief Minister to James I. The oak staircase of about 1610–12 is decorated with Renaissance strapwork motifs and carved newel figures of playful *putti*. Another, less celebrated example is the elaborately carved wooden staircase of about 1600 from Slaugham Place in Sussex, now installed in Lewes town hall. This staircase incorporates carvings of female virtues together with classical gods, the Senses, Elements and Parts of the World (Fig. 87).[52] Such figurative carving was probably relatively common in staircases of this date although complete staircases are rare survivals. A carved post with the figures of Adam and Eve dating from about 1600–20 was possibly part of a newel staircase (Fig. 88).[53] It is likely that many carved wooden panels and posts that once formed part of early seventeenth-century staircases were removed in subsequent centuries and have since been lost.

As a focal point on the ceremonial route connecting the important rooms on all the floors of the house, the formal staircase was the literal and symbolic backbone of the house and household. With its scale and grandeur, the formal staircase was a sort of room of state in itself and this new space could serve other, additional functions. In a ground-breaking study of the evolution of the Protestant country house chapel, Annabel Ricketts described how a particular type of 'assembly chapel' emerged as a response to the demands of Protestant household worship.[54] Assembly chapels made use of peripheral spaces around the core chapel, allowing the wider household to gather for daily prayers and Bible readings. Ricketts found that these subsidiary spaces were often part of main circulation routes and a significant number of houses designed or built during the Elizabethan and Jacobean period included chapels positioned close to the great stair. Examples include Hunstanton Hall in Norfolk, where a nineteenth-century description of the (now lost) chapel records that it was at the centre of the main wooden staircase, allowing those gathered on the stairs to see into the chapel through the banisters.[55] Another example is the original arrangement around the two-storey chapel at Hardwick Hall, where the upper chapel is only divided from the landing by an open-work screen, allowing an assembly area looking into the chapel from the upper floor.

The connection between chapel and staircase constitutes a unique response to two issues bearing on the design of the domestic chapel in the Protestant interior. First, it provided a practical way of ensuring enough space to gather the whole household for daily worship without the need for a disproportionately large chapel within the floor-plan. Secondly, it represents a fundamental change in attitude to the status of the private, domestic chapel in response to Protestant thought. The use of connecting, subsidiary spaces, like the staircase, served to integrate the chapel within the building, representing a radical departure from the concept of a private chapel as a 'sacred' space, separate from the rest of the interior. Rather, Protestant householders sought to maintain an atmosphere of piety throughout the whole building and at all times.

Use of the staircase as a subsidiary space for the assembly chapel might also have been influenced by contemporary ideas about the connection between physical and spiritual elevation. During the early modern period, physical ascent was conceived as symbolising moral and spiritual ascent. This association is sometimes reflected in the decoration applied to the staircase and its surrounding wall surfaces. For example, the great staircase of about 1636 at Aldermaston in Berkshire, as illustrated in Joseph Nash's *The Mansions of England in the olden time* (1839–49) was adorned with carved newel figures including female personifications of Virtues (Fig. 89).[56] Even allowing Nash a degree of poetic licence in exaggerating the scale of the figures in his drawing, these newel figures were evidently huge and imposing statues. From Nash's drawing one can identify, in addition to Peace (holding a dove) and Prudence (with a mirror), a figure holding an anchor as the Theological Virtue of Hope while another figure, in deep shadow, appears to represent Charity, another of the Theological Virtues. Similarly, C. J. Richardson's illustration of a section of the staircase at Claverton Manor in Somerset shows the carved figure of Fortitude as a newel figure.[57] This suggests that the staircase at Claverton was similar to that at Aldermaston. These images of Cardinal and Theological Virtues were perhaps intended to impress on those ascending the staircase the need for moral and spiritual self-regulation, as they rise from the lower levels of the house (associated with service and social inclusion) to the socially exclusive, high-status rooms above.

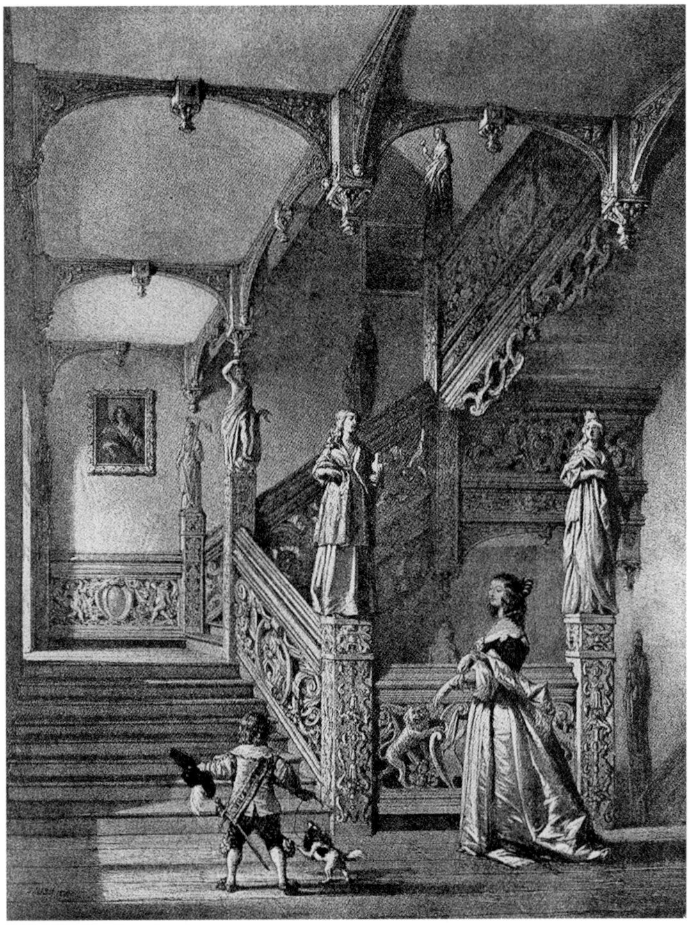

89 The great staircase of c. 1636 at Aldermaston in Berkshire, as illustrated in Joseph Nash's *Mansions of England* (1839–49)

A similar message is communicated by the carved decoration of the staircase from Rawden Hall in Hoddesdon, Hertfordshire. Rawden Hall was built by Marmaduke Rawden in the 1620s.[58] The staircase, which must date from that decade, incorporates carved figures and panels, including a scene of Samson and Delilah which is curiously repeated twice on the first-floor landing. This depicts a sleeping Samson, with his head resting on the lap of the seated Delilah, who is dressed in loose drapery with her breasts exposed (Fig. 90). The panel represents the moment when Samson lies sleeping and powerless at Delilah's feet, having been seduced and enticed into confiding the secret of his strength to her, and just before his hair is cut, thus robbing him of his strength. Seduction as a theme is picked up in another of the carved panels where two *putti* each play a different type of horn.[59] One *putto* carries an arrow and so may be identified as the classical god of love, Cupid. In other sections of the balustrade two *putti* are shown exchanging amorous looks and another naked, grotesque figure blows a horn. The carved panels of the staircase therefore suggest a sexual theme and this is taken up again in a carved stone chimneypiece (probably from the great chamber) which was removed from Rawden in

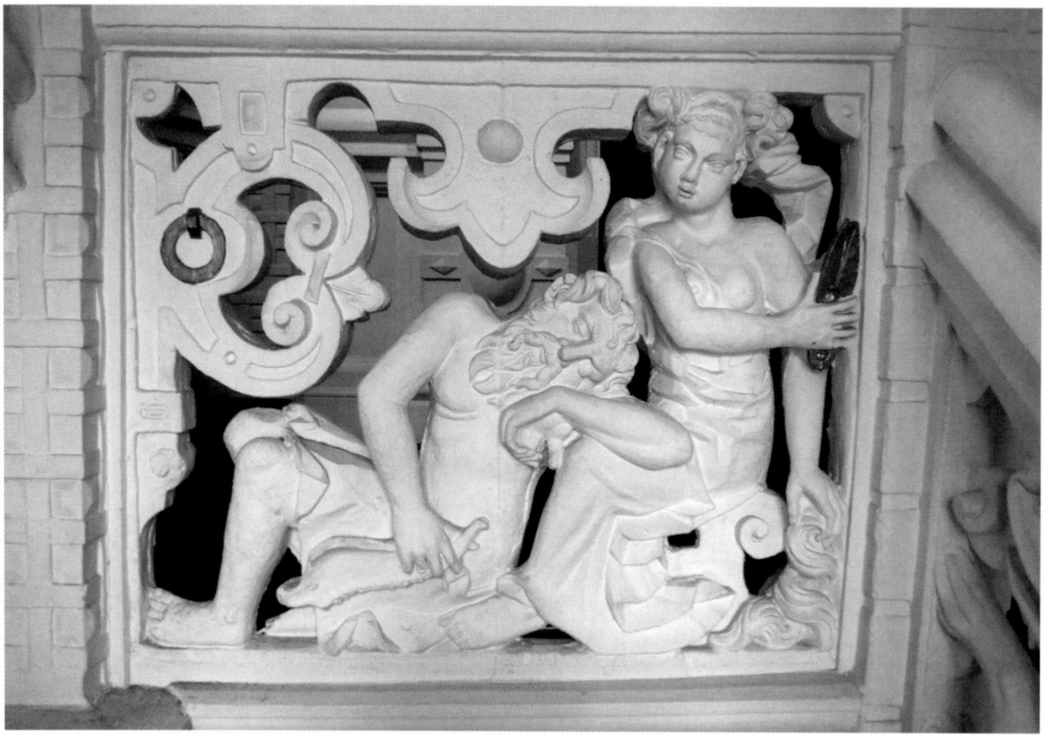

90 Samson and Delilah, detail of the carved staircase of 1622 at Rawden Hall, Hoddesdon, Hertfordshire

about 1900 and is now installed at Rothamsted Manor in Hertfordshire.[60] Its overmantel depicts scenes of satyrs playing musical instruments with caryatids of a satyr and nymph. While this overmantel, viewed in isolation, might be understood to reflect the use of the room for musical entertainments in a celebration of the association between music and sexuality (as symbolised by the satyrs), it is significant that before viewing this chimneypiece in the great chamber, visitors would have first encountered the two scenes of Samson and Delilah as they ascended the great staircase. As a vivid depiction of Samson at the mercy of Delilah, this image served as a cautionary reminder of the dangers of music as an enticement to lust, and its dire consequences, thus regulating the social activities about to take place in the great chamber.

It has also been argued that the programme of wall paintings of about 1608 that decorate the great staircase at Knole in Kent alludes to the spiritual ascent of man away from bodily preoccupations, towards higher moral and spiritual virtues (Fig. 91). On the lower levels of the staircase the paintings depict the Four Ages of Man and the Senses, with images of pleasurable pastimes involving the fulfilment of the body, while the moral victory over the temptations of the senses is represented by various Virtues, and Virtues conquering Vices, at the top.[61] Thus, the spiritual journey of the soul is symbolically mirrored in the physical ascent up the stairs. That such an analogy between physical and

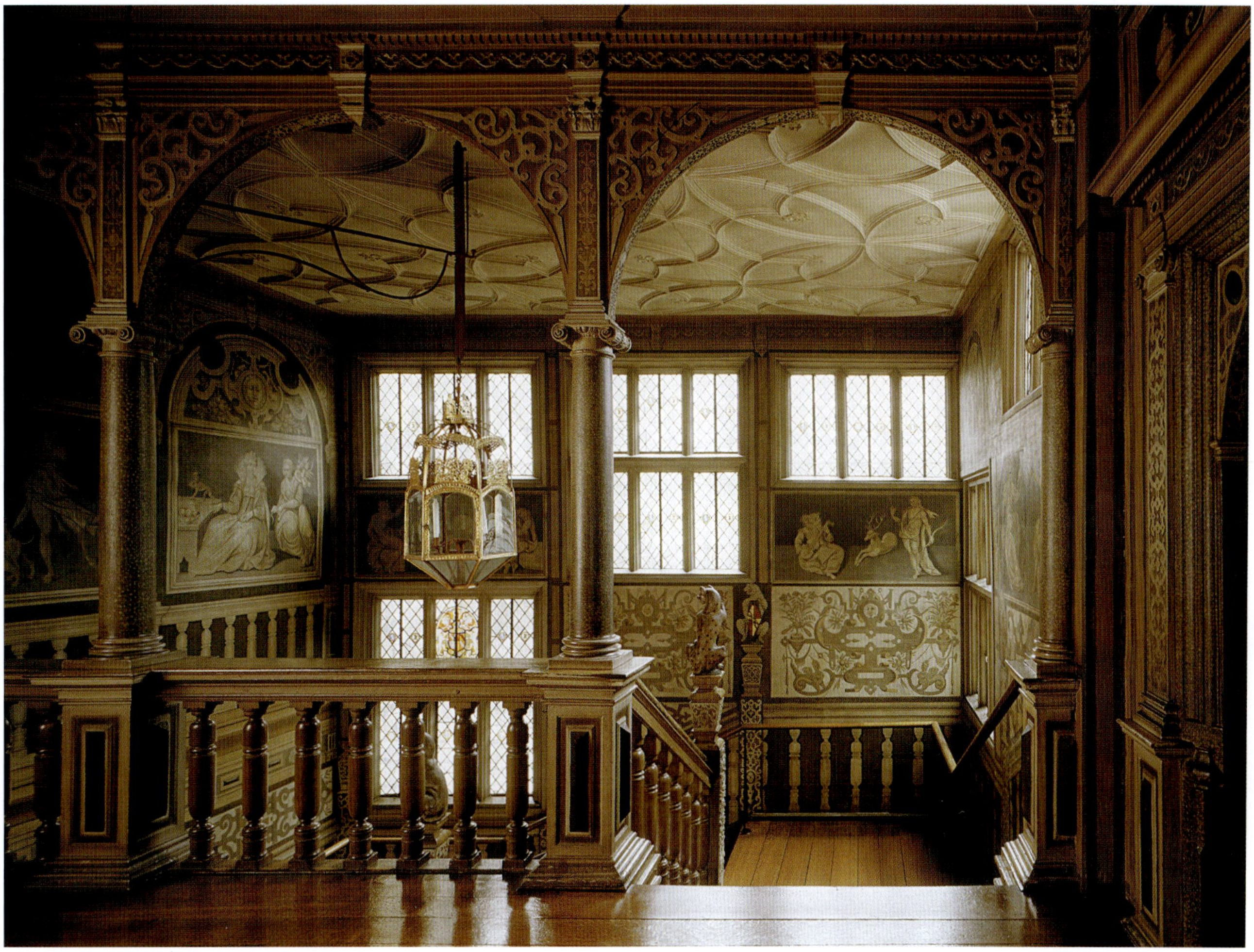

91 View of the great staircase at Knole, Kent, with wall paintings of c. 1608

spiritual ascent would have been recognised by contemporary viewers is supported by a spiritual meditation written in 1634 by Lucy Robartes, a Puritan and the wife of Lord Robartes, of Lanhydrock House in Cornwall. The meditation is one of three written in the blank flyleaves of her Geneva Bible, and records her thoughts prompted by a walk to the top of the house to take in the prospect. It begins with an appreciation of the view: 'Here is a fair prospect. With what ease do my eyes survey that which would tyre my feete to compasse'. But her thoughts quickly turn to spiritual matters:

> What a contended [*sic*] solitude doth this place afford mee where I am neerer in place to heaven and in affection. I overlooke the world and seem to be scarce now a partie in it. It is not amisse to travale out of the worlde in a figure and a thought; one journey which in earnest we must undertake will be more facile.[62]

THE GREAT CHAMBER

On the first floor, at the head of the main staircase, was the most prestigious room in the early modern house. The principal first-floor chamber was usually positioned above the hall (in houses with a single-storied hall) or above the parlour. In larger country houses in England this principal first-floor room was known as the great chamber or (great) dining chamber. As the name suggests, its main function was for formal dining and associated after-dinner entertainment but, as the room with the highest status in the house, it was also the location for other formal and ceremonial activities. It was conceived as the room of presence, where the owner of the house sat in whatever state he was entitled to (or that he assumed) and where he received guests in full pomp and ceremony. The great chamber was the location for all special and public events involving the owner or his family. It was the setting both for marriages and the lying-in-state of a family member prior to burial. It was, therefore, the symbolic heart of the household, a space for the performance of social interaction and the public discharge of responsibilities.

Given its status as the foremost room of state, it is unsurprising that the principal first-floor chamber was usually the most richly decorated room in the early modern house. In smaller farmhouses and town houses, the main first-floor chamber was often the only room with applied, permanent decoration. In larger houses, the quality and quantity of decoration in the great chamber tended to be superior to that in other rooms, with the possible exception of the gallery. As with other high-status rooms, decoration was often located on the chimneybreast and ceiling but in the great chamber the walls too were usually decorated; walls were often painted or panelled or covered with textile hangings. In houses owned by the wealthy many art forms were included; this could result in an abundance of decoration in different media. The layering and excess of materials (textiles on painted walls or wooden panelling, with plasterwork ceilings above) signified great wealth and opulence. Perhaps the most famous example is the High Great Chamber at Hardwick Hall where painted and carved wooden panelling, wall painting, plasterwork, marble, and tapestry are brought together to create a visual feast. For those outside the elite class the display of worldly wealth and luxury was less excessive. The cost and quality of the decoration was supposed to be commensurate with the owner's station in life, as well as appropriate to his religious calling as the spiritual leader of his family.

Perhaps the most significant additional function that the first-floor chamber came to perform in many Protestant households was as a venue for collective prayers. As discussed in the previous chapter, daily prayers were often held in one of the main rooms, where the whole household could gather with ease. While the great hall was the most socially inclusive, the parlour or great chamber on the first floor were nobler in status and therefore offered more fitting spaces for communicating with God. In merchant town houses, which usually lacked a sizeable reception hall, the only room large enough for this purpose was the main first-floor chamber. Gatherings of the whole household for prayer would take place daily, often twice daily. Meanwhile, associated religious activities involving sub-groups in the household would have taken place at other points in the day and, once again, the most convenient venue for gathering people together in most larger houses was the parlour or great chamber. After-dinner recreation, in a good Protestant household, comprised Bible readings, lectures (based on passages from scripture) and the singing of psalms. For example, in her diary entry for 6 December 1599, Lady Margaret Hoby recorded: 'I went to supper: after, to publeck praers, then I talked and song a psalm with divers that were with me, and lastly, praied privatly, and so went to bed'.[63]

Considering the status of the great chamber as the most grand and solemn reception space in the house and these various functions relating to the practice of household religion, it seems fitting that biblical imagery was often the subject of decoration. The character and appearance of the great chamber expressed symbolically the identity of the owner and by implication the character of his household. Representing Bible stories in this room served to demonstrate publicly the owner's knowledge and understanding of scripture and his concern to communicate this understanding to his household, thus fulfilling his role as a good Protestant householder. Nevertheless, religious imagery employed as decoration in the principal first-floor chamber should also be considered in relation to practical and spiritual activities that took place in the room: first, formal dining and after-dinner recreation such as Bible study and the singing of psalms and second, daily or twice-daily meetings of the whole household for collective prayer and devotions. In this section, the subject matter and visual character of decoration in the great chamber is described with reference to specific surviving examples. Discussion of the symbolic meaning and theological significance of particular iconography is reserved for the next chapter.

In houses of any circumstance the creation of an ornate plasterwork ceiling in the great chamber immediately added a sense of status and splendour. These ceilings were usually highly decorated with enriched ribs and interlaced geometric patterns containing floral or heraldic motifs, and often incorporated drop pendants. Less common, and far more elaborate, were plasterwork ceilings encompassing figural imagery. Images of exotic beasts and birds, and some standard motifs such as roundel portraits of heroic 'worthies', were usually cast from moulds and set in an otherwise ornamental design. At its most accomplished, figural subject matter consisted of series of large-scale narrative scenes, which were hand-modelled by the craftsman in sections on the floor before being set into position on the ceiling.

For example, in the great chamber at Boston Manor House in Brentford, Middlesex, is a sophisticated scheme of figural decoration, with an elaborate plasterwork ceiling in which female personifications of the Elements, Senses and Theological Virtues are depicted alongside exotic beasts and birds (Fig. 92). Within the design of the plasterwork ceiling is the date '1623' and the initials 'MR', which announce that the decoration must have been carried out for the female owner, Lady Mary Reade, the widow of Sir William Reade, just before she remarried in that same year.[64] This biographical information might explain the presence of a charming little detail in the ceiling design. A miniature Father Time, holding his scythe to reap the souls of the deceased, is attacked on each side by cupids, who aim their arrows in a threatening manner. This little tableau's message seems to be that love combats death.

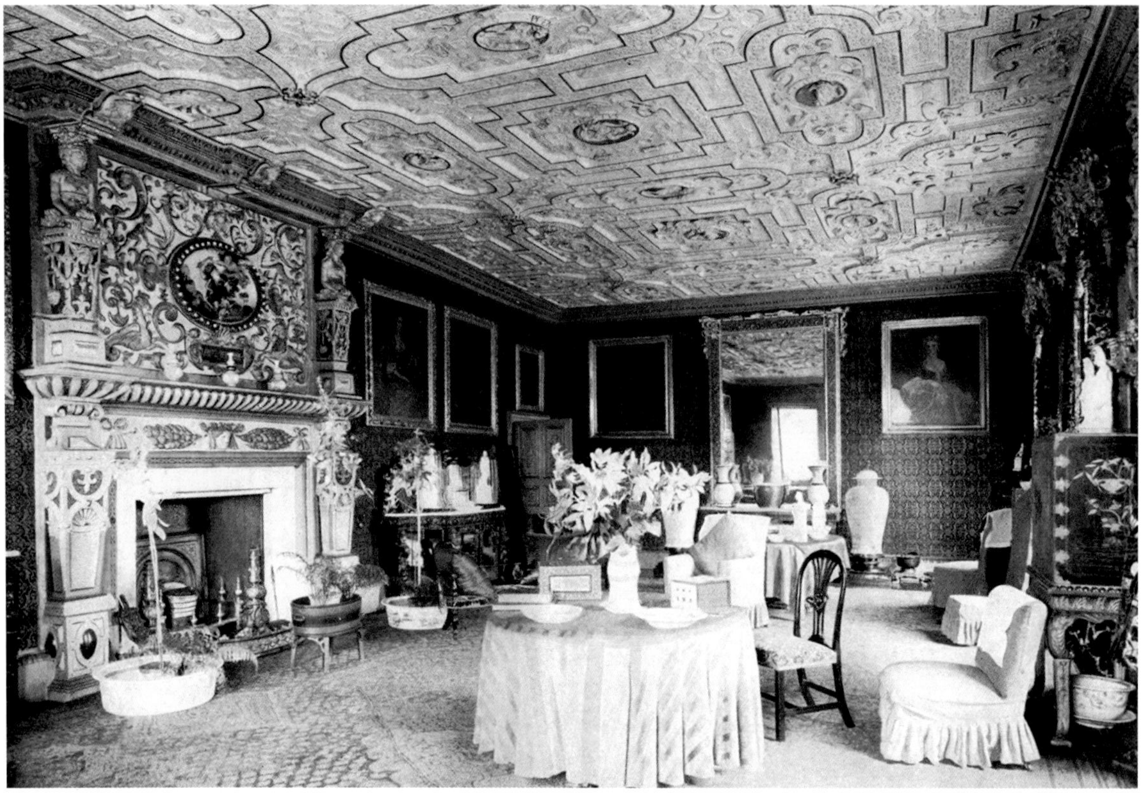

92 The great chamber at Boston Manor House, Brentford, Middlesex, photographed in 1918

93 Diagram showing the design of the plasterwork ceiling dated 1623 at Boston Manor House

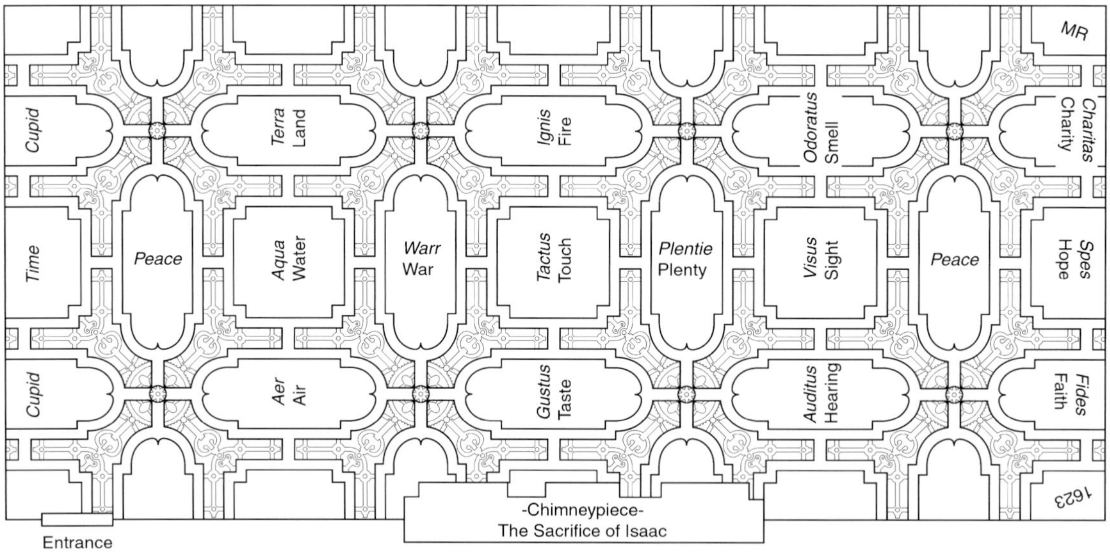

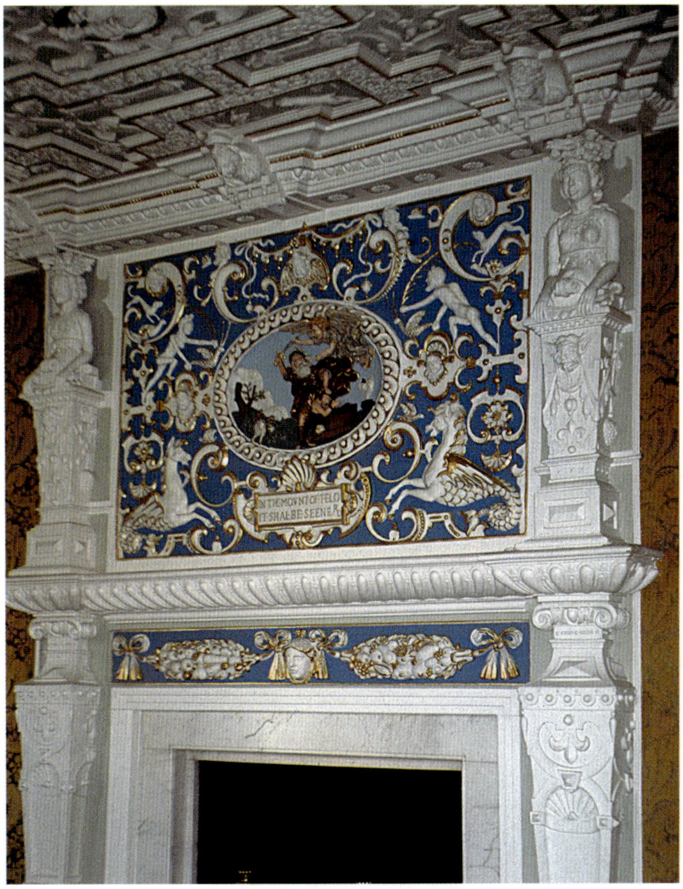

94 The Sacrifice of Isaac, chimneypiece of 1623 in the great chamber at Boston Manor House

The distribution of the principal figures on the ceiling suggests that the overall scheme was given careful consideration (Fig. 93). On entering the great chamber, the viewer can see personifications of the Elements (the physical components of man); on moving further into the room the viewer next encounters images of the Five Senses (as the sensory and perceptual faculties of man). Only once the viewer has progressed through the room to the end farthest from the entrance may they view depictions of the Three Theological Virtues, symbolising the spiritual route to salvation. The ceiling can therefore be understood as a visual representation of the physical, sensory and spiritual apparatus of man.

At Boston Manor the focal point of the decoration in the great chamber is the magnificent chimneypiece (Fig. 94). In the centre of the overmantel, framed by an oval cartouche, is a scene of Abraham sacrificing Isaac. This scene was by far the most common biblical subject in decorative art throughout the period 1560–1660. Another example of this subject at the centre of a chimneypiece in a great chamber is at Hardwick House in Whitchurch, Oxfordshire, where it is flanked by allegorical personifications of Hope and Faith and surmounted by the arms of Richard Lybbe (1582–1658; Fig. 95). Yet the scene

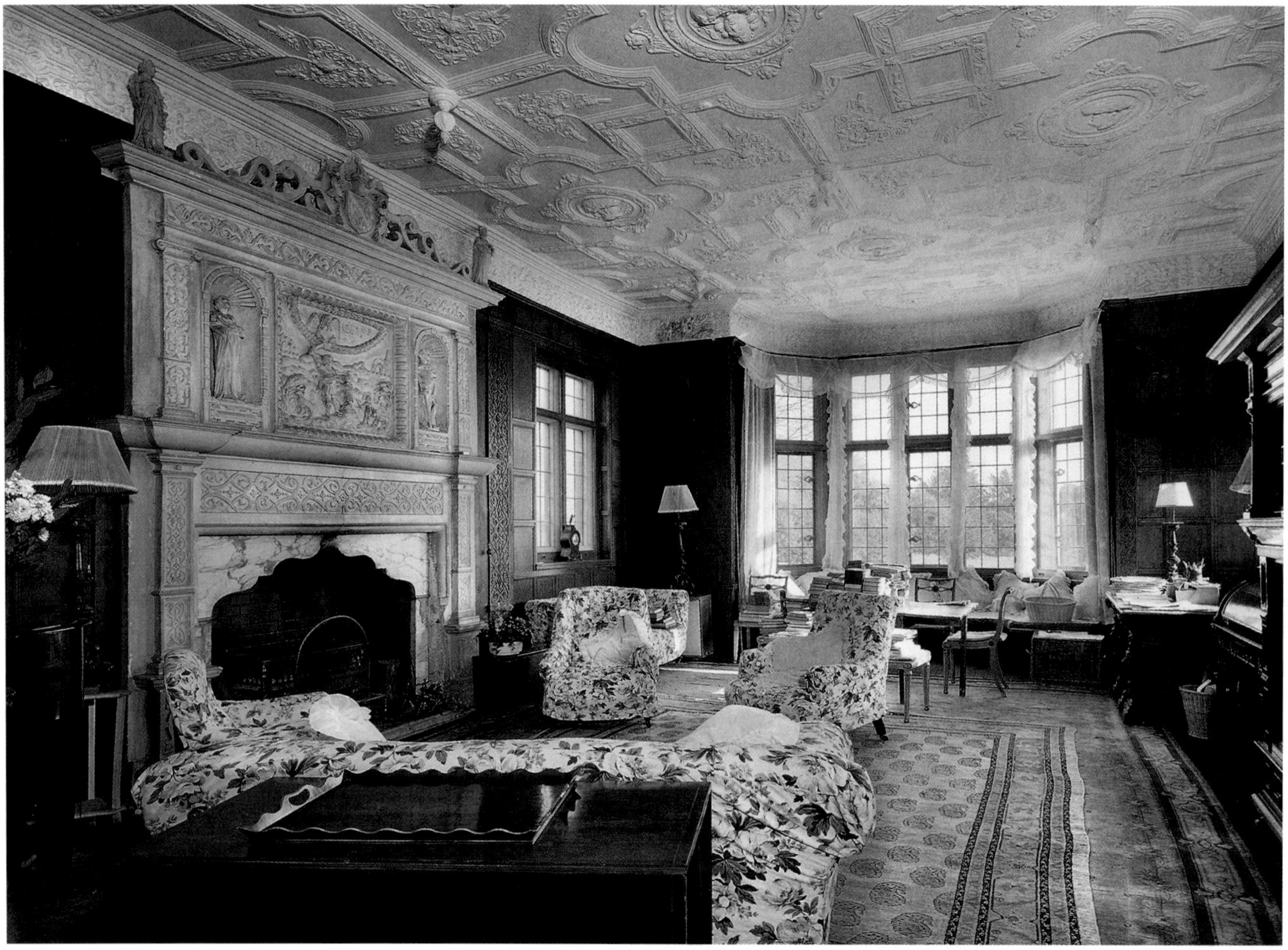

95 View of the great chamber at Hardwick House, Whitchurch, Oxfordshire. The Sacrifice of Isaac is at the centre of the chimneypiece

appears in houses of widely differing status and evidently appealed to a broad section of the population. An explanation for its widespread popularity is provided in the next chapter.

The second most popular subject to appear in the decorative arts of early modern Britain was the scene of Adam and Eve's fall from grace. At the Manor Court House in Cotton End, Bedfordshire, a plasterwork ceiling in the old great chamber depicts the scene of Adam and Eve's fall, not once but twice, surrounded by scenes of a shepherd with his flock, a woman with a distaff and a man with a rake in a vineyard (Fig. 96).[65] The building is now reduced in scale but was once a substantial house on an H-plan and built in red brick with stone dressings. At some stage the single large room that this ceiling decorates was divided into several smaller rooms and this has made it hard to identify the overall scheme of iconography. I propose that the scheme represents Adam's family work-

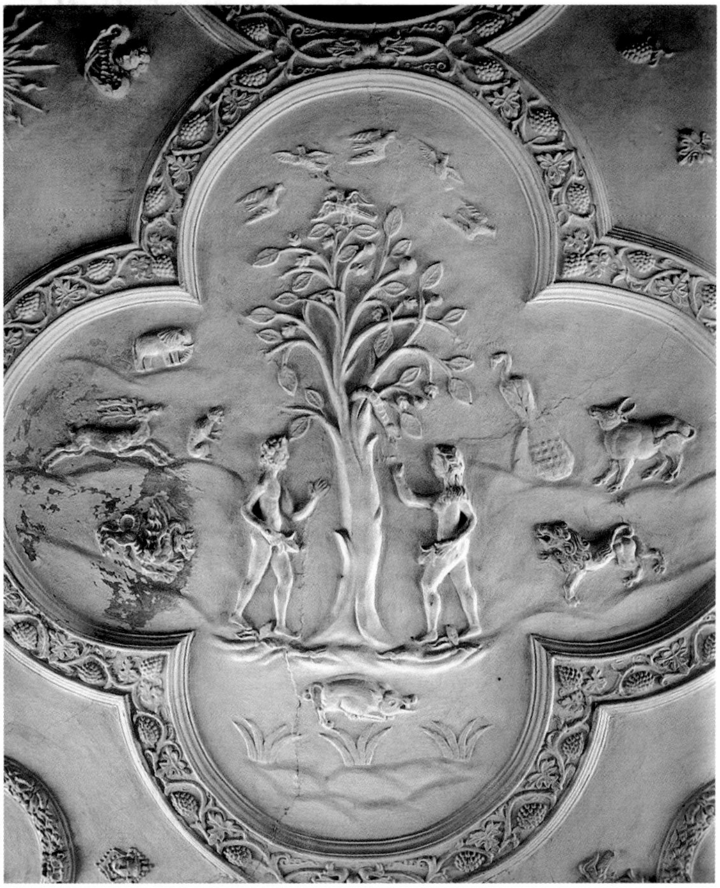

96 Adam and Eve, detail of the plasterwork ceiling of c. 1620–50 at the Manor Court House, Cotton End, Bedfordshire

ing the land as the consequence of the fall from grace, a subject appropriate for a manor house whose owner made his living (however indirectly through rents) by working his lands. The design includes a coat of arms which has proved difficult to identify with any of the known owners of the manor during the seventeenth century.[66] Yet the presence of this shield as proof of gentility (and therefore a symbol of worldly status) is assuaged by the theme of the imagery, which can be understood as a gesture of humility in acknowledging the sinfulness of man.

Another great chamber decorated with elaborate figural plasterwork is at Prideaux Place in Cornwall. Prideaux Place was built late in the sixteenth century but the plasterwork in the great chamber seems to have been executed about thirty years later, when the house was owned by John Prideaux, the Sheriff of Cornwall.[67] The principal subject of the decoration, as depicted in the main body of the barrel-vaulted ceiling, is the story of Susannah and the Elders (Fig. 97). It is illustrated in eight consecutive scenes, starting with Susannah walking in the garden with her maids and ending with the Elders being stoned to death (Fig. 98). This same story's depiction in the parlour at Little Moreton Hall was considered earlier in this chapter. The choice of Susannah and the Elders

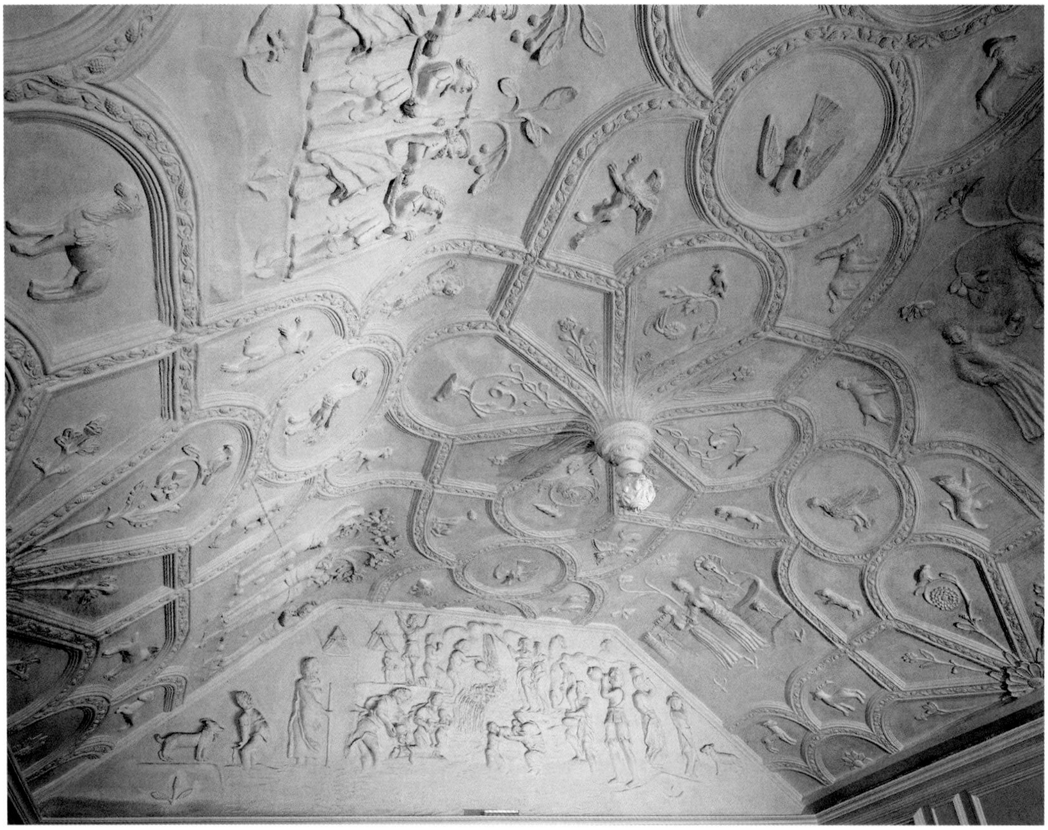

97 View of the plasterwork ceiling of c. 1630 in the great chamber, Prideaux Place, Cornwall

as the subject of decoration in the great chamber at Pridaeux Place was no doubt intended to communicate the same warnings about the need for sexual restraint and moral self-regulation. However, the inclusion of another scene from an unrelated story in the tympanum – Moses striking the rock and bringing forth water, illustrating Exodus 17.6 – indicates that there is a wider, thematic, meaning to the decorative scheme (Fig. 99). It is revealing that both subjects, one from the Apocrypha and one from the Old Testament, have a common theme. Both narratives have water as a common factor: Susannah is spied on by the elders while bathing in her garden, while Moses miraculously produces water from a rock in order to nourish the Israelite refugees in the desert. Yet water is not the only connection between the two subjects. Susannah's rescue from a death sentence by the intercession of God acting through the boy Daniel, and the story of Moses bringing forth water in the desert through the power of God and thus saving his people from dying of thirst, share the same essential theme of salvation through faith.

The imagery at Prideaux can therefore be seen to operate on two levels: narrative, presenting an edifying *exemplum* in the virtues of Chastity and Constancy, and symbolic, ex-

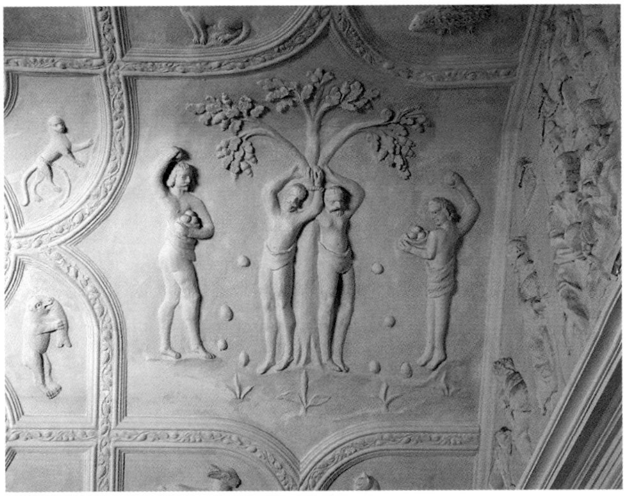

98 The Stoning of the Elders, detail of the plasterwork ceiling of c. 1630 in the great chamber, Prideaux Place

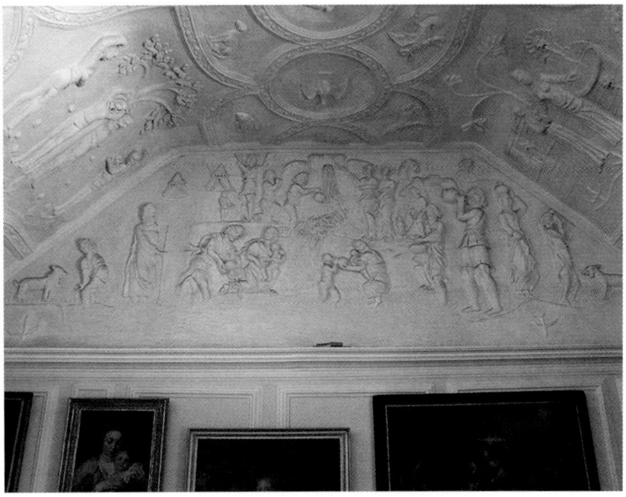

99 Moses striking the rock, detail of the plasterwork ceiling of c. 1630 in the great chamber, Prideaux Place

pressing the Christian concern with the nature of salvation. In this way, the story of Susannah and the Elders communicated messages that were especially pertinent in both a domestic and a godly context. The representation of the story in art also offered great dramatic potential, with images of attempted rape and the graphic death of the elders. Other biblical subject matter employed as decoration in great chambers also combines lively and dramatic storylines, domestic and familial themes and underlying spiritual meanings. An example is the parable of the Prodigal Son from Luke 15, as depicted in the wall paintings of about 1600 which decorate the first-floor chamber at Knightsland Farm in Hertfordshire (Fig. 100).[68] Five sections of narrative painting are divided by painted classical-style columns in an attempt to create a *trompe l'oeil* effect, as if the viewer were looking out at these scenes from under a colonnade. The first section of the painting is obliterated but must have shown the Prodigal's departure, as the surviving imagery picks up with his feasting and womanising in a tavern (Fig. 101). His decline is charted in the rest, with the Prodigal asking for work and feeding the swine (Fig. 102), and his ignominious return, where he is embraced by his father. The final, damaged, section shows the feast in celebration of the Prodigal's return.

These paintings call to mind a reference to the story of the Prodigal Son as a subject for painted decoration in Shakespeare's *The Merry Wives of Windsor*, where the Host of the Garter describes Falstaff's chamber at the Garter Inn as 'painted about with the story of the Prodigal, fresh and new' (Act 4, Scene 5, 8). This subject is highly appropriate to Falstaff – overspending on the joys of loose living – but the reference might also reflect the popularity of the subject in the decorative arts of the period. Indeed, it appeared frequently in moveable decorative arts, such as cushion covers, throughout Europe. Although Catholics and Protestants differed on points of theological interpretation, the

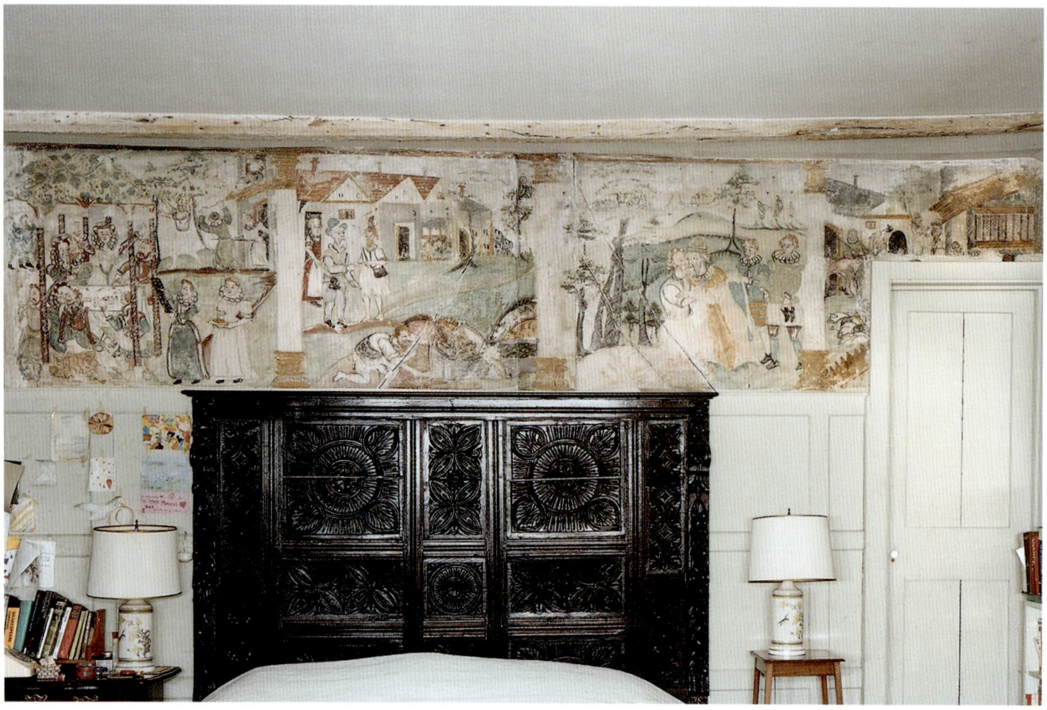

100 View of the wall paintings of c. 1600 at Knightsland Farm, Hertfordshire

101 The Feast of the Prodigal, detail of the wall paintings of c. 1600 at Knightsland Farm

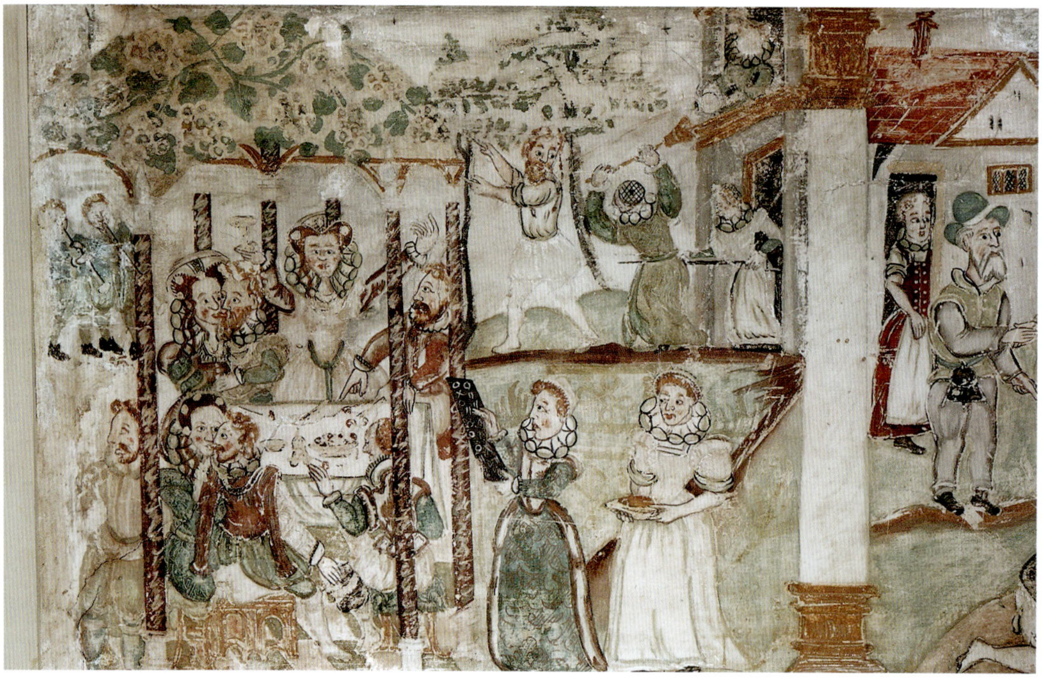

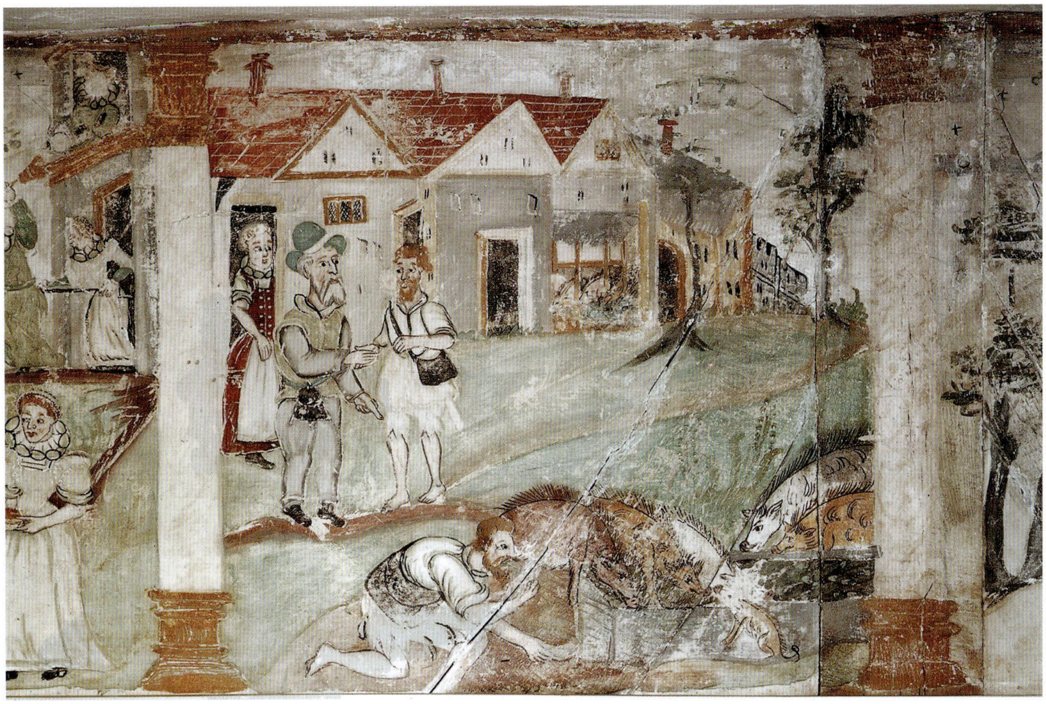

102 The Prodigal tending swine, detail of the wall paintings of c. 1600 at Knightsland Farm

story could appeal to both as its primary message was God's willingness to forgive repentant sinners.[69] Thus, Flemish tapestry cushion covers of the subject were copied by London-based workshops in the later part of the sixteenth century.[70]

As Tessa Watt has commented in her discussion of the wall paintings at Knightsland Farm, the popularity of the Prodigal Son for a Protestant audience was probably due to the fact that it was flexible in the purposes it served.[71] It combined a moral warning against indulgence in the pleasures of the flesh with more profound spiritual meanings. Godly literature elaborated on the original meaning of the parable as an example of God's mercy in forgiving remorseful sinners. As Samuel Gardiner explains in his address 'To the Religious Reader' in his book *The Portraitur of the prodigal sonne* (1599): 'The spirit speaketh evidently throughout this whole discourse how as the Lord is just in punishing of sinners: so is hee as mercifull unto those that doe repent'.[72] To what extent the entertainment value of lively scenes of feasting and whoring was enjoyed over and above contemplation of the moral and spiritual meanings of the parable is not clear.

In many ways the story of Joseph, from Genesis 37–45, is analogous to the story of the Prodigal Son, involving the separation of a son and a loving father during which the son endures a period of humility before being reunited with his family. Joseph provided the subject for a series of wall paintings in the main first-floor chamber of the early seventeenth-century town house at 5 Widemarsh Street in Hereford. The scheme of decoration is, sadly, lost but two scenes, of Joseph interpreting Pharaoh's dream and Joseph

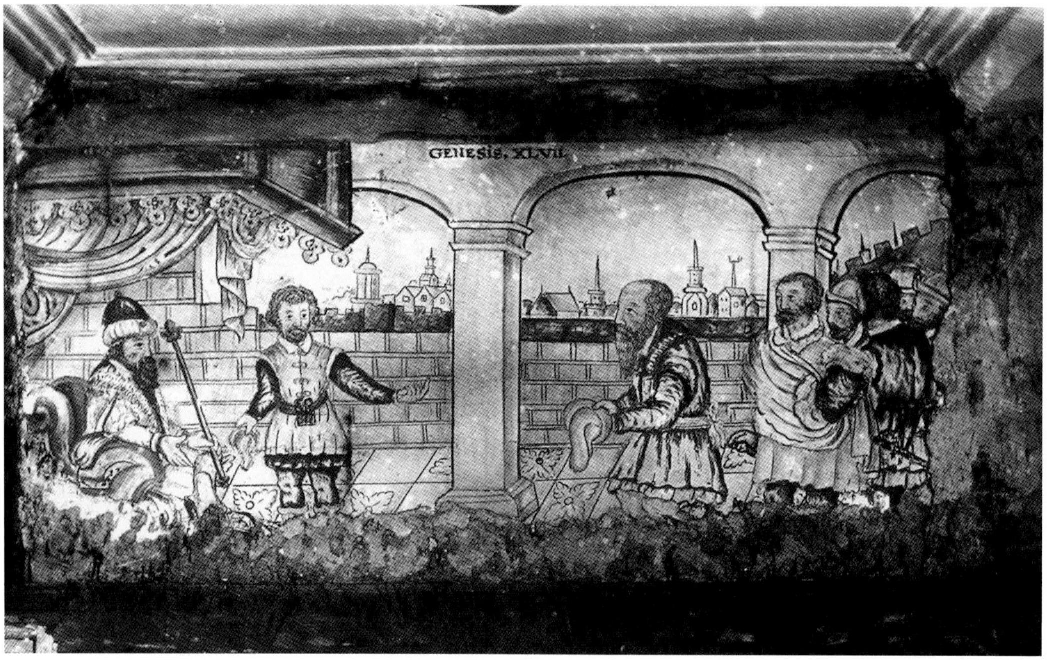

103 Joseph presenting Jacob to Pharaoh, detail of wall paintings of c. 1600 from 5 Widemarsh Street, Hereford

presenting Jacob to Pharaoh, have survived, having been moved to the Old House Museum in Hereford. A photograph taken in 1888 gives some sense of the appearance of the paintings as a frieze in their original location (Fig. 103). Like the parable of the Prodigal Son, the story of Joseph combines great dramatic and visual potential with familial subject matter and spiritual symbolism. The story charts the abuse and betrayal of Joseph at the hands of his own brothers, his various tribulations as a slave, his rise to fame and fortune, his reunion with his family and his forgiveness of their sins against him. Key moments in the narrative, such as Joseph being cast into the well and the attempted seduction of Joseph by Potiphar's wife, offer superb dramatic potential especially when depicted on a large scale. However, the essential meaning of the story in Protestant literature was to praise Joseph as a model of godly behaviour and as an Old Testament parallel to or 'type' of episodes from the life of Christ.[73] Once again, the story contains the essential themes of faith, endurance of trials and eventual deliverance.

It is clear from these examples that the choice of biblical subject matter employed as decoration in the principal first-floor chamber was carefully considered. Specific stories from the Apocrypha and Old Testament were particularly popular because they provided *exempla* and spiritual consolation for godly viewers. While Old Testament subject matter was relatively unproblematic in Protestant image theory, it might seem more surprising to find New Testament imagery decorating the great chamber of houses in a post-Reformation context. The depiction of imagery from the New Testament in the main public room, a room potentially used for household prayer, seems at odds with Protestantism's concerns about the potential abuse of religious images. As was discovered in Chapter 1, the permissibility of religious art hinged on issues of subject matter, media, context and use. Images of Christ, and of the Virgin Mary, were widely condemned in a church setting and yet, as will be seen, were not unusual in post-Reformation domestic decoration.

From the extant evidence it seems that New Testament subject matter was particularly common in the first-floor chamber of town houses belonging to merchants. Given that these houses were usually too small to contain a chapel and lacked sufficient space on the ground floor for a formal reception hall, the 'great' first-floor chamber was almost certainly the room used for household prayers and associated activities. It is also significant that New Testament imagery tended to be depicted in the medium of plasterwork, a relatively inexpensive and unadorned art form.[74] There is a concentration of surviving examples in the southwest of England which reflects the fact that figural plasterwork is found mainly, though not exclusively, in this region.

My first example of such New Testament imagery is the plasterwork ceiling in the principal first-floor chamber in the town house at 62 Boutport Street in Barnstaple, Devon (Fig. 104). The house was built by an unidentified merchant early in the seventeenth century and the plasterwork is dated 1620. Four biblical scenes within framed circular cartouches decorate the ceiling: Adam and Eve (the Temptation/Fall from Grace), the Sacrifice of Isaac and, more surprisingly, two scenes from the New Testament, the Annunciation and the Nativity (Fig. 105). It appears that a workshop in the area was catering to a demand for biblical imagery in plasterwork.[75] A virtually identical ceiling design with the same four biblical scenes was salvaged from a first-floor room at 7 Cross Street in Barnstaple, while fireplace overmantels depicting the Annunciation and Nativity were recorded at 69 High Street in the same town.[76] This house was subsequently destroyed but the plasterwork overmantel of the Annunciation dating from about 1620 was salvaged and is now in the Museum of North Devon (Fig. 106). The Annunciation tells of possibly the most significant moment in the Christian story apart from the Crucifixion: the moment of the Incarnation, when Mary conceives via the power of the Holy Spirit and God becomes man. This scene was ubiquitous in church art and devotional imagery throughout the medieval period but was problematic in reformed art because it involved representation of the divine presence.[77] Nevertheless, the iconography depicted in the plasterwork overmantel is conventional and includes the dove, as a symbol of the Holy Spirit, descending amid rays of light, as well as the Angel Gabriel and Virgin Mary. Another depiction of the Annunciation appears in the ornate painted chimneypiece in the great chamber of the Charterhouse in London, where it is paired with a scene of the Last Supper. These scenes were probably painted in 1626 when Rowland Buckett was employed in gilding and painting work. Also included are the arms and cipher of Charles I with images of the Evangelists, Apostles and Prophets.[78]

Such controversial images of the Virgin Mary and the Holy Spirit in the form of a dove also appear in the decoration of a merchant's house in the Butterwalk in the harbour town of Dartmouth in Devon. The row of houses forming the Butterwalk was built

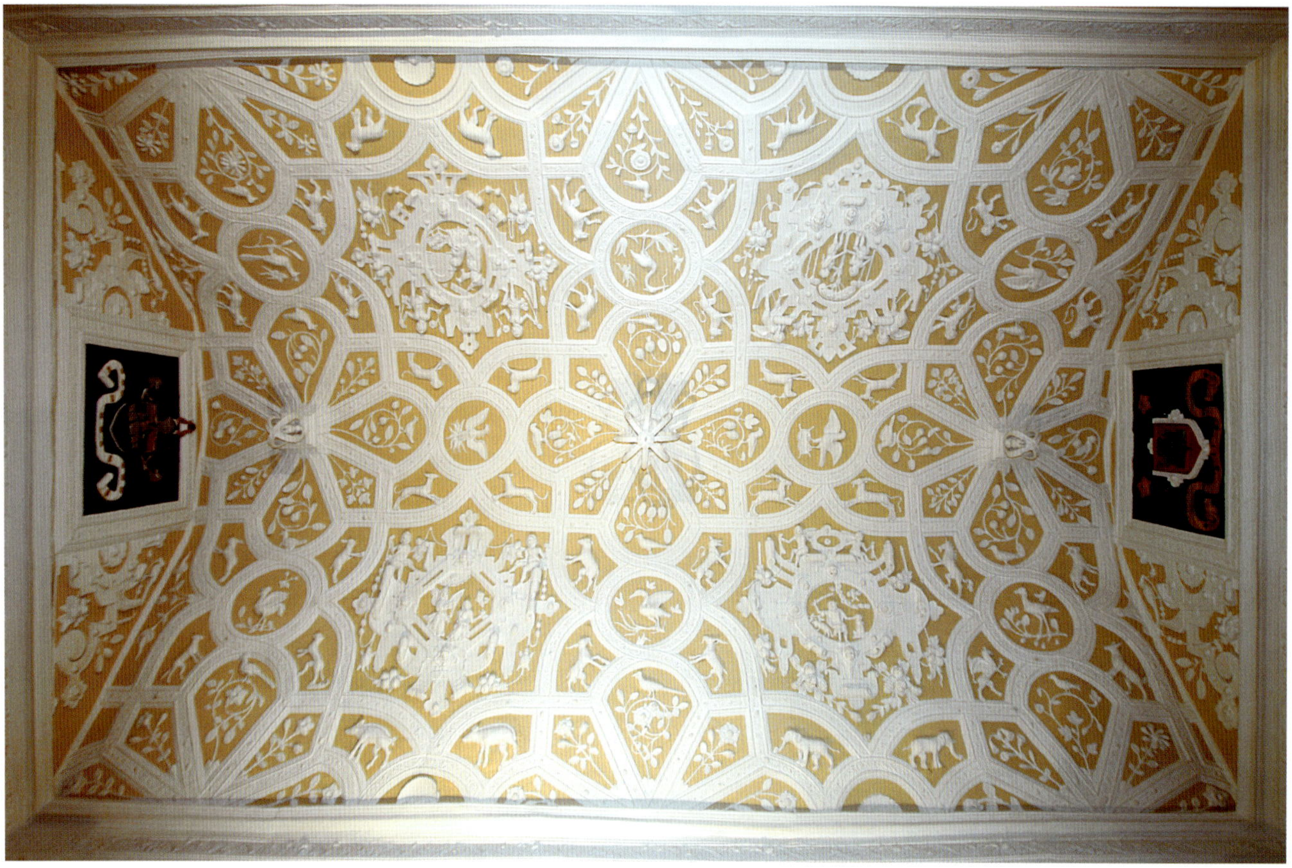

104 View of the plasterwork ceiling of 1620 at 62 Boutport Street, Barnstaple

between 1634 and 1640 by a fish merchant named Mark Hawkins. As noted earlier, he was a prominent townsman and a member of the Town Corporation during the 1630s, when its hierarchy was staunchly Puritan.[79] Above the fireplace in the largest first-floor chamber of the house at number 12 is a large plasterwork overmantel, approximately six feet across and three feet in height (183 and 91 centimetres; Fig. 107). At the centre is an image of the Descent of the Holy Spirit at Pentecost. This scene is flanked by two large figures: Moses holding the tablets of the law and King David playing his harp. The central scene depicts the episode that took place ten days after the Ascension of Christ, when the Virgin and disciples met together at the festival of Pentecost and received the blessing of the Holy Spirit. At the centre of the scene is the Virgin Mary, with the Apostles arranged round her. The Holy Spirit, represented according to tradition in the form of a dove, descends within a cloud from the top centre, directly above the head of the Virgin. Floating above the heads of all the figures is a shape suggesting a flame, representing the 'tongues of fire', from the biblical account. Raised lettering at the base of the scene gives the scriptural reference 'ACTES.2..1.2.3.4'.

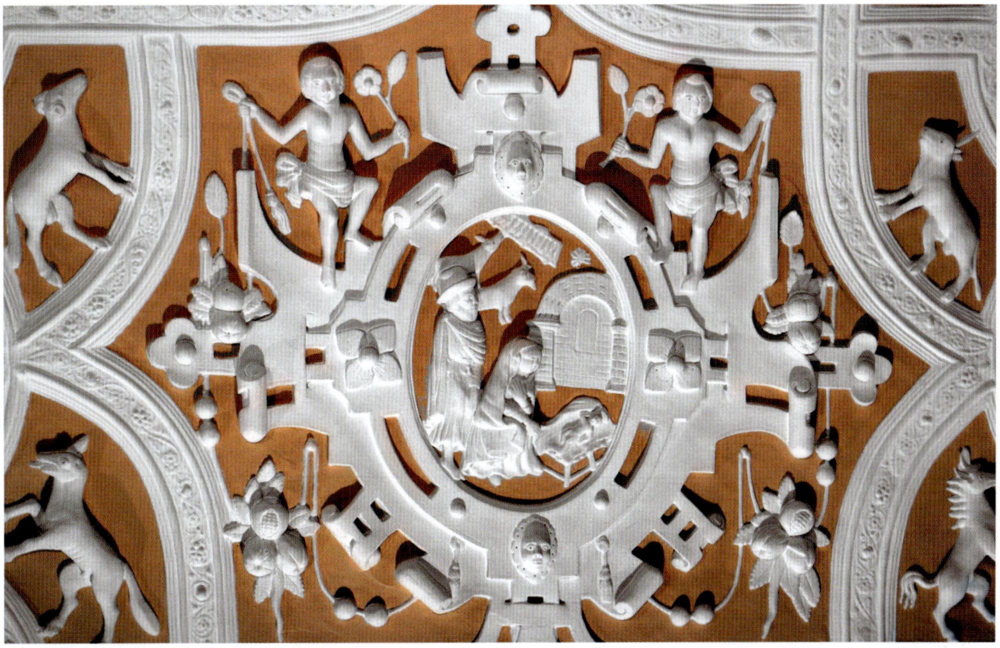

105 The Nativity, detail of the plasterwork ceiling of 1620 at 62 Boutport Street, Barnstaple

106 The Annunciation, plasterwork overmantel of c. 1620 from 69 High Street, Barnstaple

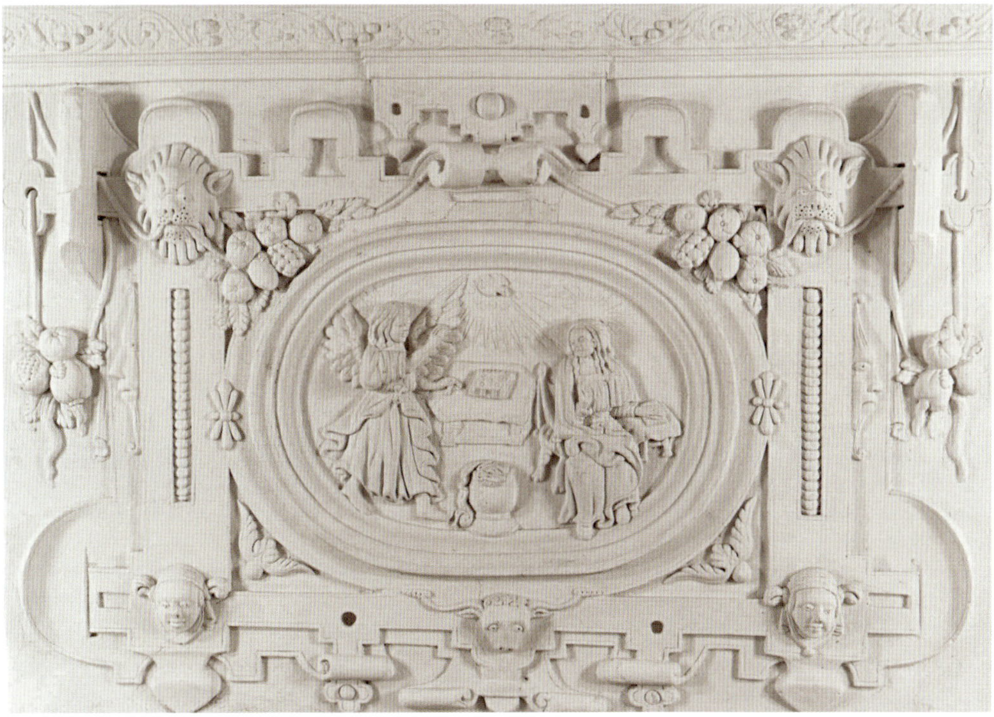

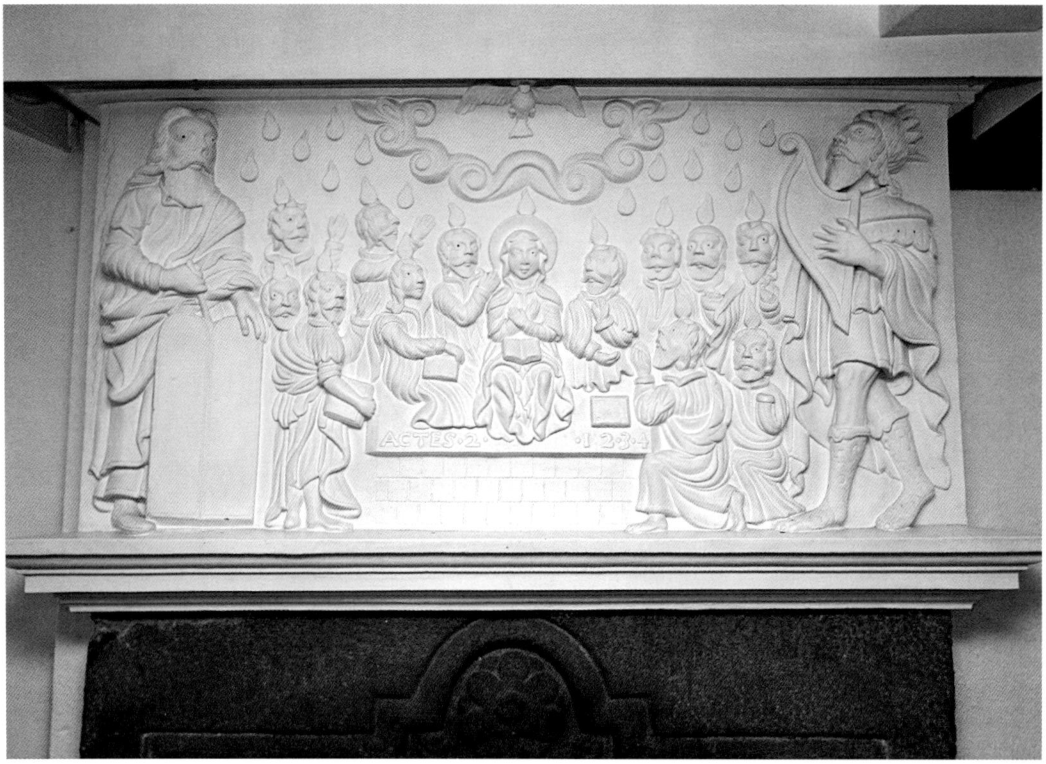

107 Pentecost, plasterwork overmantel of c. 1635 in the Butterwalk, Dartmouth, Devon

The descent of the Holy Spirit upon the Apostles at Pentecost renewed the nascent Christian religion. This gift of the Holy Spirit, the 'tongues of fire', signified the ability to speak in different languages. It was due to this divine intervention that the Apostles were able to spread Christ's teachings across the world. This scene is therefore an allusion to the importance of preaching. An emphasis on preaching, of God's Word and on sermons, was a cornerstone of the Protestant faith and, as has been discussed, was realised within the household through daily gatherings for prayer and guided Bible readings. It is surely no coincidence that this plasterwork overmantel depicting a gathering of the first Christian evangelicals who were blessed by God with a holy gift, is at the centre of a room used for gatherings of the household for religious observance. In this way the imagery mirrors the use of the room by a community of Protestants meeting together to worship and hoping for a similar divine blessing.[80] The figures of Moses and David also reflect the use of the room. Moses holding the tablets engraved with the Ten Commandments represents divine law, while King David playing the harp represents the godly singing of psalms. However, this decoration presents potent and profoundly spiritual imagery. It depicts one of the key moments in the formation of the early Christian Church and includes images of holy figures such as the Apostles and the Virgin Mary, as well as the controversial image of the Holy Spirit in the form of a dove.

Perhaps the most surprising subject matter to be depicted in public rooms in a post-Reformation context is that of the Virgin Mary because it had been expressly singled out for criticism by reformers; but there are other examples. The town house known as Mary Somerville's House in Burntisland, Fife, once contained painted ceilings dating from about 1620 in two rooms on the second floor. As noted earlier, the usual internal arrangement of Scottish houses had the formal reception rooms on the first and second floor, so it is likely that these two rooms served as the great chamber and bedchamber. In the larger of the two rooms a painted ceiling included images of the Virgin Mary, Christ as Saviour of the World (Salvator Mundi), the Agnus Dei and St Matthew as well as numerous sibyls (Fig. 108). While the ceiling was in a fragmentary condition when it was uncovered and recorded in 1957, the identity of the figures depicted was confirmed by the inscriptions beneath each figure.[81]

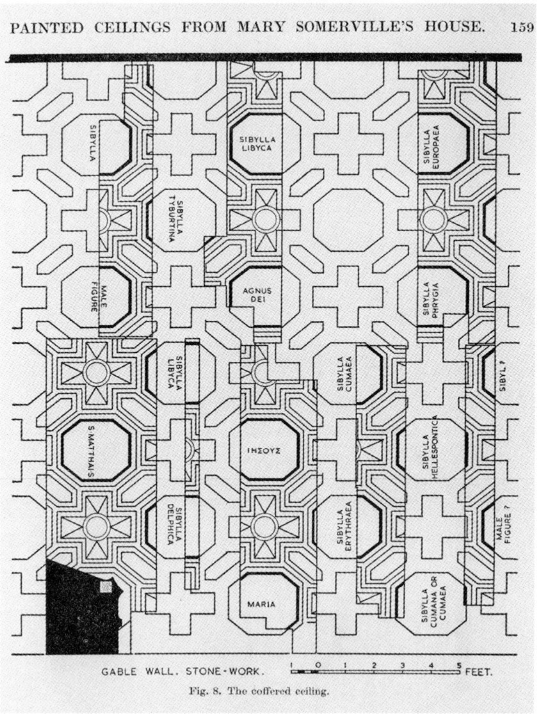

108 Diagram of the painted ceiling of c. 1620 from a house in Burntisland, Fife

The sibyls were celebrated in Christian belief for their legendary prophesying of the coming of Christ. Other examples include the six sibyls with accompanying inscriptions painted on a wooden screen of 1629 for Wester Livilands House in Stirling (now in the National Museums of Scotland) and the set of sibyls and prophets painted on panelling at Cheyney Court in Herefordshire.[82] The scheme of iconography at Burntisland can be understood as a celebration of the Christian message and portrays figures central to the promise of Christ (sibyls), the Incarnation (Virgin), Christ's life and ministry (St Matthew, as the principal Evangelist), his sacrifice (the Agnus Dei as the symbol of sacrifice) and his role as Saviour (Salvator Mundi). Early in the seventeenth century the house was owned by a family of merchants named Watson but there is no indication that they were recusant Catholics. While the images of the Virgin and Christ as Saviour might seem unexpected in a post-Reformation context, it appears that such imagery was acceptable as part of a decorative scheme celebrating the Christian message.

These various case studies provide an overview of the type and character of religious imagery commonly employed as decoration in the main first-floor chamber of many gentry and merchant houses in the late sixteenth and early seventeenth centuries. When one imagines these rooms filled with a gathering of the whole household for daily prayers and associated activities, it is clear that the decoration served as an appropriate backdrop to such spiritual activity. However, it is curious that Protestants should choose to have religious imagery in such a setting. Given that Protestant ideology focused on the nature of the subject matter and the context and use of religious imagery to determine its permissibility, having any biblical imagery as the subject of permanent decoration in rooms used regularly for the devotional activity of prayer is remarkable. Why it was depicted and how it was actually looked at and thought about are issues addressed in the next chapter. First, to complete the tour of the public rooms in the Protestant domestic interior, I move on to the bedchamber.

THE BEDCHAMBER

Although it should be considered an important part of the suite of formal rooms in the early modern interior, the bedchamber was a less public space, as access was restricted to only the most privileged, or familiar, guests. In larger houses, the bedchamber was often reached through a withdrawing room, which could be used as a sitting room away from wider company. This liminal space separated the bedroom from the rest of the interior and emphasised the significance of moving from the public reception space of the great chamber to the more intimate surroundings of a room used for domestic activities such as sleeping and dressing. Despite its practical nature, the bedchamber was not thought of as a personal space. For true privacy or seclusion, the owner could retire to a closet, which was increasingly provided as an extra, close space beyond the bedchamber.[83] While the ideal suite of rooms consisted of withdrawing chamber, bedchamber and closet, many smaller houses had to manage with just one room that contained a bed but also accommodated other functions, serving as a bed-sitting room.

Most large gentry houses had more than one bedchamber, with the principal bedchambers dedicated to the owner and his wife. An additional 'state' bedchamber was sometimes provided, although this often doubled as the householder's own chamber. The depiction of the royal arms displayed prominently in the decoration of many state bedchambers indicates that if a monarch chose to visit, this is the room in which they would have been lodged. However, even given Elizabeth I's infamous love of progressing round the country, it seems unlikely that householders lower down the social scale could realistically expect their monarch to come calling. In such cases the depiction of the royal arms in a bedchamber was a gesture of loyalty to the crown but also served to invoke the virtual presence of the monarch. The common claim advertised by historic houses and hotels throughout England that 'Queen Elizabeth slept here' perhaps derives from the fact that a room was named as the Queen's chamber because it contained her royal arms and in this way evoked her social identity and presence.

In the early modern interior, physical activities involving the body were not necessarily kept private. For example, the practical activity of getting dressed was, in upper-class circles, elaborated into a ritual performance attended by servants and commonly involving an audience of high-status guests. This long-standing tradition evolved into the fashionable morning levees of the eighteenth century, famously depicted by William Hogarth in his satirical narrative series *Marriage à la Mode*. Moreover, it was not unusual for activities that we in the modern age would consider intensely private, such as undressing and going to bed, to be observed by others if the activity had consequence for wider society. An example of such socially approved voyeurism is the bedding ceremony of a newly married couple. This ritual actively involved the wedding guests in preparations for the consummation of the marriage: the bedchamber and bedstead were decorated with flowers and the guests might drink the health of the couple before or after they had physically assisted them into their bedclothes and led them to the bed.[84] The guests withdrew from the room only once the couple was seen together in the bridal bed. This bedding was observed at all levels of society but the degree of ribaldry no doubt varied according to the social status and religious beliefs of the family.

An association between the bedchamber and intimate activities involving the body meant that the bedchamber was conceived as an extension of the physical presence of its occupant. To name a bedchamber after the usual occupant was common during this period.[85] The close connection between the identity of the owner and the physical environment of their bedchamber is illustrated by the convention of depicting the owner's coat of arms (as the heraldic symbol representing their social identity) within the decoration of their room. In this way the environment inhabited by the physical body was linked to the idea of the social body.

It is clear that while people spent much of their personal time in their bedchamber, they were still available to meet select guests. In their diaries, Lady Margaret Hoby and Lady Anne Clifford both recorded keeping to their chambers on a regular basis. In the case of Lady Hoby this was due to periodic bouts of sickness, usually lasting a few days. While she was confined to her room, she would receive select guests to keep her company. The entry for 26 March 1601 indicates the varied use of the bedchamber: 'this day I kept my chamber, and, as I was able, I wrought [embroidery] and reede [read] and had Mr Ardington to read to me and Mr Rhodes: some time we sung psa: [psalms] and, att my accustomed times, I went to [the closet for] privat praier and medetation'.[86] These male guests were ministers attached to the household; no doubt they were called on to provide spiritual consolation to comfort Lady Margaret through her illness.

Lady Clifford, in contrast, chose to keep to her chamber in order to sulk. For this lady, withdrawing her presence from the social world of the household was one of the few ways she could express her distress and frustration at the ongoing campaign of intimidation imposed by her husband, male relatives and even King James I as they sought, unsuccessfully, to compel her to renounce her claim to her inheritance. On 29 October 1618 she recorded dining in the drawing chamber with her husband but that: 'After this I never stirr'd out of my own Bed Chamber till the 23rd of March'. During her voluntary disengagement from society she nevertheless received many visitors, who were entertained in her chamber. A revealing entry from December 1619 suggests a hint of victory when her tactics produced a response from her husband: 'The 18th. My Lord came & supped with me in my Chamber, which he had not done since his coming from London, for I determined to keep to my Chamber & did not so much as go over the Threshold of the Door.'[87]

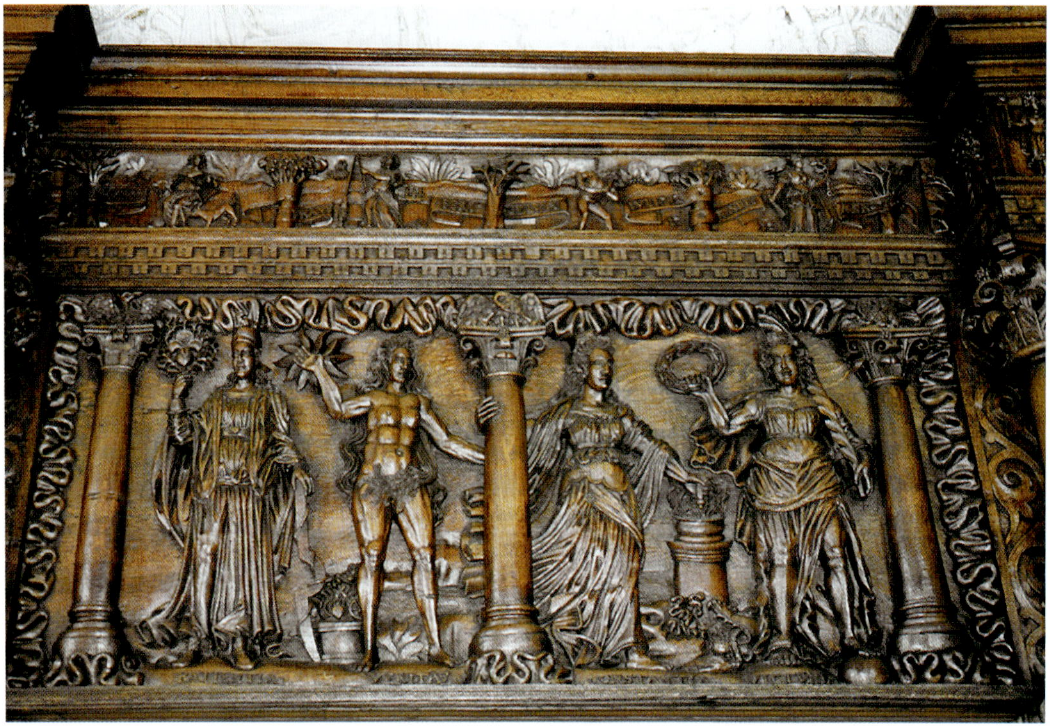

109 Allegory of the Victory of Virtue, carved wood overmantel of c. 1610 in the 'Queen's State Bedroom' at Burton Agnes Hall, East Yorkshire

In general there is less surface decoration extant in rooms used as bedchambers than in the other formal rooms in the early modern interior, which suggests that this room was not a prime location for religious imagery. This is possibly due to the semi-private nature of the space. Religious imagery in this context might be considered suspect as it would be viewed in a more intimate environment, away from the gaze of the wider household, which served to regulate the viewer's response.

Among the few examples of figurative decoration still *in situ* in the bedchamber is the carved decoration of about 1610 in the so-called 'Queen's State Bedroom' at Burton Agnes Hall in Yorkshire. I have already discussed the decoration of the great hall at Burton Agnes but the religious and allegorical imagery encountered in the hall was just part of a scheme of decoration throughout the state rooms. The bedchamber in question was almost certainly that used by the owner's wife, Elizabeth Throckmorton, who married Henry Griffith in 1584, two decades before he undertook the building of Burton Agnes Hall.[88] Elizabeth's bedchamber contains a programme of carved imagery relating to her gender, including biblical figures as exemplars of feminine virtues and allegorical personifications of those virtues considered desirable in a woman.

In the large carved overmantel three Corinthian columns divide two pairs of female figures (Fig. 109). Three of the figures are personifications of virtues, identified by inscriptions at their feet as Patience, Truth and Constancy. These figures walk from the left towards the figure of Victory, on the right, who raises her laurel wreath to crown them as a reward for their virtue. Within the narrow frieze above the overmantel smaller carved figures represent three vices – Tribulation, Fraud and Danger – as the antitheses to the virtues, while a figure identified as Reason appears above the head of Victory. The message of the imagery is relatively straightforward in its praise of those particular virtues often identified as ideal feminine qualities in contemporary literature, found especially in funerary sermons and epitaphs on tomb monuments to women. But the scheme of exemplary females is not confined to the overmantel. In the pediment of a carved internal porch are figures of Judith (labelled 'S.Judith') and 'Eternity'. At the other end of the room in the carved pediment above the doorway to a small closet, is a figure of St Barbara who, in Christian tradition, symbolised the virtue of Chastity (Fig. 110). While the figure of 'Saint' Judith represented the Old Testament heroine who killed the tyrant Holofernes to liberate her people, the carved figure of a female saint such as Barbara, a focus of veneration in the pre-Reformation church, is a particularly striking instance of the use of contested imagery in the decoration of a Protestant household.

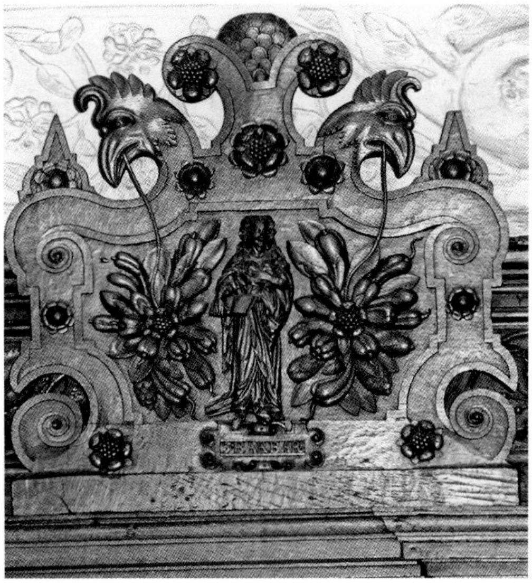

110 St Barbara, carved pediment of c. 1610 in the 'Queen's State Bedroom' at Burton Agnes Hall

It might be wondered to what degree the choice of these particular virtues and saints expressed the self-fashioned identity of the lady of the house or, rather, served as an imposition of certain ideal values and models considered appropriate by the male householder for his wife. In the absence of commission documents relating to the programme of decoration at Burton Agnes it is unclear who made decisions about the iconography in the decoration. Sir Henry Griffith's own chamber is decorated with a carved chimneypiece displaying his coat of arms, flanked by the Four Cardinal Virtues of Prudence, Justice, Fortitude and Temperance. The message of that decoration is that Sir Henry's social identity, represented by the coat of arms, encompassed these four virtues. In his wife's chamber the relationship between its extended programme of decoration and her social identity is more ambiguous.

The most significant item of furniture in the bedchamber was the bed, which became the primary focus for display. In all larger houses during the period 1560–1660, beds in the principal bedchambers were embellished and dressed with textile hangings. As with the development of joined and carved staircases, the bed was transformed from a piece of practical furniture to a status symbol expressing wealth and luxury. Until the sixteenth century most people outside the nobility slept on pallets that could be stored away during the day. By the mid-1500s, changes in architectural design were facilitating a more permanent style of living. It was only with the elaboration and specialisation of rooms that a piece of monumental furniture could be allowed to occupy a given space and define its use in such a dominant manner.

As the size and material splendour of household furniture came to denote the status or aspirations of the owner, people from all ranks of society scrambled to invest in a suitably impressive bed. William Harrison, recording his observations on Elizabethan society in the 1570s for his *Description of England*, described the rapidity and impact of this change in wider society. He relates the tales of old men from his village who recalled: 'our fathers, yea, and we ourselves also, have lien oft upon straw pallets, on rough mats covered only with a sheet . . . and a good round log under their heads instead of a bolster or pillow.' Yet Harrison's chronicle of his own time records that costly furniture was found in the houses of 'even the inferior artificers and many farmers, who . . . have for the most part learned also to garnish their cupboards with plate, their joint beds with tapestry and silk hangings, and their tables with carpets and fine napery'.[89]

The 'joint beds' mentioned by Harrison refers to more ornamental beds made by joiners, rather than carpenters.[90] Elaborately carved wooden bedsteads became fashionable in the Elizabethan period and remained in vogue through the seventeenth century. Such beds were monumental in scale and cost and were created with a sense of posterity in mind. Beds were passed down from generation to generation and they usually stand at the top of lists of goods bequeathed in wills.

In addition to the bed's significance as an expensive status symbol and vehicle for conspicuous display, its extravagant carvings and dressings were two of the clearer signs of a more general rise in domestic comfort during the early modern period. The status, wealth and luxury conveyed by the rich and ornate materials of the carved and dressed bed must have made it all the more inviting as a vehicle for rest and repose. Wooden bedsteads' carved decoration created undulating lines and smooth curves, which must have encouraged a desire to touch the warm wooden surface. Meanwhile an excess of fabric in the drapery and hangings, especially the velvet and silk materials used in elite beds, must have seemed the height of luxury but also intimated a snug and sumptuous sanctuary.

This degree of material comfort, even sensual pleasure, associated with rest and relaxation, perhaps suggests why Protestant commentators were keen to emphasise the spiritual significance of going to bed. In the domestic handbook for Protestants, the *Christian Prayers and Meditations* of 1569, the prayer to be said on going to bed contains the following reflection: 'When the day is ended, we geve our selves to rest in the night: so when this life is ended, we rest in deth. Nothing resembleth our life more the[n] the day, nor death more then sleepe, nor the grave, more then the bed.'[91] Lewis Bayly repeated this association between the bed and the grave and reminded his readers:

> When thou seest thy bed, let it put thee in minde of thy grave; which is now the bed of Christ: For Christ by laying his holy body to rest three daies and three nights in the grave; hath sanctified, and as it were warmed it for the bodies of his Saints to rest and sleepe in till the morning of the resurrection.[92]

Bayly developed the metaphor to include the bedclothes: 'Let therefore thy bed-cloathes represent unto thee, the mould of the earth that shall cover thee: thy shetes, thy winding sheete: thy sleepe, thy death: thy waking, thy resurrection.'[93] While the instruction to meditate on death when looking at, and lying in, your bed might seem odd in the modern age, such an association was obviously considered necessary for a society concerned about the pleasures of material comfort as a path to moral corruption and neglect of spiritual duty. The function of the bed as a location for, or prompt to, prayer is commemorated in the three pious ladies at prayer carved on the headboard of the seventeenth-century bedstead now on display at Red Lodge in Bristol. These figures look identical to a pilaster of about 1575–1600 carved with a woman in an attitude of prayer, suggesting that she too once graced the headboard of a bed (Fig. 111).

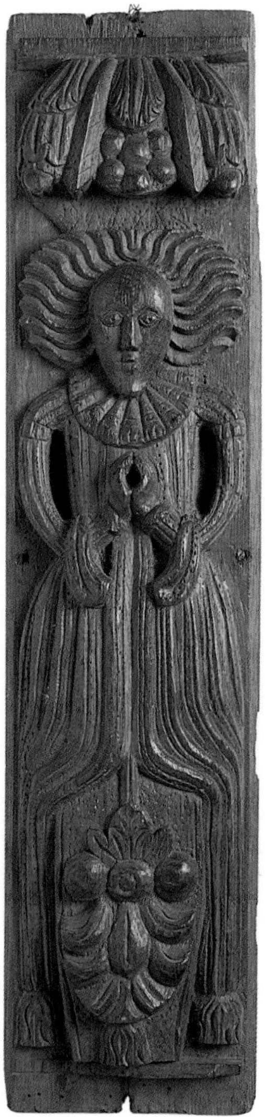

111 Woman at prayer, carved pilaster, possibly from a bed-head, 1575–1600. Victoria and Albert Museum, London

In a similar manner to the prescriptive instructions in Protestant conduct literature, religious symbols could be incorporated within the decoration of the bed, as a visual reminder of spiritual concerns even in this agent of comfort. A carved bed now displayed at Falkland Palace in Fife, Scotland, incorporates a sophisticated programme of motifs and meanings relating to the various functions and associations of the bed (Fig. 112). The decoration of the bed includes the date '1618' above the headboard, along with a comprehensive scheme of spiritual iconography.[94] Round the outside of the canopy an inscription reads: 'Fear God his will obey/For to heaven it is the way'. An association between the canopy and the idea of heaven is suggested by the numerous carved cherubim arranged round the outer side of the canopy, and the running vine and grape pattern (a traditional symbol of Christ) on the underside of the canopy. The headboard (Fig. 113) includes numerous carved figures including personifications of four virtues: Faith (with her attributes of book and anchor), Charity (with three infants), Justice (holding her scales) and Prudence (with her attribute of a snake coiled round her arm). In addition there are two satyrs, one at each end of the headboard. These traditional symbols of male virility are depicted tugging their beards, a rather crude suggestive gesture alluding to sexual desire. Carvings representing baskets of fruit and foliage above the heads of the figures suggest fertility and fecundity and, once again, relate to the bed as a site for procreation.

A similar combination of spiritual and sexual meanings is communicated by the decoration of another carved wooden bedstead now in the Ancient High House Museum in

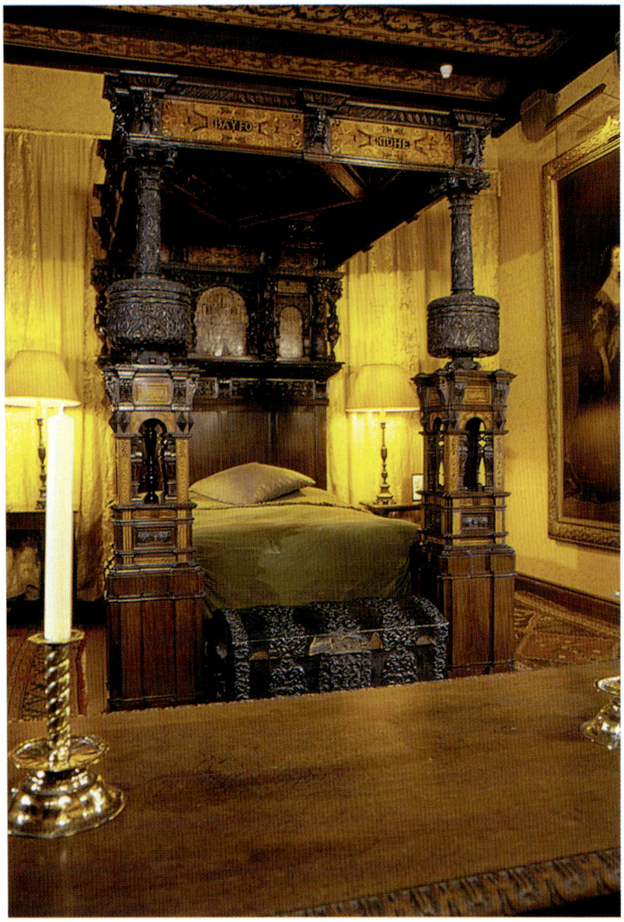

112 Carved bedstead now in the 'Keeper's Bedroom' at Falkland Palace, Fife, upper parts original (dated 1618) with later additions

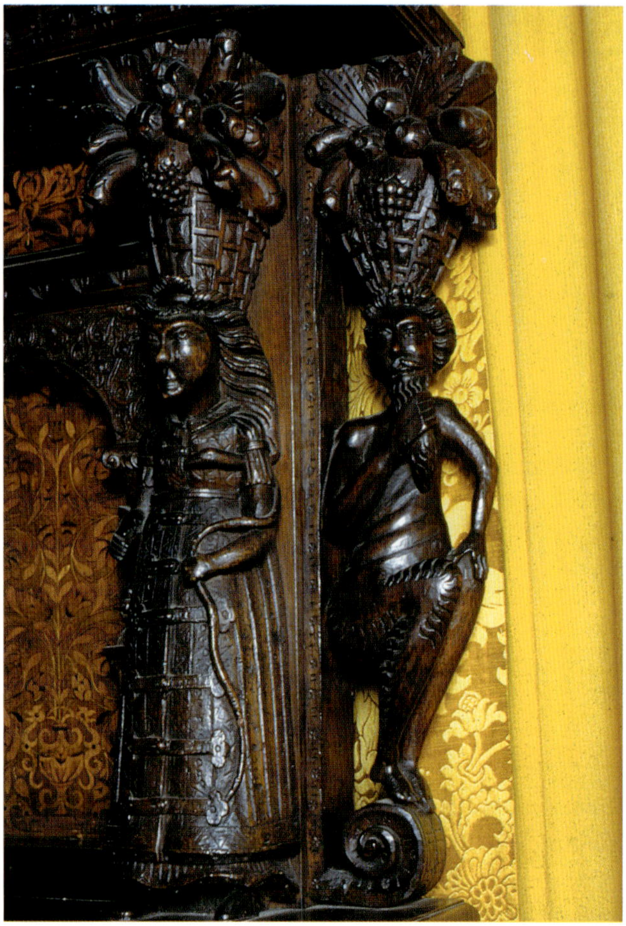

113 The Virtue of Prudence alongside a suggestive satyr, detail of the headboard of the bed dated 1618, now in the 'Keeper's Bedroom' at Falkland Palace

Stafford. The headboard includes the standing figures of Adam and Eve at each side, with two panels in the centre depicting the Tree of Life and the Tree of Knowledge. In the branches of the Tree of Knowledge is the coiled form of the serpent. The inclusion of the serpent signals the episode of the Fall, when Adam and Eve broke their promise to God not to eat the forbidden fruit and were expelled from paradise. In the background behind the figure of Adam are the tools of his labour after the expulsion, while at his feet is a tiny skull. This *memento mori* detail serves as a reminder that sin leads to death, and recalls Bayly's instruction to think of the bed as a symbol of the grave.

The story of Adam and Eve is particularly appropriate for the decoration of beds because it makes explicit the significance of the bed as a site for conjugal relations. In her study of the carved decoration of Elizabethan and Jacobean elite beds, Sasha Roberts has observed that the use of motifs such as satyrs, atlantes, grotesques and caryatids, relate to the idea of the bridal bed and the use of the bed for procreation.[95] This illustrates, once again, that the decoration of fixtures and furniture within the interior was rarely neutral but reflected and engaged with the social activities relating to their use. For members of the godly, decorating the bed with religious imagery could communicate similar messages about the bed as a site for conjugal relations but with the added edge of morality and spiritual significance.

Indeed, the story of Adam and Eve's fall from grace was quite common in the decoration of beds and associated marriage furniture, such as marriage chests, during this period. When studying the construction of family values in early modern culture, Catherine Belsey identified a group of material artefacts that explicitly link the iconography of Adam and Eve's fall from grace with the institution of marriage through the inclusion of the couple's initials within the iconography. Belsey argues that the episode of the Fall was chosen, rather than the pre-Fall paradise, as a manifestation of 'a precariousness in the early modern account of marriage, an instability in the cultural meaning of the institution itself', which is also manifest in contemporary literature.[96] If marriage is a perfect state instituted by God, as the framework for sexual pleasure and desire it also endangers the immortal soul.

Among the several examples discussed by Belsey, the Ruthven marriage valances perhaps best encapsulate this sense of ambivalence about the state of marriage as expressed in the visual and material paraphernalia of the bed (Fig. 114). The three sections of narrow embroidered cloth are designed to hang round the edge of a tester bed, with the im-

114 The Ruthven valances, embroidery of c. 1550 in the Burrell Collection

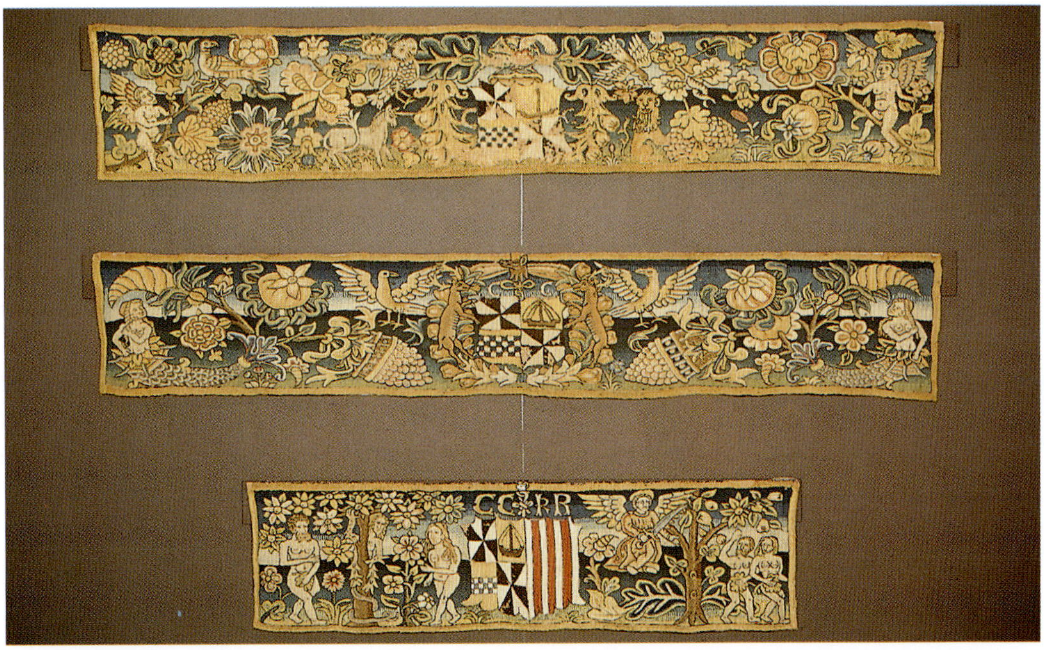

agery facing outwards on display to the room. In the section intended for the end of the bed, a shield bearing the Campbell and Ruthven arms is surmounted by the initials of Sir Colin Campbell and his wife, Katherine Ruthven. The couple married in 1550 and it is possible that the valance was created as part of the decorations for the bridal bed. On the left of the shield is a scene of the Temptation and Fall with Adam and Eve standing either side of the Tree of Knowledge. A particularly grotesque serpent, with the face of a woman, is coiled round the trunk. Further left is a scene of the Expulsion, with Adam and Eve being chased out of Eden by an angel bearing a sword. This iconography unites the marriage of the couple (represented by the shield and initials) with the episode of the Fall. The two longer sections present sexual motifs; in one section cupids are depicted astride the stalks of burgeoning flowers, while mermaids, traditional symbols of female sexuality, are depicted in the other. Their lively and playful imagery seems at odds with the moral gravitas of the imagery in the end section. The iconography represents a cohesive scheme of imagery only when understood in the context of contemporary concerns about the sexual side of marriage.

That there was also concern about sexual relations outside marriage is indicated by a depiction of Joseph and Potiphar's wife in a plasterwork panel in a first-floor room at Ludstone Hall in Claverley, Shropshire. The house was rebuilt from 1607 by one John Whitmore and the room with this plasterwork was described in modern times as a dressing room but its size and position on the first floor suggest that it might originally have served as a bedchamber.[97] An image of Joseph fleeing the bed of a seductress seems a fitting subject for the decoration of a bedroom, serving as a warning against adultery and an exemplar of sexual restraint (Fig. 115).

If the image of Adam and Eve's fall from grace provided a theologically ambiguous representation of the institution of marriage, a carved alabaster overmantel now in the Blue Bedroom at Hardwick Hall in Derbyshire provides a similar comment on the potential pitfalls of matrimony. The overmantel was either part of the original fixtures of Hardwick Hall, built in the 1590s, or is possibly part of the original decoration of Elizabethan Chatsworth dating from the 1570s, removed at some point in the seventeenth century and installed at Hardwick.[98] Either way, it was created for Elizabeth, Countess of Shrewsbury, otherwise known as Bess of Hardwick. The subject matter is taken from the Old Testament, this time from the apocryphal book of Tobit, and depicts the marriage of Tobias and Sarah (Fig. 116). Tobias set out to collect a debt in Media and on his travels acquired a servant, who was in fact the Angel Raphael in disguise. Raphael directed Tobias to harvest the heart and liver of a huge fish that miraculously appeared on the banks of a river. On arrival in Media Tobias stayed with a cousin, whose daughter Sarah was under the power of a demon. She had been married seven times but the demon had killed all the previous husbands on their wedding nights. Tobias followed Raphael's advice that burning the innards of the fish would destroy the demon. Then Tobias married Sarah himself and was able to consummate the marriage safely.

The message of the story is therefore concerned with a marriage sanctioned by God but not without an element of danger. It is thus analogous to the meanings communi-

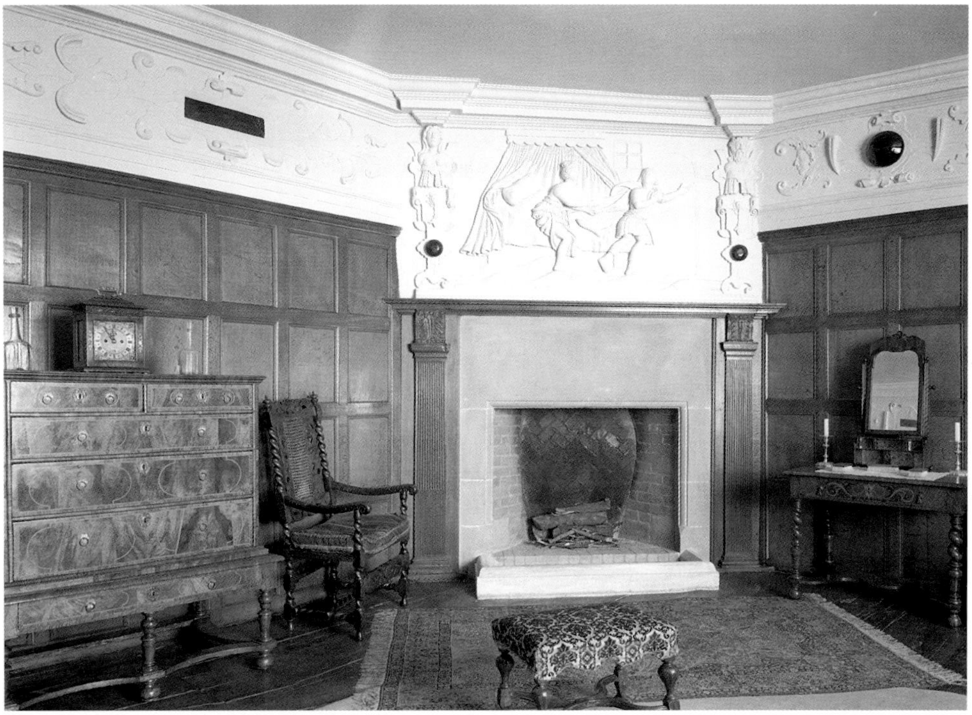

115 Joseph and Potiphar's wife, plasterwork overmantel of c. 1620 in a first-floor room at Ludstone Hall, Claverley, Shropshire

116 The marriage of Tobias and Sarah, carved alabaster overmantel of the 1570s, now in the Blue Bedroom at Hardwick Hall, Derbyshire

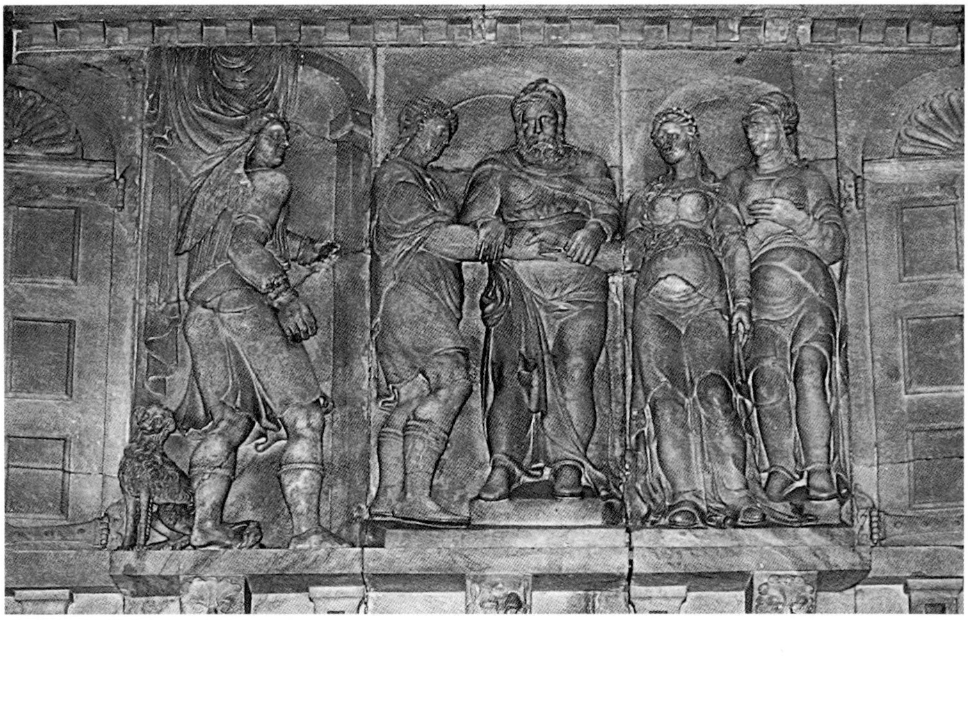

cated by the story of Adam and Eve's fall in suggesting a degree of insecurity about the dangers of conjugal relations. An overmantel dating from the 1620s in the great chamber at Langleys in Essex also alludes to this episode, with a scene in the central cartouche depicting Tobias and the Angel removing the innards from the fish.[99] Distributed round this central scene are large figures personifying the Five Senses but it is significant that presiding over the scheme is the figure of Touch. It was the innards of the fish that allowed the enjoyable exercise of this particular sense on Tobias's wedding night. The depiction of this story in decorative art can therefore be understood as part of a wider preoccupation with the nature of marriage, as the institution at the heart of the household.

One might also consider whether the image in the Hardwick overmantel had a personal resonance for its patron. That Bess of Hardwick married her way to great fortune through four husbands is a celebrated aspect of her biography. Also famous is the ignominious estrangement between Bess and her last husband, George Talbot, Earl of Shrewsbury, whom she married in 1567.[100] If the overmantel was created in the 1570s as part of Bess's renovations at Chatsworth then it perhaps represents a desire to represent the most recent of her marriages in a favourable light. If so, it seems ironic that her excessive spending at Chatsworth contributed towards the breakdown of this marriage.

In conclusion, the decoration of the bedchamber should be understood in the context of contemporary concerns about two aspects of domestic life: material comfort and the institution of marriage. The common use of Adam and Eve iconography, in particular, seems to reflect a widespread insecurity about the use of the bed as a location for the pleasurable vices of Sloth and Lust. Religious imagery in the bedchamber served as a moral warning about the spiritual consequences of the sin of excessive indulgence of the body.

THE GALLERY

A vogue for galleries as an essential component of the ideal suite of formal rooms reached a peak late in the sixteenth and early in the seventeenth century in Britain.[101] The character of the gallery as an elongated and sparsely furnished space came in part from its evolution from the covered passageways that connected the important rooms of state in medieval greater houses. Their usefulness as spaces to promenade for exercise in poor weather encouraged the development of the 'long' gallery as an independent room dedicated to this purpose.[102]

In early modern thought, walking was widely approved as 'a commendable exercise' and while strenuous walking in the fresh air was recommended for the daily exercise of fit men, those of more delicate constitution (including women) were cautioned to use only moderate exercise.[103] As Sir Thomas Elyot explained in his manual on health written in the 1530s and reprinted in 1595: 'They which are leane and cholerike must walke softly, and exercise themselves very temperatly.'[104] Physicians also recommended periods of gentle walking as an aid to digestion between meals, for 'a little soft walking, that by an upright moving, the meat being stirred may descend.'[105] The gallery, easily accessible from the main rooms of the house, was perfectly suited to such regular but brief strolling for the purposes of health and recreation. As a space used for daily walking at regular intervals, it was desirable to alleviate the potential for boredom by providing pleasant things to look at. Galleries were often situated to take advantage of views of the gardens and for this reason were built with ample provision of large windows. In this way galleries were closely related to open loggias which served to connect the house with the formal gardens.[106] As well as the views available through the windows, the interior of the gallery was decorated with an abundance of imagery that could stand repeated viewing.

The design specification for galleries was straightforward: the longer the better. Its physical dimensions were considered to be commensurate with the social status and dignity of the builder, since ownership of land and the enclosure of space was the principal indicator of social rank. The character of decoration in galleries was directly related to the impression created by such vast and imposing spaces. In his comments on the types of pictures appropriate for display in particular rooms, quoted in Chapter 2, it has been seen how Sir Henry Wotton recommended '*Graver Stories in Galleries*'.[107] This advice indicates how a contemporary audience would have conceptualised the gallery. In this way the inherent grandeur of the awe-inspiring space was enhanced by the serious atmosphere of the 'grave' subjects in imagery displayed within it.

As it evolved in France during the sixteenth century, the gallery was usually reserved for the use of the owner as part of his private rooms and was often connected to his study.[108] These galleries were decorated according to the patron's own intellectual interests and taste. The *galerie* of the Château d'Oiron, for example, was decorated in the 1540s with frescoes depicting scenes from the Aeneid. Such subject matter was intended to divert and stimulate the mind of the owner as he paced around this space in peace and solitude from the hubbub of the household. A similar concept of galleries as the outward expression of the owner's mental space developed in Britain. Here too, the gallery was inextricably connected with the social and individual identity of the householder. Its size reflected the social rank and wealth of the builder, while its decoration indicated his education, knowledge, intellectual concerns and taste.

Patrons within the elite class could certainly afford to dedicate a gallery to their own use, as a relatively private area for walking, contemplation and conversation.[109] Most members of the aristocracy would have travelled extensively in Europe, where they would have seen, or certainly known about, the famous *Galerie François I* at Fontainebleau, with walls decorated in 1534–36 with a lavish profusion of fresco and stucco depicting scenes from classical mythology.[110] In the same fashion elite patrons in Britain adorned their galleries with complex schemes of iconography derived from classical literature, often with witty or wise inscriptions in Latin. The lost gallery built in the mid-1570s by Nicholas Bacon, Keeper of the Great Seal and trusted advisor to Elizabeth I, was painted with thirty-seven pairs of Latin *sententiae*.[111] Still extant is the painted ceiling in the gallery at Pinkie Castle in Musselburgh, Scotland, which was built in 1613 for Alexander Seton, the Lord Chancellor of Scotland and First Earl of Dunfermline. The decoration of the ceiling consists of seventeen panels of emblems, taken from a selection of continental emblem books.[112] An emblem, a combination of image and text, was a rhetorical device intended to encapsulate profound wisdom. At Pinkie the emblems employ Latin mottos derived from classical authors. It is clear that this decoration was aimed at the owner's social equals, equipped with the education and cultivated taste to appreciate such intellectual devices.

These elite galleries spawned a host of imitations among the middling classes later in the sixteenth and early in the seventeenth century. Most members of the gentry building new country houses during this period tried to incorporate as 'long' a gallery as possible, while others remodelled existing properties in order to add an elongated, open space as an extension to the existing suite of rooms. However, these 'lesser' galleries were usually more modest in scale, reflecting the limitations bearing on members of the gentry in attempting to realise their social and architectural ambitions.

It was not always easy to find sufficient space within existing buildings to dedicate to a gallery and patrons often had to compromise in the scale or situation of the room. At Little Moreton Hall, John Moreton's determination to accommodate this new fashion regardless of the limited capacity of his timber-framed moated house, resulted in a new gallery of about 1570 being created, somewhat fantastically, as the top floor of a three-storey gatehouse wing (see Fig. 38). At Haddon Hall in Derbyshire a new wing to house the gallery of 110 feet (about 33 metres) was added in about 1600 to the medieval sprawl of buildings. This wing, built in the modern style with large windows spaced at regular intervals along the length of the structure, expresses the transformation in architectural design that had taken place over the course of the sixteenth century.

Even in new building projects, the problem of how and where to house this awkward space resulted in several design solutions.[113] As part of the ideal suite of public rooms, the gallery needed to be readily accessible from the great chamber and 'state' bedchamber so, where possible, it was on the same floor, often occupying the whole length of a lateral wing. In the more compact houses of the gentry, however, this arrangement was not always possible. At Montacute and Burton Agnes, the gallery stretches the length of the house on the second, top floor and is connected to the first-floor suite of rooms by the great stair. In the Scottish tower castles at Craigevar and Crathes, a long gallery runs the full length of the fifth floor at the very top of the building. It was a common strategy in the houses of the gentry to utilise the attic space, as for example at Eastbury Manor in Barking (of about 1570s) and Chastleton House in Oxfordshire (of about 1610).

The location of these galleries reflects not just the limitations on design but also the slightly different character and function of the room in gentry houses. Writing in the 1690s, but reflecting prevailing habits of thought from the preceding century, Roger North suggested that patrons of middling social rank should observe the rule of decorum in creating more modest galleries:

> But as the state of a gentleman, or at least his company, may be of a midle condition, or he desires by his entertainment to raise them above their order, which is allwais pleasing, I should propose a gallery of a midle sort, not wholly dedicated to parade, nor

to private use, but such as may serve reasonably to both porposes . . . And I doe not know any superfluity in a house more desirable than this, for it pleaseth all, and is useful to all . . . And a sort of moderation may be allow'd as to the decoration, and position of it, with respect to the offices of the family, being supposed for the use of the master and his family, and his indulgent friends onely, and not for proud and ambitious enterteinements of grandure.[114]

In this way galleries in the houses of the gentry were more flexible in nature, as they were required to serve a mixture of practical functions and were used by a wider audience of family and friends. However, these lesser galleries retained a close association with the identity, dignity and learning of the householder, as part of his own self-fashioning. The decoration of galleries still reflected the serious, intellectual concerns of the owner but the more public character of these lesser galleries meant that imagery was aimed not just at the owner's social equals but was also directed towards his social inferiors within the household. As a vehicle for the patron's self-fashioning the gallery still needed to impress but for the daily use of members of the family it could be employed as part of the owner's attempt to provide for the welfare of his household, by creating an uplifting, inspirational space.

Acting as a means of communication between the owner and his family, galleries were a tool for instruction. Given that it was provided, at least notionally, by the owner to benefit his family and friends, the gallery was one of the few areas in the house where it was considered acceptable to show off unapologetically the owner's knowledge and possessions. This was considered legitimate because the works of art displayed in the gallery were understood to perform an educative and improving function.

Collections of pictures were the principal form of decoration for the walls of galleries during this period. In Act 2, Scene 1 of Ben Jonson's play *Poetaster*, first performed in 1601, the citizen Albius pesters his increasingly irritated wife, Chloe, with instructions on furnishing their house in preparation for a visit from the court. One of his directions concerns the gallery as the appropriate venue for the display of pictures: '(by heaven) wife: hang no pictures in the hall, nor in the dyning-chamber, in any case, but in the gallerie onely, for 'tis not courtly else'.[115] Similarly, Sir Henry Wotton's advice on the disposition of pictures within his vision of the ideal building suggests that the gallery was the only room in the house in which it was considered appropriate to display a large quantity of pictures: 'I will onely adde a caution or two, about the disposing of *Pictures* within [the house]. First, that no *Roome* bee furnished with too many, which in truth were a *Surfet* of *Ornament*, unlesse they bee *Galleries*, or some peculiar *Repository* for *Rarities* of *Art*.'[116] Certainly, the sheer size of the room demanded a huge quantity of pictures to fill the wall space. Perhaps it was a fear of seeming to have only a meagre collection that resulted in over-compensation so that galleries came to be appreciated for a profusion of imagery. It is therefore no coincidence that the popularity of galleries and the fashion for large picture collections developed concurrently in the second half of the sixteenth century.

Contemporary documents such as letters and inventories reveal that portraits, in particular, were desired and admired as an illustration of family ties and ancestry but also as worthy examples from history to inspire the viewer to emulate the sitter's virtue and noble deeds. This concept of portraits was part of the wider Renaissance interest in reviving classical conventions.[117] In his study of *The Painting of the Ancients*, published in English in 1638, Franciscus Junius explained that in the ancient world, statues and images of great men were set up with 'this alwayes the chiefest motive, That generous spirits seeing Vertue so much honoured, should likewise be provoked unto vertuous actions.'[118] The improving function of portrait collections is also indicated by a scene in Thomas Heywood's *If You Know Not Me, You Know Nobody* (1606) where Alexander Nowell, the Dean of St Paul's, London, shows his guests through the picture gallery of his town house, 'wherein', he tells them, 'I keepe the pictures of many charitable Citizens that . . . You may by them learne to refresh your soules'.[119]

However, ownership of large collections of portraits was rare outside the elite class, at least until the mid-seventeenth century. Householders of lower status commissioned or bought pictures only very occasionally and so had no existing sizeable collection to display in their new galleries. A desire to remedy this situation is illustrated by the many crude copies of historical portraits which were created as complete sets in this period. These paintings were apparently churned out by workshops catering to a demand for the appearance of a portrait collection acquired over centuries and therefore the impression of an ancient pedigree.[120]

There was an advantage to commissioning or buying whole sets of portraits in one transaction, as it allowed the patron to collect pictures in thematic groupings which formed comprehensive and unified programmes of imagery. The collection of pictures acquired by Edward Alleyn, the actor, businessman and founder of Dulwich College, early in the seventeenth century reveals a taste for comprehensive groupings of historical and religious figures.[121] His diary of accounts for the period 1617 to 1622, in which he recorded his purchase of pictures, decorative objects and the costs of workmen for decorative carving work for his own house as well as for the new College, provides an insight into the collecting habits and taste of an up-and-coming London citizen. Over two years, 1618–20, Alleyn bought four sets of portraits of English kings and queens, eventually forming a complete set of twenty-six portraits from William the Conqueror to James I. On 3 November 1620 he bought a new set of twelve portraits of the sibyls, the prophets of Christ from the ancient world. Just a week later, on 10 November, Alleyn recorded his purchase of a set of fourteen pictures of the twelve Apostles, Christ and the Virgin, now lost.

This tantalising reference to new pictures depicting Christ and the Virgin is particularly revealing about attitudes to the production of religious imagery in the century following the establishment of the Protestant faith. Many inventories of the picture collections of members of the upper classes record religious subjects, such as the 'Christ taken from the Cross' noted in the Earl of Leicester's house at Wanstead.[122] It is likely that for the most part these were pre-Reformation paintings that remained on display as part of wider collections. However, the acquisition of new pictures of Christ, the Virgin and the Apostles by Alleyn is striking because it suggests that there was a demand for new religious pictures as well as a toleration of the old. The fact that these paintings were portraits is also significant, as images of single figures were considered to present a greater danger of idolatry than a narrative scene with many figures as an illustration of scripture. Yet it is clear that single portraits of Christ were being created in painting and in print late in the sixteenth and into the seventeenth century. Richard L. Williams has shown that one particular portrait type, professing to be the 'true likeness' of Christ, which exists in several versions following the same face pattern, must have been produced in some quantity.[123] These portraits of Christ in profile against a gold background were evidently considered acceptable for display in Protestant England; a visitor to Hampton Court Palace in about 1610 records that a version of this portrait type of Christ was on display in the galleries there.[124] It seems likely that the particular context of the gallery as an exhibition space for historical portraits allowed this type of image to be appreciated, even by committed Protestants, for its antiquarian interest.

In addition to these portraits of historical and religious figures, it is probable that a group of five portraits of the Protestant Reformers in the collection at Dulwich was also part of Alleyn's collection. Portraits of the Protestant Reformers circulated widely in print and seem to have been a relatively common subject in paintings.[125] A single portrait of 'Dante' in the Dulwich collection suggests that Alleyn might also have owned a set of great literary figures. In any case, Alleyn's portrait collection consisted of at least fifty-seven pictures and probably many more.

The visual impact of these great picture collections is captured in the play *The Roaring Girle* by Thomas Middleton and Thomas Dekker, first published in 1611. In the early stages of the play the host, Sir Alexander Wengrave, shows off his house to his guests and boasts about the excessive nature of the decoration in his galleries:

> Nay when you looke into my galleries,
> How bravely they are trim'd up, you all shall sweare
> Yare highly pleas'd to see whats set downe there:
> Stories of men and women (mixt together
> Faire ones with foule, like sun-shine in wet wether)
> Within one square a thousand heads are laid
> So close, that all of heads, the roome seemes made,
> As many faces there (fill'd with blith lookes)
> Shew like the promising titles of new bookes.[126]

This analogy between a multitude of heads and faces and the titles of books indicates that the imagery in galleries operated as a sort of visual library communicating knowledge of historical and heroic themes. Alleyn's type of portrait series was also printed in books produced during this period; indeed, it seems likely that published engravings provided the source for some of Alleyn's paintings.[127]

The encyclopaedic quality of the picture collections displayed in galleries could be enhanced and extended by similar imagery in interior decoration. Surface decoration could stand in for portrait collections or, as part of a carved frieze or decorated ceiling, could supplement a picture collection and enhance the overall visual impact and grandeur of the space. The painted ceiling dated 1620 in the gallery at Earlshall in Leuchars, Scotland, is decorated with dozens of coats of arms of classical and biblical worthies, European royalty and Scottish nobility. These coats of arms function as the heraldic equivalent of portraits, while other parts of the ceiling depict an array of virtues, devices, animals and birds. As Michael Bath has shown, most of the imagery is copied from emblem literature and other contemporary books.[128] Many of the animals painted in the ceiling are fantastical creatures copied from Edward Topsell's *Historie of Foure-Footed Beasts* published in 1607. According to the title page this book professed to provide the 'true and lively figure of every beast' and claimed to be 'Necessary for all Divines and students, because the story of every Beast is amplified with Narrations out of Scriptures, Fathers, Phylosophers, Physitians, and Poets'. This underlines the scholarly quality of the book and, by implication, the associated imagery in the ceiling at Earlshall. It is as if the contents of contemporary books were cast up to adhere to the surface of the ceiling.

By the nineteenth century the ceiling at Earlshall was in a poor state of repair and it was comprehensively restored in 1892 when damaged areas of the painting were 'recreated' in a free manner. The damage caused by the ravages of time is only part of the problem in reconstructing the original appearance of early modern galleries. Determining the character of the original decoration in this room is especially difficult because of the lack of galleries unadulterated by later alterations. Subsequent generations found the Elizabethan and Jacobean gallery, especially those on the top floor or in the attic, a particularly unwieldy space. Many galleries were divided into separate rooms in the eighteenth and nineteenth centuries, at which point the original decoration of the wall surface was usually stripped out. Montacute and Burton Agnes are examples of houses with extensive decoration still *in situ* in most of the state rooms but with bare and forlorn-looking galleries.

It seems likely that many fragments of decorative art in museum and private collections throughout Britain once formed part of the decoration of galleries. The set of carved wooden panels at Craigston Castle in Aberdeenshire must once have formed a comprehensive scheme of decoration, most probably in a gallery.[129] They form four distinct groups consisting of historical kings of Scotland (including Mary Queen of Scots), the Virtues (Cardinal and Theological), the Worthies and the Four Evangelists (Fig. 117). These groupings form a programme of imagery entirely consistent with the encyclopaedic quality of decoration in galleries. The carvings serve as a series of portraits of worthy heroes and historical characters, intended to inspire the viewer to emulate their virtues. Significantly, the odd one out among the conventional groupings is a female figure holding an open book, identified by the accompanying inscription as 'KNAVLEDG' (Knowledge). I have already observed that the concept of knowledge was integral to the character of the gallery as an expression of the owner's education and wisdom, and a similar personification of Learning (Doctrina) holding an open book is included among the emblems in the plasterwork ceiling of the gallery at Blickling Hall in Norfolk, built in 1624–26 for Sir Henry Hobart.[130]

Similarly, the set of twenty-five painted panels depicting figures from the Old Testament may once have formed part of the panelling of a gallery. The set includes a scene of Adam and Eve's fall from grace (Fig. 118), the figures of Moses and Joshua and the

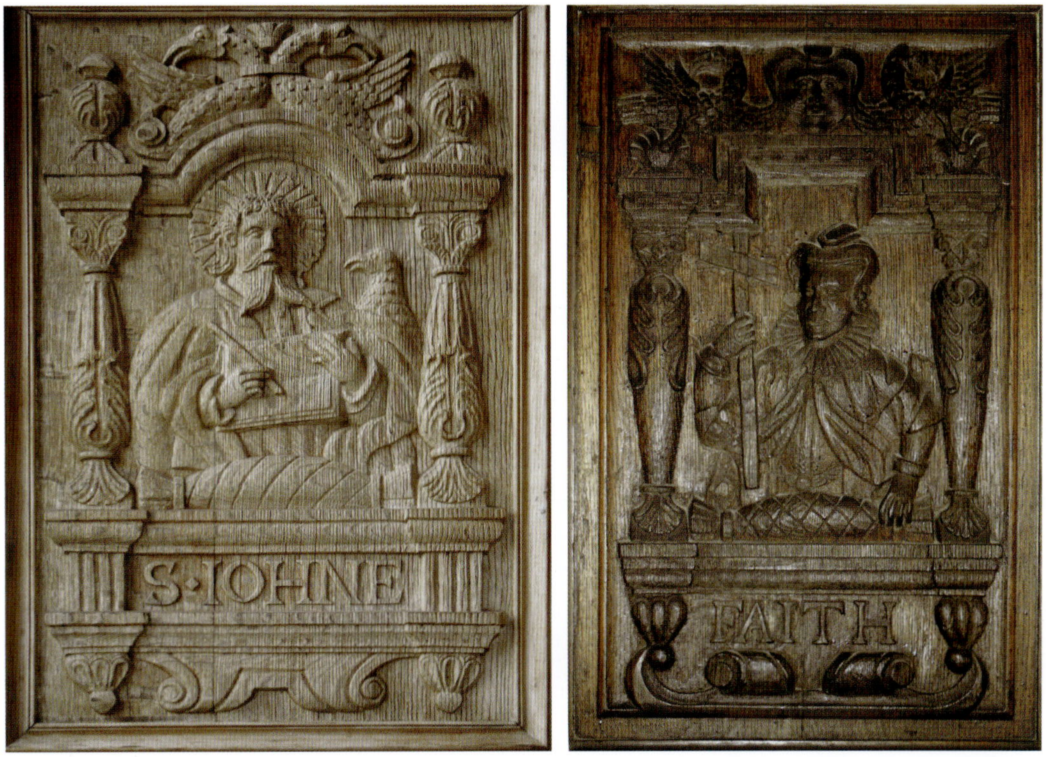

117 St John and the Virtue of Faith, c. 1610, two of the carved panels at Craigston Castle, Aberdeenshire

prophets Ezekiel and Elias. Each panel includes biblical quotations on a scroll above the head of the figures, while the name of each character is provided under their feet. These panels call to mind, and may once have resembled, the painted portraits of biblical characters and sibyls that now form a frieze in the panelling of the great chamber at Chastleton House in Oxfordshire.

A scheme of biblical imagery in the gallery not only expressed historical themes and worthy examples but had the added benefit of establishing that the owner was concerned with religious matters. It also helped to offset the potential accusations of vanity in owning a gallery. For a godly householder, keen to give the appearance of propriety and modesty as well as humility before God, the conceit of a gallery celebrating his own personal rank and learning was a visible manifestation of ambition and pride. Decorating the space with biblical imagery effectively transferred the honour to God and could be justified as the householder providing for the spiritual welfare of his family.

While the surface of walls was vulnerable to later alterations and modifications to the space of galleries, decorated ceilings were offered a degree of protection if covered at a later date with a false ceiling. Fortunately this has contributed to the survival of several decorated ceilings in galleries. The fact that three of these ceilings depict a comprehensive scheme of biblical imagery might represent a wider fashion.

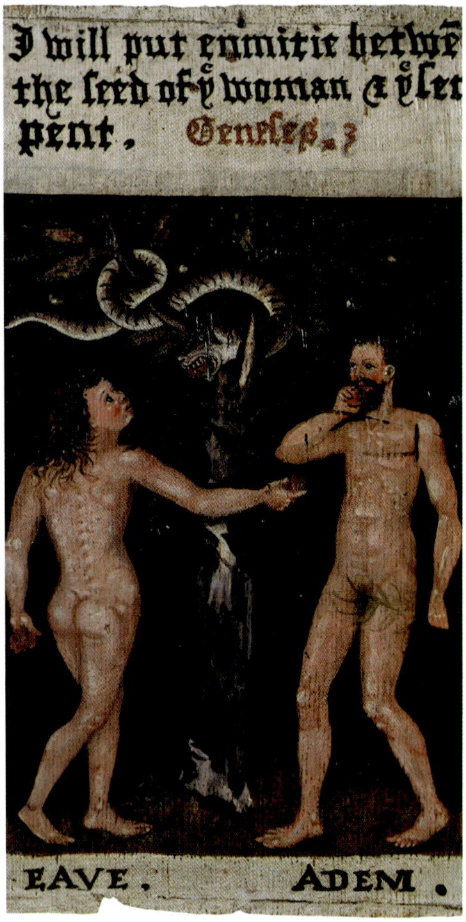

118 Adam and Eve, one of a set of painted panels with biblical figures, c. 1600. Victoria and Albert Museum, London

Lanhydrock House in Cornwall still boasts a magnificent decorated ceiling in its original seventeenth-century gallery (Fig. 119). The ceiling was probably created in 1636 for John, Lord Robartes, later created the first earl of Radnor (1606–1685).[131] John Robartes was a committed Puritan and had a profound intellectual interest in religious matters. This interest is reflected in the formidable collection of theological books still at Lanhydrock today. Several books contain annotations in Robartes's own hand which testify to his Calvinist principles.

The mansion house at Lanhydrock was almost certainly the contrivance of John's father, Richard Robartes, designed as a testimony to the new-found wealth and position of the family.[132] Land was acquired in 1620 and it seems that building work began shortly afterwards. Its scale and ambition is indicated by the fact that the house was only finished in 1642, eight years after Richard Robartes's death, with the building work and interior decoration being completed by his son. In the original layout of the building, the gallery occupied the length of the north wing of a quadrangular house. This north wing connected the entrance front of the east wing with the main block, containing the formal reception rooms of the house, on the opposite and far side of the courtyard. The gallery can therefore be described as an example of Roger North's 'middle sort' of gallery, positioned to accommodate access from the 'ordinary' and 'reserved' apartments of the house.[133] Nevertheless, there is no concession to middling status in terms of its physical dimensions; the gallery at Lanhydrock is a sizeable space, 116 feet long and 20 feet wide (about 35 by 6 metres).

An elaborate barrel-vaulted plasterwork ceiling decorates the gallery. Depicted in high relief in the main body of the ceiling are thirty-six scenes from Genesis, starting with Adam in the Garden of Eden and progressing through the stories of Adam and Eve, Cain and Abel, Noah and the Ark, the Sacrifice of Isaac and the life of Jacob. In addition there are two plasterwork overmantels depicting specific scenes from the life of David: Saul throwing the spear at David (1 Samuel 18.11) and David taking the pitcher and spear from Saul's tent (1 Samuel 26.12). In the tympanum at the west end of the gallery is a scene depicting the victory of David over Goliath, illustrating 1 Samuel 17.49.

The sheer number of separate episodes depicted in one room (thirty-nine in total) is an impressive response to the potential of the gallery as an exhibition space for a programme of imagery. That the main body of the ceiling is devoted to scenes from Gene-

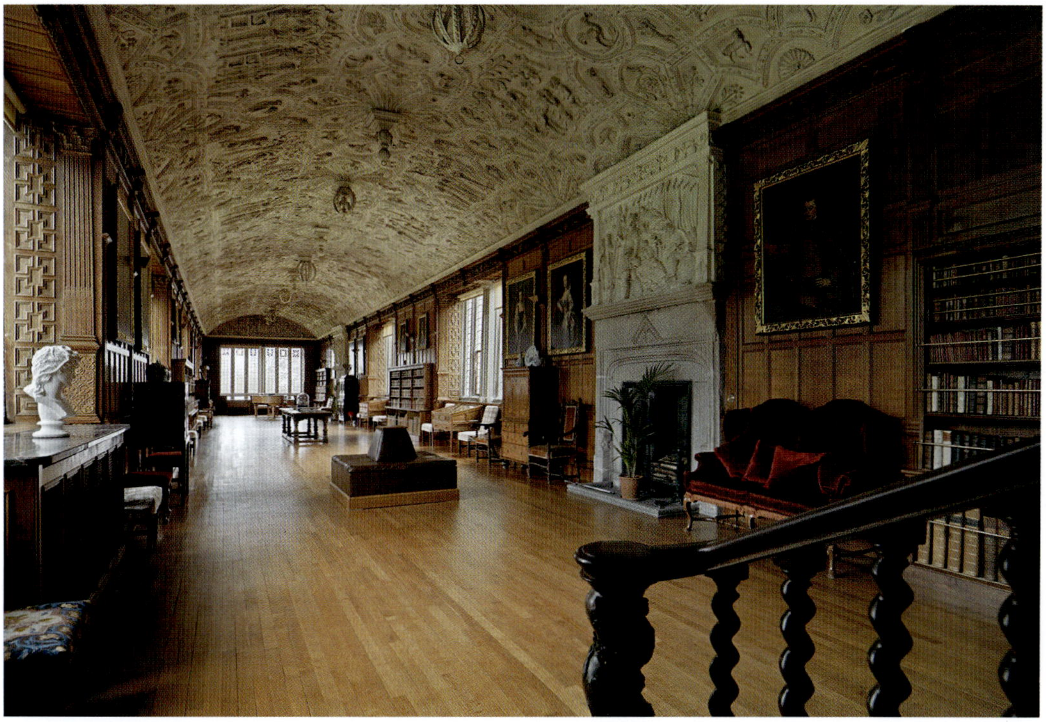

119 View of the long gallery at Lanhydrock House, Cornwall

sis suggests a particular interest in the first book of the Pentateuch and this concern is certainly evident in contemporary literature. During the sixteenth and seventeenth centuries a great number of exegetical commentaries on Genesis were published in Europe. While this output reflects a general increase in scriptural exegesis characteristic of the period, a concentration of texts dealing with Genesis has been identified as a distinct and substantial category.[134]

Various factors influenced this literary and theological concentration on Genesis. The episodes described in the first book of the Bible satisfied a popular demand for information about the creation of the world and the beginning of life. In theological terms Genesis describes some of the most significant episodes for the Christian faith. The story of the Creation attests the omnipotence of God and that the universe was created for the purposes of his design for humankind. Adam and Eve's fall from grace is one of the two crucial points of Christian history, with the sacrifice of Christ on the Cross as the other. The narrative of the Flood and the history of the patriarchs Abraham, Isaac and Jacob establish God's covenant with his chosen people, providing the foundation for the whole of Christian history. Theologians on both sides of the divide separating Catholics and Protestants vied to utilise the stories in Genesis to support their own doctrinal concerns.

John Robartes owned at least two commentaries on Genesis in English. Henry Ainsworth's *Annotations upon the first book of Moses called Genesis* (1616), and William

Whately's *Prototypes, or, The Primarie Precedent Presidents out of the booke of Genesis* (1640) are still in the collection in the gallery at Lanhydrock today.[135] Both texts are typical of their genre in the application of stories in Genesis to doctrinal and moral issues and as illustrations of the scheme of salvation, the foundation of the Church and the operations of election and grace.

In the right-hand section of the ceiling, twelve scenes depict some of the most theologically significant episodes in Genesis, covering chapters 2 to 22, including the creation of Adam and Eve, their fall and expulsion from paradise, the stories of Cain and Abel, Noah and the Flood and the Sacrifice of Isaac. What these episodes have in common is the theme of election, the mystery of the operation of Divine will in choosing some people in preference to others. It was Adam and Eve's sin of disobedience that led to God's grace being withdrawn from all humankind. Cain and Abel both made offerings to God but it was Abel, the younger brother, whose offering found favour with God, resulting in Cain's jealousy and murderous rage. Noah and his family were chosen to survive the flood while the rest of humankind was destroyed. God's covenant with Abraham and his progeny was renewed after he demonstrated his unquestioning fidelity to God in being willing to sacrifice his son Isaac at God's command.

The doctrine of election occupied a central place in the forms of Protestantism adopted in England and Scotland, which had absorbed Calvinist principles. Calvin had made the doctrine of predestination one of the cornerstones of his system, asserting that certain persons were pre-elected by God wholly without relation to faith or works and that Christ's sacrifice was intended only for the elect. While the doctrine of election was affirmed by the Scottish Confession of 1560 and the Anglican Thirty-Nine Articles of 1563, commitment to an uncompromising predestination as defined by Calvin was one of the indicators of Puritan conviction.

It is therefore significant that there is a particular emphasis on the life of Jacob in the ceiling at Lanhydrock. The left-hand section of the ceiling depicts twenty-four separate episodes, covering Genesis, chapters 27 to 35. In order to accommodate this number of separate scenes, the design of the ceiling changes in the section running the length of the north side of the gallery so that each star-shaped narrative panel contains two separate episodes (Fig. 120). It is clear that the story of Jacob must have been of particular interest for John Robartes to have endorsed this asymmetrical design. An explanation lies in the application of the story of Jacob as an exemplar for the operation of election. Jacob had cheated and lied in order to steal his father's blessing from his brother Esau and yet it was Jacob and his lineage that God chose for his covenant. According to Calvin in his own commentary on Genesis, this illustrated that election and grace were not achieved through works but through God's will.[136] Calvin elaborated this theme in his thirteen sermons 'Entreating of the Free Election of God in Jacob, and of reprobation in Esau' which were published in an English translation by John Field in 1579. Following Calvin, William Whately opened his discussion of the 'example of Jacob' with the observation:

> and in them [Jacob and Esau] the Lord did manifest the freedome of his Election, seeing he choose the younger before the elder to inherite the promises, and that before

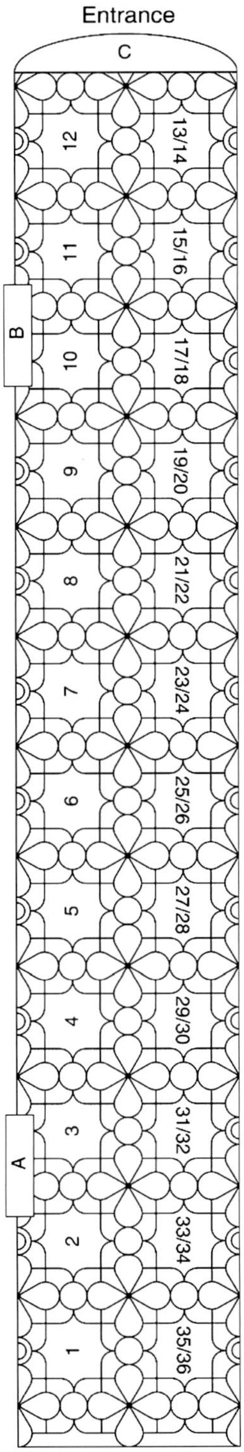

1. Adam in the Garden of Eden
2. The Creation of Eve
3. The Temptation and Fall from Grace
4. The Expulsion from Paradise
5. Adam and his family toiling after the Expulsion
6. Cain and Abel making altars to God
7. Cain killing Abel
8. Noah building the Ark
9. Boarding the Ark
10. The Flood
11. Noah and his family give thanks to God
12. The Sacrifice of Isaac
13. Rebekah speaking to Jacob
14. Jacob catching kids
15. Esau hunting
16. Isaac blessing Jacob
17. Rebekah speaking to Isaac
18. Isaac speaking to Jacob
19. Jacob praying
20. Jacob's dream of the ladder
21. Jacob anointing the stone
22. Jacob meeting Rachel at the well
23. Jacob speaking to Laban
24. Jacob working for Laban
25. Jacob with Leah and Rachel
26. Jacob, with his wives on camels, leave Laban
27. Laban searches the tent for Jacob
28. Jacob and Laban setting up a pillar
29. Jacob wrestling with an angel
30. The man of God and Jacob
31. The meeting of Esau and Jacob
32. Hamor and Jacob
33. The slaughter of Hamor and Shechem
34. Jabob leaving for Bethel
35. Jacob pouring oil upon an altar
36. The burial of Isaac

A. Saul throwing a spear at David
B. David taking the pitcher and spear from Saul's tent
C. David and Goliath

120 Diagram showing the position of biblical scenes in the plasterwork ceiling of the long gallery at Lanhydrock House (not to scale)

they had done good or evill, that the purpose of God according to election might remaine (or be firme) not of works, but of him that calleth.[137]

Clearly, therefore, the choice of scenes in the ceiling at Lanhydrock was not an indiscriminate or comprehensive pictorial rendering of Genesis. Instead, the content represents a systematic investigation and illustration of the nature of election. The quantity and content of scenes from the life of Jacob, in particular, indicate a specific interest in Jacob's calling and his covenant with God. This same emphasis is evident in Protestant literature on the subject and is entirely in keeping with the Puritan beliefs of the patron.

These Puritan beliefs determined not only the choice of particular subject matter from Genesis but also affected the content and iconography of the pictorial scenes. Some of the scenes in the main body of the ceiling have peculiar and awkward compositions. That of Adam in the Garden of Eden is especially odd, as Adam's body is depicted at a strange angle with his limbs awkwardly contorted (Fig. 121). He cannot be described as standing or lying down but instead his body appears to be half-propped against a tree. This makes the precise identification of the scene difficult – is this a depiction of Adam naming the beasts? If so, why is Adam depicted in such an unusual position? An answer is provided by comparison with printed illustrations in Bibles. In her study of the illustrations to the official Elizabethan Bible of 1568, known as the *Bishops' Bible*, Margaret Aston describes how the woodcut blocks by Virgil Solis employed for these illustrations were also used in Lutheran and Catholic Bibles printed on the continent.[138] Crucially, for the 1568 English Bible these blocks were altered to accommodate the particular demands of the Elizabethan Church so that the image of God the Father as a robed and bearded ancient was 'edited out' of several pictures and replaced with the Hebrew Tetragrammaton. Protestant theologians agreed that the image of God the Father was unequivocally forbidden by the Second Commandment, so that for the 1568 *Bishops' Bible* an attempt was made to expunge the image of God the Father wherever he occupied a central or substantial part of the composition. This required the physical alteration of the woodblock, so that the part depicting the offending figure was removed and substituted with a fresh wooden insert carved with the Tetragrammaton. As Aston describes, the censorship is most evident in the first two woodcuts for the book of Genesis, illustrating the Creation of the World and the Creation of Eve.

Nevertheless, this process of censorship was not comprehensive and many of the illustrations incorporating a smaller figure of God were not changed. This oversight provoked the fury of the Puritan lobby so that the Second Admonition to Parliament in 1572 criticised the 'sight of blasphemous pictures of God the father' in the first *Bishops' Bible*.[139] In the subsequent edition published in 1572, the process of censorship was comprehensive. A new set of illustrations eliminated all depictions of God in human form, with the Tetragrammaton deployed instead.

This censorship resulted in several unusual and pictorially incoherent compositions and one of the most anomalous outcomes is the illustration of the Creation of Adam. In medieval iconography, the figure of God the Father as a robed and bearded man is de-

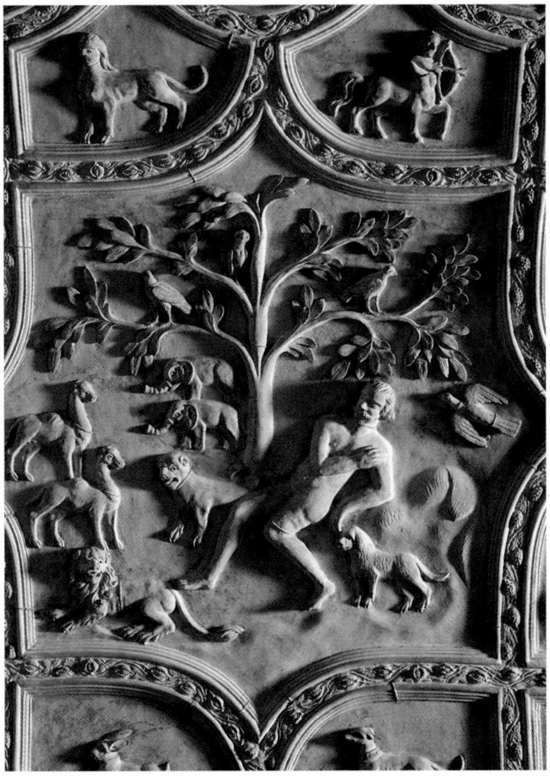

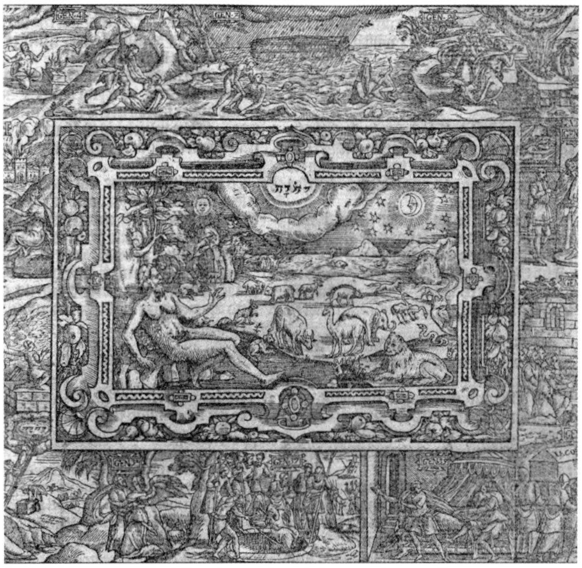

121 (LEFT) Adam in the Garden of Eden, detail of the plasterwork ceiling of the long gallery, c. 1636, at Lanhydrock House

122 (ABOVE) The Creation of Adam, woodcut illustration from the *Bishops' Bible* of 1572

picted in the Garden of Eden reaching out to give life to the inert Adam. This is the incident depicted in the iconic scene from Michelangelo's painted ceiling in the Vatican's Sistine Chapel. In the 1572 *Bishops' Bible* illustration of the Creation, the previously central and substantial figure of God is missing, so that there is no visual explanation for the strange position and posture of Adam's body (Fig. 122). The 1572 illustration is close to the corresponding scene in the ceiling at Lanhydrock with the same awkward positioning of the body of Adam propped against a tree, though reversed, so that Adam is on the right-hand side of the scene rather than the left. This suggests that the figure of God has been 'edited out' in a similar manner to the process employed to expunge the offending subject in the Bible illustrations. It is certainly apparent from comparison with the corresponding illustration in the 1572 *Bishops' Bible* that the first scene in the gallery ceiling is also intended to represent the Creation of Adam, an identification not obvious from the image alone. The second scene in the ceiling, the Creation of Eve, has also been subject to censorship. Again, comparison with the *Bishops' Bible* illustrations is instructive. The large figure of God the Father shown extracting Eve from the body of Adam in the woodcut in the Lutheran and Catholic Bibles is conspicuously absent from the same illustration in the 1568 English Bible. Instead, the figure of Eve emerges from the side of Adam and looks upwards to the Tetragrammaton (Fig. 123).[140] In the Lanhydrock version, even the Tetragrammaton is absent, so that Eve emerges as if spontaneously from the

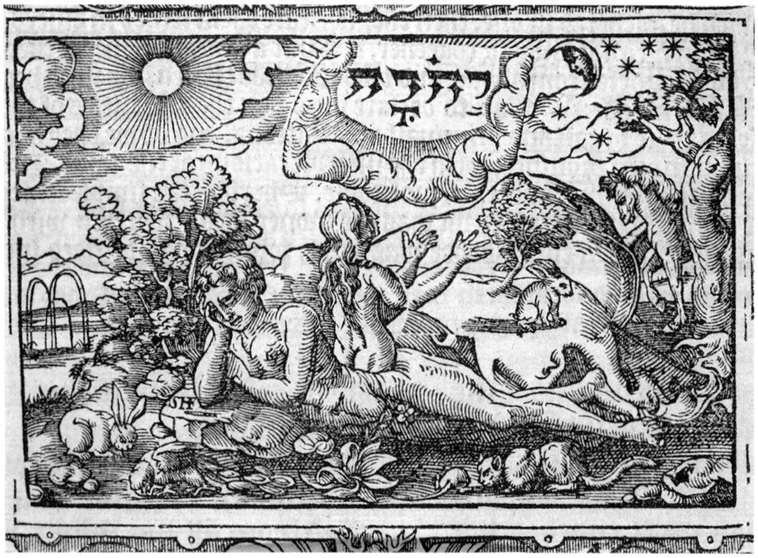

123 (ABOVE) The Creation of Eve, woodcut illustration from the *Bishops' Bible* of 1568

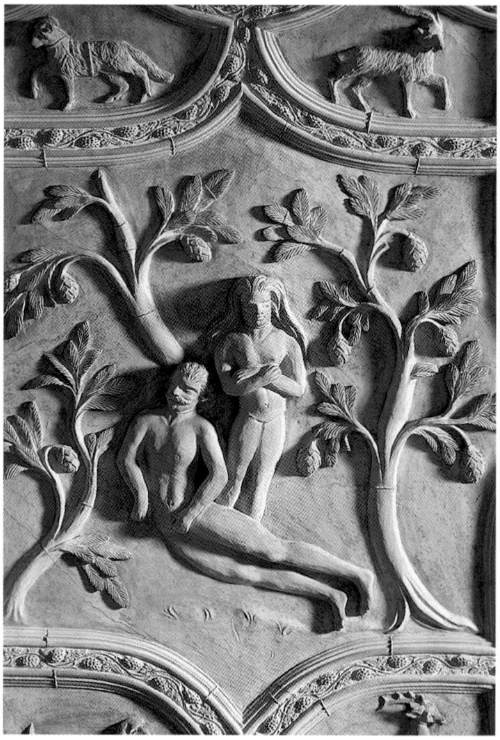

124 (RIGHT) The Creation of Eve, detail of the plasterwork ceiling of the long gallery, c. 1636, at Lanhydrock House

body of Adam, presenting an edited, and thereby simplified, version of the traditional iconography (Fig. 124). Other scenes in the ceiling at Lanhydrock show signs of similar expurgation and adaptation. That of Jacob's dream of the ladder, for example, lacks the traditional figure of God in heaven in the 1568 *Bishops' Bible* illustration and instead the ladder ascends into a swirl of clouds and stars.

The removal of God the Father from the otherwise conventional iconography in the ceiling at Lanhydrock proves that the choice of particular imagery for the decoration was carefully considered and, where necessary, purged of any offensive elements. This level of critical attention to the pictorial content of so-called 'ornament' demonstrates that decorative art was understood to be subject to the same controls and prohibitions as other forms of imagery. The decoration of the gallery at Lanhydrock with a scheme of biblical scenes demonstrates that even a strict Puritan like John Robartes approved of large-scale religious imagery within the domestic sphere. However, the steps taken to ensure that the imagery was purified of objectionable elements underlines that patrons might be concerned that such imagery had the potential to corrupt the thoughts and behaviour of its audience.

No single printed source has yet been identified for the scheme of scenes in the main body of the ceiling at Lanhydrock. The similarities with the *Bishops' Bible* illustrations of 1568 and 1572 are striking but there are various omissions and discrepancies that rule these illustrations out as a single source. Of course, it is possible that a number of different printed sources were employed to construct such an extensive programme.

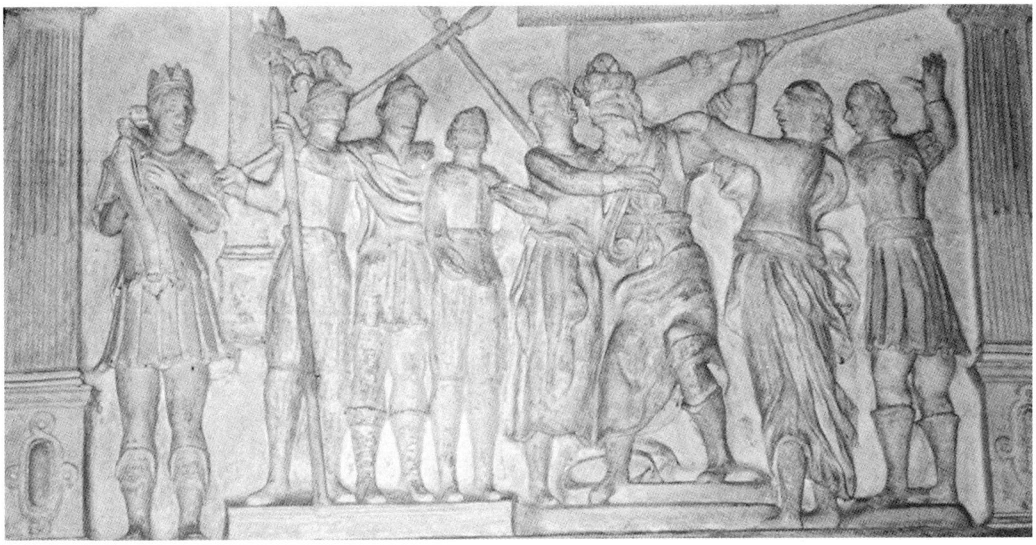

125 Saul throwing the spear at David, plasterwork overmantel in the long gallery, c. 1636, at Lanhydrock House

A single printed source has, however, been identified for the three scenes in the fireplace overmantels and in the tympanum. As Anthony Wells-Cole has demonstrated, these scenes were all copied from the *Thesaurus Sacrarum Historiarum Veteris Testamenti* published by Gerard de Jode in Antwerp in 1585.[141] All three scenes are concerned with incidents from the life of King David, a particularly popular character as a subject for decorative art during this period. As has been seen, David, then understood to be author of the Psalms, is often shown playing his harp, an example of legitimate music-making as a vehicle for praising God. In one of the overmantels in the gallery at Lanhydrock, David is shown playing his harp to entertain King Saul (Fig. 125).

King David playing his harp is also the subject of a carved overmantel of about 1622–24 in the long gallery of Apethorpe Hall in Northamptonshire (Fig. 126). An inscription underneath extols the virtues of music to dispel melancholy and evil spirits but the iconography at Apethorpe also has an allegorical meaning. The statue of David has features resembling King James I and the harp alludes to the harmony brought about by his reign. This central figure of David playing his harp stands in a niche and is flanked by reclining female personifications of Justice (on the left) and Fortitude (on the right). In low relief on the panel above Justice is the head of Goliath pierced through with David's sword and above the figure of Fortitude are the sling and stones used by David to defeat the giant. The overmantel is part of a programme of allegorical decoration throughout a newly built suite of state apartments intended to celebrate the benefits of King James's rule. James I was often compared to David in the literature of the period and the James-as-David iconography in the long gallery at Apethorpe was a politically motivated compliment to the king by a loyal supporter.[142]

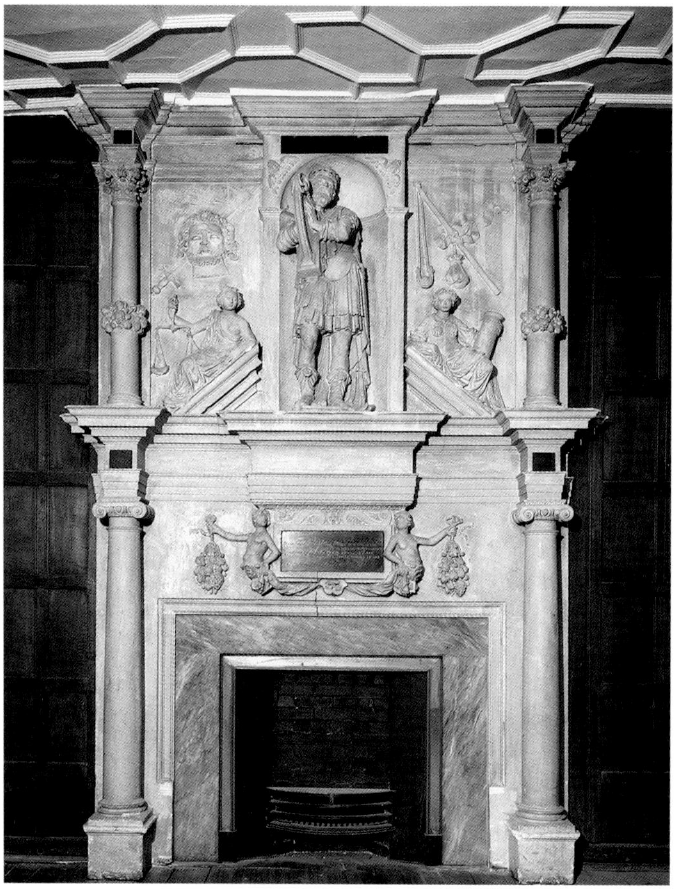

126 King David playing his harp, chimneypiece of c. 1622–24 in the long gallery at Apethorpe Hall, Northamptonshire

The selection of three particular scenes from the life of David in the gallery at Lanhydrock also suggests a political message but represents the other side of the political divide. In the chimneypieces and the tympanum, the imagery taken from the first book of Samuel stands apart from the scenes in the main body of the ceiling. The subject matter for these three scenes is taken from a different book of the Old Testament and the imagery is copied from a set of printed engravings not employed for the other scenes in the main body of the ceiling. Considered together, these three scenes suggest an allusion to contemporary politics.

When the decoration of the gallery at Lanhydrock was created, in about 1636, the personal rule of Charles I had exacerbated the political and religious divide between the Puritan Parliamentary faction and the Crown. The conflict between King Saul and the young David, as illustrated in the two overmantels at Lanhydrock, can be understood as an allegory of this growing rift. These particular scenes emphasise Saul's tyranny (Saul throwing the spear at David) and David's diplomacy and military restraint (David taking the pitcher and spear from Saul's tent). David's resolution not to kill the crazed King Saul, who was trying to kill him, was widely understood as a scriptural endorsement of the divine right of kings. Indeed, in the Elizabethan Homily, *An Exhortation concerning good Order, and obedience to Rulers and Magistrates*, the same two episodes from the book of Samuel are recounted as evidence that no amount of tyranny or persecution can justify the overthrow of an anointed king by his subjects:[143]

> Holy David also teacheth us a good lesson . . . who was many times most cruelly and wrongfully persecuted of king Saul, and many times also put in jeopardie and danger of his life by king Saul and his people, yet hee neither withstood, neither used any force or violence against king Saul his mortall and deadly enemie, but did ever to his liege Lord and Master king Saul, most true, most diligent, and most faithfull service (1 Samuel 18.11)
>
> . . . when the most unmercifull and most unkinde King Saul did persecute poore David, GOD did againe give king Saul into Davids handes, by casting of king Saul and his whole armie into a dead sleepe, so that David and one Abisai with him, came in the night into Sauls host, where Saul lay sleeping, and his speare stacke in the ground at his head: then said Abisai unto David, GOD hath delivered thine enemie into thy hands at this time, now therefore let me smite him once with my speare to the earth . . . And David answered and said to Abisai, Destroy him not, for who can lay his hands on the Lords anointed, and be guiltlesse? And David sayd furthermore, As sure as the Lord liveth, the Lord shall smite him, or his day shall come to die, or he shall descend or goe downe into battaile, and there perish, the Lord keepe me from laying my handes upon the Lords anoynted. But take thou now the speare that is at his head, and the cruse of water, and let us goe . . . Here is evidently prooved that we may not withstand, nor in any wise hurt an anointed King, which is GODS lieftenant, vice-gerent, and highest minister in that countrey where he is King.

In creating a pictorial version of this subject for his gallery Robartes was perhaps expressing his dismay at the political and religious policies of the king during the personal rule, while underlining the need for restraint and trust in providence. As the scenes in the two overmantels illustrate, God and righteousness was with David (the Godly) but the Godly must not take action against the king, as God's anointed, but should trust in God's will. However, the large scene of David victorious over Goliath in the tympanum, a traditional allegory of Virtue over Vice, served as a reminder that God assists the righteous to triumph over the forces of oppression (Fig. 127).

The decoration of the gallery at Lanhydrock may thus be understood as an expression of religious and political ideology on behalf of a Puritan opponent to the policies of the Crown in the turbulent decade leading up to the outbreak of civil war. This fusion of political and religious belief expressed through biblical metaphor is typical of the age. As Christopher Hill has demonstrated, during the seventeenth-century Revolution the Bible was used to justify both resistance to and defence of the king.[144] The use of biblical imagery in the decoration of the gallery at Lanhydrock was part of this trend and testifies to the function of the gallery as a tool for exhibiting the education, beliefs and politics of the owner.

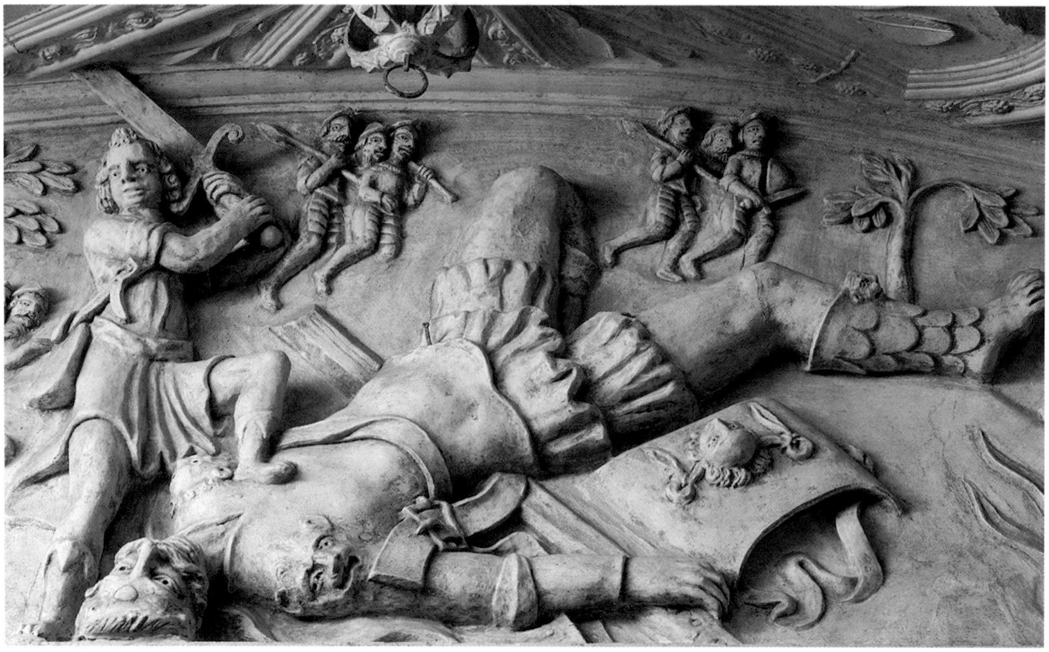

127 David victorious over Goliath, detail of the plasterwork in the long gallery, c. 1636, at Lanhydrock House, Cornwall

Lanhydrock's scheme of Old Testament scenes in the plasterwork ceiling of its gallery once had a close parallel towards the other end of Britain. There is a striking similarity between the work at Lanhydrock and the lost painted ceiling from the gallery at Dean House in Edinburgh, the mansion house of Sir William Nisbet. The house was demolished in 1845 but some of the painted panels from the barrel-vaulted ceiling in the long gallery were salvaged. Most of these salvaged panels are now in the collection of the National Museums of Scotland, with two further panels on display at the John Knox House Museum.

William Nisbet served as the Lord Provost of Edinburgh in 1616 and again in 1622. He was knighted by James I and VI in 1617 and the painted ceiling in the gallery of his grand house appears to have been carried out in 1627.[145] Like John Robartes of Lanhydrock, William Nisbet rose from the ranks of the gentry to a position of social and political prominence. Given their similar backgrounds and careers in public office, it is perhaps no coincidence that both men chose to embellish their galleries with decorated ceilings depicting a similar selection of biblical scenes.

The surviving panels from Dean House are painted with three stories from Genesis: Cain and Abel (Genesis 4; Fig. 128); Lot and his daughters (Genesis 19)[146] and Abraham and Isaac (Genesis 22), while another panel shows Judith and Holofernes, from the Apocrypha. Two further panels depict King David playing the harp (Fig. 129) and St Luke, shown reading in his study (Fig. 130). Another three extant panels depict three of the Five Senses (Hearing,

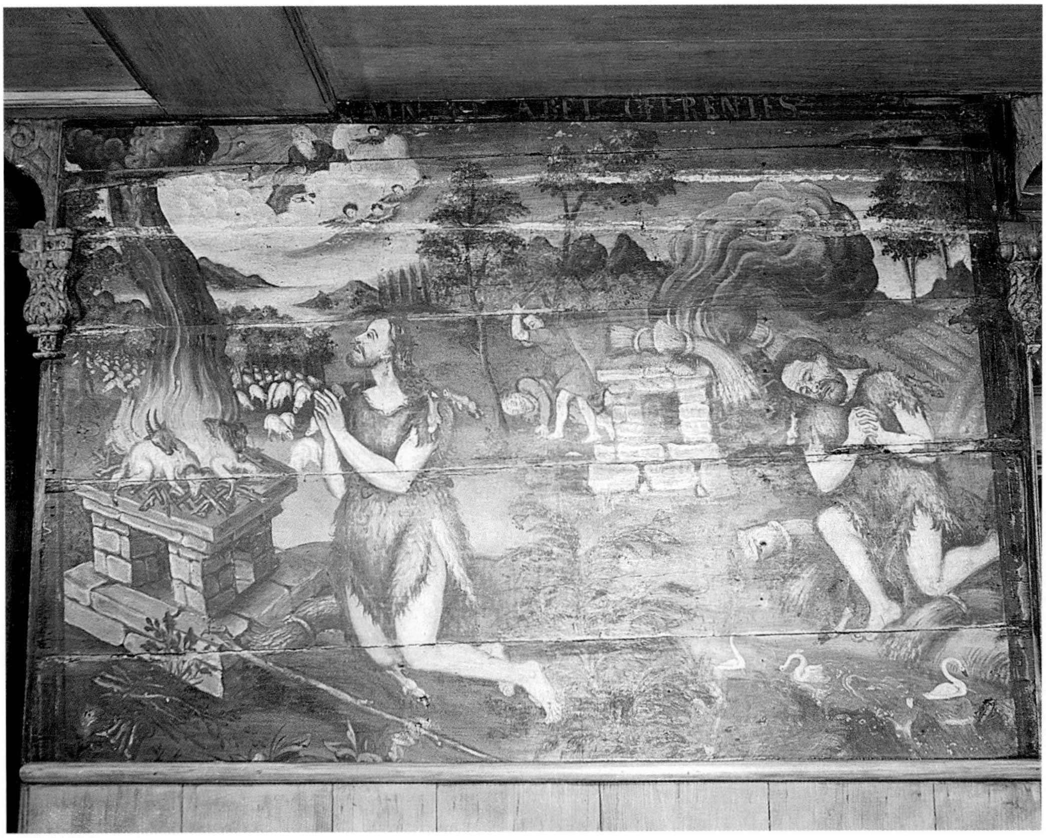

128 Cain and Abel sacrificing to God, painted panel of 1627 from the long gallery ceiling at Dean House, Edinburgh, now on display at John Knox House Museum

Sight and Taste). A further panel was recorded in a description of 1848, although its present whereabouts is not known. The painting was described as a group of musicians, including a lutenist and horn player with music books in front of them.[147]

It is obviously impossible to reconstruct the entire programme of iconography in the painted ceiling at the Dean, based on just nine extant panels. It is possible, however, to speculate about what allied scenes might have been included. To complete the set of Five Senses and Four Evangelists, and to include the lost 'musicians' panel, requires that the ceiling must have included at least fifteen distinct sections and, for a gallery of any length, probably many more. The scenes from Genesis and the image of King David playing his harp recall the choice of subject matter in the ceiling and overmantels at Lanhydrock. The figure of Judith holding the decapitated head of Holofernes has a closely similar iconography and message to the victory of David over Goliath, as depicted in the tympanum at Lanhydrock. If the painted ceiling at the Dean resembled its cousin in plasterwork at Lanhydrock then it probably also included several other scenes from Genesis. Based on its popularity in decorative art more widely, and as the first story told in Genesis, we may

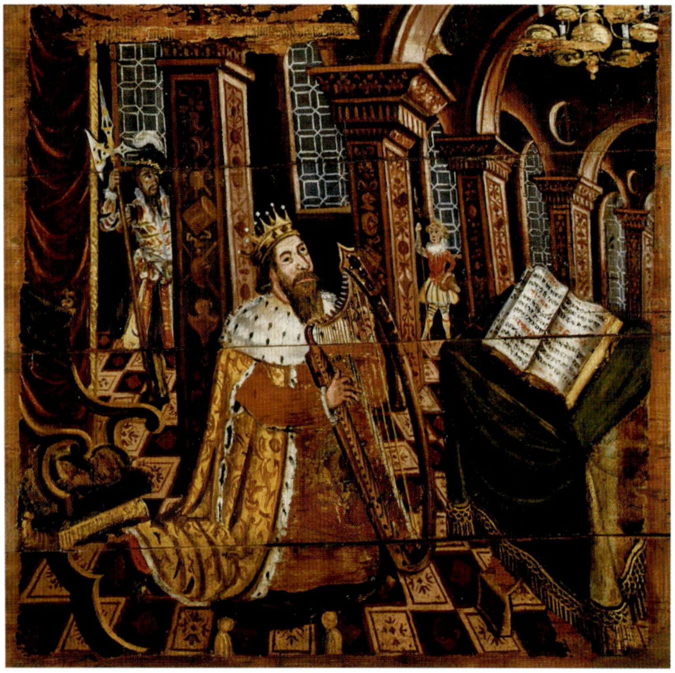

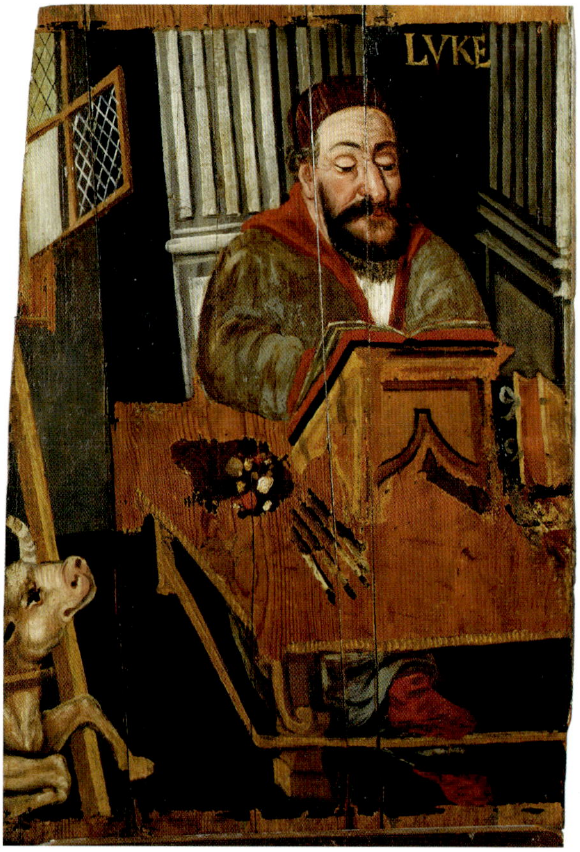

129 (ABOVE) King David, painted panel of 1627 from the long gallery ceiling at Dean House

130 (RIGHT) St Luke, painted panel of 1627 from the long gallery ceiling at Dean House

assume that the story of Adam and Eve must surely have been included at the Dean, as it is at Lanhydrock. If the ceiling presented a chronological sweep through the book of Genesis then it may be assumed that an intermediary scene between Cain and Abel and Lot and his daughters was included, and another between Lot and his daughters and Abraham and Isaac. The story of Noah and the Ark, included in the series in the ceiling at Lanhydrock, is an obvious candidate.

Since Nisbet was a figurehead for the city, the interior of his house would have been on open display to dignitaries within the urban community as well as figures on the national stage. The decoration of Nisbet's gallery, in particular, would have been understood as part of the process of self-fashioning his personal and political identity. As a civic leader on a local level, a scheme of biblical imagery in such a space established his credentials as a godly and moral man. More particularly, scenes from Genesis expressed knowledge of the origins of the world and the foundation of the Christian Church. I have noted that early Reformers and the first Protestant generations identified themselves with the patriarchs of the Old Testament. This certainly seems to be the message in emphasising the life of Jacob, the arch-patriarch and father of the twelve tribes of Israel, in the ceiling at Lanhydrock.

Given that the gallery in gentry houses tended to be for the use of family and friends, it may also be significant that most of the extant panels from the Dean House ceiling articulate familial relationships: Cain and Abel (brothers), Abraham and Isaac (father and son), Lot and his daughters (father and daughter), Judith and Holofernes (man and woman). However, far from representing ideal familial relationships, these particular scenes represent examples of unnatural or aberrant relations, with a sinister edge. Cain was brutally murdered by his brother Abel. Lot was seduced into incest with his own daughters who fell pregnant as a result. Abraham would have killed his own son if the angel had not prevented it. The story of Judith and Holofernes, as with the story of the seduction of Lot by his daughters, is based around the wiles of feminine seduction and ends in the murder and decapitation of Holofernes. Furthermore, inebriation was the common factor in the seduction of Lot and the downfall of Holofernes, so these images have another thematic link. Bringing together this group of scenes might therefore be understood as a moral warning about the dangers of corrupting the natural order within familial relationships. The imagery articulates the strengths and weaknesses of men in fulfilling or neglecting their obligations to their family and to God.

Despite the similarities in the choice of subject matter, there is a significant difference in the detail of the imagery as depicted at Lanhydrock and Dean House. The Cain and Abel panel from the Dean includes at top left the figure of God the Father emerging through clouds accompanied by cherubim (see Fig. 128). As noted earlier, this figure was 'edited out' of several scenes at Lanhydrock, resulting in several crude and awkward compositions. If a growing tolerance of imagery over the period 1620–40 explains the presence of this controversial detail in the painted ceiling at the Dean, its careful omission in the plasterwork at Lanhydrock suggests where a dividing line might be drawn between Protestants of different temper on the issue of images in the 1620s and 30s.

It is difficult to imagine the overall visual impact of the painted ceiling when in its complete form in the gallery at the Dean but it must have resembled the painted ceiling still *in situ* in the gallery at Provost Skene's House in Aberdeen. This painted ceiling is extraordinary in representing a scheme relating to the life, Passion, Resurrection and Ascension of Christ (Fig. 131).[148] The large town house, named after its late seventeenth-century owner, incorporates a wing which was remodelled by Matthew Lumsden, the owner of the building from 1622 to 1644. Lumsden was a prominent citizen and became a baillie of Aberdeen in 1634. His arms and initials together with the initials of his wife and the date 1626 are depicted on the façade of this wing and the same arms appear in the painted decoration of the gallery on the second floor. The painted decoration was discovered in 1951, when it was extensively restored. Unfortunately, all the painting at the east end of the gallery was in a poor condition and only part of the original programme of imagery survives today. The ceiling design incorporated ten rectangular panels, each containing a narrative scene: four scenes on each of the sloped sides and a further two scenes in rectangular panels in the central, flat section of the ceiling. At the centre of the whole design is a single circular panel which now contains only clouds but which might originally have depicted Christ in heaven.[149] Five of the narrative scenes survive in good

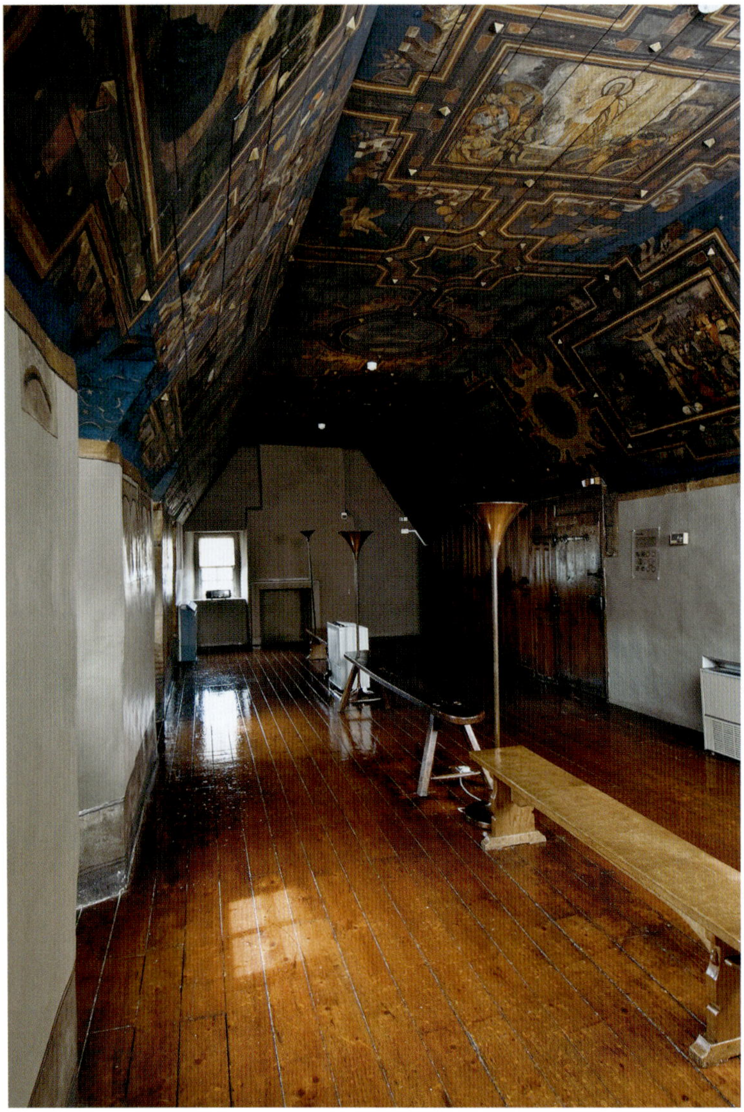

131 View of the painted ceiling of c. 1626 in the gallery at Provost Skene's House in Aberdeen

condition: the Annunciation (Fig. 132), Nativity, Crucifixion (Fig. 133) and Entombment on the four sloping faces at the western end of the room, and the Resurrection on the flat portion of the ceiling in between. Another, badly damaged, panel on the flat portion of the ceiling at the eastern end of the gallery contains fragments of painting, whose composition and situation suggest that it represented the Ascension. The four scenes on the sloping faces at the eastern end of the gallery are now completely blank. As these four panels must have represented the key episodes from the life of Christ between the Nativity and the Crucifixion, it is possible to speculate that they most probably depicted Christ in the Temple, the Baptism, the Last Supper and the Agony in the Garden. As well as these narrative scenes, the spaces round the panels in the central section of the ceiling contain numerous *putti*, each holding a symbol associated with the Passion. In addition,

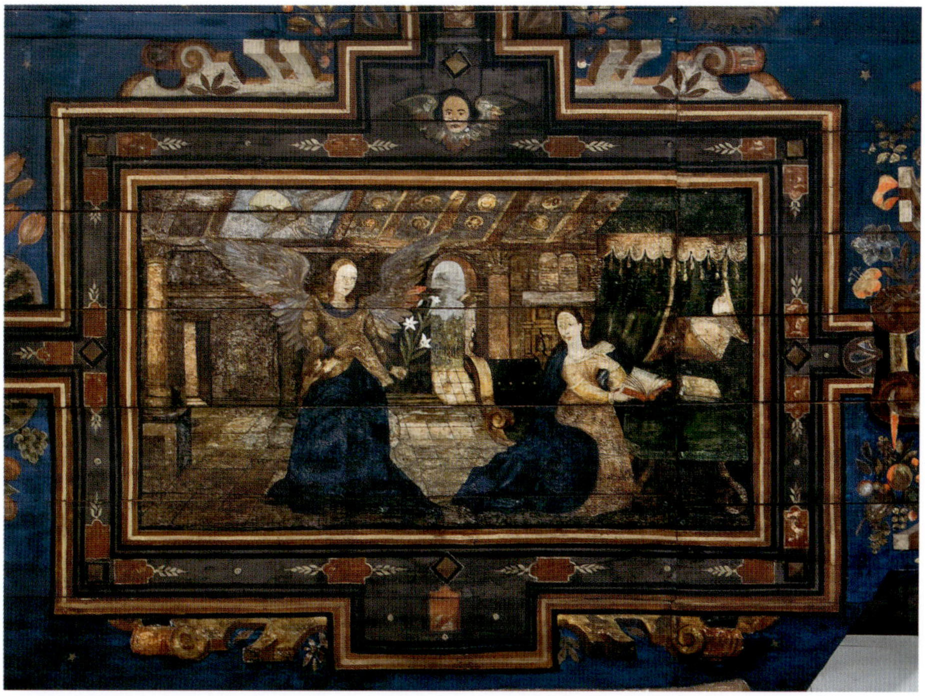

132 The Annunciation, detail of the painted ceiling of c. 1626 in the gallery at Provost Skene's House

133 The Crucifixion, detail of the painted ceiling of c. 1626 in the gallery at Provost Skene's House

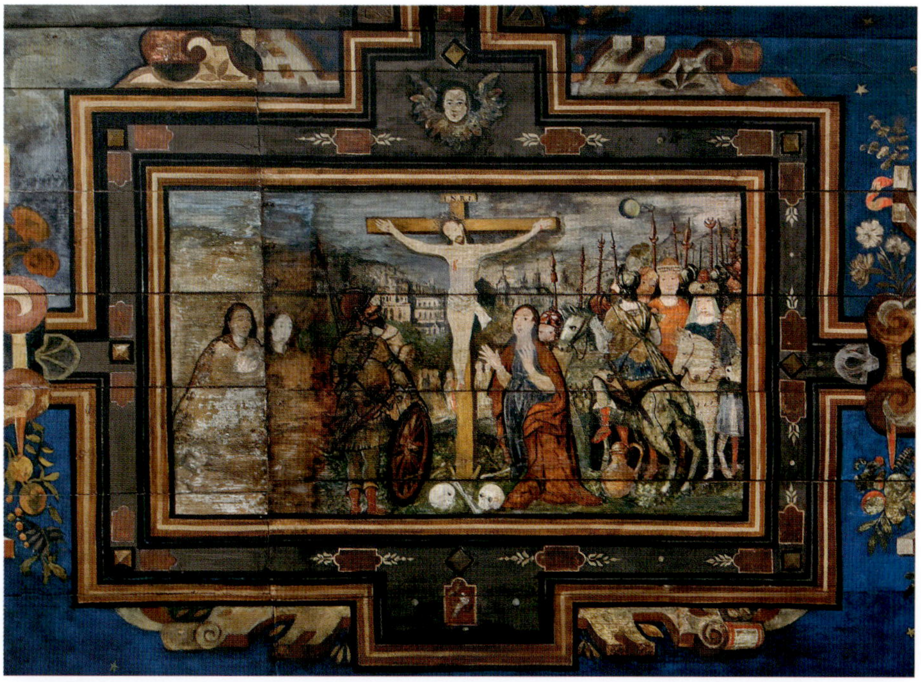

three of the six roundels which intersperse the rectangular panels along the sloping faces still contain their original decoration; one depicts the symbolic Five Wounds of Christ, while the other two have the sacred monograms IHS and XPS.

That scholars have found it difficult to reconcile the decoration of this painted gallery with the concept of a Protestant patron is understandable. It has been suggested that Lumsden must have been a crypto-Catholic and it has even been claimed that this room served as his secret Catholic chapel.[150] Such claims have been unable to unearth any evidence in support of the hypothesis that Lumdsen was Catholic and have instead had to grapple with the awkward historical evidence to the contrary. Indeed, Margo Todd in her authoritative study of the culture of Protestantism in early modern Scotland has described Lumsden as 'a vigorous Protestant who would later take up arms for the Covenant in the Bishops' Wars'.[151] Given the evidence presented throughout this volume proving that Protestant culture was not incompatible with religious imagery, the claim that the very existence of the painted decoration at Provost Skene's House is itself 'definite proof' of Lumsden's Catholicity must now be discounted.[152] While it was certainly unusual for such a traditional scheme of religious iconography to have been created within a Protestant context, it was not unique.[153] Its narrative scenes adhere to the rule of scriptural fidelity and could have been justified as an illustration of the account of Christ's life provided in the New Testament. The symbols of the Passion are certainly unusual but as a lesser part of a scheme of religious imagery it is unlikely that they would have become the focus of improper worship. From a Protestant viewpoint, the most problematic aspect of the iconography is the cultic Five Wounds, a focus of veneration in late medieval religion.[154] Yet similar depictions of this iconography in early seventeenth-century decoration can be found elsewhere. It appears in plasterwork at Woodlands Farmhouse in Holford, Somerset,[155] and at the apex of a scheme of wall painting of about 1610 in a house in Church Street in Beaumaris, Anglesey.[156]

These three examples of decorated ceilings in long galleries provide a microcosm of the wider context in representing the range of approaches adopted by patrons who were clearly firm Protestants but of different sorts, during the period 1620–40. It is likely that the imagery at the Dean and especially at Provost Skene's House would have shocked good Calvinists like John Robartes who was careful to avoid the inclusion of contentious subject matter in his own commission. The burgeoning tolerance of disputed imagery in some Protestant circles in this period goes some way to explain the ferocity of the renewed and more comprehensive attack on images by the Puritan government in the 1640s.

FURNISHINGS AND DECORATED OBJECTS

This book focuses on large-scale, fixed surface decoration that can be identified with a particular location and/or patron because this allows the reconstruction, to some extent, of the original context in which this imagery was produced and viewed. However, religious imagery also adorned a range of moveable objects displayed in the domestic interior. These objects are harder to document because they usually have little or no provenance and are often assigned to a broad date range. From the surviving material it is difficult to assess how widely these objects circulated or how typical religious imagery was as the subject of decoration. It is also hard to be precise about where or how these objects were displayed and therefore how they might have been viewed and used. With these caveats, what follows provides a brief discussion of some of the types of objects decorated with religious imagery that could be seen in the houses of post-Reformation Britain.

The visual effect of imagery in applied decoration was enhanced by the relatively sparse furnishing of rooms in early modern Britain. Despite a general rise in living standards and increased investment in household goods, the interiors of most houses during the period 1560–1660 would seem plain and meagrely furnished in comparison with modern tastes. Larger items of furniture and decorative objects for the purposes of display were major investments, so that most households possessed only a few such items, which were highly prized and passed down through the generations.

Evidence from probate inventories reveals that even in the wealthiest houses furniture consisted of a few key pieces in each room. These items of furniture were supplemented by occasional stools, for larger gatherings, which could be kept at the sides of the room or on landings to be brought in by servants when required. In the great dining chamber of Sir Henry Sharington's mansion at Lacock in Wiltshire in 1575 was one long table, three tressells, one square table, one 'cupborde of waynscotte', one 'brusshinge boarde and 2 tressells', five chairs and twenty stools. This provides only the furniture necessary for the function of the room: a table and seats for dining, a cupboard for display or serving and a gaming board and seats for after-dinner entertainment. The walls were adorned with a set of six hangings illustrating the story of Jephthah (Judges 11) and two large embroidered hangings.[157]

There was also a degree of formality to the way smaller decorative objects and material goods were displayed. Moveable items were not scattered throughout the house but were stored or displayed as collections in specific locations. The impermanence and communality of medieval domestic life had encouraged a security-conscious attitude to the ownership of goods. In the medieval period it was usual for belongings to be stored in wooden chests that could be locked and moved when necessary. Habits had not yet adjusted to the more permanent and stable living conditions of the early modern period, so that it remained usual to store goods away, out of sight and under lock and key.

Gold, silver or pewter plate was stored in chests or cupboards and displayed on special occasions, usually on a cupboard or sideboard in the hall or dining room, as depicted in the *Memorial Portrait to Sir Henry Unton* of 1596 (Fig. 134). The scene of Sir Henry presiding over a feast in his great chamber at Wadley House in Berkshire shows a company of guests ranged round a table served with food. In the background is a sideboard on which is displayed a collection of silverware. This is not the functional plate used during the meal but a symbolic expression of Unton's wealth and social position.

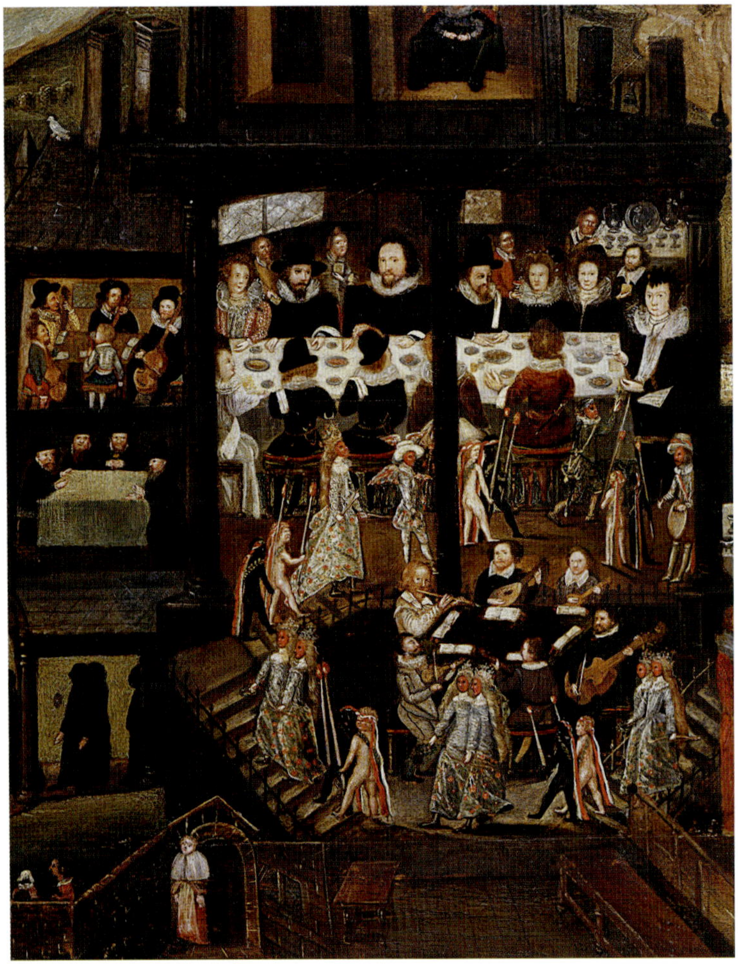

134 Detail of the *Memorial Portrait to Sir Henry Unton* of 1596, showing Sir Henry and guests dining in his house at Wadley

Textiles were also stored in chests or linen cupboards and brought out for display or when need arose. The development of free-standing, monumental linen cupboards (or wardrobes) in the course of the seventeenth century created an impressive focal point for the household's collection of textiles such as table linen, bed linen, clothing. These were equated with the practical aspects of domestic life and so the linen cupboard came to be associated with the identity, status and size of the household. In the Netherlands these *linnenkast* occupied a central place in the physical and conceptual space of the domestic interior, symbolising the wealth, decorum and moral virtue of the household.[158] For this reason *linnenkast* were sometimes decorated with carvings of Virtues or religious figures and occasionally with religious scenes. The linen cupboard did not acquire the same degree of prominence in the domestic interior in Britain but it did serve to showcase the size and importance of the textile collection and, by implication, the status of the household.[159]

In wealthy households, expensive *objets d'art*, such as portrait miniatures, medals, gems and small-scale sculpture, were acquired as part of a collection that was housed in an exotic decorative cabinet (usually imported) or, for really sizeable collections, in a specific room, usually a closet or study. These so-called 'cabinets' of collectables were the preserve of the elite but the process of acquisition involved in collecting, storing and exhibiting these treasures only on specific occasions is illustrative of wider cultural habits in relation to the ownership and display of luxury material goods.

The display of furnishings and decorated objects should thus be understood as part of a deliberate and conscious strategy of visual communication. Such moveable forms of decoration were intended to enhance and extend the messages and atmosphere of imagery depicted in applied decoration. However, they could be deployed or concealed depending on audience or circumstance. The smaller scale of the pictorial imagery and the occasional nature of display, on specific occasions and within orchestrated contexts, suggest a degree of intimacy encouraging personal engagement with the iconography. Moreover, as some of these objects were associated with gift-giving and exchanged in social rituals, the meanings communicated by pictorial iconography would be nuanced by the nature of the occasion prompting the gift.

Fixtures and Furniture

Wooden architectural fixtures were sometimes embellished with carvings of biblical subject matter. In the collection of the National Museums of Scotland is a carved oak door from Amisfield Tower in Dumfriesshire dated 1600 and depicting Samson wrestling with the lion.[160] This may allude to the concepts of strength and fortitude required of the door itself in offering solid protection from the outside world. Samson wrestling with the lion also appears in a wooden carving of about 1635 on the exterior of number 12 the Butterwalk in Dartmouth, Devon. It was common in the architectural vocabulary of the period to associate the exterior of buildings with the concept of strength. The classical order of Doric was personified in John Shute's *First and Chief Grounds of Architecture* (1563) with Samson's *alter ego*, Hercules, another muscled hero who wore the skin of the lion he defeated. Such symbolic allusions on the exterior of buildings might actually include sculptures of biblical or classical heroes associated with superhuman strength, so that a massive sculpture of Hercules supports the balcony at Bolsover Castle in Derbyshire, while statues of the Nine Worthies are ranged along the west front of Montacute House in Somerset.

Within the house, larger cupboards and chests were a semi-permanent addition to a room and were treated as display pieces in themselves. I have already considered the significance of the bed as a vehicle for the display of meaningful imagery. Other items of monumental furniture were similarly embellished, sometimes with religious figures or scenes. For example, a late sixteenth-century court cupboard of oak in the Burrell Collection, Glasgow, includes supports to the upper section consisting of two carved caryatid figures; one is Judith with the head of Holofernes.[161] However, it is difficult to ascertain if this kind of religious motif was at all common in carved British furniture. Much early

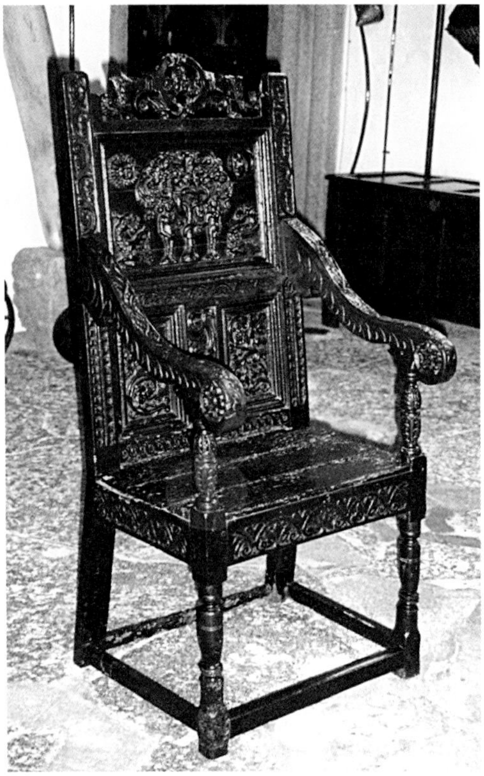

135 Adam and Eve, carved chairback at Cotehele House, Cornwall, 1630s

furniture with carved panels was imported from the Netherlands or France. Few original pieces of native furniture survive and the situation is complicated by extravagant Victorian confections incorporating carvings from continental pieces of similar date.

The popularity of the story of Adam and Eve has been described as a subject of decoration for marriage furniture: a wooden chest carved with this subject and an inscription referring to the marriage of Izaak Walton and Rachel Floud in 1626 has been discussed by Catherine Belsey in her study of concepts surrounding the institution of marriage in early modern culture.[162] Another carved wooden chest dating from the late sixteenth or early seventeenth century at Craigston Castle in Scotland is decorated with a scene of Adam and Eve's Fall on one end.[163] The predilection for this subject evidently extended to other items, such as the joined armchair dating from the 1630s now at Cotehele House in Cornwall (Fig. 135).[164] A scene of Adam and Eve's fall from grace is depicted in a carved panel in the upper part of the chair back. In a culture in which it was usual, even in the grandest houses, to sit on benches and stools, such an impressive chair with back and armrests was primarily a display piece signifying the position and authority of the master or mistress of the house. Adorning the chair with religious imagery enhanced its status even further and marked it out as an extraordinary object among the other domestic furniture.[165]

Plate and Pottery

Buffet, or 'court', cupboards were used to display decorative objects, especially sets of plate. Silver plate was the preserve of the extremely wealthy and was sometimes engraved with religious scenes. A set of twelve silver-gilt plates engraved with illustrations of the story of the Prodigal Son, with the hallmark for 1568–69, might represent an ironic comment on the nature of the objects as a safe form of investment commodity.[166] While the Prodigal Son squandered his inheritance on loose living, the owner of these plates chose to invest his money wisely in prestigious material goods. Another set of six Elizabethan silver-gilt spice bowls in the collection of the Victoria and Albert Museum is engraved with scenes from the life of Isaac, illustrating Genesis 17–27.[167] The religious scenes are engraved at the centre of each bowl of this set, while the well is engraved with marine creatures and the rim with birds and beasts and scrolling foliage. These bowls were luxury

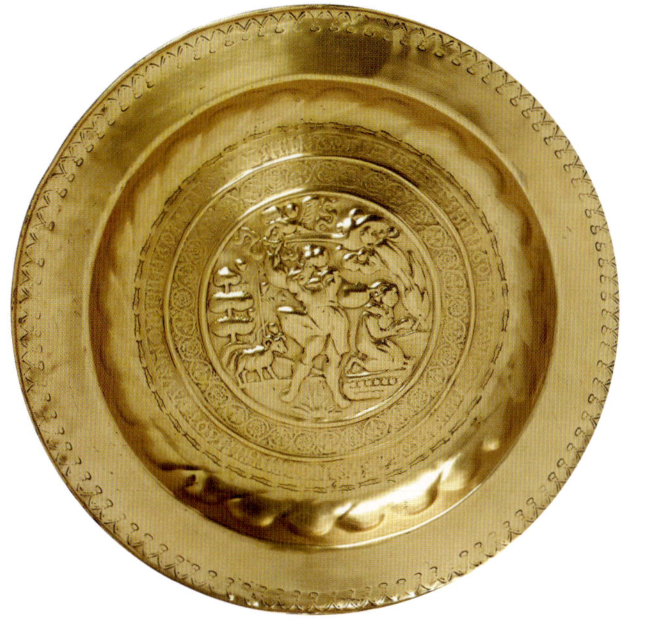

136 The Sacrifice of Isaac depicted in a brass bowl, German, early sixteenth century. Victoria and Albert Museum, London

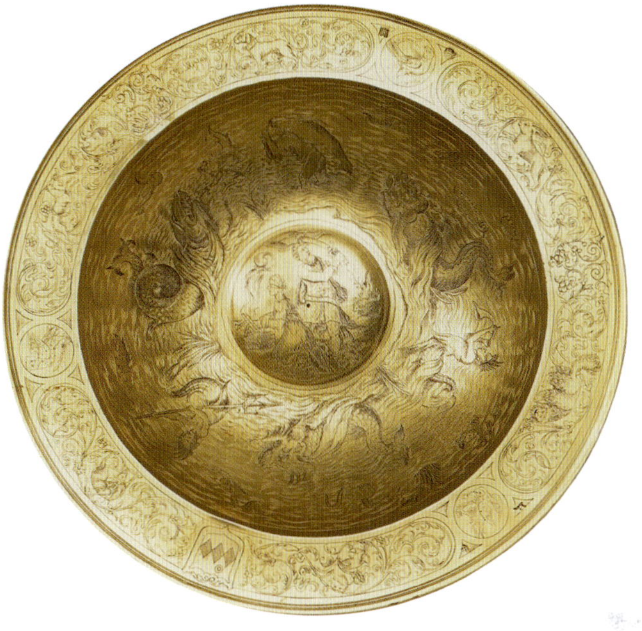

137 The Sacrifice of Isaac, one of a set of six silver-gilt spice bowls, hallmarked 1573–74. Victoria and Albert Museum, London

items intended for dessert or 'banqueting' – a stand-alone and luxurious sweet course usually experienced in whimsical locations such as a banqueting turret on the roofscape or in a garden building. When displayed on a court cupboard these luxury objects denoted great wealth and alluded to their occasional use within the extreme indulgence of a banquet. When in use the religious scene is revealed only after the delicacies have been consumed. In the context of display and use the biblical scenes provide a timely reminder of the need to moderate excess with spiritual reflection. The size, shape and decoration of these bowls adopt a traditional form that had been popular since medieval times. They resemble northern European brass basins produced from the fifteenth century and exported to Britain throughout the 1500s. The whole of the bottom of the inside of these basins was covered with relief decoration and often depicted scenes from the Old or New Testament. This perhaps explains why they were sometimes used in Britain as alms dishes. One can compare, for example, an early sixteenth-century brass bowl of German origin, decorated with a scene of the Sacrifice of Isaac[168] and the Elizabethan silver-gilt spice dish depicting the same episode (Figs 136 and 137). This comparison underlines the high degree of continuity in tradition, despite the strictures on decorated church plate imposed by the Protestant authorities. These imported brass dishes almost certainly remained on display within many domestic houses in Britain throughout the period 1560–1660.

Related to collections of plate with relief or engraved religious scenes is the 'Apostle spoon'. As described in Chapter 1, these spoons were part of pre-Reformation material culture. While there are examples from the continent, Apostle spoons were especially

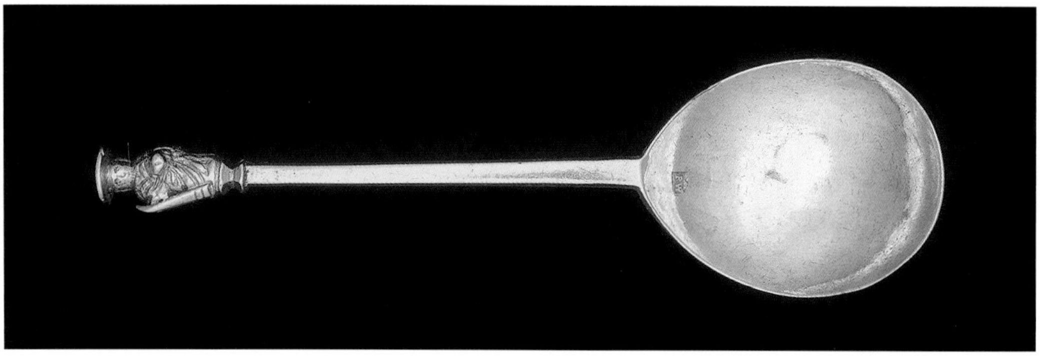

138 'Apostle' spoon with the figure of St James the Less on the finial, dated 1635. Victoria and Albert Museum, London

popular in Britain from around 1500 to the end of the seventeenth century. A post-Reformation example is a silver spoon with the figure of St James the Less on the finial (the decorative end of the handle) (Fig. 138). It is inscribed on the back of the bowl with the initials 'TA' and the date '1635'. This traditional form of gift, associated with the sacramental ritual of baptism, seems to have been largely unaffected by the process of the Reformation and Apostle spoons were often left as bequests in wills. For example, one Henry Aldey, a gentleman from Canterbury, at his death in 1590 bequeathed to a cousin a silver spoon 'which was his aunt's with the ymage of Christ upon the top of the same'.[169] Apostle spoons therefore represent another form of object decorated with traditional religious imagery that continued to be produced, given and displayed in Protestant Britain.

In the first half of the seventeenth century the development of English delftware produced a new vehicle for religious imagery. The native production of tin-glazed earthenware pottery created a new material for a range of utilitarian objects. However, large decorated plates, known as chargers, were intended for display purposes and could be exhibited on cupboards or sideboards or hung on the wall. Indeed, holes in the base of many extant examples indicate that suspending these plates from hooks on the wall was the most usual method of display. These chargers were acquired mainly by the middle classes and lesser gentry and must have been made to order; the painted decoration often includes initials in a triangular arrangement together with the date of manufacture. The inclusion of three initials (for a patron and his wife) with a particular date suggests that chargers were acquired on the occasion of a marriage. This is further supported by the popularity of images of Adam and Eve's Temptation and Fall as the subject of the decoration. An early example dated 1635, with the initials T/TM and a particularly accomplished painted scene of the Fall copied from a print by Crispin van de Passe, must have been produced for a wealthy patron (Fig. 139).[170] This new form of native pottery was no doubt appreciated for its novelty as well as for its narrative message and colourful ornament. As the seventeenth century wore on more factories opened in London and in other

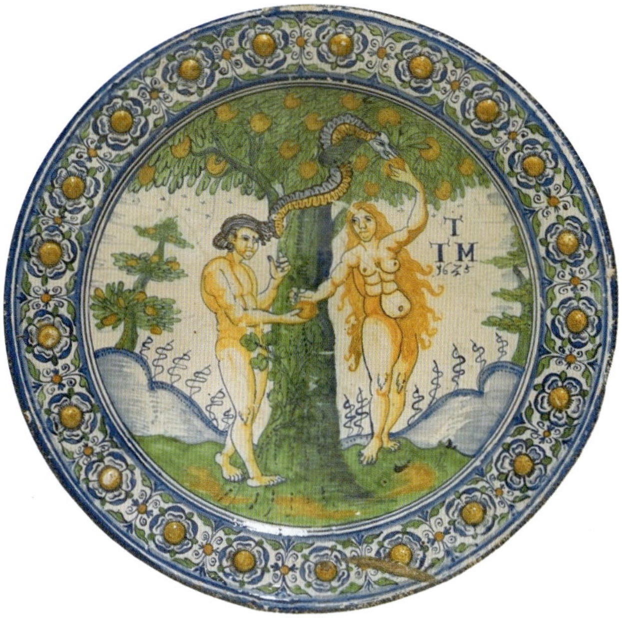

139 Adam and Eve, tin-glazed earthenware charger, dated 1635. Victoria and Albert Museum, London

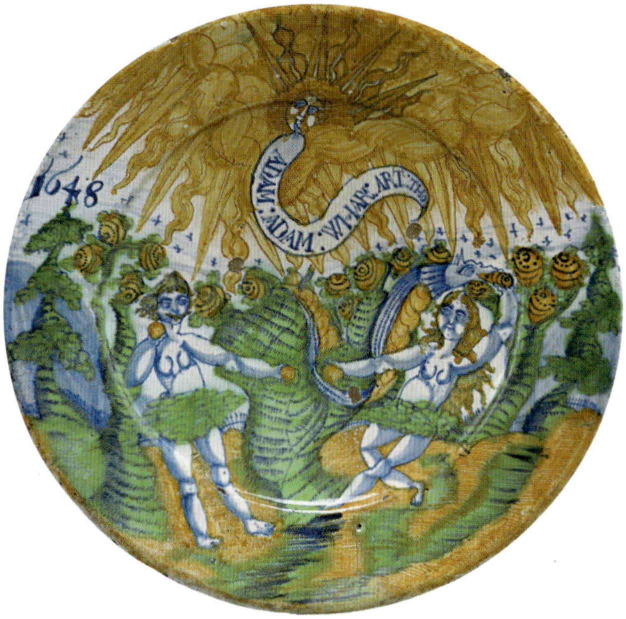

140 Adam and Eve, tin-glazed earthenware charger, dated 1648. British Museum, London

areas of the country so that there was a decline in the novelty, rarity and cost of these objects. Less sophisticated versions of the Adam and Eve design as depicted on the 1635 charger were churned out throughout the seventeenth and eighteenth centuries so that most collections of decorative art in the country possess an example of this type.[171]

A smaller and cheaper plate is dated 1648, with a free and lively depiction of Adam and Eve's fall from grace (Fig. 140). The avoidance of images of God the Father as an old and bearded man in Protestant art is here manifest through the substitution of a flaming sun bearing facial features. An inscription issuing from the mouth of God/the sun on the plate reads 'ADAM: ADAM: WHARE: ART THO[U]'. Using the image of the sun as an alternative way of depicting God may have been suggested by Psalm 84.11: 'For the Lord God is the sun and shield'. The spirited portrayal of the subject means that the exuberant figures of Adam and Eve seem far from repentant, although this is the effect of naive painting and cannot be intended.

While images of Adam and Eve predominate, a broad range of other religious scenes were depicted in English delftware chargers. Extant examples of Old Testament scenes include Jacob's Ladder, dated 1660 (British Museum) and the Sacrifice of Isaac, dated 16[55] in the Victoria and Albert Museum.[172] A charger in the National Museums Liverpool (M1874), painted with a scene of the Feast of the Prodigal and dated 1657, alludes to the functional associations of the object and when displayed on a sideboard in the dining room would have mirrored the activities taking place in the room. New Testament scenes as the subject for chargers include a scene of the Nativity, dated 1652, and a rather enig-

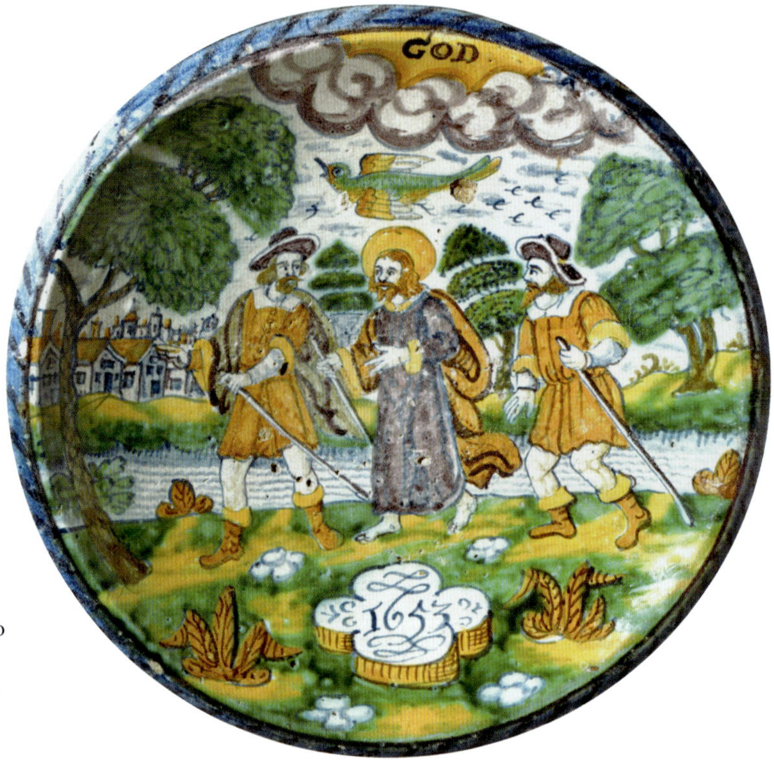

141 Christ on the Road to Emmaus, tin-glazed earthenware charger, dated 1653. Victoria and Albert Museum, London

matic illustration of Salome on her way to the sepulchre, dated 1637. The precise subject of this plate was identified only through comparison with the printed source for the illustration.[173] It seems that the charger was occasioned by the marriage of John Clarke, a Merchant Taylor and citizen of London, and Ann Pierce, who married in 1637.[174] While this might seem an unusual, and morbid, choice of subject to commemorate a marriage, the image – which evokes the entombment and Resurrection of Christ – must have carried profound spiritual meanings for a Christian audience.

Another New Testament episode is depicted in a plate dated 1653, with a scene of Christ on the Road to Emmaus (Fig. 141).[175] This charger is of particular interest because it offers a Protestant revision of the traditional image of the Godhead. The ancient iconography of the Trinity was condemned by Reformers because it included the forbidden image of God the Father in human form and the Holy Spirit in the form of a dove, which was criticised as unscriptural. While images of Christ in his humanity were considered tolerable, the story of Christ accompanying his disciples on the road to Emmaus was potentially problematic to represent in Protestant art because it took place after the Resurrection, when Christ was no longer human. This charger therefore alludes to the presence of the Godhead on the road to Emmaus. That this is an image of the risen Christ is suggested by the presence of a halo. Hovering above the figure of Christ is the dove of the Holy Spirit, although it is represented in such an equivocal manner (and painted green) that it could simply be any bird, perhaps a duck, flying overhead. Within a cloud in the sky above is written the word 'GOD'. The adaptation of traditional iconography as depicted on this charger demonstrates that there was still a demand for spiritually potent imagery almost a century after the Protestant faith had been officially established in Britain. However, the sensitivities surrounding certain types of image, especially images of the Godhead, resulted in the studious modification of pictorial content to expunge or circumscribe prohibited and controversial elements.

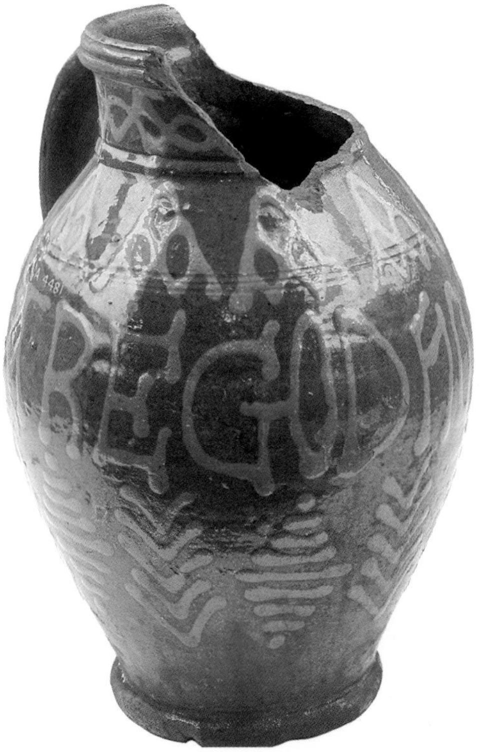

142 Metropolitan-ware earthenware jug with slip-trailed decoration, undated but c. 1650

More utilitarian pieces of pottery might also exhibit the piety of the owner. A group of earthenware items of seventeenth-century date thought to have been made in Essex but known as 'metropolitan ware' often includes slip-trailed inscriptions. The message on one single-handled cup simply commands 'FEARE GOD 1630'. This sentiment is expanded to 'BE NOT HY MINDED BUT FEARE GOD 1638' on a jug. A more lengthy inscription on another jug reads 'FAST AND PRAY/AND PITTY THE POOR AMEND THY/LIFE AND SENNE NO MOR 1656', which is similar to one of the mottos included in the Pittleworth Manor wall paintings of 1580. An undated jug simply states 'FEARE GOD HONOR GOD' (Fig. 142). The presence of this jug, and similar ware, on the dining table of Protestant houses served as a reminder of the need to show due respect and honour to the ultimate authority during periods of relative relaxation. Other objects could offer more profound food for thought: a metropolitan-ware chamber pot dated 1656 is inscribed 'EART I AM ET TES MOST TRU DES DA/N ME NOT FOR SO EAR YOU', while an undated jug of about 1650 bears the more abbreviated 'FOR EARTH I AM'. In this way a connection is made between the material from which the object is made and pious thinking in the *memento mori* tradition.[176]

Textiles

In early modern interiors the most striking decorative feature must have been the abundant textile hangings and coverings. William Harrison's *Description of England* first published in 1577 describes how 'the walls of our houses on the inner sides in like sort be either hanged with tapestry, arras work, or painted cloths, wherein either divers histories, or herbs, beasts, knots, and suchlike are stained . . . whereby the rooms are not a little com-

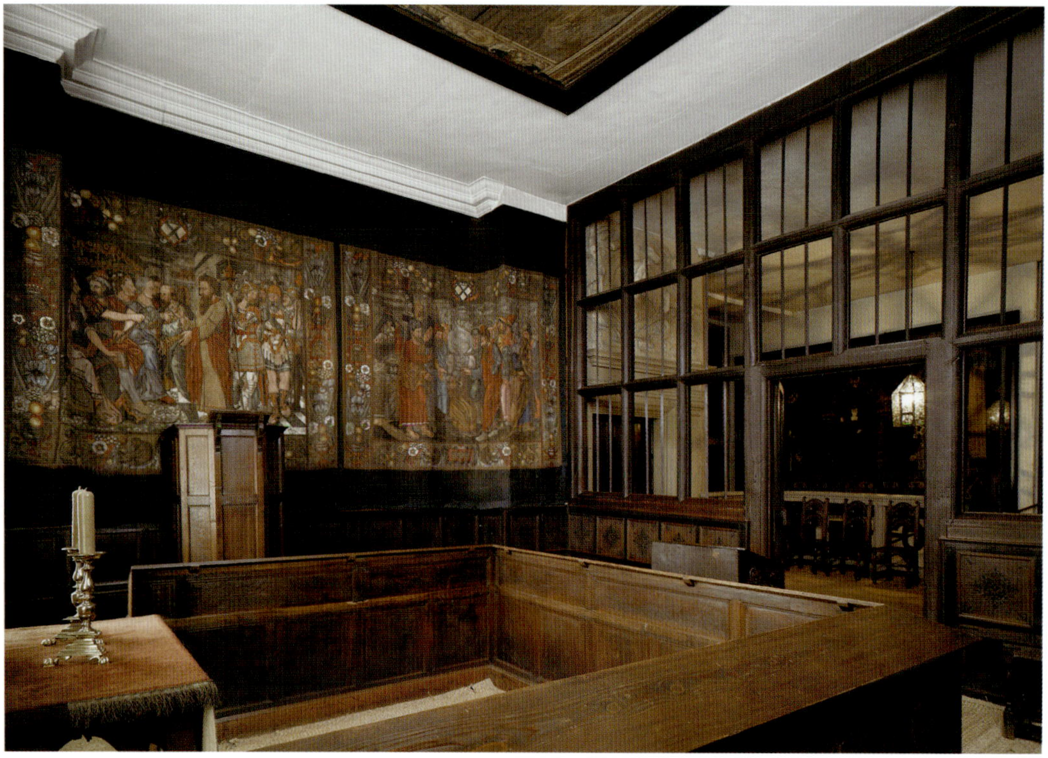

143 Two of the set of painted cloths depicting the story of St Paul, c. 1600–01, now displayed in the chapel at Hardwick Hall, Derbyshire

mended, made warm, and much more close than otherwise they would be.'[177] Harrison's comment suggests the practical appeal of such hangings as insulation against the British climate and perhaps explains the ubiquity of this form of furnishing. While woven tapestries were generally restricted to houses belonging to the wealthy, references to painted cloths in literature of the period indicate that such hangings were common even in relatively modest dwellings. These textiles were painted in bright colours and sometimes included large-scale figurative and narrative decoration. Although the designs on painted cloths resembled the patterns and subjects found in tapestry, the art form is more closely related to wall painting than weaving. Both were carried out by members of the Company of Painter-Stainers and, unlike tapestry, were relatively affordable.[178]

The type of subject matter painted on cloths is indicated by references in the plays of Shakespeare. There are allusions in several to the 'wise' or witty sentences in painted cloths.[179] In *Henry IV Part I* Act 4 Scene 2, lines 23–31, Falstaff refers to the type of imagery that must have been relatively common:

> my whole charge consists of ensigns, corporals, lieutenants, gentlemen of companies – slaves as ragged as Lazarus in the painted cloth, where the glutton's dogs licked his sores – and such as indeed were never soldiers, but discarded unjust servingmen,

> younger sons to younger brothers, revolted tapsters, and ostlers trade-fallen, the cankers of a calm world and a long peace, ten times more dishonourable-ragged than an old feazed ensign . . .

This cloth's image of dogs licking the sores of poor Lazarus recalls the Pittleworth Manor wall paintings of 1580, described earlier in this chapter.

Hardly any of these once common painted hangings have survived to the present day, due to the thin and perishable nature of the linen. A set of four hangings depicting scenes from the life of St Paul probably created in 1600 for Bess of Hardwick and still on display at Hardwick Hall in Derbyshire represents the highest quality that could be achieved in the art of the painted cloth (Fig. 143).[180] The type of painted cloths on display in lesser houses throughout the period is represented by a rare survival of a scheme of late seventeenth-century painted cloths at Owlpen Manor in Gloucestershire.[181] Their lively and brightly coloured scenes depict Joseph and his brothers. Although a century later in date, these cloths recall the wall paintings of the same subject from 5 Widemarsh Street in Hereford (see Fig. 103), illustrating the strength of tradition in the choice of subject matter. Bridging the gap in this date span are mid-seventeenth-century wall paintings with scenes from the life of Joseph at a house in Hadleigh, Suffolk.[182] Another set of late seventeenth-century painted cloths in the Shakespeare Birthplace Trust possibly depict the story of Isaac and Rebecca. They include a scene of figures at a well, which could be the meeting of Eliezer (Isaac's servant) and Rebecca (Fig. 144). The significance of this story for a contemporary audience may well have been its allusions to a felicitous marriage.

High-quality Flemish tapestry was found only in the houses of the elite, although second-hand tapestries made their way into the houses of the middle classes. In the later part of the sixteenth century, a certain amount of tapestry was produced by native weavers. A group of tapestry-ware items of English manufacture has long been associated with the so-called 'Sheldon workshop' established at Bordesley in Worcestershire and Barcheston in Warwickshire in about 1561 by a local gentleman-entrepreneur called William Sheldon. The attribution of this large body of work to a single workshop has recently been disputed in a convincing reassessment by Hilary L. Turner and the status and extent of the Sheldon enterprise is now called into doubt.[183] Given the uneven nature of the material, including work of widely differing competence in styles and sizes, it seems much more likely, as Turner suggests, that many of the tapestry-ware objects long associated with the Sheldon workshop were produced in London by émigré Flemish weavers. Native tapestry production made these luxury objects more accessible and available to an expanded clientele but these English-made tapestries were still expensive and larger pieces were made to order, so that the initials of the patron might be included within the design.

A set of four tapestries depicting the story of Judah and Tamar, illustrating Genesis 38 were created in 1595 for Walter Jones of Chastleton House in Oxfordshire. The second in the series, depicting Judah giving the seal, cord and staff to Tamar at Timnath, is currently on display at Aston Hall (Fig. 145). This morally ambiguous story seems an unusual

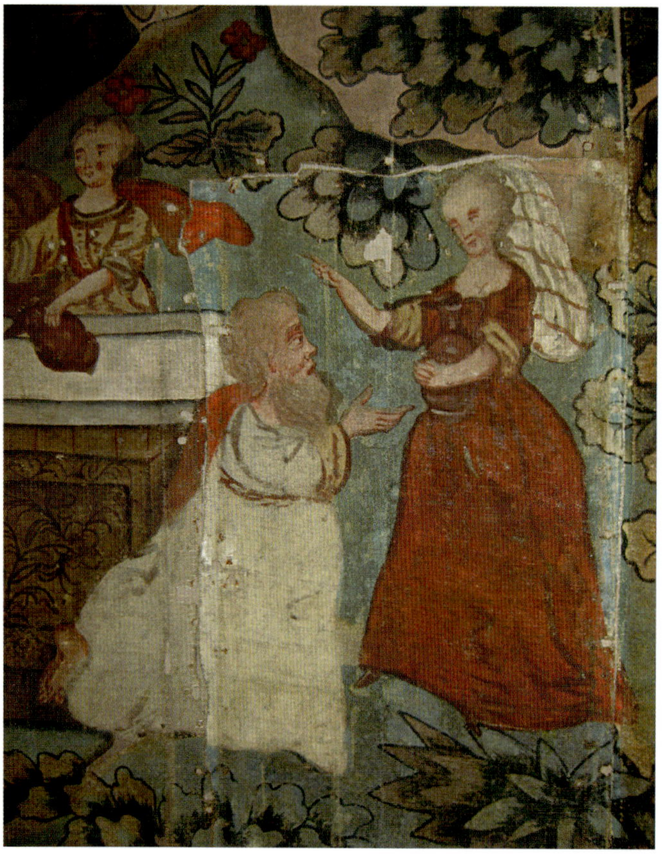

144 (?)Eliezer and Rebecca at the well, detail of a set of painted cloths possibly depicting the marriage of Rebecca and Isaac, late seventeenth century

choice of subject. When two of Judah's sons were struck down dead after failing to fulfil their conjugal obligations to Tamar, Judah was obliged to marry his third son to Tamar so that she could have a child of Judah's line. Fearing for his son, Judah delayed the nuptials. Thus wronged, Tamar disguised herself as a harlot to trick Judah into intercourse. Judah paid Tamar with a signet-seal, cord and staff and she fell pregnant. When Judah discovered the pregnancy, unaware that he was responsible, he denounced Tamar for harlotry and condemned her to death. She sent him the signet-seal, cord and staff to prove his culpability and, realising his fault, Judah repaired the injustice by marrying Tamar himself. All four tapestries in the Judah and Tamar series include the initials WJ and EJ for Walter Jones and his wife Elinor and it seems likely that the significance of this subject lay in its allusions to marital obligations and honour, as well as procreation and inheritance (the last in the series depicts the birth of Tamar and Judah's twins). Since the theme of Judah and Tamar is rare in the decorative arts of early modern Britain it suggests a particular interest in the story. Early modern rituals of courtship often involved the exchange of gifts as 'proofs' of commitment between couples.[184] Details of these gifts or tokens could be presented in legal proceedings as evidence of an intention to wed. In this story, the evidence of the material goods exchanged between Judah and Tamar prior

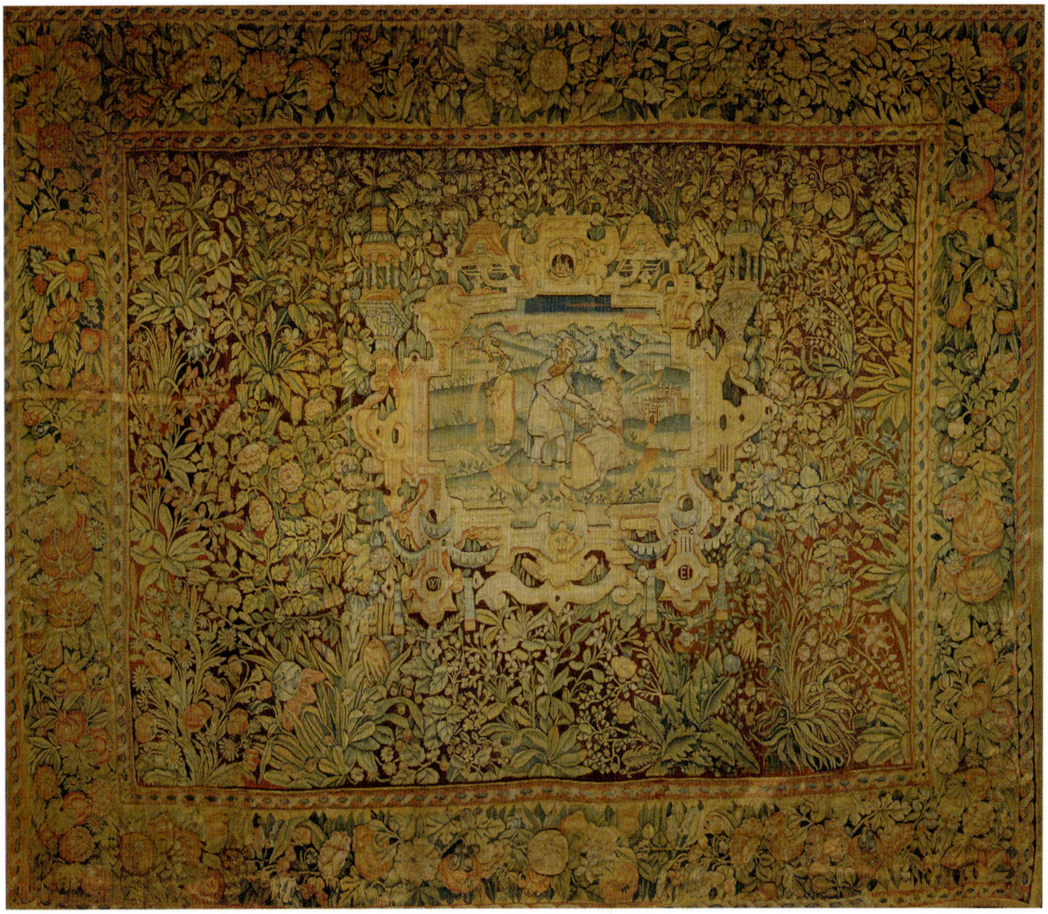

145 Judah and Tamar, one of a set of English tapestries, dated 1595, with the initials of Walter Jones from Chastleton, Oxfordshire

to intercourse proves and seals their alliance. This therefore seems a suitable subject for depiction in a set of tapestries that served, through the initials of the couple, to commemorate the union through marriage of Walter and Elinor Jones.

Tapestry cushion covers were more affordable than large hangings. These could be bought as individual pieces or, more usually, as a series of cushions depicting a specific story. It seems that cushion covers formed the greater part of the output of the native tapestry workshops.[185] Two types of cushion cover were produced: 'short' cushion covers, for use on un-upholstered chairs or stools, usually depict a single scene in the centre; 'long' cushion covers, for benches, often incorporate three pictorial subjects, typically divided by columns as if the scenes are viewed through a colonnade. To judge from extant examples, religious subject matter seems to have been fairly common as decoration for tapestry cushions and a set of cushions could provide a whole narrative with each cushion depicting a single episode. Short cushion covers depicting episodes from the story of

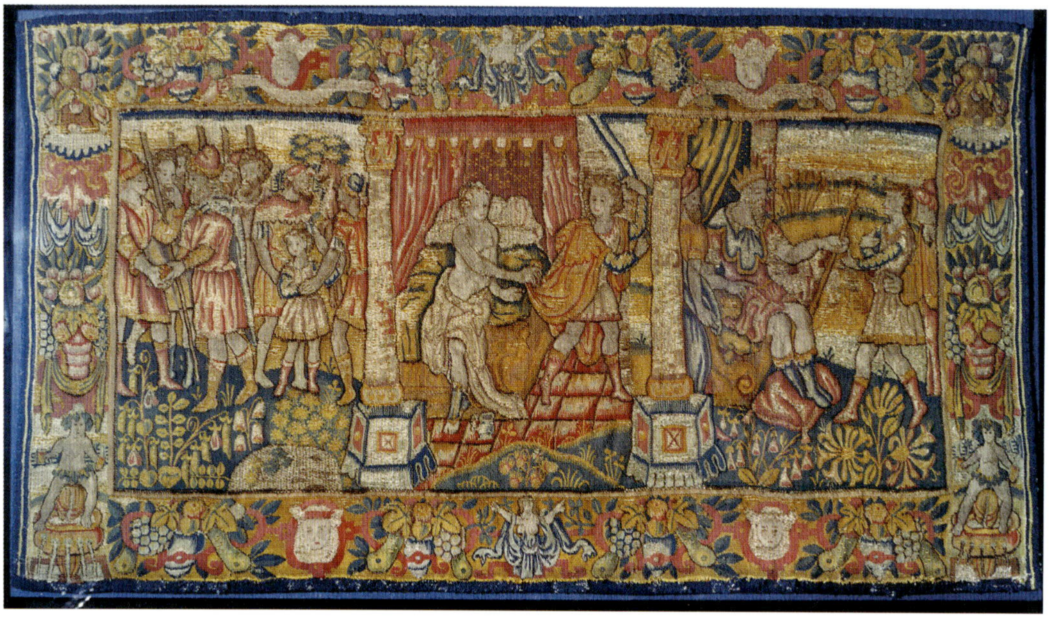

146 Scenes from the story of Joseph, long cushion cover, English manufacture, late sixteenth century. Shakespeare Birthplace Trust

Susannah and the Elders (in the Shakespeare Birthplace Trust) and the Prodigal Son (Victoria and Albert Museum) suggest that stories from the Apocrypha and parables were popular.[186] A tapestry panel for a long cushion cover depicts three scenes from the Old Testament story of Joseph (Fig. 146). This dates from the last quarter of the sixteenth century and includes depictions of Joseph sold into captivity (left), Joseph and Potiphar's wife (centre) and Joseph before Pharaoh (right).[187] Additional short cushion covers might once have extended the narrative.

It is clear that there was also a demand for New Testament subject matter in tapestry cushions. Narrative sequences depicting scenes from the life of Christ appear on at least two sets of English tapestry cushion covers, both dating from around 1600. One set long identified as a 'Sheldon' product depicts four scenes from the early life of Christ; a long cushion cover now in the Metropolitan Museum in New York depicts the Annunciation, Nativity and Adoration of the Magi.[188] An associated short cushion cover adds the Flight into Egypt (Fig. 147). Both items include the initials of the patron and his wife, creating an association between holy imagery and patron reminiscent of portraits of donors in medieval altarpieces. Another two sections of embroidered work dating from the late sixteenth century are probably the remains of a once extensive set of cushions depicting the Passion of Christ. The two extant sections depict the placing of the crown of thorns on Christ's head and the Crucifixion (Fig. 148).[189] These contain a textual inscription of the scriptural reference for the subject in the top left-hand corner. Apart from this concession to the Protestant emphasis on scriptural fidelity, the iconography is traditional. The

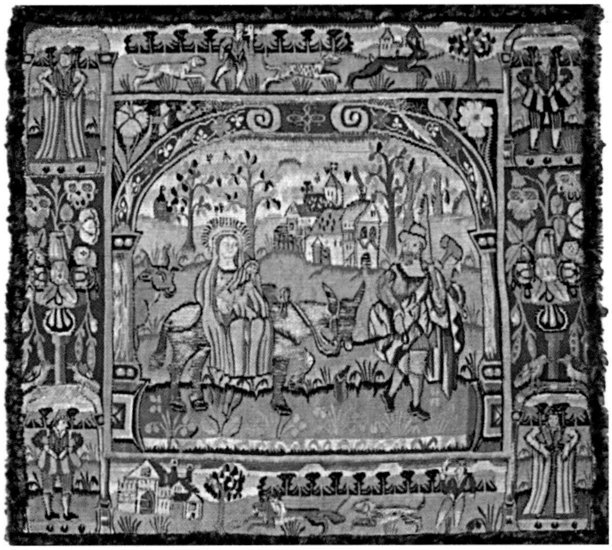

147 The Flight into Egypt, short cushion cover, English manufacture, c. 1600–15. Victoria and Albert Museum, London

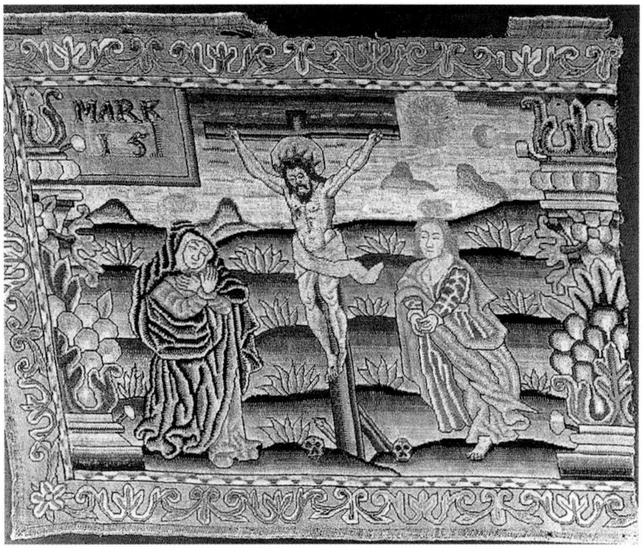

148 The Crucifixion, embroidered cushion cover [?], English manufacture, late sixteenth century. Victoria and Albert Museum, London

scene of Christ on the Cross includes the traditional attendant figures of Mary and John. There is a question surrounding how such cushions might actually have been used. What did it mean to sit on or prop the body against an image of Christ? It is perhaps an unanswerable question and it seems likely, though this can only be conjecture, that these pieces were carefully stored and only displayed on occasion lest the physical treatment of the object suggested any disrespect for the spiritual nature of the subject matter.

As with other decorated objects, cushions were not scattered through the house but displayed in specific locations. Probate inventories show that decorated cushions were displayed in the largest, public rooms and were often positioned in the seating areas created by window bays. The inventory of goods at Hardwick Hall in 1601 is particularly revealing in recording the precise location of objects within rooms, including that cushions with figurative imagery were often displayed in the window seats of the grandest rooms. In the Best Bed Chamber, 'too [sic] nedleworke quitions for the windowes', while in the long gallery the inventory lists 'nyntene long quitions whereof one for the Chare [sic] the rest for the windowes'.[190] Among these nineteen long cushions displayed in the window bays of the gallery was the pair of embroideries depicting the Sacrifice of Isaac and the Judgement of Solomon.[191] However, there may have been some concerns about the propriety of conspicuous display of cushions, as luxurious agents of comfort. In Ben Jonson's play *Poetaster*, first published in 1602, one of Albius's fussy directions to his wife Chloe in preparing their house to receive the court concerns the distribution of cushions: 'Heare me but one thing; let not your maides set Cushions in the Parlor windowes; nor in the dining Chamber windowes; nor upon stooles, in either of them in any case; for tis Taverne like; but lay them one upon the other, in some out Roome, or corner of the dining Chamber.'[192] The reference to cushions disposed around the room being 'tavern-like' suggests that an appearance of too much comfort or furnishings was equated with vulgarity. Cushions could be stacked discreetly away out of sight or in the corner to be deployed when needed.

An alternative to professionally produced woven cushion covers was embroidered ware.[193] While there was a professional trade in embroidery, much of the surviving work was produced by amateurs within the home. All ladies of status were trained in the art of embroidery from a young age. Embroidered linen was not only used as a covering for furnishings like cushions but also to decorate devotional books such as Bibles and prayer books. Towards the end of the period, in the mid-seventeenth century, it became usual to create embroidered pictures as independent works of art. The resulting objects or pictures were given as gifts and/or displayed within the home.

To practise embroidery filled long hours of confinement within the home and was considered to be beneficial in preventing idleness. Among the godly the studious working of religious imagery in embroidery could contribute to religious instruction and contemplation. Lady Margaret Hoby mentioned spending time working at embroidery in her diary of spiritual activities, which suggests that this was how she perceived the nature of this pursuit. Indeed, the process and experience of creating this art was perhaps more significant than its eventual display in the home. Lady Dorothy Davenport spent twenty-six years creating embroidered coverings for the headboard and tester of her bed, with scenes from the story of Adam and Eve and devotional texts. The result, completed in 1636, is on display at Capesthorne Hall in Cheshire.

A set of four embroidered long cushion covers in the Victoria and Albert Museum are decorated with sixteen scenes from Genesis 1–28, from the Creation of Adam to Jacob's Dream (Fig. 149). This set is a further indication of the particular interest in depicting series of scenes from Genesis, also manifest in the decoration of ceilings in the galleries at Lanhydrock House and Dean House (see Figs 119–21, 124 and 128). In the case of cushion covers, the intimate context for display is analogous to the close and personal engagement required for viewing illustrations in books. Indeed, there are strong similarities between the design and iconography of the embroidered scenes on the cushions and woodcut illustrations in sixteenth-century Bibles. For various reasons, Genesis was the section that was illustrated most liberally in sixteenth-century Bibles. These illustrations must have enhanced the theological significance of the first book of the Pentateuch for a contemporary audience. As these cushions appear to date from the later sixteenth or early seventeenth century, it is surprising to find the controversial image of God the Father as an old man in robe and crown included in many of the embroidered scenes. However, illustrated Bibles with this contested image were circulating in the decades after 1560. Archbishop Parker's official *Bishops' Bible* of 1568 includes a series of woodcuts with similar content to the scenes in the cushion covers, including the image of God in human form. Although this controversial element was expunged from the subsequent, 1572 edition, the earlier version must have remained in circulation[194] and potentially led to some confusion surrounding the permissibility of such iconography.

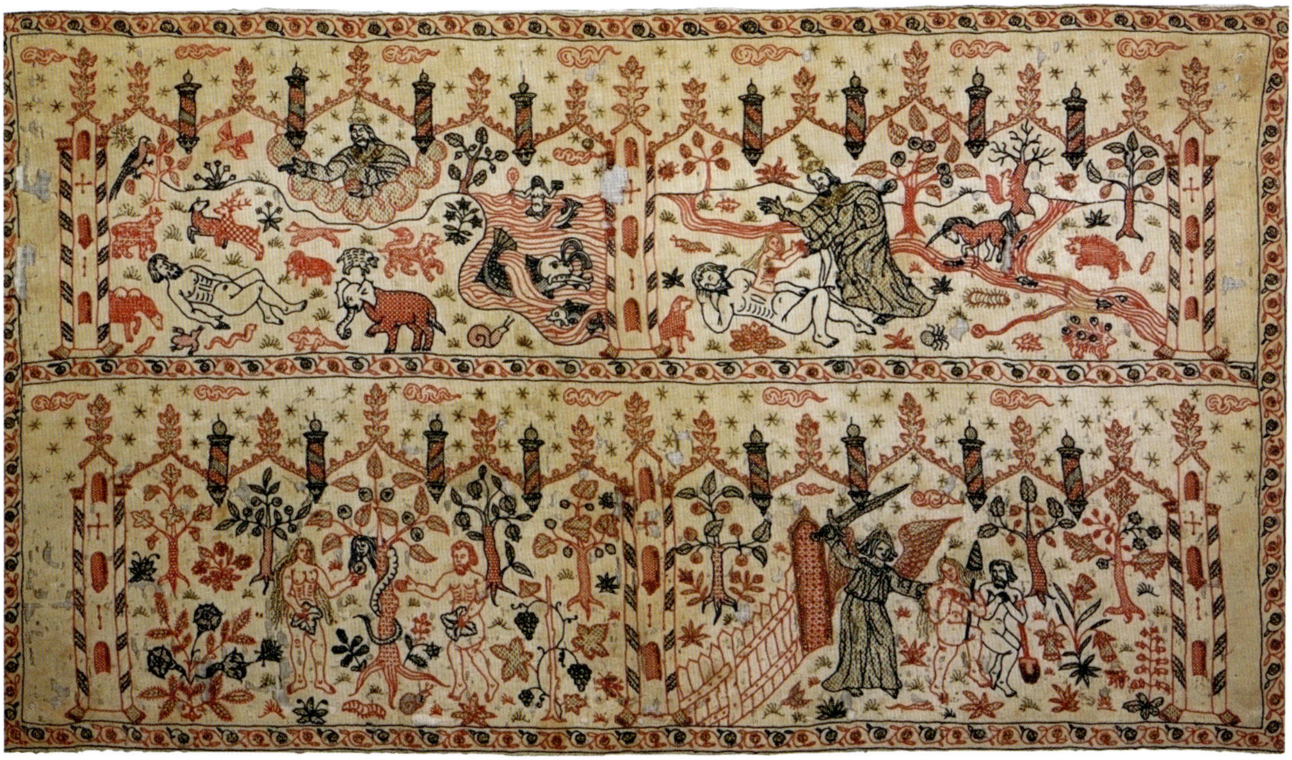

149 Scenes from Genesis, one of a set of four embroidered long cushion covers, early seventeenth century. Victoria and Albert Museum, London

Old Testament scenes predominate in early modern embroidery and certain subjects and themes recur. Considering that this was an art practised by women, and was an essential part of the education of girls, it is unsurprising that the most commonly depicted subject matter represents biblical heroines or subjects pertinent to key rites of passage in a woman's life.[195] The institution of marriage was explored through depictions of Adam and Eve, Solomon and the Queen of Sheba and Esther and Ahasuerus, while the virtue of Chastity in marriage was reinforced by the stories of Susannah and the Elders, Joseph and Potiphar's wife and David and Bathsheba. Motherhood was explored through the finding of Moses and the highly popular Judgement of Solomon. Several examples of this subject can be seen in the collection of needlework at Parham House in Sussex. The theme of parenthood also explains the popularity of images from the story of Abraham and Isaac. This is the subject of a long cushion cover of about 1640–70 featuring two principal episodes: Abraham entertaining the angels announcing the birth of Isaac, and Abraham being prevented from sacrificing Isaac (Fig. 150).[196]

New Testament subject matter was considerably rarer, although the subjects chosen again reveal a predilection for women playing key roles. Two small cushion covers in the Victoria and Albert Museum with scenes of Christ and the woman of Samaria and Mary

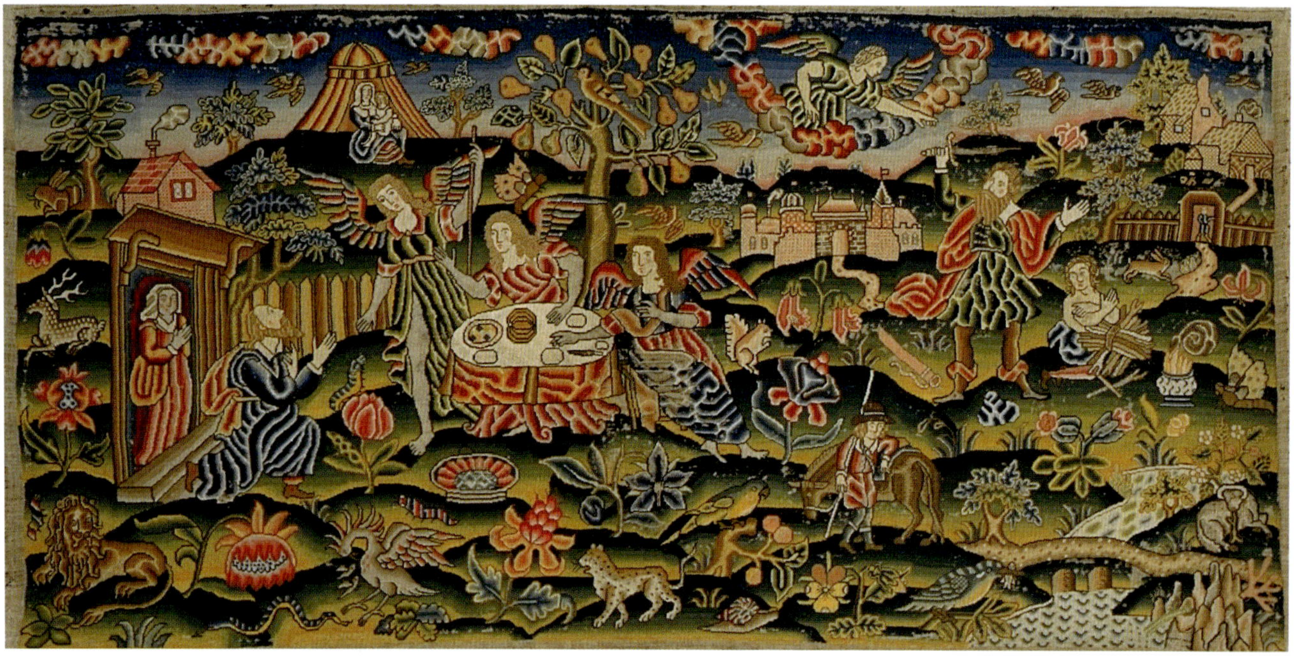

150 Scenes from the story of Abraham and Isaac, embroidered long cushion cover, c. 1640–70. Victoria and Albert Museum, London

Magdalen's meeting with the risen Christ after the Resurrection, provide exemplars of women who recognised the divinity of Christ.[197] The embroiderer was thus encouraged to contemplate Christ's role as Saviour. For pious Protestants, the detailed process of working an image of Christ must have been a moving spiritual experience.

The recurrence of specific subject matter in domestic embroidery illustrates that particular iconography was invested with meanings relating to social conduct, moral values and devotional habits. That certain iconography might also be associated with sectarian and political ideology is illustrated by an embroidery of about 1660–70, worked by Damaris Pearse, the daughter of a Puritan minister. Her raised work picture depicts the drowning of Pharaoh in the Red Sea (Fig. 151).[198] An insight into the personal significance of this subject is provided by a small volume dedicated to Damaris, written by her father following her death at the age of twenty and published in 1683. The book records that Damaris once:

> talked long concerning the Israelite bondage in Egypt, and miraculous deliverance from thence, and their passage thorow the Red Sea, and preservation and supportment in the wilderness, and safe conduct into Canaan: (As she proceeded besides other hints, she made some observation on Aarons making the Molten Calf, both condemning the sin, and likewise, showing how people now living should improve it, that it should teach all to be watchful against sin, not only inferiors, but also those in high place and dignity: Considering what Aaron was, and yet how grievously he sinned.)[199]

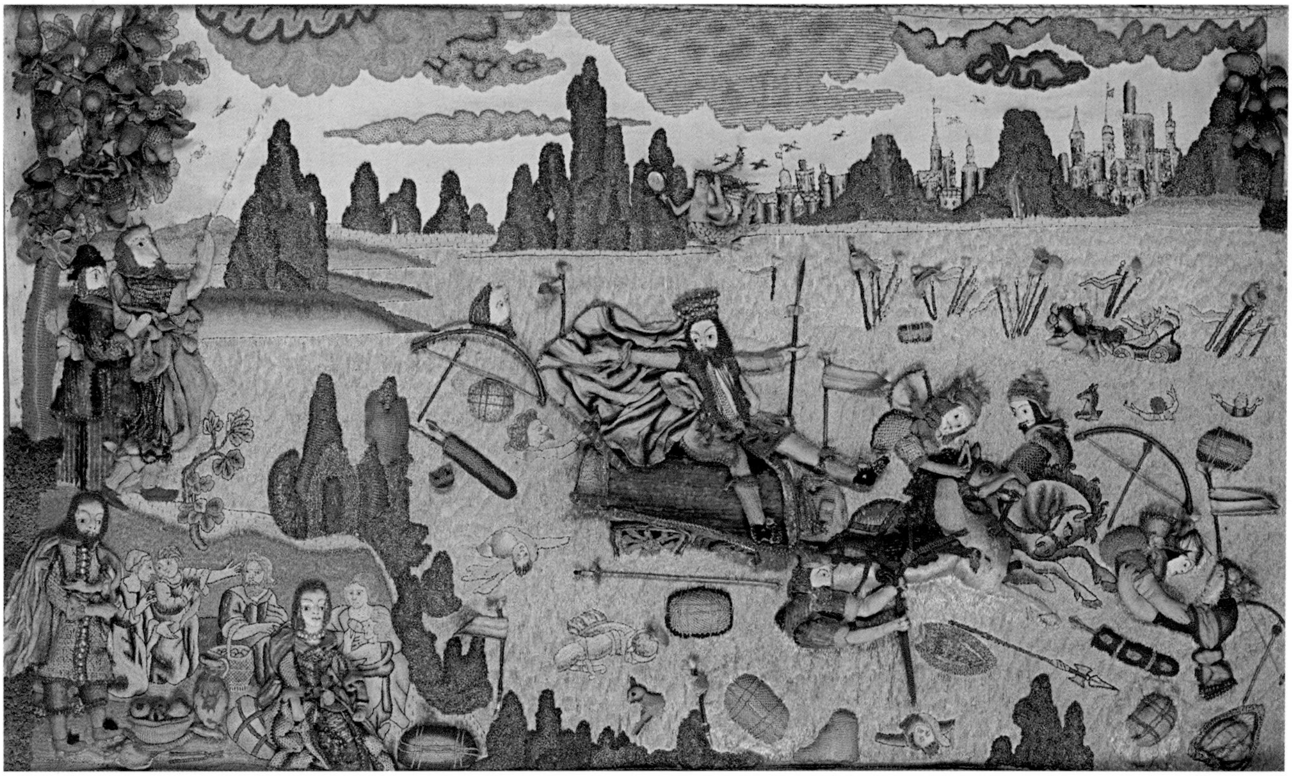

151 The drowning of Pharaoh, embroidered picture of c. 1660–70, worked by Damaris Pearse. Lady Lever Art Gallery

From this, one is given to understand that Damaris, presumably schooled by her father, identified the hardship and subsequent deliverance of the Israelites with the suppression of Puritanism following the Restoration in 1660. Her image of the drowning of the Pharaoh can therefore be understood as a comment on the worldliness and sin of Charles II's court and the righteousness and eventual salvation of members of the true, Puritan, faith.

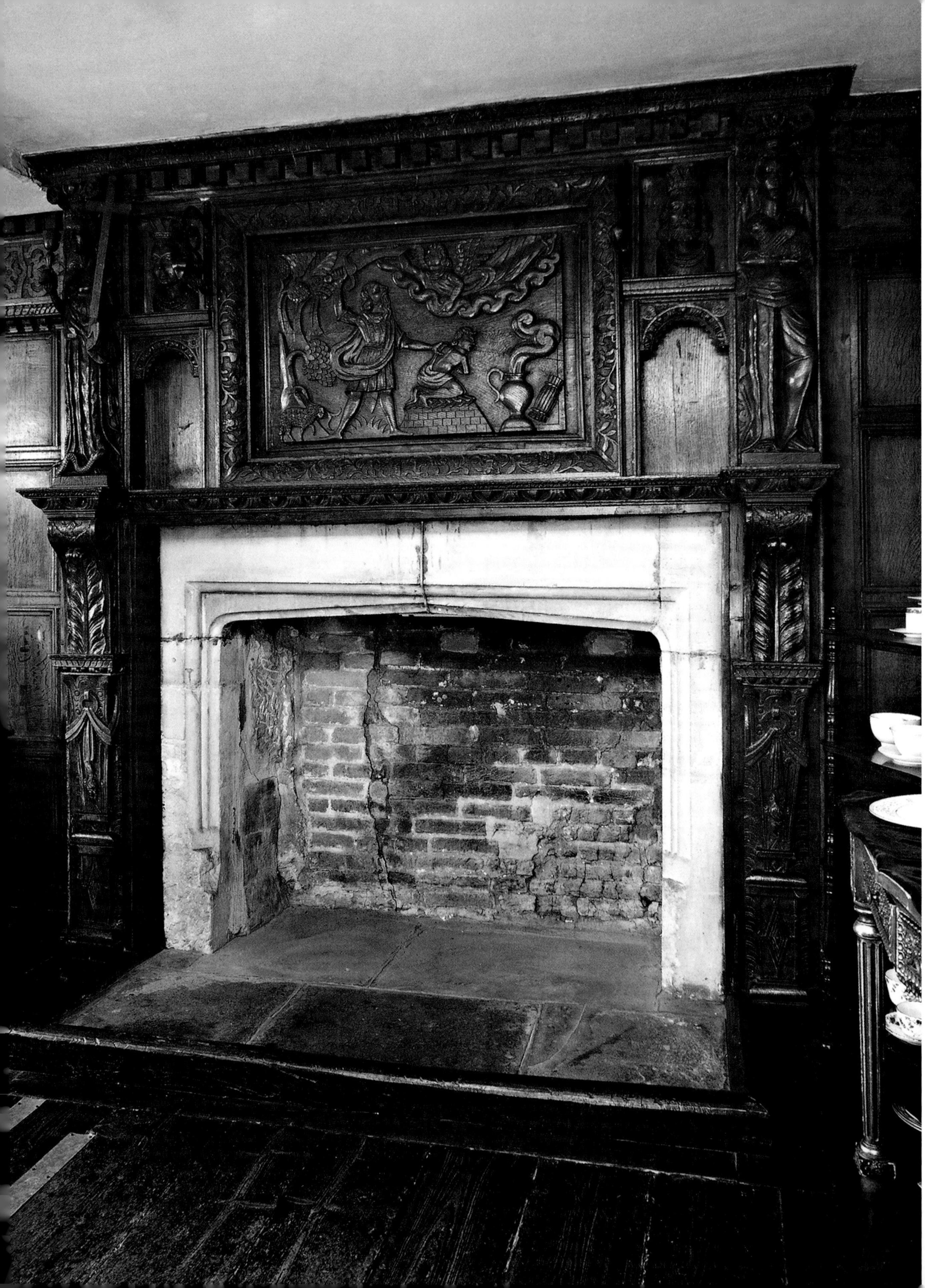

5

Images for Meditation

The previous two chapters have focused on the role of religious imagery in relation to social activities taking place within domestic space, that is, in creating an appropriate setting for collective religious observance and as a form of social control to regulate behaviour during communal gatherings. This chapter considers whether another function of religious imagery in the home was concerned with more private and internalised religious activity, as prompt and guide to the practice of spiritual meditation. As Susan Foister has observed in relation to medieval practice, it is virtually impossible accurately to reconstruct the nature of personal devotion because it 'is an elusive pastime, by its nature hard to document'.[1] It is possible, however, to assess how people were instructed to conduct their own personal devotions, from contemporary literature and the popular guides to Protestant piety circulating at the time. This chapter explores how the location, form and subject matter of decoration around fireplaces suggest that traditional religious imagery had a specific role in the devotional habits of individuals in the home.

In discussing the impact of the Reformation on the visual arts, most scholars have agreed that the Protestant emphasis on the sin of idolatry caused a replacement of objectionable forms of imagery with less objectionable alternatives. Most accept the premise that New Testament imagery on the whole was avoided in favour of 'histories' from the Old Testament and Apocrypha which were used to point a moral. This ongoing process of replacing controversial subject matter with safer alternatives has been described by Tessa Watt and others as a 'ladder of sanctity' which affected drama as well as the visual arts.[2] As Watt explained it: 'In England there were obstacles to the popularisation of the Bible through the direct portrayal of scriptural characters and events . . . Painters and printers continued to cater to the demand for religious figure subjects, but

152 (FACING PAGE) The Sacrifice of Isaac, carved wood chimneypiece at 8 Queen Street, Salisbury

saints were replaced by Old Testament scenes; then by Apocrypha and parables; then by allegorical and classical figures'.[3] While the 'ladder of sanctity' idea is catchy it may be too simplistic to reflect accurately the nature and significance of any process of change. In particular, I want to question the implication that a move from New to Old Testament imagery reflects a distinct shift in emphasis from a spiritual concern with sacred subjects to a secular interest in moral themes. In his 1965 study of interior decoration in Elizabethan and Jacobean England (still used by many as the standard account), Eric Mercer argued that 'iconography and subject-matter had a pronounced ethical and moralising character which determined both the predominance of biblical themes and the marked partiality for a particular selection of them.'[4] Although it is clear that much biblical imagery was chosen and depicted because it offered exemplary models of behaviour, it is not clear if contemporaries would have understood any separation between 'moral' and 'spiritual' meanings. It is equally doubtful whether Old Testament imagery was less spiritually resonant than scenes or characters from the New Testament. Here I shall suggest that the popularity of certain Old Testament scenes in domestic decoration can be explained in relation to their traditional symbolic role as 'types' for episodes from the life of Christ. In this way the process of replacement should be understood as a creative response to a continued desire for visual aids to support traditional spiritual concerns and practices.

THE SIGNIFICANCE OF THE HEARTH

The chimneybreast was one of the more common areas for the application of decoration in the early modern domestic interior in Britain. As has been described, fireplace overmantels in the most important rooms often depicted large-scale narrative and figurative imagery including religious subject matter. Overmantels were crafted in various media, such as carved wood, stone and plasterwork, but painted imagery might also be applied directly to the surface of the chimneybreast. This visual emphasis on the area of the chimneybreast reflects the practical and social significance of the fireplace in early modern architecture.

Chimneys were still a relative novelty in the sixteenth and early seventeenth centuries. In the medieval period most houses had an open hearth in the centre of the main room, used for cooking and heating, and the smoke would escape through an opening in the roof. Only the grandest houses had fireplaces in other rooms. From about 1500 chimneys became more common in response to the increased availability of brick which allowed the creation of chimneystacks and flues. This development marked a revolution in living conditions. The relatively smoke-free fires made possible by enclosed flues encouraged the construction of additional fireplaces in other rooms. This contributed to the elaboration and division of domestic space and the practical and symbolic decline of the central hall. Other rooms could then benefit from smokeless fires, making them warmer and more usable.

It is because chimneys were associated with improved living conditions that they were celebrated as a status symbol. On the exterior of buildings chimneystacks were emphasised as an architectural feature and were often unnecessarily broad to call attention to the expense involved in building them. Early Tudor mansions such as Compton Wynyates in Warwickshire were adorned with numerous over-sized and ornately decorated chimneys in order to proclaim the luxury of a building comprehensively heated by so many enclosed flues. By the 1570s, however, the building of chimneys was no longer the preserve of the rich. William Harrison's much quoted remark about the 'multitude of chimneys lately erected' in his *Description of England* reported the gossip of old men living in Radwinter, Essex, in the 1570s. They remembered:

> in their young days [that is, about 1510–20] there were not above two or three [chimneys], if so many, in most uplandish towns of the realm (the religious houses and manor places of their lords always excepted, and peradventure some great personages), but each one [man] made his fire against a reredos [wooden board] in the hall, where he dined and dressed his meat.[5]

Harrison's account of this dramatic transformation of the built environment is presented as an indication of the prosperity of Elizabethan England. The perceived relationship between the quantity of fireplaces in a house and the wealth and social status of the owner was formalised by the introduction of the Hearth Tax in 1662, which taxed householders a shilling for each hearth in their property.

If the exterior stack and pots of chimneys were embellished as status symbols, so too was the surface of the chimneybreast in the interior. Enhancing the visual impact of the fireplace drew attention to this prized architectural feature. The application of decoration to the chimneybreast also underlined the symbolic significance of the fireplace itself. Anthropologists have long recognised the importance of the hearth in domestic life. The fireplace provides a natural gathering point for individuals and groups seeking warmth and so functions as the symbolic centre of social interaction and as a focal point for domestic rituals. Although the shift away from a communal hearth in the hall to multiple fireplaces in many rooms signalled a change in the nature of social experience within the wider household, the fireplace was still the practical and symbolic centre of each room.

Members of the household must have sat beside the fire in groups or alone, facing and in proximity to the chimneybreast. In Shakespeare's *Taming of the Shrew*, Act 5 Scene 2, Bianca and the widow 'sit conferring by the parlour fire'. In his study of Protestant culture, Patrick Collinson described a social meeting of about ten godly neighbours in the Essex parish of Aythrop Roding on a Sunday in the 1580s: 'After supper, some "attended to one that read in the Booke of Martyrs", and the rest to a minister "in company with them", *who was reading by the fireside* [author's italics] 'a peece of a catechisme . . . which he had then in his hand" '.[6] In such contexts, the fireplace is a centre of attention for long periods of time and it is possible to imagine people looking down into the fire and up at any imagery depicted in the overmantel. It is therefore sensible to speculate that imagery above a fireplace might serve as a site for prolonged viewing, contemplation and possibly discussion.

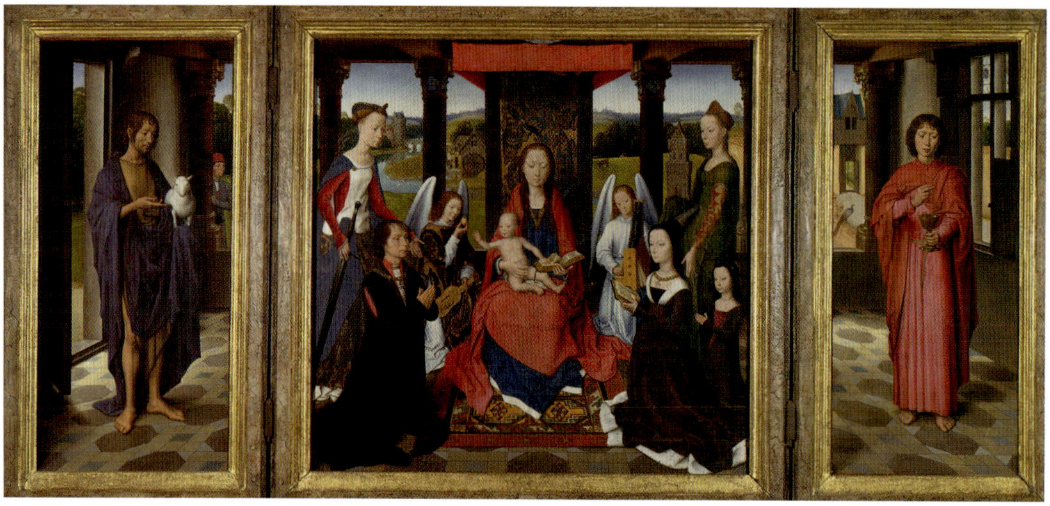

153 Hans Memling, *The Virgin and Child with Saints and Donors* (the Donne Triptych), oil on oak, c. 1478

Turning now to the appearance of decorative imagery above fireplaces, it may be noted that while a range of media was employed – overmantels with religious imagery were crafted in wood, stone and plasterwork while painted imagery was applied direct to the wall surface as well as to wooden panels – the form and appearance of decoration in this location conformed to certain types. The carved wood chimneypiece dating from the 1620s from Woodston Manor near Peterborough is typical.[7] It includes three main panels: a coat of arms at the centre and a biblical scene at each side, on the left the Sacrifice of Isaac and on the right the presentation of the head of John the Baptist to Salome. These panels are interspersed with standing figures of the Four Continents. Such a three-panel arrangement is found in larger overmantels, while smaller chimneypieces often have just one central scene depicting a passage from scripture, with standing figures at either side. An example of the latter is the carved wood chimneypiece dating from about 1620 from the town house at 8 Queen Street in Salisbury, possibly crafted by the local joiner Humphrey Beckham. This has the Sacrifice of Isaac at the centre flanked by female personifications of the virtues of Faith with her cross and chalice and Humility holding a lamb (Fig. 152). A similar chimneypiece but in plasterwork is in the old great chamber of a town house at 18 Fore Street in Taunton, Somerset, where a central scene of the Sacrifice of Isaac is flanked by figures personifying the virtues of Hope and Justice. The supporting figures at the sides of biblical scenes are usually specific Virtues but, as seen in the previous chapter, biblical characters were also depicted in this position.

These compositional arrangements recall the structure and appearance of medieval altarpieces, with panels of narrative imagery interspersed or flanked by figures of saints. For example, the plaster overmantel of about 1635 in a merchant's house in the Butterwalk in

Dartmouth, Devon (see Fig. 107), recalls the format and compositional arrangement of a medieval triptych altarpiece. The large standing figures of Moses and King David resemble attendant saints in the outer panels of an altarpiece, as in Hans Memling's so-called Donne Triptych (c. 1478; Fig. 153). Memling's central panel depicts the Virgin and Child in Majesty, enthroned in heaven and surrounded by a group of figures comprising angels, female saints and portraits of the donor's family. Although the scene depicted in the centre of the plaster overmantel is a different subject (the Descent of the Holy Spirit at Pentecost), this image also includes the Virgin depicted at the centre, surrounded by a group of figures, in this case disciples. The scene of Pentecost was a potent spiritual image and served as the focus of devotion in medieval times. It is, for example, depicted on a small fifteenth-century painted diptych from southern Germany, now in the British Museum.[8] The pictorial composition in this devotional object is virtually identical to the plasterwork version of the seventeenth century.

An allied plaster overmantel removed in the nineteenth century from another seventeenth-century town house in Dartmouth also depicts Pentecost, Moses and David but with four additional scenes arranged round the central subject (Fig. 154). On the left-hand side are two episodes from the Old Testament book of Kings: Elijah bringing the widow's son back to life and Elijah being taken up to heaven in a chariot of fire. On the right-hand side are two scenes depicting New Testament episodes: the Baptism and a scene combining the Resurrection and Ascension. The shape, compositional arrangement and iconography of this extended overmantel are also conventional and recall earlier polyptych altarpieces in paint, but also in alabaster. Carved alabasters were produced in great quantities in medieval Britain and larger altarpieces included numerous episodes from the life of a given saint. Altarpieces with scenes from the life of Christ or the Virgin were especially common.[9] The arrangement of narrative scenes in the larger plaster overmantel may be compared with the so-called Swansea Altarpiece (about 1460–90; Fig. 155).[10] As with the plaster overmantel, the Swansea Altarpiece comprises four narrative scenes arranged either side of a central image, with flanking figures (of saints) at each end. The overall visual impact is markedly similar. There are also similarities in the detail of iconography and composition: the Resurrection in the plaster overmantel is virtually identical to depictions of the subject in numerous devotional alabasters. If one compares the plaster version of about 1635 with another alabaster panel of the late fourteenth century, it is notable that both compositions centre on the figure of Christ rising from the tomb, holding a victory banner in one hand with the other raised (originally in blessing), and figures of sleeping soldiers ranged around the tomb (Figs. 156 and 157).[11] The scene of the Resurrection in the overmantel also refers to the Ascension, with Christ's feet disappearing into a cloud at the top. This imagery too is taken from medieval pictorial convention, as depicted in the Swansea Altarpiece (here the Assumption of the Virgin) and numerous other extant alabasters, including an early fifteenth-century panel re-cased in a wooden frame in the seventeenth century.[12] Such continuity illustrates the enduring strength of tradition in the pictorial content and composition of religious images despite the upheavals of the Reformation.

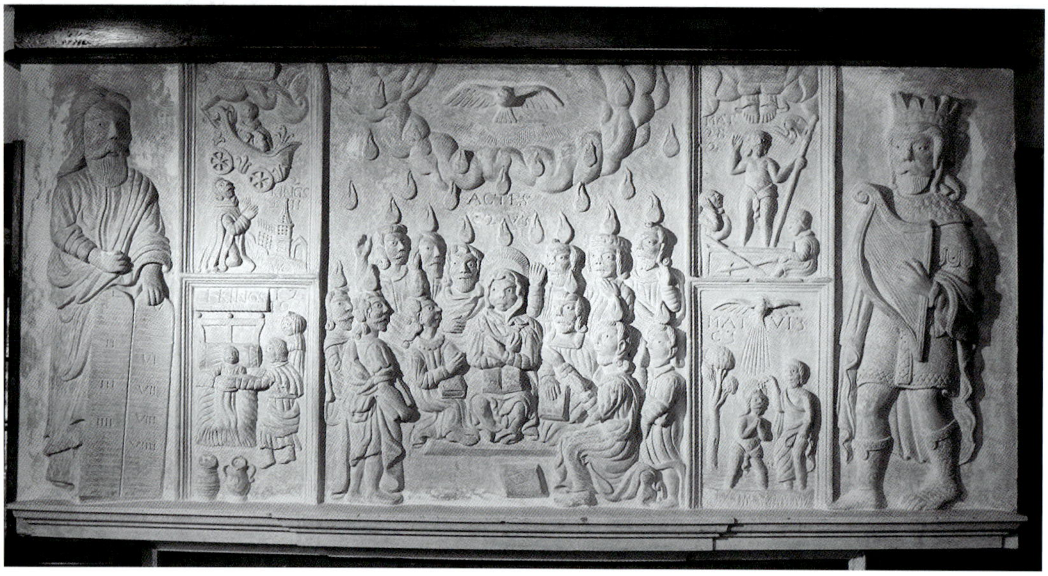

154 Plasterwork overmantel with Old and New Testament scenes, of c. 1635, from a house in Lower Street, Dartmouth, Devon, now in a private collection

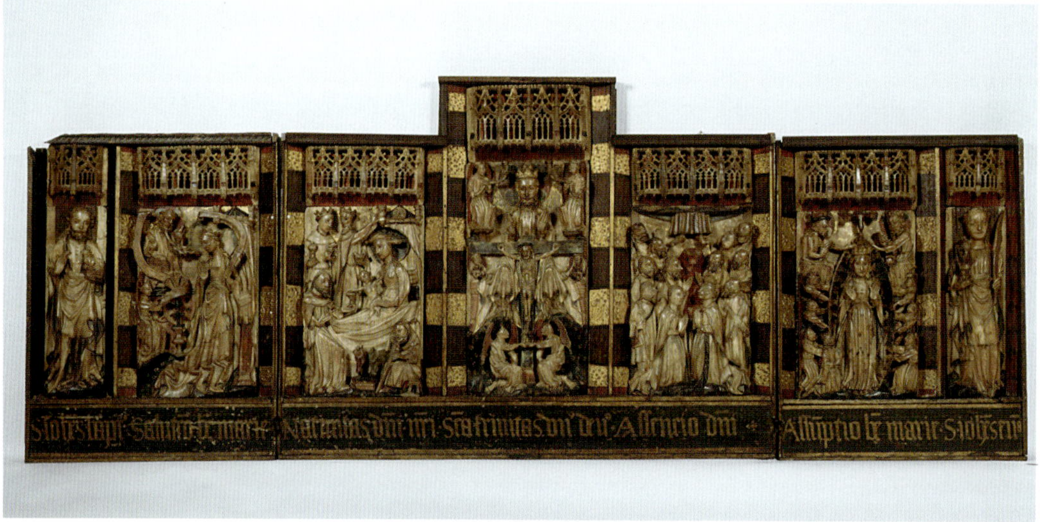

155 The Swansea Altarpiece, carved alabaster, English, c. 1460–90. Victoria and Albert Museum, London

To give yet another example, it is useful to compare the three carved wooden panels formerly in the chapel of a nunnery in Dundee, dating from about 1540, with the carved wood overmantel formerly in the Mansion House in Newcastle, dating from about 1630.[13] The pre-Reformation panels from the devotional context of a nunnery depict the Annunciation, Adoration and Judgement of Solomon (Fig. 158).[14] The seventeenth-cen-

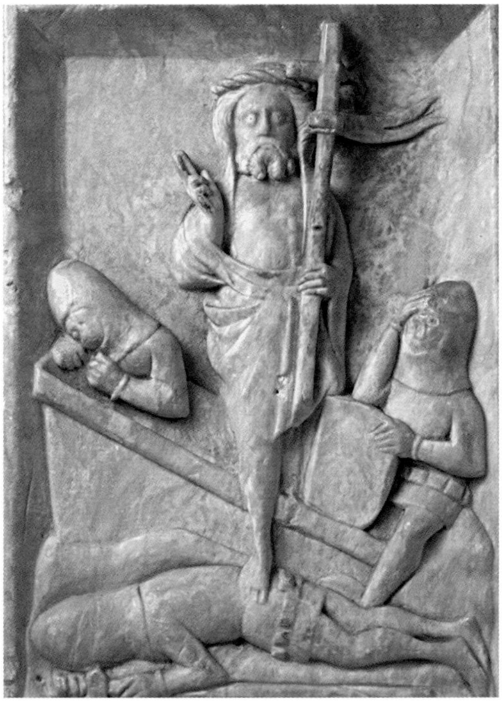

156 The Resurrection, alabaster panel, late fourteenth century. Victoria and Albert Museum, London

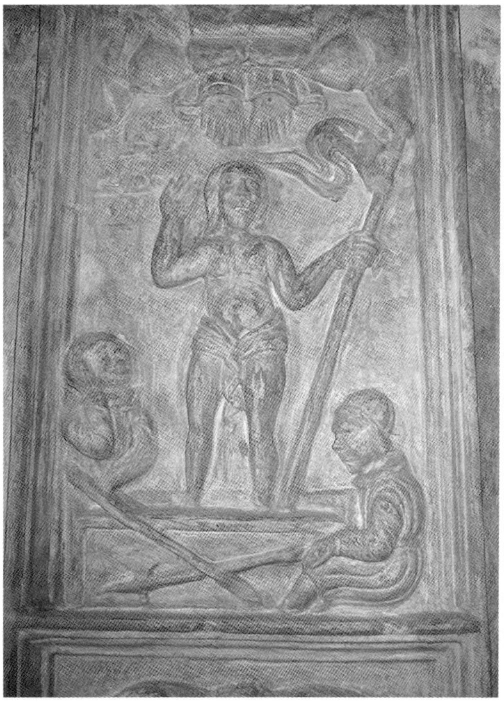

157 The Resurrection, detail from plasterwork overmantel from a house in Lower Street, Dartmouth, Devon, now in a private collection

tury domestic overmantel has much in common with this earlier work. It depicts the Adoration and the Presentation in the Temple. In composition and iconography, the Adoration, with kneeling figures adoring the infant Christ, recalls the earlier work. A significant departure evident in the later panels, however, is the addition of textual inscriptions (in Latin) beneath the scenes to underline the scriptural fidelity of the imagery.[15]

It is now well established that earlier visual forms, including the triptych format, were appropriated and modified for portraiture and royal iconography following the break with Rome in the 1530s. Several authors have noted the similarities between the famous portrait of *The Family of Henry VIII* of about 1545 in the Royal Collection and the triptych arrangement of devotional altarpieces: Henry VIII and his son at the centre take the place of the heavenly family while the two princesses at the sides recall attendant saints. It seems likely that familiarity with the devotional associations of this traditional format would predispose viewers to respond to the portrait of the royal family as an image of majesty, authority and power. Triptychs were also used for the great paintings of family dynasty, most extravagantly represented by Lady Anne Clifford's 'Great Picture' of 1646.[16] Similarly, triptychs continued to be displayed in churches after the Reformation but the form was adapted to Protestant requirements, to exhibit the texts of the Ten Commandments (see Fig. 21) or the Royal Arms.[17]

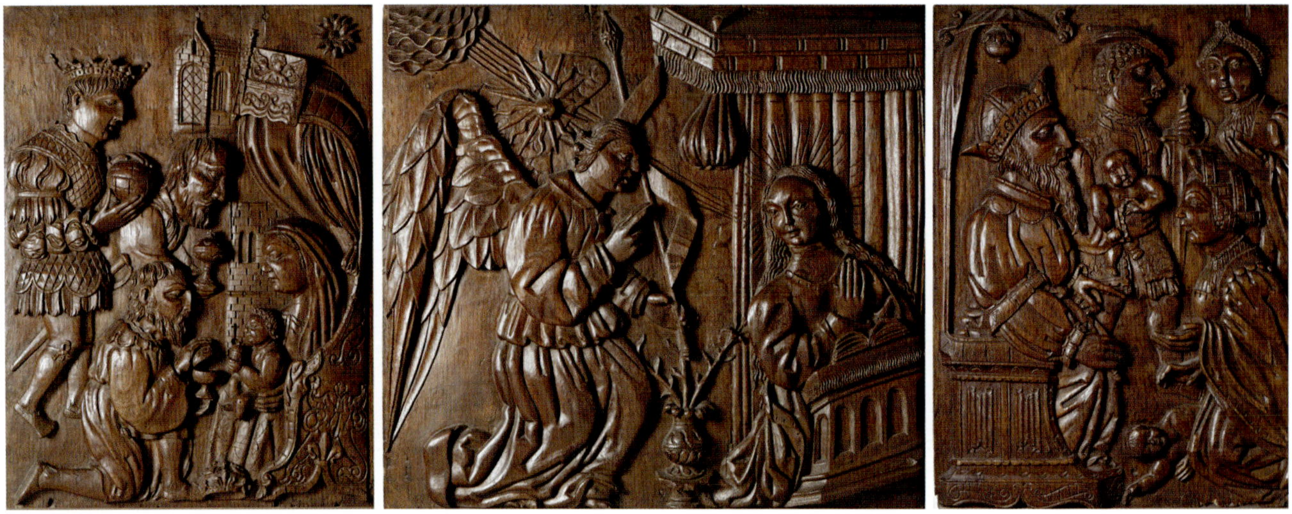

158 The Annunciation, Adoration and Judgement of Solomon, carved wood panels of c. 1540, from the chapel of a nunnery in Dundee

It has not, however, been recognised that this traditional triptych format was also appropriated and employed for religious imagery in post-Reformation domestic decoration. The traditional associations of this format as a focus for devotional activity raise many questions about the function of these overmantels in the context of the reformed domestic interior. Similarities between the general form and iconography of pre-Reformation devotional altarpieces and some post-Reformation fireplace overmantels suggest an allied function, as a focus for devotion. However, it is commonly assumed that religious images had no place in Protestant religious practice. Certainly, religious images and objects for devotional use were condemned by reformers and prohibited by the Elizabethan Injunctions of 1559. As observed in Chapter 1, Injunction 35 stated that 'no persons [shall] keep in their houses any abused images, tables, pictures, paintings and other monuments of feigned miracles, pilgrimages, idolatry, or superstition'.[18] This ordered the removal of 'abused' images from private houses and was probably intended to refer to devotional objects from private chapels and oratories as well as salvaged images from churches. Less clear is the status of religious imagery as the subject of large-scale domestic decoration and in the context of less regulated forms of everyday spiritual practices taking place outside formal worship in church. Is it possible that these overmantels operated in relation to aspects of Protestant devotional activity?

THE PROTESTANT PRACTICE OF MEDITATION

As discussed in previous chapters, the home was the location for day-to-day religious observance. Alongside weekly visits to church and daily prayer meetings, the godly were instructed to pray and meditate continuously, in response to the biblical command to 'pray without ceasing' (1 Thessalonians 5.17). As Ian Green has discussed, a strong meditative tradition never developed in Protestant Britain.[19] The term meditation itself was used loosely by authors of the period and there was no clear consensus on the nature of the relationship between prayer and meditation. It was generally accepted that there were different types and levels of meditation. At a basic level it involved thinking seriously and often about things 'which may tend to your spiritual good and edification' and there was broad agreement among Protestant authors that this practice was desirable and beneficial.[20]

Meditation undertaken by individuals, as with prayer, was defined in two distinct forms: 'ordinary' or 'deliberate' meditation was formal and subject to routine, while 'extraordinary' or 'occasional' meditation was a spontaneous response to particular stimuli or events at points throughout the day, week or year.[21] According to Protestant advice manuals, ordinary meditation should be performed as a solemn and solitary ritual at least twice a day, ideally in the morning and evening. This kind of meditation should include an examination of conscience and pious contemplation of points of scripture as a preparation for formal prayer. For members of the family, this activity would usually take place in intimate and private spaces, such as a closet. As Downame in *A Guide to Godlynesse* observed:

> this private place must be such, as in our experience we find freest from distraction, and fittest to further us in our devotion. In which regard . . . those places are most convenient, wherein there are fewest objects to draw away the senses with unusual delights, seeing they are ready to carry to the imagination, what they observe with pleasure, and that being distracted, withdraweth also the mind and heart from this exercise. And consequently our closet and chamber, or our ordinary and usual walke abroad, where nothing is to be observed but that which is common and often seene, are to be preferred before such places, wherein there is variety of new and pleasing objects.[22]

According to Downame, familiar locations in a domestic setting were especially appropriate for the practice of meditation because there was little risk of distraction; that 'which is common and often seene' was unlikely to capture the imagination and interfere with concentration.

The ideal practice of this kind of solitary, personal devotion is depicted in decorative art at Montacute House in Somerset. Sir Edward Phelips built Montacute in the last years of the sixteenth century with the decoration in the principal reception rooms completed during the first decade of the seventeenth century. In one of the high-status rooms on the first floor, called the 'garden room' in an inventory taken in 1638, is an overmantel modelled in plasterwork with a scene of King David at prayer (Fig. 159). This iconography bears a striking resemblance to a woodcut that appeared in various editions of Thomas Rogers's English translation of Thomas à Kempis's *Of the Imitation of Christ*, first published in 1580.[23] The woodcut – which itself recalls the frontispiece image of Queen Elizabeth at prayer in the 1569 and 1578 editions of the *Christian Prayers* pub-

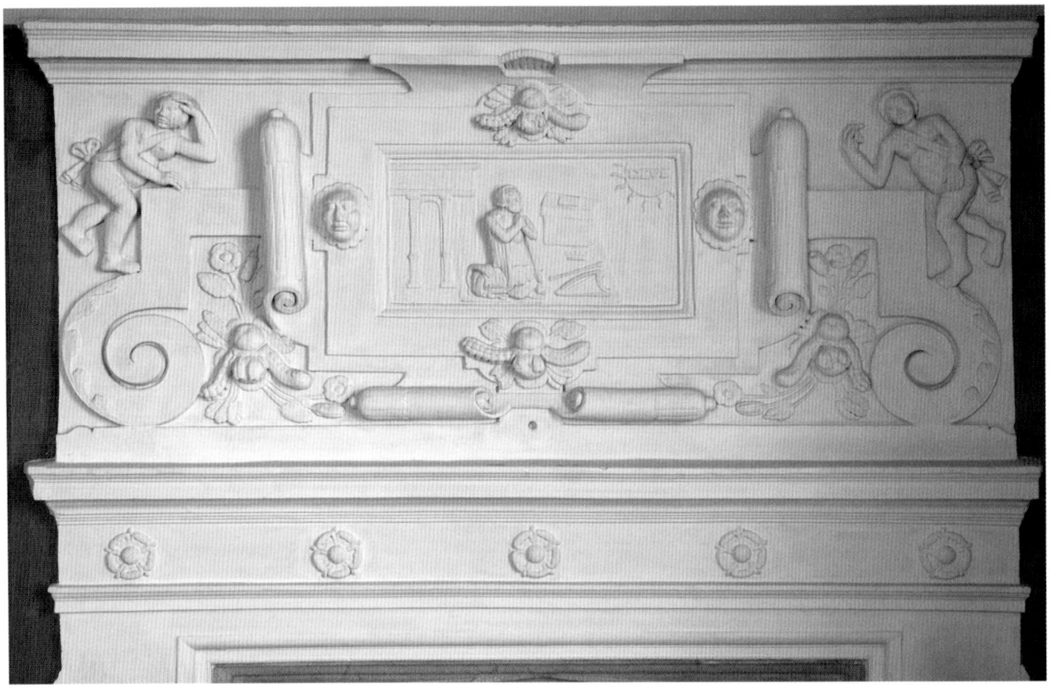

159 King David at prayer, plasterwork overmantel of c. 1610, Montacute House, Somerset

lished by Daye – shows David kneeling with his hands together in prayer (Fig. 160). He looks up to a vision of God (in the form of the Hebrew Tetragrammaton) depicted within a cloud emitting rays of light in the top right of the scene. An open book rests on a table and David's harp is laid down at his feet. In the version at Montacute, the setting has changed: David now appears to be outside the classical-style building on the left. The figure of the kneeling David is, however, close to the woodcut, with his harp on the ground and the open book on a table to his side. While the cloud with the Tetragrammaton is replaced with an image of the sun containing the word 'DEUS', the vision occupies the same position in both versions. Although the slight differences indicate that this particular woodcut was not a direct source for the decoration at Montacute, the similarities between the two underline, once again, that the same stock of imagery was used to decorate the pages of devotional books and the spaces of Protestant houses. Both images communicate an atmosphere of quiet piety: King David provides an exemplar for the practice of private prayer.

Unlike 'ordinary' prayer and meditation, which was planned, subject to a set routine and solitary, 'extraordinary' meditation was a spontaneous activity practised at any time and could be performed in company or while engaged in some practical activity. Downame described this extraordinary sort of meditation as 'sudden, and continuously in use, when any occasion or opportunity is offered and observed, by outward objects presented to our senses, especially the sight and hearing'.[24] Most authors recommended the

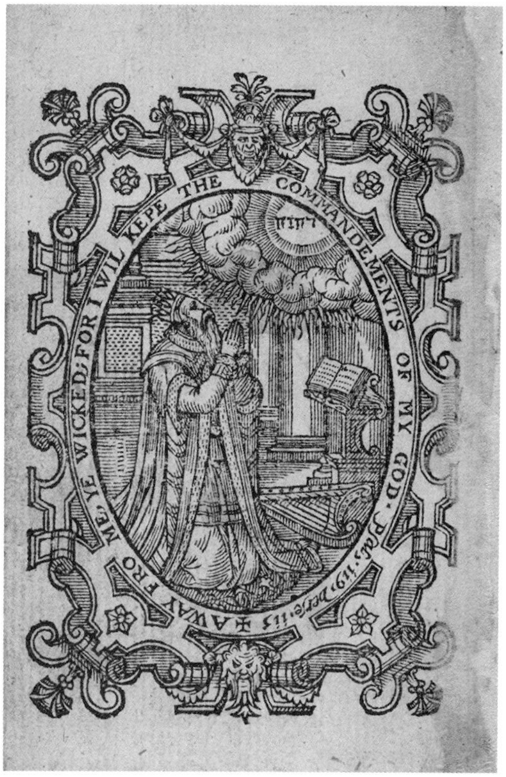

160 King David at prayer, woodcut from Thomas Rogers's translation of Thomas à Kempis's *Of the Imitation of Christ*, 1585 edition

natural world or God's 'creatures' as the most suitable source to prompt this sort of spontaneous meditation, so that the observation of stars, plants and rivers could 'make everie sight a lesson'.[25] In emphasising the role of visual objects in the environment, these Protestant advice manuals left room for the possibility that visual art might also be employed to trigger extraordinary meditation. In his discussion of the Second Commandment published in 1639, Edward Gurnay acknowledged the traditional arguments that images serve to instruct and to act as reminders. He wrote:

> And so, no doubt these Images may occasion good meditations, and serve to put us in mind of things most excellent and divine; even as the sight of a stable or a manger may move us to think upon our Saviour, and the consideration of sinne or Satan may incline us unto devotion and thanksgiving. But that Images are speciall good to give instruction, (which is the question) that we deny.[26]

Several other authors also mentioned crafted artefacts being used as a stimulus to meditation in the context of warning their readers against the use of 'false' images or man-made devices which might corrupt the imagination. Downame was careful to point out that the godly must avoid the use of such matter of meditation as God had expressly forbidden, 'as namely, Images, to put us in mind of him, or any essential part of his worship; seeing they leade us into idolatry, will-worship and superstition and teach us nothing but vanity and lyes, namely to conceive of him as visible and corporall, who is incorporeall and invisible'.[27] Similarly, Joseph Hall offered this warning in relation to extemporal meditation:

> caution is to be had, that our Meditations be not either too farre fetcht, or savoring of Superstition . . . Superstitious, [is] when we make choice of those grounds of Meditation, which are forbidden us as Teachers of Vanitie; or imploy our owne devices (though well grounded) to an use above their reach; making them upon our owne pleasures, not only furtherances, but parts of Gods worship; in both which, our Meditations degenerate, and growe rather perilous to the soule.[28]

Images of God in bodily or visible form were therefore expressly prohibited while Hall's comments indicate that the devices of man, which may be used to further God's worship, must not be used as part of worship. This seems an important, if ambiguous, distinction. It suggests that 'well grounded' devices of man (which might include images) may be used with caution, as long as they do not become abused to a 'use above their reach' – as a focus of worship rather than as a prompt to pious thoughts. It is possible therefore that decorative art was intended at least in part to serve as a reminder or spur to meditate on the subject depicted.

While the practice of extraordinary meditation should make use of whatever sensory prompts occurred in daily life, Protestant authors anchored that of ordinary meditation in the study of God's Word. In discussing the range of approved subject matter for meditation, Downame recommended 'the Scriptures themselves, or else the things revealed in them'.[29] He described in detail two 'abundant matters for meditation' arising from scripture: the nature of sin and punishment and 'our Redemption by Christ', which Downame claimed 'doth above all other parts of Divinity, minister unto us most plentifull and fit matter for our meditations'.[30] In this way, the godly were encouraged to understand and use stories from the Bible to meditate on doctrines or specific propositions of scripture.

It is suggestive therefore that despite the ubiquity of religious imagery in domestic decoration throughout a period of approximately a hundred years from the start of Elizabeth's reign to the Restoration of Charles II, the range of subject matter employed was relatively limited and tended to concentrate on certain key episodes from the Bible. The underlying theological meaning of these recurring episodes falls into two general categories and symbolises either the nature of sin or of salvation.

Despite attempts by reformers to purify the practice of public and private worship by eliminating any dependence on the ritual use of visual and material props, the theological focus providing the substance for personal devotion in Protestant practice remained essentially unchanged from medieval tradition. While there were shifts in doctrinal emphasis, the role of Christ as Saviour remained a focus for personal devotion in Protestant England as it had in late medieval practice.[31] The godly were instructed to meditate on the Incarnation, birth, Passion and Resurrection of Christ as evidence of God's love and forgiveness of sin, and as the means of the operation of election – the salvation of God's chosen people.[32] This emphasis is evident in Protestant devotional texts. Daye's *Booke of Christian Prayers* of 1578 included fourteen prayers on 'the minding of Christes passion'. The first of these prayers evoked traditional Crucifixion imagery: 'What man is this whom I behold all bloudy, with skin all to torn, with knubs and wales of stripes, hanging down his head for weakenes towards his shoulder, crowned with a garland of thornes pricking through his skull to the hard brayne, and nayled to a crosse?' A broadsheet printed in 1630 offered 'A Meditation on the Passion' with texts describing the Crucifixion in gory detail. The text celebrated Christ as 'A living sacrifice our soules to free/from sinne, death, hell, to live eternally', and is arranged in and around the shapes of three crosses.[33] The pictorial arrangement of text in this sheet suggests the persistence of a desire for imagery relating to Christ's sacrifice as a visual focus to assist Protestants in the practice of mediation.

Some post-Reformation decorative overmantels include imagery relating to Christ's Incarnation, birth and sacrifice, as remarked earlier. The Annunciation is depicted in a plasterwork overmantel from a merchant's house in Barnstaple, Devon (now in the Museum of North Devon). The Adoration of the Christ Child formed part of the carved wood overmantel formerly in the Mansion House in Newcastle, as well as the painted overmantel formerly in a house in Uckfield (see Fig. 1). This overmantel also included the Crucifixion in the right-hand panel. As explained earlier, the image of Christ on the Cross was technically permissible according to Protestant image theory because it was an illustration of a historical event described by scripture. Nevertheless, it was generally avoided; it carried associations of idolatry because of its history of use as a focus of worship in the pre-Reformation church. Where scenes of Christ's Passion were included the imagery was treated with some care. Charlton House in Greenwich, built between 1607 and 1612 for Sir Adam Newton, contains a chimneypiece in the 'White Room' which has as its centrepiece a scene of Perseus with the head of Medusa and Pegasus, but the frieze level below includes a depiction of the Triumph of Christ with tiny scenes of Christ carrying the Cross, the Crucifixion and Resurrection (Fig. 161). In this position in the chimneypiece these scenes are best viewed close up, and could serve as the focus of meditation when sitting by the fire, but the iconography is so small and simplified that it seems unlikely that it would worry iconomachs. It is in any case faithful to the historical account as described in scripture and therefore justifiable.[34] The Deposition, as depicted in an overmantel at the Court House in Somerset (see Fig. 53), avoids the depiction of the actual sacrifice but even an image of the Descent from the Cross might provoke criticism, so that the stained-glass panel from a domestic chapel dated 1629 (see Fig. 31) includes an inscription informing the viewer that 'The truth here of is historicall devine and not superstissious'. This suggests a perceived need to explain the validity of any Christocentric imagery and many patrons chose to avoid any appearance of impropriety. In seeking a less controversial alternative it seems that some patrons employed biblical prototypes of Christ's sacrifice taken from the Old Testament.

As the moment when humankind became corrupted by sin, Adam and Eve's fall from grace served as a warning to monitor your own behaviour but it was also the theological and iconographical counterpart to the eventual redemption of that sin by Christ's sacrifice on the Cross. This is made explicit in a wall painting of seventeenth-century date from 'The Springs' farmhouse in Buckinghamshire (Fig. 162). As I have shown elsewhere,[35] the iconography is loosely copied from the first illustration in John Speed's diagrammatic *The Genealogies of Holy Scriptures*, first published in 1611 and inserted in editions of the new, authorised Bible. An inscription in a panel between Adam and Eve at the centre of both the printed and painted versions declares that 'As by one mans disobedience many were made sinners, so by the obedience of one shall many be made righteous'. This image of Adam and Eve's original sin is also, therefore, a reminder of Christ's sacrifice as the source of salvation. It is significant that it was this particular scene, Adam and Eve's Fall, that was common in decorative art of the period 1560–1660 and any assessment of the meaning attached to this imagery by contemporaries should take its spiritual significance into account.[36] Similarly, it was also possible to evoke the sacrifice of Christ through the depiction of other biblical episodes that were understood as symbolic prefigurations or 'types' of Christ's Crucifixion. In this way, scenes from the

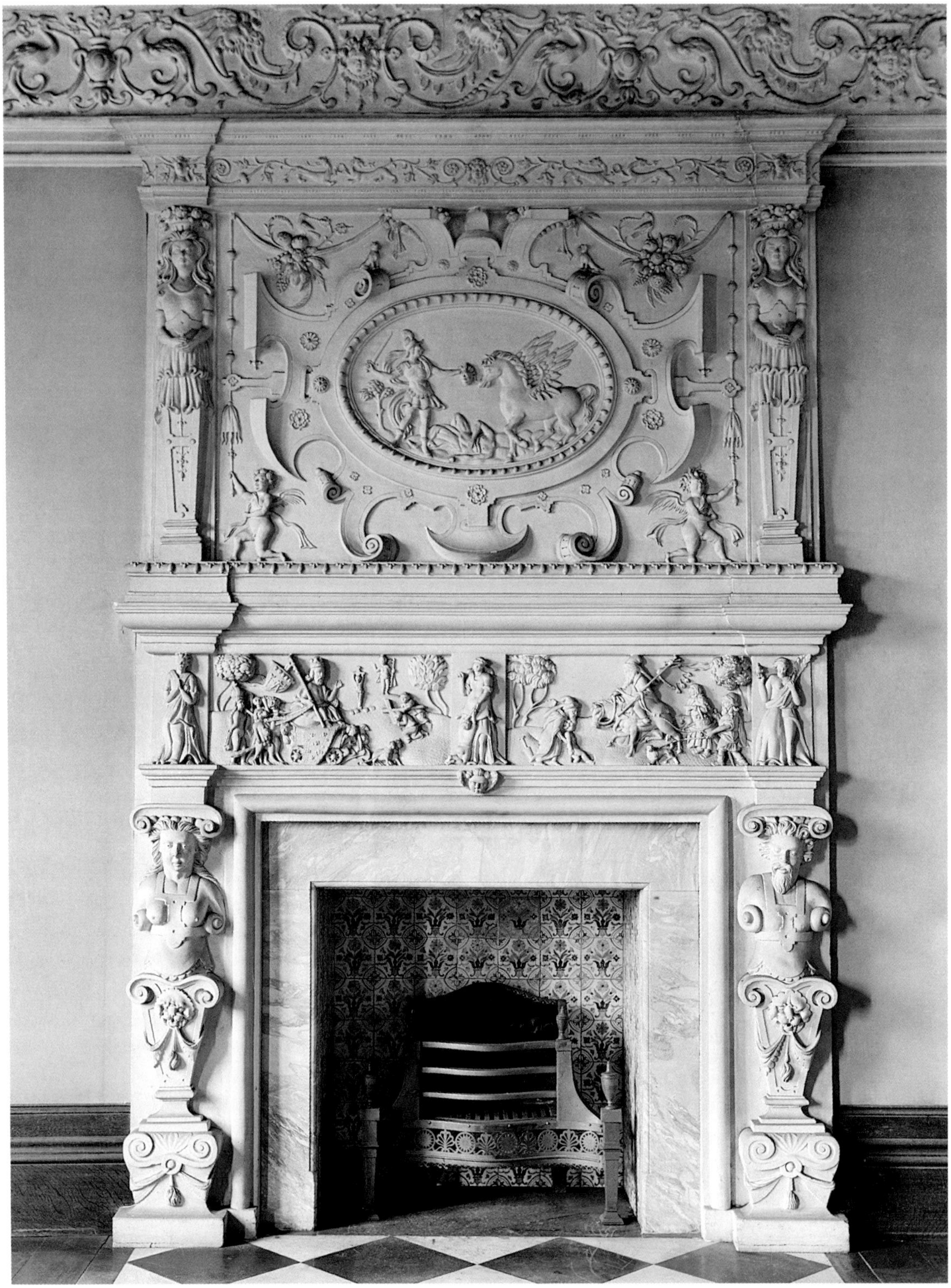

161 Chimneypiece of c. 1612 in the 'White Room' at Charlton House, Greenwich

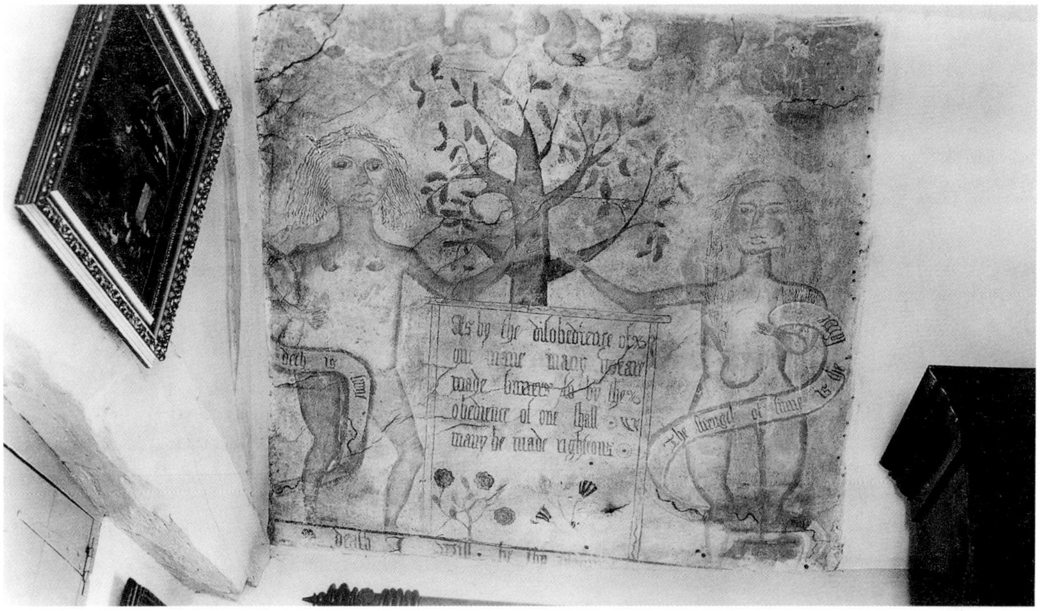

162 Adam and Eve (The Temptation or Fall from Grace), wall painting from a farmhouse in Buckinghamshire, first half of the seventeenth century

Old Testament could serve to prompt and guide spiritual meditation on the key points of Christian doctrine – the great scheme of sin brought in by Adam and redeemed through the sacrifice of Christ.

TYPES AS 'SURROGATE IMAGES'

Typology is an ancient form of biblical interpretation that assumes that God placed anticipations of Christ throughout the Old Testament. In this way personages and events in the Old Testament are prefigurations (types) of corresponding personages and events in the New Testament (antitypes). This method of exegesis was employed by Jesus himself, as recorded in Matthew 12.40, when he compared himself to Jonah in the belly of the whale as a symbol of his death and Resurrection. The concept of the Bible as a mystically cohesive text was fundamental to Christian belief and was popularised during the later medieval period through the influence of the *Biblia Pauperum* and the *Speculum Humanae Salvationis*, which illustrated New Testament events alongside their Old Testament types. These works originated early in the fourteenth century in the form of illuminated manuscripts and the printed versions with woodcuts produced in the second half of the fifteenth century were hugely influential. As mentioned in Chapter 1, the typological programmes of these books are shared by many other forms of medieval art, especially stained-glass windows.

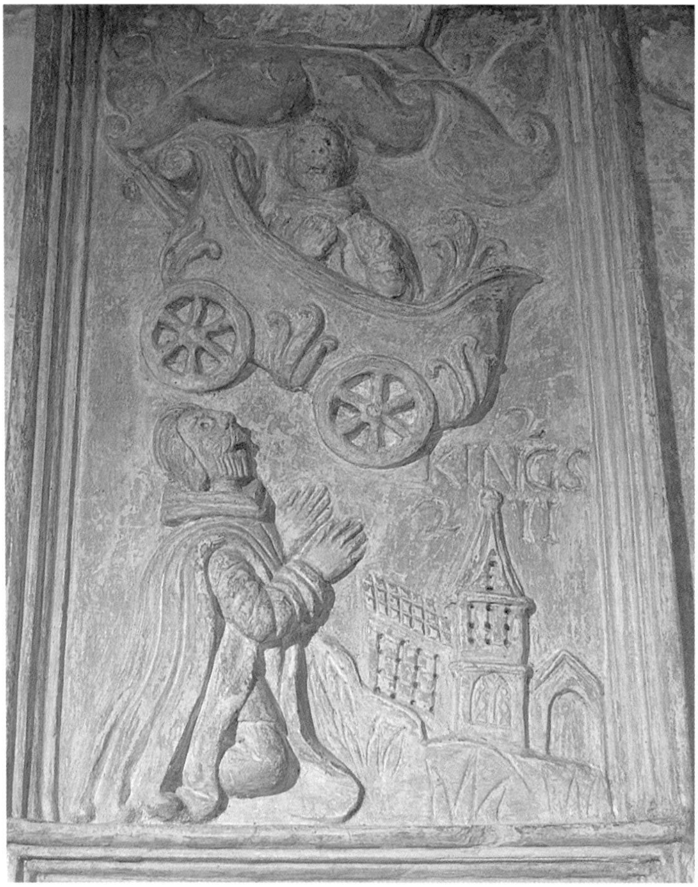

163 Elijah in the fiery chariot, detail from the plasterwork overmantel from a house in Lower Street, Dartmouth, Devon, now in a private collection

In post-Reformation texts, the identification of types with explanations of their symbolism was emphasised, drawing attention to and raising the profile of this ancient theological device. This method of exegesis was enumerated in the countless biblical commentaries produced throughout the period, evident especially in texts such as Edward Vaughan's *Method, or briefe instruction, verie profitable and speedy, for the reading and understanding of the old and new testament. The one expounding the other* . . . published in 1590 and the Scottish minister William Guild's *Moses Unveiled or Those figures which served unto the patterne and shadow of heavenly things, pointing out the Messiah Christ Jesus*, first published in 1620. Meanwhile, the juxtaposition of types and antitypes in visual art survived the Reformation to be depicted in the margins of Daye's *Christian Prayers* published in 1569 and 1578.[37]

The larger of the two plasterwork overmantels from Dartmouth in Devon (see Fig. 154) depicts types and antitypes in a similar manner to the illustrations in *Christian Prayers*. Indeed, the two Old Testament episodes depicted on the left-hand side of the overmantel might even derive from woodcuts in this prayer book. These illustrate events described in the book of Kings: Elijah bringing the widow's son back to life and Elijah being taken

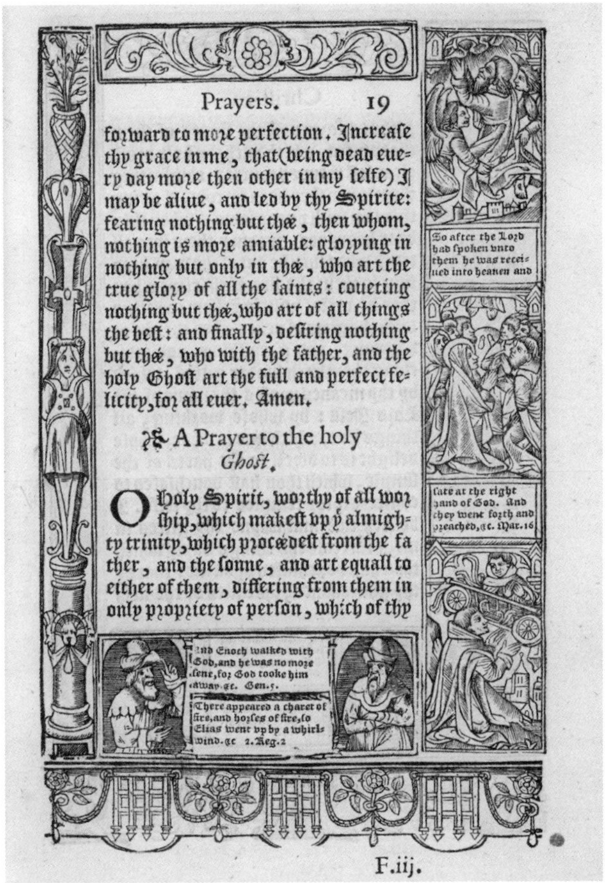
Prayers. 19

forward to more perfection. Increase thy grace in me, that (being dead every day more then other in my selfe) I may be aliue, and led by thy Spirite: fearing nothing but thee, then whom, nothing is more amiable: glorying in nothing but only in thee, who art the true glory of all the saints: coueting nothing but thee, who art of all things the best: and finally, desiring nothing but thee, who with the father, and the holy Ghost art the full and perfect felicity, for all euer. Amen.

A Prayer to the holy *Ghost.*

O Holy Spirit, worthy of all worship, which makest vp ẏ almighty trinity, which procedest from the father, and the sonne, and art equall to either of them, differing from them in only propriety of person, which of thy

So after the Lord had spoken vnto them he was receiued into heauen and

sate at the right hand of God. And they went forth and preached, &c. Mar. 16

And Enoch walked with God, and he was no more seene, for God tooke him away. &c. Gen. 5.

There appeared a charet of fire, and horses of fire, so Elias went vp by a whirlwind. &c 2. Reg. 2

F.iij.

164 Page from *A Booke of Christian Prayers* (1578), with woodcut illustrations of Elijah in the fiery chariot and the Ascension of Christ

up to heaven in a chariot of fire (Fig. 163). They are balanced on the right-hand side by two scenes depicting New Testament episodes: the Baptism and a scene combining the Resurrection and Ascension. The juxtaposition of these scenes relies on the device of types. Thus Elijah raising the widow's son prefigures Christ's spiritual and physical rebirth in the form of the Baptism and Resurrection, depicted opposite.[38] Meanwhile, Elijah being carried to heaven in a fiery chariot is paired, in line with ancient typological exegesis and as depicted in Daye's *Christian Prayers*, with the Ascension of Christ (Fig. 164). The use of types reveals the extent to which this seventeenth-century overmantel depends on, and continues, a much older tradition of biblical interpretation and visual symbolism.

William Perkins, the influential theologian, explicitly identified the representation of types as a permissible form of Protestant visual art. In a treatise on the 'civill use of images' from 1598, Perkins expressed his belief that:

> In one case it is lawful to make an image to testifie the presence or the effects of the Majestie of God, namely when God himselfe gives any special commandment so to do.

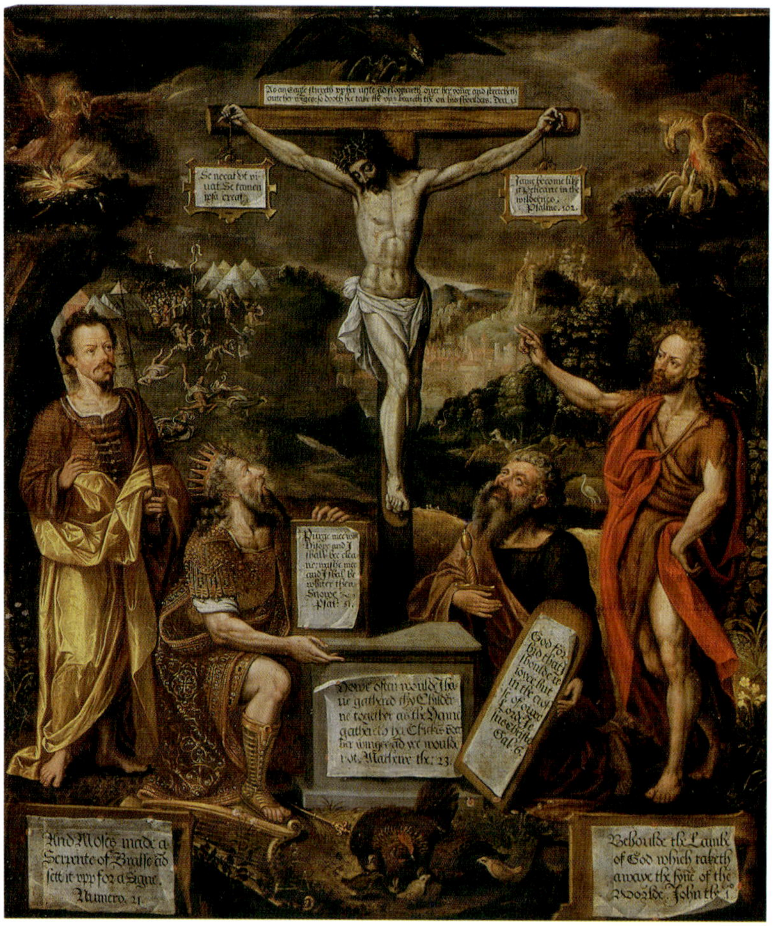

165 The Crucifixion with English texts, oil on canvas, c. 1600. Victoria and Albert Museum, London

> In this case Moses made and erected a brazen serpent, to be a type, signe, or image to represent Christ crucified. Joh.3.14.[39]

That is, Perkins is stating that the image of the brazen serpent, erected by Moses at the command of God as recounted in Numbers 21, was a way of 'lawfully' representing Christ's Crucifixion. As indicated by the reference to John 3.14 at the end of this passage, the traditional association between the brazen serpent and the Crucifixion of Christ was founded on Christ's own words as recorded in scripture: 'And as Moses lifted up the serpent in the wilderness, even so must the Son of man be lifted up: That whosoever believeth in him should not perish, but have eternal life.' The brazen serpent thus became a favourite type for the Crucifixion in art and literature. A painted panel of the Crucifixion with English texts of about 1600 incorporates complex allegories showing quotations and parallels between the Old and the New Testament (Fig. 165). The brazen serpent is depicted in the background on the left-hand side of Christ's crucified body.[40] In Thomas Trevelyon's illustrated manuscript of 1608, a citation from Numbers 21.8–9 is written underneath an image of the Crucifixion: 'And the Lord sayd unto Moses, Make

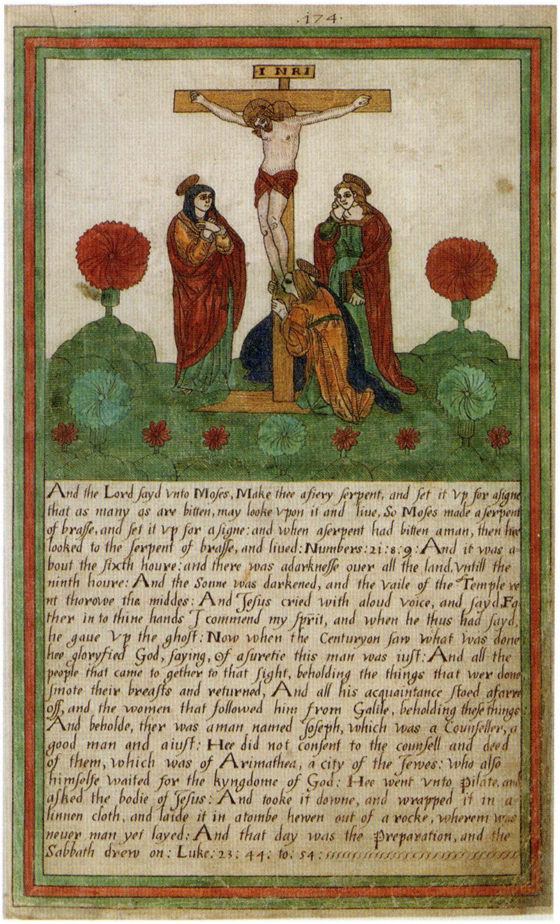

166 The Crucifixion, page from Thomas Trevelyon's illustrated miscellany of 1608

thee afiery serpent, and set it up for asign that as many as are bitten, may looke upon it and live, So Moses made a serpent of brasse, and set it up for a signe: and when aserpent had bitten aman, then he looked to the serpent of brasse, and lived' (Fig. 166).[41]

In this context it seems probable that a scene of Moses and the Brazen Serpent in a plasterwork overmantel of about 1590 at Holcombe Court in Devon was intended to allude to the Crucifixion.[42] The role of this story as a type would certainly be familiar to an early modern audience and so the image could operate as a symbolic substitute for the more controversial image of the Crucifixion. It would be reasonable therefore to expect to find other instances of the brazen serpent in post-Reformation decorative art but in fact this particular iconography is rare. It is possible, however, to explain why the brazen serpent was not widely employed as an alternative image to refer to Christ's sacrifice on the Cross. The story of the brazen serpent does not end with the passage from Numbers 21. Another section of the Old Testament describes how, over time, the brazen serpent became abused as a focus for idolatry and was consequently destroyed by King Hezekiah. The example of Hezekiah as an Old Testament iconoclast was invoked as a paradigm for the iconoclasm of the Protestant Reformation and both Henry VIII and Elizabeth I were

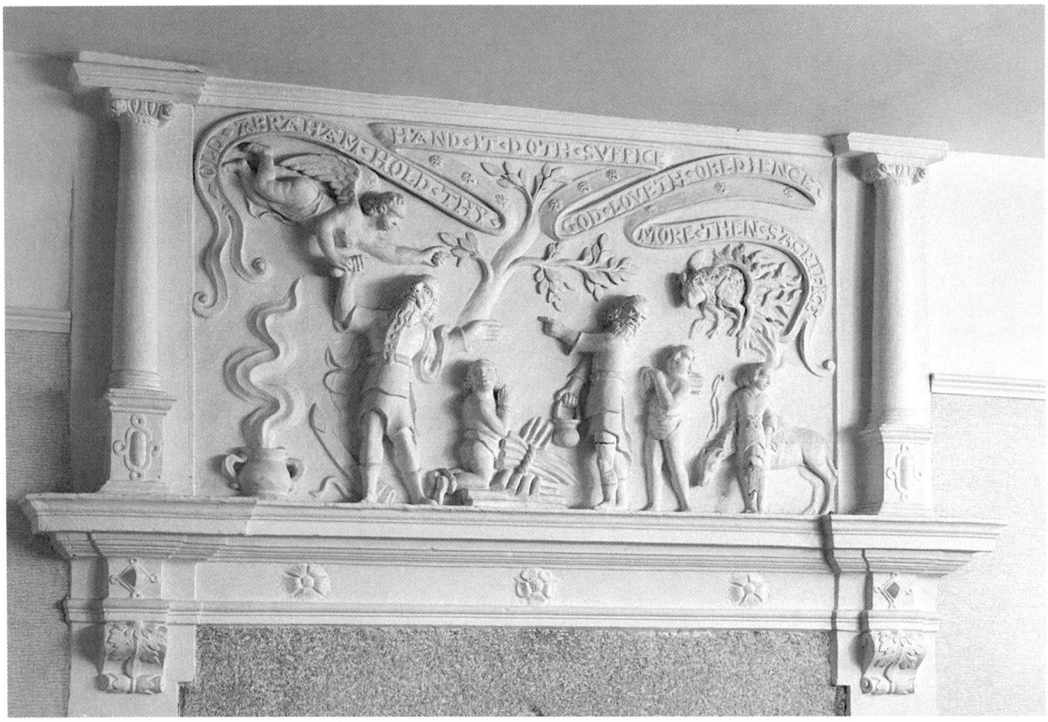

167 The Sacrifice of Isaac, plasterwork overmantel of c. 1635 at Trewane Manor, Cornwall

described as a new Hezekiah. Hezekiah provided the subject of a cycle of wall paintings of about 1570 at Hill Hall in Essex which includes a scene of image destruction.[43] Thus, as Margaret Aston has observed: 'In the repertoire of Old Testament examples the brazen serpent's patterning of the true cross was overlaid by the pattern of the properly destroyed idol'.[44] The image of the brazen serpent was therefore also contaminated by abuse.

There were, however, other Old Testament types for the sacrifice of Christ that could be employed without associations of idolatry. One particularly ancient and common Old Testament type for the Crucifixion was the Sacrifice of Isaac from Genesis 22. This was a natural type for the Crucifixion because of the obvious parallel between the two events: as Abraham was willing to sacrifice his only son to prove his love for God, so God sacrificed his only son out of love for humankind. As Andrew Willet explained in his commentary on Genesis of 1605: 'There seeme to have beene two principall ends of this commandment of God. 1. That thereby Abrahams faith and obedience might be tried: as the Apostle saith, Heb. I.I.17. by faith Abraham offered up Isaack. 2. The other end was, to be a lively type and representation of the sacrifice of Christ'.[45] Willet's first explanation of this event as a test of obedience is the subject of a plasterwork overmantel dating from about 1635 at Trewane Manor in Cornwall (Fig. 167).[46] An inscription at the top of the scene specifies the intended moral of the imagery: 'OLD ABRAHAM HOLD THY HAND IT DOTH SUFFICE GOD LOVETH OBEDIENCE MORE THEN SACRIFICE'. There is little mystery about why the quality of obedience should be celebrated in a domestic overmantel. Unquestioning obedience was necessary to preserve household order as well as to secure God's blessing.

Willet's other explanation of the episode as a type for the sacrifice of Christ is made explicit in a carved wood overmantel above a fireplace in 90 High Street in Oxford, a grand town house built from 1613 by an apothecary named John Williams. The overmantel of c. 1620 is in a large second-floor chamber and it includes representations of two consecutive episodes from the story of the Sacrifice of Isaac (Fig. 168). A panel on the left depicts Abraham and Isaac climbing the mountain, while on the right is a representation of the moment of near-sacrifice, where Abraham's hand is grasped by an angel just as he is about to strike his son with his sword. A lengthy inscription beneath these scenes provides a detailed explanation as to the intended meaning and function of the imagery:

> BEHOLD THE FATHER OF THE FAITHFULL SEEDE
> WAS HEERE APROVED TO BE SOUND INDEEDE
> FOR BEING WARND OF GOD TO SACRIFICE
> HIS SONNE ISAACK MOST PRETIOUS IN HIS EYES
> FORTHWITH OBEDIENT WAS AT HIS COMMAND
> AND SLAYES HIS SON HAD NOT GOD STAYD HIS HAND
>
> THE ANTITIPE OF CHRIST WAS HE IN THIS
> FOR GOD HIS ONLY SONN DID SLAY FOR [US]
> AND IF CHRIST CRUCIFIED THOU DESIRST TO SEE
> THIS TO A CHRISTIAN CRUCIFIX MAY BEE
> NOT FOR TO WORSHIP AS [PAPISTS] INTENT
> BUT ONLY FOR THY CHAMBERS ORNAMENT[47]

This inscription spells out the spiritual meaning of the story as an alternative image for the crucified Christ but it also specifies, possibly as a warning for its Protestant viewers, that the image is 'not for to worship'. In this way, the Old Testament story represents Christ's sacrifice in a safe form for display in a Protestant house and is distinguished from idolatrous use of the Crucifix by 'papists'.

The image of the Sacrifice of Isaac is extremely common in decorative art throughout the period under investigation. It is possible to state with confidence that this subject occurs more often than any other biblical scene; it can be found in all decorative media across most geographical areas and in houses of varying status. The imagery invariably focuses on the dramatic climax in depicting the angel halting the fall of Abraham's raised sword and thus resolves the (positive) outcome of the story.[48] A singular and charming exception is the version at Marshwood Farm in Somerset, where Abraham's sword is still sheathed and the angel has yet to appear. There is the suggestion of fatherly pride and affection in the way Abraham places his hand on the head of his son (Fig. 169). Generally, though, depictions of the Sacrifice of Isaac adopt the standard iconography and it is possible that an explanation for the popularity of this image is its role as a type; it func-

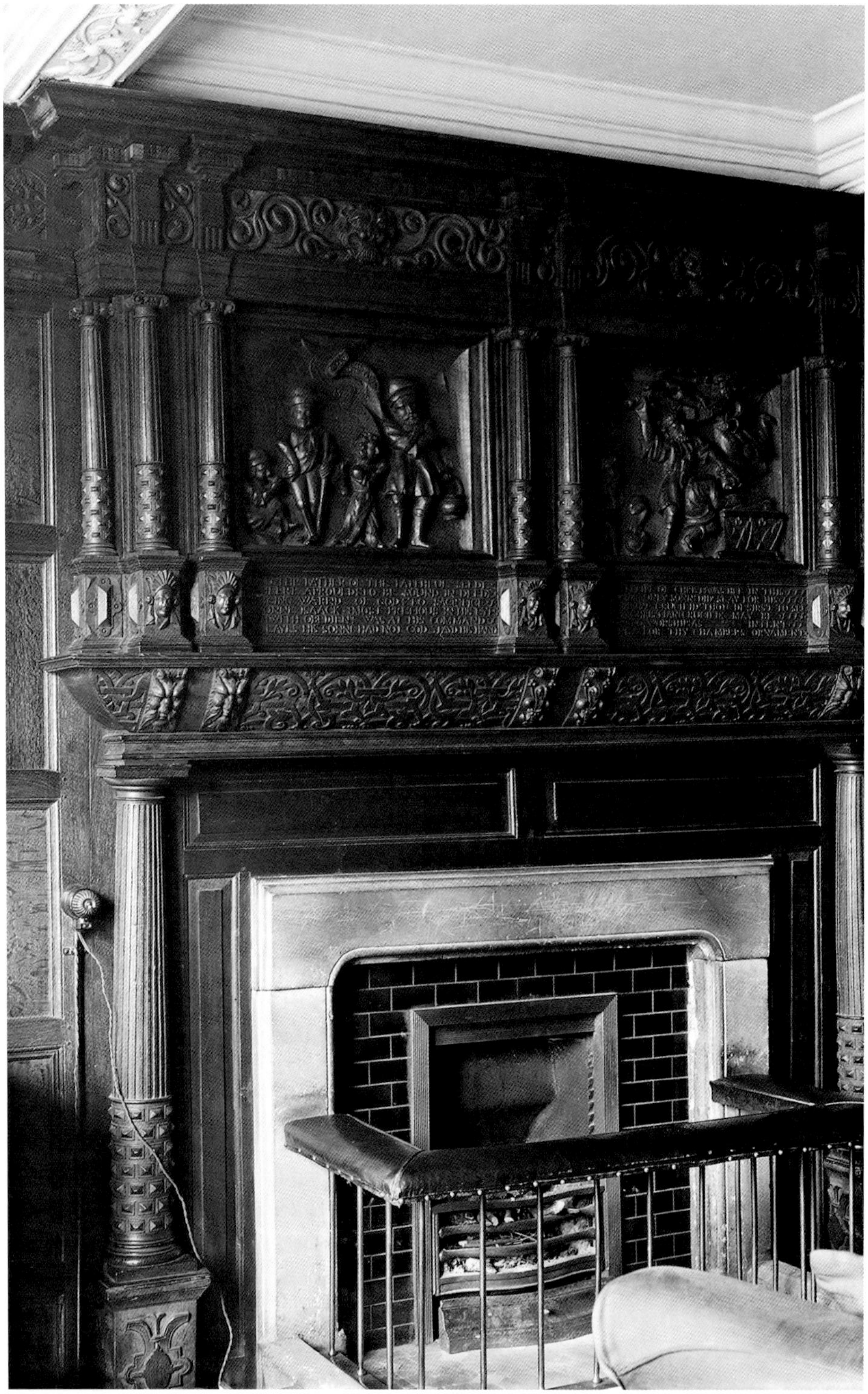

168 Scenes from the Sacrifice of Isaac with accompanying inscriptions, carved wood chimneypiece of c. 1620 from 90 High Street, Oxford

tioned as a symbolic substitute or 'surrogate image' where the signified meaning was the sacrifice of Christ on the Cross.[49]

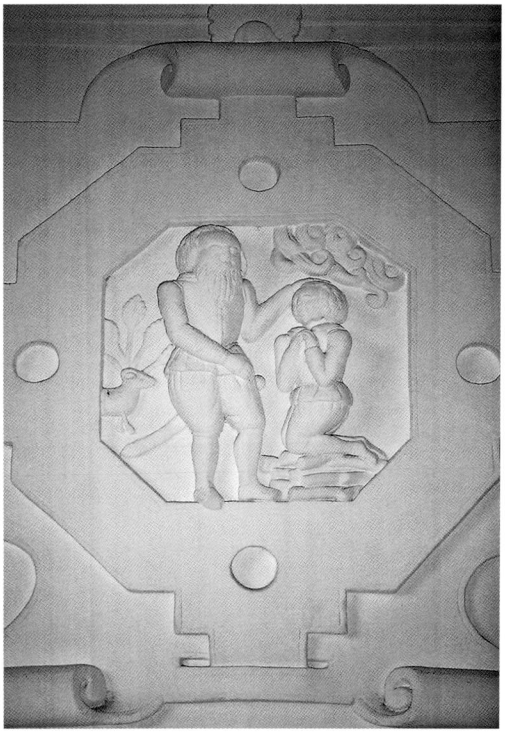

169 This unusual variation on the standard iconography for the Sacrifice of Isaac in plasterwork at Marshwood Farm, Somerset (c. 1630), depicts with some poignancy the pregnant moment before Abraham raises his sword to kill his son

If this reading is accurate then it appears that one result of the ongoing controversy surrounding the legitimacy of religious images was the use of types as alternatives to represent key moments in Christ's life, especially the Crucifixion. It seems that although certain religious images were expressly prohibited while others were viewed as questionable, a desire for traditional imagery remained. This resulted in a process of substitution in which the controversial iconography was replaced with a 'safe' Old Testament type. In discussing this method of depicting one story in order to refer symbolically to another, associated story, Erwin Panofsky – the father of the iconographical method for interpreting works of art – observed that such 'superimposed meaning', as he termed it, might not enter the content of the work at all; that is to say, it may not be discernible through analysis of only the visual elements of the image itself but is, rather, an additional message which operated through the association of ideas within specific cultures.[50] Certainly, the significance of Old Testament scenes as types is only rarely made explicit in domestic decoration by accompanying texts; rather, the association relies on the tradition of conventional usage and exegesis, which made such an association an automatic response. The content and appearance of such scenes lends support to the theory that they functioned as a symbolic signifier, rather than as a straightforward pictorial rendering of the biblical narrative. Images designed to operate as types are characterised by highly simplified and formulaic iconography so that the image is pared down to the elements essential for its symbolic, indexical function. Some scholars have dismissed the unsophisticated and simple nature of British decorative art during this period as the result of a lack of artistic invention or a reliance on printed sources. It is possible that the symbolic function of the image resulted in the stripping away of extraneous detail to aid the process of association. Where 'extra' visual detail is included in such images, such information usually emphasises aspects of the story which reinforce its function as a type.

For example, the fairly frequent inclusion of an additional scene from the story of the Sacrifice of Isaac, where Isaac carries the sticks for his own funerary pyre up the hill, can be shown to reinforce and expand the typological meaning. In biblical commentaries, the description of this part of the story was interpreted as another prefiguration of the events

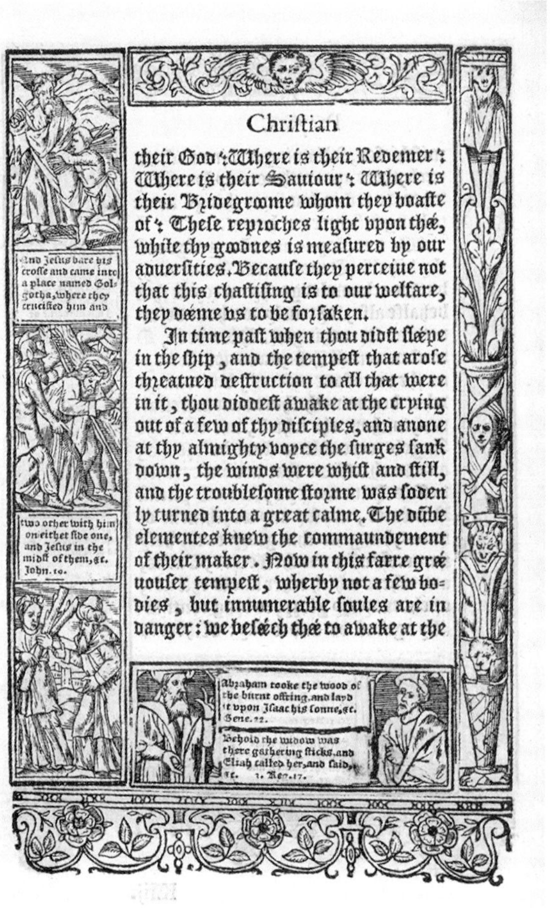

Chriſtian

their God? Where is their Redemer? Where is their Sauiour? Where is their Bridegrome whom they boaſte of? Theſe reproches light vpon thee, while thy goodnes is meaſured by our aduerſities. Becauſe they perceiue not that this chaſtiſing is to our welfare, they deeme vs to be forſaken.

In time paſt when thou didſt ſleepe in the ſhip, and the tempeſt that aroſe threatned deſtruction to all that were in it, thou diddeſt awake at the crying out of a few of thy diſciples, and anone at thy almighty voyce the ſurges ſank down, the winds were whiſt and ſtill, and the troubleſome ſtorme was ſodenly turned into a great calme. The dube elementes knew the commaundement of their maker. Now in this farre greuouſer tempeſt, wherby not a few bodies, but innumerable ſoules are in danger: we beſeech thee to awake at the

And Jeſus bare his croſſe and came into a place named Golgotha, where they crucified him and

two other with him on either ſide one, and Jeſus in the midſt of them, &c. John. 19.

Abraham tooke the wood of the burnt offring, and layd it vpon Iſaac his ſonne, &c. Gene. 22.

Behold the widow was there gathering ſticks, and Elias called her, and ſaid, &c. 3. Reg. 17.

170 Page from *A booke of Christian Prayers* (1578), with woodcut illustrations of Isaac carrying the wood for his sacrificial pyre and Christ carrying the Cross

of the Crucifixion: as Isaac carried the sticks for his own funerary pyre, so Christ carried the Cross to Calvary for his Crucifixion. Thus Gervase Babington, in a text published in 1592, commented: 'Abraham tooke the wood of the burnte offring, and layde it upon Isaac his sonne, to goe towards the place of death that God had appointed. Behold a lively figure of Jesus Christ, bearing his owne crosse towards the place of execution even as yong Isaac dooth beere the wood to burne himselfe withal'.[51] A scene of Isaac carrying the sticks up the hill is included above an image of Christ carrying the Cross in the margins of the *Christian Prayers* of 1569 and 1578 (Fig. 170). In the same way the prominence of a ram caught up in a bush in the standard iconography was listed by Andrew Willet in 1605 as one of the numerous symbolic parallels: 'the ramme is entangled in a thicket, [and] Christ was crowned with thornes'.[52]

A carved wooden plaque dating from about 1600 from Yeovil in Somerset depicts the story of the Sacrifice of Isaac in the main body of the panel.[53] The iconography includes only these essential elements (Fig. 171). On the left, Isaac is shown carrying the sticks while Abraham points the way up the mountain, while to the right is the scene of near-

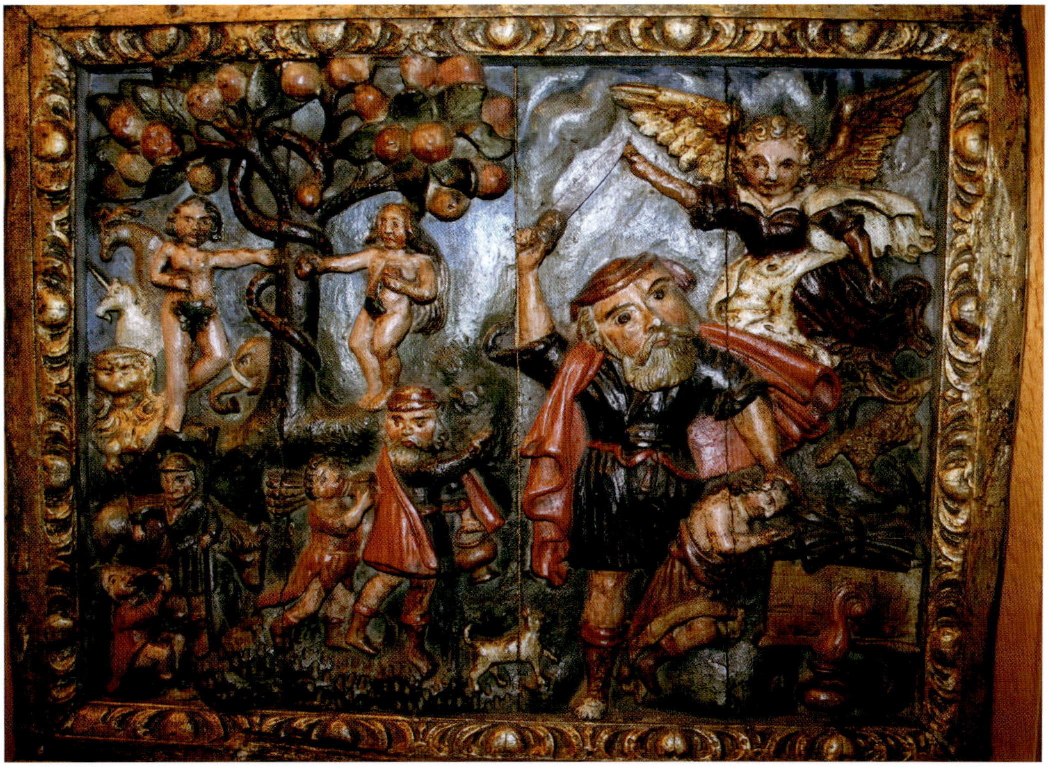

171 Carved and painted wooden panel of the Sacrifice of Isaac and Adam and Eve, c. 1600. Museum of South Somerset

sacrifice with a lamb caught in the thicket squeezed in under the body of the angel. The servants waiting with the donkey in the bottom left corner also contribute to the meaning of the story as a type: Abraham and Isaac travelled to their destination on a donkey, in the same way that Christ entered Jerusalem. Also included is a scene of Adam and Eve's fall from grace in the top left-hand corner. To pair these two Old Testament episodes only makes sense in relation to the significance of the Sacrifice of Isaac as a type for the sacrifice of Christ; the imagery illustrates the Christian scheme of sin and salvation.

The meaning of the Sacrifice of Isaac as a type for Christ's sacrifice might explain the use of this scene as the centrepiece of a plasterwork ceiling dating from about 1620 in the chapel of Sir Paul Pindar's mansion house in Bishopsgate, London. Pindar was an extraordinarily wealthy merchant and served as a diplomat and financier to James I, for which he received his knighthood.[54] The chapel ceiling was destroyed along with the house in 1890 but there exists a record of its appearance in a drawing made in 1840 by C. J. Richardson.[55] From this drawing it can be seen that the central scene of the Sacrifice of Isaac was the only figurative iconography within the ceiling (Fig. 172). The use of this particular image in the context of a domestic chapel suggests that it had significance within devotional practices. As has been noted, imagery in churches and other places of

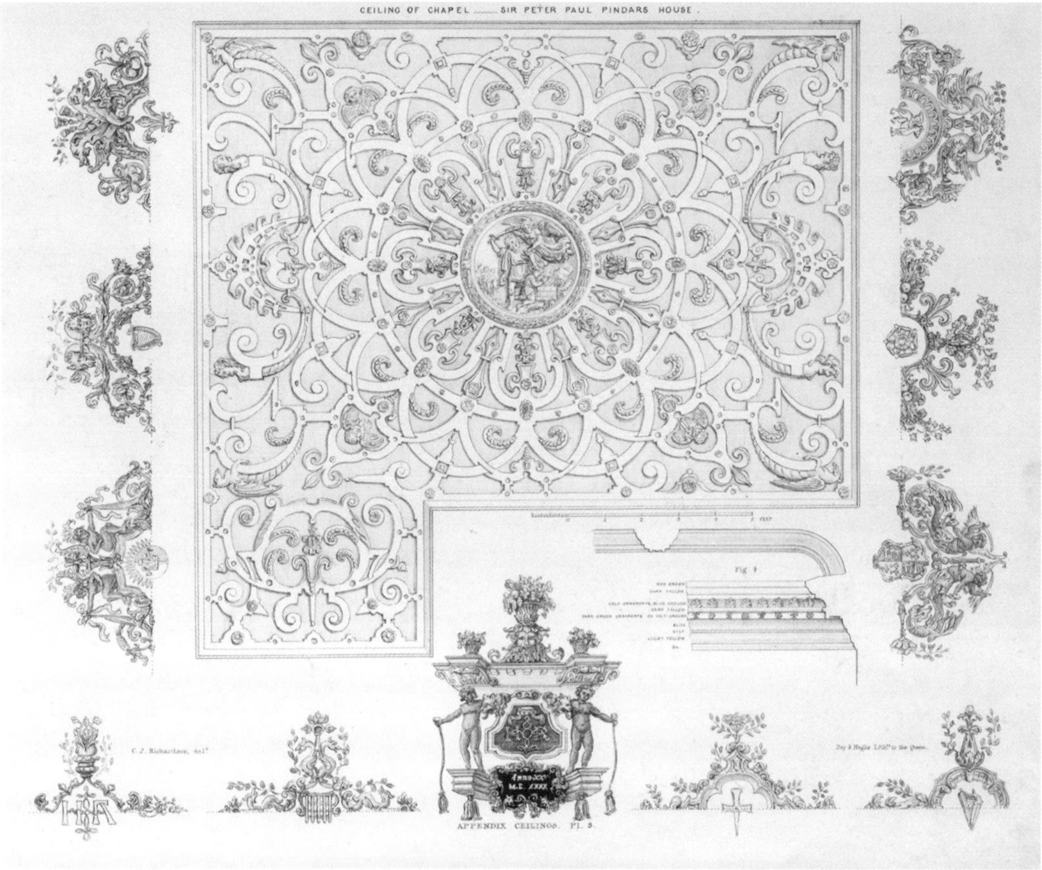

172 The Sacrifice of Isaac at the centre of the plasterwork ceiling in the chapel of Sir Paul Pindar's house in Bishopsgate, London. Drawing by C. J. Richardson, 1840

worship was especially vulnerable to accusations of idolatry, and images of Christ's sacrifice in this context were explicitly vetoed by the 'Homily against peril of idolatry' and most subsequent Protestant texts. At the same time a process of de-sanctifying church space meant that the altar had lost much of its previous power as the traditional focus of worship. Criticised by reformers in the mid-sixteenth century because of its idolatrous associations with the Catholic mass, the altar was removed from the holy chancel area and repositioned within the nave to be treated merely as practical church furniture until its status was restored under the Laudian reforms of the 1630s. With the removal of this traditional focal point and its accompanying adornments and imagery, the ceiling provided another natural focus during devotions. Looking up and raising the hands towards heaven during prayer were gestures approved by Protestant authors of devotional conduct literature such as Bayly and Downame. In this context the image of the Sacrifice of Isaac makes sense at the centre of a ceiling in a Protestant chapel. As a substitute for Christ's Crucifixion it provides both a physical and symbolic focus for prayer.

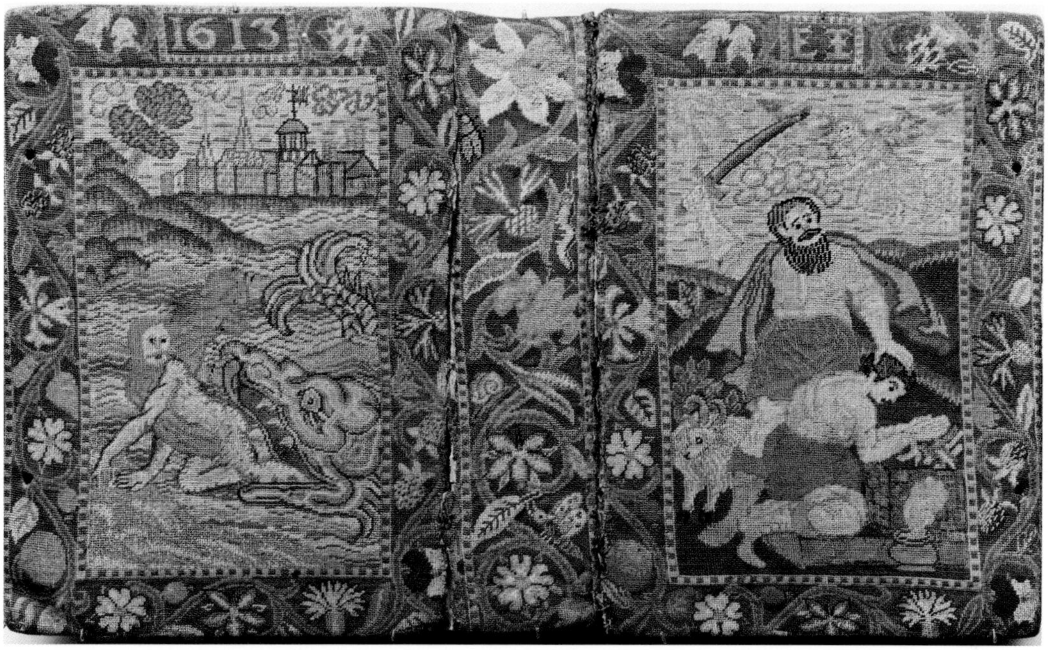

173 The Sacrifice of Isaac and Jonah emerging from the whale, Bible cover embroidered by Elizabeth Illingworth, dated 1613. Victoria and Albert Museum, London

Similarly, the use of the scene of the Sacrifice of Isaac as embroidery for a Bible cover suggests another way in which this 'surrogate imagery' might have functioned within the spiritual practices of individuals. The cover was embroidered by Elizabeth Illingworth and her initials are included along with the date 1613 (Fig. 173).[56] Isaac appears on the front while a scene of Jonah being expelled from the whale's mouth is depicted on the back. As mentioned earlier, the story of Jonah and the Whale was understood as a prefiguration of Christ's death and Resurrection, based on Matthew 12.40: 'For as Jonas was three days and three nights in the Whale's belly: so that the sonne of man bee three days and three nights in the heart of the earth'. The two scenes chosen to decorate the Bible therefore act as surrogate images for the Crucifixion and Resurrection. The location of this imagery as part of the hand-worked adornment of her Bible suggests that Elizabeth Illingworth desired imagery to help with her meditations on the sacrifice and Resurrection of Christ during her religious reading and associated devotions.

Jonah and the whale is the subject of a wall painting originally from a house in Waltham Abbey in Essex. Just one scene was recovered from its original location in a first-floor room of a town house on Highbridge Street and is now in the Museum of London.[57] The scene depicts the moment when Jonah was thrown overboard by his fellow sailors, while the whale waits open-mouthed ready to swallow him (Fig. 174). This particular image therefore refers to the moment when Jonah was sacrificed in order to save the lives of the other men on the ship – a clear parallel with Christ's sacrifice on the Cross.

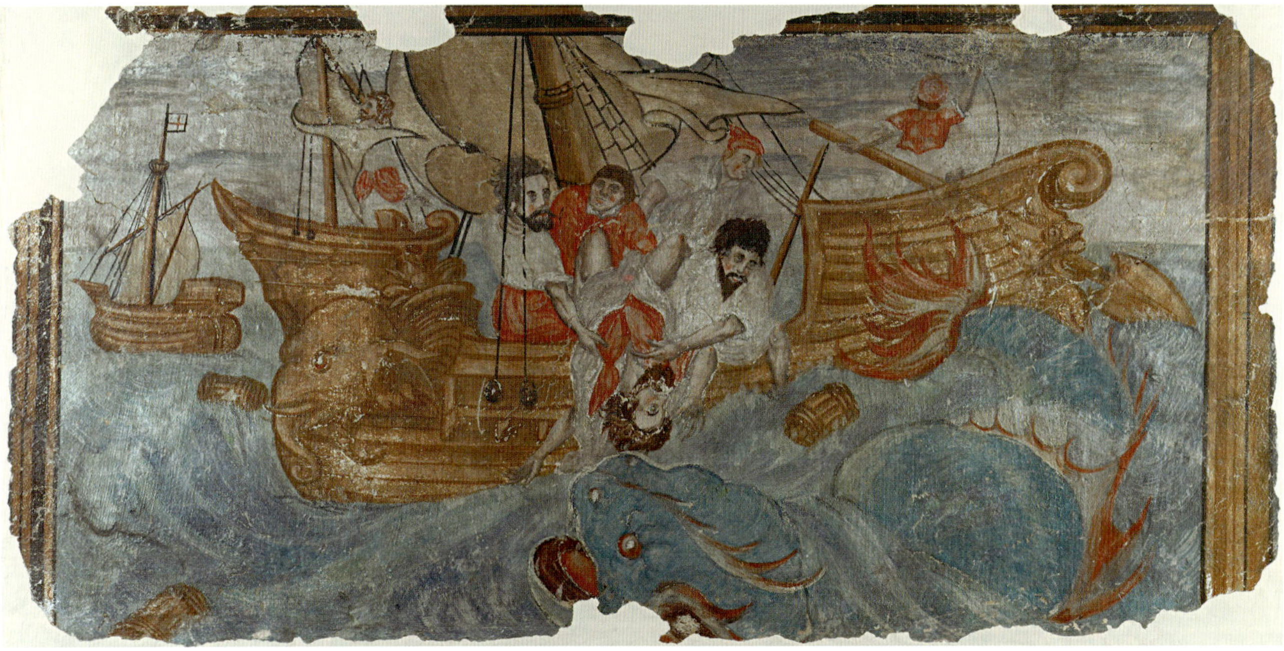

174 Jonah being cast into the sea, wall painting of c. 1600 salvaged from a house in Waltham Abbey, Essex. Museum of London

An illustration of Jonah being cast into the sea is paired with the Entombment in the *Booke of Christian Prayers* of 1578 (Fig. 175). It is not clear if the Waltham Abbey scene was once part of a series of wall paintings depicting the whole story of Jonah and the whale. No other paintings were identified or preserved but the early records documenting the discovery of the mural are fairly vague.[58] If this scene existed as part of a wider scheme then one might suspect that the programme of imagery served as an allusion to the death and Resurrection of Christ. As John Andrewes spelt out in his treatise, *Christ his crosse* of 1614, '*Jonah*, lying three daies in the whales belly; is a *Type* and figure of *Christ* dying, buried, and rising againe the third day'.[59] English sermons of the period used the story to elaborate on the Protestant conception of divine mercy and the remission of sin but the essential typological meaning of this image as a symbol of sacrifice and salvation operated on a more basic level and had a long tradition in the visual arts.[60] Indeed the typological reading of the story is supported by the nearly contemporary programme of imagery in the enamelled glass of the east window in Lincoln College chapel in Oxford, created in 1629–31 by Abraham van Linge. There, six scenes from the life of Christ are paired with types from the Old Testament and a vivid depiction of Jonah emerging from the whale appears as the companion to the Resurrection.

The examples discussed so far suggest that the depiction of certain Old Testament stories and scenes served as direct substitutes for controversial Christological imagery and especially images of the Crucifixion and Resurrection. Obviously, not all Old Testament

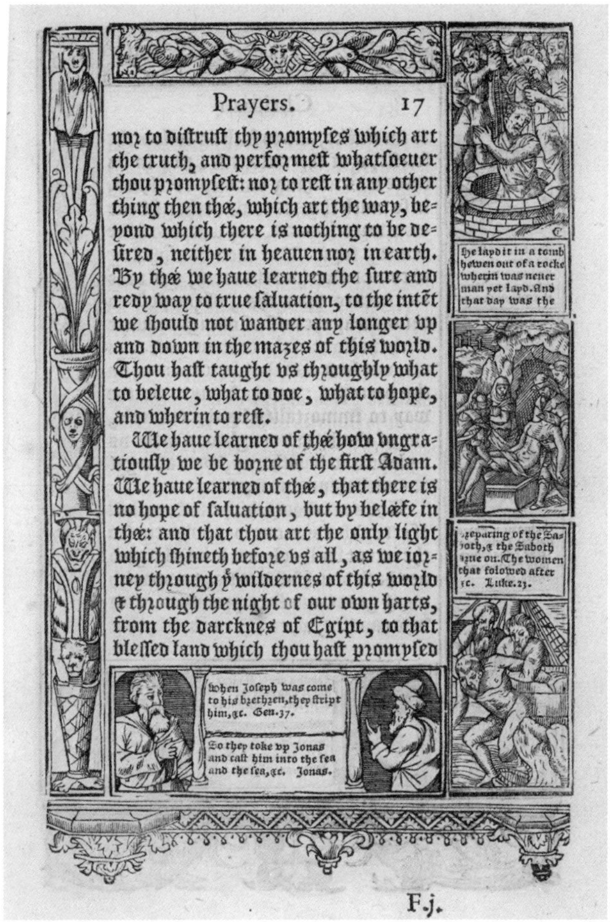

Prayers. 17

noꝛ to diſtruſt thy pꝛomyſes which art the truth, and perfoꝛmeſt whatſoeuer thou pꝛomyſeſt: noꝛ to reſt in any other thing then thée, which art the way, beyond which there is nothing to be deſired, neither in heauen noꝛ in earth. By thée we haue learned the ſure and redy way to true ſaluation, to the intẽt we ſhould not wander any longer vp and down in the mazes of this woꝛld. Thou haſt taught vs thꝛoughly what to beleue, what to doe, what to hope, and wherin to reſt.

We haue learned of thée how vngratiouſly we be boꝛne of the firſt Adam. We haue learned of thée, that there is no hope of ſaluation, but by beléefe in thée: and that thou art the only light which ſhineth befoꝛe vs all, as we ioꝛney thꝛough ẏ wildernes of this woꝛld & thꝛough the night of our own harts, from the darcknes of Egipt, to that bleſſed land which thou haſt pꝛomyſed

175 Page from *A Booke of Christian Prayers* (1578), with woodcut illustrations of Jonah being cast into the sea and the Entombment

subject matter was intended to function in this way. Yet, although other biblical scenes in domestic decoration might not operate as direct surrogates for Christ's sacrifice, it is possible that they were selected as another means to represent the soteriological message of the Christian faith. Many Old Testament scenes included in Protestant decorative art share the theme of tests or trials of faith, with divine intervention resulting in eventual salvation.

Chapter 4 included a description of the plasterwork ceiling in the great chamber of Prideaux Place in Padstow, Cornwall. Its principal subject as depicted in the main body of the ceiling is the story of Susannah and the Elders from the Apocrypha. The story, represented in eight consecutive scenes, culminates in Susannah's reprieve and the stoning of the guilty Elders. This can be understood to function as a warning against the sins of lust, fornication and false witness and as praise for the virtues of chastity and constancy. Yet the inclusion of another biblical scene from an unrelated story indicates that there is another, thematic meaning to the ceiling decoration. The tympanum depicts Moses striking the rock and bringing forth water, illustrating Exodus 17.6 (Fig. 99). This story of

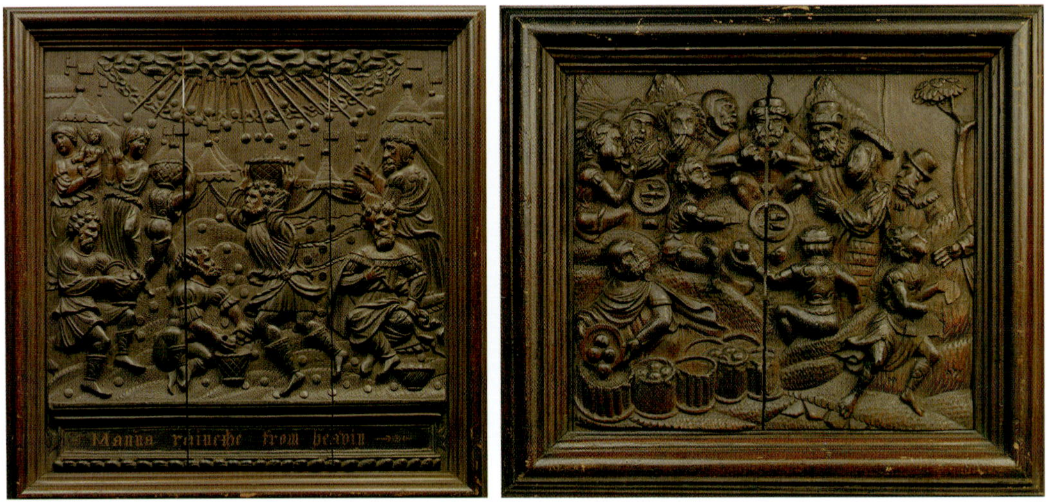

176 Manna from Heaven and Feeding the Five Thousand, carved panels of the late sixteenth century from Lanfine House in Sornhill, Ayrshire

Moses providing water in the desert and thus saving his people from dying from thirst underlines God's gift of salvation to his chosen people. In this way the miracle performed by Moses was understood as another type for Christ, as noted by Edward Vaughan: 'The water out of the stone 17.6 signified Christ 1 Cor. 10.3'.[61] In the *Biblia Pauperum* the scene of Moses striking the rock was allied with Longinus spearing the side of Christ on the Cross. The inclusion of this particular episode in the tympanum at Prideaux shifts the meaning of the Susannah narrative from an edifying *exemplum* in the virtues of chastity and constancy to a symbolic expression of divine intervention and salvation. Moses striking the rock was also depicted as one of a series of carved panels from Lanfine House in Sornhill, Ayrshire. Five panels which must have formed part of a wider set are now in the NMS.[62] The extant panels seem to suggest pairings of Old and New Testament subject matter: thus the panel of Manna from Heaven has a natural companion in the Feeding of the Five Thousand (Fig. 176). Here again the programme of decorative imagery uses typology to express the core theme of deliverance and salvation.

The decorative scheme of the plasterwork in the great chamber of the Manor Court House in Chard, Somerset, also suggests a soteriological theme. This building was once a large manor house in the centre of the town, possibly owned in the first half of the seventeenth century by a family of clothiers by the name of Cogan.[63] In the great chamber the plasterwork dates from about 1620 and in the barrel-vaulted tympanum on the east wall are three scenes from the Old Testament separated by large standing figures of Justice and Mercy. The imagery is in shallow relief and is thus hard to photograph but the tympanum is illustrated in a drawing published in the *Proceedings of Somersetshire Archaeological and Natural History Society* of 1882 (Fig. 177). From left to right the narrative scenes depict the Judgement of Solomon, Shadrach, Meshach and Abednego in the

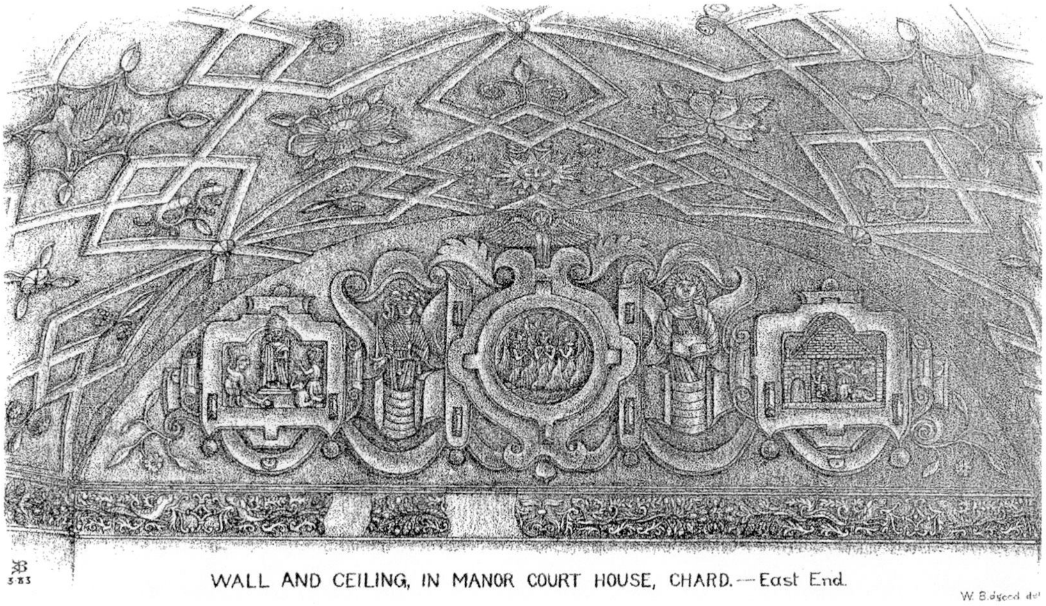

177 Drawing of the plasterwork tympanum in the old great chamber of the Manor Court House in Chard, Somerset, published in 1882

fiery furnace and Daniel in the lion's den. These three scenes share the theme of tests of faith during persecution, resulting in deliverance. Solomon ordered that a child claimed by two mothers should be cut in half in order to cause its true mother to reveal herself; thus the child was saved and justice prevailed. The three men were condemned to the fiery furnace by the wicked King Nebuchadnezzar for refusing to worship a golden idol but, due to their faith in God, they emerged from the furnace completely unharmed. Daniel was cast into the lion's den as punishment for worshipping God against the orders of King Darius but was saved from harm by an angel of God. It is clear therefore that all three stories depicted in the tympanum illustrate trials and deliverance.

Shadrach, Meshach and Abednego in the fiery furnace is also the subject of a plasterwork overmantel above a fireplace at Stockton House in Wiltshire (Fig. 178). Stockton House was built in the last years of the sixteenth century by John Topp, a London merchant tailor, and it seems there were two phases of decoration; the earlier prior to 1603 and the second sometime between 1603 and 1625.[64] The overmantel is in a room on the first floor; it depicts the three men in the furnace, surrounded by flames. On the right of the scene is a small architectural feature, which resembles a brick tower, and looking out from an opening in the tower is King Nebuchadnezzar. Another figure, holding a two-pronged staff, stands upright at the centre of the composition and this seems to be an attempt at representing the textual inscription above the scene which reads: 'LOE.I. SEE.FOURE/MEN.LOOSE.WALKI/NG.IN.THE.MIDST./OF.THE.FIRE./DANIEL 3.25'. This scriptural quotation refers to Nebuchadnezzar's vision of a fourth man walking in the midst

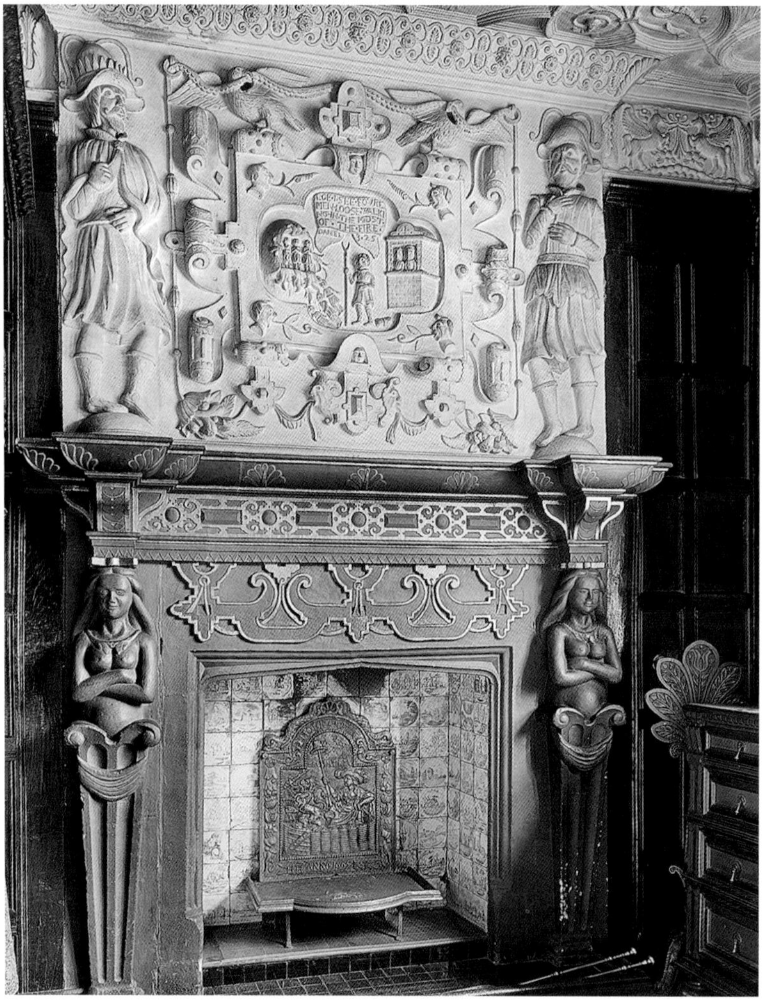

178 Shadrach, Meshach and Abednego in the fiery furnace, plasterwork overmantel of c. 1603–25 at Stockton House, Wiltshire

of the fire which he described as 'like the Sonne of God'. Thus this scene depicts the protective presence of the divine angel and the salvation of the faithful.

To return to the decoration at the Manor Court House: at the opposite end of the room from the tympanum is a plasterwork overmantel above a fireplace (Fig. 179). At the centre of the overmantel is a phoenix rising from the flames which, as a symbol of life emerging from death, served as a traditional allegory of Christ's Resurrection. Indeed, the phoenix in flames is part of the symbolism included with the Crucifixion in the painted panel of about 1600 mentioned earlier (see Fig. 165). It is significant that the image of the phoenix on the west wall of the chamber at the Manor Court House faces the image of the three men in the fiery furnace at the centre of the tympanum at the opposite end of the room. The opposition of these two images reminds the viewer of their similar meaning; both images share the theme of salvation from flames and both allude to the sacrifice and Resurrection of Christ.

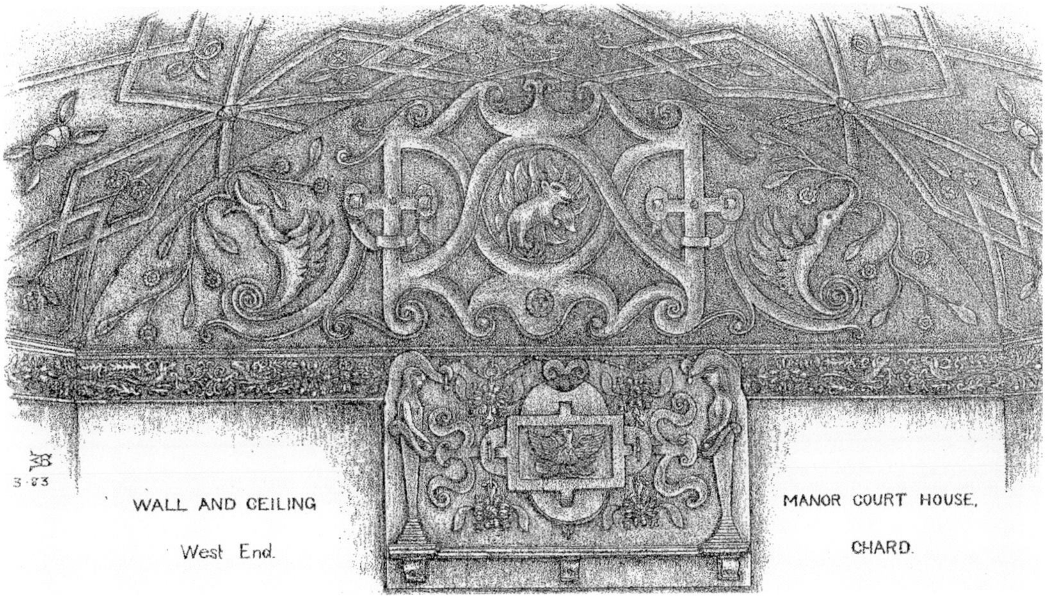

179 Drawing of the plasterwork overmantel in the old great chamber of the Manor Court House in Chard, Somerset, published in 1882

Imagery involving fire and flames is obviously appropriate for the centre of an overmantel above a fireplace. The phoenix at the Manor Court House is positioned directly above the fireplace and thus refers to the function of the object it adorns. In the same way, the decoration of a cast-iron fireback dated 1649 combines an appropriate reference to fire with a soteriological message (Fig. 180). Cast-iron slabs were placed on the wall at the back of the fireplace in order to protect the brickwork, and also to radiate heat into the room. Given this function, fireback decoration often included stories involving fire but sometimes there was also a political theme. The royal arms were a common subject and several firebacks are extant with the date 1588 which suggests a reference to the victory over the Armada. As the example here is dated 1649 the choice of subject matter may refer to the execution of Charles I. The image of a snake rising from flames to bite an outstretched hand refers to Acts 28. 3–6, which describes St Paul being shipwrecked on the island of Malta. On landing he lit a fire and as he did so a viper emerged from the flames and bit him. The fact that he was unhurt allowed the people of the island to realise that he must be a holy man. In Geoffrey Whitney's *A Choice of Emblemes* (Leyden, 1586) the same design appears with the title 'If God be with us, who can be against us?' and with the verse: 'His servauntes God preserves, thoughe they in danger fall: Even as from vipers deadlie bite, he kept th' Appostle Paule.' This same image was employed on a medal struck in 1562 to celebrate Elizabeth I's recovery from smallpox.[65] The inscriptions on both sides of the medal give the credit for her deliverance to divine protection. In this way, the iconography operated as a symbol of salvation. It is possible therefore to imagine people gazing

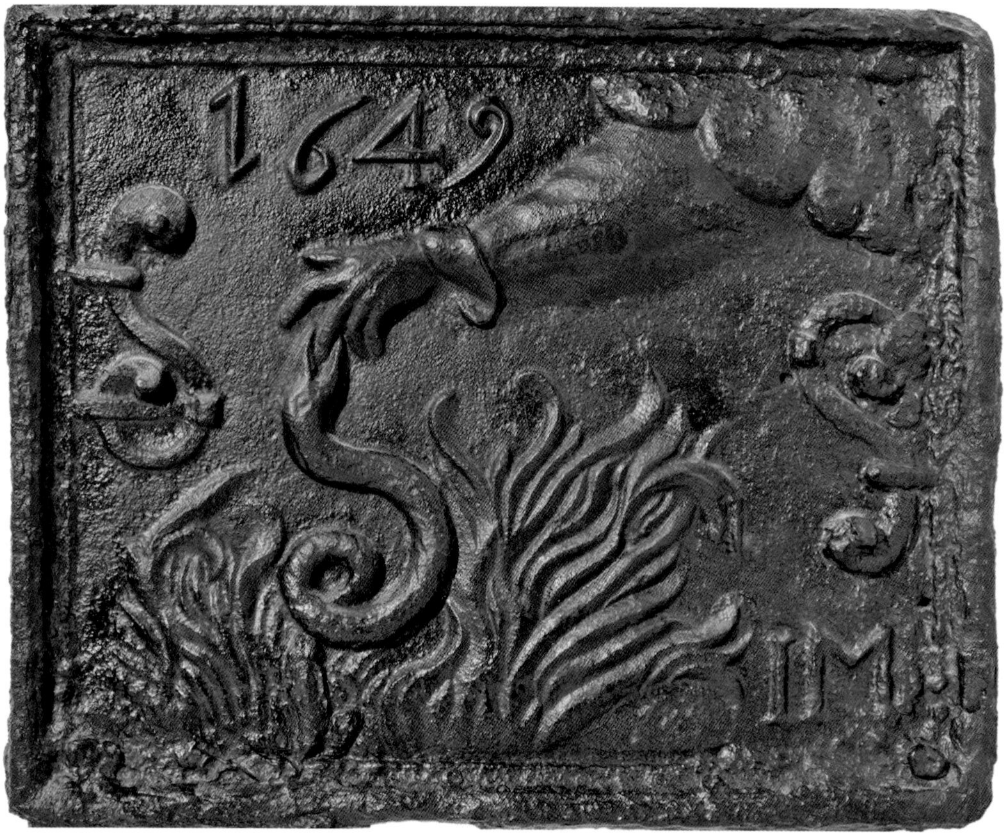

180 Cast-iron fireback, dated 1649. Victoria and Albert Museum, London

down into the fire and using the imagery depicted on this fireback to prompt contemplation on the nature of Christian salvation.

In conclusion, imagery in and around the fireplace was likely to receive more prolonged and concentrated attention than imagery in other positions within the domestic interior. The physical form of overmantels in the post-Reformation period often recalled the traditional shape and appearance of pre-Reformation devotional altarpieces, which indicates that a taste for traditional visual forms endured and that the imagery had an allied function as the focus of prolonged visual attention. Meanwhile, the choice of subject matter shows a predilection for stories and themes illustrating the soteriological message of the Christian faith, which suggests that imagery in this position served to prompt and guide meditation on the fundamentals of Christian doctrine. The popularity of certain Old Testament stories, in particular, suggests that the traditional device of types was employed in order to refer to New Testament episodes requiring the depiction of controversial scenes and figures. In this way, the decoration of chimneypieces with religious imagery could provide a visual focus for the practice of Protestant meditation, while the risk of idolatry was minimised by substituting safe alternatives for potentially problematic images.

Another way to reduce the risk of idolatry was to pare down the amount of visual detail. The relatively simple appearance of what I have termed 'surrogate imagery' implies a recognition that the function of the religious image as sign was purely and immediately as a referent; there was no inherent substance or value within the image to absorb the viewer; rather, the image referred (and deferred) to the vastly superior authority of the Word, which it served to evoke. The use of images as visual reminders in this way is close to the Catholic justification of religious images as reminders of holy things. As described in Chapter 1, the twenty-fifth session of the Council of Trent in 1563 restated the traditional justification of sacred images for the purposes of instruction and as aids to pious thoughts: 'by means of the histories of the mysteries of our Redemption, portrayed by paintings or other representations, the people is instructed, and confirmed in [the habit of] remembering, and continually revolving in mind the articles of faith'. Although they may have served this traditional function, the form, subject matter and appearance of 'surrogate images' conform to the emphasis in Protestant image theory on the authority of the Word and the rejection of the aesthetic, seductive quality of art that would distract the viewer from the pure and invisible spiritual sphere. Several Protestant authors repeated a warning that if images were too beautiful or moving they distracted the viewer from religious thoughts. As the moderate bishop Symon Patrick observed, 'there is too much of sense in the tragical and theatrical representations which are made by some papists of Christ's sufferings . . . The eye and ear are so fully possessed, that their objects work of their natural strength, and not by the soul's considering and meditating powers'.[66] Surrogate images avoided the distracting, even perilous, depiction of Christ's Passion that aroused the senses and emotions and diverted thoughts to bodily and material concerns when the end goal was to attain a pure, spiritual understanding.

It is possible to speculate therefore that certain kinds of biblical imagery in the household were provided to remind its inhabitants of their religious duty to meditate and reflect on Christ's sacrifice as the route to salvation. The householder provided these images for his family because he could not rely on their ability to meditate on appropriate subject matter without visual prompts, but he also could not be sure that such visual depictions would not seduce viewers into improper forms of response. The idea was to liberate the mind from worldly things, not to get bogged down in them. Images were supposed to lead the godly to pure worship and not put barriers in the way. What I have termed 'surrogate images' in domestic decoration therefore represent a particular kind of response to Protestant theories about the utility and dangers of religious art. This use of Old Testament types can also perhaps be understood as the response of a particular kind of Protestant – the more godly among the conforming majority who were sensitive to the potential pitfalls of depicting sacred subject matter but who nevertheless desired and utilised traditional forms of imagery to promote and prompt pious thoughts.

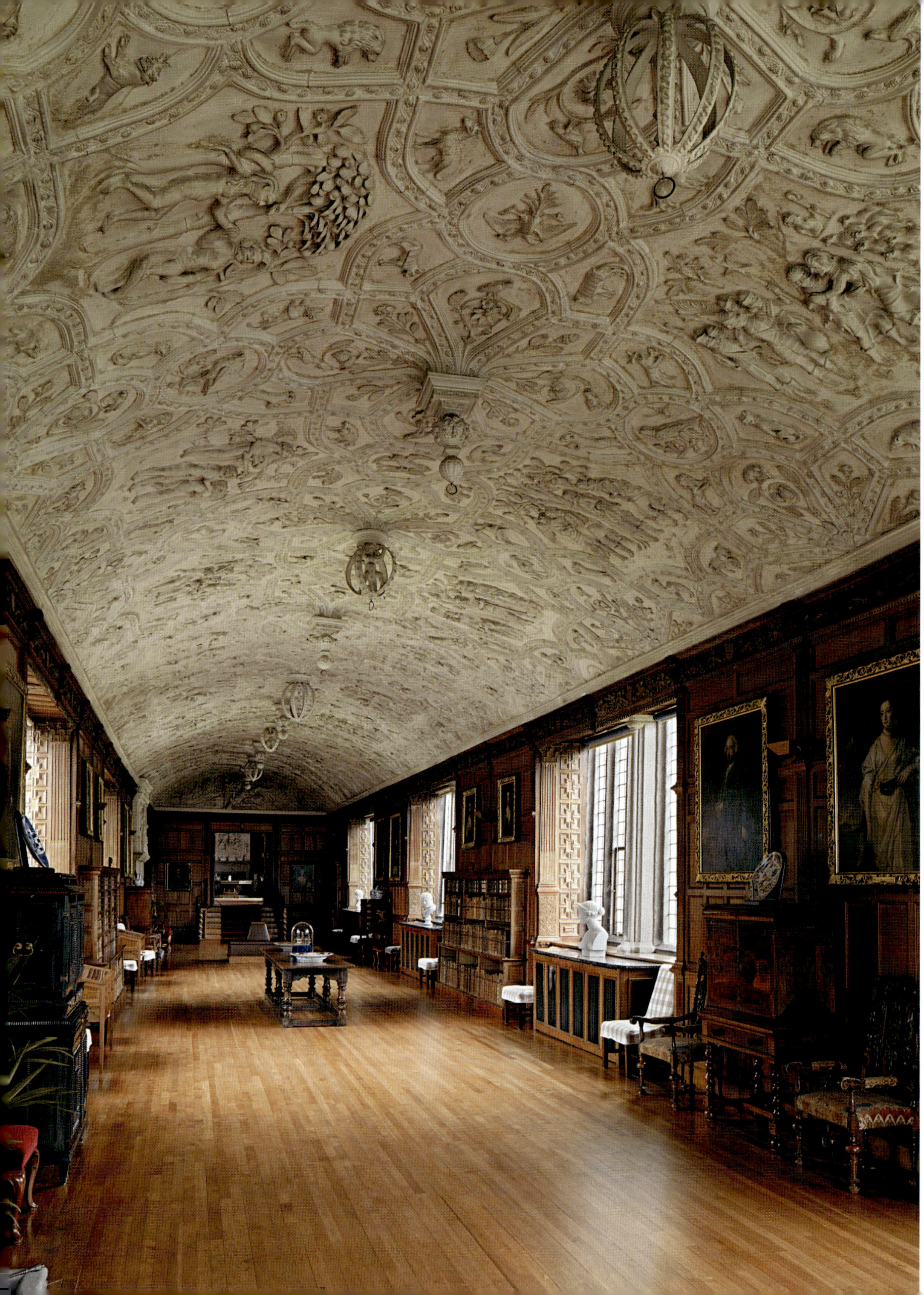

6

The Presence of Religious Imagery in the Godly Household

The prominent position of religious images above fireplaces in the principal rooms of early modern houses suggests two things: that the imagery was meant to be noticed and that a certain level of engagement was expected and encouraged. In this chapter I will reverse this argument to suggest that religious imagery depicted in other areas of the interior was *not* meant to be viewed or engaged with in a prolonged or focused manner, at least not on a regular basis. Much of the study so far has been concerned with the spiritual meanings of iconography. This chapter moves away from the issue of content to explore the impact of form. The creation of large-scale religious imagery as a permanent addition to domestic space made tangible a spiritual presence in everyday life and this chapter speculates about the psychological effect of this presence on human thought and behaviour.

The area above the fireplace seems a natural place for the application of decoration, providing a physical and symbolic focal point in the room. Fireplaces were usually positioned at the half-way point along the longer side of any given room and were therefore conspicuous and highly visible wherever the occupant of the room might be situated. They provided a natural gathering point for individuals and groups seeking warmth from the fire so they were also the symbolic centre of social interaction. It is therefore reasonable to assume, as in the previous chapter, that imagery above a fireplace might serve as a site for prolonged viewing and associated contemplation and/or discussion. This kind of viewing experience is familiar to modern society, as we are used to looking at works of art conveniently positioned at eye-level on the walls of art galleries. While there may be questions about the meanings and functions of imagery depicted above a fireplace, the physical position does not seem problematic in considering the nature of the process of viewing. This is also the case for imagery depicted in wall decoration, such as the painted

181 (FACING PAGE) View of the plasterwork ceiling of c. 1636 in the long gallery of Lanhydrock House, Cornwall

surfaces of great chambers in merchants' houses including the Black Lion in Hereford, or the parlour of farmhouses such as 'Roger's Farmhouse' in Suffolk. This imagery is within comfortable line of sight and may be viewed easily by occupants of the room whether they are standing or seated.

However, many other examples of religious imagery in decorative art displayed within the post-Reformation domestic interior resist prolonged and concentrated viewing. For example, the carved wood and plasterwork screen of about 1610 in the great hall at Burton Agnes Hall in Yorkshire (see Figs 73 and 74) includes complex iconography that reaches high into the ceiling space. The upper sections of this detailed iconographical scheme are effectively beyond viewing range, with the content and meaning of the imagery difficult to discern from the ground. Furthermore, the imagery incorporates tiny textual inscriptions depicted so high up in the frieze of the carved wood section of the screen that they are impossible to read, or even to detect their presence, without erecting scaffolding to enable the viewer to study the text at close quarters. This decorated screen therefore raises several questions. How should one approach complex figurative iconography, like this elaborate scheme at Burton Agnes, if the experience of viewing such imagery is impeded by its scale, location and level of detail? What was the purpose of including textual inscriptions within decorative art if it is virtually impossible to read them? How should one interpret narrative and figurative imagery that is situated beyond the normal and natural range of view?

To explore these questions, this chapter focuses on the decoration of ceilings with complex iconography. Most of the examples have already been discussed in previous chapters but here I want to focus on how, exactly, the original inhabitants of these houses might have viewed or experienced these images on an everyday basis. It is proposed that due to inherent physical difficulties in the process of viewing, the study of imagery on ceilings requires an interpretative approach which places the visual qualities of the imagery second to the impact of its presence. In short, the meaning of the imagery is less important than its effect. In pursuing this argument, the chapter draws on ideas and approaches from the interdisciplinary project of visual studies: specifically, an interest in the physical dynamics of viewing and the mechanics of visual perception allied with an awareness of the specificity of visual experience according to historical and cultural context. This focus on questions of the visual is allied with anthropological and archaeological approaches focusing on the relationship between art, belief and behaviour. I conclude that placing religious imagery on ceilings within the domestic interior allowed Protestant patrons to exploit the power of the visual in the service of reformed faith while minimising the risk of idolatrous abuse.

The first case study is the plasterwork ceiling in the long gallery of Lanhydrock House in Cornwall, executed in about 1636 for John, Lord Robartes (Fig. 181); the work is described in detail in Chapter 4. Its decoration has been little studied but most scholars who have considered or mentioned it tend to assume that the ceiling was created for a didactic purpose, so that the series of scenes from Genesis form a narrative sequence to be 'read' in a manner analogous to text.[1] According to this interpretation, the imagery provides a kind of picture-Bible and is explained as serving the purposes of religious instruction.[2] In questioning this interpretation it is necessary to reconstruct the experience of viewing the scenes depicted in the ceiling at Lanhydrock.

The scenes do follow a continuous sequence but with the orientation of each one directed towards the centre of the room (see Fig. 120). This format of presentation means that to view the imagery as a sequence of scenes in the biblical order, the viewer is required to progress down the length of the gallery but must stop and make a ninety-degree turn to the side as they encounter each new scene, in order to view it from the correct angle. An alternative mode of viewing the scenes in a progressive sequence is for the viewer to walk sideways, crab-style. Even if such sideways perambulation was not highly implausible, the physical challenge of looking up at these images for any length of time has to be taken into account. Since the imagery at Lanhydrock is positioned on the ceiling and not on the walls, it requires the viewer to look heavenwards. While this may be considered appropriate to the religious nature of the subject matter, it is extremely problematic for the process of viewing. Firstly, the required stop-start, turn-and-face movement is physically awkward and is not in keeping with the primary function of long galleries during this period as a space for walking. Secondly, it is impossible to view this ceiling for any length of time without getting severe neck-ache. Indeed, the National Trust, now responsible for managing the property, distributes mirrors to enable visitors to view the imagery on the ceiling. This ceiling therefore presents a conundrum. Why depict such a sophisticated and detailed scheme of religious iconography, the kind of narrative iconography one expects to communicate meaningful messages requiring time to interpret, if its positioning on the ceiling makes it almost impossible, certainly highly uncomfortable, to view? An alternative, and less problematic, position for such imagery is the frieze level.

My second case study, which raises a similar set of questions, is the 'Jesse' ceiling in one of two seventeenth-century merchant houses known as the Butterwalk in the harbour town of Dartmouth in Devon. As noted before, this house was built in 1635 as the new residence of the fish merchant and town receiver Mark Hawkins. In the street-facing, first-floor room of Hawkins's house, which was probably the parlour, or best chamber, is an elaborate plasterwork ceiling depicting the Tree of Jesse and the Four Evangelists (Fig. 182). As with the ceiling at Lanhydrock, this post-Reformation decoration employs a common pre-Reformation iconography. The Tree of Jesse, illustrating Isaiah 11.1 and Matthew 1.6–16, which describes the genealogy of Christ, is an ancient and traditional religious image, employed throughout the medieval period in churches, most often in stained-glass windows but sometimes in sculpture, as for example in the north wall of the chancel at Dorchester Abbey (about 1340; Fig. 183). The Tree of Jesse in the Butterwalk adopts the conventional iconographical format, depicting the recumbent figure of Jesse at the base (although I use the word 'base' here out of convenience as it is not in fact an appropriate term in this case, a point to which I will return). From the body of Jesse sprouts a vine and encircled among the branches and leaves are twenty-eight figures, some holding identifying attributes, others wearing crowns. At the top of the tree is a rose-shaped cartouche framing a depiction of the Virgin and Child and at the four corners of

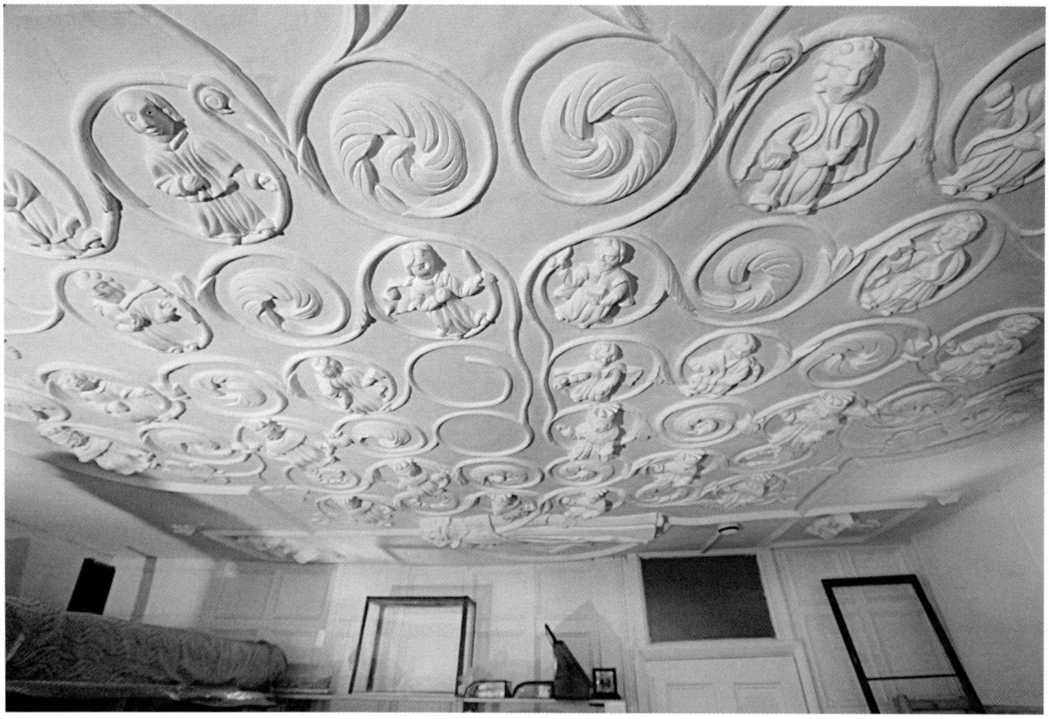

182 Tree of Jesse, plasterwork ceiling of c. 1635–40 in the Butterwalk, Dartmouth, Devon

the design are images of the Four Evangelists with their symbolic creatures. Again, it is striking to find such traditional pre-Reformation iconography in a post-Reformation domestic context.

The controversial nature of such imagery during this period is illustrated by the fact that many depictions of the Tree of Jesse were attacked by reformers during iconoclastic purges of churches. For example, the sculpted Tree of Jesse made in 1470 for the Lady Chapel of St Cuthbert's Church in Wells, Somerset, was stripped of its twenty statues of kings, leaving only empty niches, while the figure of Jesse at the base was defaced. It is likely that the location of the Jesse sculpture in the sensitive space of St Cuthbert's Church, rather than the particular subject matter, prompted the attack. Still, there are clear iconographical similarities between this carved depiction of Jesse and the plasterwork version in the Butterwalk. Yet, while the Jesse iconography employed in the Butterwalk is highly traditional, the positioning is markedly unconventional. One of the striking features about this version of the Tree is the incongruity of representing this particular iconography on a flat ceiling. The Tree by its very nature requires a vertical format for representation with the tree rising upwards, through the chronology of Christ's ancestors, to the depiction of Christ at the apex. Viewers accustomed to this iconography would expect to view the image from the base upwards, with the eyes gradually being raised heavenwards and the obvious symbolic connotations of spiritual ascent. This representation,

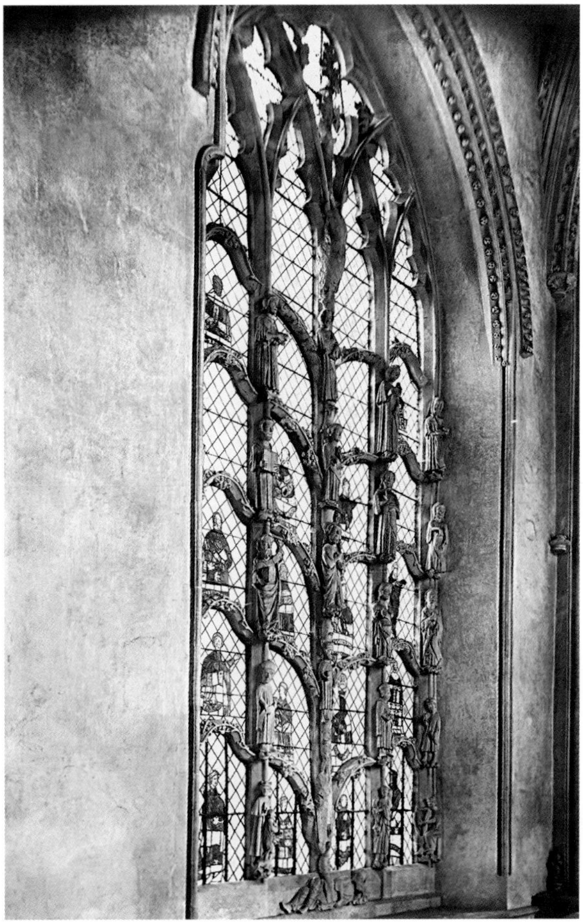

183 Tree of Jesse window, carved stone and stained glass, c. 1340, in Dorchester Abbey, Oxfordshire

however, is on a horizontal plane, making it difficult to determine the starting point for viewing the imagery in a logical manner, if such a logical 'reading' of the imagery is intended. Moreover, the incongruity of the flat representation is compounded by the dimensions of the space. The room is relatively small (approximately fifteen feet or five metres square) and the ceiling is so low that the entire iconography cannot be seen unless the viewer lies down flat on the floor. Therefore, it seems that the imagery is not supposed to be viewed as an entirety or engaged with in a detailed manner.

It is notable that both of these decorated ceilings, at Lanhydrock and the Butterwalk, are located in the larger and more public areas of the house, that is, the long gallery at Lanhydrock and the principal, first-floor chamber in the Butterwalk. These are rooms in which guests would have been entertained, where business transactions would have taken place and, in the case of the chamber in the Butterwalk, was probably the location for family dining. These rooms were therefore semi-public, often communal and multi-purpose spaces. I have indicated that due to the positioning on the ceiling, viewing these works of decorative art for any length of time would be physically uncomfortable and would require rather odd movements within the room (sporadic viewing-and-walking combinations or walking sideways, lying down flat on the floor) in order to view the entirety of the imagery from the correct angle. Clearly none of these movements would be compatible with social interaction or domestic activities. This positioning therefore reveals a problem with traditional, Panofskian-style approaches to complex iconography which tend to assume a static viewer, engaging with images for prolonged periods of time. The location of the imagery on the ceilings of principal, semi-public areas of the house also indicates that prolonged viewing of a concentrated nature was unlikely, as it is known that these works of decoration were experienced repeatedly by members of the household and regularly by frequent guests. This constant exposure to the imagery, presumably often on the move through the house or in company, again suggests that any prolonged or engaged form of viewing was unlikely, certainly on a regular basis.

Furthermore, the physical act of viewing imagery on a ceiling, that is, looking upwards, might in itself be considered problematic in this particular historical context. As observed in Chapter 1, some Protestant commentators argued that raising the eyes heavenward was one of the outward forms of devotion proscribed by the Second Commandment. As William Perkins explains: 'Adoration in generail, is an outward Worship, signifying and testifying the inward worship of the heart. More specially, by it we must conceive, the bowing of the head, and knee; the bending and prostrating of the bodie; *the lifting up of the hands, eyes*, and such like' (my italics).[3] Henry Ainsworth's annotations on the Ten Commandments include a definition of the Second Commandment's ban on the worship of images. He observed: 'not bow down or, not worship: under this one, all other gestures of reverence are forbidden; as bowing the knee, 1 King. 19.18. kissing, Hos.13.2. *lifting up of the eyes*, Ezek.18.6. spreading out of the hands, Psal. 44.23. and the like' (my italics).[4] While these proscriptions were primarily intended for contexts where outward gestures of worship were most likely to occur (such as in churches and chapels), it is clear that good Protestants were cautioned to be mindful of their bodily movements to avoid any appearance of impropriety. Thus, raising the eyes heavenward to look at religious imagery on a ceiling might, in the context of post-Reformation anxiety about the dangers of image-worship, be considered an idolatrous gesture of reverence. It seems therefore that these images were problematical to view, both in terms of physical discomfort and lest the actual gesture required to view was taken as an outward sign of improper worship.

Other examples of figurative imagery on ceilings include the plasterwork at 62 Boutport Street in Barnstaple which depicts the New Testament scenes of the Annunciation and Nativity. This building is now used as a restaurant and at some point in the past the floor between the ground and first-floor level was removed so that the barrel-vaulted plasterwork ceiling is now viewed at some distance. The ceiling originally adorned the principal first-floor chamber and the closer proximity to the ceiling would have required a much greater arch of the neck to view the narrative scenes. A near-identical ceiling was removed from 7 Cross Street in the same town and is now re-installed in a private house. At Manor Court House in Cotton End, Bedfordshire, a plasterwork ceiling depicts the

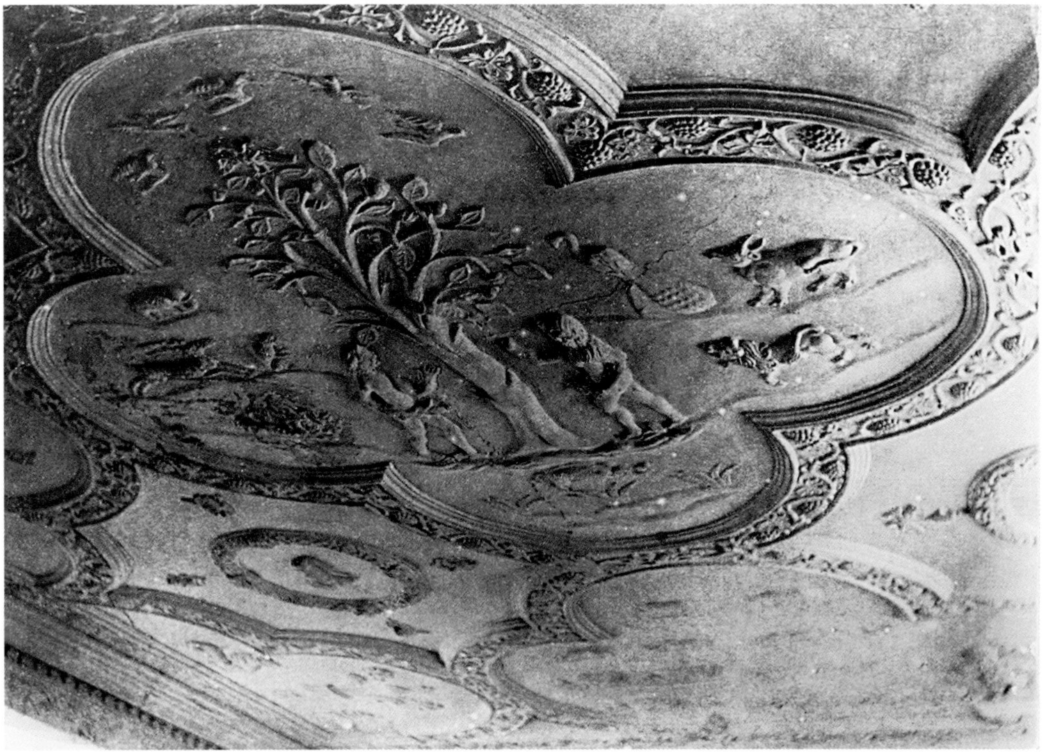

184 View of the plasterwork ceiling of c. 1620–50 at Manor Court House, Bedfordshire

scene of Adam and Eve's fall, which is duplicated twice with other imagery relating to Adam's family toiling after the expulsion. The single large room that this ceiling decorates has at some stage been divided into several smaller rooms which has not only made it hard to identify the overall scheme of iconography but has diminished the effect of such large-scale sculptural work on the ceiling of a single space. The huge figures depicted in high relief are not only a looming presence above the head but intrude into the space of the room (Fig. 184).

Alongside these examples of plasterwork ceilings in England is a group of Scottish painted ceilings, which has been comprehensively documented and analysed by Michael Bath.[5] This includes the painted ceiling of the building known as Mary Somerville's House in Burntisland, Fife, which incorporates the symbolic Agnus Dei and portraits of Christ and the Virgin Mary; the long gallery at Dean House (now destroyed) and the painted gallery at Provost Skene's House in Aberdeen which includes scenes of the Crucifixion, Resurrection and, originally, the Ascension. Another ceiling design with complex religious iconography adorned the ceiling of one of the merchant houses in Blyth's Close in Edinburgh, of which a brief discussion provides the final case study for this chapter.

Blyth's Close was demolished in 1845 and shortly afterwards the antiquary Daniel Wilson provided a detailed description of the decorated interiors of the various buildings on the site. One of the painted ceilings described by Wilson was in a tenement at the head of Blyth's Close on Castle Hill. The exterior of this block was inscribed with the motto LAUS DEO ('Praise be to God'), the initials RM and the date 1591. Wilson's description of the iconography of the ceiling includes some biblical scenes (the Baptism of Christ, Jacob's Ladder) but also some curious, unidentified allegories. A recent study by Michael Bath has now elucidated the nature of these allegories and in so doing he has revealed the religious and political meanings of the entire scheme.[6] Bath discovered a set of coloured drawings in the RCAHMS which he attributes to the antiquary and architect A. W. Lyons. These drawings correspond with Wilson's description of the Blyth's Close ceiling but provide the pictorial detail to identify the precise nature of the iconography. Bath's account reconstructs the ceiling as consisting of eight separate sections. Two circular compartments at the centre contained images of the Apostle John and Christ holding an orb. On either side of these compartments, lower down the coved ceiling, were six rectangular panels, three on each side. These depicted Jacob's Ladder, the Baptism of Christ and Christ asleep in the Storm, two allegories (the Four Horsemen of the Apocalypse and Death, Persecution and the Devil), and possibly a scene showing four musicians. Bath convincingly reads the two allegories as a comment on the triumph of Protestantism over Apocalyptic destruction. The Four Horsemen are depicted with the symbols of the Evangelists (representing the Gospels), suggesting that the Word will triumph over the Horsemen at the end of things. In the allegory of Death, Persecution and the Devil, the Ship of Faith is guided by the hand of God, with Christ as helmsman. The ship sails away from the burning City of Destruction (identified with Babylon and thus a figure of the Church of Rome). In its entirety, the meaning of the iconography is revealed as a statement about Protestant righteousness in the face of apocalyptic destructive forces.

The focus of Bath's study is on the meanings of the allegorical images but these provide a clue to reading the biblical scenes within what emerges as a sophisticated iconographical concept. Jacob's Ladder and Christ's Baptism can be grouped together since both depict moments of connection between Heaven and Earth and represent the route to heaven through Christ. Indeed these two scenes are visually similar in that they both depict the heavens opening to reveal God (represented by the Tetragrammaton). The scene of Christ asleep in the storm – a parable about faith in the face of potential destruction – can be paired with the Ship of Faith allegory: again, both are visually similar with the depiction of a ship at sea. This leaves the Four Horsemen and the four musicians as a group which, as Bath points out, is plausible given that Revelation 18.22 forecasts the destruction of Babylon 'and the voice of harpers and musicians, and of pipers, and trumpeters, shall be heard no more in thee'. One might note that the religious subject matter of the ceiling described by Wilson led to the theory, restated enough to become accepted as fact, that the apartment must have been part of the Catholic Mary of Guise's palace. Bath's discoveries crush that fiction; as he observes, 'if we were looking for biblical painting that entirely fitted the ideology of pious Protestant middle-class householders in early modern Scotland, we could hardly do better'.[7]

Bath was able to reconstruct the iconography and meaning of this painted ceiling through the study of coloured drawings that recorded its appearance. However, viewing pictorial iconography in drawings – which are presumably laid flat on a table before the viewer and thus within close range – is a fundamentally different experience from viewing the same iconography when it is depicted above the head in a ceiling still *in situ* in a domestic room. It is interesting to consider whether the communicative richness of the iconography could have been appreciated to the same extent in this position and context. As the house at Blyth's Close no longer survives it is not possible to determine the height of the ceiling or the degree of curve so that it is not clear if the viewer had only to tilt their head upwards or arch it back a full ninety degrees in order to view the imagery on a flat ceiling. If the relatively low ceiling at Provost Skene's House is used as a comparison, the imagery extends from the sloping sides of the ceiling to culminate with images on its flat centre. To view this imagery the viewer must arch their neck to the point where considerable discomfort is felt after a relatively short period of time. There is also the question of how the viewer would move about the space in order to appreciate each image at the correct angle and in sequence, which is required if the complex dynamic between the paired images and the overall message of the entire scheme is to be understood. It is quite possible that the ceiling's imagery was read in this way on special occasions by guests who shared the owner's religious sympathies. Perhaps they were aided in their interpretation by the patron's explication of the iconography. In such situations the patron is able to monitor interpretation and response and ensure that the intended, correct understanding is achieved. Yet the fact remains that the process of viewing imagery on a ceiling is unnatural and thus physically uncomfortable. So: why depict complex religious iconography in a position that serves to discourage prolonged and concentrated viewing?

In addressing this question it is necessary to examine the specificity of the nature of vision in this particular historical context. The discussion that follows first considers contemporary beliefs concerning the nature and operation of the bodily senses, with particular focus on religious and folk beliefs about the potency of the sense of sight. This leads on to a discussion of the dynamics of viewing in relation to the cases studied in this chapter and, more specifically, a questioning of the dominant assumption about the relationship between object and subject in relation to the act of vision. The second section revisits the responsibilities of the godly householder in disciplining his household and protecting it from sin and shame. It then focuses on the role of material and visual culture in sanctifying the domestic interior, thus fortifying it against malevolent forces.

Early modern society held a complicated and ambivalent understanding of how vision operated. A certain preoccupation with the bodily senses in the early modern period is evidenced by the popularity of the Senses as subject matter for domestic decoration. Images of the Senses usually adopted the conventional iconography, which depicted each of them personified as a woman dressed in classical drapery and holding an identifying attribute. This is how they are found, for example, in the plasterwork ceiling dated 1623 in the great chamber at Boston Manor House in Middlesex (Fig. 185). Representation of the Senses in decorative art can be understood as highly appropriate for a domestic con-

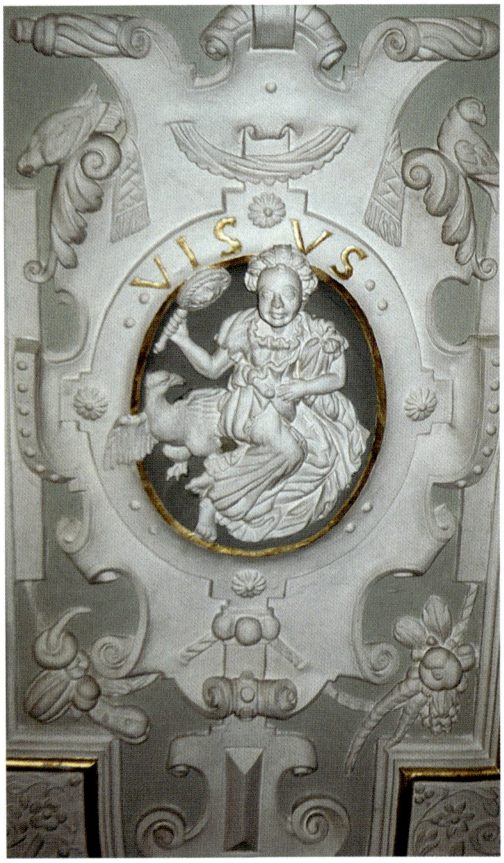

185 The Sense of Sight, detail of the plasterwork ceiling of 1623 at Boston Manor House, Middlesex

text, as the imagery alludes to sensory pleasures experienced in the domestic sphere: eating and drinking (taste and smell), music-making and theatrical entertainment (hearing and sight) and love-making (touch). However, their presence within decorative art during this period is more likely to have served as a warning than a celebration because indulgence of the senses was feared by Protestant commentators as the path to sin and corruption. Thus Richard Brathwaite, writing in 1620, warned that 'the five senses be those five gates, by which the world doth besiege us, the Devill doth tempt us and the flesh ensnare us'.[8] He went on to identify the sense of sight as the most dangerous of the senses for, he said, 'there is no passage more easie for the entry of vice than by the cranie of the eye'.[9] In his *Treatise of Mans Imaginations*, Perkins directed his readers:

> David prayed the Lord to direct and keepe his eies from beholding vanitie: Now looke how these holy men dealt with their eyes, so must wee proportionably deale for all the outward senses of our body; bynding them all, after their example, from being the meanes of provocation to any sinne: This dutie is most necessarie, for the outward senses be the doores & windowes of the soule, and unlesse good care be had thereto, the devill will enter in by them and fill the soule with all corruption.[10]

A key concern was the seductive nature of the visual sense. Stephen Egerton was convinced that a desire for visual pleasure would lead to the misuse of riches and the sin of pride: 'By the lust of the eyes, I understand a greedy desire of wealth & riches, which are as thornes & briers to the covetous man'.[11] Meanwhile Anthony Nixon, writing in 1616, reflected on the question: 'What is the use of the eyes?'. He concluded: 'To behold the works of God, and therefore we ought to beware that we feed them not with the sight of prophane and dishonest things, lest they poison the soule, whose messangers they ought to be to declare unto it vertuous and healthful things.'[12] What these comments help to reveal is an understanding that sight could be both disabling and enabling in the quest for spiritual purity. As a door to the soul, eyesight could be the means of corruption or grace. In order not to poison the soul, it was necessary to look only at virtuous and 'healthful' things. While commentators attempted to define what one might and might not look at, in practice there was an obvious problem in controlling what was seen. How might a good Protestant know where to look? How might a godly man 'bynd' his senses, in Perkins's words, 'from being the meanes of provocation to any sinne'?

Not only was the act of seeing considered dangerous as a potential provocation to sin but being seen might also be cause for concern. During the sixteenth and seventeenth century and concomitant with the process of the Reformation, there was a dramatic surge in witch trials. Belief in *maleficium* – the ability of one person to hurt others through occult means – reached a peak in this period and one of the most acknowledged methods of *maleficium* was the 'evil eye' whereby the witch gave out an invisible emanation from her eyes, thus afflicting the subject of her sight. In such cases the victim was said to be 'fascinated' or 'overlooked'.[13] Belief in the power of the evil eye was described by William Perkins in his *Discourse of the Damned Art of Witchcraft* of 1608. He explained: 'Witches by malitious and wrie looks in anger and displeasure, may and doe hurt those upon whome they looke whether they be men or other creatures'. Although Perkins dismissed this popular belief as unproven, he acknowledged it as an old received opinion, 'as fond as it is old'.[14] George Hakewill, the author of a treatise on eyesight, devoted a chapter to the subject 'Of bewitching by the eie'. He wrote:

> Some write that women that have a double pupill in their eie, doe most harme this way; but upon what certaine grounds of experience, I cannot affirme; only in this, I finde most of auncient heathen Philosophers to concur, & some of the latter christian Physitions, that not only men and women, doe interchangeably hurt one an other in this kinde (as hath already beene shewed,) but both of the unreasonable creatures, and they againe, both men, and women.[15]

John Gaule, writing in 1646, provided a list of methods used to exercise the power of bewitching. The evil eye is listed as number three (of twelve), after the power of thought and the use of familiars. He described the evil eye thus: 'Some by Inspecting, or looking on, but to glare, or squint, or peep at with an envious and evill eye, is sufficient to effascinate.'[16] Belief in the power of the look to 'effascinate' helps explain why the eyes of saints and religious figures in medieval paintings were often targeted in acts of iconoclasm. The removal of the eyes, often through scratching and gouging, removed the potency of the image as a spiritual agent as well as diminishing its affective power.

In concluding this section, it is clear that there was a certain ambivalence around the power of the visual sense during this period. The primacy of this sense, as the most efficient of the bodily senses, was acknowledged but Protestants feared the facility of their own sense of sight as a potential point of entry for sin and vice. Anxiety surrounding the act of vision stemmed from two contemporary beliefs. First, that viewing sensuous objects could lead to the sins of covetousness, lust, greed, vanity and idolatry. Secondly, that being the object of sight might lead to a malignant infection caused by emanations issuing from the eyes of another person. Both beliefs concern the idea of infection from outside and underline the immediacy and potency of vision. Concern about the potentially corruptive power of visual artefacts may explain why religious imagery in plasterwork is not coloured but left plain and white.[17] This decorative art does not feed the visual sense, it does not stimulate or encourage visual pleasure, so it is less likely to encourage idolatry and poison the soul. Yet the Scottish ceilings are richly painted so perhaps it should be questioned if imagery on ceilings was meant to be viewed intently at all; perhaps it is the decoration itself that does the viewing.

DETECTING THE GAZE FROM ABOVE

Placing figurative imagery on a ceiling puts it in a powerful position in relation to the act of vision. Over the past few decades, the development of a scholarly interest often termed 'gaze theory' has established that looking – whether gazing, glancing, glimpsing or peeping – involves the operation of power. The 'gaze' (defined as a prolonged look) is characterised as an especially potent act of looking. As Jonathan Schroeder has noted, 'to gaze implies more than to look at – it signifies a psychological relationship of power, in which the gazer is superior to the object of the gaze'.[18] This power dynamic between gazer and gazed-at is graphically illustrated by Michel Foucault's seminal discussion of Panopticism and the regulatory and reformatory effects of surveillance.[19] In the context of my study, while it is awkward and uncomfortable for the human viewer to look up at the ceiling, the imagery on the ceiling occupies an optimum viewing position down into the room. Thus the painted or sculpted figures of Christ, Jesse and the other biblical characters are able to survey the room constantly, while the occupant of the room may only glance at the ceiling occasionally. Therefore, if it is the 'gazer' with the power, then the gaze is performed by the figures on the ceiling.

Numerous anthropological studies have established that art and objects are often invested with agency and power. For example, in his influential book, *Art and Agency*, Alfred Gell has argued against the passivity of art and instead focused on the making of art objects as a means of affecting the thoughts and actions of others.[20] He proposed that art works embody complex webs of intentionalities and mediate social agency. What is striking and exciting about Gell's thesis is, as Shirley Campbell has observed, that the art object can be understood as 'a social actor, merging with and standing for human agents and/or other supernatural "agency" given anthropomorphic vitality by significant human actors.'[21] In this way the art object becomes an active participant in human social relationships and behaviours.

While Gell's theory concerns the way that agency operates through and around art objects, W. J. T. Mitchell went a step further in his discussion of the active, 'animate' quality of art to suggest that images can have a will and a purpose of their own. In his article 'What do Pictures Really Want?' Mitchell shifted the location of desire away from the producers and consumers of imagery to the images themselves to ask what they want or desire from us.[22] He highlighted the 'personhood' of images and concluded that the magical, pre-modern attitude to images as animate, powerful beings is just as alive in the modern world as it was in traditional societies.

One of the ways that humans attribute animism and intentionality is through the language of the eyes. It has long been recognised that eyes play a crucial role in social interaction, particularly in relation to communication and courtship.[23] However, eye contact is often assigned a more sinister character. For example, in his reflection on the nature of seeing, *The Object Stares Back*, James Elkins reflected on the instinctive sense of the presence of objects, which seem to watch you. He used the example of the child's fear that the bedroom at night comes to life and the toys become sinister as they stare back at the child in bed.[24] Indeed, it is now accepted that there is a solid foundation for this infantile fear which stems from the fact that humans are biologically sensitive to the perception of gaze. The ability to detect and follow eye or eye-like stimuli in the environment appears early in human development. In 1995 the psychologist Simon Baron-Cohen argued that the human mind must include a system which deals explicitly with gaze detection and interpretation and plays a critical role in the development of social cognition.[25] In summary, the proposed system has three basic functions: it (a) detects the presence of eyes or eyelike stimuli in the environment, (b) computes whether the eyes are directed towards it or towards something else and (c) attributes the mental state of 'seeing' to the gazer.

Subsequently, researchers in neuroscience, cognitive science and psychobiology have been able to substantiate the existence of a gaze detection system in the human brain. Various methods have been employed to prove that particular areas of the brain respond to the perception of gaze.[26] Numerous studies have found that specific cells in the superior temporal sulcus (STS) region are activated in response to eye gaze. In particular, whereas some cells are tuned to detect eye contact, others are tuned to detect averted gaze. These cells are part of a broader system that is dedicated to the detection of social attention. Other researchers have found that the processing of gaze perception significantly activates those regions of the amygdala involved in detecting threat.[27] These investigations have demonstrated that the neuronal activity triggered by the perception of gaze is a biological, reflexive response, which supports the importance of gaze detection in our perceptual framework. Furthermore, gaze detection is triggered both by living eyes and images that resemble eyes. The brain activity occurs regardless of whether the 'gazer' is real or represented (as long as the image has realistic eyelike characteristics).[28] This neuronal response to any eyelike image provides an explanation for the animate quality we often assign to inanimate objects. As Elkins has observed, 'Each object has a presence – a being and a face of its own – and if we take that seriously (not as a vague intuition but as a fact of vision), then the world is full of eyes. Seeing is being seen.'[29]

All the examples of decorated ceilings discussed in this chapter include images of faces and, more significantly, eyes. At the Butterwalk, for instance, thirty-five pairs of eyes stare down from all parts of the ceiling to scrutinise every part of the room. Painted faces are arguably even more realistic and the twenty pairs of eyes belonging to the figures of saints and sibyls in the painted ceiling at Mary Somerville's House in Fife suggest a daunting sense of being surveyed by figures of authority. If one accepts the premise that it is the ceiling decoration that does the gazing, and that the human audience is the subject of the gaze, the next step is to consider the purpose of this surveillance.

As discussed in Chapter 3, one of the principal duties of the good Protestant householder was the maintenance of order and discipline. Yet the patriarch could not always be present to monitor the activities of his extended family. I have suggested that one way that the patriarch could attempt to regulate that behaviour was to appeal to a higher authority and invoke the watchful presence of God. George Hakewill's comment on the all-seeing God is pertinent:

> Hee that is present with them sitting in their Thrones, is likewise present with them lying in their Beds: as he is with them in their Chappels, so is he in their most secret Cabinets and withdrawing roomes. *Like a well-drawne picture that eyeth each in the room*, hee eyeth in that manner each one in the world; and all the waies of each one, as if his eye were upon him alone [my italics].[30]

Hakewill's metaphor of the well-drawn picture eyeing each member of the room suggests an understanding of the power of crafted imagery to mimic the act of vision. There was broad agreement among Protestant authors that the figure of God the Father could not be represented in any form or context without breaking the Second Commandment, so the pictorial representation of God in domestic decoration was generally avoided.[31] Nevertheless, the biblical personages depicted on ceilings act as divine agents, as well as agents for the worldly householder. Most of the ceilings discussed here include formidable authority figures such as biblical patriarchs, saints or sibyls; these figures doing the surveying act as a proxy for the 'real' patriarch and serve to bolster his authority. In this way a link is made visible from the heavenly Deity above, to the patriarchs on the ceiling and the worldly patriarch below. This kind of ceiling decoration was thus a metaphor for the spiritual hierarchy and worked to justify and reinforce the authority of the male householder.

Sculpted and painted figures that gaze down on daily life in the godly household serve as a reminder of God's constant gaze over all humankind. The sense of being watched, especially by religious figures, acts as a form of constant surveillance, regulating both behaviour and thought. If a gaze detection system in areas of the human brain concerned with threat awareness and social interaction does indeed make humans biologically sensitive to the perception of gaze, then it could be argued that these ceilings, full of eyes and placed in a position that puts the object of gaze at a disadvantage, manipulate that effect to create a perceptual response: a sensation of heightened social awareness, even anxiety. As a form of constant surveillance this imagery could therefore serve to inhibit sinful behaviour. This might be especially useful during periods when the real patriarch was absent from the house. In this context one might also wonder if the location of decoration on ceilings provided a convenient way to limit the quality and quantity of individuals' engagement with religious imagery on an everyday basis when the patriarch was not on hand to supervise the nature of interpretation and response. Like the 'surrogate images' of the previous chapter, imagery on ceilings could also have discouraged the prolonged and emotional engagement associated with devotional behaviour but through different means: the physical discomfort of the viewing process worked to discourage the devout gaze.

I have suggested that a perceptual awareness of the physical presence and watchful gaze of these biblical characters might produce a discomforting sensation. Yet the presence of these figures with their watchful gaze might also offer comfort. As Hakewill observes:

> True it is, that the eyes of the Lord are sayd to be in every place, beholding the evill and the good . . . yet they are in a special manner set upon those places and persons that hee hath a tender care of and respect unto, and loves in a speciall maner . . . The eyes of the Lord are over the righteous, 1 Pet. 3.12: and they are so over them that hee withdrawes not his eyes from them, Job 36.7.[32]

This indicates that the sense of being watched over, especially by such familial figures, was perhaps a comforting experience for members of the household. Prior to the Reformation saints were often depicted in domestic decoration, presumably because the presence of images of intercessionary figures helped to provide a tangible connection between people and God, but it is also possible that images of saints were employed as talismans. Supporting this interpretation is evidence that members of early modern society felt spiritually vulnerable in their homes to the extent that certain protective rituals were widely employed. A brief diversion into protective practices in the home is instructive in revealing a wider cultural preoccupation with the nature of the home as a spiritual, as well as physical, shelter.

PRACTICES FOR PROTECTION

Only in recent years has academic scholarship begun to consider the long-neglected subject of folk ritual in Britain, including cultural practices relating to magical forms of protection. That the subject has been neglected is no doubt due to the almost complete lack of documentary evidence to support interpretation, although a certain reluctance to consider superstition and magic is probably a significant factor in discouraging scholarly work in this area. However, a huge body of extant artefacts and visual signs testifies to the once widespread belief in the efficacy of material objects and imagery to ward off danger and a burgeoning interest in the area has recently produced some provocative literature on various aspects of the subject.[33]

Protective practices in the home included the making of so-called ritual marks on timber and stone (incised or burned) and the deliberate concealment of certain objects within buildings, including shoes and other garments, horseshoes or skulls, mummified cats and so-called 'witch bottles'.[34] It seems most likely that these marks and objects were intended as apotropaic devices to deflect or capture evil spirits and malevolent forces. The greatest concentration of these objects and signs date from the mid-sixteenth and seventeenth century at a time when, as I have already discussed, belief in witchcraft reached a peak. A notable feature of witchcraft lore was the belief that witches, their animal familiars and other evil spirits could travel through the air. This was by no means restricted to lower-class 'folk' belief but was shared by all sectors of society as a mainstay of Protestant religion. The ubiquity of such beliefs is demonstrated by evidence of ritual protection found in high-status houses as well as in more humble dwellings. William Perkins warned:

> For Sathan contenteth not himselfe, to have manifested his malice in afflicting mens persons, but he also enlargeth the same to the molestation of the places where they dwell, by infecting the ayre, and such like. The onely effectuall meanes to remedie this evill, is the Sanctification of the places of our habitation. Looke as we are wont to sanctifie our meate and drinke, by Gods word, and by praier, and thereby procure his blessing upon his owne ordinance for our refreshing: so in like manner may we sanctifie the places of our aboad, and thereby both procure the blessing which we want, and also avoid many curses and dangers, which otherwise would fall upon us.[35]

Perkins was suggesting that sanctification of places of habitation could be achieved through prayer but it is likely that fearful members of the household resorted to other, traditional practices in order to protect themselves from the 'many curses and dangers'.

The nature of ritual marks and concealed objects is highly symbolic. Series of crosses, composed of just two roughly incised lines, lines forming the initial M and V (referring to the Virgin Mary) are among the most common ritual marks. Circles are also common, symbolising the eternal God, and three interlocking circles represent the Trinity. Another common motif is the six-petalled flower or 'daisy wheel' which is often found in English churches and is usually identified as a consecration mark.[36] A daisy wheel in such a context is found in the chancel of St Mary's Church in Cerne Abbas, Dorset, where it marks the left wall directly above the traditional position of the altar rail and may act as a mystical divide between the nave and the holy area of the chancel. These symbols were also employed in a domestic context. One is incised on top of decorative wall painting from late in the sixteenth century, formerly from a house in Fittleworth and now in the Weald and Downland Open Air Museum in West Sussex. Another daisy wheel symbol is incised on the ceiling of the withdrawing room of Little Moreton Hall in Cheshire (Fig. 186).[37] Similar daisy wheel symbols are inscribed into the woodwork of the screen dividing the entrance passage from the great hall at Chastleton House in Oxfordshire.

There are two aspects to protective practices in the home that are of particular relevance for this chapter: first, the usual location of these objects and marks within certain areas of the house and second, the significance of concealment. Concealed objects were hidden in the fabric of buildings and the space was intentionally sealed up afterwards. In her discussion of shoes concealed in buildings, June Swann has described the location of a shoe dating from the 1620s which had been found embedded in the plaster halfway up a wall at Leigh Barton in Devon, which could not have been plastered over by accident.[38] While objects are often found in wall cavities or buried in the earth under floors, by far the most common location for concealed objects is the chimney or fireplace, while the second most common location is under the floor or above the ceiling.[39] Similarly, ritual marks are also usually found in the attic space, on ceilings, on or near doors, windows and stairs but are most often located on the chimney bressumer.[40] It seems that marks and objects were positioned to protect those liminal areas of the building that were considered the most vulnerable to assault from outside. This explains why the most common location for all forms of ritual marks and objects is the chimney. The chimney and ceiling/attic space are the two areas of the household that are open to the sky and therefore offered potential access points for malevolent forces in the air. These areas therefore became invested with ritual importance. Can it be mere coincidence that these two areas are also the most common areas for the application of surface decoration, often with religious imagery? It is only a short step from casually etching a ritual mark into a stone or fireplace wooden mantel to the more formal inscribing of mottos, such as 'MY.HOYP[HOPE].IS.IN.YE.LORD' as found carved across a fireplace mantel at Delgatie Castle in Aberdeenshire along with the sacred monogram IHS and the date 1570, and then to the application of associated imagery.

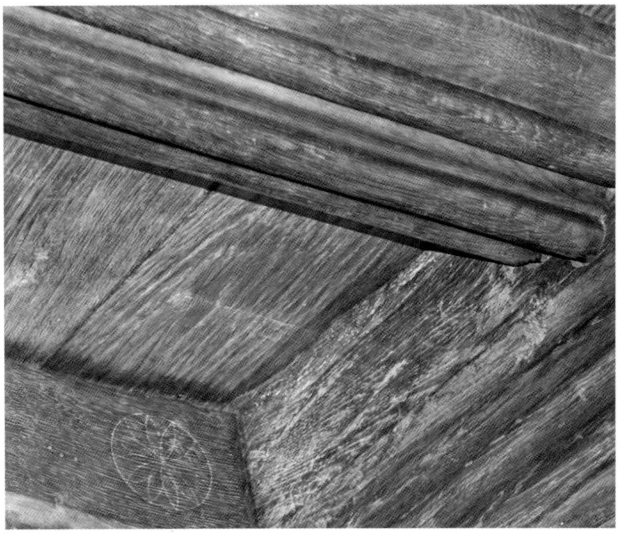

186 'Daisy wheel' ritual mark etched into the wooden ceiling of the withdrawing room at Little Moreton Hall, Cheshire

The fact that these apotropaic marks and objects were deliberately concealed is also significant. It appears that their efficacy relied on the fact that they were out of sight. Certainly it is clear that the act of concealment was part of the ritual. The efficacy of these marks and objects relied on their (non-visible) presence within the household, not on their visual properties. Knowing that these devices were present was comforting to members of the household but they did not need to be visible to be efficacious in offering protection. As Edward Roberts has observed in his discussion of marks in houses in Hampshire: 'Although the marks are now clearly visible, the entire fireplace as well as its plaster overmantel may originally have been painted, concealing the marks but not affecting their protective value'.[41] Similarly, images of figures, faces and eyes on ceilings may not need to be readily visible or looked at properly to provide a sense of a protective presence in the room.

It is possible that ritual marks, deliberately concealed objects and decoration with religious subject matter are all manifestations of the same belief system that considered the household as a spiritual shelter but one that was under attack from outside forces. The perceived permeability of the building resulted in a range of devices intended to invoke the power of God to sanctify or spiritualise the household against evil spirits. While prayer could be employed at certain points during the day, it is possible that visual and material signs were employed to offer constant protection. The appearance of cherubim as a common motif in plasterwork and painted ceilings can be seen as an appropriate

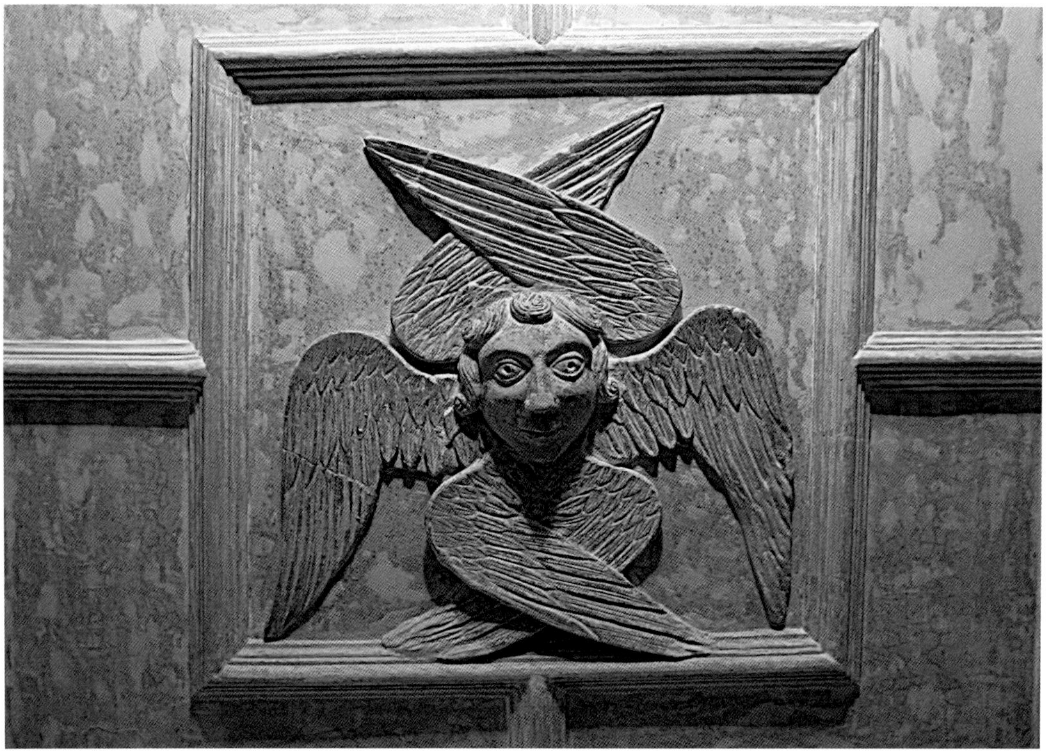

187 Cherubin, detail of plasterwork ceiling from a house in Lower Street, Dartmouth. Private collection

subject for the decoration of ceilings but perhaps these angelic faces can also be understood as a benevolent watchful presence to bring comfort to the inhabitants of the building (Fig. 187).

❀

To conclude this chapter, I have suggested that certain forms of decoration in post-Reformation houses were not intended to be viewed in a concentrated or intelligent manner. The positioning and design of decoration on the ceiling indicates that it was not intended to be the focus of prolonged viewing. Rather, engagement with the iconographical content is secondary to the effect created by the physical, and mystical, presence of the imagery. The cases studied in this chapter suggest that domestic decoration had a key role in promoting and regulating godly behaviour within the Protestant household. The desired atmosphere of domestic piety and spirit of constant religious observance was reinforced by the presence of traditional, spiritual imagery positioned within areas of domestic space used for social interaction and recreation – activities that might prompt lapses in godly thought and behaviour. A serious spiritual mood, coupled with the disquieting sensation caused by the alien presence of such large-scale and oppressive imagery, served to discourage immorality. The constant gaze of the figures encouraged the perception of an animate presence which functioned to suggest a sense of surveillance. In this way such decoration is an active agent, defining and controlling the use of the space it inhabits. However, it might also serve as a comforting, protective presence, invoking the power of traditional religious imagery against sin and malevolent spirits. Yet there was a tension between the power of the image itself to survey and therefore control human behaviour and the potential power of religious imagery to corrupt the faithful into acts of idolatry. By placing this imagery on the ceiling the godly householder could exploit the power of the art's agency, while curbing the viewing experience and thus discouraging the intent gazing associated with devotional response.

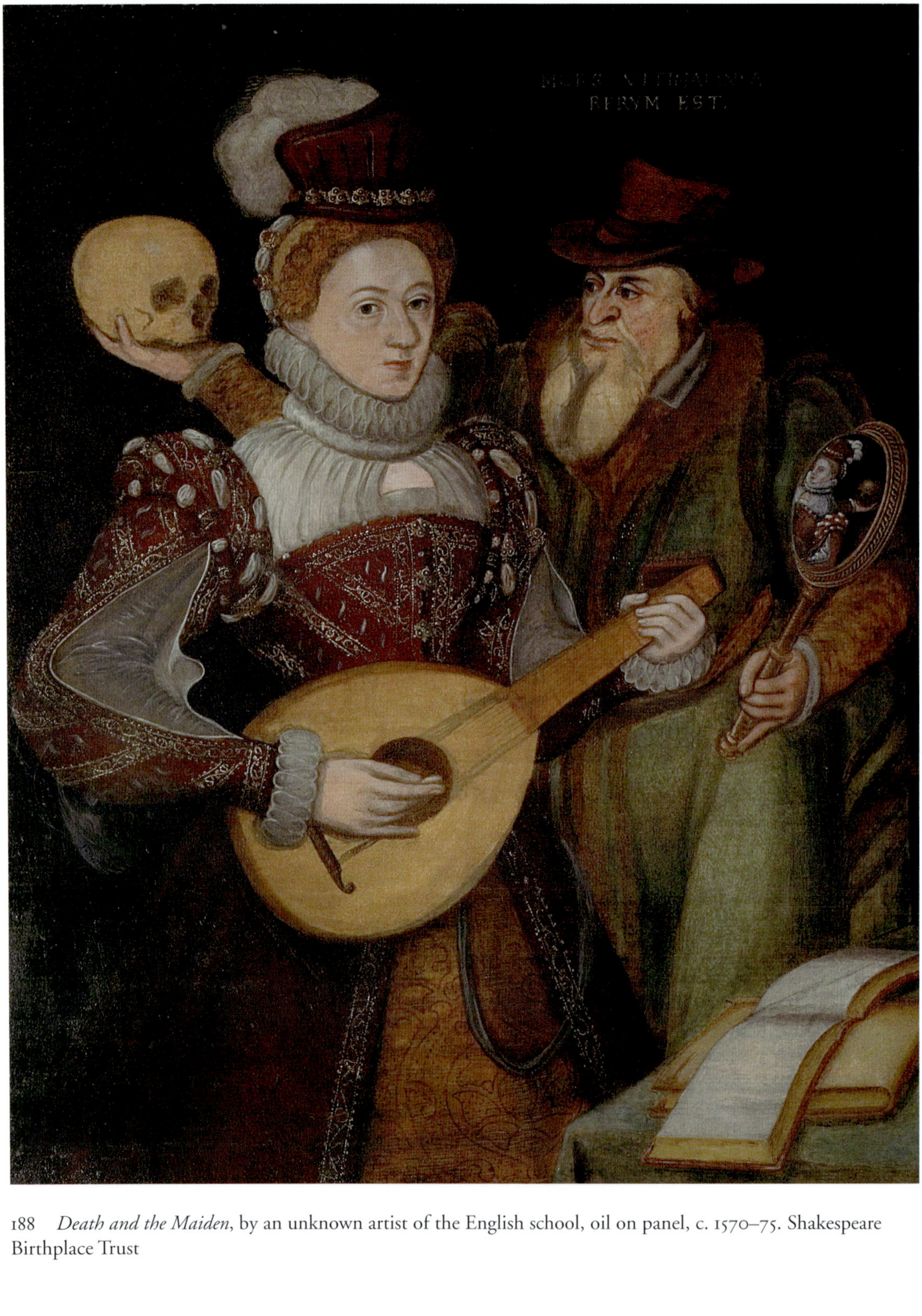

188 *Death and the Maiden*, by an unknown artist of the English school, oil on panel, c. 1570–75. Shakespeare Birthplace Trust

Conclusion ❀ Last Judgements

It is generally acknowledged to be bad practice to introduce new material in a conclusion but in bringing this study to a close I want briefly to consider one last group of iconographies on the *memento mori* theme which appear in post-Reformation domestic decoration; this could be said to provide an appropriate subject for a conclusion in dealing with the end of things. A brief account of this category of imagery is provided here because it suggests, once again, that decorative imagery in the home functioned to provide spiritual reminders to prepare the viewer for the afterlife. It also serves to emphasise that religious imagery in the form of biblical scenes was not viewed in isolation in the domestic interior; this space was also adorned with other images, symbols and objects which all connected with and commented on the various aspects of domestic life, including the impending arrival of death.

I have shown that religious imagery in domestic decoration seems to have been favoured especially by the gentry and prosperous middle class of merchants, citizens and yeoman farmers. However, other categories of imagery were also used to decorate the houses of these social groups: heraldry and floral and animal motifs were especially common. In terms of figurative and narrative imagery a fairly restricted range of subjects proved popular: Virtues and Worthies and occasionally scenes from Ovid's *Metamorphoses*. It is surely significant that most of the stories from classical mythology depicted in decorative art were derived from this one source. Perhaps the importance of Ovidian subjects for a contemporary audience lay in the spiritual dimension propagated through the medieval period in the form of the *Ovide moralisé* and associated edifying texts.[1] By the time Arthur Golding published his English translation of the *Metamorphoses* in 1565–67, an allegorical reading of Ovid's tales as a compendium of Christian truth and morality was firmly established. It seems therefore that at this level of society the trend in interior decoration was for long-standing subjects and themes that could serve as exemplars of virtue and vice within a traditional Christian moral framework. In support of this is another pre-Reformation category of imagery which gained ascendancy alongside biblical scenes as the subject of domestic decoration during this period, as this also expressed spiritual concerns.

THE PASSING OF TIME AND THE PRESENCE OF DEATH

The development and popularity of *memento mori* imagery in post-Reformation visual culture has been described and discussed by other scholars, notably by Nigel Llewellyn and Tarnya Cooper.[2] This theme – a reminder to meditate on mortality even during the prime of life – had a long history prior to the Reformation, becoming popular through the visual tradition of the Dance of Death and associated iconography such as the Three Living and the Three Dead.[3] Attitudes to death were redefined in Protestant thought in response to the abolition of the last rites and prayers for the soul together with the new Calvinist emphasis on predestination. Individuals could no longer rely on the sacred rituals surrounding their last moments to prepare them for the afterlife, so images in various forms operated to encourage and exhibit continual readiness for judgement. Symbols of mortality were omnipresent in funeral monuments in churches but were also present in everyday life; they were worn on the body in the form of jewellery and the so-called 'remembrance rings' often decorated with a skull were a common bequest in wills.[4] This period also witnessed the development of the *memento mori* portrait, characterised by the inclusion of symbols alluding to the passing of time such as an hourglass or reminders of mortality such as a skull. It seems that this type of portrait appealed to the more godly members of society who were anxious to balance the vanity implied by portraiture with an expression of humility and an acknowledgement of the brevity of (earthly) life.[5] These portraits were displayed in a domestic context alongside other symbols of mortality in pictures and in large-scale surface decoration.

For example, a painting of about 1570–75 by an unknown English artist in the Shakespeare Birthplace Trust shows a woman playing a lute while a bearded male figure, probably meant to represent Time, holds a skull over her shoulder and a looking-glass to reflect her ultimate fate (Fig. 188). An inscription in Latin at the top right of the picture reads 'MORS ULTIMA LINEA/RERUM EST' (Death is everything's final limit), which is taken from Horace's *Epistles* (I, 16, 79). The imagery continues the tradition of the Death and the Maiden iconography which circulated widely in print form throughout Europe early in the sixteenth century.[6]

Another painted picture of about 1600 in the collection of Norwich Castle Museum and Art Gallery includes personifications of Youth and Age along with the figures of Time, holding a scythe and an hourglass, and Death as a skeleton in a coffin.[7] The moral is explained by detailed inscriptions:

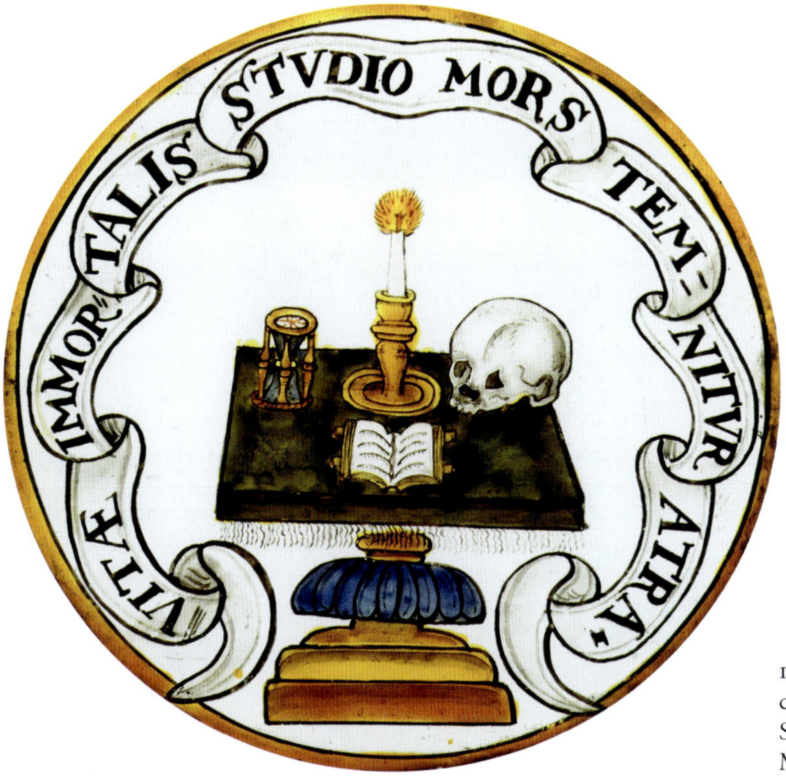

189 Painted glass roundel of c. 1600 from Preston Hall, Suffolk. Victoria and Albert Museum, London

Consyder man howe tyme doth passe
And lykewyes knowe all fleshe is grasse
For tyme consumes the strongeste oke [oak]
So deathe at laste shall stryke the stroke.

Yet this bleak message is balanced by one of hope for salvation through Christ:

The heavenlye joyes at lengthe to see
Lett faith in Chryste thyne Ancor bee

Such pictures were probably created as ready-made objects for sale on the open market and are likely to have been based on single-sheet prints also available to purchase for domestic display. Alongside these moveable items examples have survived of similar imagery in fixed surface decoration, a more permanent addition to the interior of a household.

A painted glass roundel of about 1600 from Preston Hall near Lavenham in Suffolk depicts a table with various *memento mori* symbols: a skull, hourglass, an open Bible as the route to salvation and at the centre a candle which symbolised the fragility of life because both could be snuffed out in an instant (Fig. 189). The roundel belongs to a group of glass panels painted with moralising images and accompanying Latin inscriptions

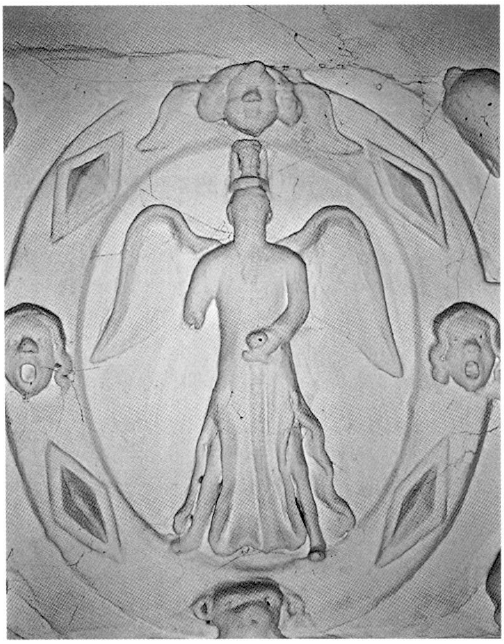

190 Figure of Time, plasterwork overmantel, mid-seventeenth century, in a house on the Prideaux Estate, Cornwall

which were probably commissioned by the antiquary Robert Reyce (1555–1638) who was part of a group of prosperous local gentry of Puritan persuasion. In his description of the county of Suffolk published in 1618, Reyce observed approvingly that many of the county's gentry were 'crowned with the purity of true religion and godly life'.[8] Religious scenes in painted glass roundels for domestic display were exported from the Netherlands throughout Europe in the 1520s and 30s but it is not clear how widely this glass was collected in Britain or if it remained visible in houses after the Reformation. The fragile nature of the medium means that few examples survive, especially *in situ*. Nevertheless, it is clear that at least some painted glass was newly made, even for the stricter kind of Protestant, in the post-Reformation period. The Preston Hall roundels suggest that some patrons chose to avoid traditional religious imagery in favour of allied iconographies on a spiritual theme.

The figure of Time or Death, personified as a bearded and robed man holding a scythe, was a familiar presence in the visual culture of early modern Britain and he could often be found presiding over domestic life. A print of the *Good Housewife* first produced about 1600 shows the figure of Time depicted in an overmantel at the heart of the household.[9] This idealised vision of the dutiful housewife shows her busy at work having achieved a state of domestic harmony around her. The message is similar to that presented in the image of the Wise and Foolish Virgins in the great hall at Burton Agnes; industriousness is rewarded at the end of time. In this print the figure of Time appears to be painted on a board above the fireplace. Although the print was intended as an allegory and should not be taken to reflect the appearance of real domestic interiors, the subject matter in this overmantel might reflect actual trends in the subject matter of decoration. A closely similar figure of Time with his scythe stands at the centre of a plasterwork overmantel from the mid-seventeenth century in a farmhouse on the Prideaux Estate in Cornwall (Fig. 190). The menacing presence of this figure in the permanent decoration of domestic space mirrored the looming presence of death in daily life.

An allegory of the Triumph of Time over Fame, where Time races through life on his chariot, is depicted in plasterwork overmantels at four different locations in the West Country. This allegory of the passing of time, which includes the charming detail of an infant in a baby walker, suggests the pointlessness of pursuing earthly fame, which Time will erase.[10] The figure of Time also takes centre stage in an allegory of Industry and Idleness which appears in the carved parlour at Crewe Hall in Cheshire (Fig. 191) and again, in a much later work, at Tackbeare Manor on the Cornwall–Devon border.[11] This iconog-

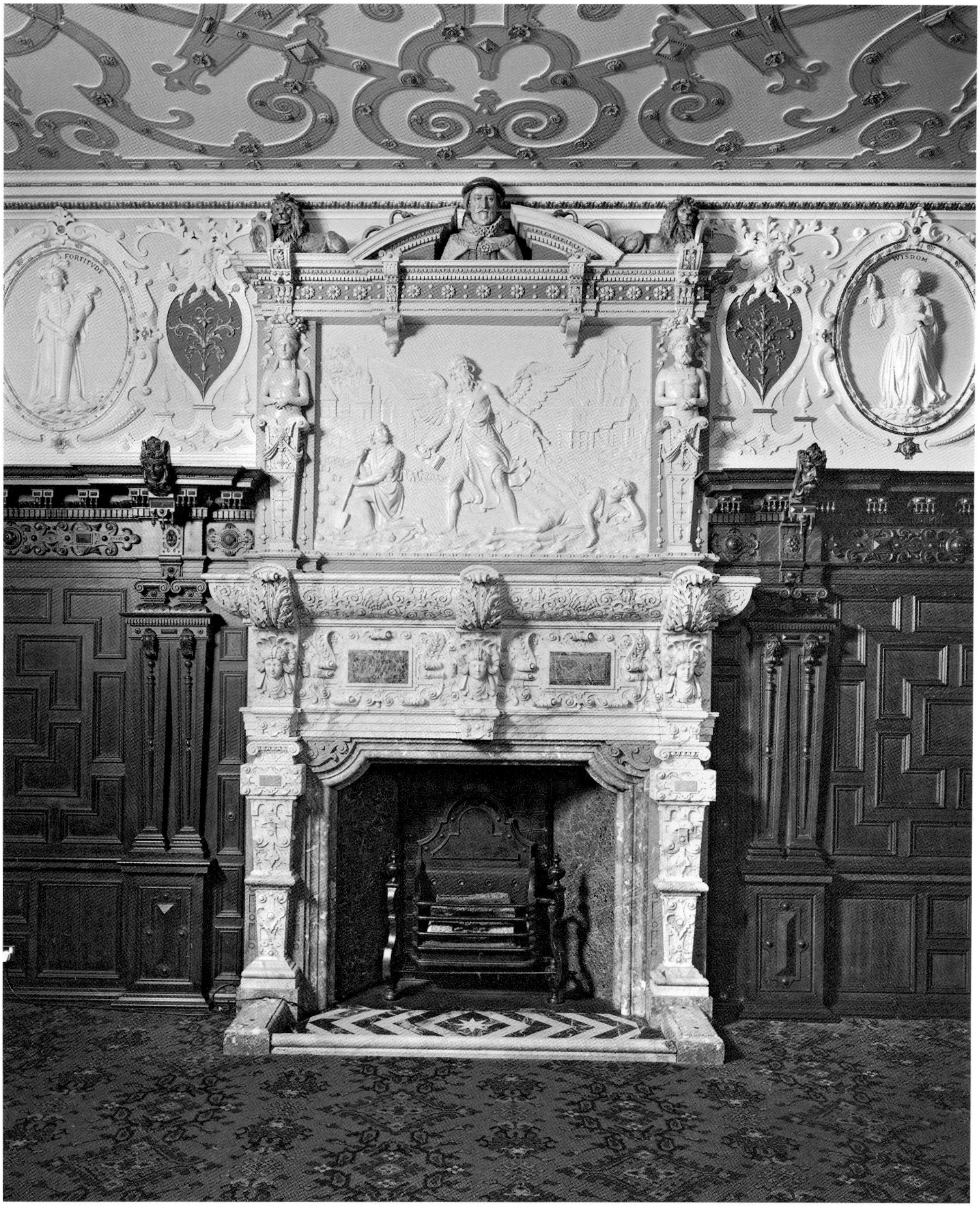

191 Allegory of Time between Industry and Idleness, plasterwork chimneypiece in the carved parlour at Crewe Hall, Cheshire. This is a Victorian reconstruction of a Jacobean original

raphy also appears in the 'Abbott' sketchbook of plasterwork designs and this drawing possibly informed the late seventeenth-century work at Tackbeare.[12] The imagery depicts Time at the centre with personifications of Industry on one side and Idleness on the other. Time rewards Industry with the crown of heaven while Idleness receives a whip. This iconography, which derives from a print published in 1582, appears to adapt the traditional imagery of the Last Judgement, dividing the deserving from the undeserving, the righteous from the reprobate.[13] It communicates a similar message and serves an analogous function to Last Judgement iconography in warning viewers to ready themselves for divine judgement. Although the imagery depicts Industry engaged in physical labour which might suggest that material actions in life determine the outcome of judgement, Protestant doctrine rejected the Roman Catholic belief in the efficacy of good works or actions during life and held that salvation was secured through faith alone (*sola fide*). According to the Calvinist tenet of predestination, God had pre-determined who was destined for heaven and who was not. Although Calvinist theologians maintained that it was impossible to identify the elect during the course of life (because the reprobate could appear faithful, while the elect could fall into sin), for devout Protestants exemplary Christian behaviour could tentatively be taken as an indication of elect status. In consequence, the outward display of virtue and the demonstration of industry, especially in relation to spiritual activities, was a necessary form of self-fashioning for the godly.

As discussed in Chapter 1, depictions of the Last Judgement, known as Doom paintings, were positioned above the chancel arch of parish churches in the late medieval period. This iconography included an image of Christ in his heavenly glory dividing the saved from the damned and so fell foul of the reformers' proscriptions. The wall painting of the Doom on the chancel arch in the guild chapel at Stratford-upon-Avon was whitewashed over under the supervision of John Shakespeare (the father of the playwright) between 1563 and 1564 but it seems that some other paintings survived this first phase of removal and a *Dance of Death* was still visible in 1571 when it was mentioned by John Stow.[14] While the great Doom paintings in churches were eradicated, imagery related to the theme of the Last Judgement endured in post-Reformation art.[15] Some of the imagery discussed in this book deals explicitly with the subject: the painted ceiling in the chapel at Grandtully; the Wise and Foolish Virgins at Burton Agnes in Yorkshire; the Angel sounding the last Trumpet above a skeleton in the ceiling at Gaulden Manor in Somerset. All these iconographies function in the *memento mori* tradition to remind viewers of their own mortality and thus to ensure spiritual preparedness for the day of judgement.

An overmantel in the old parlour or Low Dining Room at Burton Agnes Hall presents a creative reworking of Last Judgement imagery (Fig. 192).[16] This carving may not have been part of the original decorations of the house; it was possibly removed from another house and brought to Burton in the eighteenth century. But the message of the imagery is remarkably similar to the parable of the Wise and Foolish Virgins depicted in the overmantel in the hall, which suggests that both pieces of work might be original to the house. The panel depicts a skeletal figure of Death brandishing an enormous scythe at the cen-

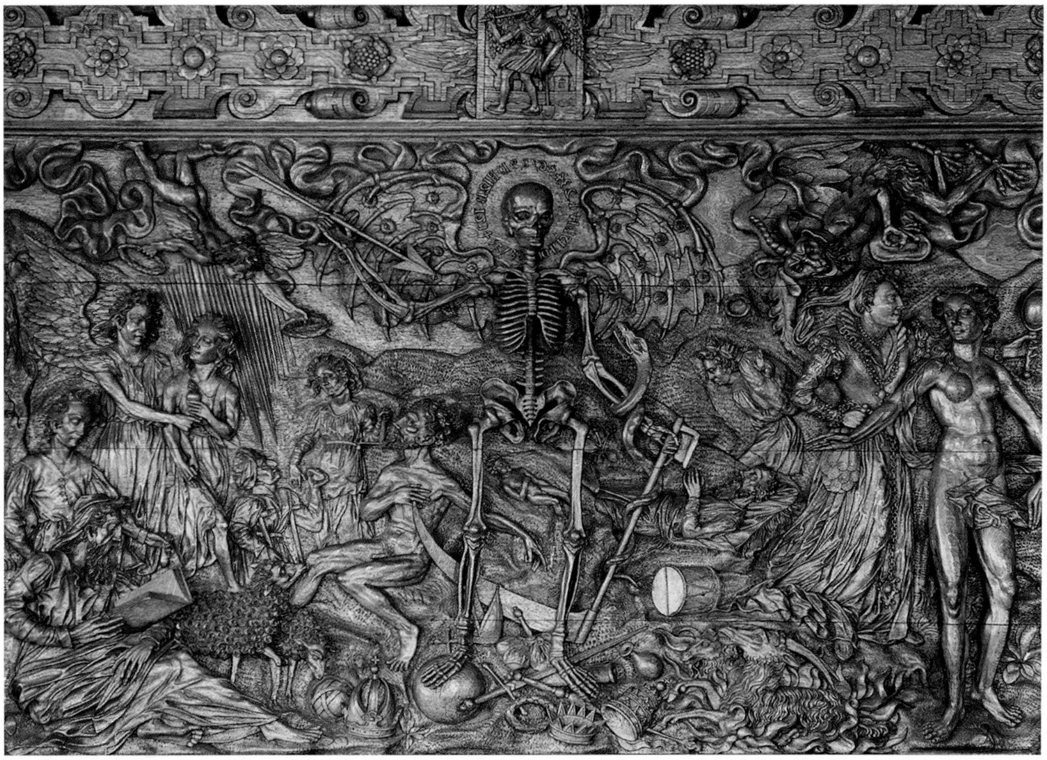

192 Allegory of Judgement, carved wood overmantel of c. 1600–10 in the parlour at Burton Agnes Hall, East Yorkshire

tre of the composition. At his feet are earthly symbols of power and authority (including a papal tiara and bishop's mitre). He divides the Just, on the left, from the Unjust on the right. The Unjust are represented mainly by a woman personifying the sin of pride. She is depicted twice: dressed in all her finery and holding a mirror and then again as a naked soul (in line with traditional Judgement iconography). A grotesque devil hovers menacingly above her head. On the opposite side, an angel swoops from heaven to crown the saved soul of a naked man. The figure of Death at the centre is spectacularly terrifying. Like traditional Last Judgement scenes, the imagery is intended to shock and awe, and thus bring about the reformation of character and aid the path to salvation.

Allied to Last Judgement imagery in traditional pre-Reformation art was the iconography of the Weighing of Souls. In the painted schemes and altarpieces of churches, the Weighing of Souls was often included as an integral part of the Last Judgement – as for example in the late Doom of about 1500 painted on wooden boards at Wenhaston church in Suffolk – but some Weighings of Souls were presented as detached, if not actually separate, subjects. In the traditional iconography the archangel St Michael holds the scales or balance to judge how individual souls are weighed against their sins. At one end of the scale the Virgin Mary may intervene on behalf of an endangered soul by putting her

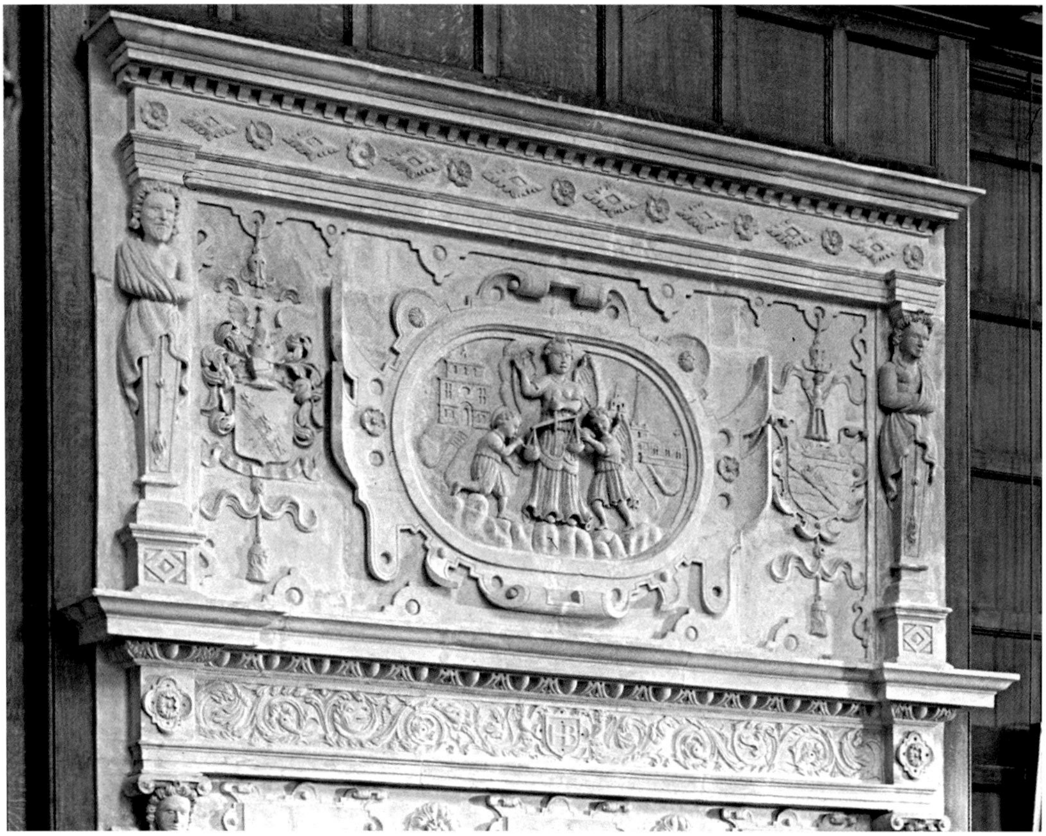

193 Allegory of Judgement, carved stone chimneypiece now installed in the great hall of Sutton Place, Surrey

hand on the balance or her rosary in the scale-pan, while at the other end the devil or devils try to counteract the Virgin's influence by pulling frantically on their pan. There is a particularly fine fifteenth-century version of this traditional iconography in wall paintings at South Leigh church in Oxfordshire. An example of the Weighing of Souls from a domestic context prior to the Reformation survives in a carved wood mantel which was probably above the doorway of Millington Hall in Weobley, Herefordshire. The carving, now in Hereford Museum and Art Gallery, dates from around 1500 and shows St Michael holding scales, while the Virgin Mary uses her rosary to tip the balance in her favour.

A remarkable reworking of this traditional Weighing of Souls iconography in post-Reformation domestic decoration is depicted in a carved stone chimneypiece recently installed in the great hall of Sutton Place in Surrey.[17] The chimneypiece is associated with the Bristol workshop and looks to date from the mid-seventeenth century but unfortunately its original location is not known. In an oval panel at the centre of the chimneypiece is a large winged figure holding a pair of scales (Fig. 193). On one side a boy blows through a straw to create a bubble in one of the scale pans, which drops downwards. At the other end another winged figure appears to be adding objects to his pan as he smiles out at the viewer. Depicted in the background on the left is a grand mansion, while on the right is a church.

It is possible to identify the source of this iconography as an illustration in Francis Quarles' *Emblemes* first published in 1635, a book designed to aid pious meditation of a moderate Protestant variety.[18] Although the imagery in the Sutton Place chimneypiece is very close to the printed illustration there are some significant modifications. In Quarles the 'angels' are cupids with quivers of arrows to symbolise Profane and Sacred Love (Sacred, or Divine, Love in the centre is identified by his halo), but in the chimneypiece the central 'cupid' lacks a quiver and is transformed into a larger, adult, winged figure. The two buildings in the background are an addition; in the printed version there is just one tiny building on the horizon. Most significantly, the chimneypiece does not incorporate any of the accompanying explanatory text on which emblems rely for their meaning, although it is possible that texts were applied to the original surface but were subsequently erased.[19]

Quarles explains the meaning of the emblem as follows:

> LORD, what a world is this; which, day and night,
> Men seek with so much toyle, with so much trouble!
> Which, weigh'd in equall Scales, is found so light,
> So poorely over-balanc'd with a Bubble.

This iconography is intended, then, as an allegory of the fleeting, ephemeral nature of worldly experience, which is of such little substance that it weighs lighter than a bubble. Profane Love, in the printed illustration, adds all worldly pleasure, achievement and possessions into his pan but this 'bubble-world' of vanity is still lighter than a thought.[20] The addition of the two buildings in the background of the chimneypiece suggests an elaboration of the central concept to emphasise the inconsequence of worldly existence. The message seems to be that the immortal soul is endangered when enjoyment of worldly, material things (symbolised by the mansion) outweighs spiritual concerns (symbolised by the church). It is not clear to what extent a contemporary audience could have understood this message from the image alone. Large in scale and apparently lacking the supporting text to explicate the more sophisticated elements of the allegory, it seems likely that the imagery in the Sutton Place chimneypiece operated primarily through the visual impact of its component parts. Changes made to the appearance of the central figure, in particular, strengthen associations with an older iconography from which the printed illustration ultimately derives. The image of a Divine Angel holding the scales of judgement to weigh the vanities of worldly life recalls the traditional iconography of the Weighing of Souls, prompting, we may assume, similar thoughts about the transience of this life and the need to reform the soul. In this way the imagery, though extracted from a contemporary printed text, is anchored in the traditions of the pre-Reformation past.

These examples of iconography on the Last Judgement theme indicate the extent to which traditional eschatological imagery from pre-Reformation church art endured in a domestic context for roughly a century after the establishment of the Protestant faith in Britain. It also shows how subject matter was tweaked, modified and revised to remove those elements that were no longer consistent with reformed ideals and faith.

❦

This book set out to prove that the Reformation did not bring about an abrupt and wholesale rejection of the artistic traditions of the medieval past. The body of visual evidence presented here supports a view of the long post-Reformation period as one of assimilation, adaptation and transformation. It is evident that, far from being hostile towards images, a great many Protestant patrons continued to desire and commission religious art to decorate their houses. While the choice of materials, forms and iconography represents a significant degree of continuity with the pre-Reformation past, the imagery was modified where necessary to remove objectionable elements and used to express and support specifically Protestant habits of thought and behaviour.

Consistent with the wide range of opinion on the issue of images evident in published commentaries of the period, the extant visual and material evidence suggests that there was no uniform or consistent approach to the use of religious imagery as decoration in the home. Religious art appealed to different kinds of Protestants for different reasons, and attitudes changed and diverged dramatically over the course of the period. Although it is clear that some high-church patrons desired imagery to 'beautify' spaces used to honour God, which led to the resurgence of imagery in some churches and private chapels, I think it is fair to say that most of the imagery presented in this book was not created or appreciated primarily for its aesthetic quality. This decoration should not be understood as mere ornament to spruce up the walls of houses but intrinsically meaningful comments on religious and social concerns. It could also serve a range of functions in relation to daily life in the pious Protestant household. Decorating the godly household with religious imagery defined and exhibited the faith and humility of the owner and his household. It could provide an appropriate backdrop to the daily patterns of religious observance and support the instruction of the patriarch. It could also reinforce and extend the periods of active instruction throughout the day by providing reminders to meditate on spiritual matters at all times. The atmosphere created by the presence of large-scale religious imagery could operate to prevent dishonourable behaviour that would ruin the reputation of a family and imperil the souls of its members.

Religious imagery was not employed, however, without considerable care and caution. Concessions were made in the form and appearance of imagery to accommodate the Protestant emphasis on the strictures of the Second Commandment. The images that had proved most popular as the focus of devotional activity in the pre-Reformation church were phased out (although a considerable amount of pre-Reformation material survived for much of the period and could be displayed in neutral contexts). Depictions of individual holy figures – God, Christ, the Virgin and saints – were generally avoided, especially in the form of sculpture, along with the a-scriptural cultic images of the Trinity, Pieta and Man of Sorrows. Instead there was a clear preference for narrative depictions that adhered to the scriptural account and could be justified as the illustration of history. This meant that New Testament imagery was not intrinsically problematic, as long as it was not abused by worship. The location of such imagery in the semi-public, reception areas of domestic houses where response could be monitored secured its legitimacy. But other patrons chose to play it safe and avoided New Testament subject matter. I have argued that certain Old Testament iconographies proved especially popular because they encapsulated the great Christian scheme of sin and salvation, functioning as types to symbolise Christ's sacrifice on the Cross. These different responses to the choice of subject matter and the manner of its depiction can be seen to reflect the range of perspectives within Protestantism during this period.

The 'fashion' for religious imagery in decorative art that I have charted in this book continued until the mid-seventeenth century. A print-seller, Peter Stent, issued a series of advertisements in the 1650s and 60s listing his stock and it is interesting to see that the Sacrifice of Isaac, Adam and Eve and the Ten Commandments were among the few biblical subjects on sale in print form at this date.[21] It is no doubt significant that these subjects were the most common in decorative art throughout the period 1560–1660; their longevity confirms that these subjects were the most potent and pertinent iconographies to support Protestant thought and religious practice. Traditions also endured for longer in some regions and social groups but in general terms it is fair to take 1660 as a turning point which inaugurated a pronounced shift in the nature and style of iconography chosen for depiction in domestic decoration. The ascent of Charles II to the throne introduced a cosmopolitan taste for foreign fashions and the period of exile in France had shaped courtly taste for baroque art in the grand manner.

Part of the reason for the decline of the fashion I have described here also lies in a gradual move from a traditional, symbolic understanding of pictorial iconography to a more rational conception and interpretation of art. The reformers had provided the groundwork for this shift. By advocating imagery that adhered to the literal description of stories from scripture and critiquing the a-scriptural inventions of man's imaginations as false or deceitful corruptions of the Word or fanciful attempts to picture the unknowable heavenly sphere, they advanced a new theoretical framework for appreciating, judging and critiquing images. It took time for this new way of thinking to permeate wider society but this shift towards a more rational appreciation of imagery is represented by a series of essays by Sir Thomas Browne, 'Of many things questionable as they are commonly described in Pictures', within the *Pseudodoxia Epidemica*, commonly known as 'Vulgar Errors' published in 1646.[22] In this text, Sir Thomas exposed the historical inaccuracies and inconsistencies within various forms of traditional iconography, including the scene of the Temptation of Eve and the Sacrifice of Isaac. The depiction of the serpent with a human face in the scene of the Temptation was found to be unreasonable while the depiction of Isaac as a young boy at the time of the Sacrifice was criticised as unhistorical. Browne's criticism of the scene of the Sacrifice of Isaac as lacking in accuracy suggests that its traditional symbolic language and spiritual potency as a type for the Crucifixion of Christ was waning, certainly among educated circles. This episode in the history of British art was drawing to a close. Religious subject matter fell from favour in native art production after 1660 and other genres – group portraiture, landscapes, sporting art and modern moral subjects – developed to cater to the social and cultural concerns of the gentry and aspiring middle class in the eighteenth century.

Notes

INTRODUCTION

1 I am grateful to Nigel Llewellyn for bringing the records concerning this chimneypiece to my attention. The chimneypiece was first described in *Sussex Archaeological Collections* vol. 12 (1859–60), p. 16, when it was still *in situ* in a panelled room in a 'cottage' in Uckfield, Sussex (exact address not provided). It is described as consisting of three painted oak panels depicting the Adoration, the Judging of Souls and the Crucifixion. By the time of the subsequent note in *Sussex Notes and Queries* of 1929 (vol. 2, pp. 120–21), the panels had been removed from their setting and belonged to a private owner who intended to 'dispose' of them.

2 The official iconoclasm of the 1560s re-enacted the purges of churches which took place in 1548 under Edward VI and this previous wave of reform set the stage for Elizabethan policy.

3 Yet the pressure on images can be seen as a more targeted campaign of scrutiny restricted to known Catholic sympathisers. On how pictures and other objects were read as subversive because of their association with Catholic individuals see Richard L. Williams, 'Contesting the Everyday: The Cultural Biography of a Subversive Playing Card', in Tara Hamling and Catherine Richardson (eds), *Everyday Objects: Medieval and Early Modern Material Culture and its Meanings* (Aldershot, 2010).

4 This conservative strain in the English church has been described as 'English Arminianism' by Nicholas Tyacke who argued that the movement was in opposition to the general Calvinist consensus of the English church; *Anti-Calvinists: The Rise of English Arminianism, c. 1590–1640* (Oxford, 1987, 1990 edn). It has been argued that this limited acceptance of certain images extended beyond the circle of anti-Calvinists, particularly by Peter Yorke, 'Iconoclasm, Ecclesiology and "the beauty of holiness": Concepts of Sacrilege and the "peril of idolatry" in Early Modern England, c. 1590–1642', PhD dissertation (University of Kent, 1997). Yorke's argument is summarised in Julie Spraggon, *Puritan Iconoclasm during the English Civil War* (Woodbridge, 2003), p. 21.

5 William Perkins, *A Reformed Catholike: or A Declaration shewing how neere we may come to the Present Church of Rome in sundrie points of Religion: and wherein we must for ever depart from them* (Cambridge, 1598), p. 172.

6 Following the OED definition of 'godly' as 'Devoutly observant of the laws of God; religious, pious' (second edn, 1989).

7 On the contemporary terminology for 'the hotter sort of Protestant' see John Spurr, *English Puritanism, 1603–1689* (Basingstoke, 1998), ch. 2; Christopher Durston and Jacqueline Eales (eds), *The Culture of English Puritanism, 1560–1700* (Basingstoke, 1996) and Patrick Collinson, *Godly People: Essays on English Protestantism and Puritanism* (London, 1983).

8 Richard Humphreys, *The Tate Britain Companion to British Art* (London, 2001), p. 23. Despite this rather bleak overview, the author acknowledges later that wall painting such as that at Knightsland Farm in Hertfordshire, which depicts the story of the Prodigal Son, 'is quite typical of what could be seen' (p. 33).

9 For authoritative studies of iconoclasm see Margaret Aston, *England's Iconoclasts: Volume I, Laws against Images* (Oxford, 1988); John Phillips, *The Reformation of Images: Destruction of Art in England, 1535–1660* (Berkeley, Los Angeles and London, 1973) and Spraggon, *Puritan Iconoclasm*. See also the many excellent articles and chapters by Margaret Aston including her contributions to Clifford Davidson and Ann Eljenholm Nichols (eds), *Iconoclasm vs. Art and Drama* (Kalamazoo, Mich., 1989) and Durston and Eales, *Culture of English Puritanism*.

10 There is a growing literature on the relationship between Protestantism and the visual arts; these are some of the key studies: Maurice Howard, *The Building of Elizabethan and Jacobean England* (New Haven and London, 2007) details how monasteries were converted into private dwellings and ecclesiastical fabric was incorporated within secular buildings. On how printed wares responded to Protestant thought see Tessa Watt, *Cheap Print and Popular Piety, 1550–1640* (Cambridge, 1991); Sheila O'Connell, *The Popular Print in England* (London, 1999); and Peter Lake with Michael Questier, *The Antichrist's Lewd Hat: Protestants, Papists and Players in Post-Reformation England* (New Haven and London, 2002). Nigel Llewellyn in *The Art of Death: Visual Culture in the English Death Ritual, c. 1500–c. 1800* (London, 1991) has described the wider visual culture and his *Funeral Monuments in Post-Reformation England* (Cambridge, 2001) is a comprehensive account of an art form which flourished after the Reformation. On portraits see Robert Tittler, *The Face of the City: Civic Portraiture and Civic Identity in Early Modern England* (Manchester, 2007) and Tarnya Cooper 'Memento Mori Portraiture: Painting, Protestant Culture and the Patronage of Middle Elites in England and Wales, 1540–1630', D.Phil. thesis (University of Sussex, 2001). Her monograph on this subject is forthcoming with Yale University Press. On Protestant ceremony see David Cressy, *Bonfires & Bells* (London, 1989). The development of Protestant private chapels is the subject of Annabel Ricketts, *The English Country House Chapel: Building a Protestant Tradition*, ed. Simon Ricketts (Reading, 2007). A recent overview of these various forms is provided by Maurice Howard, 'Art and the Reformation' in Tim Ayers (ed.), *The History of British Art, 600–1600* (London, 2008), pp. 231–45. For an overview of how the processes of continuity, adaptation and innovation can be seen in virtually every visual medium across a wide geographical and social range see Tara Hamling and Richard L. Williams (eds), *Art Re-formed: Re-assessing the Impact of the Reformation on the Visual Arts* (Newcastle, 2007).

11 While Richard Humphreys is right to point out that many wealthy Protestants would have found this sort of religious iconography acceptable 'as an aid to prayer and right thinking', it is hard to agree with his assertion that they would have placed such a painting on a side wall in a chapel or in a small room set aside for their devotions (*Tate Britain Companion*, p. 26). In fact this context for display would be more likely to render the painting unacceptable according to Protestant thought because the location suggested it might be used as the focus of worship.

12 E.g. Michael Archer, *Delftware: The Tin-Glazed Earthenware of the British Isles* (London, 1997); Philippa Glanville, *Silver in Tudor and Early Stuart England: A Social History and Catalogue of the National Collection* (London, 1990); Andrew Morrall and Melinda Watt (eds), *English Embroidery from the Metropolitan Museum of Art, 1580–1700* (New York, New Haven and London, 2008).

13 Patrick Collinson, 'From Iconoclasm to

Iconophobia: The Cultural Impact of the Second English Reformation', Stenton Lecture, 1985 (Reading, 1986) and Patrick Collinson, *The Birthpangs of Protestant England: Religious and Cultural Change in the Sixteenth and Seventeenth Centuries* (Basingstoke, 1988).

14 Collinson, *Birthpangs of Protestant England*, pp. 117–19.

15 Challenges to this notion of 'iconophobia' include William A. Dyrness, *Reformed Theology and Visual Culture: The Protestant Imagination from Calvin to Edwards* (Cambridge, 2004) as well as those listed in n. 10 above. The concept of iconophobia also influenced the study of literature of this period: see e.g. Ernest B. Gilman, *Iconoclasm and Poetry in the English Reformation: Down went Dagon* (Chicago and London, 1986).

16 James Ayres, *Domestic Interiors: The British Tradition, 1500–1850* (New Haven and London, 2003). Existing studies of the domestic interior tend to focus on the evolution of design and fittings and to neglect the meanings and functions of narrative imagery in the home.

17 Instrumental in raising the profile of the domestic interior as a subject for serious study, the AHRC-funded Centre for the Study of the Domestic Interior (2001–06) focused on how the domestic interior has been represented from the Renaissance to the present day, rather than on the physical and material realities of that environment. For the interest in 'Renaissance' themes in domestic contexts see Patricia Fumerton and Simon Hunt (eds), *Renaissance Culture and the Everyday* (Pennsylvania, 1998); Flora Dennis and Marta Ajmar-Wollheim (eds), *At Home in Renaissance Italy* (London, 2006) and Flora Dennis, Marta Ajmar-Wollheim and Ann Matchette (eds), *Approaching the Italian Renaissance Interior: Sources, Methodologies, Debates* (Oxford, 2007).

18 On England see Christopher Haigh, *English Reformations: Religion, Politics, and Society under the Tudors* (Oxford, 1993). On Scotland, Jane E.A. Dawson, *Scotland Re-formed, 1488–1587* (Edinburgh, 2007). For England and Scotland in the context of Europe see Diarmaid MacCulloch, *Reformation: Europe's House Divided* (Harmondsworth, 2004). For comparison and connections between the processes of reform in the two countries leading up to the settlements of 1559 and 1560 see Clare Kellar, *Scotland, England, and the Reformation 1534–1561* (Oxford, 2003).

19 See Anthony Wells-Cole, *Art and Decoration in Elizabethan and Jacobean England: The Influence of Continental Prints, 1558–1625* (New Haven and London, 1997) and Michael Bath, *Renaissance Decorative Painting in Scotland* (Edinburgh, 2003).

20 Jane Dawson, 'Anglo-Scottish Protestant Culture and Integration in Sixteenth-Century Britain' in Steven G. Ellis and Sarah Barber (eds), *Conquest and Union: Fashioning a British State, 1485–1725* (London and New York, 1995), p. 92.

21 Andrew Morrall, 'Protestant Pots: Morality and Social Ritual in the Early Modern Home', *Journal of Design History*, vol. 15, no. 4 (2002), p. 268.

22 David R. M. Gaimster, *German Stoneware, 1200–1900: Archaeology and Cultural History* (London, 1997).

23 Ilja M. Veldman has suggested how Calvinism can be judged to have made a positive contribution to the visual arts in the Netherlands, 'Protestantism and the Arts: Sixteenth- and Seventeenth-Century Netherlands' in Paul Corby Finney (ed.), *Seeing beyond the Word: Visual Arts and the Calvinist Tradition* (Grand Rapids, Mich., and Cambridge, 1999), pp. 397–425.

24 I gratefully acknowledge the award of a British Academy Small Grant which allowed me to conduct fieldwork in the Netherlands to investigate evidence for a body of decorative fixtures or material comparable to that in England and Scotland. In fact it seems that the fabric of walls and ceilings in Dutch middle-class houses were relatively unadorned, apart from the generous display of paintings, which could include numerous pictures on a single wall. Biblical subject matter was sometimes depicted in panels on the great oak cupboards used to store linen which came into fashion from the mid-seventeenth century. These were also exported throughout Europe and formed substantial display pieces in some British houses.

25 By gentry I mean the landed classes below the nobility without claim to hereditary title and those who styled themselves as 'gentlemen'. The term 'the gentry' embraces a large section

of landed society and is often subdivided as 'upper' and 'lesser' gentry to indicate the extent of wealth and status. See Felicity Heal and Clive Holmes, *The Gentry in England and Wales, 1500–1700* (Basingstoke, 1994, reprinted 2002). For an analysis of the constitution and development of the 'middle sort of people' see Jonathan Barry and Christopher Brooks (eds), *The Middling Sort of People: Culture, Society and Politics in England, 1550–1800* (Basingstoke, 1994) and H. R. French, *The Middle Sort of People in Provincial England, 1600–1750* (Oxford, 2007).

26 Important studies of the larger country houses include Mark Girouard, *Life in the English Country House: A Social and Architectural History* (New Haven and London, 1978), Maurice Howard, *The Early Tudor Country House: Architecture and Politics* (London, 1987), Mark Girouard, *Elizabethan Architecture* (New Haven and London, 2009) and Charles McKean, *The Scottish Chateau: The Country House of Renaissance Scotland* (Stroud, 2001). Nicholas Cooper in *The Houses of the Gentry, 1480–1680* (New Haven and London, 1999) examines a much broader range of country houses owned by different ranks within the gentry.

27 See John Harris, *Moving Rooms: The Trade in Architectural Salvages* (New Haven and London, 2007).

28 Muriel Carrick, 'Sixteenth and Seventeenth Century Wall Paintings in the County of Essex', 3 vols, M.Phil. thesis (University of Essex, 1990) and *Essex Domestic Wall Paintings, 14th–18th Century*, exh.cat., University Gallery, University of Essex (Colchester, 1993). Kathryn Davies, *Artisan Art: Vernacular Wall Paintings in the Welsh Marches, 1550–1650* (Almeley, Herefordshire, 2008); this study includes the old English counties of Shropshire, Herefordshire, Worcestershire, Cheshire, Staffordshire and Gloucestershire and the old Welsh counties of Denbighshire, Flintshire, Montgomeryshire, Radnorshire, Breconshire, Monmouthshire and Glamorganshire. Davies identifies a 'high incidence of wall paintings' in this area which she associates with its relative prosperity (p. 1).

29 E. Clive Rouse, 'Domestic Wall and Panel Paintings in Hertfordshire', *The Archaeological Journal* 146 (1989): 423–50.

30 Bath, *Renaissance Decorative Painting in Scotland.*

31 For plasterwork with religious subject matter across the region see Tara Hamling, 'Decoration and Devotion: Religious Representation in West Country Decorative Plasterwork c. 1590–c. 1660', M.Phil. thesis (University of Birmingham, 1999). For plasterwork in Devon see Kathleen and Cecil French, 'Devonshire Plasterwork', *Transactions of the Devonshire Association for the Advancement of Science, Literature and Art* 89 (1957): 124–44 and John Thorp, 'Wall Painting and Lime-Plaster Decoration' in Peter Beacham (ed.), *Devon Building: An Introduction to Local Traditions* (Exeter, 1990), pp. 129–49. On plasterwork in Somerset see John and Jane Penoyre, *Decorative Plasterwork in the Houses of Somerset, 1500–1700* (Taunton, 1994). A study of decorative plasterwork in Cornwall over the period 1550–1670 by Stephen Tyrrell is eagerly awaited.

32 Wells-Cole, *Art and Decoration.*

33 Claire Gapper, 'Plasterers and Plasterwork in City, Court and Country, c. 1530–c. 1640', Ph.D. dissertation, 2 vols (University of London, 1998), pp. 298–301.

34 Davies, *Artisan Art*, p. 67.

35 Victor Chinnery, *Oak Furniture: The British Tradition, A History of Early Furniture in the British Isles and New England* (Woodbridge, 1979), p. 45.

36 C. J. Charles, *Old English Interiors*, 3rd edn (New York, 1919). The illustration is between pp. 24 and 25.

37 Heath Old Hall was demolished in 1961 and the chimneypiece is now installed at Hazlewood Castle Hotel, Tadcaster. Louis Ambler's description of the chimneypiece still *in situ* at Heath in 1913 stated that the work was 'dated 1584', *The old halls and manor houses of Yorkshire, with some examples of other houses built before the year 1700* (London, 1913), p. 51. The hall was built in the 1560s by John Kaye whose arms were depicted above the entrance surmounted by those of Queen Elizabeth. This indicates the patron's loyalty to the Elizabethan government so it is tempting to speculate about the possible political meanings of this image as a comment on the reign of Mary Tudor or, more likely, as a call to arms in response to growing concerns about the threat

of a Catholic uprising in support of Mary Queen of Scots (the Throckmorton plot was discovered in 1584).

38 Wells-Cole, *Art and Decoration*, pp. 185–92.

39 *Ibid.*, figs 314 and 315, p. 190.

40 The Joiners' Company of Salisbury was founded in 1617. Humphrey and John Beckham are both recorded as chamberlains and wardens in the 1620s; 'Salisbury Trade Companies since 1612', *A History of the County of Wiltshire: Volume 6* (1962), pp. 136–38.

41 'The Design Book of John Abbott', Devon Record Office, Exeter, MS 404M/B1.

42 The origin of this idea may be the piece by Margaret Jourdain, 'Plasterer: John Abbott of Barnstaple and his Sketch Book', *Country Life* 434 (2 March 1940), pp. 222–25.

43 Michael Bath, 'The Sources of John Abbott's Pattern Book', *Architectural History* 41 (1998), pp. 49–66.

44 Davies points out that the greater number of examples found in the counties of the south-east reflects research which has been undertaken as well as incidence of wall painting, *Artisan Art*, p. 120.

45 Bath, *Renaissance Decorative Painting in Scotland*, p. 6.

46 Bath presents Pinkie House as an example where the early plasterwork is almost certainly contemporary with the painted decoration of the long gallery (*ibid.*). The plasterwork, however, includes no figurative imagery but reproduces motifs from moulds.

47 C. L. Kingsford (ed.), *A survey of London by J. Stow; reprinted from the text of 1603, with intro. and notes*, 2 vols (Oxford, 1908).

48 Gapper, 'Plasterers and Plasterwork', p. 272.

49 Sir Henry Wotton, *The Elements of Architecture* (London, 1624), p. 108.

50 Indeed, R. Machin identified the period 1620–39 as a significant peak in an uneven chronology of building activity; 'The Great Rebuilding: A Reassessment', *Past & Present*, vol. 77, no. 1 (1977): 33–56.

51 Although it relates to a church rather than a domestic commission, it is known for example that the plasterer Robert Brockway, who created the plasterwork at East Knoyle church in Wiltshire in the late 1630s, was provided with 'a model or draughte thereof in paper' with all the imagery mapped out by the patron for the craftsmen to execute. However, this evidence comes from Brockway's deposition to a Parliamentary commission in 1647 and his testimony shows him anxious to avoid personal responsibility for a programme of contentious imagery. He may have exaggerated the patron's involvement to distance himself from blame. See Louise Durning and Clare Tilbury, '"Looking into Jesus": Image and Belief in a Seventeenth-Century English Chancel', *Journal of Ecclesiastical History* vol. 60, no. 3 (July 2009): 490–513.

52 Wells-Cole, *Art and Decoration.*

53 As pointed out by Francis W. Reader, 'Tudor Domestic Wall Paintings, Part 2', *The Archaeological Journal* vol. 93 (1936), p. 246.

54 Malcolm Airs, *The Making of the English Country House, 1500–1640* (London, 1975); rev. as *The Tudor & Jacobean Country House: A Building History* (Stroud, 1995).

55 I am grateful to Claire Gapper for sharing the information provided by Kate Harris about this remarkable drawing and for providing a photocopy with a transcription of the handwritten inscription. The drawing is discussed in her thesis, 'Plasterers and Plasterwork', pp. 361–62. Kate Harris's research on this document will shortly be published in the journal of the Wiltshire Archaeological and Natural History Society.

56 It is possible that the craftsman's inability to draw the patron's arms was the result of not knowing what they were; some contracts for funeral monuments indicate that the arms will be supplied to the craftsman before he commences work. My thanks to Richard Cust for pointing this out.

57 Mrs Baldwin-Childe, 'The Building of the Manor House of Kyre Park, Worcestershire (1588–1618)', *The Antiquary* vol. 21 (1980), pp. 202–05, 261–64 and vol. 22, pp. 24–26, 50–53. In the entry for 1590, under the heading 'Titles for my House', there are several verses in English and Latin, including a four-line verse in Latin entitled 'For Mars & Venus Story' (p. 25).

58 Catherine Richardson, *Domestic Life and Domestic Tragedy in Early Modern England: The Material Life of the Household* (Manchester, 2006).

59 Paul S. Seaver, *Wallington's World: A Puritan Artisan in Seventeenth-Century London* (Stanford, 1985), p. 79. See also David Booy, *The*

Notebooks of Nehemiah Wallington, 1618–1654: A Selection (Aldershot, 2007). The range of godly texts consulted by Wallington is detailed by Seaver, p. 5.

1 RELIGIOUS IMAGERY IN BRITAIN

1 For a single-volume study bringing together recent scholarship on the relationship between religious reform and the visual arts in Britain see Tara Hamling and Richard L. Williams (eds), *Art Re-formed: Re-assessing the Impact of the Reformation on the Visual Arts* (Newcastle, 2007).

2 See e.g. Kathleen Kamerick, *Popular Piety and Art in the Late Middle Ages: Image Worship and Idolatry in England, 1350–1500* (Basingstoke, 2002); Richard Marks, *Image and Devotion in Late Medieval England* (Stroud, 2004); Richard Marks and Paul Williamson (eds), *Gothic: Art for England, 1400–1547* (London, 2003); Richard Deacon and Philip Lindley, *Image and Idol: Medieval Sculpture* (London, 2001); Eamon Duffy, *The Stripping of the Altars: Traditional Religion in England, c. 1400–c. 1580* (New Haven and London, 1992); Margaret Aston, *England's Iconoclasts: Volume 1, Laws against Images* (Oxford, 1988); Robert Whiting, *Local Responses to the English Reformation* (Basingstoke, 1998); a useful chapter-length overview is provided by Phillip Lindley, 'The Visual Arts and their Functions in the English Pre-Reformation Church' in Hamling and Williams, *Art Re-formed*, pp. 15–45.

3 On the wider European context see Robert N. Swanson, *Religion and Devotion in Europe, c. 1215–c. 1515* (Cambridge, 1995).

4 For imagery on rood screens see Eamon Duffy, 'Late Medieval Religion' in Marks and Williamson, *Gothic*, pp. 56–67.

5 Duffy, *Stripping of the Altars*, pp. 29–37, figs 7–10.

6 See E. W. Tristram, *English Medieval Wall Painting*, 3 vols covering the twelfth, thirteenth and fourteenth centuries published in 1944, 1950 and 1955.

7 The Three Living and Three Dead was a popular story thought to have originated in thirteenth-century Flanders. Three kings while hunting encounter three corpses who castigate them for their preoccupation with pleasure and worldly things, adding the ominous words 'as you are, we once were; as we are, so shall you be'. Paintings of the subject on walls and in manuscripts followed and it proved popular in England in the fourteenth and fifteenth centuries. Fragments of this imagery can still be seen in fourteenth-century wall paintings in the chapel at Haddon Hall, Derbyshire.

8 Richard Marks, *Stained Glass in England during the Middle Ages* (London, 1993), p. 67.

9 Marks and Williamson, *Gothic*, cat. 261; see also cats 262 and 263 for other roof corbels carved as angels.

10 *Ibid.*, cat. 121.

11 A forthcoming monograph by Alexandra Walsham will examine the way in which the complex religious changes of the sixteenth and seventeenth centuries left their imprint on the wider physical landscape; *The Reformation of the Landscape: Religion, Identity and Memory in Early Modern Britain and Ireland* (Oxford).

12 Maurice Howard and Edward Wilson, *The Vyne: A Tudor House Revealed* (London, 2003), pp. 111, 147–48.

13 Susan Foister, 'Private Devotion', in Marks and Williamson, *Gothic*, pp. 334–36; Susan Foister, 'Paintings and Other Works of Art in Sixteenth-Century English Inventories', *Burlington Magazine* 123 (1981): 273–82.

14 Foister, 'Paintings and Other Works of Art'.

15 Foister, *ibid.*, p. 280, states that the popularity of alabaster reliefs of religious subjects was greatest c. 1480–1520. See also Francis Cheetham, *English Medieval Alabasters* (Oxford, 1984).

16 David Gaimster, 'Pots, Prints and Protestantism: Changing Mentalities in the Urban Domestic Sphere, c. 1480–1580' in David Gaimster and Roberta Gilchrist (eds), *The Archaeology of Reformation, 1480–1580* (Leeds, 2003), pp. 122–44.

17 Robert Campin, *The Annunciation*, c. 1420–40, oil on panel, Musées Royaux des Beaux-Arts, Brussels, and Robert Campin or Rogier van der Weyden, wing panels from the Werl Altarpiece, c. 1434–38, oil on panel, Museo del Prado, Madrid.

18 Eamon Duffy, *Marking the Hours: English People & their Prayers, 1240–1570* (New Haven and London, 2006).

19 British Museum no. M&ME 1894, 7–29, 1.
20 For hat pins with scenes from the Old and New Testaments see Diana Scarisbrick, *Tudor and Jacobean Jewellery* (London, 1995), p. 46; for other types of jewellery with devotional imagery see p. 42. For pilgrim badges see Geoff Egan, *Material Culture in London in an Age of Transition: Tudor and Stuart Period Finds c. 1450–c. 1700 from Excavations at Riverside Sites in Southwark*, MoLAS Monograph 19 (London, 2005), pp. 204–10.
21 Marks and Williamson, *Gothic*, cats 98 and 211.
22 Hugo Blake, Geoff Egan, John Hurst and Elizabeth New, 'From Popular Devotion to Resistance and Revival in England: The Cult of the Holy Name of Jesus and the Reformation' in Gaimster and Gilchrist, *Archaeology of Reformation*, pp. 175–203, fig. 5.
23 The provenance of this chest is not known, so it is unclear whether it was created as a domestic or church item.
24 David H. Caldwell, 'The Beaton Panels: Scottish Carvings of the 1520s or 1530s', in John Higgitt (ed.), *Medieval Art and Architecture in the Diocese of St Andrews*, British Archaeological Association, Conference Transactions, 14 (London, 1994), pp. 174–84.
25 Christopher Hussey, 'Cothay, I – Somerset', *Country Life* (22 October 1927): 596–604, figs 13 and 15; the discussion mistakenly identifies the Annunciation as the Immaculate Conception.
26 Edward Croft-Murray, *Decorative Painting in England, 1537–1837: Early Tudor to Sir James Thornhill*, 2 vols (London, 1962), vol. 1, p. 175.
27 James S. Richardson, 'Sixteenth and Seventeenth Century Mural Decorations at the House of Kinneil, Bo'ness, West Lothian', *Proceedings of the Society of Antiquaries of Scotland* vol. 75 (1941): 184–204, pls 25–47; Bath, *Renaissance Decorative Painting*, pp. 272–74.
28 Marker's Cottage, near Killerton, Devon, is managed by the National Trust.
29 Cullacott Farmhouse, Werrington, Launceston, Cornwall. The building is privately owned but with opening arrangements through English Heritage Grant-Aided Properties listings. The wall paintings include the Tudor arms so they must date after 1485.
30 The Church's position on images was formally established at the second Council of Nicaea in AD 787; see Aston, *England's Iconoclasts*, pp. 47–61.
31 For the issues involved in defining devotional imagery see Marks, *Image and Devotion*, pp. 11–37.
32 Eamon Duffy, 'Devotion to the Crucifix and Related Images in England on the Eve of the Reformation' in Bob Scribner (ed.), *Bilder und Bildersturm im Spätmittelalter und in der frühen Neuzeit* (Wiesbaden, 1990), pp. 21–36; Duffy, *Stripping of the Altars*, pp. 234–48.
33 The Wounds of Christ decorate a bench back at Ashmanhaugh church in Norfolk. The symbols of the Passion can be seen on a sixteenth-century bench end at St Andrew's Church in Trent, Dorset. The Image of Pity is the subject of the Coventry Ring, described earlier in this chapter. A woodcut of the Pieta with an indulgence defaced after the Reformation is illustrated in Tessa Watt, *Cheap Print and Popular Piety, 1550–1640* (Cambridge, 1991), p. 133, fig. 9. For discussion of the Image of Pity/Man of Sorrows iconography in the context of indulgences see R. N. Swanson, 'Two texts and an image make an object: a devotional sheet from pre-Reformation England' in Tara Hamling and Catherine Richardson (eds), *Everyday Objects: Medieval and Early Modern Material Culture and its Meanings* (Aldershot, 2010).
34 For discussion and examples of this image in various media see Marks, *Image and Devotion*, pp. 123–43.
35 See Duffy, *Stripping of the Altars*, pp. 256–65.
36 On devotions to the saints see *ibid.*, pp. 155–205 and Marks, *Image and Devotion*, pp. 86–120.
37 A useful overview of the ideological framework for the assault on images by reformers is provided by Carlos M. N. Eire, 'The Reformation Critique of the Image' in Scribner, *Bilder und Bildersturm*, pp. 51–68.
38 For Luther's theology of religious art see Carl Christensen, *Art and the Reformation in Germany* (Athens, OH., 1980), pp. 42–65. For the impact of Lutheran theology on the production of religious art see Joseph Leo Koerner, *The Reformation of the Image* (London, 2004).
39 On Calvin's attack on idolatry see Carlos M. N. Eire, *War against the Idols: The Reformation of Worship from Erasmus to Calvin* (Cambridge, 1986).

40 Calvin's *Institutes* of 1559 was originally published in Latin. The first English translation was published in 1561. The quotation here is from Henry Beveridge's translation of 1599 (London), Book 1, Chapter 11, 'The setting up of idols a defection from the true God'.

41 *The Canons and Decrees of the Sacred and Oecumenical Council of Trent*, ed. and trans. by J. Waterworth (London, 1848), pp. 233–36.

42 On European iconoclasm, popular and official, see Eire, *War against the Idols* and Lee Palmer Wandel, *Voracious Idols and Violent Hands: Iconoclasm in Reformation Zurich, Strasbourg, and Basel* (Cambridge, 1999).

43 See Koerner, *Reformation of the Image.*

44 See Aston, *England's Iconoclasts*, pp. 298–302 for comparison of the Elizabethan and Edwardian Injunctions.

45 Injunctions quoted from Henry Gee and W. H. Hardy (eds), *Documents Illustrative of English Church History* (New York, 1896), pp. 417–42.

46 All quotes from the Homily taken from John Griffiths (ed.), *The Two Books of Homilies Appointed to be Read in Churches* (Oxford, 1859), pp. 167–272.

47 For accounts of this in Elizabeth's reign see Duffy, *Stripping of the Altars*, pp. 565–93 and for an episode in 1643 see Aston, *England's Iconoclasts*, pp. 85–86.

48 For useful overviews on the process and impact of the Scottish Reformation see Julian Goodare, 'Scotland' in Bob Scribner, Roy Porter and Mikuláš Teich (eds), *The Reformation in National Context* (Cambridge, 1994), pp. 95–110 and Michael F. Graham, 'Scotland' in Andrew Pettegree (ed.), *The Reformation World* (London, 2000), pp. 410–29. Ian Cowan's *The Scottish Reformation* (London, 1982) provides a standard introduction with discussion of regional variations. On Popular Protestantism see Margo Todd, *The Culture of Protestantism in Early Modern Scotland* (New Haven and London, 2002).

49 Alexandra Walsham, *Church Papists: Catholicism, Conformity and Confessional Polemic in Early Modern England* (Woodbridge, 1993).

50 Peter Lake, *Moderate Puritans and the Elizabethan Church* (Cambridge, 1982).

51 Judith Maltby, *Prayer Book and People in Elizabethan and Early Stuart England* (Cambridge, 1998, 2000 edn).

52 For definition and discussion of the term 'parish Anglicans' see Christopher Haigh, *English Reformations: Religion, Politics, and Society under the Tudors* (Oxford, 1993).

53 Anthony Milton's *Catholic and Reformed: The Roman and Protestant Churches in English Protestant Thought, 1600–1640* (Cambridge, 1995) provides a comprehensive analysis of how Protestant writers described the position of the English Church relative to the Roman Catholic Church and continental Protestantism. It highlights the areas of ideological tension within the Established Church.

54 This conservative strain in the English Church has been described as 'English Arminianism' by Nicholas Tyacke who argued that the movement was in opposition to the general Calvinist consensus of the English Church; *Anti-Calvinists: The Rise of English Arminianism, c. 1590–1640* (Oxford, 1987, 1990 edn). Tyacke's argument has attracted many supporters but also some critics, including Peter White who has maintained that Arminianism and Calvinism were not clearly defined positions set against each other but fell within a broader spectrum of belief; *Predestination, Policy and Polemic: Conflict and Consensus in the English Church from the Reformation to the Civil War* (Cambridge, 1992). See also the exchange between Tyacke and White in *Past and Present*, no. 115 (May 1987), pp. 201–29.

55 For a case study of how the tensions between conservative Anglicans and the godly in relation to church decoration and images played out in the 1620s in a particular parish, see Matthew Reynolds, *Godly Reformers and their Opponents in Early Modern England: Religion in Norwich, c. 1560–1643* (Woodbridge, 2005), ch. 7.

56 On the processes that led to the creation of the Protestant Second Commandment see 'The Structure of the Decalogue' in Aston, *England's Iconoclasts*, pp. 371–91.

57 William Perkins, *The whole treatises of the cases of conscience* (Cambridge, 1608), Book II, p. 150. He goes on to distinguish between religious and 'civill' adoration.

58 Henry Ainsworth, *Annotations upon the Second book of Moses, called Exodus*, ([Amsterdam] 1617), n.p.

59 Edward Elton, *God's Holy Mind Touching*

Matters Morall, which himself uttered in Tenne Words, or Tenne Commandments (London, 1625), p. 28.

60 The subject of the painting was identified by Edward Croft-Murray and published in an article by John Cornforth in *Country Life*, 15 March 1962. This identification was accepted by E. Clive Rouse in a report dated 30 September 1975 held in the NMR archive. For information about the house see RCHME Original Investigator's Notes for Queen Hoo Hall, Tewin, Hertfordshire, 1909; RCHME Inventory for Hertfordshire, 1910; Floor plans in NMR archive (MD48/377 and MD93/2316); W. H. H. Van Sickle, 'Queen Hoo: The Story of the Manor and the Hall c. 1060–2003', report of 1987 published by the Hatfield Local History Society, 2003.

61 Oliver Garnett, *Canons Ashby, Northamptonshire* (London, 2004).

62 I have explored the possible significance of leaving religious images 'plain' or without rich colours in relation to Protestant thought in 'The Appreciation of Religious Images in Plasterwork in the Protestant Domestic Interior' in Hamling and Williams (eds), *Art Re-formed*, pp. 147–68.

63 John Donne, *The Sermons*, ed. Evelyn Simpson and George Potter (Berkeley and Los Angeles, 1954–62), VII, pp. 431–32 and X, pp. 90–91.

64 Lancelot Andrewes, *The pattern of catechistical doctrine at large, or, A learned and pious exposition of the Ten Commandments* (London, 1650), p. 214.

65 The visitation articles comprised detailed questions by officials to ask church wardens in order to assess reform at a local level. As such the articles represent public statements of official policy.

66 William Fulke, *D. Heskyns, D. Sanders and M. Rastell . . . overthrowne, and detected of their severall blasphemous heresies* (London, 1579), p. 598.

67 William Perkins, *A Reformed Catholike: or, A Declaration shewing how neere we may come to the Present Church of Rome in sundrie points of Religion: and wherein we must for ever depart from them* (Cambridge, 1598), p. 172.

68 William Perkins, *A Warning against the Idolatrie of the last times. And an instruction touching religious or Divine Worship* (Cambridge, 1601), p. 58.

69 Simon Birckbek, *The Protestants evidence taken out of good records; shewing that for fifteene hundred yeares next after Christ, divers worthy guides of Gods Church, have in sundry weightie points of religion, taught as the Church of England now doth* (London, 1635), p. 42.

70 See 'Graven Images: More Realism, More Danger?' in Aston, *England's Iconoclasts*, pp. 401–08.

71 Ainsworth, *Annotations upon . . . Exodus*, sig. O3v.

72 James Calfhill, *An Answere to the Treatise of the Crosse* (London, 1565), p. 16.

73 Gervase Babington, *A very fruitfull Exposition of the Commaundments by way of Questions and Answers for greater plainnesse* (London, 1583), p. 92.

74 Peter Barker, *A judicious and painefull exposition upon the Ten Commandments* (London, 1624), p. 89.

75 Henry Peacham, *The Gentlemans Exercise* (London, 1612), p. 9.

76 Edmund Gurnay, *Toward the Vindication of the Second Commandment* (Cambridge, 1639), p. 131.

77 Perkins, *A Warning*, p. 15.

78 Andrewes, *Pattern of catechistical doctrine*, p. 214.

79 Calfhill, *Answere to the Treatise*, p. 16.

80 Andrew Willet, *Hexapla in Exodum: That is, A Sixfold Commentarie upon the 2nd booke of Moses called Exodus* (London, 1608), p. 340.

81 Peacham, *Gentlemans Exercise*, p. 12.

82 Margaret Aston, 'Puritans and Iconoclasm, 1560–1660', in Christopher Durston and Jacqueline Eales (eds), *The Culture of English Puritanism, 1560–1700* (Basingstoke, 1996), p. 95.

83 Peacham, *Gentlemans Exercise*, p. 13.

84 Maurice Howard, *The Building of Elizabethan and Jacobean England* (New Haven and London, 2007), see esp. ch. 1.

85 Maurice Howard, 'Afterword: Art Reformed: Spiritual Revolution, Spatial Relocation' in Hamling and Williams, *Art Re-formed*, pp. 267–74.

86 Annabel Ricketts, *The English Country House Chapel: Building a Protestant Tradition*, ed. Simon Ricketts (Reading, 2007), p. 139.

87 Santina M. Levey, *An Elizabethan Inheritance: The Hardwick Hall Textiles* (London, 1998), p. 70, fig. 69.

88 On the Laudian reforms and their impact on the appearance of churches see Kenneth Fin-

cham and Nicholas Tyacke, *Altars Restored: The Changing Face of English Religious Worship, 1547–c.1700* (Oxford, 2007), esp. chs 4–6, pp. 227–73 and Graham Parry, *The Arts of the Anglican Counter-Reformation: Glory, Laud and Honour* (Woodbridge, 2006).

89 Aston, 'Puritans and Iconoclasm', pp. 92–121; Margaret Aston, 'Iconoclasm in England: Official and Clandestine' in Peter Marshall (ed.), *The Impact of the English Reformation, 1500–1640* (London, 1997), pp. 167–91.

90 See Julie Spraggon, *Puritan Iconoclasm during the English Civil War* (Woodbridge, 2003), ch. 2, pp. 33–60, and Appendix 1. The Ordinance of 9 May 1644 extended the proscriptions to include 'any Angel or Saint'.

91 Trevor Cooper (ed.), *The Journal of William Dowsing: Iconoclasm in East Anglia during the English Civil War* (Woodbridge, 2001).

92 The inscription, though much damaged, seems to provide the same text as that in the carved wood overmantel from 90 High Street, Oxford, discussed below, Ch. 5. If so, the inscription spells out the meaning of the Old Testament episode as a type of the Crucifixion of Christ.

93 It is not clear if the Muchelney ceiling was over-painted and embellished during 'restorations' in the past. On angels in early modern belief see Peter Marshall and Alexandra Walsham (eds), *Angels in the Early Modern World* (Cambridge, 2006), esp. chs 4 and 6.

94 Another depiction of an angel in post-Reformation church decoration is that above the chancel arch of St Peter's Church in Pebworth, Worcestershire. The angel accompanies an inscription and probably dates from early in the seventeenth century.

95 See Parry, *Arts of the Anglican Counter-Reformation*, p. 92 and fig. 23.

96 The iconography has recently been interpreted in relation to Christ's sacrifice as the ladder between man and God. The authors suggest that the visual focus on the altar, the spiritual focus on the propitiatory sacrifice of communion and the emphasis on the reciprocity of prayer and grace can be read as 'Laudian' in their theology; Louise Durning and Clare Tilbury, '"Looking into Jesus": Image and Belief in a Seventeenth-Century English Chancel', *Journal of Ecclesiastical History* vol. 60, no. 3 (July 2009): 490–513.

97 Michael Bath, *Renaissance Decorative Painting in Scotland* (Edinburgh, 2003), pp. 22, 123, 264–65.

98 The ceiling was heavily 'restored', including much re-painting in c. 1944. Its appearance prior to this intervention was recorded by A. Graham, 'The Painted Ceiling in the Church of St Mary, Grandtully', *Proceedings of the Society of Antiquaries of Scotland* (1942–43): 147–54.

99 Aston, 'Puritans and Iconoclasm', pp. 107–08.

100 Aston, *England's Iconoclasts*, pp. 306–14.

101 Lindsay Boynton (ed.), *The Hardwick Hall Inventories of 1601* (London, 1971), p. 30.

102 Ricketts, *English Country House Chapel*, p. 140 and Annabel Ricketts with Claire Gapper and Caroline Knight, 'Designing for Protestant Worship: The Private Chapels of the Cecil Family' in Sarah Hamilton and Andrew Spicer (eds), *Defining the Holy: Sacred Space in Medieval and Early Modern Europe* (Aldershot, 2005), pp. 115–37.

103 Pauline Croft, 'The Religion of Robert Cecil', *The Historical Journal* vol. 34, no. 4 (December 1991): 773–96.

104 As described by Parry, *Arts of the Anglican Counter-Reformation*, p. 101.

105 Richard L. Williams, 'Collecting and Religion in Late Sixteenth-Century England' in Edward Chaney (ed.), *The Evolution of English Collecting: Receptions of Italian Art in the Tudor and Stuart Periods* (New Haven and London, 2003), p. 164 and 174. See p. 175 for other examples of religious pictures owned by Protestants in the last decades of the sixteenth century.

106 Will of John Donne, Doctor of Divinity, Dean of Saint Paul's Cathedral, City of London, 1631. PROB 11/159.

107 Samuel Torshell, *The hypocrite discovered and cured* (London, 1644), p. 13.

108 Autobiography of Mary Pennington, c. 1640–80. West Sussex Record Office, Chichester, record ref. 31145.

109 'A report of the search made at Hoggesden [Hoxton] by order from hir Majestie & the Council, by Mr Justice Smith'. National Archives, Kew, PRO, State Papers Domestic, 12/172, fol. 113: 27 August 1584.

110 Watt, *Cheap Print*, esp. ch. 4.

111 *ibid.*, pp. 174–77, pl. 25.

112 Facsimiles available through the English

Broadside Ballad Archive, University of California, Santa Barbara (http://emc.english.ucsb.edu/ballad_project/). Originals in Pepys Library, Magdalene College, Cambridge.

113 Anthony Wells-Cole, *Art and Decoration in Elizabethan and Jacobean England: The Influence of Continental Prints, 1558–1625* (New Haven and London, 1997).

114 Chris Tabraham, *Huntly Castle* (Edinburgh, 1995), p. 11.

2 BUILDING 'GORGEOUS' BUT GODLY HOUSES

1 Queen Elizabeth, quoted in Margaret Aston, *England's Iconoclasts: Volume I, Laws against Images* (Oxford, 1988), p. 317.

2 W. G. Hoskins, 'The Rebuilding of Rural England, 1570–1640', *Past & Present* vol. 4 (1953): 44–59.

3 Subsequent scholars have refined Hoskins's discussion of the 'great rebuilding' to include regional and dating qualifications but also to argue that the transformation of the built environment which began in Elizabeth's reign was not confined to domestic housing, but affected a range of building types in town and country as well as the physical alteration of the landscape itself. See R. Machin, 'The Great Rebuilding: A Reassessment', *Past & Present* vol. 77, no. 1 (1977): 33–56; Colin Platt, *The Great Rebuildings of Tudor and Stuart England: Revolutions in Architectural Taste* (London, 1994); Maurice Howard, *The Building of Elizabethan and Jacobean England* (New Haven and London, 2007).

4 Phillip Stubbes, *The Anatomie of Abuses* (London, 1583), p. 34.

5 Peter Thornton, *Seventeenth-Century Interior Decoration in England, France and Holland* (New Haven and London, 1978), p. 97.

6 The evolution and repetition of patterns in country house design over this period has been charted in Andor Gomme and Alison Maguire, *Design and Plan in the Country House: From Castle Donjons to Palladian Boxes* (New Haven and London, 2008).

7 See John Summerson, *Architecture in Britain, 1530–1830* (New Haven and London, 9th edn, 1993), ch. 6, 'Building in Town and Country 1570–1640', pp. 51–60 and Malcolm Airs, *The Buildings of Britain: Tudor and Jacobean, A Guide and Gazetteer* (London, 1982).

8 The 'gentry' refers to a broad group in the upper levels of society who owned land or property and/or could live without manual labour. Their status and material circumstances could vary greatly, as Felicity Heal and Clive Holmes have observed, 'Flexible definitions of gentility were a necessary feature of the rather mobile society of early modern England'; *The Gentry in England and Wales, 1500–1700* (Basingstoke, 1994, reprinted 2002), p. 7.

9 For a comprehensive study of this class of building see Nicholas Cooper, *The Houses of the Gentry, 1480–1680* (New Haven and London, 1999). Eric Mercer's article of 1954 is still particularly useful on the different plans adopted by courtier and gentry builders; 'The Houses of the Gentry', *Past & Present* vol. 5, no. 1 (1954): 11–32.

10 According to J. T. Cliffe, in the first half of the seventeenth century the major county families commanding an income of £1000 a year or more had between ten and thirty servants in receipt of annual wages; *The World of the Country House in Seventeenth-Century England* (New Haven and London, 1999), p. 82.

11 The standard account of the social functions of each of these state rooms is Mark Girouard, *Life in the English Country House: A Social and Architectural History* (New Haven and London, 1978), ch. 4, pp. 81–118. For more detailed discussion of these rooms in gentry houses specifically, see Cooper, *Houses of the Gentry*.

12 For studies of the Scottish tower house plan see Deborah Howard, *Scottish Architecture from the Reformation to the Restoration, 1560–1660,* Architectural History of Scotland (Edinburgh, 1995) and Charles McKean, *The Scottish Chateau: The Country House of Renaissance Scotland* (Stroud, 2001).

13 See Nicholas Cooper, 'Rank, Manners and Display: The Gentlemanly House, 1500–1750', *Transactions of the Royal Historical Society* vol. 12 (2002): 291–310, for the ways in which the architectural form and use of ornament for gentry houses expressed the owners' aspirations and education.

14 Henry Wotton, *The Elements of Architecture, collected by Henry Wotton Knight, from the best authors and examples* (London, 1624), p. 119.

15 *Wentworth Papers, 1597–1628*, ed. J. P. Cooper, Camden Fourth Series, vol. 12 (London, 1973), p. 14.

16 Christopher Hussey, 'Fountains Hall, Yorkshire', *Country Life* (15 August 1931): 180–86.

17 Improving an older manor house also underlined the ancient pedigree of the family, an important claim to superior status in an age of widespread social mobility.

18 It is not clear if this frieze was part of the original decoration of the room or was a slightly later addition. The painted roundels were certainly in place by 1633 when they were listed in an inventory. A transcript was made in Anon., 'Excursion to Barton on the Heath, the Rollwrights, and Chastleton, June 15th 1888', *Transactions of the Birmingham and Midland Institute* vol. 15 (1888).

19 My thanks to Maurice Howard for bringing this period room at the Speed Art Museum to my attention. For other examples and discussion of scenes from Ovid in decorative art in England see Tara Hamling, 'Narrative and Figurative Imagery in the English Domestic Interior, c. 1558–c. 1640', D.Phil. thesis, 2 vols (University of Sussex, 2002).

20 Mildred Campbell, *The English Yeoman in the Tudor and Stuart Age* (new edn, Whitstable, Kent, 1990).

21 Philip B. Chatwin, *Stratford House, Camp Hill, Reprinted from the Transactions of the Birmingham Archaeological Society: Vol. 71, 1953* (Birmingham, 1955).

22 Admittedly both these houses were built in relatively undeveloped areas where space was available for this kind of building. Culross only developed into a town in the late sixteenth century; the town house was built in 1625.

23 Robert Hurd, *Gladstone's Land: The Story of an Old Edinburgh House* (Edinburgh, 1966).

24 Summerson, *Architecture in Britain*, p. 91.

25 George Vertue sketched the appearance of 'New Place' based on the memory of townsmen in 1737. The sketch survives in the British Library, Portland Papers.

26 Percy Russell, *Dartmouth: A History of the Port and Town* (Dartmouth, 1982) related that the eastern pair of houses were built for and leased to John Budley in 1640. The initials 'MH' and the date '1635' are carved in a capstone of one of the supporting piers on the exterior of the building at the western end and the date '1640' is carved in a capstone at the east end.

27 A plasterwork overmantel depicting the Judgement of Solomon was recorded *in situ* in 1950 in the easternmost house of the Butterwalk by Russell, *ibid.* but this has since been removed. An overmantel with this subject dated 1640 now installed at Stafford Barton in Devon (a private residence) may be the one from the Butterwalk.

28 Wotton, *Elements*, p. 99.

29 William Harrison, *The Description of England: The Classic Contemporary Account of Tudor Social Life* (1577), ed. Georges Edelen (Washington, D.C., and New York, 1994), p. 200.

30 *Ibid.*, p. 197.

31 *Ibid.*

32 Susan Foister's analysis of sixteenth-century domestic inventories from the Probate Court of Canterbury is a useful introduction to the use of inventories as documentary evidence; 'Paintings and Other Works of Art in Sixteenth-Century English Inventories', *The Burlington Magazine* vol. 123, no. 938 (May 1981): 277–78. Collections of inventories of citizens in towns have been published in recent decades in regional records, e.g. Michael Reed (ed.), *The Ipswich Probate Inventories 1583–1631* (Woodbridge, 1981); Dorothy Marion Herridge, *Surrey Probate Inventories, 1558–1603*, Surrey Record Society, 39 (Woking, 2005); Jeanne Jones (ed.), *Stratford-upon-Avon Inventories, 1538–1699*, Dugdale Society Publications, 40 (Stratford-upon-Avon, 2003); Edwin and Stella George (eds), *Bristol Probate Inventories. Pt. 1: 1542–1650*, Bristol Record Society, 54 (Bristol, 2002). Maurice Howard has discussed the use of inventories for reconstructing the architectural form and internal layout of great houses; 'Inventories, Surveys and the Histories of Great Houses, 1480–1640', *Architectural History* vol. 41 (1998): 14–29.

33 John Gough Nichols, *The Unton Inventories, relating to Wadley and Faringdon, co. Berks, in the years 1596 and 1620* (London, 1841), p. 5.

34 Inventory of Thomas Lord Wharton (1568), transcribed by Joan Evans and published in *The Archaeological Journal* vol. 102 (1945): 135–50.

35 Inventory of Sir Henry Sharington (1575), transcribed by Thelma E. Vernon and published in *Wiltshire Archaeological Society Magazine* vol. 63 (1968): 72–82.

36 Inventory of William Lovelace, Serjeant at Law, Canterbury (1577), transcribed in Foister, 'Paintings and Other Works of Art', pp. 273–82. The term 'table' might also refer to painting on panel.

37 Lindsay Boynton (ed.), *The Hardwick Hall Inventories of 1601* (London, 1971), pp. 29 and 33.

38 William Hinde, *A faithfull remonstrance of the holy life and happy death of John Bruen of Bruen-Stapleford, in the county of Chester, Esquire* (London, 1641), p. 85.

39 Gervase Babington, *A verie fruitfull Exposition of the Commaundements* (London, 1583, reprinted 1590), p. 9.

40 Richard Greenham, *The workes of the reverend and faithfull servant of Jesus Christ M. Richard Greenham* (London, 1612), p. 673.

41 *Ibid.*

42 Stephen Egerton, *Indecorum: or A brief treatise upon one of Salomons proverbs* (London, 1613), 'The Epistle Dedicatorie'.

43 William Gouge, *Of Domesticall Duties: Eight Treatises* (London, 1622), pp. 255–56.

44 Stubbes, *Anatomie*, pp. 27–28.

45 William Perkins, *The whole treatises of the cases of conscience* (Cambridge, 1608), pp. 96 and 102.

46 This sobriety in dress was not necessarily inexpensive or lacking in luxury. Puritan dress could consist of expensive black silks and imported linen, as Aileen Ribeiro pointed out in *Dress and Morality* (London, 1986), p. 85 and in *Fashion and Fiction: Dress in Art and Literature in Stuart England* (New Haven and London, 2005), p. 191.

47 James Durham, *The law unsealed, or, A Practical exposition of the Ten Commandments with a resolution of several momentous questions and cases of conscience* (Edinburgh and Glasgow, 1676), p. 309.

48 William Perkins, *Whole treatises*, pp. 66–67.

49 Egerton, *Indecorum*, p. 175.

50 The Alleyn panels are currently incorporated in a wooden chimneypiece in the masters' library of Dulwich College and their location prior to the nineteenth century is not known. It has been suggested that the panels were originally part of 'ye queens owld barge' that Alleyn acquired in 1618 and had made up into a chimneypiece the following year, but the diary does not provide any evidence to verify this theory and the allegorical figures are entirely consistent with the character of domestic decoration of this period. Indeed, Alleyn's diary for 1617–22 records many payments for decorative painting work, including several chimneypieces, for his house. My suggestion that the panels were part of a chimneypiece from Alleyn's house seems just as plausible as the idea that they were salvaged from a royal barge, especially since the nature of the barge's decoration is not even known. For discussion see Susan Foister, 'Edward Alleyn's Collection of Paintings' in Aileen Reid and Robert Maniura (eds), *Edward Alleyn: Elizabethan Actor, Jacobean Gentleman* (London, 1994), pp. 33–61.

3 THE SPIRITUALISATION OF THE HOUSEHOLD

1 Anthony Wells-Cole, *Art and Decoration in Elizabethan and Jacobean England: The Influence of Continental Prints, 1558–1625* (New Haven and London, 1997).

2 Bowes Museum, Barnard Castle, County Durham. Museum Accession No. Founders/W.95.

3 The panel falls within a genre of family portrait common in northern Europe, which derives from sixteenth-century German prints advocating good manners in children at the dinner table, hence their popular name, *Tischzucht* (Table Discipline). The *Tischzucht* by Georg Pencz (c. 1534) with an accompanying poem by Hans Sachs, is one of the best-known examples of this genre. The poem exhorts children to be models of good behaviour at the table; moreover, they are 'not to commence eating until a blessing is said'. These popular prints spawned a genre of family portraits depicting the saying of grace before the meal. See Wayne Franits, 'The Family

Saying Grace: A Theme in Dutch Art of the Seventeenth Century', *Simiolus* vol. 16, no. 1 (1986): 36–49.

4 The marriage agreement and settlement deeds recorded Silvestra Capps as one of the daughters of James Capps late of Jewes in Wiveliscombe. There is no record of a previous marriage and Silvestra is not identified as a widow. The marriage papers are in the Somerset Record Office, Taunton, DD/L 23/45/1–4. The daughters are identified by their mother's maiden name in Luttrell's will, in which he bequeathed them each £500 at the age of 21 or on marriage. F. Brown, *Abstracts of Somersetshire Wills*, vol. 6 (1887–90), p. 17.

5 It is not certain when these overmantels were created. They may date from an earlier phase of improvements; another (carved) overmantel in an upstairs room is dated 1616. It seems more likely, however, that the biblical overmantels were added at the same time as the plasterwork chimneypiece in the hall, which is dated 1629. This is also the most likely period for hand-modelled figural work of this level of sophistication, based on analysis of comparable examples in other areas of the West Country: at Barnstaple and Dartmouth in Devon (1620s and 30s) and Lanhydrock House and Prideaux Place in Cornwall (1630s).

6 I wish to record my gratitude to the late Col. Sir Walter Luttrell for his kind permission to study, photograph and reproduce the overmantels at the Court House, East Quantoxhead.

7 Sir H. C. Maxwell Lyte, *A History of Dunster and of the Families of Mohun and Luttrell*, 2 vols (London, 1909), vol. 1, p. 177.

8 *Ibid.* Evidently, the attempt at intervention failed because in the same year Elizabeth married Thomas Arundel of Chideock in Dorset, from a noted Catholic family.

9 Wells-Cole, *Art and Decoration*, pp. 106–11. The overmantels and corresponding engravings are illustrated as figs. 150–57.

10 Will of Sir Edmund Skory of Saint Giles without Cripplegate, City of London, 20 July 1632, PROB 11/162.

11 Lewis Bayly (d. 1631) was the bishop of Bangor. He was a moderate Puritan but with a respect for the authority of the Church. Subsequent editions of the *Practise of Pietie* usually ran to about 800 pages. J. Gwynfor Jones and Vivienne Larminie, 'Bayly, Lewis (c. 1575–1631)', ODNB, September 2004; online edn, January 2008 [http://www.oxforddnb.com/view/article/1766], accessed 27 July 2008.

12 A discussion of the idiosyncrasies of Bayly's text in relation to Puritan thought is provided by Ian Green, *Print and Protestantism in Early Modern England* (Oxford, 2000), pp. 348–49. As Green observes, this handbook is not straightforwardly 'puritan' in that it endorses some aspects of traditional ceremony.

13 F. Brown, *Abstracts of Somersetshire Wills*, vol. 5 (1887–90), p. 66.

14 Maxwell Lyte, *History of Dunster*, vol. 1, p. 178.

15 William Perkins, *Christian Oeconomie: or, A short survey of the right manner of erecting and ordering a familie* (London, 1609), p. 164.

16 Christopher Hill, *Society and Puritanism in Pre-Revolutionary England* (London, 1964). Surprisingly little scholarly literature on the spiritualised household has been published subsequent to Hill's study. Historians have tended to focus on specific aspects including the emphasis on education, the role of women and master–servant relations. Less attention has been paid to the spiritual aims and actual practices of household religious observance.

17 Margo Todd argued that the roots of the spiritualised household pre-date Puritanism and that the key precepts were first propounded by the Christian humanists; 'Humanists, Puritans and the Spiritualised Household', *Church History* vol. 49, no. 1 (March 1980): 18–34.

18 Richard Greenham, *The workes of the reverend and faithfull servant of Jesus Christ M. Richard Greenham* (London, 1612), p. 799.

19 Perkins, *Christian Oeconomie*, p. 670.

20 William Gouge, *Of Domesticall Duties: Eight Treatises* (London, 1622), p. 18. Like Perkins and Greenham, Gouge was a conformist Calvinist, having emphases in common with Puritanism, but worked within the Established Church.

21 John Downame, *A Guide to Godlynesse or a Treatise of a Christian Life* (London, 1622, 1629 edn), p. 329. Downame was another churchman of Puritan persuasion.

22 Perkins, *Christian Oeconomie*, p. 164.

23 Gouge, *Of Domesticall Duties*, p. 258.

24 The paintings have been described in Muriel Carrick and Charlotte Ryder, *The Forge Much Hadham Hertfordshire: 16th & 17th Century Wall Paintings* (Hertford, 2000). The story of their discovery and unconventional conservation history is recounted by Jane Rutherford, 'Sixteenth-Century Wall Paintings at The Forge, Much Hadham, Hertfordshire', in Robert Gowing and Robyn Pender (eds), *All Manner of Murals: The History, Techniques and Conservation of Secular Wall Paintings* (London, 2007), pp. 121–31.

25 The paintings are associated with the queen's 1578 visit to the area in Carrick and Ryder, *The Forge*, p. 23.

26 Zillah Dovey, *An Elizabethan Progress: The Queen's Journey into East Anglia, 1578* (Stroud, 1996), pp. 130–37.

27 R. A. Houston, 'Bruce, Sir George (c. 1550–1625)', ODNB, September 2004; online edn January 2008 [http://www.oxforddnb.com/view/article/47923], accessed 8 September 2009.

28 Catherine Collinson, 'Procter, Sir Stephen (bap. 1562, d. 1619)', ODNB, September 2004; online edn, January 2008 [http://www.oxforddnb.com/view/article/65801], accessed 8 September 2009; Edith Mary Walker, *Stephen Proctor, the Builder of Fountains Hall* (Ripon, 1952).

29 Mary Anne Everett Green (ed.), 'James I – volume 76: February 1614', *Calendar of State Papers Domestic: James I, 1611–18* (1858), pp. 222–25.

30 A stone fireplace in another room was certainly installed by Strode at this time. It includes the arms of the Strode and Barnard families to commemorate Strode's marriage to a local heiress, Joan Barnard. For a short history of the building see Christopher Hussey, 'Barrington Court, Somerset (Parts I–II)', *Country Life* (17 and 24 March 1928): 370–77, 404–12.

31 Bayly, *Practise of Pietie* (London, 1613, 2nd edn), p. 437.

32 William Hinde, *A faithfull remonstrance of the holy life and happy death of John Bruen of Bruen-Stapleford, in the county of Chester, Esquire* (London, 1641), p. 64. Bruen, who died in 1625, was held up by his biographer as one of the leading lights of the reformed religion in Cheshire. Hinde, who was related to Bruen by marriage, ministered in Cheshire and published other works besides the biography of Bruen. Hinde died in 1629 and his biography of Bruen was published in 1641 under the direction of his son. See Steve Hindle, 'Bruen, John (1560–1625)', ODNB, September 2004; online edn, January 2008 [http://www.oxforddnb.com/view/article/3767], accessed 27 July 2008.

33 Harley (Brilliana), 3rd wife of Sir R. Harley, Letters to her husband 1626–43, n.d. British Library, Add. MS 70110. I am very grateful to Fiona Bowler for this reference.

34 Autobiography of Mary Pennington, c. 1640–80, West Sussex Record Office, Chichester, Record Ref. 31145.

35 Annabel Ricketts, 'The Evolution of the Protestant Country House Chapel, c. 1500–c. 1700', Ph.D. thesis (University of London, 2003), published as *The English Country House Chapel: Building a Protestant Tradition*, ed. Simon Ricketts (Reading, 2007), see esp. ch. 4, pp. 58–83.

36 Ricketts's discussion of innovations in the design of spaces for specifically Protestant forms of domestic worship focused on the Elizabethan period. As she explained, while Elizabethan designs for Puritan worship survived into the 1620s, in the early Stuart period many high-church patrons built new chapels in the traditional form of the double-cell chapel; *English Country House Chapel*, pp. 84–85.

37 Hinde, *Faithfull remonstrance*, pp. 68–74.

38 As transcribed in Joanna Moody (ed.), *The Private Life of an Elizabethan Lady: The Diary of Lady Margaret Hoby 1599–1605* (Stroud, 1998).

39 Alan Macfarlane, *The Family Life of Ralph Josselin, a Seventeenth Century Clergyman: An Essay in Historical Anthropology* (Cambridge, 1970) and Alan Macfarlane (ed.), *The Diary of Ralph Josselin, 1616–1683* (Oxford, 1991).

40 Historians have tended to focus on the educational and disciplinary functions of household religion, rather than its spiritual aims although these are, of course, interrelated. For a comprehensive account of the variety of catechetical forms in circulation and methods of catechising in the home see Ian Green, *The Christian's ABC: Catechism and Catechizing in*

England, c. 1530–1740 (Oxford, 1996), esp. ch. 4. A useful article on master–servant relations is R. C. Richardson, 'Social Engineering in Early Modern England: Masters, Servants, and the Godly Discipline', *Clio* vol. 33, no. 2 (Winter 2004), pp. 163–87.

41 Hinde, *Faithfull remonstrance*, p. 123.

42 Richard Brathwaite, *The English Gentleman* (London, 1630), p. 161.

43 Robert Cleaver, *A godlie forme of householde government* (London, 1598), pp. 24–25.

44 Illustrated in Juliet Fleming, *Graffiti and the Writing Arts of Early Modern England* (London, 2001), p. 65, fig. 15.

45 I am very grateful to Nigel Llewellyn for bringing the Hangleton panels to my attention.

46 L. F. Salzman (ed.), *A History of the County of Sussex* vol. 7 (1940), pp. 277–81.

47 Green, *Christian's ABC*, esp. ch. 10.

48 'St Martin's Priory' has always been a domestic mansion; the ecclesiastical name is a poetic invention of the nineteenth century. I am grateful to Catherine Richardson for bringing this work to my attention and to Jacqueline Eales who showed us round and kindly arranged permission to reproduce the photograph.

49 Illustrated in Fleming, *Graffiti*, p. 31, fig. 7.

50 These and other examples are described and discussed in P. M. Johnston, 'Mural Paintings in Houses: With Special Reference to Recent Discoveries at Stratford-upon-Avon and Oxford', *Journal of the British Archaeological Association* vol. 37 (1931): 75–100 and E. Clive Rouse, 'Domestic Wall and Panel Paintings in Hertfordshire', *The Archaeological Journal* vol. 146 (1989): 423–50.

51 Fleming, *Graffiti*, ch. 1, pp. 29–72; examples of these posies are quoted on pp. 170–71.

52 Deborah Howard, *Scottish Architecture from the Reformation to the Restoration, 1560–1660*, Architectural History of Scotland (Edinburgh, 1995), p. 149, fig. 4.40.

53 The Delgatie ceiling is one of a group of similar ceilings in Scotland discussed in detail by Michael Bath, *Renaissance Decorative Painting in Scotland* (Edinburgh, 2003), ch. 8, 'Grave Sentences'.

54 Cleaver, *Godlie forme* (1603 edn), p. 52. Cleaver provided a comprehensive list of activities worthy of correction, from profaning the Sabbath with frivolous pastimes to intemperance in diet.

55 Gouge, *Of Domesticall Duties*, p. 666.

56 Edward Dering, *Godly private praiers, for householders to meditate upon, and to say in theyr families* (London, 1578), sigs Eiv–Eiir.

57 George Hakewill, *King Davids vow for reformation of himselfe, his family, his kingdome. Delivered in twelve sermons before the Prince his Highnesse upon Psalm 101* (London, 1621), p. 66.

58 Green, *Print and Protestantism*, pp. 346–51.

59 The imagery seems to illustrate the interpretation of this passage as given by Calvin: 'So Paule teacheth, that he doth not consider who he is, nor what he hath done, but only that he endevour unto the appointed marke, and that with such earnestnesse, *as if with stretched armes* he were carried thether'(my italics); Jean Calvin, *A commentarie of M. Iohn Caluine uppon the Epistle to the Philippians . . . Translated out of Latine by W.B.* (London, 1584), p. 73.

4 DECORATING THE PROTESTANT HOUSEHOLD

1 Note on terminology: I have standardised the names assigned to particular rooms based on generic English designations and have indicated Scottish variations. Contemporary sources use a variety of names and the same room in terms of location on the floor plan often has a different name in different sources, especially given regional variations and the status of the building. For more information on room types and terminology see Maurice Barley, 'A Glossary of Names for Rooms in Houses of the Sixteenth and Seventeenth Centuries' in I. L. L. Foster and L. Alcock (eds), *Culture and Environment: Essays in Honour of Sir Cyril Fox* (London, 1963), pp. 479–501.

2 For a 'virtual' tour of the early modern town house and its furnishings see Catherine Richardson, *Domestic Life and Domestic Tragedy in Early Modern England: The Material Life of the Household* (Manchester, 2006), pp. 1–3.

3 Deborah Howard, *Scottish Architecture from*

the Reformation to the Restoration, 1560–1660, Architectural History of Scotland (Edinburgh, 1995), p. 68; Charles McKean, *The Scottish Chateau: The Country House of Renaissance Scotland* (Stroud, 2001).

4 See Mark Girouard, *Life in the English Country House: A Social and Architectural History* (New Haven and London, 1978) and Maurice Howard, *The Early Tudor Country House: Architecture and Politics* (London, 1987).

5 Oliver Fairclough, *The Grand Old Mansion: The Holtes and their Successors at Aston Hall, 1618–1864* (Birmingham, 1984).

6 A photograph of the Kilravock overmantel is in the archive of Nairn Museum, Scotland.

7 The ritual often included punishment of both the man and the woman concerned; see D. E. Underdown, 'The Taming of the Scold: The Enforcement of Patriarchal Authority in Early Modern England' in A. Fletcher and J. Stevenson (eds), *Order and Disorder in Early Modern England* (Cambridge, 1985), pp. 116–36. The Montacute panel is discussed in the wider context of charivaris in Martin Ingram, 'Ridings, Rough Music and the "Reform of Popular Culture" in Early Modern England', *Past & Present* no. 105 (November 1984): 79–113.

8 This case is discussed in Underdown, 'The Taming'.

9 *Ibid.*

10 Margaret Imrie, *The Manor Houses of Burton Agnes and their Owners* (Beverley, 1993).

11 Eamon Duffy, *The Stripping of the Altars: Traditional Religion in England, c. 1400–c. 1580* (New Haven and London, 1992), p. 158. See also Eamon Duffy, 'Late Medieval Religion' in Richard Marks and Paul Williamson (eds), *Gothic: Art for England, 1400–1547* (London, 2003), pp. 56–67.

12 Lewis Bayly, *The Practise of Pietie: Directing a Christian how to walk that he may please God* (London, 1613, 2nd edn), p. 437.

13 John Downame, *A Guide to Godlynesse or a Treatise of a Christian Life* (London, 1622, 1629 edn), p. 279.

14 This is the theme of, for example, 'a praier made upon the similitude of the ten virgins' in Thomas Bentley's devotional manual aimed specifically at women, *The Sixt Lampe of Virginitie; Containing a Mirror for Maidens and Matrons* (London, 1582).

15 Bayly, *Practise*, p. 452.

16 The estate at Gaulden, Tolland, in Somerset, was part of the marriage settlement between John Turberville and Bridget Willoughby in October 1639 and it is assumed that the decorative work to the house was carried out around the time of this marriage. Turberville Correspondence, Somerset Record Office, Taunton, 54/5/2–17.

17 Translations as provided in John and Jane Penoyre, *Decorative Plasterwork in the Houses of Somerset, 1500–1700* (Taunton, 1994), pp. 19, 27, 81.

18 Phillip Stubbes, *The Anatomie of Abuses* (London, 1583), p. 168.

19 C. S. Gilbert, *An Historical Survey of the County of Cornwall*, 2 vols (London, 1817–20), vol. 2, p. 668.

20 *Ibid.*, p. 611.

21 This workshop is commonly identified as the 'Abbott family' workshop from Frithelstock in Devon, based on similarities between extant plasterwork in the West Country and designs in a sketchbook owned by the plasterer John Abbott who was active in the second half of the seventeenth century. As discussed in the Introduction above, there is no actual evidence that any of John Abbott's ancestors were members of the trade so the existence of an earlier workshop associated with the Abbott name remains pure conjecture.

22 Details on the history of Horsepits House are provided in Janey Copper (ed.), *A History of the County of Essex*, Victoria County History, vol. 10 (Woodbridge, 2001), p. 25. Two painted cartouches were found in 1944 at the gable ends of another room on the first floor of the building. One enclosed the initials 'TDS' for Thomas Dibney and his wife Sarah and the other contained the date '1628'. It is logical to assume that these dated paintings and the biblical wall paintings on the ground floor were executed at the same time. These paintings have since been painted over but photographs recording their appearance are illustrated by Muriel Carrick, 'Sixteenth and Seventeenth Century Wall Paintings in the County of Essex', M.Phil. thesis, 3 vols (University of Essex, 1990), vol. 1, pp. 137–39.

23 *Ibid.*

24 Here I refer to the 'great' or principal parlour. Larger houses often had multiple parlours,

each serving a particular function. It was common for another, smaller room to adjoin the parlour, which created a suite of hall, parlour and bedchamber, mostly for use by guests, as indicated in Gervase Markham's ideal plan (see fig. 41).

25 With the exception of the 'low parlour', which was situated at the opposite end of the house from a high-end parlour, to make use of warmth from the kitchen. See Nicholas Cooper, *The Houses of the Gentry, 1480–1680* (New Haven and London, 1999), pp. 290–91.

26 Thomas Wilson, *Saints by calling; or Called to be saints. A godly treatise of our holy calling to Christ, by the gospell* (London, 1620), p. 370.

27 According to evidence from probate inventories. See Cooper, *Houses of the Gentry*, p. 289 and Girouard, *Life in the English Country House*, p. 103.

28 All quotations from Shakespeare are taken from *William Shakespeare: The Complete Works*, edited by Stanley Wells and Gary Taylor (Oxford, 1988).

29 John Deacon, *Dialogicall discourses of spirits and divels declaring their proper essence, natures, dispositions, and operations, their possessions and dispossessions* (London, 1601), p. 131.

30 *Ibid.*, p. 262.

31 This is the usual arrangement in houses with double-height halls.

32 See Cooper, *Houses of the Gentry*, p. 290.

33 'Account of John Willoughby, autumn 1604' as provided in Todd Gray (ed.), *Devon Household Accounts, 1627–59*, Part I (Exeter, 1995), p. 241.

34 Unknown [A.E.H.], 'The Pittleworth Frescoes', *Country Life* (11 November 1922): 606–07.

35 Paul Slack, *Poverty and Policy in Tudor and Stuart England* (London and New York, 1988), p. 18.

36 *Ibid.*, p. 19.

37 Tessa Watt, *Cheap Print and Popular Piety, 1550–1640* (Cambridge, 1991), pp. 208–09.

38 E. Clive Rouse, 'Elizabethan Wall Paintings at Little Moreton Hall' in Gervase Jackson Stops (ed.), *National Trust Studies* (1979–80), pp. 113–18.

39 Originally the frieze continued round the rest of the parlour, but the second half of the story is obscured by later panelling and it is not clear if any of the paintings survive underneath. The last scene in the exposed section (Daniel intervening to free Susannah) is part-covered by later panelling round the fireplace.

40 The Moreton family and estate papers are in the British Library, Add. MSS 33935–42 and Add. Ch 37035–92.

41 See e.g. Robert Aylett, *Susanna, or the arraignment of the two unjust elders* (London, 1622), pp. 41–42.

42 Lawrence Weaver, 'Bradninch Manor, Devon', *Country Life* (16 September 1916): 321–28. Four other rooms at Bradninch Manor also contained mid-seventeenth-century carved woodwork but these rooms were illegally stripped in the 1980s and the 'Job room' and staircase are all that remain of the original scheme. Pre-1980 photographs show that the cardinal virtues were depicted in a carved overmantel in the library.

43 William Cowper, *The Triumph of a Christian* (London, 1608), p. 51.

44 The Rev. G. Montagu Benton, 'Domestic Wall-paintings, dated 1623, at Newton, Suffolk' in 'Notes' section of *The Antiquaries Journal* vol. 21 (1941), pp. 68–72.

45 The current condition of the paintings at Newton is not known. The NMR and regional record office do not hold any materials relating to the building apart from the listed buildings entry of 1972 which confirms that the paintings were still visible at that date. They are also noted in the revised Pevsner volume of 1974.

46 Walter H. Godfrey, *The English Staircase: An Historical Account of its Characteristic Types to the End of the XVIIIth Century* (London, 1911).

47 James Ayres, *Domestic Interiors: The British Tradition, 1500–1850* (New Haven and London, 2003), p. 117.

48 Sir Henry Wotton, 'Of Staire-cases' from *The Elements of Architecture* (London, 1624), p. 57.

49 The most characteristic Scottish arrangement was a spacious public staircase with shallow treads leading only to the first floor, with other smaller, circular stairs leading from the first to the upper floors. Craigevar (see Ch. 2, above) exemplifies this arrangement. See McKean, *Scottish Chateau*, p. 74 and D. Howard, *Scottish Architecture*, pp. 72–75.

50 The stone pier at the centre of the staircase at Montacute is decorated with shell-headed niches but it is not known if these niches ever

held statuary. Only the ceiling of the staircase at Burghley is decorated with architectural ornament. Hardwick's inventory of 1601 indicates that the great stone staircase was not originally adorned with tapestries, as it is seen now.

51 Francis Bacon, 'Of Building' from *The essayes or counsels, civill and morall, of Francis Lo. Verulam, Viscount St. Alban* (London, 1625), p. 261.

52 Thomas Sergison brought this staircase to Lewes town hall, then a hostelry, from his dismantled mansion of Slaugham Place in about 1732.

53 V&A Museum no. W.25-1959. Alternatively, it might have formed part of a bedstead. See the discussion of carved beds later in this chapter.

54 Annabel Ricketts, *The English Country House Chapel: Building a Protestant Tradition*, ed. Simon Ricketts (Reading, 2007), see esp. ch. 4, pp. 58–83.

55 *Ibid.*, p. 266.

56 The seventeenth-century Aldermaston Court burnt down in 1843 but parts of the staircase including the newel figures were saved and were re-installed in 1848 in the new Aldermaston Court, now 'The Manor Court' hotel.

57 C. J. Richardson, *Observations on the Architecture of England during the Reigns of Queen Elizabeth and King James I* (London, 1837), V&A National Art Library, pressmark 34.A.4.

58 Rawden Hall is now used for commercial purposes. The staircase is still *in situ* but has at some stage been coated in thick white paint. I am very grateful to Simon Foden for his generous help in providing me with photographs.

59 As illustrated in Godfrey, *English Staircase*, pl. XX.

60 Nikolaus Pevsner, *The Buildings of England: Hertfordshire*, 2nd edn rev. Bridget Cherry (Harmondsworth, 1977), p. 160.

61 Robert Sackville-West, *Knole, Kent* (London, 1998), p. 14.

62 The Geneva Bible owned by Lucy Robartes and containing her writings is held in the archives at Lanhydrock House in Cornwall. Lucy Robartes's 'Meditations' are transcribed and discussed by Gwyn Howells, 'Cobwebs in the Temple of God: The Brief Life of Lady Lucy Robartes 1615/6 to 1645/6', *Lanhydrock House Journal* vol. 1 (2001): 11–20.

63 As transcribed in Joanna Moody (ed.), *The Private Life of an Elizabethan Lady: The Diary of Lady Margaret Hoby, 1599–1605* (Stroud, 1998), p. 42. Lady Margaret here distinguishes between the public prayers of the whole household and her own private prayers and meditations.

64 Arthur Oswald, 'Boston Manor House, Middlesex', *Country Life* (18 March 1965): 603–07; Janet McNamara, *Boston Manor, Brentford: A History and Guide* (Hounslow, 1998).

65 I am very grateful to Claire Gapper for bringing this work to my attention and to staff at the Bedfordshire and Luton Archives and Records Service, Bedford, for forwarding a copy of their records on the building (Sites and Monuments Record No. 1696).

66 The manor was acquired in 1616 by Sir Arthur Savage who had earlier that year married his second wife Sara, the widow of George Smithes, a goldsmith of London, and it seems that this manor was intended as her jointure. Sir Arthur died in 1633 and Sara in 1653. The period 1633–53 seems the most probable dating for the plasterwork but it is unlikely that the work should have been carried out during the tenure of a widow. It is possible that the Manor Court House was occupied during this time by a member of the Forster family, who were resident in an unspecified property in Cotton End and made the leap from 'yeoman' to 'gent' in documents around the turn of 1600. The coat of arms in the plasterwork ceiling, with a chevron ermine between three hunting horns, can be associated with Forster ancestry.

67 John Cornforth, 'Prideaux Place, Cornwall', *Country Life* (February 1962): 226–29 and 274–78.

68 A possible printed source for these paintings is suggested by Muriel Carrick, 'The Prodigal Son Wall Painting at Knightsland Farm, South Mimms', *Hertfordshire Archaeology* 12 (1994): 104–10.

69 Barbara Haeger, 'The Prodigal Son in Sixteenth and Seventeenth-Century Netherlandish Art: Depictions of the Parable and the Evolution of a Catholic Image', *Simiolus* 16 (1986): 128–38.

70 A useful comparison is provided by the dis-

play in the V&A British Galleries. The English (so-called 'Sheldon') cushion cover of c. 1600–10 (T.1-1933) copies the pictorial design of the Flemish cushion cover of c. 1575 (T.278-1913).

71 Watt, *Cheap Print*, p. 204.

72 Samuel Gardiner, *The Portraitur of the prodigal sonne livelie set forth in a three-fold discourse* (London, 1599).

73 See e.g. Henry Ainsworth, *Annotations upon the first book of Moses, called Genesis* ([Amsterdam], 1616); Gervase Babington, *Certain plaine briefe, and comfortable notes upon everie chapter of Genesis* (London, 1592); Robert Aylett, *Joseph, or Pharoah's favourite* (London 1623).

74 On this issue see Tara Hamling, 'The Appreciation of Religious Images in Plasterwork in the Protestant Domestic Interior' in Tara Hamling and Richard L. Williams (eds), *Art Re-formed: Re-assessing the Impact of the Reformation on the Visual Arts* (Newcastle, 2007), pp. 147–68.

75 Much of the plasterwork of the region recorded in local society publications of the first half of the twentieth century no longer survives. See Kathleen and Cecil French, 'Devonshire Plasterwork', *Transactions of the Devonshire Association for the Advancement of Science, Literature and Art* vol. 89 (1957): 124–44 and Bruce W. Oliver, 'The Early Seventeenth-Century Plaster Ceilings of Barnstaple', *Transactions of the Devonshire Association for the Advancement of Science, Literature and Art* vol. 49 (1917): 189–99. For a more recent survey see John Thorp, 'Wall Painting and Lime-Plaster Decoration' in Peter Beacham (ed.), *Devon Building: An Introduction to Local Traditions* (Exeter, 1990), pp. 129–49.

76 The plasterwork ceiling from 7 Cross Street was removed from its original location and is now at Stafford Barton in Dolton, Devon (a private house). The 69 High Street overmantel with what appears to be a scene of the Nativity is illustrated *in situ* in G. P. Bankart, *The Art of the Plasterer* (London, 1908), p. 79. It must have been removed by 1961, when it goes unmentioned in an RCHME inspector's report of that date.

77 The Annunciation does appear in small-scale illustrations in printed books during this period, e.g. among the numerous biblical scenes illustrated in the margins of John Daye's *Booke of Christian Prayers* (London, 1569, rev. edn 1578) and on the title page of Thomas Bentley, *The Monument of Matrones* (London, 1582). It is, however, rare.

78 A monograph about the history of the Charterhouse by Philip Temple is forthcoming with Yale. I am grateful to him for sharing his photographs and ideas about the painted decoration of the chimneypiece.

79 According to Percy Russell, *Dartmouth: A History of the Port and Town* (Dartmouth, 1982), p. 97, Mark Hawkins paid a fee of £80 on taking up an eighty-year lease for the plot in 1634 and commenced building in 1635. Hawkins was appointed town receiver for the year 1635 (Records of the Dartmouth Corporation, Devon Record Office, DD 12133).

80 Anthony Wells-Cole has shown that this central scene of Pentecost derived from an engraving in Christopher Plantin's *Biblia Sacra*, published in Antwerp in 1583, while the figures of Moses and David were copied from the illustrated title page to an English Bible printed in Cambridge in 1629; *Art and Decoration in Elizabethan and Jacobean England: The Influence of Continental Prints, 1558–1625* (New Haven and London, 1997), p. 163. The use of two different printed sources suggests the considered selection of particular iconography for the imagery in the overmantel.

81 M. R. Apted, 'Two Painted Ceilings from Mary Somerville's House, Burntisland', *Proceedings of the Society of Antiquaries of Scotland* vol. 91 (1957–58), pp. 144–75. See also Michael Bath, *Renaissance Decorative Painting in Scotland* (Edinburgh, 2003), pp. 190–93 and 257–58.

82 The painted decoration at Cheyney Court was described by T. Galton Moillet in *Notes and Queries* vol. 125 (1840), p. 494. According to this account, the figures of Diana and John the Baptist were depicted either side of a coat of arms above the fireplace. I am grateful to Jessica Malay for alerting me to the Cheyney Court sibyls.

83 This secondary room adjoining the bedchamber was sometimes used as an attendant's bedroom. N. Cooper, *Houses of the Gentry*, p. 296.

84 Sasha Roberts, 'Lying among the Classics: Ritual and Motif in Elite Elizabethan and Jacobean Beds' in Lucy Gent (ed.), *Albion's*

Classicism: The Visual Arts in Britain, 1550–1660 (New Haven and London, 1995), pp. 325–58.

85 N. Cooper, *Houses of the Gentry*, p. 296.

86 Moody, *Private Life*, p. 140. Lady Margaret here recorded that having kept to her chamber during the day she 'went' to her private prayers, indicating that for true privacy she retired to a closet.

87 D. J. H. Clifford (ed.), *The Diaries of Lady Anne Clifford* (Stroud, 1990, 1998 edn), p. 82.

88 It is likely that this room, the second bedroom in a suite of chambers leading from the great chamber, was also intended to serve as part of the guest lodgings for visitors of higher social standing than the householder. On such rare occasions the owner and his wife might give up their own lodgings as a gesture of deference.

89 William Harrison, *The Description of England: The Classic Contemporary Account of Tudor Social Life* (1577), 2nd edn 1587, ed. George Edelen (Washington, D.C., and New York, 1994), pp. 200–01.

90 See Victor Chinnery, *Oak Furniture: The British Tradition, A History of Early Furniture in the British Isles and New England* (Woodbridge, 1979), pp. 384–96.

91 Daye, *Christian Prayers* (1569), sig. C. iiir.

92 Bayly, *Practise*, p. 427.

93 *Ibid.*, p. 428.

94 This bed is not original to the palace and its provenance prior to being acquired by the National Trust is not known. It is not clear to what extent the bed was altered in the nineteenth century but the style of the carved decoration in the upper section appears to be consistent with an early seventeenth-century date and suggests that this part of the bed is original. Another early seventeenth-century carved bedstead with a similar headboard with personifications of the virtues is at Berkeley Castle, illustrated in Eric Mercer, *Furniture 700–1700* (London, 1969), fig. 136.

95 Roberts, 'Lying among the Classics'.

96 Catherine Belsey, *Shakespeare and the Loss of Eden: The Construction of Family Values in Early Modern Culture* (Basingstoke, 1999), p. 61.

97 Arthur Oswald, 'Ludstone Hall, Shropshire II', *Country Life* (18 January 1952), pp. 154–57; 'Ludston Hall, Claverley, Shropshire', *The Antique Collector* (December 1965), pp. 235–44.

98 Mark Girouard, *Hardwick Hall* (London, 1996), p. 75.

99 Illustrated in Wells-Cole, *Art and Decoration*, p. 167, fig. 272.

100 David N. Durant, *Bess of Hardwick: Portrait of an Elizabethan Dynast* (London, 1999).

101 For discussion of the evolution and functions of the gallery in England see M. Howard, *Early Tudor Country House*, p. 116, Girouard, *Life in the English Country House*, pp. 112–16, N. Cooper, *Houses of the Gentry*, pp. 300–04 and esp. Rosalys Coope, 'The 'Long Gallery': Its Origins, Development, Use and Decoration', *Architectural History* vol. 29 (1986): 43–84. For the gallery in Scotland see D. Howard, *Scottish Architecture*, pp. 83–84.

102 The term 'long gallery' became the common designation for this room only from the eighteenth century. See Rosalys Coope, 'The Gallery in England: Names and Meanings', *Design and Practice in British Architecture: Studies in Architectural History presented to Howard Colvin*, Special Issue of *Architectural History* vol. 27 (1984), pp. 446–55.

103 William Vaughan, *Approved directions for health, both naturall and artificiall derived from the best physitians as well moderne as auncient* (London, 1612), p. 66.

104 Sir Thomas Elyot, *The castell of health* (London, 1595), p. 77.

105 *Ibid.*, p. 64.

106 A loggia was a long covered walkway open on one or both sides, which offered a cool, shaded space for use during hot weather. Grander houses usually provided both a loggia and a gallery, for hot and cold weather respectively, and the allied function of these rooms was often reflected in the design, with the gallery positioned above the loggia. See Paula Henderson, 'The Loggia in Tudor and Early Stuart England: The Adaptation and Function of Classical Form' in Gent, *Albion's Classicism*, pp. 109–46.

107 Wotton, *Elements of Architecture*, pp. 99–100.

108 Mark Girouard, *Life in the French Country House* (London, 2000).

109 The greater houses of noblemen could accommodate several galleries, with more public and communication galleries provided elsewhere. Lena Cowen Orlin has shown how

galleries provided one of the few spaces in the early modern house where a degree of privacy could be achieved and thus the space leant itself to conversation, especially on sensitive matters; *Locating Privacy in Tudor London* (Oxford, 2007), ch. 6, pp. 226–61.

110 See Henri Zerner, *Renaissance Art in France: The Invention of Classicism*, English edn (Paris, 2003), ch. II.

111 Elizabeth McCutcheon, 'Sir Nicholas Bacon's Great House Sententiae', *English Literary Renaissance Supplements* 3 (Claremont, Cal., 1977).

112 The painted decoration at Pinkie and similar ceilings with emblematic decoration have been discussed in a group of publications by Michael Bath: 'Applied Emblematics in Scotland: Painted Ceilings, 1550–1650', *Emblematica: An Interdisciplinary Journal for Emblem Studies* no. 7 (1993): 259–305; 'Alexander Seton's Painted Gallery', in Gent, *Albion's Classicism*, pp. 79–108 and *Renaissance Decorative Painting in Scotland*, pp. 79–103.

113 The situation of the gallery within the house plan is discussed in detail by Coope, 'Long Gallery', pp. 52–59 and N. Cooper, *Houses of the Gentry*, pp. 300–04.

114 Roger North, *Of Building: Roger North's Writings on Architecture*, ed. Howard Colvin and John Newman (Oxford, 1981), p. 137.

115 Ben Jonson, *Poetaster or The arraignment as it hath beene sundry times privately acted in the Blacke Friers, by the children of her Maiesties Chappell* (London, 1602).

116 Wotton, *Elements*, p. 98.

117 See Susan Foister, 'Sixteenth-Century English Portraiture and the Idea of the Classical' in Gent, *Albion's Classicism*, pp. 163–80.

118 Franciscus Junius, *The Painting of the Ancients in three bookes; declaring by historicall observations and examples, the beginning, progresse, and consummation of that most noble art* (London, 1638), p. 146.

119 Robert Tittler, 'Thomas Heywood and the Portrayal of Female Benefactors in Post-Reformation England', *Early Theatre* vol. 11, no. 1 (2008): 34.

120 Robin Gibson, 'The National Portrait Gallery's Set of Kings and Queens at Montacute House', *The National Trust Year Book* (1975–76): 81–87.

121 See Susan Foister, 'Edward Alleyn's Collection of Paintings' in Aileen Reid and Robert Maniura (eds), *Edward Alleyn: Elizabethan Actor, Jacobean Gentleman* (London, 1994), pp. 33–61.

122 Susan Foister, 'Paintings and Other Works of Art in Sixteenth-Century English Inventories', *The Burlington Magazine* vol. 123, no. 938 (May 1981): 273–82.

123 Richard L. Williams, 'The Reformation of an Icon: 'Portraits' of Christ in Tudor England' in Hamling and Williams, *Art Re-formed*, pp. 69–84.

124 Cited in full in *ibid.*, p. 73.

125 See Margaret Aston, 'Gods, Saints, and Reformers: Portraiture and Protestant England' in Gent, *Albion's Classicism*, pp. 181–220 and Pamela Tudor-Craig, 'Group Portraits of the Protestant Reformers' in Hamling and Williams, *Art Re-formed*, pp. 87–103.

126 Thomas Middleton and Thomas Dekker, *The Roaring Girle or Moll Cut-Purse As it hath lately beene acted on the Fortune-stage by the Prince his Players* (London, 1611).

127 As suggested by Foister, 'Edward Alleyn's Collection'.

128 Bath, *Renaissance Decorative Painting in Scotland*, ch. 7, pp. 147–67.

129 The panels are now set in the shutters and doors of the Drawing Room and the Lobby Ante-Room. It is not clear if the panels were part of the original decoration of Craigston Castle or were brought from elsewhere. The castle was built between 1604 and 1607, which fits with the style of the carvings and there was a 49ft long gallery on the third floor, which seems a probable location. In his report on the castle, H. Gordon Slade assumed that the panels belonged to the castle and suggested that their original position was either in a great screen in the hall or as panelling in the gallery; 'Craigston Castle, Aberdeenshire', *Proceedings of the Society of Antiquaries of Scotland* (1976–77): 262–99.

130 The figure of Doctrina in the Blickling ceiling is copied from Henry Peacham's *Minerva Britanna* (London, 1612), as identified by Wells-Cole, *Art and Decoration*, p. 165. The figure in the Craigston panel is quite different and must derive from another source.

131 The assumption that John Robartes was the patron for the decorative scheme in the gallery at Lanhydrock is based on two pieces of physical evidence. First, the lintel above a ground-floor entrance to the north wing

housing the gallery is carved with the initials 'I: L: R: L.' and the date 1636, which presumably marks the date of completion of this wing. These initials must refer to John, Lord Robartes and the extra 'L' probably refers to Lucy Rich, his first wife (m. 1630). Secondly, the arms of John Robartes impaling those of Lucy Rich are depicted in plasterwork in the tympanum at the east end of the gallery.

132 There are no extant documents from the period that provide historical information about the building of Lanhydrock House. It is therefore difficult to judge the relative roles of father and son in determining the design and final appearance of the house. For some of the more puzzling aspects of the building history see Paul Holden, '"Situation, Contrivance, Receipt, Strength and Beauty": The Building of Lanhydrock House, 1620–51', *Journal of the Royal Institution of Cornwall* (2005): 32–44.

133 According to William Borlase's description of the house recorded in 1756, the east wing (demolished c. 1784) was 'one large anti-chamber a handsome apartment communicating with the Gallery which is the length of the whole Eastern Front' (Borlase MSS book, 1756, Courtney Library, Truro). It appears that visitors were expected to view the series of scenes in the ceiling on entering the gallery from this east wing, as the sequence begins with Adam in the Garden of Eden at the eastern corner of the gallery, directly below the original doorway connecting the east wing.

134 Arnold Williams, *The Common Expositor: An Account of the Commentaries on Genesis, 1527–1633* (Chapel Hill, N. C., 1948). Williams examined 35 commentaries on Genesis in Latin and 6 in English.

135 The books on display in the gallery at Lanhydrock today are only part of the original collection. A number of mid-seventeenth-century books were sold at auctions in 1721 and 1954.

136 Calvin's commentary on Genesis in Latin was first published in Geneva in 1563 and was translated into English by Thomas Tymme as *A Commentarie of John Calvine, upon the first Booke of Moses* (London, 1578).

137 William Whately, *Prototypes, or, The Primarie Precedent Presidents out of the booke of Genesis* (London, 1640), p. 41.

138 Margaret Aston, 'The Bishops' Bible Illustrations' in Diana Wood, ed., *The Church and the Arts*, Studies in Church History, vol. 28 (Oxford, 1992, 1995 edn), pp. 267–85.

139 Cited in *ibid.*, p. 272.

140 The woodcut was subsequently altered back to re-insert the figure of God for publication in later Bibles. See *ibid.*, pp. 278–79 for comparison of the various states of the woodcut, from the version printed in the German Bible published in Cologne in 1565, the changed version as included in the first *Bishops' Bible* in 1568, and then the version with the figure of God re-inserted, as in a Bible published in Antwerp in 1570.

141 Wells-Cole, *Art and Decoration*, p. 162.

142 For full discussion see Adam White, 'The Iconography of the State Apartment at Apethorpe Hall', *English Heritage Historical Review* vol. 3 (2008): 63–85.

143 This connection between the subject of the overmantels and the content of the Homily was first suggested by Gwyn Howells in 'The Great Creation Ceiling in the Long Gallery', *Lanhydrock House Journal* vol. 2 (2002): 4–17.

144 Christopher Hill, *The English Bible and the Seventeenth-Century Revolution: Uses of the Bible in 17th-Century England* (Harmondsworth, 1994).

145 Antiquarian records state that the date 1627 was included in one of the panels, although this is no longer visible. See Bath, *Renaissance Decorative Painting in Scotland*, p. 241.

146 This panel is inscribed 'Genesis XIX', perhaps included to avoid doubt that the seduction of Lot by his Daughters was intended. These two panels are now held at the John Knox House Museum.

147 Daniel Wilson, *Memorials of Edinburgh in the Olden Time*, 2 vols (Edinburgh, 1848), vol. 1, p. 157.

148 I am grateful to Victoria Ward, Assistant Keeper (Applied Art) at Aberdeen Art Gallery, for forwarding her notes on the history and conservation of the ceiling.

149 See n. 81 above for the image of Christ as Salvator Mundi included in a decorated ceiling on the second floor of Mary Somerville's House in Burntisland, Fife.

150 David McRoberts, 'Provost Skene's House, in Aberdeen, and its Catholic Chapel', *The Innes Review* vol. 5 (1954): 119–24. This theory is ac-

cepted by Bath, *Renaissance Decorative Painting in Scotland*, p. 126.

151 Margo Todd, *The Culture of Protestantism in Early Modern Scotland* (New Haven and London, 2002), p. 330.

152 As argued in McRoberts, 'Provost Skene's House', p. 122.

153 The same assumption that the presence of decoration with religious imagery signalled Roman Catholic belief led to the theory that an apartment in Blyth's Close in Edinburgh which had a ceiling painted with complex religious iconography must have been part of the Catholic Mary of Guise's palace. This ceiling is discussed in Ch. 6.

154 Duffy, *Stripping of the Altars*, pp. 238ff.

155 Illustrated in Penoyre, *Decorative Plasterwork*, p. 65.

156 Illustrated in Ayres, *Domestic Interiors*, p. 45, fig. 76.

157 Thelma E. Vernon, 'Inventory of Sir Henry Sharington, Contents of Lacock House, 1575', *Wiltshire Archaeological Society Magazine* vol. 63 (1968): 72–82.

158 Hester C. Dibbits, 'Between Society and Family Values: The Linen Cupboard in Early-Modern Households' in Anton Schuurman and Pieter Spierenburg (eds), *Private Domain, Public Inquiry: Families and Life-Styles in the Netherlands and Europe, 1550 to the Present* (Hilversum, uitg. Verloren, 1996), pp. 125–45.

159 Netherlandish *linnenkast* were exported throughout Europe and some must have found their way into greater houses in England and Scotland.

160 Amisford Tower was built by a member of the Charteris family, c. 1600. The door includes this date and a shield bearing the arms of Charteris and Herries. NMS Museum no. H.KL 41.

161 Illustrated in Chinnery, *Oak Furniture*, figs 2:169 and 4:33. The figure on the left-hand side has suffered damage to the arm and has thus lost her identifying attribute. My thanks to Patricia Collins, Curator of Medieval and Renaissance Collections at the Burrell, for providing information about this piece.

162 Belsey, *Shakespeare and the Loss of Eden*, pp. 60–61.

163 An inscription on the Craigston chest records that it belonged to John Urquhart, Tutor of Cromartie, who lived between 1547 and 1631.

164 The chair appears to have been at Cotehele since the eighteenth century. Its provenance before this is unknown. It is dated by comparison with similar examples illustrated in Chinnery, *Oak Furniture*, pp. 248–55. I am very grateful to Victor Chinnery for his help in confirming that this chairback seems to be part of a genuine piece of furniture dating from the first half of the seventeenth century.

165 This chair is discussed in further detail in my chapter, 'Reconciling Image and Object: Religious Imagery in Protestant Interior Decoration' in Tara Hamling and Catherine Richardson (eds), *Everyday Objects: Medieval and Early Modern Material Culture and its Meanings* (Aldershot, 2010).

166 In the collection of the Duke of Buccleuch, Boughton House, Northamptonshire. For discussion and illustrations see Charles Chichele Oman, *English Engraved Silver, 1150 to 1900* (London and Boston, 1978), pp. 141–46.

167 London hallmark 1573–74. V&A accession no. M.55-1946.

168 V&A accession no. M.340-1924.

169 Cited in C. Richardson, *Domestic Life and Domestic Tragedy*, p. 71.

170 V&A accession no. C.26–1931. See Michael Archer, *Delftware: The Tin-Glazed Earthenware of the British Isles* (London, 1997), p. 81.

171 In the V&A collection are numerous plates dating from 1660 to 1730 which represent the gradual degeneration of the pictorial scene away from the original print.

172 V&A accession no. C.73-1951. The last two digits of the date are unclear due to blurred pigment.

173 V&A accession no. C.278-1919. The printed source used for the illustration of the plate is an engraving by Marten de Vos of 'Maria Salome', included in *Icones Illustrium Feminarum*. As identified by Archer, *Delftware*, p. 102.

174 See discussion in *ibid.*

175 V&A accession no. 3861-1901.

176 All these examples are described by Leslie Grigsby, 'Some Dated English Drinking Vessels with Trailed-Slip Decoration, 1612–1752', *Magazine Antiques* vol. 147, no. 6 (June 1995): 874–83. Also documented in John Eliot Hodgkin and Edith Hodgkin, *Examples of Early English Pottery: Named, Dated, and Inscribed* (1891; Wakefield, 1973).

177 Harrison, *Description of England*, p. 197.

178 Nicholas Mander, 'Painted Cloths: History, Craftsmen and Techniques', *Textile History* vol. 28, no. 2 (1997): 119–48.

179 *As You Like It* Act 3 Scene 2 and *The Rape of Lucrece*: 'Who fears a sentence or an old man's saw/Shall by a painted cloth be kept in awe.'

180 Detailed images of each of these cloths are provided in Wells-Cole, *Art and Decoration*, figs 477, 482, 487 and 494.

181 For the painted cloths at Owlpen and the few surviving pieces elsewhere see Mander, 'Painted Cloths' and F. E. Matley Moore, 'Painted Cloths', *Transactions of the Worcestershire Archaeological Society*, 3rd series, vol. 8 (1982): 73–79.

182 Anthony Wells-Cole, 'Elusive Sources for Renaissance Wall Paintings' in Robert Gowing and Robyn Pender (eds), *All Manner of Murals: The History, Techniques and Conservation of Secular Wall Paintings* (London, 2007), p. 8, fig. 5.

183 Hilary L. Turner, 'Tapestries once at Chastleton House and their Influence on the Image of the Tapestries called Sheldon: A Reassessment', *The Antiquaries Journal* vol. 88 (2008), pp. 313–46.

184 Diana O'Hara, *Courtship and Constraint: Rethinking the Making of Marriage in Tudor England* (Manchester, 2000), esp. ch. 2, 'The Language of Tokens and the Making of Marriage'.

185 John Humphreys, 'Elizabethan Sheldon Tapestries', *Archaeologia* (1923–24): 181–202 and George Wingfield Digby, *The Tapestry Collection: Medieval and Renaissance* V&A Museum catalogue (London, 1980), pp. 71–82.

186 SBT 1993-31/304; V&A accession no. T.1-1933.

187 SBT 1993-31/299.

188 Illustrated in Wells-Cole, *Art and Decoration*, p. 232, fig. 393.

189 V&A accession nos T.282-1894 and T.203-1911.

190 Lindsay Boynton (ed.), *The Hardwick Hall Inventories of 1601* (London, 1971), pp. 26–27.

191 Santina Levey in *The Embroideries at Hardwick Hall: A Catalogue* (London, 2007) speculates that these embroideries, previously thought to be French or Flemish, may have been worked in London. The needlework long cushion with the Sacrifice of Isaac is illustrated in Santina M. Levey, *An Elizabethan Inheritance: The Hardwick Hall Textiles* (London, 1998), p. 48, fig. 38.

192 Jonson, *Poetaster*, Act 2 Scene 1.

193 On domestic embroidery see Andrew Morrall and Melinda Watt (eds), *English Embroidery from the Metropolitan Museum of Art, 1580–1700* (New York, New Haven and London, 2008); Mary Brooks, *English Embroideries of the Sixteenth and Seventeenth Centuries in the Collection of the Ashmolean Museum* (Oxford, 2004); Xanthe Brooke, *The Lady Lever Art Gallery Catalogue of Embroideries* (Stroud, 1992); Judith Doré, *Needlework and Tapestry at Parham Park, Pulborough, West Sussex* (Pulborough, 2002).

194 The circulation would have been limited, however, as the *Bishops' Bible* was intended for use by clergy in churches, not for domestic ownership.

195 On the significance of biblical narratives in the context of virtuous exemplars for good Protestant women, and particularly the story of Adam and Eve as exemplars of marriage, see chs 4 and 5 in Morrall and Watt, *English Embroidery*.

196 V&A Museum accession no. 443-1865. For a similar piece in the Metropolitan Museum of Art see *ibid.*, p. 227, cat. 58.

197 The cushion cover with Christ and the woman of Samaria (V&A accession no. T.86-1913) is illustrated in Wingfield Digby, *Tapestry Collection*, p. 80, fig. 103C.

198 Lady Lever Art Gallery, no. LL5229 (WHL2795).

199 As quoted in Brooke, *Lady Lever Art Gallery Catalogue of Embroideries*, pp. 59–61.

5 IMAGES FOR MEDITATION

1 Susan Foister, 'Private Devotion' in Richard Marks and Paul Williamson (eds), *Gothic: Art For England, 1400–1547* (London, 2003), p. 334.

2 Tessa Watt, *Cheap Print and Popular Piety, 1550–1640* (Cambridge, 1991). Watt acknowledged Murray Roston, *Biblical Drama in England* (1968), for the 'ladder of sanctity' theory (p. 185).

3 Watt, *Cheap Print*, pp. 150 and 135. Watt identified a resurgence of New Testament imagery in printed books and church furnishings during the period of Laud's influence, although

she did not discuss in any depth the implications of this in relation to imagery in decorative art.

4 Eric Mercer, *English Art, 1553–1625* (Oxford, 1965), p. 126.

5 William Harrison, *The Description of England: The Classic Contemporary Account of Tudor Social Life* (1587), ed. Georges Edelen (Washington, D.C., and New York, 1994), p. 201.

6 Patrick Collinson, *The Religion of Protestants: The Church in English Society, 1559–1625* (Oxford, 1982, reprinted 2003), p. 266.

7 Illustrated in Anthony Wells-Cole, *Art and Decoration in Elizabethan and Jacobean England: The Influence of Continental Prints, 1558–1625* (New Haven and London, 1997), p. 123, fig. 184.

8 British Museum cat. no. MLA 1934, 11-8, 1-2. The other panel depicts Mary Magdalen mistaking the risen Christ for a gardener.

9 See Francis Cheetham, *English Medieval Alabasters* (Oxford, 1984).

10 V&A accession no. A.89-1919.

11 V&A accession no. A.61-1926.

12 V&A accession no. A.112-1946.

13 The overmantel was installed at Clervaux Castle in Yorkshire in the mid-nineteenth century. This building was demolished in 1950–51 and the panels are now in a private collection. The overmantel and panels are discussed and illustrated in Wells-Cole, *Art and Decoration*, pp. 189–90, figs 313–15.

14 John Sheill, 'Notice of Carved Oak Panels which were formerly in the Chapel of the Franciscan Nunnery in Dundee', *Proceedings of the Society of Antiquaries of Scotland* vol. 20 (8 February 1886): 108–25.

15 These texts are copied faithfully from the printed source. See Wells-Cole, *Art and Decoration*, p. 189.

16 On Anne Clifford's 'Great Picture' see Alice T. Friedman, 'Constructing an Identity in Prose, Plaster and Paint: Lady Anne Clifford as Writer and Patron of the Arts' in Lucy Gent (ed.), *Albion's Classicism: The Visual Arts in Britain, 1550–1660* (New Haven and London, 1995), pp. 359–76. On the use of the triptych form for post-Reformation dynastic portraits see Jane Eade, 'The Triptych Portrait in England, 1575–1646', *The British Art Journal* vol. 6, no. 2 (Autumn 2005): 3–11.

17 See also the painted triptych with the Royal Arms of Elizabeth I of c. 1550s, illustrated as cat. 52 in Susan Doran, ed., *Elizabeth: The Exhibition at the National Maritime Museum* (London, 2003). Both are from Preston St Mary Church, Suffolk.

18 As given in *Visitation Articles and Injunctions of the Period of the Reformation*, ed. Walter Howard Frere, 3 vols (London, 1910), vol. 3 (1559–75), p. 21.

19 Ian Green, *Print and Protestantism in Early Modern England* (Oxford, 2000), p. 278. Green focuses on England but the same can be said for Scotland.

20 The quotation is from Sir William Dawes, *The Duties of the closet* (1695), cited in *ibid.*, p. 285.

21 Joseph Hall in *The arte of divine meditation profitable for all Christians to knowe and practise* (London, 1606), distinguished between 'Extemporall, and occasioned by outward occurrences offered to the mind, or Deliberate, and wrought out of our own heart' (1609 edn, p. 7).

22 John Downame, *A Guide to Godlynesse or a Treatise of a Christian Life* (London, 1622, 1629 edn), p. 552.

23 Rogers was careful to edit and alter the text of this pre-Reformation devotional work wherever it ran counter to Protestant ideology. His reformed version ran through fourteen editions between 1580 and 1640.

24 Downame, *Guide to Godlynesse*, p. 539.

25 Hall, *Arte of divine meditation*, p. 20.

26 Edward Gurnay, *Toward the Vindication of the Second Commandment* (Cambridge, 1639), p. 108.

27 Downame, *Guide to Godlynesse*, p. 541.

28 Hall, *Arte of divine meditation*, pp. 17–18.

29 Downame, *Guide to Godlynesse*, p. 560. On the range of opinions as to the most suitable subjects for meditation see Green, *Print and Protestantism*, p. 280.

30 Downame, *Guide to Godlynesse*, p. 563.

31 See Eamon Duffy, 'Devotion to the Crucifix and Related Images in England on the Eve of the Reformation' in Bob Scribner (ed.), *Bilder und Bildersturm im Spätmittelalter und in der frühen Neuzeit* (Wiesbaden, 1990), pp. 21–36 for the complexities and forms of devotion to the Crucified Christ in late medieval personal piety.

32 Ian Green points out that even high-Calvinist thinking had a degree of Christocentricity in that Christ was generally acknowledged as the mediator of the covenant between God and man. Some of the more popular works by Puritan authors encouraged readers not only to meditate on Christ's saving sacrifice but also to apply his example to their own lives; *Print and Protestantism*, pp. 322–25.

33 Illustrated in Watt, *Cheap Print*, p. 233, pl. 41.

34 There may be a thematic link between the classical subject matter at the centre and the religious subject matter in the lower section. The victory of Perseus over Medusa could be understood as an analogy for Christ's triumph over sin/death (as depicted allegorically in the frieze section), and the emergence of Pegasus from the neck or blood of the slain Medusa may symbolise the Resurrection.

35 Tara Hamling, 'Guides to Godliness, from Print to Plaster' in Michael Hunter (ed.), *Printed Images in Early Modern Britain: Essays in Interpretation* (Aldershot, 2010), pp. 65–85. The wall painting is also discussed and illustrated in Watt, *Cheap Print*, p. 201, fig. 30.

36 This is not to ignore the wider meanings surrounding Adam and Eve imagery but it seems that the typological significance of the scene has been little explored compared with discussion of cultural ideas about nature, sex and marriage. See Andrew Morrall, 'Regaining Eden: Representations of Nature in Seventeenth-Century English Embroidery' in Andrew Morrall and Melinda Watt (eds), *English Embroidery from the Metropolitan Museum of Art, 1580–1700* (New York, New Haven and London, 2008). pp. 79–98 and Catherine Belsey, *Shakespeare and the Loss of Eden: The Construction of Family Values in Early Modern Culture* (Basingstoke, 1999), ch. 3.

37 Eamon Duffy, *Marking The Hours: English People & their Prayers, 1240–1570* (New Haven and London, 2006), pp. 171–74. For the modifications to the religious illustrations in Daye's 1578 version, made in response to Protestant ideology, see Samuel Chew, 'The Iconography of A Book of Christian Prayers (1578) Illustrated', *Huntington Library Quarterly* vol. 8 (1944–45): 293–305.

38 In fact, this is an unusual typological pairing in visual art. In the printed *Biblia Pauperum* and Daye's *Christian Prayers* of 1569 and 1578 Elijah raising the widow's son is depicted as a type for Christ raising Lazarus. However, the parallel with Christ's own Resurrection was ubiquitous in theological exegesis.

39 William Perkins, *A Reformed Catholike: or A Declaration shewing how neere we may come to the Present Church of Rome in sundrie points of Religion: and wherein we must for ever depart from them* (Cambridge, 1598), p. 172.

40 V&A accession no. P.1-1938. The painting's provenance prior to 1938 when it entered the V&A is unknown so it is impossible to determine the identity of the patron or the original location and setting of this work. The iconography is based on a print that the engraver Jerome Wierix derived from a composition by Crispin van den Broeck. Both Wierix and Broeck produced numerous prints with Counter-Reformation themes that were commissioned and disseminated by the Jesuits throughout Europe as propaganda. This association suggests that the painting might have been commissioned by an English Catholic but the imagery is not incompatible with Protestant image theory; in fact the inscriptions emphasise the reformed position that the text of the Bible was the only sure source of salvation.

41 Thomas Trevelyon, 'Pictorial Commonplace Book', 1608, Folger Shakespeare Library, Washington, D.C., MS v.b.232 (film F.83.1), fol. 174r.

42 The house is privately owned. The overmantel is illustrated in Kathleen and Cecil French, 'Devonshire Plasterwork', *Transactions of the Devonshire Association for the Advancement of Science, Literature and Art* vol. 89 (1957): 124–44.

43 Richard Simpson argued that the life of Hezekiah was chosen by the patron, Sir Thomas Smith, because of his role in the reforming process; Richard Simpson, 'Sir Thomas Smith and the Wall Paintings at Hill Hall, Essex: Scholarly Theory and Design in the Sixteenth Century', *Journal of the British Archaeological Association* vol. 130 (1977): 1–20; 'Images and Ethics in Reformation Political Discourse: The Paintings at Sir Thomas Smith's Hill Hall' in Tara Hamling and Richard L. Williams (eds), *Art Re-formed: Reassessing the Impact of the Reformation on the Visual Arts* (Newcastle, 2007), pp. 127–46 and

Paul Drury and Richard Simpson, *Hill Hall: A Singular House devised by a Tudor Intellectual* (London, 2009).

44 Margaret Aston, *The King's Bedpost: Reformation and Iconography in a Tudor Group Portrait* (Cambridge, 1993, reprinted 1996), p. 119.

45 Andrew Willet, *Hexapla in Genesin: That is A Sixfold Commentarie upon Genesis* (Cambridge, 1605), p. 236.

46 This overmantel is all that remains of a once extensive programme of biblical imagery. A description from 1820 records that the hall was 'ornamented with some curious carved work, and many composition figures' including 'Justice, Abraham and King Solomon with numerous attendants'; C. S. Gilbert, *An Historical Survey of the County of Cornwall*, 2 vols (London, 1817–20), vol. 2, p. 611.

47 RCHME MS: 'Original field-notes for 90 High Street, Oxford' (recorder R. W. McDowall), 1937, NMR archive. The letters forming the inscription were cut out in wood and stuck on to the overmantel; the word 'papists' was removed at some point in the past but the marks made by the letters are still visible.

48 Among the numerous other examples that I have not had space to describe in detail here, I would like to mention a version of the subject in wall painting at 'The Batch' in Sidbury, Shropshire, to illustrate that it was indeed depicted in all media. The painting, which dates from 1600–25 and includes Abraham and Isaac walking up the hill and the scene of near-sacrifice, has been lost but a photograph is included in Kathryn Davies, *Artisan Art: Vernacular Wall Paintings in the Welsh Marshes, 1550–1650* (Almeley, 2008), p. 174.

49 The typological significance of the Sacrifice of Isaac was also popularised through drama. Abraham and Isaac was one of the more commonly told stories among the English mystery plays and the extant play texts follow contemporary exegesis in emphasising the role of Isaac as a type for Christ; Rosemary Woolf, 'The Effect of Typology on the English Mediaeval Plays of Abraham and Isaac', *Speculum* vol. 32, no. 4 (October 1957): 805–25. The typological meaning continued to be emphasised in Protestant versions of the story. The French Huguenot Theodore de Beza's play on the subject was a huge success, going into ten editions in the sixteenth century and being translated into Italian, Latin and English. Arthur Golding's English translation was published in 1577.

50 Erwin Panofsky, *Studies in Iconology: Humanistic Themes in the Art of the Renaissance* (1939; New York and London, 1962), p. 6.

51 Gervase Babington, *Certaine plaine, briefe, and comfortable notes upon everie chapter of Genesis* (London, 1592), sig. N2v.

52 Willet, *Hexapla in Genesin*, p. 236.

53 The original location of this panel is not known and it is here assumed that it was created as a domestic overmantel or panel. Based on its known provenance the museum refers to this as the 'Angel Inn' panel, which might be misleading in suggesting that it functioned as an inn sign. In fact the Angel Inn in Yeovil had a great iron figure of an angel as its sign (also held in the Museum of South Somerset). A description of the town in 1856 helpfully recorded that 'an oak panel, representing Abraham offering up Isaac [had] for many years adorned the kitchen of the Angel Inn', confirming that the panel was displayed there for some time but suggesting that this was not its original setting; Daniel Vickery, *A Sketch of the Town of Yeovil* (Yeovil, 1856). It is unlikely that the paintwork is original, although the panel was possibly always painted.

54 C. W. F. Goss, *Sir Paul Pindar and his Bishopsgate Mansion* (Cambridge, 1930). For Pindar's role and activities as 'the leading benefactor of Laudian beautification' see Kenneth Fincham and Nicholas Tyacke, *Altars Restored: The Changing Face of English Religious Worship, 1547–c. 1700* (Oxford, 2007), p. 257.

55 C. J. Richardson, *Architectural Remains of the Reigns of Elizabeth and James I* (London, 1840), V&A, National Art Library, pressmark 51.H.101.

56 V&A accession no. T.134-1929.

57 Natalie Mears has documented her painstaking research into the likely location of the original dwelling which she has identified as a property known as 'Swift', possibly the house of a tanner. She has also read the meaning of the imagery in relation to English sermons on the subject and interpreted the painting in relation to the Protestant doctrine of *sole fide*; 'Location, Location, Location? Place, Patronage and Meaning of the Wall Painting of "Jonah and the Whale" at Waltham Abbey',

Essex Archaeology and History vol. 38 (2007): 136–47.

58 Francis W. Reader, 'Tudor Domestic Wall Paintings, Part 1', *The Archaeological Journal* vol. 92 (1935): p. 255. According to Reader, early records reporting the discovery of the painting noted that some text in a floriated border accompanied the painting. The text was not transcribed and it was destroyed along with the house. See Wells-Cole, *Art and Decoration*, p. 104 and Mears, 'Location', p. 137 for identification of the printed source.

59 John Andrewes, *Christ his crosse or The most comfortable doctrine of Christ crucified and joyfull tidings of his passion* (Oxford, 1614), p. 72.

60 See the quotations from Gwalter and Abbott in Mears, 'Location', p. 145.

61 Edward Vaughan, *A Method, or briefe instruction . . . for the reading and understanding of the old and new testament* (London, 1590), p. 66.

62 The other extant panels depict Aaron's rod/the Drowning of Pharaoh and Mary Magdalen meeting the Risen Christ ('Noli me tangere').

63 Unknown, 'Manor Court House', *Proceedings of Somersetshire Archaeological and Natural History Society* vol. 8 (1882): 23–27.

64 The interior decoration of one of the bedrooms incorporates both the initials of Elizabeth I in the ceiling design and the arms of James I at the centre of the chimneypiece overmantel. If the chimneypiece with biblical imagery was created at the same time it must date from sometime between 1603 and 1625.

65 Illustrated in Doran, *Elizabeth*, p. 85, cat. 63.

66 Quoted in Keith Thomas, 'Art and Iconoclasm in Early Modern England' in Kenneth Fincham and Peter Lake (eds), *Religious Politics in Post-Reformation England: Essays in Honour of Nicholas Tyacke* (Woodbridge, 2006), p. 38.

6 THE PRESENCE OF RELIGIOUS IMAGERY IN THE GODLY HOUSEHOLD

1 See e.g. John Thorp, 'The Ornamental Plasterwork of the Long Gallery at Lanhydrock, Cornwall: Puritan Images for Changing Times', *Apollo* vol. 434 (1998): 30–34 and Michael Bath, 'The Sources of John Abbott's Pattern Book', *Architectural History* vol. 41 (1998): 49–66.

2 This interpretation is no doubt influenced by medievalists' discussion of similar imagery in stained glass in terms of narrative and didactic function. See e.g. Norman Bryson on the iconographic programme in the stained glass of the apse at Canterbury Cathedral, in the opening chapter of his *Word and Image: French Painting of the Ancien Régime* (Cambridge, 1981).

3 William Perkins, *The whole treatises of the cases of conscience* (Cambridge, 1608), p. 150.

4 Henry Ainsworth, *Annotations upon the Second book of Moses, called Exodus* (Amsterdam, 1617), sig. O3v.

5 Michael Bath, *Renaissance Decorative Painting in Scotland* (Edinburgh, 2003).

6 Michael Bath, 'Was there a Guise Palace in Edinburgh?' in Robert Gowing and Robyn Pender (eds), *All Manner of Murals: The History, Techniques and Conservation of Secular Wall Paintings* (London, 2007), pp. 11–22.

7 *Ibid.*, p. 19.

8 Richard Brathwaite, *Essaies upon the Five Senses with a pithie one upon detraction* (London, 1620), p. 57.

9 *Ibid.*

10 William Perkins, *A treatise of mans imaginations. Shewing his naturall evill thoughts* (Cambridge, 1607), p. 182.

11 Stephen Egerton, *Indecorum: or A briefe treatise upon one of Salomons proverbs* (London, 1613), 'The Epistle Dedicatorie'.

12 Anthony Nixon, *The dignitie of man both in the perfections of his soule and bodie* (Oxford, 1616), p. 15.

13 Keith Thomas, *Religion and the Decline of Magic: Studies in Popular Beliefs in Sixteenth- and Seventeenth-Century England* (London, 1971, reprinted 1991), p. 519.

14 William Perkins, *A discourse of the damned art of witchcraft* (Cambridge, 1608), ch. 4, p. 140.

15 George Hakewill, *The vanitie of the eie* (Oxford, 1608), p. 32.

16 John Gaule, *Select cases of conscience touching witches and witchcrafts* (London, 1646), p. 129. A related belief was that a menstruating woman could ruin a mirror simply by looking at it. Hakewill concluded his discussion of be-

witching of the eye with reference to this belief: 'But for the full clearing of this point, let us but consider the common experience of infecting one another, by bleare eies, and the spotting of a looking glass, especially if it be new, and cleare by the looking on of a menstruous woman'; *Vanitie of the eie*, p. 35. This 'infection' was thought to be caused by the same emanations as operated in instances of the evil eye. Henry Peacham explained that 'it is not the sight of the woman that infeceth the glasse, but certaine grosse and putrefacted vapors, that issue from the eies'; *The Gentleman's Exercise* (London, 1612), p. 63.

17 This idea is explored in detail in my 'The Appreciation of Religious Images in Plasterwork in the Protestant Domestic Interior' in Tara Hamling and Richard L. Williams (eds), *Art Re-formed: Re-assessing the Impact of the Reformation on the Visual Arts* (Newcastle, 2007), pp. 147–68.

18 Jonathan E. Schroeder, 'Consuming Representation: A Visual Approach to Consumer Research' in Barbara B. Stern (ed.), *Representing Consumers: Voices, Views and Visions* (London, 1998), pp. 193–223.

19 Michel Foucault, *Discipline and Punish: The Birth of the Prison*, trans. Alan Sheridan (1975; London, 1991).

20 Alfred Gell, *Art and Agency: An Anthropological Theory* (Oxford, 1998).

21 Shirley Campbell, 'The Captivating Agency of Art: Many Ways of Seeing' in Christopher Pinney and Nicholas Thomas (eds), *Beyond Aesthetics: Art and the Technologies of Enchantment* (Oxford, 2001), p. 117.

22 W. J. T. Mitchell, 'What do Pictures Really Want?', *October* vol. 77 (Summer 1996): 71–82.

23 See Chris L. Kleinke, 'Gaze and Eye Contact: A Research Review', *Psychological Bulletin* vol. 100, no. 1 (1986): 78–100.

24 James Elkins, *The Object Stares Back: On the Nature of Seeing* (London, 1996), ch. 2, pp. 46–85.

25 Simon Baron-Cohen, *Mindblindness: An Essay on Autism and Theory of Mind* (Cambridge, 1995, 7th printing 2001), esp. chs 4 and 7.

26 See Bruno Wicker *et al.*, 'Brain Regions involved in the Perception of Gaze: A PET Study', *Neuroimage* vol. 8 (1998): 221–27.

27 See Ryuta Kawashima *et al.*, 'The Human Amygdala Plays an Important Role in Gaze Monitoring: A PET Study', *Brain* vol. 122, no. 4 (April 1999): 779–83 and Reginald B. Adams Jr *et al.*, 'Effects of Gaze on Amygdala Sensitivity to Anger and Fear Faces', *Science* vol. 300 (6 June 2003): 1536–37.

28 The standard experimental stimuli used in such experiments are colour photographs of faces directing their gaze straight at the viewers (for testing direct gaze) or averted to one side (for testing averted gaze). See e.g. Teresa Farroni *et al.*, 'Eye Contact Detection in Humans from Birth', *Proceedings of the National Academy of Sciences of the United States of America* vol. 99, no. 14 (9 July 2002): 9602–5, fig. 1. One study investigating the difference between straight-gaze detection and averted-gaze detection found that the visual system responded faster to straight-gaze stimuli 'that were realistically drawn renditions of pairs of human eyes, as well as with similar schematic stimuli representing pairs of human eyes'; see M. von Grunau and C. Anston, 'The Detection of Gaze Direction: A Stare-in-the-Crowd Effect', *Perception* vol. 24, no. 11 (1995): 1297–313.

29 Elkins, *Object Stares Back*, p. 12.

30 George Hakewill, *King Davids vow for reformation of himselfe, his family, his kingdome* (London, 1621), p. 98.

31 For some notable exceptions see Ch. 4.

32 Hakewill, *King Davids vow*, pp. 102–03.

33 Ralph Merrifield, *The Archaeology of Ritual and Magic* (London, 1987) was the first serious examination of practices relating to ritual protection in England.

34 This fascinating but little-understood practice was the subject of a major research project; *The Deliberately Concealed Garments Project* at the Textile Conservation Centre, University of Southampton (1998–2007). The project aimed to locate, document, research and present instances of deliberately concealed garments in buildings. The project's website includes a comprehensive database, <www.concealedgarments.org>.

35 Perkins, *A discourse of the damned art*, p. 225.

36 John Dean, 'Ritual Protection Marks on Norfolk Buildings: A Recent Survey', paper compiled for the Vernacular Architecture Group, Spring Conference, Norwich, April 1997.

37 It is, of course, impossible to be precise about the dating of these marks which could have

been added long after the object or surface they adorn was first created.

38 June Swann, 'Shoes Concealed in Buildings', *Costume* no. 30 (1996): 56–69.

39 Dinah Eastop, 'Garments Deliberately Concealed in Buildings' in R. Wallis and K. Lymer (eds), *A Permeability of Boundaries? New Approaches to the Archaeology of Art, Religion and Folklore*, BAR International Series (Oxford, 2001), pp. 79–84.

40 Dean, 'Ritual Protection Marks'.

41 Edward Roberts, with contributions by John Crook, Linda Hall and Daniel Miles, *Hampshire Houses, 1250–1700: Their Dating and Development* (Winchester, 2003), p. 103.

CONCLUSION: LAST JUDGEMENTS

1 The development and significance of the *Ovide moralisé* and associated texts in the medieval period was discussed by Jean Seznec, *The Survival of the Pagan Gods: The Mythological Tradition and its Place in Renaissance Humanism and Art* (Princeton, N.J., 1981), pp. 91–96. On the impact of this trend on the visual arts see Nigel Llewellyn, 'Illustrating Ovid' in Charles Martindale (ed.), *Ovid Renewed: Ovidian Influences on Literature and Art from the Middle Ages to the Twentieth Century* (Cambridge, 1988), pp. 151–276.

2 Nigel Llewellyn, *The Art of Death: Visual Culture in the English Death Ritual, c. 1500–c. 1800* (London, 1991); Tarnya Cooper, 'Memento Mori Portraiture: Painting, Protestant Culture and the Patronage of Middle Elites in England and Wales, 1540–1630', D.Phil. thesis (University of Sussex, 2001); Tarnya Cooper, '"Frail flesh, as in a glass": The Portrait as an Immortal Presence in Early Modern England and Wales' in Mary Rogers (ed.), *Fashioning Identities in Renaissance Art* (Aldershot, 2000), pp. 197–212; Tarnya Cooper, 'Predestined Lives? Portraiture and Religious Belief in England and Wales, 1560–1620' in Tara Hamling and Richard L. Williams (eds), *Art Re-formed: Re-assessing the Impact of the Reformation on the Visual Arts* (Newcastle, 2007), pp. 49–64. Tarnya Cooper's monograph on this category of *memento mori* portrait will be published by Yale University Press.

3 See Ch. 1, n. 7.

4 See e.g. Tarnya Cooper (ed.), *Searching for Shakespeare* (London, 2006), pp. 196–97, cats 93–95.

5 See publications by Cooper listed above, n. 2.

6 E.g. the etching *Death and the Devil Surprise Two Women* by Daniel Hopfer, Augsburg, c. 1520; reprinted in the late seventeenth century (V&A accession no. 26153).

7 Norwich Castle Museum and Art Gallery, no. NWH COL: 1953.134.2:F. Illustrated and discussed in Cooper, *Searching for Shakespeare*, p. 107, cat. 31, which states that there are at least five different versions of this composition still extant.

8 Cited in J. T. Cliffe, *The Puritan Gentry: The Great Puritan Families of Early Stuart England* (London, 1984), pp. 172–73.

9 Illustrated in Sheila O'Connell, *The Popular Print in England* (London, 1999), p. 109, fig. 4.43.

10 Binham Farm, Old Cleeve in Somerset; Dean Head, Swimbridge in Devon; Manor House, West Down in Devon and 103 High Street in Barnstaple, Devon (now destroyed?). The subject also appears as a crude drawing in the Abbott sketchbook of plasterwork designs. For illustrations and discussion see Anthony Wells-Cole, *Art and Decoration in Elizabethan and Jacobean England: The Influence of Continental Prints, 1558–1625* (New Haven and London, 1997), p. 162 and Michael Bath, 'The Sources of John Abbott's Pattern Book', *Architectural History* vol. 41 (1998): 49–66.

11 Crewe Hall was rebuilt between 1615 and 1636 by Sir Randolph Crewe (1558–1646). This overmantel is a nineteenth-century re-creation by E. M. Barry of a Jacobean original after a fire destroyed much of the old house in 1866. Another post-fire re-creation in a room on the second floor muddles the iconographies of two biblical subjects: Samson killing a Philistine and Cain and Abel. Tackbeare Manor was owned by Samuel Gilbert (1636–1728). The plasterwork allegory is in a first-floor room and from the costume of the figure of Industry looks to date from the 1670s or 80s. The figure of Idleness is naked. The iconography was adapted so that Industry lost his attribute of a spade in the print and instead holds a book.

12 'The Design Book of John Abbott', Devon Record Office, Exeter, MS 404M/B1.

13 The 1582 print, by Raphael Sadeler after Maarten de Vos, was identified by Wells-Cole, *Art and Decoration*, pp. 113–16, fig. 171 as the source for the overmantel at Crewe Hall.

14 Clifford Davidson, *The Guild Chapel Wall Paintings at Stratford-upon-Avon* (New York, 1988), p. 11.

15 There are rare examples of Last Judgements in post-Reformation prints. A traditional version of the subject is depicted in ovals at the top and bottom of a print of c. 1600 by William Rogers, 'A Godly Meditation day and night to be exercised', although in a second state of the same plate the figure of Christ in Glory at the top has been replaced by a triangle labelled 'Eternitie'. This and other examples are discussed by Tessa Watt, *Cheap Print and Popular Piety, 1550–1640* (Cambridge, 1991), pp. 238–41.

16 Wells-Cole explained that this work utilised several different printed sources; *Art and Decoration*, pp. 178–79.

17 The chimneypiece was purchased and installed at Sutton Place by Frederick Kock who acquired the property in 1986 and carried out an extensive programme of remodelling to showcase his art collections. See Michael Hall, 'Sutton Place, Surrey', *Country Life* (13 June 1996): 112–17.

18 Francis Quarles, *Emblemes* (London, 1635), Book 1, IV, p. 16. Many of Quarles' illustrations, including this one, are copied from a Jesuit emblem book, the *Typus mundi* of 1627, but the accompanying texts are by Quarles and reflect his Protestant, if high church, faith. I owe this discovery to David Griffith whose identification of Quarles' *Emblemes* as the source for a scheme of seventeenth-century painted imagery in a house in York led me to examine the other illustrations in this book. A study of these paintings in the context of the cultural impact of Quarles' *Emblemes*, co-authored by Hugh Adlington, David Griffith and Tara Hamling, is in preparation.

19 Three blank panels set in decorative cartouches are carved within a lower section of the chimneypiece. It is possible these panels were originally painted with text, or were intended for that purpose but never completed.

20 Quarles, *Emblemes*, Epigram 4, p. 19.

21 As listed in the broadside 'A Catalogue of Plates and Pictures that are printed and sould by Peter Stent', c. 1655. Alexander Globe, *Peter Stent, London Printseller, c. 1642–65* (Vancouver, 1985).

22 Charles Sayle (ed.), *The Works of Sir Thomas Browne*, 3 vols (Edinburgh, 1927), vol. 2, pp. 202–76.

Select Bibliography

MANUSCRIPT SOURCES

Abbott, John. 'The Design Book of John Abbott'. Devon Record Office, Exeter. MS 404M/B1.

Donne, John. Will of John Donne, Doctor of Divinity, Dean of Saint Paul's Cathedral, City of London, 1631. PROB 11/159.

Luttrell Family of Dunster Manuscripts. Somerset Record Office, Taunton. DD/L 23/45/1–4.

Pennington, Mary. Autobiography of Mary Pennington, c. 1640–80. West Sussex Record Office, Chichester. Record Ref. 31145.

Skory, Sir Edmund. Will of Sir Edmund Skory of Saint Giles without Cripplegate, City of London, 20 July 1632. PROB 11/162.

Trevelon, Thomas. 'Pictorial Commonplace Book', 1608. Folger Shakespeare Library, Washington, D.C., MS v.b.232 (film F.83.1).

Turberville Correspondence. Somerset Record Office, Taunton. DD/WO 54/5/1–17.

PRINTED PRIMARY SOURCES

Ainsworth, Henry. *Annotations upon the first book of Moses, called Genesis.* [Amsterdam]: Imprinted [by Giles Thorp], 1616.

—. *Annotations upon the Second book of Moses, called Exodus.* [Amsterdam]: Imprinted [by Giles Thorp], 1617.

Andrewes, John. *Christ his crosse or The most comfortable doctrine of Christ crucified and joyfull tidings of his passion.* Oxford: Joseph Barnes, 1614.

Andrewes, Lancelot. *The pattern of catechistical doctrine at large, or, A learned and pious exposition of the Ten Commandments.* London: Imprinted by Roger Norton, 1650.

Aylett, Robert. *Susanna: or the arraignment of the two unjust elders.* London: Printed for John Teage, 1622.

—. *Joseph, or Pharoah's favourite*. London: B. A[lsop] for Matthew Law, 1623.

Babington, Gervase. *A very fruitfull Exposition of the Commaundements by way of Questions and Answers for greater plainnesse*. London: Printed by Henry Middleton for Thomas Charde, 1583, reprinted 1590.

—. *Certain plaine, briefe, and comfortable notes upon everie chapter of Genesis*. London: Printed [by A. Jeffes and P. Short] for Thomas Charde, 1592.

Bacon, Francis. *The essayes or counsels, civill and morall, of Francis Lo. Verulam, Viscount St. Alban*. London: Printed by John Haviland for Hanna Barret, 1625.

Ballard, George. *The History of Susanna, Compiled according to the Prophet Daniel, amplified with convenient Meditations*. London: Printed by Thomas Harper for William Hope, 1638.

Barker, Peter. *A judicious and painfull exposition upon the Ten Commandments*. London: [by J. Beale?] for Roger Jackson, 1624.

Bayly, Lewis. *The Practise of Pietie: Directing a Christian how to walk that he may please God*. London: Printed [by T. Snodham] for John Hodgets, 1613.

Bentley, Thomas. *The Sixt Lampe of Virginitie conteining a mirrour for maidens and matrons*. London: Thomas Dawson [and Henry Denham], 1582.

Bèze, Théodore de. *A tragedie of Abrahams sacrifice, written in French by Theodore Beza, and translated into Inglish, by A.G.* London: Thomas Vautroullier, 1577.

Birckbek, Simon. *The Protestants evidence taken out of good records; shewing that for fifteene humdred yeares next after Christ, divers worthy guides of Gods Church, have in sundry weightie points of religion, taught as the Church of England now doth*. London: Augustine Mathewes and Thomas Cotes for Robert Milbourne, 1635.

Brathwaite, Richard. *Essaies upon the Five Senses with a pithie one upon detraction. Continued with sundry Christian resolves, full of passion and devotion, purposely composed for the zealously-disposed*. London: Printed by E. G[riffin] for Richard Whittaker, 1620.

—. *The English Gentleman*. London: John Haviland, 1630.

Calfhill, James. *An Answere to the Treatise of the Crosse*. London: Henry Denham for Lucas Harrison, 1565.

Calvin, Jean. *A Commentarie of John Calvine, upon the first Booke of Moses* (Latin, Geneva, 1563). Trans. Thomas Tymme. London: [by Henry Middleton] for John Harrison and George Bishop, 1578.

—. *A commentarie of M. Iohn Caluine uppon the Epistle to the Philippians . . . Translated out of Latine by W.B.* London: John Windet for Nicolas Lyng, 1584.

—. *Institutes of the Christian Religion*, trans. Henry Beveridge. London: Printed by Arnold Hatfield for Bonham Norton, 1599.

Carr, John. *The Ruinous fal of Prodigalitie: with the notable examples of the best aprooved authours which hath bin written of the same*. London: Imprinted by William How for Henry Kirkham, 1573.

Carr, Roger. *A Godly Form of Householde Governement: for the ordering of private families, according to the direction of Gods word*. London: Imprinted by Thomas Creede for Thomas Man, 1598.

Cleaver, Robert. *A godlie forme of householde government*. London: Imprinted by Thomas Creede for Thomas Man, 1598.

Colet, John. *A Right Fruitful Monition concerning the order of a good Christian man's life very profitable for all manner of estates and others to behold and look upon*. London: Martinus Nijhoff, 1534. Reprinted in Elizabeth M. Nugent, ed., *The Thought and Culture of the English Renaissance: An Anthology of Tudor Prose, 1481–1555*. Cambridge University Press, 1956.

Cowper, William. *The Triumph of a Christian*. London: [T. East] for John Budge, 1608.

Daye, Richard. *Christian Prayers and Meditations in English, French, Italian, Spanish, Greeke and Latine*. London: John Daye, 1569.
—. *A Booke of Christian Prayers, collected out of the auncie[n]t writers, and best learned in our tyme, worthy to be read with an earnest mynde of all Christians, in these daungerous and troublesome dayes, that God for Christes sake will yet still be mercyfull unto us*. London: John Daye, 1578.
Deacon, John. *Dialogicall discourses of spirits and divels declaring their proper essence, natures, dispositions, and operations, their possessions and dispossessions*. London: George Bishop, 1601.
Dering, Edward. *Godly private praiers, for householders to meditate upon, and to say in theyr families*. London: John Charlewood, 1578.
Donne, John. *The Sermons*. 10 vols, ed. Evelyn Simpson and George Potter. Berkeley and Los Angeles: University of California Press, 1954–62.
Downame, John. *A Guide to Godlynesse or a Treatise of a Christian Life*. London: Printed by Felix Kingstone [and William Stansby] for Ed. Weuer & W. Bladen, 1622, 1629 edn.
Durham, James. *The law unsealed, or, A Practical exposition of the Ten Commandments with a resolution of several momentous questions and cases of conscience*. Edinburgh and Glasgow: Robert Sanders, 1676.
Egerton, Stephen. *Indecorum: or A briefe treatise upon one of Salomons proverbs. Chap. 11.22 Wherein is shewed, how ill-beseeming all common gifts and worldly blessings are to all such, as are not furnished with some answerable measure, or spirituall and saving grace*. London: Felix Kyngston for Richard Boyle, 1613.
Elton, Edward. *God's Holy Mind Touching Matters Morall, which himself uttered in Tenne Words, or Tenne Commandments*. London: Augustine Mathewes and J[ohn] N[orton] for Robert Mylbourne, 1625.
Elyot, Sir Thomas. *The castell of health*. London: Printed by the Widdow Orwin, 1595.
Estey, George. *Certaine Godly and Learned Expositions upon divers parts of Scripture. As they were preached, and afterwards more briefly penned by that worthy man of GOD, Maister George Estey*. London: Printed by I. R. for Richard Banckworth, 1603.
Fenner, Dudley. *The Order of Houshold, in Certain godly and learned treatises*. Edinburgh: Robert Waldegrave, 1592.
Fulke, William. *D. Heskyns, D. Sanders and M. Rastell . . . overthrowne, and detected of their severall blasphemous heresies*. London, Henry Middleton for George Bishop, 1579.
Gardiner, Samuel. *The Portraitur of the prodigal sonne livelie set forth in a three-fold discourse*. London, P. S[hort] for Nicholas Ling, 1599.
Gaule, John. *Select cases of conscience touching witches and witchcrafts*. London: Printed by W. Wilson for Richard Clutterbuck, 1646.
Gouge, William. *Of Domesticall Duties: Eight Treatises*. London: Printed by John Haviland for William Bladen, 1622.
Greenham, Richard. *The workes of the reverend and faithfull servant of Jesus Christ M. Richard Greenham*. London, Thomas Snodham and Thomas Creede for William Welby, 1612.
Guild, William. *Moses Unveiled or Those figures which served unto the patterne and shadow of heavenly things, pointing out the Messiah Christ Jesus*. London: Printed by G[eorge] P[urslowe] for John Budge, 1620.
Gurnay, Edmund. *Toward the Vindication of the Second Commandment*. Cambridge: Thomas Buck, 1639.
Hakewill, George. *The vanitie of the eie First beganne for the comfort of a gentlewoman bereaved of her sight, and since upon occasion inlarged & published for the common good*. Oxford: Printed by Joseph Barnes, 1608.

—. *King Davids vow for reformation of himselfe, his family, his kingdome. Delivered in twelve sermons before the Prince his Highnesse upon Psalm 101*. London: [by Humphrey Lownes] for Matthew Lownes, 1621.

Hall, Joseph. *The arte of divine meditation profitable for all Christians to knowe and practise*. London: Humfrey Lownes, 1606, 1609 edn.

Harrison, William. *The Description of England: The Classic Contemporary Account of Tudor Social Life* (1577, 2nd edn 1587), ed. Georges Edelen. Washington, D.C., and New York: Folger Shakespeare Library and Dover Publications, 1994.

Hinde, William. *A faithfull remonstrance of the holy life and happy death of John Bruen of Bruen-Stapleford, in the county of Chester, Esquire*. London: Printed by R. B. for Philemon Stephens and Chrisopher Meredith, 1641.

Jonson, Ben. *Poetaster or The arraignment as it hath beene sundry times privately acted in the Blacke Friers, by the children of her Maiesties Chappell*. London: Printed [by R. Bradock] for M. L[ownes], 1602.

Junius, Franciscus. *The Painting of the Ancients in three bookes; declaring by historicall observations and examples, the beginning, progresse, and consummation of that most noble art*. London: Richard Hodgkinson, 1638.

Kingsford, C. L., ed. *A survey of London by J. Stow; reprinted from the text of 1603, with intro. and notes*. 2 vols. Oxford: Clarendon Press, 1908.

Markham, Gervase. *The English Husbandman*. London: T[homas] S[nodham] for John Browne, 1613.

Middleton, Thomas and Thomas Dekker. *The Roaring Girle or Moll Cut-Purse As it hath lately beene acted on the Fortune-stage by the Prince his Players*. London: Nicholas Okes for Thomas Archer, 1611.

Nixon, Anthony. *The dignitie of man both in the perfections of his soule and bodie. Shewing as well the faculties in the disposition of the one: as the senses and organs, in the composition of the other*. Oxford: Printed by Joseph Barnes, 1616.

North, Roger. *Of Building: Roger North's Writings on Architecture*, ed. Howard Colvin and John Newman. Oxford University Press, 1981.

Peacham, Henry. *The Gentlemans Exercise*. London: Printed for John Browne, 1612.

Perkins, William. *A Reformed Catholike: or A Declaration shewing how neere we may come to the Present Church of Rome in sundrie points of Religion: and wherein we must for ever depart from them*. Cambridge: Printed by J. Legat, 1598.

—. *A Warning against the Idolatrie of the last times. And an instruction touching religious or Divine Worship*. Cambridge: Printed by J. Legat, 1601.

—. *A treatise of mans imaginations. Shewing his naturall evill thoughts: His want of good thoughts: The way to reforme them*. Cambridge: Printed by John Legat, 1607.

—. *A discourse of the damned art of witchcraft so farre forth as it is revealed in the Scriptures, and manifest by true experience*. Cambridge: Printed by Cantrel Legge, 1608.

—. *The whole treatises of the cases of conscience*. Cambridge: Printed by John Legat, 1608.

—. *Christian Oeconomie: or, A short survey of the right manner of erecting and ordering a familie*. London: Felix Kyngston, 1609.

Quarles, Francis. *Emblemes*. London: Printed by G[eorge] M[iller], 1635.

Shakespeare, William. *The Complete Works*, ed. Stanley Wells and Gary Taylor. Oxford University Press, 1988.

Stubbes, Phillip. *The Anatomie of Abuses: contayning A Discoverie, or briefe Summarie, of such Notable Vices and Imperfections, as now raigne in many Christian Countryes of the Worlde, but (especiallie) in a verie famous Ilande called Ailgna: Together with most fearefull Examples of Gods

Judgementes, executed upon the wicked for the same . . . verie godly to be read of all true Christians everie where, but most needful to be regarded in Englande. London: Printed by Richard Jones, 1583.
Torshell, Samuel. *The hypocrite discovered and cured.* London: G. M. for John Bellamy, 1644.
Vaughan, Edward. *A Method, or briefe instruction, verie profitable and speedy, for the reading and understanding of the old and new testament. The one expounding the other according to the sence and meaning of our Lord and Saviour Jesus Christ.* London: Imprinted by T. Orwin for W. Holme, 1590.
Vaughan, William. *Approved directions for health, both naturall and artificiall derived from the best physitians as well moderne as auncient.* London: T. S[nodham] for Roger Jackson, 1612.
Visitation Articles and Injunctions of the Period of the Reformation, ed. Walter Howard Frere. 3 vols. London, 1910, vol. 3 (1559–75).
Wentworth Papers, 1597–1628, ed. J. P. Cooper. Camden Fourth Series, vol. 12. London: The Royal Historical Society, 1973.
Whately, William. *Prototypes, or, The Primarie Precedent Presidents out of the booke of Genesis.* London: G. M. for George Edwards, 1640.
Willet, Andrew. *Hexapla in Genesin: That is A Sixfold Commentarie upon Genesis.* Cambridge: John Legat, 1605.
—. *Hexapla in Exodum: That is, A Sixfold Commentary upon the 2nd booke of Moses called Exodus.* London: Imprinted by Felix Kyngston for Thomas Man and John Norton, 1608.
Wilson, Thomas. *Saints by calling; or Called to be saints. A godly treatise of our holy calling to Christ, by the gospell.* London: W. Jaggard, 1620.
Wotton, Sir Henry. *The Elements of Architecture, collected by Henry Wotton Knight, from the best authors and examples.* London: Printed by John Bill, 1624.

SECONDARY SOURCES

Airs, Malcolm. *The Making of the English Country House, 1500–1640.* London: Architectural Press, 1975.
—. *The Buildings of Britain: Tudor and Jacobean, A Guide and Gazetteer.* London: Barrie & Jenkins, 1982.
—. *The Tudor & Jacobean Country House: A Building History.* Stroud: Sutton Publishing, 1995.
Ambler, Louis. *The old halls and manor houses of Yorkshire, with some examples of other houses built before the year 1700.* London: B. T. Batsford, 1913.
Apted, M. R. 'Two Painted Ceilings from Mary Somerville's House, Burntisland', *Proceedings of the Society of Antiquaries of Scotland* vol. 91 (1957–58): 144–75.
Archer, Michael. *Delftware: The Tin-Glazed Earthenware of the British Isles.* London: Victoria and Albert Museum, 1997.
Aston, Margaret. *England's Iconoclasts: Volume I, Laws against Images.* Oxford: Clarendon Press, 1988.
—. 'The Bishops' Bible Illustrations' in Diana Wood, ed. *The Church and the Arts.* Studies in Church History, vol. 28. Oxford University Press, 1992, 1995 edn, pp. 267–85.
—. *Faith and Fire: Popular and Unpopular Religion, 1350–1600.* London: Hambledon Continuum, 1993.
—. *The King's Bedpost: Reformation and Iconography in a Tudor Group Portrait.* Cambridge University Press, 1993, reprinted 1996.
Avray Tipping, H. *English Homes: Period III, Late Tudor and Early Stuart, 1558–1649.* Vol. 2. London: Country Life, 1922–29.

Ayres, James. *Domestic Interiors: The British Tradition, 1500–1850*. New Haven and London: Yale University Press, 2003.
Baldwin-Childe, Mrs. 'The Building of the Manor House of Kyre Park, Worcestershire (1588–1618)', *The Antiquary* vol. 21 (1980): 202–05, 261–64 and vol. 22: 24–26, 50–53.
Bankart, G. P. *The Art of the Plasterer*. London: B. T. Batsford, 1908.
Barley, Maurice. 'A Glossary of Names for Rooms in Houses of the Sixteenth and Seventeenth Centuries' in I. L. L. Foster and L. Alcock, eds. *Culture and Environment: Essays in Honour of Sir Cyril Fox*. London: Routledge & Kegan Paul, 1963, pp. 479–501.
Barry, Jonathan and Christopher Brooks, eds. *The Middling Sort of People: Culture, Society and Politics in England, 1550–1800*. Basingstoke: Palgrave Macmillan, 1994.
Bath, Michael. 'Applied Emblematics in Scotland: Painted Ceilings, 1550–1650', *Emblematica: An Interdisciplinary Journal for Emblem Studies* vol. 7 (1993): 259–305.
—. 'The Sources of John Abbott's Pattern Book', *Architectural History* vol. 41 (1998): 49–66.
—. *Renaissance Decorative Painting in Scotland*. Edinburgh: National Museums of Scotland Publishing, 2003.
Beard, Geoffry. *Decorative Plasterwork in Great Britain*. London: Phaidon, 1975.
Belsey, Catherine. *Shakespeare and the Loss of Eden: The Construction of Family Values in Early Modern Culture*. Basingstoke: Palgrave Macmillan, 1999.
Booy, David. *The Notebooks of Nehemiah Wallington, 1618–1654: A Selection*. Aldershot: Ashgate, 2007.
Bostwick, David. 'Plaster to Puzzle Over', *Country Life* (12 July 1990): 90–93 and 'Plaster Puzzle Decoded', *Country Life* (26 July 1990): 76–79.
—. 'Decorative Plasterwork of the Yorkshire Region, 1570–1670'. Ph.D. dissertation, University of Sheffield, 1993.
Boynton, Lindsay, ed. *The Hardwick Hall Inventories of 1601*. London: Furniture History Society, 1971.
Brooke, Xanthe. *The Lady Lever Art Gallery Catalogue of Embroideries*. Stroud: Alan Sutton, 1992.
Brooks, Mary. *English Embroideries of the Sixteenth and Seventeenth Centuries in the Collection of the Ashmolean Museum*. Oxford: Ashmolean Museum, 2004.
Brown, Lesley, ed. *The New Shorter Oxford English Dictionary on Historical Principles*. 2 vols. Oxford: Clarendon Press, 1993.
Campbell, Mildred. *The English Yeoman in the Tudor and Stuart Age*. Whitstable, Kent: The Merlin Press Ltd, new edn, 1990.
Carrick, Muriel. 'Sixteenth and Seventeenth Century Wall Paintings in the County of Essex'. 3 vols. M.Phil thesis, University of Essex, 1990.
—. *Essex Domestic Wall Paintings, 14th–18th Century*. Exh. cat., 1989. Colchester: University of Essex, 1993.
—. 'The Prodigal Son Wall Painting at Knightsland Farm, South Mimms', *Hertfordshire Archaeology* vol. 12 (1994): 104–10.
— and Charlotte Ryder. *The Forge Much Hadham Hertfordshire: 16th and 17th Century Wall Paintings*. Hertford: Hertfordshire Building Preservation Trust, 2000.
Cescinsky, Herbert, and Ernest R. Gribble. *Early English Furniture and Woodwork*. 2 vols. London: Waverly Book Company, 1922.
Chaney, Edward, ed. *The Evolution of English Collecting: Receptions of Italian Art in the Tudor and Stuart Periods*. New Haven and London: Yale University Press, 2003.
Charles, C. J. *Old English Interiors*. New York: John Lane Company, 3rd edn, 1919.
Cheetham, Francis. *English Medieval Alabasters, with a Catalogue of the Collection in the Victoria and Albert Museum*. Oxford: Phaidon; Christie's, 1984.

Chenevix Trench, John. 'John Abbott's Manual of Limming', *Association for Studies in the Conservation of Historic Buildings* vol. 2 (1986): 19–25.
Chew, Samuel. 'The Iconography of A Book of Christian Prayers (1578) Illustrated', *Huntington Library Quarterly* vol. 8 (1944–45): 293–305.
Chinnery, Victor. *Oak Furniture: The British Tradition, A History of Early Furniture in the British Isles and New England*. Woodbridge: Antique Collectors Club, 1979.
Cliffe, J. T. *The Puritan Gentry: The Great Puritan Families of Early Stuart England*. London: Routledge & Kegan Paul, 1984.
—. *The World of the Country House in Seventeenth-Century England*. New Haven and London: Yale University Press, 1999.
Clifford, D. J. H., ed. *The Diaries of Lady Anne Clifford*. Stroud: Sutton Publishing, 1990, 1998 edn.
Collinson, Patrick. *The Religion of Protestants: The Church in English Society, 1559–1625*. Oxford: Clarendon Press, 1982, reprinted 2003.
—. *Godly People: Essays on English Protestantism and Puritanism*. London: Hambledon Continuum, 1983.
—. 'From Iconoclasm to Iconophobia: The Cultural Impact of the Second English Reformation' (Stenton Lecture, 1985). University of Reading, 1986.
—. *The Birthpangs of Protestant England: Religious and Cultural Change in the Sixteenth and Seventeenth Centuries* (third Anstey Memorial Lecture, University of Kent, Canterbury). Basingstoke: Palgrave Macmillan, 1988.
— and John Craig. *The Reformation in English Towns*. Basingstoke: Palgrave Macmillan, 1998.
Coope, Rosalys. 'The Gallery in England: Names and Meanings', *Design and Practice in British Architecture: Studies in Architectural History Presented to Howard Colvin*. Special Issue, *Architectural History* vol. 27 (1984): 446–55.
—. 'The "Long Gallery": Its Origins, Development, Use and Decoration', *Architectural History* vol. 29 (1986): 43–84.
Cooper, Nicholas. *The Houses of the Gentry, 1480–1680*. New Haven and London: Yale University Press, 1999.
—. 'Rank, Manners and Display: The Gentlemanly House, 1500–1750', *Transactions of the Royal Historical Society* vol. 12 (2002): 291–310.
Cooper, Tarnya. '"Frail flesh, as in a glass": The Portrait as an Immortal Presence in Early Modern England and Wales' in Mary Rogers, ed., *Fashioning Identities in Renaissance Art*. Aldershot: Ashgate, 2000, pp. 197–212.
—. 'Memento Mori Portraiture: Painting, Protestant Culture and the Patronage of Middle Elites in England and Wales, 1540–1630', D.Phil. thesis, University of Sussex, 2001.
—, ed. *Searching for Shakespeare*. London: National Portrait Gallery, 2006.
Cooper, Trevor, ed. *The Journal of William Dowsing: Iconoclasm in East Anglia during the English Civil War*. Woodbridge: Boydell Press, 2001.
Cornforth, John. 'Prideaux Place, Cornwall', *Country Life* (February 1962): 226–29 and 274–78.
Cowan, Ian. *The Scottish Reformation*. London: Weidenfeld and Nicolson, 1982.
Croft, Pauline. 'The Religion of Robert Cecil', *The Historical Journal* vol. 34, no. 4 (December 1991): 773–96.
Croft-Murray, Edward. *Decorative Painting in England, 1537–1837: Early Tudor to Sir James Thornhill*, vol. 1. London: Country Life, 1962.
Cross, F. L., and E. A. Livingstone, eds. *The Oxford Dictionary of the Christian Church*. Oxford University Press, 2nd edn, 1978.

Cust, Lionel. 'Notes on the Collections formed by Thomas Howard, Earl of Arundel and Surrey, K.G. – II'. *The Burlington Magazine* (1911): 97–100, 233–36, 341–43.
—. 'The Lumley Inventories'. *The Walpole Society* vol. 6 (1918): 15–35.
Davidson, Clifford, and Ann Eljenholm Nichols, eds. *Iconoclasm vs. Art and Drama*. Kalamazoo: University of Western Michigan Press, 1989.
Davies, Kathryn. *Artisan Art: Vernacular Wall Paintings in the Welsh Marshes, 1550–1650*, Almeley: Logaston Press, 2008.
Dawson, Jane. 'Anglo-Scottish Protestant Culture and Integration in Sixteenth-Century Britain' in Steven G. Ellis and Sarah Barber, eds. *Conquest and Union: Fashioning a British State, 1485–1725*. London and New York: Longman, 1995, pp. 87–114.
Dawson, Jane E. A. *Scotland Re-formed, 1488–1587*. Edinburgh University Press, 2007.
Deacon, Richard and Philip Lindley. *Image and Idol: Medieval Sculpture*. London: Tate Publishing, 2001.
Digby, George Wingfield. *Victoria and Albert Museum: The Tapestry Collection, Medieval and Renaissance*. London: Her Majesty's Stationery Office, 1980.
Doran, Susan, ed. *Elizabeth: The Exhibition at the National Maritime Museum*. London: Chatto & Windus, 2003.
Drury, Paul and Richard Simpson. *Hill Hall: A Singular House devised by a Tudor Intellectual*. London: Society of Antiquaries of London, 2009.
Duffy, Eamon. *The Stripping of the Altars: Traditional Religion in England, c. 1400–c. 1580*. New Haven and London: Yale University Press, 1992.
—. *Marking the Hours: English People & their Prayers, 1240–1570*. New Haven and London: Yale University Press, 2006.
Durant, David N. *Bess of Hardwick: Portrait of an Elizabethan Dynast*. London: Peter Owen, 1999.
Durning, Louise and Clare Tilbury. '"Looking into Jesus": Image and Belief in a Seventeenth-Century English Chancel', *Journal of Ecclesiastical History* vol. 60, no. 3 (July 2009): 490–513.
Durston, Christopher and Jacqueline Eales, eds. *The Culture of English Puritanism, 1560–1700*. Basingstoke: Palgrave Macmillan, 1996.
Dyrness, William A. *Reformed Theology and Visual Culture: The Protestant Imagination from Calvin to Edwards*. Cambridge University Press, 2004.
Eade, Jane. 'The Triptych Portrait in England, 1575–1646', *The British Art Journal* vol. 6, no. 2 (Autumn 2005): 3–11.
Eire, Carlos M. N. *War against the Idols: The Reformation of Worship from Erasmus to Calvin*. Cambridge University Press, 1986.
Elkins, James. *The Object Stares Back: On the Nature of Seeing*. London: Thomson Learning, 1996.
Evans, Joan. 'An Inventory of Thomas Lord Wharton, 1568', *The Archaeological Journal* vol. 102 (1945): 135–50.
Fairclough, Oliver. *The Grand Old Mansion: The Holtes and their Successors at Aston Hall, 1618–1864*. Birmingham Museums and Art Gallery, 1984.
Fenlon, Jane. 'The Decorative Plasterwork at Ormond Castle: A Unique Survival', *Architectural History* vol. 41 (1998): 67–81.
Fincham, Kenneth, ed. *The Early Stuart Church, 1603–1642*. London: Palgrave Macmillan, 1993.
— and Peter Lake, eds. *Religious Politics in Post-Reformation England: Essays in Honour of Nicholas Tyacke*. Woodbridge: The Boydell Press, 2006.
— and Nicholas Tyacke. *Altars Restored: The Changing Face of English Religious Worship, 1547–c. 1700*. Oxford: Oxford University Press, 2007.

Finney, Paul Corby, ed. *Seeing beyond the Word: Visual Arts and the Calvinist Tradition.* Grand Rapids, Mich., and Cambridge: W. B. Eerdmans Publishing, 1999.

Fleming, Juliet. *Graffiti and the Writing Arts of Early Modern England.* London: Reaktion Books Ltd, 2001.

Foister, Susan. 'Paintings and Other Works of Art in Sixteenth-Century English Inventories', *The Burlington Magazine* vol. 123, no. 938 (May 1981): 273–82.

Ford, Boris, ed. *The Cambridge Guide to the Arts in Britain, Volume 3: Renaissance and Reformation.* Cambridge University Press, 1989.

—. *The Cambridge Guide to the Arts in Britain, Volume 4: The Seventeenth Century.* Cambridge University Press, 2nd edn, 1992.

Fouracre, J. T. 'Ornamental Lime-Plaster Ceilings and the Plasterer's Craft in Devonshire', *Transactions of the Devonshire Association for the Advancement of Science, Literature and Art* vol. 41 (1909): 256–62.

French, H. R. 'The Search for the "middle sort of people" in England, 1600–1800', *The Historical Journal* vol. 43, no. 1 (2000): 277–93.

—. *The Middle Sort of People in Provincial England, 1600–1750.* Oxford University Press, 2007.

French, Kathleen and Cecil. 'Devonshire Plasterwork', *Transactions of the Devonshire Association for the Advancement of Science, Literature and Art* vol. 89 (1957): 124–44.

Friedman, Alice T. *House and Household in Elizabethan England: Wollaton Hall and the Willoughby Family.* University of Chicago Press, 1988.

—. 'Did England Have a Renaissance? Classical and Anticlassical Themes in Elizabethan Culture' in Susan J. Barnes and Walter S. Malion, eds. *Cultural Identity in the Visual Arts.* Hannover and London: National Gallery of Art, Washington, D.C., 1989, pp. 95–110.

—. 'Inside/Out: Women, Domesticity, and the Pleasures of the City' in Lena Cowen Orlin, ed., *Material London ca. 1600.* Philadelphia: University of Pennsylvania Press, 2000, pp. 232–50.

Gaimster, David R. M. *German Stoneware, 1200–1900: Archaeology and Cultural History.* London: British Museum Press, 1997.

— and Gilchrist, Roberta, eds. *The Archaeology of Reformation, 1480–1580.* Leeds: Maney Publishing, 2003.

Gapper, Claire. 'Plasterers and Plasterwork in City, Court and Country, c. 1530–c. 1640'. 2 vols. Ph.D. dissertation, University of London, 1998.

—. 'What is "Stucco"? English Interpretations of an Italian Term', *Architectural History* vol. 42 (1999): 333–43.

Garner, F. H. *English Delftware.* London: Faber and Faber, 1948.

Gee, Henry and W. H. Hardy, eds. *Documents Illustrative of English Church History.* New York: Macmillan, 1896.

Gell, Alfred. *Art and Agency: An Anthropological Theory.* Oxford: Clarendon Press, 1998.

Gent, Lucy. *Picture and Poetry 1560–1620: Relations between Literature and the Visual Arts in the English Renaissance.* Leamington Spa: James Hall, 1981.

—, ed. *Albion's Classicism: The Visual Arts in Britain, 1550–1660.* New Haven and London: Yale University Press, 1995.

— and Nigel Llewellyn, eds. *Renaissance Bodies: The Human Figure in English Culture, c. 1540–1660.* London: Reaktion Books, 1990.

George, Edwin and Stella, eds. *Bristol Probate Inventories. Pt. 1: 1542–1650.* Bristol Record Society, 54. Bristol Record Society, 2002.

Gibson, Robin. 'The National Portrait Gallery's Set of Kings and Queens at Montacute House', *The National Trust Year Book* (1975–76): 81–87.

Gilbert, C. S. *An Historical Survey of the County of Cornwall.* 2 vols. Plymouth: J. Congdon, 1817–20.
Girouard, Mark. 'Renaissance Splendour in Decay, the Ruins of Slaugham Place, Sussex', *Country Life* 9 (January 1964): 70–73.
—. *Life in the English Country House: A Social and Architectural History.* New Haven and London: Yale University Press, 1978.
—. *Elizabethan Architecture.* New Haven and London: Yale University Press, 2009.
Glanville, Philippa. *Silver in Tudor and Early Stuart England: A Social History and Catalogue of the National Collection.* London: Victoria and Albert Museum, 1990.
Godfrey, Walter H. *The English Staircase: An Historical Account of its Characteristic Types to the End of the XVIIIth Century.* London: Batsford, 1911.
Gombrich, E. H. *Symbolic Images: Studies in the Art of the Renaissance II.* Oxford: Phaidon Press, 3rd edn, 1985.
Gomme, Andor and Alison Maguire. *Design and Plan in the Country House: From Castle Donjons to Palladian Boxes.* New Haven and London: Yale University Press, 2008.
Goss, C. W. F. *Sir Paul Pindar and his Bishopsgate Mansion.* Cambridge: W. Heffer & Sons, 1930.
Gowing, Robert and Robyn Pender, eds. *All Manner of Murals: The History, Techniques and Conservation of Secular Wall Paintings.* London: Archetype Publications, 2007.
Gray, Todd, ed. *Devon Household Accounts, 1627–59*, Part I. Exeter: Devon and Cornwall Record Society, 1995.
Green, Ian. *The Christian's ABC: Catechism and Catechizing in England, c. 1530–1740.* Oxford University Press, 1996.
—. *Print and Protestantism in Early Modern England.* Oxford University Press, 2000.
Griffiths, John, ed. *The Two Books of Homilies Appointed to be Read in Churches.* Oxford University Press, 1859.
Grigsby, Leslie. 'Some Dated English Drinking Vessels with Trailed-Slip Decoration, 1612–1752', *Magazine Antiques* vol. 147, no. 6 (June 1995): 874–83.
Haeger, Barbara. 'The Prodigal Son in Sixteenth and Seventeenth-Century Netherlandish Art: Depictions of the Parable and the Evolution of a Catholic Image', *Simiolus* vol. 16 (1986): 128–38.
Haigh, Christopher. *English Reformations: Religion, Politics, and Society under the Tudors.* Oxford University Press, 1993.
—. *The Plain Man's Pathways to Heaven: Kinds of Christianity in Post-Reformation England, 1570–1640.* Oxford University Press, 2007.
Hamilton, Sarah and Andrew Spicer, eds. *Defining the Holy: Sacred Space in Medieval and Early Modern Europe.* Aldershot: Ashgate, 2005.
Hamling, Tara. 'Decoration and Devotion: Religious Representation in West Country Decorative Plasterwork, c. 1590–c. 1660'. M.Phil. thesis, University of Birmingham, 1999.
—. 'Narrative and Figurative Imagery in the English Domestic Interior, c. 1558–c. 1640'. D.Phil. thesis, 2 vols, University of Sussex, 2002.
—. 'To see or not to see? The Presence of Religious Imagery in the Protestant Household', *Art History* vol. 30, no. 2 (April 2007): 170–97.
— and Catherine Richardson, eds. *Everyday Objects: Medieval and Early Modern Material Culture and its Meanings.* Aldershot: Ashgate, 2010.
— and Richard L. Williams, eds. *Art Re-formed: Re-assessing the Impact of the Reformation on the Visual Arts.* Newcastle: Cambridge Scholars Publishing, 2007.
Harris, John. *Moving Rooms: The Trade in Architectural Salvages.* New Haven and London: Yale University Press, 2007.

Heal, Felicity. 'The Idea of Hospitality in Early Modern England', *Past & Present* vol. 102 (1984): 66–93.
—. 'Reputation and Honour in Court and Country: Lady Elizabeth Russell and Sir Thomas Hoby', *Transactions of the Royal Historical Society*, 6th series, vol. 6 (1996): 161–78.
— and Clive Holmes. *The Gentry in England and Wales, 1500–1700*. Basingstoke: Palgrave Macmillan, 1994, reprinted 2002.
Henderson, Paula. *The Tudor House and Garden: Architecture and Landscape in the Sixteenth and Early Seventeenth Centuries*. New Haven and London: Yale University Press, 2005.
Herridge, Dorothy Marion. *Surrey Probate Inventories, 1558–1603*. Surrey Record Society, 39. Woking: Surrey Record Society, 2005.
Hill, Christopher. *Society and Puritanism in Pre-Revolutionary England*. London: Martin Secker & Warburg, 1964.
—. *The English Bible and the Seventeenth-Century Revolution: Uses of the Bible in 17th-Century England*. Harmondsworth: Penguin, 1994.
Hodgetts, Michael. *Harvington Hall*. Birmingham: Archdiocese of Birmingham Historical Commission, 1998.
Holden, Paul. '"Situation, Contrivance, Receipt, Strength and Beauty": The Building of Lanhydrock House, 1620–51', *Journal of the Royal Institution of Cornwall* (2005): 32–44.
Holly, Michael Ann. *Panofsky and the Foundations of Art History*. Ithaca and London: Cornell University Press, 1984.
Hoskins, W. G. 'The Rebuilding of Rural England, 1570–1640', *Past & Present* vol. 4 (1953): 44–59.
Howard, Deborah. *Scottish Architecture from the Reformation to the Restoration, 1560–1660*. The Architectural History of Scotland. Edinburgh University Press, 1995.
Howard, Maurice. *The Early Tudor Country House: Architecture and Politics*. London: Hamlyn, 1987.
—. 'Inventories, Surveys and the Histories of Great Houses, 1480–1640', *Architectural History* vol. 41 (1998): 14–29.
—. *The Building of Elizabethan and Jacobean England*. New Haven and London: Yale University Press, 2007.
—. 'Art and the Reformation' in Tim Ayers, ed., *The History of British Art, 600–1600*. London: Tate Publishing, 2008, pp. 231–45.
— and Michael Snodin. *Ornament: A Social History since 1450*. London: Tate Gallery, 1996.
— and Edward Wilson. *The Vyne: A Tudor House Revealed*. London: National Trust Enterprises, 2003.
Howells, Gwyn. 'Cobwebs in the Temple of God: The Brief Life of Lady Lucy Robartes, 1615/6 to 1645/6', *Lanhydrock House Journal* vol. 1 (2001): 11–20.
—. 'The Great Creation Ceiling in the Long Gallery', *Lanhydrock House Journal* vol. 2 (2002): 4–17.
Humphreys, John. 'Elizabethan Sheldon Tapestries', *Archaeologia* (1923–24): 181–202.
Humphreys, Richard. *The Tate Britain Companion to British Art*. London: Tate Publishing, 2001.
Hunter, Michael, ed. *Printed Images in Early Modern Britain: Essays in Interpretation*. Aldershot: Ashgate, 2010.
Hussey, Christopher. 'Cothay, I – Somerset', *Country Life* (22 October 1927): 596–604.
—. 'Barrington Court, Somerset (Parts I–II)', *Country Life* (17 and 24 March 1928): 370–77 and 404–12.
Imrie, Margaret. *The Manor Houses of Burton Agnes and their Owners*. Beverley, E. Yorkshire: Hutton Press, 1993.

Ingram, Martin. 'Ridings, Rough Music and the "Reform of Popular Culture" in Early Modern England', *Past & Present* no. 105 (November 1984): 79–113.

Jackson-Stops, Gervase, ed. *Treasure Houses of Britain: 500 Years of Private Patronage and Art Collecting*. New Haven and London: Yale University Press, 1986–7.

Johnston, P. M. 'Mural Paintings in Houses: With Special Reference to Recent Discoveries at Stratford-upon-Avon and Oxford', *Journal of the British Archaeological Association* vol. 37 (1931): 75–100.

Jones, Jeanne, ed. *Stratford-upon-Avon Inventories, 1538–1699*. Dugdale Society Publications, 40. Stratford-upon-Avon: Dugdale Society, 2003.

Jourdain, Margaret. *English Decorative Plasterwork of the Renaissance*. London: B. T. Batsford, 1926, 1933 edn.

—. 'Plasterer: John Abbott of Barnstaple and his Sketch Book', *Country Life* (2 March 1940): 222–25.

—. *English Interior Decoration, 1500–1830: A Study in the Development of Design*. London: B. T. Batsford, 1950.

Kamerick, Kathleen. *Popular Piety and Art in the Late Middle Ages: Image Worship and Idolatry in England, 1350–1500*. Basingstoke: Palgrave Macmillan, 2002.

Katzenellenbogen, Adolf. *Allegories of the Virtues and Vices in Medieval Art: From Christian Times to the Thirteenth Century*. London: Warburg Institute, University of London, 1939; New York: W. W. Norton, 1964.

Kellar, Clare. *Scotland, England, and the Reformation, 1534–1561*. Oxford: Clarendon Press, 2003.

Koerner, Joseph Leo. *The Reformation of the Image*. London: Reaktion Books, 2004.

Lake, Peter. *Moderate Puritans and the Elizabethan Church*. Cambridge University Press, 1982.

— with Michael Questier. *The Antichrist's Lewd Hat: Protestants, Papists and Players in Post-Reformation England*. New Haven and London: Yale University Press, 2002.

Levey, Santina M. *An Elizabethan Inheritance: The Hardwick Hall Textiles*. London: National Trust Enterprises, 1998.

—. *The Embroideries at Hardwick Hall: A Catalogue*. London: National Trust Books, 2007.

Llewellyn, Nigel. *The Art of Death: Visual Culture in the English Death Ritual, c. 1500–c. 1800*. London: Reaktion Books, 1991.

—. 'Cromwell and the Tombs: Historiography and Style in Post-Reformation English Funeral Monuments', *L'Art et les révolutions* vol. 4 (1992): 193–204.

—. 'Honour in Life, Death and in the Memory: Funeral Monuments in Early Modern England', *Transactions of the Royal Historical Society* vol. 6 (1996): 179–200.

—. *Funeral Monuments in Post-Reformation England*. Cambridge University Press, 2001.

Longfellow, Erica. 'Public, Private, and the Household in Early Seventeenth-Century England', *Journal of British Studies* vol. 45, no. 2 (April 2006): 313–45.

MacCulloch, Diarmaid. *Reformation: Europe's House Divided*. Harmondsworth: Penguin, 2004.

Macfarlane, Alan. *The Family Life of Ralph Josselin, a Seventeenth Century Clergyman: An Essay in Historical Anthropology*. Cambridge University Press, 1970.

—, ed. *The Diary of Ralph Josselin, 1616–1683*. Oxford University Press, 1991.

Machin, R., 'The Great Rebuilding: A Reassessment', *Past & Present* vol. 77, no. 1 (1977): 33–56.

Maltby, Judith, *Prayer Book and People in Elizabethan and Early Stuart England*. Cambridge University Press, 1998, 2000 edn.

Mander, Nicholas. 'Painted Cloths: History, Craftsmen and Techniques', *Textile History* vol. 28, no. 2 (1997): 119–48.

Marks, Richard. *Stained Glass in England during the Middle Ages*. London: Routledge, 1993.

—. *Image and Devotion in Late Medieval England.* Stroud: Sutton Publishing, 2004.
— and Paul Williamson, eds. *Gothic: Art For England, 1400–1547.* London: V&A Publications, 2003.
Marshall, Peter, ed. *The Impact of the English Reformation, 1500–1640.* London: Edward Arnold, 1997.
— and Alexandra Walsham, eds. *Angels in the Early Modern World.* Cambridge University Press, 2006.
Martin, A. R. *Charlton House, Kent: An Historical and Architectural Guide.* London: Blackheath Press, 1929.
Martindale, Charles, ed. *Ovid Renewed: Ovidian Influences on Literature and Art from the Middle Ages to the Twentieth Century.* Cambridge University Press, 1988.
Matley Moore, F. E. 'Painted Cloths', *Transactions of the Worcestershire Archaeological Society* 3rd series, vol. 8 (1982): 73–79.
Maxwell Lyte, Sir H. C. *A History of Dunster, and of the Families of Mohun and Luttrell.* 2 vols. London: St Catherine Press, 1909.
McCutcheon, Elizabeth. 'Sir Nicholas Bacon's Great House Sententiae'. *English Renaissance Supplements* 3. Claremont, Cal.: University of Hawaii and Sir Francis Bacon Foundation and Library, 1977.
McKean, Charles. *The Scottish Chateau: The Country House of Renaissance Scotland.* Stroud: Sutton Publishing, 2001.
McNamara, Janet. *Boston Manor, Brentford: A History and Guide.* Hounslow: Heritage Publications, 1998.
McRoberts, David. 'Provost Skene's House, in Aberdeen, and its Catholic Chapel', *The Innes Review* vol. 5 (1954): 119–24.
Mears, Natalie. 'Location, Location, Location? Place, Patronage and Meaning of the Wall Painting of "Jonah and the Whale" at Waltham Abbey', *Essex Archaeology and History* vol. 38 (2007): 136–47.
Mercer, E. 'The Houses of the Gentry', *Past & Present* vol. 5, no. 1 (1954): 11–32.
—. *English Art, 1553–1625.* Oxford: Clarendon Press, 1965.
—. *Furniture 700–1700.* London: Weidenfeld & Nicolson, 1969.
Merrifield, Ralph. *The Archaeology of Ritual and Magic.* London: Batsford, 1987.
Milton, Anthony. *Catholic and Reformed: The Roman and Protestant Churches in English Protestant Thought, 1600–1640.* Cambridge University Press, 1995.
Mitchell, W. J. T. 'What do Pictures Really Want?' *October* vol. 77 (Summer 1996): 71–82.
Montagu Benton, the Rev G. 'Domestic Wall-paintings, dated 1623, at Newton, Suffolk', Notes Section, *The Antiquaries Journal* 21 (1941): 68–72.
Moody, Joanna, ed. *The Private Life of an Elizabethan Lady: The Diary of Lady Margaret Hoby, 1599–1605.* Stroud: Sutton Publishing, 1998.
Morrall, Andrew. 'Protestant Pots: Morality and Social Ritual in the Early Modern Home', *Journal of Design History* vol. 15, no. 4 (2002): 263–73.
— and Melinda Watt, eds. *English Embroidery from the Metropolitan Museum of Art, 1580–1700.* New York, New Haven and London: Yale University Press, 2008.
Mowl, Timothy. *Elizabethan and Jacobean Style.* London: Phaidon Press, 1993.
National Trust and National Trust for Scotland Guide Books (various authors). Individual volumes as cited in the notes.
Nevinson, J. L. 'English Domestic Embroidery Patterns of the Sixteenth and Seventeenth Centuries', *The Walpole Society* 28 (1939–40): 1–13.

—. *Victoria and Albert Museum Catalogue of English Domestic Embroideries of the Sixteenth and Seventeenth Centuries.* London: HMSO, 1950.
—. 'The Embroidery Patterns of Thomas Trevelyon', *The Walpole Society* 41 (1966–68): 1–38.
Nichols, John Gough. *The Unton Inventories, relating to Wadley and Faringdon, co. Berks, in the years 1596 and 1620.* London: Berkshire Ashmolean Society, 1841.
Nordenfalk, Carl. 'The Five Senses in Late Medieval and Renaissance Art', *Journal of the Warburg and Courtauld Institutes* 48 (1985): 1–22.
—. 'The Five Senses in Flemish Art before 1600', *Netherlandish Mannerism, Nationalmusei Skriftserie* 4 (1985): 135–54.
O'Connell, Sheila. *The Popular Print in England.* London: British Museum Press, 1999.
O'Hara, Diana. *Courtship and Constraint: Rethinking the Making of Marriage in Tudor England.* Manchester University Press, 2000.
Oliver, Bruce W. 'The Early Seventeenth-Century Plaster Ceilings of Barnstaple', *Transactions of the Devonshire Association for the Advancement of Science, Literature and Art* vol. 49 (1917): 189–99.
Oman, Charles Chichele. *English Engraved Silver, 1150 to 1900.* London and Boston: Faber & Faber, 1978.
Orlin, Lena Cowen. *Private Matters and Public Culture in Post-Reformation England.* Ithaca, N.Y., and London: Cornell University Press, 1994.
—. *Locating Privacy in Tudor London.* Oxford University Press, 2007.
Oswald, Arthur, 'Ludstone Hall, Shropshire II', *Country Life* (18 January 1952): 154–57.
—. 'The Dartmouth Butterwalk Restored', *Country Life* (26 August 1954): 652–53.
—. *The London Charterhouse Restored.* London: Country Life, 1959.
—. 'Boston Manor House, Middlesex', *Country Life* (18 March 1965): 603–07.
Panofsky, Erwin. *Studies in Iconology: Humanistic Themes in the Art of the Renaissance* (1939). New York and London: Harper & Row, 1962.
—. *Meaning in the Visual Arts.* Harmondsworth and Ringwood: Penguin, 1955, 1970 edn.
Parry, Graham. *The Golden Age Restor'd: The Culture of the Stuart Court, 1603–42.* Manchester University Press, 1981.
—. *The Arts of the Anglican Counter-Reformation: Glory, Laud and Honour.* Woodbridge: Boydell Press, 2006.
Peck, Linda Levy. *Consuming Splendour: Society and Culture in Seventeenth-Century England.* Cambridge University Press, 2005.
Penoyre, John and Jane. *Decorative Plasterwork in the Houses of Somerset, 1500–1700.* Taunton: Somerset County Council, 1994.
Pettegree, Andrew, ed. *The Reformation World.* London: Routledge, 2000.
Pevsner, Nikolaus *et al. The Buildings of England.* 46 vols. Harmondsworth: Penguin, 1951–74; rev. edns by Simon Bradley, Bridget Cherry *et al.*, 1974–2002; New Haven and London: Yale University Press, 2002–, as cited in the notes.
Phillips, John. *The Reformation of Images: Destruction of Art in England, 1535–1660.* Berkeley, Los Angeles and London: University of California Press, 1973.
Pinney, Christopher and Nicholas Thomas, eds. *Beyond Aesthetics: Art and the Technologies of Enchantment.* Oxford: Berg Publishers, 2001.
Platt, Colin. *The Great Rebuildings of Tudor and Stuart England: Revolutions in Architectural Taste.* London: UCL Press, 1994.
Puloy, Monika. 'Decorative Plasterwork in Hertfordshire', *Hertfordshire Archaeology* vol. 8 (1983): 144–99.

Raylor, Timothy. '"Pleasure Reconciled to Virtue": William Cavendish, Ben Jonson, and the Decorative Scheme of Bolsover Castle', *Renaissance Quarterly* vol. 52 (1999): 402–39.
Reader, Francis W. 'Tudor Domestic Wall Paintings, Part 1', *The Archaeological Journal* vol. 92 (1935): 243–86.
—. 'Tudor Domestic Wall Paintings, Part 2', *The Archaeological Journal* vol. 93 (1936): 220–62.
—. 'A Classification of Tudor Domestic Wall Paintings', *The Archaeological Journal* vol. 98 (1942): 181–211.
Reed, Michael, ed. *The Ipswich Probate Inventories 1583–1631*. Suffolk Record Society. Woodbridge: Boydell Press, 1981.
Reid, Aileen and Robert Maniura, eds. *Edward Alleyn: Elizabethan Actor, Jacobean Gentleman*. London: Dulwich Picture Gallery, 1994.
Reynolds, Matthew. *Godly Reformers and their Opponents in Early Modern England: Religion in Norwich, c. 1560–1643*. Woodbridge: Boydell Press, 2005.
Ribeiro, Aileen. *Dress and Morality*. London: Batsford, 1986.
—. *Fashion and Fiction: Dress in Art and Literature in Stuart England*. New Haven and London: Yale University Press, 2005.
Richardson, Catherine. *Domestic Life and Domestic Tragedy in Early Modern England: The Material Life of the Household*. Manchester University Press, 2006.
Richardson, C. J. *Observations on the Architecture of England during the Reigns of Queen Elizabeth and King James I*. London: John Weale, 1837.
—. *Architectural Remains of the Reigns of Elizabeth and James I from accurate drawings and measurements taken from existing specimens*. London: Ackerman, 1840.
Richardson, James S. 'Sixteenth and Seventeenth Century Mural Decorations at the House of Kinneil, Bo'ness, West Lothian', *Proceedings of the Society of Antiquaries of Scotland* vol. 75 (1941): 184–204.
Richardson, R. C. 'Social Engineering in Early Modern England: Masters, Servants, and the Godly Discipline', *Clio* vol. 33, no. 2 (Winter 2004): 163–87.
Ricketts, Annabel. *The English Country House Chapel: Building a Protestant Tradition*, ed. Simon Ricketts. Reading: Spire Books, 2007.
Roberts, Edward. *Hampshire Houses, 1250–1700: Their Dating and Development*. With John Crook, Linda Hall and Daniel Miles. Winchester: Hampshire County Council, 2003.
Roberts, J. F. A. 'English Wall-Paintings after Italian Engravings', *The Burlington Magazine* 78 (1941): 86–92.
Rouse, E. Clive. 'Elizabethan Wall Paintings at Little Moreton Hall' in Gervase Jackson-Stops, ed., *National Trust Studies* (1979–80): 113–18.
—. 'Domestic Wall and Panel Paintings in Hertfordshire', *The Archaeological Journal* vol. 146 (1989): 423–50.
—. *Medieval Wall Paintings*. Princes Risborough: Shire Publications, 1991.
Russell, Percy. *Dartmouth: A History of the Port and Town*. Dartmouth: Friends of the Dartmouth Museum Association, 1982.
Saxl, Fritz. 'A Spiritual Encyclopaedia of the Late Middle Ages', *Journal of the Warburg and Courtauld Institutes* vol. 5 (1942): 82–142.
Sayle, Charles, ed. *The Works of Sir Thomas Browne*. 3 vols. Edinburgh: John Grant, 1927.
Scarisbrick, Diana. *Tudor and Jacobean Jewellery*. London: Tate Publishing, 1995.
Scott, Andrew. 'Henry Unton's Little Lives: Inscription and Suture in the Elizabethan Portrait', *Word & Image* vol. 13 (1997): 1–22.

Scribner, Bob, ed. *Bilder und Bildersturm im Spätmittelalter und in der frühen Neuzeit.* Wiesbaden: Otto Harrassowitz, 1990.
—, Roy Porter and Mikuláš Teich, eds. *The Reformation in National Context.* Cambridge University Press, 1994.
Seaver, Paul S. *Wallington's World: A Puritan Artisan in Seventeenth-Century London.* Stanford, Cal.: Stanford University Press, 1985.
Seznec, Jean. *The Survival of the Pagan Gods: The Mythological Tradition and its Place in Renaissance Humanism and Art.* Princeton University Press, 1981.
Sheill, John. 'Notice of Carved Oak Panels which were formerly in the Chapel of the Franciscan Nunnery in Dundee', *Proceedings of the Society of Antiquaries of Scotland* vol. 20 (8 February 1886): 108–25.
Simpson, Richard. 'Sir Thomas Smith and the Wall Paintings at Hill Hall, Essex: Scholarly Theory and Design in the Sixteenth Century', *Journal of the British Archaeological Association* vol. 130 (1977): 1–20.
Slack, Paul. *Poverty and Policy in Tudor and Stuart England.* London and New York: Longman, 1988.
Slade, H. Gordon 'Craigston Castle, Aberdeenshire', *Proceedings of the Society of Antiquaries of Scotland* (1976–77): 262–99.
Spraggon, Julie. *Puritan Iconoclasm during the English Civil War.* Woodbridge: Boydell Press, 2003.
Spurr, John. *English Puritanism, 1603–1689.* Basingstoke: Palgrave Macmillan, 1998.
Stoyle, Mark. *Loyalty and Locality: Popular Allegiance in Devon during the English Civil War.* Exeter University Press, 1994.
Summerson, John. *Architecture in Britain, 1530–1830.* 9th edn. New Haven and London: Yale University Press, 1993.
Sutton, James M. 'The Decorative Program at Elizabethan Theobalds: Educating an Heir and Promoting a Dynasty', *Studies in the Decorative Arts* vol. 7, no. 1 (1999–2000): 33–64.
Thomas, Keith. *Religion and the Decline of Magic: Studies in Popular Beliefs in Sixteenth- and Seventeenth-Century England.* London: Penguin, 1971, reprinted 1991.
—. *Man and the Natural World: Changing Attitudes in England, 1500–1800.* London: Penguin, 1983.
Thornton, Peter. *Seventeenth-Century Interior Decoration in England, France and Holland.* New Haven and London: Yale University Press, 1978.
Thorp, John. 'Wall Painting and Lime-Plaster Decoration' in Peter Beacham, ed., *Devon Building: An Introduction to Local Traditions.* Exeter: Devon Books, 1990, pp. 129–49.
—. 'The Ornamental Plasterwork of the Long Gallery at Lanhydrock, Cornwall: Puritan Images for Changing Times', *Apollo* vol. 434 (1998): 30–34.
Tillyard, E. M. W. *The Elizabethan World Picture* (1943). London: Pimlico, 1998.
Tittler, Robert. *The Reformation and the Towns in England: Politics and Political Culture, c. 1540–1640.* Oxford: Clarendon Press, 1998.
—. *The Face of the City: Civic Portraiture and Civic Identity in Early Modern England.* Manchester University Press, 2007.
—. 'Thomas Heywood and the Portrayal of Female Benefactors in Post-Reformation England', *Early Theatre* vol. 11, no. 1 (2008): 33–52.
Todd, Margo. 'Humanists, Puritans and the Spiritualised Household', *Church History* vol. 49, no. 1 (March 1980): 18–34.
—. *The Culture of Protestantism in Early Modern Scotland.* New Haven and London: Yale University Press, 2002.

Tristram, E. W. *English Medieval Wall Painting: The 12th Century.* Vol. 1. London: Oxford University Press, 1944.
—. *English Mediaeval Wall Painting: The 13th Century.* Vol. 2. London: Oxford University Press, 1950.
— and Monica Bardswell. *English Wall Painting of the Fourteenth Century.* London: Routledge & Paul, 1955.
Turner, Hilary L. 'Tapestries once at Chastleton House and their Influence on the Image of the Tapestries called Sheldon: A Reassessment', *The Antiquaries Journal* vol. 88 (2008): 313–46.
Tyacke, Nicholas. *Anti-Calvinists: The Rise of English Arminianism, c. 1590–1640.* Oxford: Clarendon Press, 1987, 1990 edn.
Underdown, D. E. 'The Taming of the Scold: The Enforcement of Patriarchal Authority in Early Modern England' in A. Fletcher and J. Stevenson, eds, *Order and Disorder in Early Modern England.* Cambridge University Press, 1985, pp. 116–36.
Unknown. 'Craigston Castle, Aberdeenshire', *Country Life* (17 and 24 October 1963): 944–47.
Unknown. 'Manor Court House', *Proceedings of Somersetshire Archaeological and Natural History Society* vol. 8 (1882): 23–27.
Unknown [A. E. H.]. 'The Pittleworth Frescoes', *Country Life* (11 November 1922): 606–08.
Unknown. 'Salisbury Trade Companies since 1612', *A History of the County of Wiltshire: Volume 6* (1962): 136–38.
Vallance, Aymer. *Art in England during the Elizabethan and Stuart Periods.* London, Paris and New York: Offices of the Studio, 1908.
Vernon, Thelma E. 'Inventory of Sir Henry Sharington, Contents of Lacock House, 1575', *Wiltshire Archaeological Society Magazine* vol. 63 (1968): 72–82.
Victoria History of the Counties of England 1900– (VCH); individual volumes as cited in the notes.
Vivian, J. L., ed. *The Visitations of Cornwall, comprising the Heralds Visitations of 1530, 1573 and 1620.* Exeter: William Pollard & Co., 1887.
Walsham, Alexandra. *Church Papists: Catholicism, Conformity and Confessional Polemic in Early Modern England.* Woodbridge: Boydell and Brewer, 1993.
Wardle, Patricia. *Guide to English Embroidery: Victoria and Albert Museum Catalogue.* London: HMSO, 1970.
Watt, Tessa. *Cheap Print and Popular Piety, 1550–1640.* Cambridge University Press, 1991.
Weaver, Lawrence. 'Bradninch Manor, Devon', *Country Life* (16 September 1916): 321–28.
Wells-Cole, Anthony. *Art and Decoration in Elizabethan and Jacobean England: The Influence of Continental Prints, 1558–1625.* New Haven and London: Yale University Press, 1997.
White, Adam. 'The Iconography of the State Apartment at Apethorpe Hall', *English Heritage Historical Review* vol. 3 (2008): 63–85.
White, Peter. *Predestination, Policy and Polemic: Conflict and Consensus in the English Church from the Reformation to the Civil War.* Cambridge University Press, 1992.
Whiting, Robert. *Local Responses to the English Reformation.* Basingstoke: Macmillan, 1998.
Williams, Arnold. *The Common Expositor: An Account of the Commentaries on Genesis, 1527–1633.* Chapel Hill: University of North Carolina Press, 1948.
Williams, Richard L. 'A Catholic Sculpture in Elizabethan England: Sir Thomas Tresham's *Reredos* at Rushton Hall', *Architectural History* vol. 44 (2001): 221–27.
—. 'Religious Pictures and Sculpture in Elizabethan England: Censure, Appreciation and Devotion'. Ph.D. thesis, University of London, 2003.
Wilson, C. Anne, ed. *"Banquetting Stuffe": The Fare and Social Background of the Tudor and Stuart Banquet.* Edinburgh University Press, 1991.

Wilson, Daniel. *Memorials of Edinburgh in the Olden Time*. 2 vols. Edinburgh: Hugh Paton, and London: Simpkin, Marshall & Co., 1848.
Wingfield Digby, George. *The Tapestry Collection: Medieval and Renaissance* (Victoria and Albert Museum Catalogue). London: HMSO, 1980.
Woolf, Rosemary. 'The Effect of Typology on the English Mediaeval Plays of Abraham and Isaac', *Speculum* vol. 32, no. 4 (October 1957): 805–25.
Yorke, Peter. 'Iconoclasm, Ecclesiology and "the beauty of holiness": Concepts of Sacrilege and the "peril of idolatry" in Early Modern England, c. 1590–1642'. Ph.D. dissertation, University of Kent, 1997.

Photograph Credits

Reproduced with permission of Sussex Past (The Sussex Archaeological Society): 1; © The British Library Board: 2 (G.4099), 41 (G.2383), 160 (IX.Eng.65); Reproduced by permission of The Huntington Library, San Marino, California: 3 (RB 20116), 65 (RB 438000:004), 122 (RB 97054), 123 (RB 99900), 164 (RB 438000:004), 170 (RB 438000:004), 175 (RB 438000:004); Photograph: © V&A Images / Victoria and Albert Museum: 4, 18, 20, 31, 88, 96, 111, 118, 136, 137, 138, 139, 141, 147, 148, 149, 150, 155, 156, 165, 172, 173, 180, 189; © Tate, London 2009: 5; © Bill Bigge: 6, 44, 93, 120; © Country Life: 7, 115, 167, 178, 193; Photograph: author: 8, 11, 12, 24, 25, 27, 30, 46, 47, 62, 69, 169; Reproduced by permission of English Heritage. NMR: 9, 22, 60, 63, 64, 71, 80, 81, 95, 100, 101, 102, 126, 152, 161, 162, 168, 191; © Courtauld Institute of Art, London: 10, 183; © The Trustees of the British Museum, London: 13, 15, 16, 54, 70, 140; © Museum of London: 14, 142, 174; © SCOTLANDSIMAGES.COM / National Museums Scotland: 17, 129, 130, 158, 176; Bodleian Library, University of Oxford MS. Rawl. D. 403, fol. 2v: 19; Reproduced courtesy of The Friends of Preston St Mary Church: 21; Photograph: © The National Trust: 23, 34, 38, 39, 58, 59, 72, 91, 119, 121, 124, 127, 143, 159, 181; Photograph: © David Ross/www.Britainexpress.com: 26; © Crown Copyright Reproduced Courtesy of Historic Scotland: 28, 33; This work is licensed under the Creative Commons Attribution-Share Alike 2.0 Generic License. Image © Trish Steel: 29; The Pepys Library, Magdalene College, Cambridge: 32, 55; Courtesy of the National Trust: 35, 40; SCOTLANDSIMAGES.COM / © National Trust for Scotland: 36; Courtesy of the National Trust for Scotland: 37; Photograph: author. Reproduced courtesy of Birmingham Museums & Art Gallery: 42; © Weald & Downland Open Air Museum: 43; This diagram is adapted from plans held in the NMR. All reasonable attempts have been made to locate the copyright holder for the original plans that inform this diagram: 45; © Dulwich Picture Gallery, London: 48; The Bowes Museum, Barnard Castle, County Durham: 49; Photograph: author. With kind permission of the late Colonel Sir Walter Luttrell: 50, 51, 52, 53; Photograph: author. Reproduced with kind permission of The Forge Museum: 56, 57; Photograph: author with kind permission of Canterbury Christ Church University: 61; Photograph: author. Courtesy of Dartmouth Museum: 66, 182; Photograph: Sandy McMillan. Reproduced with his kind permission: 67; Photograph: Sandy McMillan. Reproduced with his kind permission. The woodcuts are reproduced by permission of The Huntington Library, San Marino, California. RB 438000:004: 68; Photograph: author. Reproduced with kind permission of the Trustees of Burton Agnes Hall: 73, 74, 75, 109, 110; Photograph: author. Reproduced with kind permission of the owner: 76, 77, 78, 79, 104, 105, 107; Photograph: author. Courtesy of the National Trust: 82, 116, 125, 135, 186; Photograph: author. Reproduced with generous permission of the owner: 83, 84, 85, 86; Photograph: author. With permission of the Town Clerk, Lewes Town Council: 87; Photograph: Simon Foden. Reproduced with his kind permission: 90; Courtesy of Chiswick Public Library: 92; Photograph kindly provided by Maurice Howard. Reproduced by permission of London Borough Hounslow: 94, 185; Photograph reproduced with kind permission of Mr and Mrs Prideaux-Brune: 97; Photograph: author. Reproduced with kind permission of Mr and Mrs Prideaux-Brune: 98, 99, 190; Photograph of 1888. Hereford Museum and Art Gallery, Herefordshire Heritage Services: 103; © Museum of Barnstaple & North Devon: 106; Reproduced from the *Proceedings of the Society of Antiquaries of Scotland* of 1960 with permission of National Museums Scotland: 108; Photograph: Harvey Wood. Courtesy of the National Trust for Scotland: 112; Photograph: Douglas MacGregor. Courtesy of the National Trust for Scotland: 113; © Culture and Sport Glasgow (Museums): 114; Photograph: author. Reproduced with kind permission of William Pratesi Urquhart: 117; © The Scotsman Publications Ltd: 128; Aberdeen Art Gallery & Museums Collections: 131, 132, 133; © National Portrait Gallery, London: 134; © Shakespeare Birthplace Trust: 144, 146, 188; Birmingham Museums & Art Gallery: 145; National Museums Liverpool, Lady Lever Art Gallery: 151; National Gallery, London: 153; Photograph generously supplied by the owner: 154, 157, 163, 187; By permission of the Folger Shakespeare Library, Washington, D.C.: 166; Photograph generously supplied by J. Lewis. With kind permission of the Heritage Team, South Somerset District Council: 171; Photograph supplied by Bedfordshire County Council: 184; Photograph generously provided by Anthony Wells-Cole, reproduced with kind permission of the Trustees of Burton Agnes Hall: 192.

Index

Note: biblical imagery discussed in the book is listed under 'biblical subjects'. Other iconography, including non-scriptural / cultic subject matter, is listed alphabetically by subject. References in *italics* are to pages where illustrations are found. Please note that only those historic houses marked with * are open to visitors or otherwise accessible to the public.

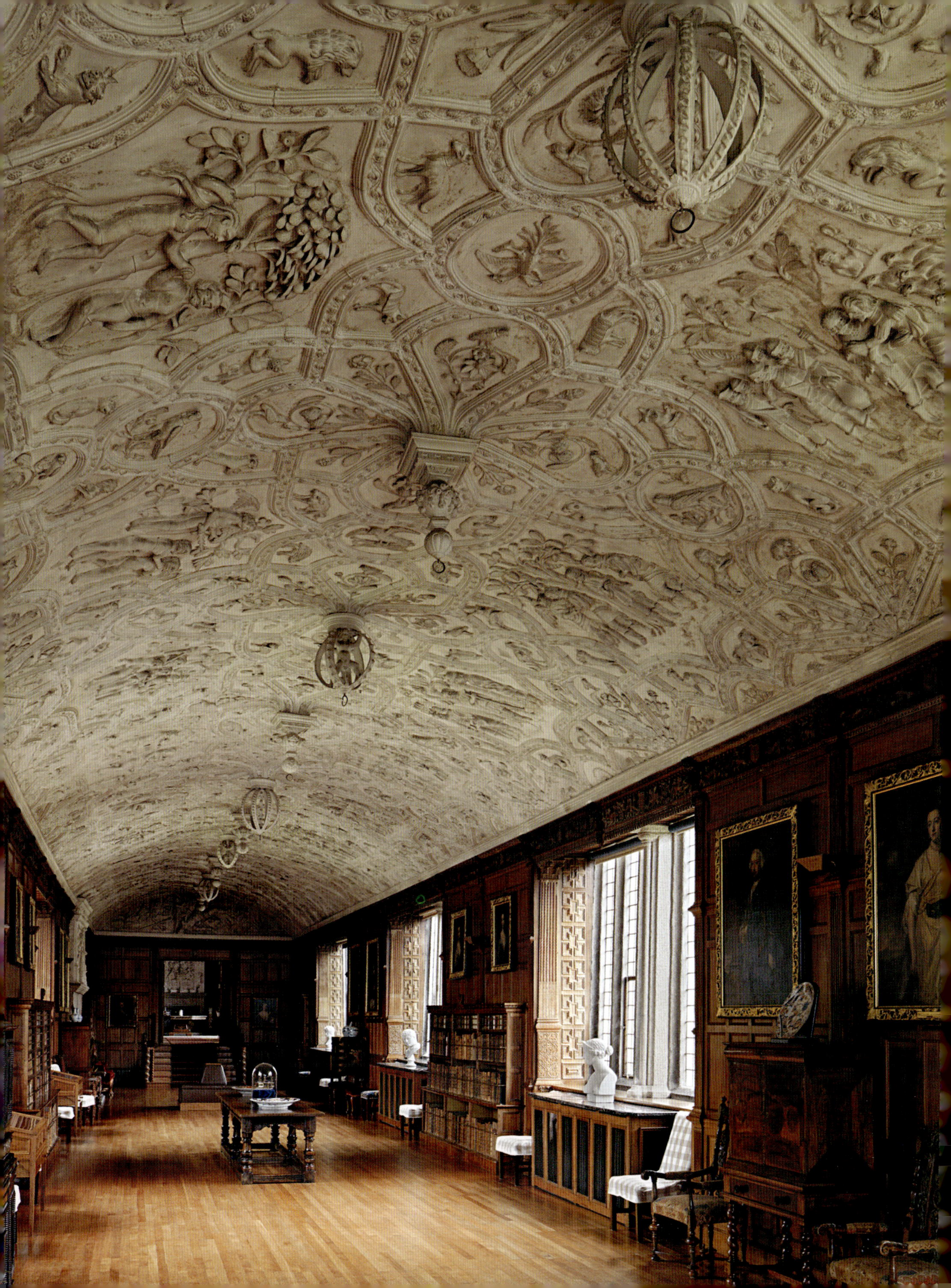

Decorating the 'Godly' Household